Network
————*and*————
Distributed
Systems
Management

Network
—— *and* ——
Distributed
Systems
Management

Edited by
Morris Sloman

Imperial College of Science, Technology & Medicine
University of London

Addison-Wesley Publishing Company

Wokingham, England · Reading, Massachusetts · Menlo Park, California
New York · Don Mills, Ontario · Amsterdam · Bonn · Sydney · Singapore
Tokyo · Madrid · San Juan · Milan · Paris · Mexico City · Seoul · Taipei

© 1994 Addison-Wesley Publishers Ltd.
© 1994 Addison-Wesley Publishing Company Inc.

The programs in this book have been included for their instructional value. They have been tested with care but are not guaranteed for any particular purpose. The publisher does not offer any warranties or representations nor does it accept any liabilities, with respect to the programs.

Many of the designations used by manufacturers and sellers to distinguish their products are claimed as trademarks. Addison-Wesley has made every attempt to supply trademark information about manufacturers and their products mentioned in this book. A list of the trademark designations and their owners appear below.

Cover designed by Hybert Design & Type, Maidenhead
and printed by The Riverside Printing Co. (Reading) Ltd.
Printed and bound in Great Britain by William Clowes, Beccles, Suffolk

First printed 1994

ISBN 0-201-62745-0

British Library Cataloguing-in-Publication Data
A catalogue record for this book is available from the British Library.

Library of Congress Cataloguing-in-Publication Data is available

Trademark Notice
DECbridge™, DECmcc™, DECnet™, ULTRIX™, OpenVMS™ and VT™ are trademarks of Digital Equipment Corporation.
DCE™, DME™, OSF™ and Motif™ are trademarks of the Open Software Foundation.
HP Open View™ is a trademark of Hewlett-Packard.
METAWINDOW™ is a trademark of MetaAccess Inc.
MS-DOS™ and Windows™ are trademarks of Microsoft Corporation.
NET/MASTER™ is a trademark of System Center Inc.
NetView™ is a trademark of International Business Machines Corporation.
OpenLook™ and SunNet Manager™ are trademarks of Sun Microsystems Inc.
TME™ is a trademark of Tivoli Systems.
UNIX™ is a trademark of UNIX Systems Laboratories Inc.

Preface

In 1989, The International Federation for Information Processing (IFIP) working group 6.6 on network management held the first International Symposium on Integrated Network Management in Boston. This grew into a series of biennual symposia which essentially provided the impetus for this book in that many of the authors were actively involved in the series. Some of the chapters are derived from papers presented at these symposia.

The contributors to the book are all experienced researchers who were invited to contribute a chapter relevant to their particular expertise.

The book is intended as a reference covering current practice and future directions for managing networks and distributed systems. The book is intended for use by:

- System managers, to determine the techniques and standards available for managing their systems. This will give them the basis for formulating their enterprise requirements, understanding what vendors have to offer and asking the right questions about future plans.

- Network and system management vendors, to understand the benefits and limitations of current standards and in the hope of influencing them to use modern distributed processing techniques for implementing their management products.

- Students and computing professionals, to learn about the important concepts and issues related to management of networks and distributed systems.

- Researchers, to obtain information about management topics complementary to their own expertise.

Acknowledgments

I would like to thank Kim Kappel who helped to formulate the proposed contents of the book and suggested potential authors for some of the chapters. I am grateful to the authors for giving up the time to write the material and for their patience in that the book took much longer to get from conception to fruition than originally planned. Many of the authors also reviewed and provided comments on other chapters. Other reviewers include:

Peter Harrison, Imperial College
Gabe Jakobson, GTE
Robert Weihmayer, GTE

   Jane Spurr did much of the editing of submitted manuscripts to fit in with the book style. Aspassia Daskalopulu helped in drawing the diagrams.
   Finally I would like to thank Ruth, Leonie and Nicole for their understanding and patience for the time I have spent in editing the book and in putting up with my ranting and raving when things did not turn out the way I had planned!

                                                            Morris Sloman

                                                            March 1994

Contents

5   OSI Structure of Management Information   95

Part IV   Management Functions

Part VII   Case Studies

22 Digital Equipment Corporation's Enterprise Management Architecture   581

Part I

Introduction

Chapter 1

Management: What and Why

Morris Sloman

Imperial College of Science Technology and Medicine,
180 Queen's Gate,
London SW7 2BZ, UK
Email: m.sloman@doc.ic.ac.uk

This chapter explains what management is in terms of the functions and services required for managing a network or distributed system and stresses the strategic importance of management to many enterprises. We advocate that management should itself be implemented as a distributed system.

1.1   The network decade

The network age is upon us. Computers are no longer used stand-alone. An office workstation is usually connected to remote printers, file servers, database servers and worldwide electronic mail facilities. A point of sale terminal will connect to in-store stock control systems, banking systems for credit validation and possibly even a remote consumer analysis organization. An automated banking teller will access customer records in their home bank anywhere in the world. A travel agent can access the on-line reservation systems of dozens of airlines, hotels or car rental companies. Even the simple home computer may have modem access to electronic mail, bulletin boards or remote computing facilities.

A typical factory or industrial plant will now have dozens of computers connected by networks cooperating to control car assembly plants, oil refineries, steel mills, food manufacturing plants or power generation.

The 1980s was the age of the computer with word processors replacing typewriters and microcomputers being built into televisions and washing machines. It is now accepted that many organizations – banks, insurance companies, telephone companies, airlines – cannot function without the computer. These organizations no longer depend upon a centralized mainframe but on the ability to rapidly and reliably exchange information between computers within their own organization as well as with other organizations.

Over the past twenty years there has been considerable research and development effort on techniques for building networks and distributed systems – network architectures, protocols, very large scale integrated circuits for communication devices, distributed programming languages, concurrency control mechanisms, and so on. We now have solutions to most of these problems (although further research is still required, for example, on faster networks or more powerful programming languages). We can build complex interconnected networks and the distributed processing systems to run on them but managing such systems is much more of a problem.

This book addresses the issues of managing networks and distributed systems. It stresses the similarities between them and advocates the use of distributed processing techniques for management.

In the next section we define distributed and networked systems and then explain what we mean by management.

1.2   Distributed versus networked systems

Interconnected computers are often referred to as a *network*. The term is often used synonymously with communication system, that is, the hardware and software that permits autonomous computers to exchange information. Chapter 2 describes the components for building networks.

A *distributed processing system* (DPS) consists of 'several autonomous processors and data stores supporting processes and/or databases which interact in order to cooperate to achieve an overall goal. The processes coordinate their activities and exchange information by means of a communication system' (Sloman and Kramer, 1987). The implication is that there is fairly close synchronization between the components of the DPS in order to achieve cooperation. The DPS is built upon the basic services of processing, storage and communication over a network. Chapter 3 covers the underlying principles of implementing a DPS.

Tanenbaum (1992) defines a distributed system as 'one that runs on a collection of machines that do not have shared memory, yet looks to its users like a single computer'. Very few systems actually fulfill this requirement of a single virtual machine image. We consider this definition to be too restrictive. Many factory automation, telecommunication and process control systems exhibit most of the properties and issues relating to distributed systems, including cooperation to achieve a common goal, but distribution is not transparent as it reflects the physical distribution of the application.

The term "networked system" implies message-based communication, potentially long delays between sending and receiving messages, loose synchronization and no overall common goal. The term "distributed system" usually implies fairly close synchronization between components in order to achieve cooperation, remote procedure calls or message passing. In reality there is no hard-and-fast distinction between networked and distributed systems. For example, users of an electronic mail service exchange messages and are generally considered to form a networked system because there is no close synchronization, although some users may be cooperating to write a paper. However, the components that implement the electronic mail service cooperate to provide a mail service to users and so are considered a DPS.

1.3 What is management?

Management of a system is concerned with supervising and controlling the system so that it fulfills the requirements of both the owners and users of the system. This includes the longer-term planning required for the system to evolve to provide improved performance, incorporate new functionality or new technology. Management may also involve accounting to make sure that resources are fairly allocated to users or to actually charge users for use of services. The management of a system may be performed by a mixture of human or automated components. We use the term *manager* to refer to any entity, human or automated, that can perform management activities.

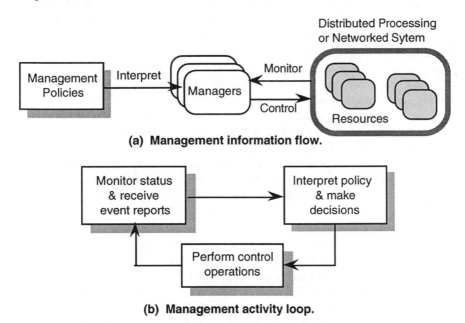

Figure 1.1 Management activities.

As part of the on-line control of a system, the managers must perform the following activities shown in Figure 1.1:

i)   Monitor the system to obtain up-to-date status information and to receive event reports;

ii)   Interpret the overall policy pertaining to the goals or requirements of the organization that owns the system in order to make decisions about what behavior is required from the system;

iii) Perform control actions on the system resources to change their behavior and implement the management decisions.

1.4   Management example

1.4.1   The scenario

We will consider the computing services used within a hypothetical large international manufacturing enterprise to see what management functions would be needed. Assume there are manufacturing sites in many countries and that products from a site may be needed as raw material at other sites. There are a number of sales offices in each country to coordinate orders from customers for products from any manufacturing site and to arrange distribution. There may be regional headquarters in each country for planning of sales and manufacturing related to that country as well as the overall corporate headquarters say in London. A corporate-wide communication system supporting voice, data and video communication is provided by a communication company as a virtual private network. This scenario is appropriate for many petrochemical, electronics, or automobile manufacturing enterprises.

At a manufacturing site computers are used for process control or factory automation, production control, stock control, "just in time" ordering of materials and design for local manufacturing. These sites must communicate with each other to schedule production and provide production information to sales offices and regional headquarters. They also a need to order materials from other manufacturers. Manufacturing sites cooperate via video and data links with other corporate and suppliers' sites in the design of components and specification of materials.

Sales offices need to interact with customers for order processing; with manufacturing sites for passing on orders and querying production schedules or stock levels; with transport companies to schedule collection from manufacturing sites or depots and deliveries to customers; and with banks for electronic funds transfer.

Regional headquarters interact with manufacturing sites to monitor production and local costs. They interact with sales offices to monitor sales and cash flow. They also coordinate transport for deliveries from overseas sites for both manufacturing and sales. They act as the interface for legal and accounting services needed by the enterprise in the country. Future planning might need interaction with architects for new buildings. Corporate headquarters performs similar functions but on a world-wide basis.

1.4.2   Required management

The overall distributed systems management would have to control the registration and issuing of identifiers for all human users and components of the system to make sure names are unique. Directory services for location of people, services and resources must be maintained.

Faults in any part of the system must be detected. Fault diagnosis may require interaction with other cooperating organizations or those providing services. Fault recovery actions have to be instigated and repairs tested.

It is necessary to specify a required quality of service (QoS) from outside suppliers such as for communications or database services and to take corrective action if that quality is not maintained. Similarly, the performance of all components of the system must be monitored to detect bottlenecks. Planning for expansion could use modeling or analysis tools to determine required characteristics of new components or services.

External services are charged for and these are passed on to the various divisions in the organization as part of the accounting function. Many internal resources are shared and so accounting is also needed to make sure they are fairly allocated to all users.

Security management is needed to specify who can access what resources or services. This is particularly important in that computers are accessed by outside organizations for order processing and design of components in collaboration with outside suppliers. It is necessary to detect and check up on security violations. Encryption keys have to be generated and distributed to permit encryption of confidential information, authentication and "signing" of payments, orders, and so on.

Monitoring of the system is needed for all these functions to determine the current status of components and react to events. This entails filtering events, and disseminating event notifications to those that require them.

Many of the applications and services within the system will consist of components running on distributed computers. The software components have to be installed and connections set up to other specific services they need. Software will have to updated in a controlled manner. All these are functions of configuration management, including keeping track of what components constitute the overall system and how they are interconnected. This information is needed to determine dependencies and diagnose faults.

Some services and components will be provided by different manufacturers so there is a need for standardization of the management interface to these components, otherwise you will end up with multiple independent management systems. This makes it difficult to interact with these components or services to obtain status information or to cooperate in diagnosing faults.

There is a need to group components for management purposes to cope with the complexity of a very large system involving multiple organizations. This can be achieved by using domains for grouping components to which a common policy applies or to partition the overall management structure to assign responsibility to multiple managers.

It is necessary to specify the policy that managers have to interpret in order to make their management decisions. Coding policy into managers makes it difficult to change their behavior without replacing the manager components.

There is a large amount of information generated by monitoring which needs to stored, analyzed and correlated. Configuration information about component location, containment relationships and relationships about physical and logical interconnections is needed for diagnostic purposes. Databases are thus an essential part of a management system.

It is not possible to fully automate all aspects of management. Humans will still be involved in monitoring and decision management. These human interfaces must be designed based on sound principles with consistent use of icons, windows, menus and color.

Another aid to coping with complexity is to use artificial intelligence techniques to help in the decision-making process for both human and automated managers. This has been particularly successful in aiding fault diagnosis.

This book covers all these aspects of management in considerable detail and then describes a few case studies to show what some vendors are providing.

1.5   Why do we need management?

As described in Section 1.1 and in the above scenario, networks and distributed systems have become critical to the working of many enterprises. For example, when their DPS systems do not provide the required service, factories cease to produce goods, banks cannot perform their normal transactions, airlines cannot make reservations, airports and railways may shut down or work at a very reduced level. Management is essential to make sure these systems continue to function to provide the service required of them. No enterprise remains static. It changes to meet new market needs and new business practices. The longer-term planning aspects of management are essential to permit the systems to evolve and adapt to these changing requirements of the enterprise (Langsford and Moffett, 1993).

This realization of the strategic importance of network and distributed systems management has resulted in a demand for management facilities which has, to some extent, outstripped the research and development needed to implement these systems. The fully integrated management systems which will cope with management of large-scale distributed applications and their underlying communication services are not available commercially. Many of the issues relating to specifying policy, structuring management and building complex management systems incorporating artificial intelligence techniques and graphical user interfaces are still research topics.

Another reason for the upsurge in interest in automated and integrated management of networks and distributed systems is that some of the systems already installed have grown so large and complex that *ad hoc*, manual management is not coping. The components to be managed are manufactured by different vendors, and may have proprietary management facilities or none at all; there are likely to be multiple interconnected networks providing the overall communication service to a distributed application; the distributed nature of the system results in delays in obtaining status information so it is not easy to get a global view of the overall state of the system; the system may be constantly changing and determining the current configuration can be difficult. The two main problems are:

i)   The complexity of management requires automation of many aspects of management;

ii)   Tools are needed to support human managers in performing their function.

This book indicates some of the protocols and techniques for implementing management, in the hope that these will be used by vendors of management systems to provide the required tools and services. In the next section we describe how some of these solutions and standards have evolved.

1.6   Evolution of management

The early work on management has been derived from three different areas.

i)   *Systems management* has been provided as part of the operating system of large mainframes and is concerned with managing the resources such as disk stores or memory, setting scheduling policies and the security information needed for controlling access to resources.

ii)   *Telecommunications management* techniques concentrated on managing hardware devices, connections and circuits.

iii)   *Network management* also concentrated on managing hardware devices such as modems, routers, multiplexors, network interfaces and connections.

Telecommunications and network management, by their very nature, involve interactions between multiple components and hence have to cope with components from different vendors. Standardization of management interactions provides obvious benefits of being able to manage multi-vendor components from a single management platform, as explained in Chapter 4. The Simple Network Management Protocol (SNMP), described in Chapter 7, emerged from the internet community and is now a *de facto* standard. This was not considered sophisticated enough to cope with the future complexities of modern communication systems and so an object-oriented approach was undertaken by the International Standardization Organization (ISO) within the Open Systems Interconnection (OSI) framework. This is described in Chapters 4 to 6, with the two approaches being compared in Chapter 8. The telecommunications community have combined with the OSI community to define a common set of standards which are applicable to both. Chapter 9 describes how these standards are used for telecommunications management network (TMN). OSI management, SNMP and TMN all concentrate on management of the communications system. Although there are lessons to be learnt from their approach, they do not really support management as a DPS.

Systems management is based on proprietary operating systems so there has been less standardization effort in this area. However, there are many similarities in the approach taken by these system vendors and the approach taken in the standards (see Chapter 22). The Open Software Foundation (OSF) has realized there is a need for vendor-independent management and so OSF is bringing out the Distributed

Management Environment (DME) as described in Chapter 23.   DME does follow the distributed processing approach advocated in this book.

Early systems, telecommunications and network management have all been based on centralized management platforms, but there has now been a growing realization that the management system itself must be automated and distributed to reflect the distribution of the system elements being managed.   As stated previously, mainframes are not isolated but are connected to networks.   General-purpose computing facilities are increasingly being provided as clusters of workstations connected by networks to servers.   Telecommunication systems are moving from analog to digital signaling and incorporate computers within the communication systems.   Intelligent networks and multiservice broadband communications systems are emerging and need sophisticated distributed systems for their implementation. Thus there is no longer a real distinction between the needs of system, network and telecommunication management.   The communication system should merely be considered one of many (distributed) services required to implement a DPS. Similar concepts and techniques are needed to implement the management of any distributed service or application.   It is for this reason that this book covers the concepts of both network and distributed systems management.

Within a single organization, a hierarchically structured distributed management system may still be appropriate.   There may be a central control room with operators responsible for overall management.   They effectively manage the automated managers.   The management system may be partitioned functionally with dedicated manager components performing configuration, fault or security management.   There may be further partitioning within each function with managers dedicated to particular local area networks.   This overall hierarchical structure is very common in all forms of control systems.   The higher-level management has responsibility for longer-term control, at a more abstract level, and the lower levels for more detailed control of individual components within shorter timescales.   The Domain framework described in Chapter 16 explains how to deal with structuring complex systems.

This strict hierarchy is inappropriate for applications that cross organizational boundaries.   There may be multiple interacting hierarchies with no top level.   Instead there is a need for peer-to-peer interactions between managers.   In fact these peer-to-peer interactions can be useful between cooperating, distributed managers which together form a management application within a hierarchical system.   A general-purpose management system must support both hierarchical and peer-to-peer management interactions.

An important benefit of treating management as a DPS is that management components can themselves have management interfaces and so the management can also be managed using the same techniques and tools as other distributed applications.

1.7   Book structure

The initial ISO work on OSI management identified five functional areas of management, namely fault management, configuration management, accounting, performance management and security management (ISO 7498-4, 1989). Monitoring was not identified as a functional area in its own right, but was subsumed within the other areas.

More recent work (Sloman *et al.,* 1993) has indicated that these functional areas should be considered as management applications, implemented as a DPS with some aspects being automated in distributed manager components but some aspects being under the control of humans. The management applications provide a (graphical) interface to human managers. Human managers interact with the management system to set policy, make management decisions that cannot easily be automated or to override automated management where appropriate.

The fact that management is itself a distributed processing system is the main theme of this book and has influenced its structure. Most of the existing work on management has been oriented towards communication systems and so there is a strong emphasis on network management as reflected in many of the examples presented in various chapters.

The book is divided into eight parts:

I: This introduces the concepts, explains what management is and why it is needed.

II: Enabling technologies consist of the network components from which communication systems are built (Chapter 2) and the basic principles for building a DPS (Chapter 3). These principles are essentially the same for implementing management or any other distributed application.

III: The various models and standards for management are covered in Chapters 4–9. The OSI management model and its related set of standards are overviewed in Chapter 4, followed by a detailed exposition of the OSI object-oriented approach in Chapter 5. The guidelines for defining OSI managed objects are explained in Chapter 6. There is a large installed base of SNMP objects and agents which are unlikely to be replaced in the short term with OSI management. Chapter 7 describes SNMP and Chapter 8 compares it to the OSI management architecture in an attempt to resolve some of the controversy between protagonists of the two approaches. Any large system will make use of telecommunication services supplied by the public carriers so Chapter 9 describes the TMN approach.

IV: The management functional applications needed in a distributed management system are covered in the next six chapters. Chapter 10 describes how to manage the namespace for managed and manager components and how a directory and name services can be used for naming. Chapter 11 explains how the specification of required QoS must be mapped onto those offered by the components implementing a service. We also discuss issues relating to negotiating a suitable QoS if that required by a user does not match that offered by a service provider. A distributed monitoring service for all aspects of management is explained in Chapter 12. The issues of planning a network to meet required performance is discussed in Chapter 13 which includes modeling and analysis of performance. Accounting methods and techniques are explained in Chapter 14. Chapter 15 describes how to provide security for management in a network environment as well as how to manage the security service itself.

V: Separating management policy from managers enables reuse of manager components in different situations and easy modification of their behavior. Chapter 16 describes the use of domains for grouping objects to which a common policy applies and Chapter 17 explains how to specify management policy with particular reference to access control policy.

VI: The implementation issues of management are covered in this part of the book. In Chapter 18 we show how the software configuration can be managed in terms of creating components, allocating them to hardware and binding the interfaces of component instances. Chapter 19 gives an example of the use of database modeling techniques to store network management information. The principles of graphical user interface design are covered in Chapter 20 and Chapter 21 surveys Artificial Intelligence techniques and tools for management.

VII: Case studies include Digital Equipment's enterprise management, in Chapter 22 and the Open Software Foundation's DME – a distributed object-oriented approach to management in Chapter 23. The MetaAccess tools for designing management in a changing environment are described in Chapter 24.

VIII: The conclusions in Chapter 25 concentrate on where do we go from here – the important issues for the future.

The overall intention of this book is to provide a source of reference for both students and practitioners as to the concepts they should understand about network and distributed system management. It also covers research topics in order to influence vendors on how management will develop in the future.

Abbreviations

DME   Distributed Management Environment
DPS   Distributed Processing System
ISO   International Organization for Standardization
OSI   Open Systems Interconnection
QoS   Quality of Service
SNMP   Simple Network Management Protocol
TMN   Telecommunications Management Network

References

ISO 7498-4. (1989). *Open Systems Interconnection – Part 4: Management Framework.*

Langsford A. and Moffett J. (1993). *Distributed Systems Management.* Addison Wesley

Sloman M. and Kramer J. (1987). *Distributed Systems and Computer Networks.* Prentice Hall

Sloman M., Magee J., Twidle K. and Kramer J. (1993). An architecture for managing distributed systems. In *Proc. 4th IEEE Workshop on Future Trends of Distributed Computing Systems,* Lisbon, Sep. 1993, 40–6

Tanenbaum A. (1992). *Modern Operating Systems.* Prentice Hall

Part II

Enabling Technologies

Chapter 2

Network Technologies

Fred Halsall

University College of Swansea,
Singleton Park,
Swansea, SA2 8PP, UK
Email: eehalsall@vax.swan.ac.uk

This chapter first identifies the different types of computer communication networks and the technology associated with them. The operation of these networks is then presented together with a description of the communication protocols associated with them. The chapter concludes with a brief introduction to network management protocols that have been developed for use with them.

2.1 Network classification and standards evolution

The past decade has seen unprecedented growth in the range of networking technology that is now available. For descriptive purposes, the networks used in different application environments are categorized according to their speed of operation and field of coverage.

Local area networks or LANs: these are used to interconnect computers (workstations, servers, and so on) that are physically distributed around a single office or building or group of buildings that all belong to the same organization. In some instances just a single LAN is used while in others multiple interconnected LANs are used. In the latter case the LANs are interconnected either by bridges, if all the LANs are of the same type, or routers if a mix of LAN types is involved. High-speed LANs are now widely used as backbones and increasingly as replacements for the basic LAN types in applications that demand very high network throughputs. A LAN is normally managed by the organization that has installed it.

Metropolitan area networks or MANs: these are used to interconnect a set of LANs that are physically distributed around a town or city. The geographical scope of MANs is similar to or greater than that of high-speed LANs. Normally, such networks are installed and managed by a public carrier and have been designed from the outset to be compatible in operation with the next generation of public networks.

Wide area networks or WANs: these are used to enable computers that are physically distributed over a wide geographical area such as a country to communicate with one another. There are two types of such networks: private networks and public networks. Private networks are used when all the computers belong to the same enterprise and there is a requirement to transfer substantial amounts of data between the various sites that make up the enterprise. Typically, there is a (private) switching system at each site and these are interconnected by digital circuits leased from one or more public carriers. They are also known as enterprise networks since they normally incorporate all enterprise-wide data and voice communications. They are installed and managed by the one enterprise.

For the interconnection of computers that belong to different enterprises, public-carrier networks must normally be used. These include the (analog) public switched telephone network (PSTN) with modems, public switched data networks (PSDNs), and integrated services digital networks (ISDNs). Public WANs are thus managed by one or more public carriers.

Internetworks or internets: in the early days of wide-area computer networking, all the (host) computers were connected directly to the wide area network termination equipment. More recently, however, with the widespread installation of LANs at most sites, the computers are now attached to their site LAN and hence computer-to-computer communication often involves communication across multiple networks, for example LAN–WAN–LAN. The device used to interconnect two networks together is known as a gateway or, in ISO terminology, an intermediate system. The total interconnected network is then known as an internetwork or internet. Their management may involve both private and public authorities depending on the ownership of each constituent network.

Standards Evolution

The various international bodies concerned with public-carrier networks have for many years formulated internationally agreed standards for connecting devices to these networks. The V-series recommendations, for example, are concerned with the connection of data terminal equipment (DTE) to a modem connected to the PSTN; the X-series recommendations for connecting a DTE to a public data network; and the I-series recommendations for connecting a DTE to the ISDNs. The recommendations have resulted in compatibility between the equipment from different vendors, enabling a purchaser to select suitable equipment from a range of manufacturers. The resulting system is then known as an open system or, more completely, as an open system interconnection environment (OSIE).

In the mid 1970s, as different types of distributed systems (based on both public and private data networks) started to proliferate, the potential advantages of open systems were acknowledged by the computer industry. As a result, a range of standards started to be introduced. The first was concerned with the overall structure of the complete communication subsystem within each computer. This was produced by the International Standards Organization (ISO) and is known as the ISO Reference Model for Open Systems Interconnection (OSI).

The aim of the ISO Reference Model is to provide a framework for the coordination of standards development and to allow existing and evolving standards activities to be set within a common framework. The aim is to allow an application process in any computer that supports a particular set of standards to communicate freely with an application process in any other computer that supports the same standards to carry out a particular (distributed) information processing task.

The logical structure of the ISO Reference Model is made up of seven protocol layers, as shown in Figure 2.1. The three lowest layers (1–3) are network-dependent and are concerned with the protocols associated with the data communication network being used to link the two communicating computers. In contrast, the three upper layers (5–7) are application-oriented and are concerned with the protocols that allow two end user application processes to interact with each other, normally through a range of services offered by the local operating system. The intermediate transport layer (4) masks the upper application-oriented layers from the detailed operation of the lower network-dependent layers. Essentially, it builds on the services provided by the latter to provide the application-oriented layers with a network-independent message interchange service.

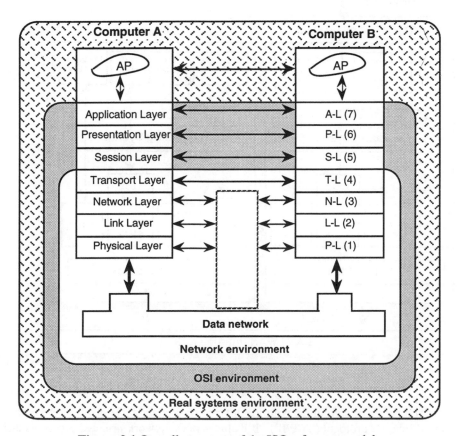

Figure 2.1 Overall structure of the ISO reference model.

The three major international bodies actively producing standards for computer communications are the ISO, the American Institution of Electrical and Electronic Engineers (IEEE) and the International Telecommunications Union (ITU). Essentially, ISO and IEEE produce standards for use by computer manufacturers while the ITU defines standards for connecting equipment to the different types of national and international public networks. As the degree of overlap between the computer and telecommunications industries increases, however, there is an increasing level of cooperation and commonalty between the standards produced by these organizations.

In addition, prior to and concurrently with ISO standards activity, the United States Department of Defense has for many years funded research into computer communications and networking through its Defense Advanced Research Projects Agency (DARPA). As part of this research, the computer networks associated with a large number of universities and other research establishments were linked to those of DARPA. The resulting internetwork, known as ARPANET, has recently been extended to incorporate internets developed by other government agencies.

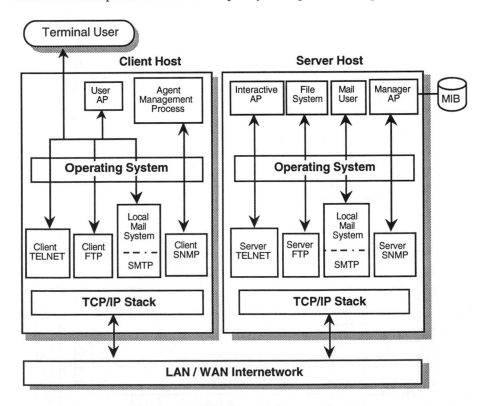

Figure 2.2 TCP/IP application protocols.

The protocol suite used with the Internet is known as Transmission Control Protocol/Internet Protocol (TCP/IP). It includes both network-oriented protocols and application-support protocols. Because TCP/IP has been in widespread use with an existing internet, many of the TCP/IP protocols have been used as the basis for ISO standards. Moreover, since all the protocol specifications associated with TCP/IP are in the public domain – and hence no license fees are payable for their use – they have been used extensively by commercial and public authorities for creating open system networking environments. In practice, therefore, there are two major open system (vendor-independent) standards: the TCP/IP protocol suite and those based on the evolving ISO standards.

Figure 2.2 shows some of the standards associated with the TCP/IP protocol suite. As can be seen, since TCP/IP has developed concurrently with the ISO initiative, it does not contain specific protocols relating to all the ISO layers. Moreover, the specification methodology used for the TCP/IP protocols differs from that used for the ISO standards. Nevertheless, most of the functionality associated with the ISO layers is embedded in the TCP/IP suite.

In the case of ISO/CCITT standards, as can be seen in Figure 2.3, there is a range of protocols associated with each layer. Collectively they enable the administrative authority that is establishing the open system environment to select the most suitable set of standards for the application.

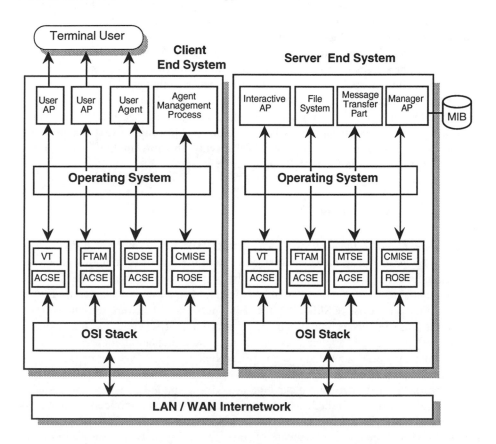

Figure 2.3 OSI application protocols.

As can been seen in the figures, in addition to a range of user application protocols – TELNET/VT for remote terminal interaction, FTP/FTAM for the control of interactions with a remote file system, and SMTP/MTSE for the submission and delivery of electronic mail – each protocol suite includes an application protocol that is concerned with network management. In the TCP/IP suite this is known as the simple network management protocol (SNMP) and in the OSI suite the common management information service element (CMISE). Each of these protocols has been defined to enable management-related information to be downloaded to and retrieved from an (agent) management process running in a computer or item of networking equipment, using the corresponding protocol stack. Typically, such transfers relate to the retrieval of performance data, the downloading of operational parameter settings, or the reporting of suspected fault conditions. In the case of transfers relating to performance or operational data, these are initiated by a manager application process (AP) running in a dedicated management computer, while fault reports are normally reported directly to the manager AP by the agent management process running in the computer or item of networking equipment where the fault is detected.

It should be noted that the two management protocols, SNMP and CMISE, only provide the means whereby management-related information can be transferred in an open way. The meaning of this information and the actions to be taken on its receipt are functions of the two communicating management processes. It can be concluded from this, therefore, that the manager AP and the collection of agent management processes perform a distributed application function in a similar way to any other distributed application – file transfer, electronic mail etc. Hence in the same way that it is necessary to define the structure of the information that is being transferred in relation to, say, a file transfer application, so it is necessary to define the structure of the information that is being transferred in relation to a management application and also to what it relates. Collectively, this information is held in the management information base (MIB) shown in the figures.

2.2   Local area networks

As LANs evolved in the late 1970s and early 1980s, some major initiatives were launched by various national standards bodies with the aim of formulating an agreed set of standards for LANs. The major contributor to this activity was the IEEE which formulated the IEEE 802 series of standards which have now been adopted by ISO as international standards. CSMA/CD bus (Ethernet) and token ring are currently in widespread use in the technical and office environment whereas the token bus is widely used in industrial applications such as manufacturing automation.

Most early LAN installations comprised just a single LAN segment to which were attached the distributed community of workstations and associated servers. The number of stations (systems) that can be attached to a single LAN segment, and also its physical length, are limited. Hence as the acceptance and applications of LANs has become widespread, most large LAN installations now comprise multiple linked segments. The three alternative means of interconnecting LANs are shown in Figure 2.4.

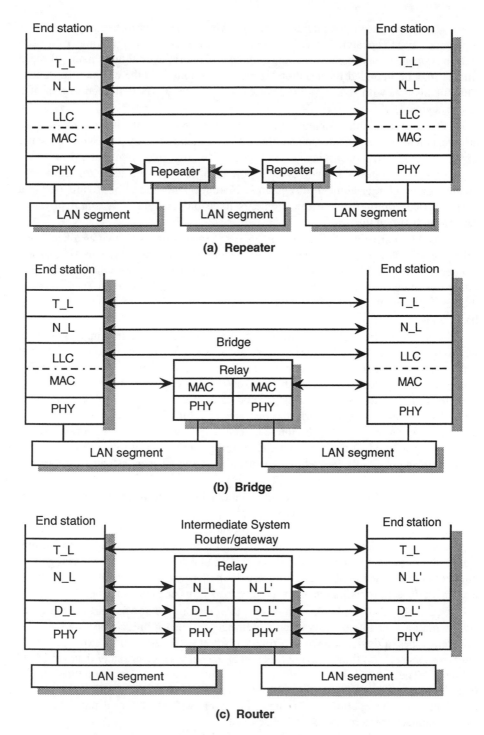

Figure 2.4 LAN interconnection schematics.

The basic means of interconnecting LAN segments is to use physical-layer repeaters. With repeaters, however, the frame transmissions originating from each station propagate (and hence load) the complete network, even though many of these frames may be intended for a station on the same segment as the originating station. This means that with repeaters the total capacity of the LAN is limited to that of a single segment.

To overcome this problem, devices known as bridges have been introduced as an alternative means of interconnecting LAN segments that operate with the same MAC method. A basic bridge interconnects just two segments, but more sophisticated bridges – known as multiport bridges – can be used for the inter-connection of a larger number of segments. Normally, multiport bridges are used in a single office complex when the segments have only a relatively small physical separation between them.

An alternative way of using bridges is to create what is known as a backbone subnetwork. Normally, no end systems (workstations, servers, and so on) are connected to a backbone and they are used solely for inter-segment traffic. For interconnecting only a small number of segments in a single building, backbones of the same type as the interconnected segments are used. They are known as building backbones.

As the number of interconnected segments increases, there comes a point at which the transmission capacity required by the backbone to meet the inter-segment traffic starts to exceed that available with the basic LAN types. To overcome this problem, backbones based on the higher-speed LAN types are used. The standard used for this function is the fiber distributed data interface (FDDI) LAN. This is an optical fiber-based ring network that operates at a bit rate in excess of 100 Mbps. Moreover, it can be used for the interconnection of segments that are spread over a wider geographical area than a single building, such as a university campus or manufacturing plant. The resulting network is then known as an establishment or site backbone.

The three LAN types mentioned in the last section each use a different maximum frame size. A serious problem can arise if a frame is first transmitted on, say, a token ring segment but is to be subsequently forwarded on a CSMA/CD segment since the latter uses a smaller maximum frame size. Assuming maximum frame sizes are being used, the only way this can be overcome is for the bridge that connects the two segments together to divide the larger frame into smaller subunits, each with the same destination and source addresses, prior to transmission.

Although this can be done in theory, this function – known as segmentation or fragmentation – is not normally offered in bridges. Thus for interconnecting LANs of different types, a device known as a router is often used. As will be expanded upon later, routers perform their relaying function at the network layer rather than the MAC sublayer. The network layer, in addition to routing, also performs segmentation and hence routers are normally used for the interconnection of LANs of different types. A description of the operation of routers, however, will be deferred until the more general subject of internetworking is discussed.

2.2.1   CSMA/CD Ethernet

The CSMA/CD standard is defined in IEEE 802.3. The general interconnection structures are shown in Figure 2.5. For historical reasons a CSMA/CD bus network is also known as **Ethernet**. Normally, it is implemented as a 10 Mbps baseband coaxial cable network although other cable media are supported in the standards documents. These include twisted pair and optical fiber, these being in the form of drop cables from a central hub.

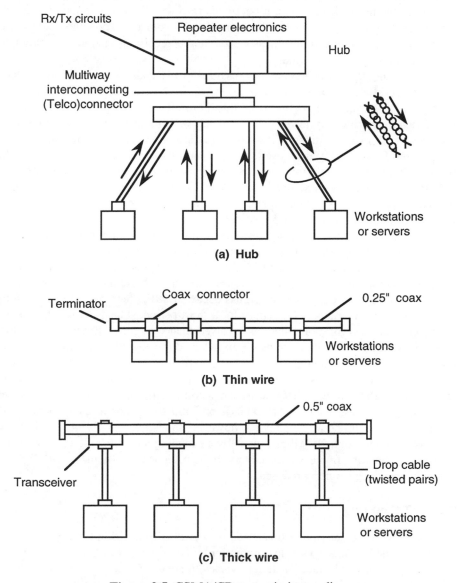

Figure 2.5 CSMA/CD transmission media.

Although different media are used, they all operate using the same medium access control (MAC) method. All the stations are connected directly to the same cable which is used, therefore, for transmitting all data between stations. The cable is thus said to operate in a **multiple access (MA) mode**. All data is transmitted by the sending station first encapsulating the data in a frame with the required destination address at the head of the frame. The frame is then transmitted on the cable. All stations connected to the cable detect when a frame is being transmitted and, when the required destination detects that the frame currently being transmitted has its own address at the head of the frame, it continues reading the data contained within the frame and responds according to the defined link protocol. The source address is included as part of the frame header so that the receiving station can direct its response to the originating station.

With this style of operation, it is possible for two stations to attempt to transmit a frame over the cable at the same time, causing the data from both sources to be corrupted. To reduce the possibility of this, before transmitting a frame, the source first **listens** electronically to the cable to detect whether a frame is currently being transmitted. If a **carrier** signal is **sensed (CS)**, the station defers its transmission until the passing frame has been transmitted, and only then does it attempt to send the frame. Even so, two stations wishing to transmit a frame may simultaneously determine that there is no activity (transmission) on the bus and hence both start to transmit their frames simultaneously. A **collision** is then said to occur since the contents of both frames will collide and hence be corrupted.

To allow for this possibility, a station simultaneously monitors the data signal on the cable when transmitting the contents of a frame on to the cable. If the transmitted and monitored signals are different, a collision is assumed to have occurred – **collision detected (CD)**. To ensure that the other station(s) involved in the collision is (are) aware that a collision has occurred, it first enforces the collision by continuing to send a random bit pattern for a short period. This is known as the jam sequence. The two (or more) stations involved then wait for a further short random time interval before trying to retransmit the affected frames. Should a collision occur a second time, a third attempt is made but this time after waiting for a longer time period. If necessary, this procedure repeats until a defined maximum number of retries has been reached, when the transmission attempt is abandoned. It can be concluded that access to a CSMA/CD bus is probabilistic and depends on the network (cable) loading. It should be stressed, however, that since the bit rate used on the cable is relatively high (10 Mbps), the network loading tends to be low. Also, since the transmission of a frame is initiated only if the cable is inactive, the probability of a collision occurring is further reduced.

2.2.2   Token ring

The principle of operation of a token ring network is illustrated in Figure 2.6. When the ring is first initialized a single (permission) token is generated that controls access to the ring. Then, whenever a station wishes to send a frame, it first waits for the token. On receipt of the token, it initiates transmission of the frame, which includes the address of the intended recipient at its head. The frame is repeated by all stations in the ring until it circulates back to the initiating station where it is removed. In addition to repeating the frame, however, the intended recipient retains a copy of the frame and indicates that it has done this by setting a pair of response bits at the tail of the frame.

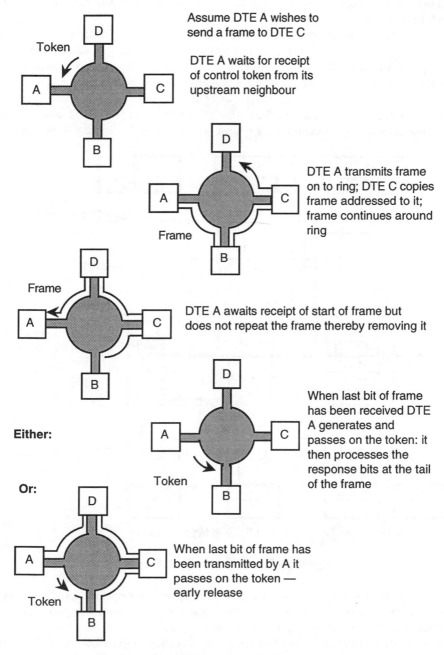

Figure 2.6 Token ring token passing alternatives.

A station releases the token in one of two ways depending on the bit rate (speed) of the ring. With slower rings (4 Mbps), the token is released only after the response bits have been received. With higher speed rings (16 Mbps), it is released after transmitting the last bit of a frame. This is known as early (token) release. The (trunk) cable medium is typically screened twisted-pair which is differentially driven at a bit rate of either 4 or 16 Mbps.

As shown in Figure 2.7, a station can be connected directly to the ring or through a concentrator. This device connects directly to the main trunk cable and, in turn, provides direct drop connections to a number of stations. A **concentrator** is often used to simplify the wiring within a building. Typically, it is located at the point where the trunk cable enters (and leaves) an office. Direct drop connections are then used to connect each station in the office to the concentrator. It is also known, therefore, as a wiring concentrator; a typical installation may use many such devices.

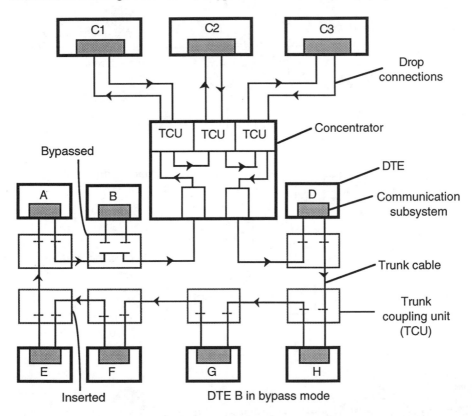

Figure 2.7 Token ring wiring schematic.

Unlike CSMA/CD, the frames to be transmitted can be prioritized; the higher the priority associated with a frame, the sooner it will be transmitted. This is accomplished by assigning a priority to the token and a station can only transmit a waiting frame if its priority is equal to or greater than that in the token. In addition, in the header of the token – and also normal information frames – is a field that allows stations to request that the priority of the token is lowered when it is next released by the current owner. In this way, each time the token is released, it will always have a priority equal to the highest priority associated with any waiting frame.

2.2.3 Token bus

The basic operation of a token bus network is shown in Figure 2.8. All stations that can initiate the transmission of a frame are first linked in the form of a **logical ring**. A single control token is then generated and this is passed around the ring using the bus as the transport means. On receipt of the token from its predecessor (upstream neighbor) on the ring, a station can transmit any waiting frames up to a defined maximum. It then passes on the token to its known successor (downstream neighbor) on the ring. As can be deduced from this, each station need only know the address of the next (downstream neighbor) station in the logical ring.

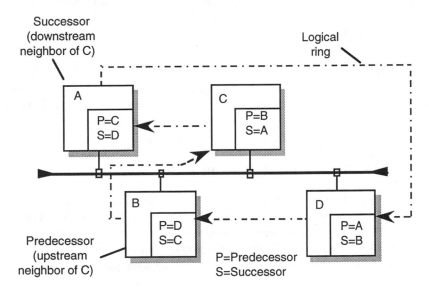

Figure 2.8 Token bus schematic.

After a station passes on the token to its neighbor, it monitors the transmission medium for a further short time interval to ensure the neighbor station initiates the transmission of a frame. Clearly, this can be either the token if it has nothing waiting to send, or an information frame if it has. If nothing is detected, however, the station uses a series of recovery procedures to find a new successor. These procedures get progressively more drastic if the station fails to evoke a response from a neighboring station. Other procedures are concerned with the initialization of the ring and maintaining its correct operation as stations enter and leave the ring.

As with a token ring, it is possible for frames to have a priority value associated with them. With a token bus, however, the order of transmission of frames is accomplished by each station maintaining three timers rather than the token having a priority associated with it. The first two are the token hold timer (THT) and the high priority token hold timer (HP–THT). When a station receives the token, it first sends any high-priority frames it has waiting up to a maximum determined by the HP-THT. Then, providing the THT has not expired, the station begins to transmit any waiting lower priority frames.

The third timer is known as the token rotation timer (TRT) and indicates the time that has expired since the station last received the token. When the station next receives the token, it first transfers the current value in the TRT into the THT and resets the contents of the TRT to zero. It then transmits any waiting high-priority frames, increasing the TRT at the same time, and computes the difference between a fixed time known as the target token rotation time (TTRT) and its current THT. If the difference is positive, the station can send any waiting lower priority frames until the TTRT is reached; if the difference is zero or negative, the station cannot send any lower priority frames on this pass of the token. Each station can transmit any waiting frames working from higher to lower priority until the TTRT is reached.

2.2.4   Protocols

The various protocol standards for LANs are defined in IEEE Standard 802. This standard defines a family of protocols each relating to a particular type of medium access control method. The three medium access control (MAC) standards discussed so far, together with their associated physical media specifications, are defined in:

IEEE 802.3/ISO 8802.3:	CSMA/CD bus,
IEEE 802.4/ISO 8802.4:	Token bus,
IEEE 802.5/ISO 8802.5:	Token ring.

In the context of the ISO Reference Model the MAC and logical link control (LLC) sublayers collectively perform the functions of the data link control layer. The functions of the latter are framing – signaling the start and end of each frame – and error detection; also, for a reliable (connection-oriented) service, error control, flow control and link management. Thus the MAC sublayer performs the framing and error detection functions, together with the medium access control function, while the LLC sublayer performs the remaining functions.

The descriptions of the three LAN types presented earlier relate only to the MAC sublayer. Although each is different in its internal operation, they all present a standard set of services to the LLC sublayer. The latter is thus used with any of the underlying MAC standards.

2.2.5   FDDI

The FDDI LAN standard is defined in ISO 9314. It uses a ring topology and operates with a token medium access control method. The physical interface to an FDDI ring, however, is different from the basic token ring. In a basic token ring network, at any instant there is a single active ring monitor which, amongst other things, supplies the master clock for the ring. Each circulating bit stream is encoded by the active monitor using differential Manchester encoding. All the other stations in the ring then frequency and phase lock to the clock extracted from this bit stream.

Such an approach with FDDI would require a baud rate of 200 M baud. Instead, therefore, each ring interface has its own local clock. Outgoing data is then transmitted using this clock while incoming data is received using a clock that is frequency and phase locked to the transitions in the incoming bit stream. To ensure adequate transitions are present in the bit stream, all data to be transmitted is first encoded using a 4-of-5 group code. This means that for each four bits of data to be transmitted, a corresponding five-bit codeword or symbol is generated by the encoder. The latter is thus known as a 4B/5B encoder.

The use of five bits to represent each of the 16 four-bit data groups means that there are a further 16 unused combinations of the five bits. Some of these combinations (symbols) are thus used for other (link) control functions, such as indicating the start and end of each frame or token. With the basic token ring, there is only a single bit delay in each station interface. This means the total ring has only a small latency – number of bits – associated with it and hence a new token is only transmitted after the last bit of a transmitted frame has circulated around the ring. With an FDDI ring, however, the use of 4B/5B encoding means that each ring interface must provide a pair of 5 bit buffers, one for encoding and the other for decoding. The latency of an FDDI ring, therefore, is much larger and hence to improve the utilization of the ring capacity, a station initiates the transmission of a new token immediately after it has transmitted the last bit of a frame. Also, because of this mode of operation, an FDDI ring uses the same priority method as a token bus rather than that used with a token ring.

2.2.6 Bridges

The function of a bridge is similar to a repeater in so much as it is used for interconnecting LAN segments. When bridges are used, however, all frames received from a segment are buffered and error checked before they are forwarded. Moreover, only frames that are free of errors and addressed to stations on a different segment from the one on which they were received are forwarded. Consequently, transmissions between stations connected to the same segment are not forwarded and hence do not load the rest of the network. A bridge thus operates at the MAC sublayer in the context of the ISO Reference Model. The resulting LAN is then known as a bridged LAN.

The two types of bridge that feature in the standards documents are transparent (also known as spanning-tree) bridges and source routing bridges, the main difference between them being how frames are routed. With transparent bridges, the bridges themselves make all routing decisions while with source routing bridges, the end stations perform the major route-finding function. The standard relating to transparent bridges is IEEE 802.1 (D) and source routing forms a part of the IEEE 802.5 token ring standard.

With a transparent bridge, as with a repeater, the presence of one (or more) bridges in a route between two communicating stations is transparent to the two stations. All routing decisions are made exclusively by the bridge(s). Moreover, a transparent bridge automatically initializes and configures itself (in terms of its routing information) in a dynamic way after it has been put into service. Each bridge maintains a forwarding database that indicates, for each port, the outgoing port (if any) to be used for forwarding each frame received at that port. Then, if a frame is received at a port that is addressed to a station on the segment (and hence port) on which it was received, it is discarded; otherwise it is forwarded via the port specified in the forwarding database. This process is known as filtering and a schematic of a bridge is shown in Figure 2.9.

When a bridge first comes into service, its forwarding database is initialized to empty. Then, whenever a frame is received, the source address within it is read and the port number on which the frame was received is entered into the forwarding database. In addition, since the forwarding port is not known at this time, a copy of the frame is forwarded on all the other ports of the bridge. During the learning phase, this procedure will be repeated for each frame received by the bridge. In this way, all bridges in the LAN rapidly build up the contents of their forwarding databases.

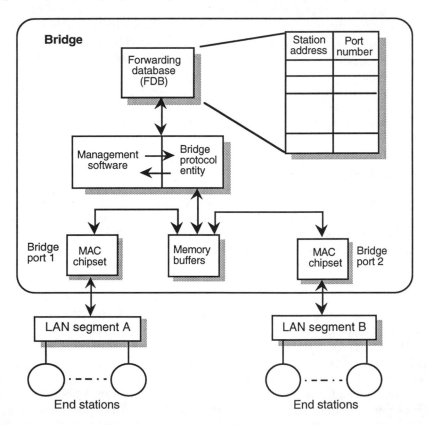

Figure 2.9 Bridge architecture.

The MAC address associated with a station is fixed at the time of its manufacture. Hence, if a user changes the point of attachment to the network of his or her workstation, the contents of the forwarding database in each bridge are periodically updated to reflect such changes. To accomplish this, an inactivity timer is associated with each entry in the database and, if this expires, the entry is removed and the learning procedure repeated when the station next becomes active.

The learning process will only work if the total bridged LAN has a simple (spanning) tree topology since, if multiple paths between two segments exist, frames will continuously circulate in a loop with the entries for each port being continuously updated. To allow for this possibility, all the bridges participate in identifying possible loops and setting selected ports into the blocked (non-forwarding) state to ensure an active tree topology. This is known as the **spanning-tree algorithm** and involves all the bridges regularly exchanging bridge protocol data units (BPDUs) first to establish a single root bridge and then a single bridge (port) for forwarding frames from each segment. After the spanning-tree algorithm has been run, all bridge ports are either root ports or designated ports – in which case they are set into the forwarding state – or they are set into the blocked state.

With **source routing**, a station ascertains the route to be followed by a frame to a required destination station before any frames are transmitted. This information is inserted at the head of the frame and is used by each bridge to determine whether a received frame is to be forwarded on to another segment or not. The routing information comprises a sequence of segment-bridge identifiers. Thus on receipt of each frame, a bridge needs only to search the routing field at the head of the frame for its own identifier and only if it is present and followed by the identifier of a segment connected to one of its ports does it forward the frame. The routing information field contained within each frame immediately follows the source address field at the head of the normal (IEEE 802.5) information frame.

To find a route, a station first creates and transmits a single-route broadcast frame. On receipt of this, a bridge simply broadcasts a copy of the frame on each of the segments connected to its other ports. Since this procedure is repeated by each bridge in the LAN, a copy of the frame will propagate throughout the LAN and thus will be received by the intended destination station. As with transparent bridges, however, if there are redundant bridges (and hence loops) in the LAN topology, multiple copies of the frame will propagate around the LAN. To prevent this, therefore, before any route-finding frames are sent, the bridge ports are configured to give a spanning-tree active topology. On the surface, this may appear to be the same procedure used with transparent bridges. With source routing bridges, however, the resulting spanning-tree active topology is used only for routing the initial single-route broadcast frames.

On receipt of a single-route broadcast frame, the destination station returns an all-routes broadcast frame to the originating station. Unlike the single-route broadcast, however, this frame is not constrained to follow the spanning tree. Instead, on receipt of such frames, the bridge simply adds a new route designator (comprising the segment identifier on which the frame was received and its own bridge identifier) to the existing routing information, and then broadcasts a copy of this on each of its other ports, providing the incoming and outgoing ports are not already present. If they are, this indicates a copy of the frame is circulating in a loop and hence is discarded.

In this way, one or more copies of the frame will be received by the originating source station via all the possible routes between itself and the required destination station. By examining the routes in each frame, the source station can select the best route to be used for transmitting a frame to that destination. This is then entered into its routing table and is used subsequently for transmitting any frames to that station. Thus a route to a given destination need only be determined once. Moreover, since most stations transmit the majority of their frames to a limited number of destinations, the number of route-finding frames is relatively small compared with normal information frames.

2.2.7   Remote bridges

Many large corporations have sites (and hence LANs) distributed around a country or over many countries. In addition to being able to exchange information between stations connected to the same LAN at a single site, therefore, there is also a requirement to exchange information between sites. Clearly this requires a facility for interconnecting the LANs at each site together.

A common solution is to interconnect the LANs by dedicated leased (private) lines. The MAC addresses used in LANs are normally unique across the total network (that is, across all the LANs). Hence it is possible to use the MAC addresses and bridges to provide the routing function. Such bridges are normally connected directly to the site-wide backbone network on one port and to the leased lines(s) on the other. A similar bridge is used at the other end of the leased line. To discriminate between these and the bridges used for the interconnection of the LAN segments at each site, they are known as remote bridges.

In many instances, the leased lines used are part of a much larger, enterprise-wide voice and data network. Hence the leased lines used for LAN interconnection are normally integrated with those used for telephony. The bit rate of the leased lines range from multiples of 56 kbps (64 kbps in Europe) to multiples of 1.544 Mbps (2.048 Mbps in Europe). In general, the reliability of these lines is significantly less than the lines used within a single site. Hence it is normal to have backup paths (lines) in the event of failures.

Although in principle it is possible to implement the spanning-tree algorithm in remote bridges (thus extending the coverage of the spanning tree across the entire network), in practice this is not always done. Normally, the entire enterprise-wide voice and data network has an integral network management facility, one of the main functions of which is to reallocate the available bandwidth to the various voice and data services in the event of failure of a leased line. A common solution, therefore, is for the network manager (via the network) to dynamically assign an alternative line (or channel) in the event of a line failure. Although this may lead to a slight degradation in performance during the reconfiguration period, it often leads to a more efficient usage of the available transmission capacity.

2.3   Metropolitan area networks (MAN)

Although leased lines are often used by large corporations for the interconnection of LANs at different sites, this is only a viable solution providing there is sufficient inter-site traffic to justify the use of dedicated (leased) circuits. Moreover, to ensure a fast response time, the latter must operate at a relatively high bit rate and hence in many instances this is not a suitable solution.

To meet this need, a number of public carriers now provide an alternative means of providing this function. The service is known as **switched multimegabit data service (SMDS)** and is based on a number of interconnected metropolitan area networks. As the name implies, such networks cover an area of a single town or city. As will be described, however, they have been designed to be compatible with the next generation of wide area networks. These are known as **broadband integrated services digital networks (B-ISDN)** or, because of their mode of operation, **asynchronous transfer mode (ATM)** networks.

A MAN provides a means for communication between LANs located within the same town or city. MANs are interconnected by high-speed digital circuits to provide the means for communication nationwide or beyond. The standard for use as a MAN is known as **distributed-queue, dual-bus** or **DQDB**. It is defined in IEEE 802.6 ATM networks have been developed not just to transmit voice (for telephony) and data, but also other types of media such as photographic quality images and moving images (video). To cater for this all media – voice, data, image and video – are first segmented into small fixed-sized cells or packets prior to transmission. This has the advantage that the available network transmission bandwidth can be used more efficiently than in the current rigid transmission hierarchy which has been developed for voice. Consequently, the next generation of wide area networks will operate using cell switching, also known as fast-packet, rather than circuit switching as is currently used. DQDB networks have been developed to be compatible with such networks.

DQDB is a multiple-access, broadcast bus similar in principle to a CSMA/CD bus. The digital circuits used to implement the bus, however, are unidirectional. Hence, in order to broadcast data, the bus is implemented in the form of two undirectional buses each comprised of a series of point-to-point segments as shown in Figure 2.10. The two buses pass data in opposite directions and hence broadcasting data involves transmitting it on both buses.

Each bus carries a continuous stream of fixed-sized slots, each the same size as a cell in an ATM network, that are generated by the corresponding slot generator. Each access control unit (ACU) simply reads each bit at its input port and repeats it one bit cell later on the corresponding output port. The slots traveling in each direction, therefore, can be considered as containers on a conveyor belt and the access control method used is based on a distributed queuing algorithm known as **queued-packet, distributed-switch (QPSX)**.

Each slot contains two bits at its head which are used in the distributed queuing algorithm: a busy or B bit and a request or R bit. A cell is then transmitted between two ACUs by the sending ACU writing it into a free slot on each of the two buses. Access to the slots on each bus is controlled by a separate request counter, one for each bus. Requests for slots on one bus are made using the R bit in slots on the other bus. Then, for each counter, whenever a slot passes with the R bit set, the contents of the corresponding counter are incremented by one. Similarly, whenever an empty slot is repeated at the interface with the opposite bus, the counter is decremented by one.

At any point in time, therefore, the request counter for each bus contains the number of outstanding requests for slots from ACUs that are downstream of the ACU on the particular bus.

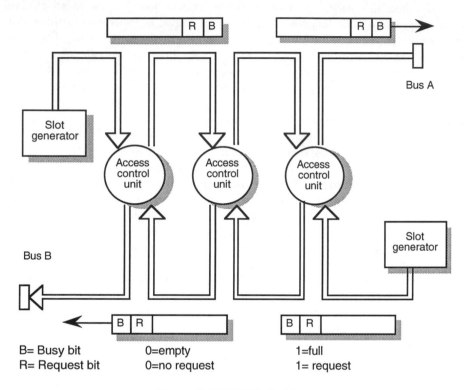

B= Busy bit   0=empty   1=full
R= Request bit   0=no request   1= request

Figure 2.10 DQDB dual bus.

To transmit a cell, the sending ACU first sets the R bit in the first slot that is repeated at each bus interface that has a zero R bit. It then transfers the current contents of the request counter for the required bus to a second counter – one for each bus – known as the countdown counter, at the same time resetting the contents of the request counter to zero. This has the effect of placing the waiting cell in the distributed queue for the two buses.

While a cell is queued for the buses, any slots that are repeated at each bus interface with their R bit set cause the appropriate request counter to be incremented as before. Slots repeated on the opposite bus with their B bit reset, however, now only cause the countdown counter for that bus to be decremented. The waiting cell is then transmitted on each bus when the related countdown counter becomes zero.

The slotted bus structure has the property that it maintains an almost constant (and very low) access delay. Also, a variable priority scheme can be used for the transmission of both asynchronous and delay sensitive data. This is controlled by the use of a separate pair of request and countdown counters, one for each priority class. In addition, for the transmission of (constant bit rate) voice traffic, slots are preallocated by the head of bus for this purpose.

Typically, each LAN is connected to the bus by means of a bridge. The forwarding (relaying) software associated with the bridge, however, is unaware of each frame being segmented into cells by the source ACU and subsequently reassembled by the receiving ACUs during its transfer across the bus. A DQDB bus is thus viewed simply as a broadcast bus similar in principle to a high-speed CSMA/CD bus. To broadcast a frame, the complete frame, including the destination and source MAC addresses and its CRC, is first segmented into a sequence of cells each with a standard ATM header. The complete set of cells is then broadcast by the source ACU (one after the other) to all the other ACUs attached to the (dual) bus.

Since the sending ACU cannot determine the position of the required destination ACU on the bus from the destination MAC address, it initiates the transmission of the complete set of cells on both buses using the broadcast access control mechanism described earlier. All the cells relating to the same frame carry two fields in their header: the first indicating the cell type in relation to the total frame – first, intermediate or last – and the second a message identifier field that enables the receiving ACUs to relate each cell to the same frame. Since multiple frames can be in transit across the bus concurrently, each ACU is allocated a different (unique) set of identifiers.

As each cell relating to a frame is received (and repeated) by an ACU, it proceeds to reassemble them into a complete frame. It then passes the frame to its local bridge which determines from the destination MAC address at the head of the frame whether it should be forwarded onto its local LAN or discarded. If any of the cells relating to a frame are found to have errors, from the additional CRC appended to the tail of each cell by the source ACU, the frame is simply discarded by the receiving ACU. It is then left to the two communicating LAN stations to determine (and recover from) the loss of the frame.

2.4   Wide area networks

The majority of data-only wide area networks operate using packet-switching principles and are known as **packet-switched data networks (PSDNs)**. In addition, a range of data services are available with the emerging ISDNs. These include two additional frame-based data services, one known as frame relay and the other as frame switching. Each will be considered separately.

2.4.1   Packet-switched networks

The international standard access protocol X.25 has been defined to interface an item of equipment (known as a DTE) to a PSDN. In practice, X.25 is a set of three protocols as shown in Figure 2.11. As can be seen, the three protocols that make up X.25 have only local significance in contrast to the transport layer which operates on an end-to-end basis.

The physical interface between the DTE and the local PTT-supplied **data circuit terminating equipment (DCE)** is defined in recommendation X.21. The DCE plays an analogous role to a synchronous modem since its function is to provide a full-duplex, bit-serial, synchronous transmission path between the DTE and the local packet switching exchange (PSE). Note also that a second standard known as X.21 (bis) has been defined for use with existing (analog) networks. This is a subset of RS.232C/V.24 thus enabling equipment that has such an interface to be more readily used.

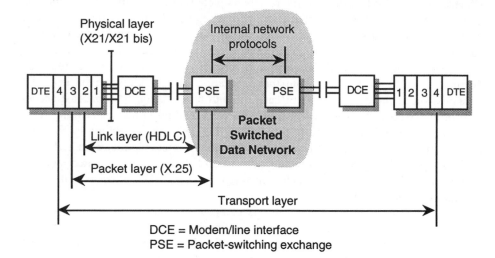

Figure 2.11 X.25 network access protocol.

The frame structure and error and flow control procedures used by the link layer are based on the HDLC protocol. It uses the asynchronous balanced mode (ABM) of operation and is referred to as LAPB in the X.25 standard. Its aim is to provide the packet (network) layer with a reliable (error free and no duplicates) packet transport facility across the physical link between the DTE and the PSE. There can be multiple packet layer calls – known as virtual calls/circuits – in progress concurrently over this link but the link layer has no knowledge of the call to which a packet relates

For historical reasons, the X.25 network layer is normally referred to as the packet layer. It is concerned with the reliable transfer of transport layer messages – transport protocol data units (TPDUs) – and with the multiplexing of one or more virtual calls onto the single physical link controlled by the link layer. Each virtual call is assigned a separate network service access point (NSAP) address since normally each involves a different destination.

A virtual call involves a logical circuit or path being established (set up) across the network and a corresponding virtual call (circuit) identifier (VCI) assigned to the call on each inter-exchange link within the network. All subsequent data packets associated with this call are then assigned the same VCIs on the corresponding links and it is thus the VCI carried in each packet that is used to perform the routing operation. Also, since HDLC is used as the packet transport mechanism, the packet layer protocol is concerned mainly with flow control over the local DTE/PSE link. The flow control algorithm used is based on a sliding window mechanism and the flow of packets is controlled separately for each virtual call and for each direction of flow. The main error recovery mechanisms are the reset and restart procedures. Both procedures are used only during the data transfer phase; the reset procedure affects just a single virtual call while the restart procedure affects all virtual calls currently in progress over the link.

2.4.2   Integrated services digital networks (ISDN)

A limited set of standard, multi-purpose user (subscriber) interfaces are available with the ISDN. These include normal telephony services – voice and, with additional equipment, video – data services and a range of additional value-added services known as **teleservices**. The latter include fast (64 kbps) teletex, facsimile and videotex.

A key feature of the ISDN is the logical separation of the signaling channel from the voice and/or data channels. The signaling channel, because it is used for call setup, is said to be part of the control or C plane, while the user channels are said to belong to the user or U plane. The basic user interface provides two 64 kbps channels, known as B channels, and the separate signaling channel, known as the D channel, that operates at 16 kbps. Both circuit-switched and packet-switched services are supported. Also, as indicated earlier, two new frame-level services: frame relay and frame switching.

With both frame-level services a virtual call/circuit, known as a virtual path, is first set up in an analogous way to a virtual circuit through a PSDN. Unlike X.25, however, the multiplexing of multiple calls is handled by the link (frame) layer instead of the packet layer. Frame switching then uses error and flow control procedures with each call while frame relay provides only a simple best-try service. Because of the high quality of service associated with the ISDN, however, frame relay is proving to be the most popular service. It is also finding widespread use in private networks since the lack of error and flow control means that higher link bit rates can be used.

2.4.3   Private networks

A schematic of a typical private network configuration is shown in Figure 2.12. As can be seen, it consists of a linked set of intelligent multiplexers (IMUXs), one per site, interconnected by circuits leased from a PTT or public carrier. Typically, these are high-speed digital circuits of 1.544 Mbps (DS1/T1) or 2.048 Mbps (E1), and form an enterprise-wide backbone network.

Each IMUX has a range of voice and data interfaces to meet the requirements at that site. In the case of voice, these can involve direct links to telephone (or videophone) equipment or, more usually, a higher bit-rate link to a PABX. In the case of data, termination equipment is available for interfacing terminals, LANs or X.25 packet-switching equipment to the IMUX. In this way a private, enterprise-wide, integrated voice and data network is formed that is used for all inter-site communications. Normally the IMUXs can all be managed from a single remote site by transferring management-related information via the network using one of the management standards introduced earlier.

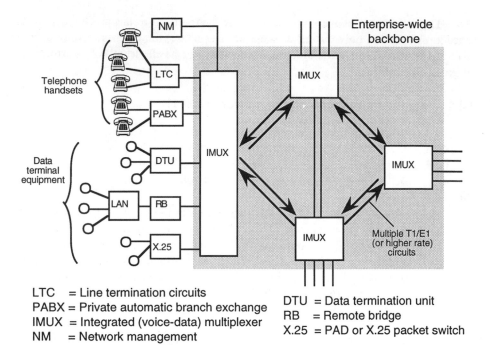

LTC   = Line termination circuits
PABX = Private automatic branch exchange
IMUX = Integrated (voice-data) multiplexer
NM   = Network management

DTU = Data termination unit
RB   = Remote bridge
X.25 = PAD or X.25 packet switch

Figure 2.12 Typical private network.

2.5   Internetworks

As indicated earlier, an internetwork (or internet) is comprised of a number of interconnected networks. Also, when part of an internet, each individual network is often referred to as a subnetwork or subnet. A simple example is a LAN–WAN–LAN although in practice any network type can be involved: CSMA/CD LAN, DQDB MAN, X.25 WAN etc. As may be concluded from the foregoing sections, such networks have different operational characteristics: maximum frame/packet size, network service (connection-oriented/connectionless) etc. It is thus not possible to perform the relaying/routing functions between networks at the data link layer (as with bridges) and instead this must be performed at the network layer. The device used to interconnect two networks/subnets is known variously as a router, a gateway or an intermediate system.

   The simplest approach to internetworking is to utilize the X.25 packet layer protocol (PLP) as the network layer protocol for all networks. To facilitate this, a standard is available for using the X.25 PLP with a LAN. It is defined in ISO 8881. Also, a variant of X.25 known as X.75 has been defined for use in the gateways that link two X.25 networks together. In practice, the gateway used to interconnect two X.25 networks is split into two halves, each half connected to its own network. Each device is thus known as a half gateway or, because its major role is concerned with call setup, a signaling terminal exchange or STE. The two STEs are then connected together by multiple point-to-point data links and a variant of HDLC known as the multi-link protocol or MLP is used to control the transfer of frames across them. A schematic showing the general approach is shown in Figure 2.13.

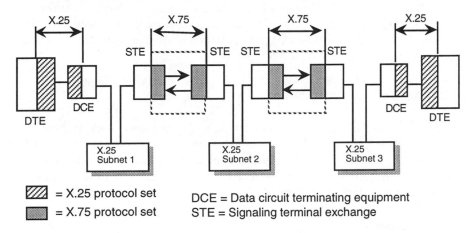

Figure 2.13 X.25 network interconnection and the X.75 protocol.

Although the adoption of X.25 throughout the internet significantly reduces the problems that arise when interconnecting networks that use different network layer protocols, there are also disadvantages with this approach. The high quality of service (QOS) associated with LANs, for example, means that a connection-oriented service like the X.25 PLP is not required. Also, the significantly better QOS associated with the newer MANs and WANs is also resulting in a movement away from X.25 to, for example, frame-based services. For these reasons, therefore, an alternative approach based on an internet-wide connectionless network protocol is also widely used. This is the approach used in the TCP/IP protocol suite, for example, and a similar protocol has also been defined for use with OSI suites. In the first it is known simply as the **internet protocol (IP)** and in the second the **connectionless network protocol (CLNP)**. The remainder of this section is concerned with the major issues relating to them.

2.5.1 Addresses

The address used to identify a user of the network layer in an end system/host is a unique network-wide address which allows that user to be uniquely identified within the total network. For a single network type, this is normally the point-of-attachment (PA) address of the system concatenated with any additional interlayer address selectors. For an internet comprising multiple network types, however, the syntax of the PA address of systems will differ from one network to another and hence it is not possible to use this as the internet-wide network address. Instead, therefore, with an internet, a completely different set of addresses is used to identify each network service (NS) user. In a TCP/IP suite it is known as the **IP address** while in an OSI suite it is known as the **network service access point (NSAP)** address.

Each IP/NSAP address is comprised of two parts: a network identifier and a host/system identifier. The first uniquely identifies the network in relation to the total internet and the second then identifies the host/system on that network. There are thus two addresses associated with each host/system: one its PA address and the second its IP/NSAP address. The first has only local meaning while the second is internet-wide. Also, each gateway/IS has multiple PA addresses – one for each network to which it is attached – but only one IP/NSAP address, which enables management information to be sent directly to it.

2.5.2   Network layer structure

The network layer in each host/end system must provide a standard, internet-wide, network service to its local NS-user(s) – transport layer entities in practice – that masks users from the presence of multiple, possibly different, network types. To achieve this, the network layer in each end system and gateway/IS is comprised of three sublayers as shown in Figure 2.14.

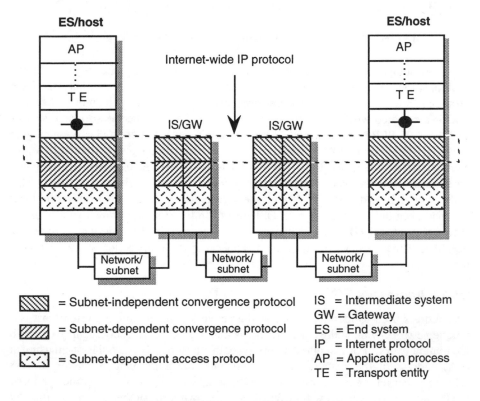

Figure 2.14 Internet-wide IP protocol.

As can be seen, the internet-wide IP protocol is known as the subnet-independent convergence protocol (SNICP). The network layer protocol associated with each network/subnet is then known as the subnet-dependent access protocol (SNDAP) and, because this is different from the IP protocol, a third protocol known as the subnet-dependent convergence protocol (SNDCP) is used to perform the necessary mapping functions between the SNICP and SNDAP.

2.5.3 Routing

When considering routing in an internet two points must be remembered: firstly, a datagram cannot be routed directly by inspecting the destination IP/NSAP address within it and secondly, since each network/subnet may use different point-of-attachment (PA) addresses to route frames/packets – MAC addresses with LANs, X.121 addresses with X.25 WANs, and so on – a system attached to one of these networks can only send a datagram directly to another system if it is also attached to the same network.

In an internet, all routing is performed by the internetwork gateways/ISs. To route datagrams, therefore, the IP in each gateway must know firstly, the PA addresses of all the hosts/end systems that are attached to the networks to which it is also attached and secondly, the PA addresses of the other gateways that are also attached to the same networks. Also, which of these should be used to forward datagrams to reach all other networks in the internet. The two sets of addresses are obtained using two separate protocols. Hosts run just the first protocol while gateways run both protocols.

It should be remembered that a host has only a single PA address while a gateway has multiple PA addresses, one for each network to which it is attached. As part of the first protocol, each host attached to a network broadcasts its own IP/PA address pair and this information is stored by all the gateways that are attached to the same network. In addition, each IS attached to a network broadcasts its own IP/PA address pair for that network which is stored by all the hosts on the network. In this way each host acquires knowledge of the IP/PA address pairs of the gateways that are attached to the same network and each gateway the IP/PA address pairs of all hosts. With non-broadcast networks, the same information must be loaded by network management.

As part of the second protocol, each gateway determines the IP/PA address pairs of the gateway attached to the same network that should be used to route datagrams to all other networks. Hence routing is carried out by a host first sending a datagram to one of its local gateways and the latter forwarding it either to the destination host directly (if it is attached to one of its local networks) or to the next gateway along the route if it is for a remote network.

In a TCP/IP suite the first protocol is known as the **address resolution protocol (ARP)** and in an OSI suite the **end system-to-intermediate system (ES-to-IS) protocol**. The second protocol is known as the interior gateway protocol (IGP) and the IS-to-IS protocol respectively. A number of routing algorithms are used with the latter, the most popular of which are the distance vector algorithm and the shortest path first algorithm.

2.6 Summary

This chapter has identified some of the different network types and items of networking equipment that are currently in use for computer-to-computer communication. Also, their operation and the communication protocols that are associated with them, all of which need to be managed via the network/internetwork using one of the two management protocols introduced earlier – SNMP and CMISE. A typical, albeit simplified, network schematic based on TCP/IP and SNMP is shown in Figure 2.15.

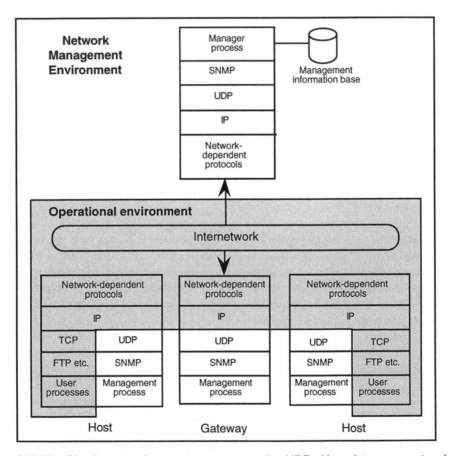

SNMP = Simple network management protocol   UDP= User datagram protocol

Figure 2.15 SNMP network management.

As can be deduced from the figure, there are two types of message transmitted over the network: those containing normal (user) data and those containing management-related information. As indicated earlier, the latter includes:

- *performance data:* packets per second passing through an X.25 PSE, frames per second on a particular bridge port/LAN segment, number of collisions per hour on a CSMA/CD LAN segment etc.

- *operational parameter settings:* retransmission timeouts associated with a protocol layer, window limit with an X.25 protocol, priority of a bridge etc.

- *fault reports:* loss of communication with a neighboring bridge, loss of contact with a neighboring gateway, attempt limit on a LAN segment expiring etc.

In conclusion, it must be stressed that the above arrangement only enables the management-related information to be exchanged in an open way across the network/internetwork and, to achieve full open systems network management, additional standards and functionality are needed above the communications layers.

Abbreviations

ACU	Access Control Unit
ATM	Asynchronous Transfer Mode
B-ISDN	Broadband Integrated Services Digital Network
CMIP	Common Management Information Protocol
CMISE	Common Management Information Service Element
CSMA/CD	Carrier Sense Multiple Access/Collision Detection
DQDB	Distributed Queue Dual Bus
DTE	Data Terminal Equipment
ES	End System
FDDI	Fiber Distributed Data Interface
IS	Intermediate System
ITU	International Telecommunications Union
LAN	Local Area Network
MIB	Management Information Base
NSAP	Network Service Access Point
OSI(E)	Open Systems Interconnection (Environment)
SMDS	Switched Multimegabit Data Service
SNMP	Simple Network Management Protocol
TCP/IP	Transmission Control Protocol/ Internet Protocol
WAN	Wide Area Network

Bibliography and further reading

The material in this chapter has been obtained entirely from the book:

Halsall F. (1992). *Data Communications, Computer Networks and Open Systems* 3rd edn. Addison Wesley.

Chapter 3

Distributed Systems

Jeff Kramer

Department of Computing,
Imperial College, 180 Queen's Gate,
London SW7 2BZ, UK
Email: jk@doc.ic.ac.uk

Distributed processing provides the most general and promising approach for the provision of computer processing. Interconnected workstations are widely used for local processing, to support user communication for interaction and cooperation, and to provide access to shared facilities. Conventional and special-purpose processors are interconnected to support a wide range of applications from chemical plants to cars, from stock market trading to student meal reservations.

Why are distributed systems so attractive? The answers are as multifarious as the applications. The users of computers, the information they require and provide and the applications themselves are often physically distributed. In addition, distributed computing offers advantages in its potential for improving availability and reliability through replication; performance through parallelism; flexibility, incremental expansion and scalability through modularity.

This chapter provides a brief overview of the principles and concepts in distributed systems, and provides some answers to the questions:

What is a distributed system?

How does it provide these advantages?

How can one construct or use such a system?

What are the major issues?

3.1   What is a distributed system?

The major advance towards distributed computing was the provision of standard and reliable serial communication networks, such as those based on the ISO Systems Interconnection Reference Model (described in Chapter 2). This led to the provision of *Networked Systems*. Autonomous computers with independent operating systems are connected to the network. There is no single system master. Interaction between the individual systems is essentially for file transfer, using long-lasting, one-to-one sessions. The interaction is thus more in the form of communication than close cooperation.

   Distributed Systems are essentially an extension of these networked systems. They can also be composed of a number of general-purpose, autonomous processors interconnected by a network. However, the interaction is expected to include close cooperation (Figure 3.1).

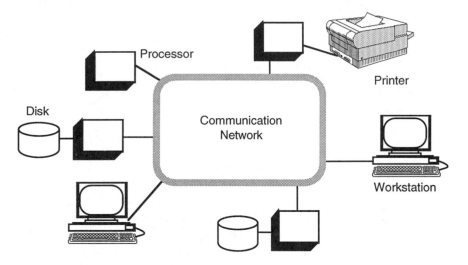

Figure 3.1 A distributed system.

   A more refined definition which emphasizes the cooperative aspect of a distributed system is as follows (Sloman, 1987):

> '*A distributed system is composed of a number of autonomous processors and/or data stores supporting processes and/or data bases which interact in order to cooperate to achieve a common goal. The processes coordinate their activities and exchange information by means of information transferred over a communications network.*'

   There is thus a need for some form of system-wide management and control. Distributed computing is complicated by the fact that interprocess communication is subject to delay and failure. Furthermore, the overall system "state" is partitioned and distributed across its constituent processors and data stores. There is no global coherent view. System management must therefore be capable of making decisions based on partial information.

The potential benefits offered by distributed systems are many. Some seek to exploit the potential for improved availability by the use of replication and the removal of single failure points. Others seek performance gains by improving the response time through local processing and/or the throughput by the use of parallel processing. Distributed systems provide a more general and modular structure for matching the application structure and user needs, and thus also provide the potential for incremental extension as needs arise. This flexibility provides obvious cost benefits. As mentioned, one of the main benefits is the ability to support resource and service sharing. Expensive resources can be accessed across the network and shared among the system users.

The challenge is to provide such benefits in a robust and transparent manner. Transparency is the provision of these shared resources and services such that the user or application programmer is unaware of their provision in a distributed fashion. Terms such as "open" and "loose coupling" are used to denote the ease with which distributed systems should support interconnection and yet maintain the autonomy and independence of their constituent components.

3.2   Distributed applications

One of the largest examples of distributed computing is perhaps that of the public packet-switched network services offered worldwide. The communications system itself is distributed, its components cooperate to provide a common service, and it is controlled by a network management system. Another common use of distributed computing is for process control. For fast response and possible independent operation, processors are placed close to the devices being monitored and/or controlled. These processors are interconnected, often via a master controller, to permit interaction and cooperation in the control of the overall plant.

The most common use of distributed systems is the provision of shared services which are provided transparently by the cooperative effort of local and remote processors. The provision of services by server processors is illustrated by a simple example from office automation. Figure 3.2 gives an outline of such a system in which users access the system services from terminals and workstations. Different services are offered by servers, which provide access to a variety of facilities such as file stores, printer services, powerful mainframe processing, and database services. Some services are provided locally at the site and accessed via a LAN, others at remote sites accessible via a gateway to a WAN.

Users and application programs act as the clients to servers in a client–server relationship. Clients make requests for service and are allocated a server which is relinquished after use. A server may well use the services of other servers in the performance of its function. A name server provides a directory service to the system to enable services to be registered and subsequently found by users and application programs.

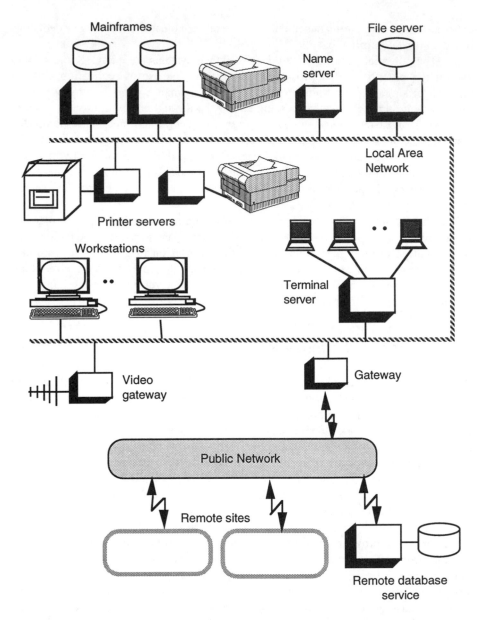

Figure 3.2 A distributed office automation system.

Sharing imposes a number of requirements on the system. Distributed systems management must ensure that it keeps track of what is allocated, to whom and for how long. The system must provide facilities for safe sharing, such as client authentication (the client is who he says he is), access control mechanisms to prevent unauthorized access and resource recovery in case of client monopoly or failure. In addition, protection mechanisms must prevent interference between different clients.

Finally there is the problem of heterogeneity: the need to support and integrate services offered by different vendors using different systems software and hardware. Communication standards (described in the previous chapter) have gone some way to alleviating this problem, but the provision of standard interfaces and interaction formats is still required.

The advantages of the client–server approach and the use of shared services in a distributed system (cost, extensibility, performance, availability) are such that many general computing systems are now provided in this way. For instance, the Athena distributed computer system implemented at MIT provides computing services to around 10 000 users. In 1990 it reportedly (Chanpine *et al.*, 1990) had about 1000 workstations in 40 clusters. It provides file servers (24 remote virtual disk, 10 NFS, and two AFS – Andrew file servers), 79 PostScript printers, three name servers (Hesiod), three post office servers for electronic mail, and two authentication servers (Kerberos). The management system, Moira, provides a centralized management service, keeping track of the hardware and software configuration, allocation, and access control lists.

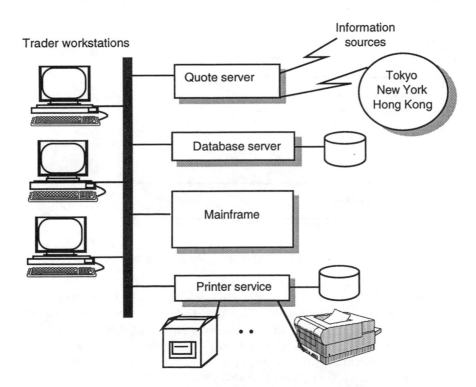

Figure 3.3 A distributed financial trading system.

Another application which provides similar facilities and uses a similar structure is that of financial trading (Massoudi, 1990) (Figure 3.3). In addition to workstations for the traders and conventional office automation services, the system includes specialized services such as a quote server for market prices. This information can be integrated with other information such as Reuters, and must be delivered in a reliable and timely manner.

3.3   Distributed system architecture

The simplest overview of the structure of a distributed system is that of a collection of physically distributed computer nodes fully interconnected by some communications network. Each computer node can perform processing and store data, and may be connected to external devices such as printers, terminals and even to other distributed systems. The communication system is responsible for supporting information communication. The software in a computer can be considered in different layers, each performing a different function (Figure 3.4). We now briefly overview the functions of each layer.

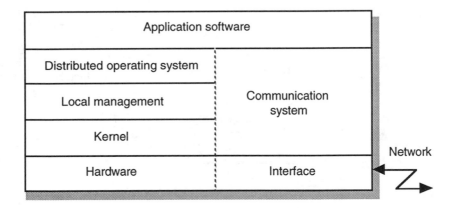

Figure 3.4 Layered software structure in a computer node.

The *application software* consists of the application functions decomposed into distributable processing components. In addition, the data may be distributed by partitioning and/or by replication. Interprocess communication (IPC) is used at this level for information communication and synchronization. The language features available for constructing distributed programs is discussed in Sections 3.4 and 3.5.

The local component of the *distributed operating system* (DOS) provides local access to and management of local and remote services, such as file access and transfer, remote execution, device services (for example, virtual terminal, printing), security services – authentication, encryption, synchronization services for atomic transactions and global scheduling of resource access. It utilizes local management for local services and cooperates with the DOS component of remote nodes to provide access to remote and distributed services. It provides the "open" access required for distribution. One of its primary responsibilities is to coordinate resource usage, providing the resource sharing, protection and recovery mentioned above. Transparency requires coherent and uniform naming and access conventions to permit local and remote resources to be accessed using identical operations and without knowledge of their physical location. For instance, users specify their required service rather than the particular server. DOS components are usually organized as cooperative but autonomous in that they can refuse requests and remain mutually suspicious in order to protect their domain. Finally, as in all operating systems, they must provide support for administration and accounting. We give some examples of DOSs below.

Local management (executive) provides the conventional local resource management, including process management, such as process creation/deletion, stop/start. In addition, the executive provides uniform access to local and remote interprocess communication. Some support programming with concurrent threads (or lightweight processes) in a shared address space. The Kernel is again conventional, providing multitasking (local processor management), local interprocess communication (IPC), memory management and protection and low level I/O and interrupt handling.

The communication system is responsible for transporting messages to/from the computer node. It can provide different services (virtual circuits, datagrams) in addition to routing, addressing, error and flow control.

Although a large number of distributed systems have been constructed and are in use, DOS is an active research topic as there is as yet no agreement as to how it should be structured, organized and managed. For instance, as described above, the Athena distributed system is based on the client–server model. The services are built on and are compatible with the Berkeley UNIX programming and user interface. The workstations act as dataless nodes. The software is loaded and cleared at the start and end of each user session, and the application processing is generally performed on the workstation itself. Hence, although the services are remote (for example, Kerberos) and there are distributed facilities such as the mail service, the processing is generally local.

At a different level, the Mach kernel (Rashid, 1986; Accetta *et al.,* 1986) is designed as a specialized kernel of a DOS to support both tightly coupled and loosely coupled multiprocessors. It provides multiple threads (tasks) in clusters (large virtual address space) with synchronous message-based communication via ports. The kernel is designed to support a variety of programming interfaces, including Berkeley UNIX. The Andrew File System (Morris *et al.,* 1986), also used in Athena, was developed for use with Mach.

Other examples of kernels and DOS facilities include the V kernel – testbed for lightweight processes and IPC experiments (Cheriton, 1988); Amoeba– threads and objects with capabilities for protection (Mullender *et al.,* 1990); Chorus – threads, clusters and ports to provide UNIX-like distributed processing (Rozier and Martinis, 1987) and the Advanced Networked Systems Architecture (ANSA platform – an object-oriented platform for open distributed processing (Oskiewicz *et al.,* 1988, ANSA 1991).

3.4   Language-level software structure

In order to write software that can be distributed and execute concurrently in a distributed environment, we need to be able to produce modular software components that do not share memory but interact by some form of interprocess communication (IPC). In this section we examine the form of these components and set out the requirements for their interconnection.

3.4.1   Software components

The software component is described here as the unit of distribution. In their simplest form, it can be a simple sequential process (for example, Conic tasks (Magee *et al.*, 1989); however, many systems provide for some form of shared data component (cf. cluster) which can contain a number of threads or light-weight processes, for example ARGUS guardians (Liskov, 1992) (Figure 3.5). Note that, if multiple threads/processes do share data in the cluster, it is necessary to provide some means for synchronizing such access, such as semaphores or monitors. The main principle is that the component *encapsulates* some resource in the form of data or devices.

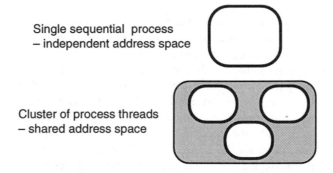

Single sequential process
– independent address space

Cluster of process threads
– shared address space

Figure 3.5 A distributable software component.

3.4.2   Interfaces

Each component provides an interface for interaction with other components and for access to its encapsulated resources. This interface describes the type of the information that can be received or transmitted by the component. In order to provide context-independent components – capable of being used in differing circumstances and interacting with other different components – they should be coded so as not to address any external entity, but rather to receive messages from local entry ports at their interface and to send messages to local exit ports at their interface. The interface thus consists of typed entry and exit ports. This approach is discussed further below in connection with the communication primitives. Furthermore, since the types of information to be communicated are expressed explicitly at the interface, this enables type checking to be performed when binding component interfaces. In heterogeneous environments in which components of different types communicate, data transforms can be invoked. A separate Interface Specification Language (ISL) is thus frequently used as a common language for interface descriptions, including data types of interaction points, for example, Matchmaker (Jones *et al.*, 1985), MLP (Hayes and Schlichting, 1987), IDL (ANSA, 1991) and REX ISL (Kramer *et al.*, 1991). They provide a basic set of primitive data types (boolean, integer, real, char); a set of constructors for building more complex data types (enumeration, arrays, sequences, records); and entry/port/operation signatures for specifying the form of communication and interaction.

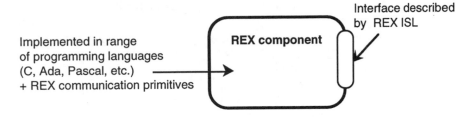

Figure 3.6 A REX primitive software component.

For instance, REX components (Figure 3.6) can be written in different programming languages. The interface is described in terms of entry ports such as

port ((int, int), char –> ()) control;

which describes a component port of an interface that can receive a record of two integers and a character, and replies with a synchronization signal. This is translated into an underlying representation called Assembled ISL (AISL) (Cheung, 1991). The AISL interface descriptor provides the information needed for validating type compatibility when binding interfaces, based on structural type compatibility. The AISL descriptor is also used for transformation of message representations across heterogeneous boundaries and to display message contents when monitoring messages sent from a component. For the port above, the AISL descriptor is

(control,{i,i},c,@())

where c is the representation for char, i for int, r for real, and <null> for a zero-length synchronization signal.

3.4.3   Component instantiation and interconnection

Languages for distributed programming usually provide a means for defining the component as a type (cf. Class) from which instances can be created. A distributed system is then constructed as a structure or configuration of interconnected instances of components. Instances must be mapped (allocated) to the physical structure of interconnected computer nodes. For instance, Figure 3.7 gives a logical configuration and allocation where the *performance* component type has an exit port *data,* the *analyzer* an entry *in* and an exit port *out* and the *reporter* an entry *print*.

Configuration information is often specified in the distributed programming language, or as operating system commands. However, work on the Conic (Kramer and Magee, 1985; Magee *et al.,* 1989) and REX system (Kramer *et al.,* 1992) suggests that there is a benefit in clarity and system management if a separate language (such as that used above) is provided specifically to express configuration structure. In Figure 3.7, a configuration language utilizes the **use** construct for the types of components, **inst** to instantiate component instances from those types, and **bind** to interconnect their interfaces. Component instantiation and interconnection (binding) can take place at compile time, but is more usually performed at configuration time before allocation and also at run time, to provide the greatest flexibility.

use	performance, analyzer, reporter;	{component types}
inst	MONITOR:performance;	
	ANALYZER: analyzer;	
	PRINTER: reporter;	{instances}
bind	MONITOR.data -- ANALYZER.in;	
	ANALYZER.out -- PRINTER.print;	{interconnection}

Logical structure:

Allocation to the physical structure:

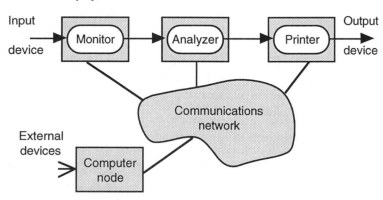

Figure 3.7 A simple system configuration.

3.4.4   Dynamic binding

Client-server binding is usually required to be performed at run time, according to client need. These bindings are based upon service need and availability and are not predefined in a configuration description. Rather, a client needs a binding to a name server or service broker to locate a server providing a particular service. For their part, servers register their interfaces, names, addresses and type/quality of service with the broker. In the example above, the ANALYZER could make a request to the service broker for connection to a printer server. The broker returns the name and address of an available server providing the required print service. The ANALYZER then uses the DOS to bind to the particular printer server before use (Figure 3.8).

Clients and servers thus use the service broker as intermediary to perform run-time binding. For instance, the ANSA platform provides a **trader** (ANSA, 1991) for this purpose. Although this provides a highly flexible form of interconnection, there are obviously execution overheads in registering and deregistering services, and in performing the lookup and dynamic bind operations. Furthermore, the broker may have to be partitioned and distributed to prevent it becoming a bottleneck.

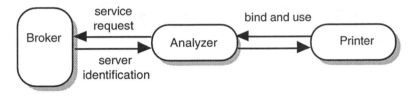

Figure 3.8 Dynamic binding using a broker.

3.5   Language-level communication primitives

Distributed components of a distributed system communicate in order to cooperate and synchronize their actions. The underlying communication service provides for messages to be sent from one component to another. This service, often referred to as a message *transaction*, is offered to the application in a number of different forms, from simple unblocked (asynchronous), unidirectional communication analogous to the datagram, to the blocked (synchronous), bidirectional **remote procedure call (RPC)** analogous to the conventional procedure call. The choice of communication primitives determines how easily systems can be designed and implemented, given that they execute in an environment that is subject to delays and failures. In this section we briefly describe message sending and receipt primitives, the associated synchronization and some failure and implementation issues.

3.5.1   Message receipt

Component processes usually offer a number of entries or ports at their interface at which they are prepared to receive messages. Different entries are usually offered for different types of message and/or different types of service. The standard form of primitive is the blocked **receive**, in which the destination process blocks if no message is available at that entry, and receives it into a target variable when it is available. If the process is busy, messages are queued at the entry. For example:

receive staff-record **from** personnel

The most common situation is for a process to be prepared to receive messages from a number of different entries. To avoid having to poll the entries to test if there are waiting messages, languages provide a **select** statement. The process is then blocked awaiting receipt of a message from any one of a number of entries and can execute code associated with the particular entry selected (cf. a case statement in conventional programming). If messages are waiting on a number of entries, selection policy can be arbitrary, nondeterministic perhaps with some fairness criteria or in lexical order of the select branches. A timeout or failure branch is also often provided to enable an application process to limit the waiting time and/or handle exceptions raised by failed communication transactions, for example:

select   receive temperature   **from** temp-sensor => ...process temperature...

   or receive pressure   **from** press-sensor => ...process pressure...

   or receive command   **from** operator   => ...process command...

   or fail (30) => ...process exception...

end

An alternative to the use of entries at the receiver is that messages are sent to separate entities from which receivers can accept messages. These are called *mailboxes* or *channels* and provide for message queuing. Senders and receivers communicate by naming the same mailbox in their send and receive statements respectively.

3.5.2   Message send

Processes can name the destination process(es) directly in the send primitives. However, this enforces a fixed binding at compile time. More often, some form of indirection is used to allow for later binding; for example, a Conic (Magee *et al.,* 1989) sender process sends to its exit ports (analogous to entries) which act as name holders for the different destinations. These are later bound to the entries of other processes at configuration or run time.

Unidirectional asynchronous send

The asynchronous **send** is an unblocked operation where the sender continues processing once the message has been copied out of the sender's address space. The message flow is unidirectional from sender to receiver (Figure 3.9). The sender and receiving processes are thus only loosely synchronized which is often useful in real-time, embedded applications. It is efficient and can be easily used for multi-destination messages, such as alarms. Since the sender has continued processing after message transmission, error reporting (such as message loss or receiver failure) to the sender is not sensible. Furthermore, since buffer exhaustion at the receiver may require messages to be discarded, asynchronous message transactions must be considered to be unreliable. Hence it is often used in periodic processes that can withstand or cater for possible message loss. Languages such as Conic (Magee *et al.,*

1989), LADY (Nehmer *et al.,* 1987), and NIL (Strom and Yemini, 1983) support asynchronous message passing.

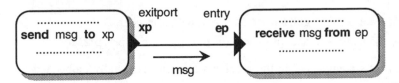

Figure 3.9 Asynchronous send.

Bidirectional request-reply

In the **request-reply** message transaction, the sender is blocked after sending a (request) message and waits until the return of a reply message. It provides a synchronization point for the sending and receiving processes, and permits the receiver to process the request (if appropriate) and return a result or reply message (Figure 3.10). This is the simplest form of message support for client–server interaction.

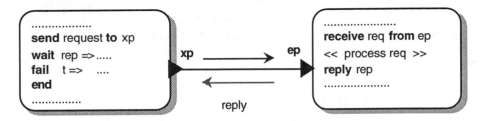

Figure 3.10 Request-reply.

As for the receive, an optional timeout or failure exception handling exit can be provided. The simplest implementation is for the sender timeout to be a local timer which is only canceled on return of the reply (completion of the transaction). This means that, should the sender timeout expire, there is no information as to what has happened: request or reply loss, receiver failure or slow response, and the exception handling must take this into account. If the reply should arrive at the sender after timeout expiry, it is discarded by the underlying system as that transaction is no longer valid. The Conic programming language supports request-reply with failure handling.

Rendezvous

The request-reply can be made to appear more like a procedure call by using out value (cf. request) and in variable (cf. reply) arguments in the client call, and vice versa for call acceptance parameters at the server entry. The calling client and server processes *rendezvous* for the duration of the transaction. Besides the difference in syntax from the request-rely, the underlying system is required to perform parameter marshaling and unmarshaling, that is, respectively collecting the values of the parameters to form a message to be sent, and assigning the values from a received message to parameter variables. Ada (US DOD, 1983) is the most widely known language supporting the rendezvous, for example:

At the client   **call** service (**out** av1, av2, ... **in** ar1,ar2, ...)
At the server   **accept** service (**in** pv1, pv2, ...**out** pr1, pr2, ...)

The accept statements, like the receive statement, is usually embedded in a select statement.

Remote procedure call (RPC)

For general client–server interaction, the RPC is now the most widely adopted and accepted approach. It is provided by most operating systems for remote communication, and embedded in languages such as Concurrent CLU (Cooper and Hamilton, 1988) and SR (Andrews *et al.,* 1988). It is a natural outcome of the desire to provide a distributed mechanism analogous to the conventional procedure call. The notion is that programmers need not be aware of the distribution but can use familiar mechanisms whether or not the invoked procedure is local. An object (or instance of a form of abstract data type) has encapsulated data and offers a number of access "procedures" to manipulate the data. An active thread is created for each occurrence of procedure invocation. Thus there can be concurrent access to the data (see clusters described above) and some form of internal synchronization is usually required. In addition, dynamic binding of client to server may be required, for example:

object x;

   <<local data>>

   proc service1 (**in** pv1, pv2, ...**out** pr1, pr2, ...); **begin** ... **end**

   proc service2 (**in** pv1, pv2, ...**out** pr1, pr2, ...); **begin** ... **end**

   ....

end.

The aim of the RPC is to provide uniform call semantics in that the behavior should be the same for remote as for local procedures. This is termed **exactly once semantics.** However, this transparency cannot be achieved in the case of server crashes. One possible semantics is **at least once** in which case the system keeps retrying the call until the server recovers or an alternative service is available; however, this may result in multiple invocations. Another alternative is **at most once** in which case the system does not retry but reports the failure. Neither of these is ideal, and it is necessary for programmers using an RPC to be aware of the possibility of failure and take measures to deal with it.

Atomic transactions provide the best semantic behavior in that they either complete successfully or not at all, leaving no side effect. However, this entails a large overhead including data checkpoints and commit protocols. Other complications are related to client crashes which can lead to **orphan** executions, where the server execution has no client. The ARGUS language (Liskov, 1988) supports atomic transactions.

In general, the implementation of an RPC is supported by having stub procedures (Figure 3.11) at the client and server ends, responsible for performing parameter marshaling and, in some cases, binding. One of the general authoritative descriptions of the implementation of RPCs is given by Birrel and Nelson (1984).

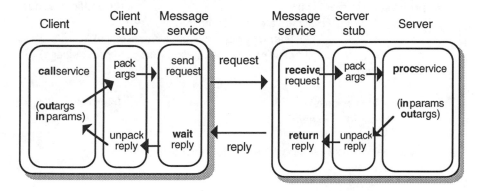

Figure 3.11 Implementation of RPC.

3.6 A simplified (network monitoring) example

Each of the gateways in a network includes a manager for monitoring and controlling the message traffic. Each manager measures and displays the current traffic. For each gateway, the desired traffic settings can be set by local command. If the current traffic readings are outside the desired limit, the manager issues a warning. A central network operator can request the current traffic readings from any gateway.

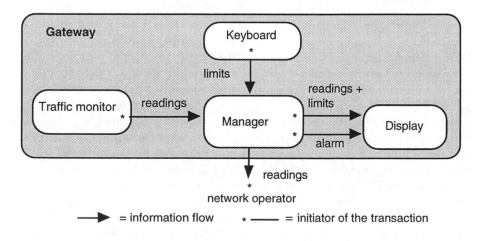

Figure 3.12 Structure for gateway management.

The overall software structure of the processes for gateway management could be as given in Figure 3.12. An outline of the behavior of the Manager process using RPCs is as follows:

```
process Manager;

        <local data: limits and traffic readings>
        proc traffic (in readings);                          {latest traffic readings}
                begin if <readings are outside limits>
                        then call display.alarm (out readings);
                        else call display.update (out readings, settings)
        end;

        proc setting (in limits);                            {new limit settings }
                begin ... end;

        proc operator (out readings);   {operator request for latest traffic}
                begin ... end;

end manager.
```

3.7   Some issues common to all layers

There are a number of issues which are common to all layers of software in a distributed computer node. In order to provide some indication of the concerns in constructing distributed software systems, we briefly summarize each of these.

3.7.1   Naming

Naming is the identification of what we seek. It can be contrasted with addressing, which indicates where it is, and routing which indicates how to get there (Shoch, 1978). The discussion so far has rather glibly referred to the need for naming other components in the distributed system in order to communicate. In fact, naming is a crucial issue with many subtle effects. Names are required to be unique (or resolvable so as to identify any component or object uniquely), should be capable of being communicated efficiently, should be location-independent to permit migration, and should support sharing. Local naming schemes support the use of concise names tailored to local use, but must then be mapped to some scheme to permit global uniqueness and interaction. Global naming schemes enforce uniqueness and uniformity but are difficult to use and maintain. Most systems use a form of hierarchical naming which is layered so as to provide uniqueness within a local context but can be extended with context names to give more global uniqueness when required; cf. telephone numbers which can be extended by area and country codes. (See Chapter 10.)

3.7.2 Synchronization

Management and control of parallel and distributed systems requires synchronization, for action ordering, to coordinate and enforce mutual exclusion during access to shared resources, and generally to preserve consistent states. For instance, consider the transfer of £1 million from an account A in London to account B in New York. Consistency requires that the sum of the balances of accounts A and B remains the same before and after the transfer. Furthermore, it should not be possible for a third party to obtain either balance while the transfer is in progress. This must be maintained despite failures and delays. One of the main techniques adopted is the use of atomic transactions, which provide both failure atomicity – either all operations complete or none – and visibility atomicity – intermediate states are not visible. A number of distributed algorithms exist for enforcing mutual exclusion, for clock synchronization and timestamping, and for related synchronization activities. In general the centralized approaches are simpler and more efficient, but less robust and more likely to be bottlenecks. The decentralized techniques overcome these problems but are more complex and impose more overheads.

3.7.3 Error control

Distributed systems potentially offer reliability and availability. However, being constructed of more entities also implies that there is a greater likelihood of the failure of one of them, such as a communications failure or the failure of a remote process. Failure detection techniques generally employ redundancy such as parity, CRC checks or replicated data, or timer-based approaches such as a timeout for lack of response. Recovery to a consistent state can involve either forward recovery, in which case the operation is repeated or some form of compensatory action performed, or backward recovery to undo unacceptable side effects and retreat to a previous consistent state. In practice the strategies vary according to error frequency and type. For example, one of the simplest strategies is to employ periodic operations where such operations are idempotent. Where this is not the case, atomic transactions may have to be employed.

3.7.4 Resource management

As described early in this chapter, shared, distributed resources provide one of the chief attractions of distributed processing. However, they must be carefully managed to prevent interference and ensure efficient allocation. One of the objectives of such management is to improve performance, through reduced response times and/or increased throughput. In many cases a compromise is required. Management must also act to prevent deadlock, congestion, starvation of access and monopoly of a resource by any client. The aim is to provide some form of fairness. As before, the techniques vary from the simpler centralized approaches which are more efficient, but less robust and more likely to be bottlenecks, to decentralized resource managers which retain local autonomy but require more complex protocols.

Resource management, security, protection and related issues are more fully discussed in other chapters.

3.8   Conclusions

This chapter has provided a brief overview of the principles and concepts in distributed systems. The descriptions have, perforce, omitted many interesting and important aspects. As is the case in the fields of networks and communications, distributed computing is achieving wide-scale use. The research is mature and much of the work is being adopted as standards, either officially or *de facto* through wide adoption.

For instance, OSF (Open Software Foundation), a consortium of more than 300 companies, have produced and made available an implementation of UNIX based on the Mach kernel. They have also produced OSF/DCE, their distributed computing environment as a software platform for supporting distributed applications. It provides facilities for threads, RPCs, a distributed directory service, a time service, distributed file system and a security service. Recently OSF have put forward OSF/DME, their proposals for a management environment. Competing software platforms are offered by each of the major computer vendors, including independent bodies such as ANSA. Other standards organizations are also very active, such as Object Management Group, Unix International, and ISO/ODP (Open Distributed Processing).

Abbreviations

AFS   Andrew File System
DCE   Distributed Computing Environment
DME   Distributed Management Environment
DOS   Distributed Operating System
IPC   Interprocess Communication
ISL   Interface Specification Language
LAN   Local Area Network
NFS   Network File System
ODP   Open Distributed Processing
OSF   Open Software Foundation
RPC   Remote Procedure Call
WAN   Wide Area Network

References

Accetta M. *et al.* (1986). Mach: A new kernel foundation for UNIX development, *Proc. of Summer* USENIX *Conf.*, 93–112

Andrews G. R., *et al.* (1988). An overview of the SR language and implementation, *ACM TOPLAS*, **10**(1), 51–86

ANSA (1991). *ANSAware 3.0 Implementation Manual*, Document RM.097.00. APM Ltd. Cambridge

Birrel A.D. and Nelson B.J. (1984). Implementing remote procedure calls. *ACM Trans. on Computer Systems*, **5**(1), 39–59

Chanpine G.A., Geer D.E. and Ruh W.N. (1990). Project Athena as a distributed computer system, *IEEE Computer*, **23**(9), 40–51

Cheriton D.R. (1988). The V distributed system, *Comm. of the ACM*, **31**, 314–33

Cheung S.C. (1991). *Assembled ISL (AISLE)*. Report REX-WP2/5-ICST-55. Imperial College

Cooper R.C.B. and Hamilton K.G. (1988). Preserving abstraction in concurrent programming, *IEEE Trans. on Software Engineering*, **14**(2), 258–63

Hayes R. and Schlichting R. (1987). Facilitating mixed language programming in distributed systems, *IEEE Transactions on Software Engineering*, **13**(8)

Jones M.B., Rashid R. and Thompson M. (1985). Matchmaker: An interface specification language for distributed processing. *Proc. of 12th Annual Symposium on Principles of Programming Lnaguages*, 225–35

Kramer J. and Magee J. (1985). Dynamic configuration for distributed systems. *IEEE Transactions on Software Engineering*, **11**(4), 242–436

Kramer J. (1990). Configuration Programming – A framework for the development of distributable systems. *Proc. of IEEE COMPEURO'90, Tel-Aviv, Israel*, 374–84.

Kramer J. *et al*. (1991). An introduction to distributed programming in REX. *ESPRIT '91 Conference proceedings*, Brussels, 207–21

Kramer J., Magee J., Sloman M. and Dulay N. (1992). Configuring object-based distributed programs in REX. *IEE Software Engineering Journal*, **7**(2), 139–49

Liskov B. and Sheifler R.W. (1992). Guardians and Actions: Linguistic support for robust, distributed programs. *ACM TOPLAS*, **5**(3), 381–404

Liskov B. (1988). Distributed programming in ARGUS. *Comm. of the ACM* **31**(3), 300–12

Magee J., Kramer J. and Sloman M. (1989). Constructing distributed systems in Conic. *IEEE Transactions on Software Engineering*, **15**(6), 663–75

Massoudi R.A. (1990). The pillars of financial services, *SunTech Journal*, Winter, 55-62

Morris J.H. *et al*. (1986). Andrew: a distributed personal computing environment. *Comm. of the ACM*, **29**(3), 184–201

Mullender S.J. *et al*. (1990). Amoeba: a distributed operating system for the 90s. *IEEE Computer*, **14**(5), 44–53

Nehmer J. *et al*. (1987). Key concepts in the INCAS multicomputer project. *IEEE Transactions on Software Engineering*, **13**(8), 913–23

Oskiewicz E., Otway D. and Sventek J. (1988). ANSA Testbench Manual. *Report* T1.28.02, ANSA Project, APM Ltd. Cambridge

Rashid R.F. (1986). From RIG to accent to mach: the evolution of a network operating system. *Fall Joint Computer Conf., AFIPS*, 1128–37

Rozier M. and Martins L. (1987). The Chorus distributed operating system: some design issues. In *Distributed Operating Systems: Theory and Practice* (Paker, Y. *et al.* eds) NATO ASI Series, vol. F28, 261–87, Springer Verlag

Shoch J.F. (1978). Inter-network naming, addressing, and routing, *COMPCON 78*, 72–79

Sloman M. and Kramer J. (1987). *Distributed Systems and Computer Networks*. Prentice Hall.

Strom R.E and Yemini S. (1983). NIL: An integrated language and system for distributed programming. *SIGPLAN Notices*, **18**(6), 73–82

US DOD (1983). US Department of Defense, *Reference Manual for the Ada Programming Language*, ANSI/MIL-STD-1815A

Part III

Models and Standards for Management

Chapter 4

OSI Management Model and Standards

Alwyn Langsford

Independent Consultant,
4 Aston Close,
Abingdon, Oxon. OX14 1EP, UK

This chapter introduces the set of Open System Interconnection (OSI) standards which has been developed for the purpose of managing the open communication environment. It shows how the standards are related both to each other and to the OSI Basic Reference Model. The chapter describes the standards for management functions and the standards by which functional operations and event reports are communicated between management entities. The importance of supporting services and functions, used by management so that management activity can itself be managed, is also examined.

4.1 Management standards in the OSI context

This chapter considers the way in which the requirements for network management are now being realized in international standards, specifically those standards developed as part of ISO's **Open Systems Interconnection** (OSI) initiative. OSI standards are concerned with more than the basic set of rules for use by equipment to transmit strings of bits efficiently. They assign application-specific syntactic and semantic significance to the bit strings. Typical applications are the transfer of files and text messages or performing transaction processing or directory inquiries. With the diversity of organizations expected to provide and use data processing and communication services, the range of information processing applications they require and the complexity of the equipment being employed, the developers of OSI standards recognized that management of the OSI communications environment is an application which can be subjected to open system standards.

The reference model for OSI (ISO 7498-1) was developed during the 1980s. It derived its principles from the practical experience from the data networks of business and research prototypes of the 1970s (Barber, 1976; Kahn, 1972). In contrast, there was little referenced work on network management from which OSI management standards could be developed. Such as there was had evolved within large organizations which had specialist internal networks and within telecommunications suppliers, often in connection with the maintenance and support of their voice networks. This lack of suitable exemplars has caused the development of standards for OSI management to progress more slowly than has been the case for many other OSI standards. Those developing the standards have had to research the management requirements and, from them, deduce an acceptable set of generic management functions and communication services. They have also had to research new ways in which to specify those functions and services.

Standards only have value when they have general applicability and it is possible to test that a product which claims to conform to a standard can have that conformance demonstrated in some way. The former constraint is set by the cost-effectiveness of the international effort to agree standards (although it does not rule out the enterprise-specific standards). Conformance testing ensures inter-operability and can protect the user and the supplier when claim and counter-claim are made concerning products meeting their specifications. Yet not everything of relevance to management is appropriate for standardization. In common with other OSI standards, no attempt is made to specify or constrain implementations. Because every enterprise and every network is configured and operated in enterprise-specific ways, there are no standards for management policies nor for standard configurations. Instead, standard functions are provided by which policies can be referenced and configurations can be determined.

Management standards have identified an abstract view of resources, the management operations which need to be performed upon them and the communications which are necessary when those resources are managed at a distance. That is, the standards are concerned with

i)   interfaces,

ii) the nature of the testable interactions that can take place across those interfaces and

iii) the presumed behavior of the resources that are accessed through the interfaces.

Figure 4.1. shows that whereas the scope of management lies both inside and outside the circular boundary, the scope of standards lies only within it. The standards are influenced by, and in turn influence, the enterprises which use management standards and the suppliers who provide management products.

OSI Management presumes that the resources that provide communication services need to be supported by management activity. It also presumes that the systems that access the communication resources also require to be managed. One of the major issues that had to be faced when developing management standards was the way in which data and control signals relating to the OSI communications environment were to be communicated by that environment. Using the protocol of a specific layer to communicate about the resources corresponding to that layer was a possible option. However, it has the disadvantage that it cannot accommodate the need to correlate management activity occurring in resources handling the activities of other OSI layers. Nor could lower layers make use of the powerful data formatting and dialogue control services provided through the upper layers. This concern can be illustrated by considering the following scenario. Suppose that a fault is discovered in a particular data link. This event needs to be communicated from the data-link protocol handler to the network layer routing algorithm so that an alternative route can be configured. It is inappropriate to use the service interface between the two layers because fault reporting is not a standard service offered by the data-link layer nor one expected by the network layer. Furthermore, when one system wishes to communicate management data that relates to or influences the operation of the resources that support communication as a whole, it is appropriate to handle this as communication between two application entities. This is to recognize that the management of communications is a distributed processing activity that requires its own application layer protocols for intercommunication.

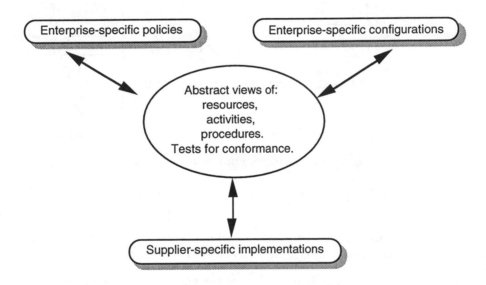

Figure 4.1 Scope of standards.

The relationship between the OSI Basic Reference Model and the way in which it is used to communicate data about the management of OSI resources is set out in the **OSI Management Framework**. This is the fourth part of the OSI Basic Reference Model standard (ISO/IEC 7498-4). It specifies that while data exchanges between entities at layers below the application layer (**layer management**) can be used in special cases for system initialization or fault recovery situations when the existence of full seven-layer protocol support cannot be guaranteed, the norm is for the application layer exchange of data between management entities. This is termed **Systems Management**.

The OSI Management Framework also provides a way to model the management data that relates to communication resources. These data are conceived as residing within the open system which provides a local interface to the resources. The data provide an abstraction of the management behavior and state of the resources. The conceptual repository of data residing within a system and required for management purposes is termed the **management information base** (see Figure 4.2). Some of the data will represent resources and their activities that are specific to one or other of OSI's seven layers. Other data will be pertinent to the communications activities of the system as a whole.

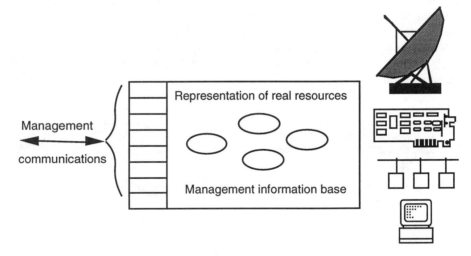

Figure 4.2 The management information base.

The OSI Management Framework also introduces the concept that management and its standards are divided into five functional areas:

i) *fault management*, to identify the existence of a fault, diagnose its cause and to carry out confidence tests to ensure that faults have been rectified;

ii) *configuration management*, to monitor the state of resources and their inter-relationships (for example, to describe network topology); to change the state of and relationships between resources either through simple commands or by downloading alternative versions of communications software or configuration tables;

iii) *accounting management*, to gather data relating to the usage of resources and the assignment of that usage to a subscriber whose use is to be accounted. Control is exercised over both the gathering of the usage data and the sharing and allocation of resource usage to subscribers;

iv) *performance management*, to gather resource usage data and to combine the data to provide performance statistics;

v) *security management,* which is concerned not with the actual provision and use of encryption or authentication techniques themselves but rather with their management, including reports concerning attempts to breach system security. There are two important aspects: (i) managing the security environment of a network including detection of security violations and maintaining security audits; (ii) performing the network management task in a secure way.

Having identified these functional areas, three things became apparent to those developing the standards.

i) Whereas the functional areas are excellent for identifying management's functional requirements, they are inappropriate as the basis of standards because the list of functions that could arise within an area is open-ended. A standard attempting to cover an area could never be known to be complete and could be subjected to continual upgrade and revision.

ii) Many entities and many of the operations performed upon entities are common across the different management functional areas. For example, both fault management and security management need to be able to respond to and control the flow of alarm data; accounting and performance management both make use of the concepts of counters; management data whether about alarms or usage is entered into logs for subsequent processing. It is therefore more appropriate to provide generic definitions of the entities, their operations and their behavior than to be concerned to assign them to a specific function.

iii) Management is a distributed processing activity which itself needs to be managed if network operation is to be effective. For example, one fault can give rise to many alarm signals as different network components are influenced by the fault. Management needs to identify which alarms are significant and to control the flow of their alarm data when excessive fault reporting threatens to cause network congestion. Also, management functions need to be able to manipulate the data that describe system configurations. Because these data may be distributed, the functions must be constrained so that the consistency of the data is maintained. Management therefore needs functions to support its self-management.

OSI standards are developed within Sub-Committees of a joint ISO and IEC Technical Committee (ISO/IEC JTC1) and in close collaboration with CCITT. The principal work is undertaken in Sub-Committees 6 and 21.

4.2   Systems management and its architecture

Three important consequences stem from these realizations. The first is the need to provide a suitable data model through which to define the abstract but common view of the management of communication resources. The breakthrough comes from the realization that the management interface to resources can readily be described in terms of an object modeling paradigm. The management interface to resources is characterized as a **managed object**. This method of describing management information is the subject of the next two chapters. The second development concerns the way in which the resulting standards are documented and the relationship between them. This has led to the development of a number of specific function standards and a set of standards specifying the management support functions. The interrelationship of the OSI management standards is outlined in Figure 4.3. The OSI Basic Reference Model is the starting point for considering the OSI Management Framework and the communication protocols that communicate Systems Management data. However, it is the **Systems Management Overview** (ISO/IEC 10040) which is the more appropriate starting point for understanding the Systems Management standards as a whole. The standards divide into two classes, those concerned with management functionality and those concerned with the representation of management information. Not shown in this figure are the specific management information definitions corresponding to the management of layer entities. Standards have been specified for the Transport (ISO/IEC 10737) and Network (ISO/IEC 10733) layers.

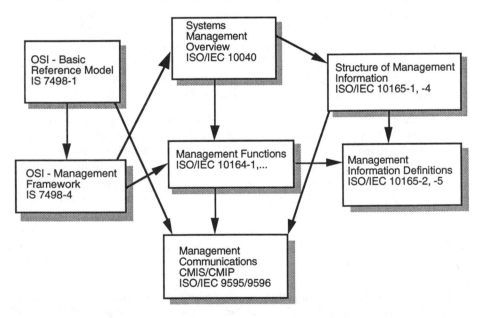

Figure 4.3 Interrelationship of OSI management standards.

The third consequence is the development of an architecture for systems management. Although this is still incomplete, that part of the architecture which is recorded in the Systems Management Overview standard assists in the comprehension of the published standards and the ways in which they can be applied. A complete OSI Management Architecture would show how all aspects of management that affect the open systems interconnection and communications environment could be realized from OSI Management Standards. It would cover the distributed processing activity of network management, showing how management interactions between systems could be coordinated and how data could be combined from many sources. It would define how the supervisory services of management could compare data from monitoring open systems activities with that expected to satisfy policy requirements. It would show how mismatches between observed and expected behavior give rise to control action, so that communications activities meet their requirements. Such an architecture would be independent of the scale of the network to be managed (large or small). Its communication services would be provided from communication channels supplied from many different carriers and these would support the interconnection of many different business enterprises each with its own management requirements. The architecture would be independent of specific computing and communications technologies. It would also be independent of the precise manner in which the management services and functions map onto those technologies though it would give guidance on efficient mappings.

Whereas some work is in progress to develop standards to meet the architectural requirements outlined above, the architecture documented in the Systems Management Overview is limited to the communication between a pair of systems management application entities. It has taken a particular style of management interaction in which a manager process interacts with a remote system in order to exercise management control over remote resources.

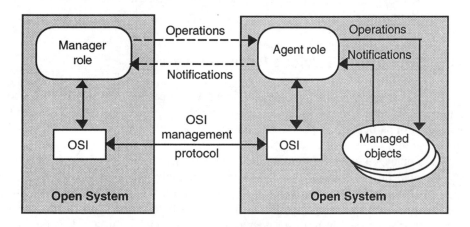

Figure 4.4 Basic system management architecture.

This simple architecture is shown in Figure 4.4. A management process in one system operates in a **manager role**. Its peer entity in the other system operates in an **agent role** to provide access to the *managed object* representation of the resources to be managed. The former system is sometimes referred to as a "managing system" while the latter is termed a "managed system". Together they provide a distributed management service. The assignment of roles to systems does not imply that the roles are permanent. It is the nature of the communication activity which provides the distinction between manager and agent role. To appreciate this distinction it is necessary to anticipate the characteristics of managed objects.

Managed objects provide a management interface through which (i) **operations** can be performed and (ii) events occurring asynchronously within the managed object can be emitted in the form of **notifications**. The entity operating in the agent role supports the communication of operations to the object and the communication of the notifications to the entity operating in the manager role. Thus, the communication channel between manager and agent supports two types of management data transfer services, **management operations** (requested by the manager of the agent) and **notifications** (sent from the agent to the manager). Thus the role taken by either of the systems management application entities is entirely dependent upon the type of management data transfer and the direction of that transfer. Both operations and notifications are communicated using OSI management protocols (see Section 4.5).

The Systems Management Overview also specifies data exchanges which can take place when two application entities form an association in order to perform management functions. Two types of information can be exchanged. The first, which establishes the **management context**, identifies whether an entity will operate only in the manager role, the agent role or in both roles for the duration of the association. The other, which identifies systems management **functional units**, is used to establish the functionality associated with the subsequent management exchanges. Functional units serve both to indicate the functional capability associated with the exchanges and also to limit the scope of the exchanges to those that are agreed between the communicating entities.

4.3   Supporting services for management

Agent processing provides management support services as well as providing the mapping between the managed object interface and the open communications interface. In particular it supports mechanisms for addressing groupings of managed objects within a system, for the synchronization of operations, and for controlling access to managed objects, features which will be describes in more detail in Section 4.5. It also provides mechanisms that can selectively filter the operation to be performed or control the flow of data arising from notifications. Where these support features provided by the agent role can themselves be managed, this management capability is expressed in terms of operations upon managed objects. It is through these supporting services that the OSI Management standards specify self-management functionality.

Two support functions were ratified as international standards in 1991. These provide management of the **event reporting function** (ISO/IEC 10164 part 5) and the **log control function** (ISO/IEC 10164 part 6). Two other functions are progressing towards international standard status. These handle **access control** (ISO/IEC 10164 part 9) and the **scheduling function** (ISO/IEC 10164 part 15). Some features of scheduling have already been incorporated into the specification of event reporting and logging and these will be described in the following paragraphs.

Figure 4.5 illustrates this view of the management of agent processing. It shows representative managed objects responding to an operation and emitting a notification, both of which are handled by the agent. The diagram also shows support managed objects which exercise local control over the agent processing (dashed lines). Scheduling is related to the time as determined by a local system clock. Figure 4.5 shows the data flow from the agent to a local log which is also accessed by the log control function object so that the latter can perform its management support activity. These activities are described in more detail in the following sections.

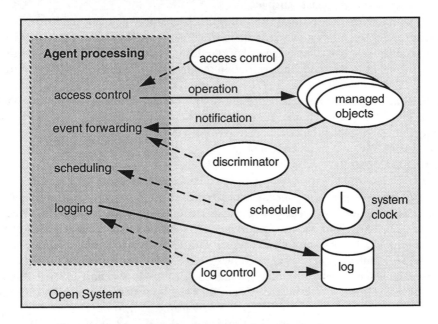

Figure 4.5 Agent processing.

4.3.1   Event handling

Event handling is outlined in the Systems Management Overview and its functional aspects are specified in the **Event Reporting Function** (ISO/IEC 10164 part 4). The purpose of the Event Reporting Function is to provide a managed mechanism by which to control the forwarding of notifications from managed objects. The model of event management is one in which all notifications can potentially give rise to management event reports. (Section 4.5 describes how these are communicated to managers as M-EVENT-REPORTs.) All the notifications arising within a system are conceptually subjected to the control of **event forwarding discriminators** whose task is to select particular notifications and forward them to appropriate destinations. A notification that is forwarded is termed an *event report*.

The event forwarding discriminator is a class of managed object. Two of its mandatory read/write attributes are a **discriminator construct** and a **destination**. The former maintains a predicate that determines the criteria under which notifications will be forwarded. Its parameters are Boolean combinations of simple constructs that test for the notification type and/or the presence, arithmetic relationship (greater than, less than or equal to), set relationships, and so on of some data generated by the notification. The destination attribute contains the chosen destination for the selected event report either as an "application entity title" or as a group address if more than one destination is chosen. The event forwarding discriminator also has a mandatory **administrative state** attribute through which the operation of the managed object can be suspended and resumed. (See Section 4.4 for more information about state attributes.)

In addition, the event forwarding discriminator may also manifest certain optional attributes. One of these can define a set of alternative destinations, ranked in priority order, that can be selected as backup destinations if it is not possible to send the event report to the location specified in the destination attribute. Another option is to set the **mode** attribute. This determines whether the event forwarding discriminator expects an acknowledgment from the chosen destination to show that it has received the event report. Although not specified as a standard procedure, this acknowledgment capability could be used in conjunction with the backup destination attribute and, say, a local timeout parameter (also not specified within the standard) to determine whether the notification had reached its target in a predefined time. If not, the notification could be reissued to a selected backup destination.

As well as providing mechanisms to report notifications selectively and to choose a destination, the event forwarding discriminator optionally supports selective reporting in time. This facility is provided by scheduling the time at which event reporting is to start and terminate together with either daily, weekly or some other specified schedules. A daily schedule gives a list of time intervals as {start time, stop time} pairs when event forwarding is enabled. A weekly schedule extends this by defining a **week mask** to show the days of the week to which a given daily schedule applies.

Because event forwarding discriminators are managed objects they can raise notifications. Those defined by the standard arise when a new event forwarding discriminator is created, when one is deleted or when the value of one of the event forwarding discriminator's attributes changes. These notifications, like all others, are submitted to all event forwarding discriminators within a system to determine if and to what destination the corresponding event report shall be sent.

4.3.2   Logging

Although the standards do not mandate the destination of event reports, one intended destination for them is a **log**. A log is a device that can selectively store event reports in **log records** and the Log Control Function standard defines how this may be done. Recognizing that management needs to be able to control the parameters that support the logging activity and the retrieval of log records, the standard specifies these aspects of logs and log records by defining both as managed objects.

A log may be located either in a system supporting the manager role or co-located with the managed objects whose notifications it has to log. For that reason, the log shares many of the characteristics of the event forwarding discriminator. The model presumes that all notifications arising within a system are passed to logs as well as to all event forwarding discriminators. Logs have a *discriminator construct* attribute in order to select which data shall be placed into log records. Like the event forwarding discriminator, the log has an *administrative state* attribute; operations on this attribute control the suspension and resumption of logging activity. Optionally, logs may be subjected to the same types of scheduling constraints as event forwarding discriminators.

Specific to the log is the recognition that it may not have an inexhaustible capacity for log records and that, after some time, the log can become full. The standard identifies two types of log:

i)   those which reset to the beginning when the log is full, and overwrite earlier records,

ii) those which halt further logging when full.

Notifications can be generated at defined thresholds as the log becomes filled in order to alert a manager that some action may be required. If the log is one that has a finite size, other attributes give the total log size (in octets) and how much of it is filled (both in octets and as a record count).

Log records are objects with read-only attributes. Their attributes include a record identifier (an integer whose value increases as records are added to the log), the time at which the record was entered into the log, and the data associated with the event report being logged.

4.3.3   Access control

Each operation upon a managed object which is requested by the manager entity can be made subject to access control. It is a function of the agent role to exercise this control through agent processing. Reading and modification of the access control parameters is again handled by defining this aspect of the agent as a managed object. In this way the agent is informed of the (sets of) objects and operations that are subject to access control together with the manager role entities that may perform the operations upon the objects.

4.4   Systems management function standards

Table 4.1 lists the set of management function standards, their ISO reference numbers and their status as of August 1993. Nine of the functions have been ratified as international standards and others are in various stages of progressing to ratified status[1]. As a guide to the standard's origins, the table also indicates (with a capital

---

[1]   A Committee Draft (CD) is the initial stage in this process, when a working draft is first regarded as having sufficient technical stability that it can be subjected to formal, international ballot procedures. A CD that is successfully balloted is then registered as a Draft International Standard (DIS). A DIS that is successfully balloted is registered as an International Standard (IS).

letter) the functional area whose requirements gave rise to the standard. It will be seen that this list includes the support functions described in the previous section.

Table 4.1 Management function standards.

ISO reference	CCITT reference	Title	FCAPS origin
IS 10164-1	X.730	Object Management Function	C
IS 10164-2	X.731	State Management Function	C
IS 10164-3	X.732	Objects and Attributes for Representing Relationships	C
IS 10164-4	X.733	Alarm Reporting Function	F
IS 10164-5	X.734	Event Report Management Function	F
IS 10164-6	X.735	Log Control Function	F
IS 10164-7	X.736	Security Alarm Reporting Function	S
IS 10164-8	X.740	Security Audit Trail Function	S
DIS 10164-9	X.741	Objects and Attributes for Access Control	S
DIS 10164-10	X.742	Usage Meter Functioning	A
IS 10164-11	X.739	Metric Objects and Attributes	P
DIS 10164-12	X.745	Test Management Function	F
DIS 10164-13		Summarization Function	P
DIS 10164-14	X.737	Confidence and Diagnostic Test Categories	F
DIS 10164-15	X.746	Scheduling Function	P

4.4.1 Configuration management

The Object Management Function standard was developed to specify a general mechanism through which to create and delete managed objects, to perform actions upon them, and to read and modify their attributes. All are generic requirements for managing the configuration of communication resources. Because these specifications can be used by other functions to pass their data communication requirements to the communication protocol, they are termed *pass through* services. The standard also defines specific notifications which can be used to signal managed object creation, managed object deletion and attribute value change. These notifications provide data to identify whether the event being reported was caused by activity internal to or external to the managed object and, for the attribute change notification, the values of the attribute prior to the change (optional) and after the change (mandatory). A common feature of the notifications defined by these and many other Systems Management standards is the ability to provide (as optional data) information relating a specific notification to others to which it could be correlated. Although this ability presumes a degree of intelligence within the managed object generating the notification, it is a facility which is of considerable value to managers when they attempt to relate event reports from one source to those from other sources which are nonetheless triggered by some common cause. For example, communication circuit reconfigurations could result from the failure of a data link.

Other than defining specific attribute change reporting services, neither of the next two parts of the standard defines any functionality associated with particular objects. Rather they define a series of attributes which can be (and are) imported into managed object specifications. The State Management Function defines two sets of attributes, those that identify a system's **state** and those that identify its **status**. Part 3 of the management function standards, as its title implies, specifies **relationship** attributes.

Three state attributes, *operational state, usage state* and *administrative state*, are defined. The first two are read-only, the values being modified by internal activity associated with the managed object. The operational state takes two values *enabled* and *disabled*. Enabled objects can have one of three usage states, *idle, active* and *busy*. The model is one of a multi-threaded object which, as it takes on work, changes from the idle to the active state. When its work has increased so that it has no further resource capacity its state changes from *active* to *busy*. Objects whose operational state is disabled must have an *idle* usage state. The administrative state is the only one whose value can be modified by operations external to the managed object. This attribute takes one of three states. It is *unlocked* when a resource is able to perform its intended activities and *locked* when these are suspended. When locked, a resource is forced into the idle state. Recognizing that this could be a drastic operation for an active system (for example, a telephone exchange or a packet switching system) the *shutting down* administrative state is also specified. In this state current activities are continued but no new ones are started. When the *usage* state changes from *active* to *idle*, the administrative state automatically changes to *locked*. Requesting a resource that is in an *idle* state to place itself in a *shutting down* state results in it being placed in the *locked* state.

Five status attributes are specified (together with the ability to indicate that status is *undefined*). Certain status values, for example the *critical, major* or *minor* **alarm status** values are used in conjunction with alarm reports. The **procedural status** attribute is used to identify when resources are *initializing* and *terminating* their activity. The **availability status** is related to the resource being tested or not available by being off-line or not powered up. This status attribute is also used by the log object class to indicate that the log is full. **Control status** is used to indicate test conditions and it can show that a device has been suspended in some way other than by being placed in a *locked* administrative state (for example by an internal action of the device or by an external *action* operation upon a managed object). Finally, the **standby status**, as its name implies, gives information as to whether some resource is in service or providing hot or cold standby capability.

Five types of relationships are defined in Part 3 of this standard:

service, peer, fallback, backup, group.

These give rise to nine relationship attributes whose relationship to the relationship type is shown in Table 4.2. Mostly, the intent of these attributes is self-evident from the names they have been given. The *backup* object and *backed-up* object attributes are found in the Event Reporting Function standard; the *user* and *provider* attributes are referenced in standards for reporting security violations. *Member* and *owner* may come to have application in the developing standards which give structure to grouping of managed objects according to management policy or authority. The others have obvious relationships to descriptions of network topology.

Table 4.2 Relationship attributes.

Relationship type	Attribute
Service	Provider
	User
Peer	Peer
Fallback	Primary
	Secondary
Backup	BackUp
	BackedUp
Group	Owner
	Member

4.4.2   Alarm reporting

There are close parallels between the **Alarm Reporting Function** (ISO/IEC 10164-4) and the **Security Alarm Reporting Function** (ISO/IEC 10164-7). Both define the types of notifications that are to be raised in the event of an error or other prohibited operation, though there are differences in the precise semantics associated with attribute values. Both have mandatory parameters that identify the *probable cause* and *perceived severity* of the alarm condition. Additionally, the security alarm report must identify the provider and user of the service. The Alarm Reporting Function also permits the (optional) reporting of trend data and, for alarms generated when values cross alarm thresholds, the threshold value. An illustration of an alarm threshold has already been provided by the log with its series of threshold levels able to report the extent to which the log has been filled (see Section 4.3.2).

Five types of alarm report:

communication, quality of service, processing, equipment, environment

and are qualified by 57 types of standard *probable causes*. There are five types of security alarm that relate to the violation of a security condition:

integrity, operation, physical intrusion, security mechanism, time domain.

The Security Alarm Reporting Function standard lists 14 types of security alarm probable causes. A time domain violation alarm, for example, would be raised if an attempt was made to perform an operation outside a scheduled time frame.

4.4.3   Fault management

Once a fault has been indicated by an alarm report (or possibly through polling managed objects to determine their behavior, the standards permit either) some follow- up test action may be required to locate the fault prior to a reconfiguration. Following reconfiguration or the repair of a failed device, the system or device may need to be further tested to establish that it is performing according to specification. Standards have been developed to assist in performing these *confidence and diagnostic* test functions. The **Test Management Function** specifies a test environment which is common to a range of **Confidence and Diagnostic Test Categories**. These include tests such as:

connectivity, data integrity, protocol integrity, loop-back, echo

and internal resource checks (sometimes referred to as *self-tests*).

4.4.4   Audit trails

Just as alarm reports generate alarm records within logs, security-related notifications can also be logged. One specific class of security-related record is the **audit trail** record and the class of event that gives rise to this record type is defined in the Security Audit Trail Function standard (ISO/IEC 10164-8).

4.4.5   Performance management

Two closely related standards have been developed to support performance management needs. They are the **Metric Objects and Attributes** and the **Summarization Function**. Both identify **metric objects**. These are managed objects which exist to control the gathering of performance data and to provide statistics on, for example, resource utilization. The former was originally titled the "Workload Monitoring Function", although it did not actually provide a standard prescription for determining "workload". (The standard implicitly relates workload to effective resource utilization.) Rather it provides a specification of an environment within which gauges can supply data at fixed sampling periods. These data can be combined using defined algorithms to provide average values over defined sampling intervals. Two algorithms have been defined. One is the *mean monitor* which maintains a true average value of given data for the previous n samples. The disadvantage of this statistic is that it requires the averaging algorithm to retain the values of the previous $n-1$ observations. The preferred algorithm determines the *exponentially weighted mean* value. This takes a weighted average of the current value and of the previous exponentially weighted mean value. Thus, only one previously obtained data value needs to be retained until the next value is determined. The greater the weighting, the less account is taken of earlier data. The standard also specifies algorithms for calculating a variance about the mean and for calculating percentiles.

These functions also take account of the concept of a **scanner**. This concept is elaborated in the **Summarization Function** which provides definitions of the attributes and permitted operations to control a scanner. A scanner is modeled as a device for periodically sampling the values of a specified set of attributes within particular objects. Not only can the sampling period be controlled but the sampling activity may be suspended and resumed according to a schedule. Scanner objects may maintain a buffer to hold the sampled data for delivery according to an independently controlled reporting period and operational schedule. One class of scanner, the *dynamic scanner*, can be activated to provide a "snapshot" of a set of attributes.

4.4.6   Accounting management

One accounting-related management function has been developed to the degree that it has been registered for ballot as a Draft International Standard, though other aspects of the accounting management functional area have been recognized as potential sources of standards. This is the **Usage Metering Function**. It shares with the performance management functions the characteristics of gathering data related to resource utilization and controlling the data gathering activity. However, there are significant differences in the standard because of the anticipated use of the data being gathered. The standard defines three classes of managed object; a **metercontrol object**, a **meter data object** and a **usage record**. The first of these provides the control over internal events, both those that lead to accounting data being recorded and those that lead to it being reported. It also identifies the types of information for which that meter may account; for example, octets, packets, units of time. The meter data object models the resource which maintains data values to be reported according to the rules identified in the accounting meter control object. Metering can be started, suspended or resumed. One control object can control several data objects. Thus the model is of a common controlling entity and a number of data recording entities. A data object is created for each user of a given resource or whenever there is a need to provide independent accounting of instances of resource utilization by a user. The standard specifies a notification that provides the corresponding data parameters for storing in a usage record.

Data objects can also provide accounting data by being polled.

An anticipated extension to the accounting management standards is to provide a means of controlling the allocation of resources to users by applying accounting constraints. An allocation of resource usage which is available to a user would be maintained by a *quota object* (ISO/IEC JTC1/SC21 N4971, 1990).

4.4.7   Other functions

Extensions to event forwarding and log control are under consideration. Other functions in a less advanced stage of standards development are **software management** and **time management**.

Software management is concerned with delivering and maintaining the programmable aspects of a communications environment. It defines software versions, enables the version in use to be identified, prescribes the way in which software may be downloaded into a device and how the software may then be activated. It defines procedures for reverting to a previous version of software in the event of problems with a current version. In this it can be expected to make use of commitment protocols being developed in conjunction with transaction processing standards (ISO/IEC 10026).

Time management is arguably not a System Management function at all but a response to a more general distributed processing requirement to maintain a common perception of time throughout a distributed processing environment. Its value to management lies in its ability to give some indication as to whether events in different systems could be causally related. It presumes that managed systems that need to be synchronized will contain clocks and that these clocks, being imperfect, will drift relative to each other in time. At any instant, a clock not only has a time reading but also a precision which should be ascribed to that reading. This standard is expected to specify appropriate time and precision attributes as well as procedures for synchronizing distributed clocks. These could include the synchronization procedures which are possible when a master clock can be used to broadcast a timing signal to all interested systems through a medium with a known propagation delay. They could also cover procedures which enable estimates to be made of the current time using timing data which can be provided over asynchronous communications networks.

4.5   Systems management communications

The main requirements for the communication of management information between two open, connected systems have already been described. Essentially, these utilize a communication channel between two management entities which is established through an application layer association with a defined management context and (optionally) identified functional units to specify the functions which are to be used within that context. Then operations and notifications are communicated by means of data interchanges.

4.5.1   The Common Management Information Service (CMIS)

All the management functions defined to date use a **Common Management Information Service** (ISO/IEC 9595) for communications between managers and agents. This service provides the conceptual access to communication mechanisms through which the operations of

> getting data,
> setting and resetting data,
> adding data to attributes which are defined as set-valued,
> removing data from attributes which are defined as set-valued,
> actions upon objects,
> object creation, and
> object deletion

can be performed and through which notifications are transmitted as event reports.

Systems Management communications requirements are simple and the service provides the essential characteristics of a *remote procedure call* in which a transmission is requested and, some time later, a response is generated to the requester should that be required. Table 4.3 shows the mapping of each of the above operations, and the notification onto the Common Management Information Service and whether the service must be confirmed (C) or whether confirmation is optional (O).

Table 4.3 Mappings between management interaction, service and protocol.

Management Interaction	Communication Service	C/O	Communication Protocol
notification	M-EVENT-REPORT	O	m-Event-Report
get data	M-GET	C	m-Get
replace	M-SET	O	m-Set
replace with default	M-SET	O	m-Set
add set value	M-ADD	O	m-Set
remove set value	M-REMOVE	O	m-Set
action	M-ACTION	O	m-Action
create	M-CREATE	C	m-Create
delete	M-DELETE	C	m-Delete
—	M-CANCEL-GET	C	m-Cancel-Get-Confirmed

It is not necessary that each management operation is completed before an independent request or notification is issued. Hence, the type of management operation (or event report) is indicated together with an identifier so that the request and any expected response can be correlated. Each request identifies the class of managed object and object instance to which the operation is targeted or by which the event report is generated. It identifies the operation or event reporting parameters and, optionally, the time of the request. For example an M-GET request will specify an *attribute identifier list* which states which attributes of the identified managed object are to be read. In response, the agent will identify the particular M-GET operation, the managed object class and instance, the time of the response (optional) and the result of the operation as a list of {attribute identifier, attribute value} pairs. Alternatively, the agent will generate an error response if the request cannot be honored, for example if the identified object does not exist or the attribute list is incorrectly specified. As stated in Section 4.3.3, operations are (optionally) subjected to access control constraints. The service also provides the ability to cancel any M-GET which has been started but not completed.

The above paragraphs describe the basic services which, with the exclusion of M-CANCEL-GET, are designated through the specification of a **kernel functional unit**. Five further categories of functional unit are available which extend the kernel service. These are negotiated through the exchange of functional units at the time the association is established. Additional functional capability is provided so that several managed objects can be selected in one operation request, so that operations upon those objects can be synchronized, and so that requests can be made according to selection criteria. Each of these is considered in turn.

In some instances, a single operational request can give rise to a series of agent replies. A typical case is provided by considering an M-ACTION performed upon a remote system. If this were to suspend the activity of a number of usage meter data objects, it could not only modify the behavior of those objects but could generate a sequence of responses, one for each object which was affected by the action. These responses would take the form of a sequence of *linked* replies, each one referencing the invoked action through a *linked reply* parameter. If use is to be made of this capability, a **multiple reply functional unit** is negotiated. All services other than the M-CREATE and M-EVENT-REPORT services offer the possibility for generating linked replies.

Provided that the *multiple reply functional unit* has been proposed and accepted it is possible to select a group of objects upon which to perform an operation and to impose synchronizing constraints upon that operation. This service is negotiated using the **multiple object selection functional unit**. With the exception of the M-CREATE service, all other operations permit the requester to specify not just the selected object class and instance but to specify some containing object instance within which the structure of the containment tree is known to both communicating parties. An example is to select records contained within a log. The level selected within this containment hierarchy is known as the **scope** of the request. The scope parameter can specify a particular level in the hierarchy or can include all contained objects down to and including that level. In this way it would be possible to reference a system and instruct all contained objects to set their administrative state to *locked*, thereby disabling normal operations. Two synchronization options are available when performing scoped operations. The operation is carried out either according to **best efforts** which is the default or, when it is important to ensure a consistent set of operations on the contained objects, as an **atomic** operation.

In those instances where it is important to be more selective of the objects upon which to perform an operation, the **filter functional unit** is negotiated. This allows a requester to specify a predicate to be true before the operation is performed. The objects and attributes referred to in the filter must be within the scope of the base managed object. The filter construct is identical to that used by both the event forwarding discriminator and the log to make selections of the notifications which will be subjected to further agent processing. The only difference in use is that the effect of the filter is transient, applying only to the operation in which it is specified, whereas discrimination of notifications is characterized by its persistence.

Of the two remaining functional units, the **cancel get functional unit** is used to signal a requirement to be able to use the M-CANCEL-GET service. The **extended service functional unit** provides a facility for Systems Management to access the services of the Presentation Layer directly in addition to using the P-DATA service required for the communication of management data.

4.5.2   The Common Management Information Protocol (CMIP)

Management communication is effected through the **Common Management Information Protocol** (ISO/IEC 9596-1). There is a simple relationship between the elements of the CMIS and the protocol data units which are used to communicate service requests and, where required, their responses. An early revision of the protocol made it possible to map the services which *add* and *remove* values to and from set-valued attributes and to *reset* attributes to their default values onto the protocol for conveying the M-SET request. Table 4.3 shows these service-to-protocol mappings.

All aspects of CMIP are provided by mappings onto other application layer protocols by giving management-specific significance to their parameter fields. The Association Control protocol (ISO 8650) is invoked to make, release and abort management associations. Operations and event reporting map onto the Remote Operation Protocol (ISO/IEC 9072-2). Requests are communicated using the elements of the remote operations *invocation* procedure (ROIV). Normal responses use the *return-result* (RORS) procedure. Error responses use the *return-errors* (ROER) procedure.

These considerations have led to various bodies identifying preferred protocol profiles in order to support Systems Management. Their characteristics tend to differ only in the set of network and lower layer protocols which fall within the profile. Figure 4.6 shows the profile proposed by the OSI Network Management Forum (see Section 4.6). It shows the use of association control and remote operations and their reliance, in turn, upon the presentation layer for which at least the kernel functional unit is required. Because there is no constraint on concurrent flow of management data between manager and agent, the profile specifies the OSI session layer protocol and requires kernel capability together with the support for *two-way simultaneous* data flow. Transport layer class 0 is normally adequate for management communication over a connection-oriented network service. Transport layer class 4 may be preferred when using a connectionless mode of network communication.

The profile also shows that not all management communications necessarily have to use CMIP. Some data transfers, for example those concerning software update, may, with advantage, be communicated using a file transfer protocol as specified in the File Transfer, Access and Management standards (ISO 8571). Some suppliers have published profiles which also include the capability of using *commitment* protocols (ISO 9804, 1990) to support distributed management transactions.

Implementations of CMIP are available from several manufacturers of computing and communications equipment. Experience to date shows that, while the protocol is a viable and valuable vehicle for communicating management data, further facilities appear desirable. These would allow additional filtering constructs to be specified and for sets of management operations to be grouped together as atomic transactions. A period of study has been initiated with the prospect of a further version of the protocol being registered as a standard around 1995.

A system which claims conformance to CMIP is expected to support the kernel functional unit and the corresponding procedures set out in that standard. However, it has been recognized that this could represent "over-kill" for some particularly simple systems; for example a system which is only required to communicate alarm reports and has its event forwarding parameters preloaded into the system. Such a system would only need to communicate event reports in the agent role.

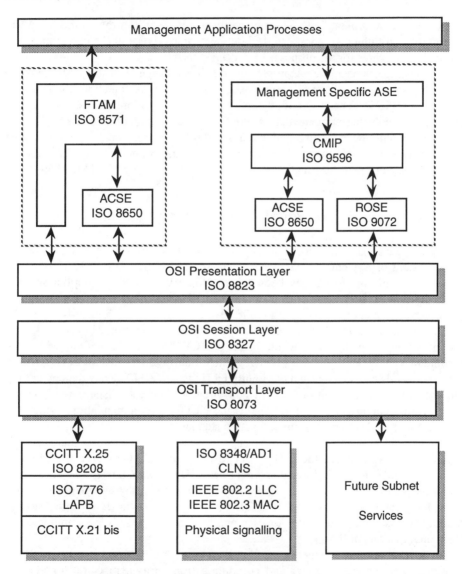

Figure 4.6 Network Management Forum profile.

 The significant issue for management is not the conformance requirements which can be placed upon protocol implementations but the requirements to be placed upon systems. Recall the point made earlier in this chapter that a standard is only of value when it is possible to test that a product conforms to its specification. For the simple system outlined above, there are no internal mechanisms to generate data or to respond to operations to allow tests to be performed on anything other than the event report. To resolve this matter, two approaches to conformance are taken. The normal case is that conformance requirements are dictated by the behavior of the managed

objects and management functions to be performed in respect of those objects. As an alternative, an implementation can declare the characteristics of the communication platform it provides for the purposes of management.

Statements concerning an implementation's conformance to standards are made through a series of standard proformas called Protocol Implementation Conformance Statements (PICS). These identify the management information, the managed objects and the protocols that implementation supports. It is a requirement that any protocol standard should be accompanied by a standard proforma setting out how the conformance statement for a given implementation has been satisfied. That for the Common Management Information Protocol has been issued as (ISO/IEC 9596-2).

4.6   Other activities relating to OSI management

A largely ISO perspective has been adopted in the above discussion, focusing on the development of Systems Management standards in ISO/IEC JTC1/SC21/Working Group 4. This approach has been taken primarily to avoid complicating the description of the standards development process. However, other organizations have made significant contributions both to the development of these standards and to the realization of products. During 1990, CCITT agreed that Question 23 of Study Group VII on network management would result in CCITT Recommendations which are technically equivalent to those of ISO. Since then, international work to develop these standards has been carried out jointly by ISO and CCITT teams thereby adding strength to the collaborations which had already been established within many participating countries. Table 4.1 shows the CCITT Recommendations which are equivalent to the ISO's management function standards.

As well as applying the OSI Management approach to systems management, CCITT has also adopted the ISO model to the Telecommunication Management Network (TMN) for digital voice and data networking (see Chapter 9). This work, undertaken in CCITT SG IV, is carried out collaboratively by telecommunications providers, for example through the T1M1 sub-group of the Exchange Carriers Standards Association in North America and by the European Telecommunications Standards Institute in Europe.

As the OSI Management model was coming to be accepted internationally, a group of equipment suppliers and communications providers came together to establish the Network Management Forum (NMF). They were motivated by two main concerns.

i)   The pace of technology development needed to be increased if management standards were to be available in time to meet the growing demands of planned network services. Traditional ways of developing international standards and recommendations do not readily provide a sufficiently managed working environment to expedite standards when there is a significant amount of technical work required for their prospective development.

ii) Recognizing the complexity of standards and hence the possibilities of failure to interwork even with agreed standards, the Forum provides an environment within which suppliers can test and demonstrate inter-operability between products.

A feature of networking conferences and exhibitions from 1990 onwards has been the presence of NMF members demonstrating the interaction between and inter-working of compatible network management systems.

4.7 Open issues

In spite of the progress which has been made, more needs to be done. One requirement is to undertake a thorough review of the architecture. Another is to classify the sort of data that network managers require to know about a system in order to be able to interact with it for the purposes of management, how to represent that knowledge and how to manage it. A third, having recognized that management is a distributed processing activity, is to apply the OSI Management approach to the management of all aspects of the distributed information processing environment and not just those parts that provide the communications infrastructure. The objective is to avoid introducing piecemeal solutions when the aim is to satisfy total systems requirements.

The representation of management knowledge and management in the scope of open distributed processing are topics for discussion in later chapters. In respect of the architecture, three things in particular need attention. One is to find ways of defining the behavior to be expected of entities operating in a manager role, say in response to event reports. This could become the starting point for defining extended management procedures like those for fault handling, software load and system reconfiguration. A second is to ensure that management and its standards can be applied to systems of any scale. The scale ranges from local area networks with a few attachments up to global systems where the communications facilities span several networking administrations. Here the concept of **management domains**, introduced as a non-normative discussion in the Systems Management Overview, could become significant. Domains result from a recognition that management does not deal with each and every resource on an individual basis but tends to group its resources according to their common characteristics and according to the management policies to which they are subjected (see Chapter 16). The third architectural need influences communications and concerns the requirement for management to exercise control over a number of systems and their resources as a single atomicaction. An architectural study is in progress to identify the applicability and relative merits of multicast transmission mechanisms or the application of transaction processing techniques which handle atomic operations with their facility for rollback and recovery when atomicity cannot be assured.

Even with these items outstanding, the open systems management approach, with the positive assistance of the NMF initiative, has begun to demonstrate its applicability. Yet it must be recognized that users and providers are only at the threshold of coherent implementations of management functionality. Many of the necessary standards have yet to be developed even to the stage of registration as Committee Drafts. There are no agreed standards for simple management procedures for testing and reconfiguration. It is still an open question whether some aspects of management can ever be made the subject of international standardization since they are concerned with system-specific configurations and enterprise-specific management policies. But OSI and OSI Management do give network managers the potential to have a powerful set of tools to use in communicating their management requirements. Although the data they communicate may be enterprise- and network-specific, the architectural framework, the method by which object classes are registered and the communications mechanisms can be common. At best, communicated data will carry sufficient qualifying information that the semantics as well as the syntax will be clear to the recipient; at worst the recipient will be able to detect that it cannot fully understand the data and be able to respond with a well-formed and fully understood error response.

Abbreviations

CCITT	International Telegraph and Telephone Consultative Committee
CD	Committee Draft
CMIP	Common Management Information Protocol
CMIS	Common Management Information Service
DIS	Draft International Standard
IEC	International Electrotechnology Commission
IS	International Standard
ISO	International Organization for Standardization
JTC1	Joint Technical Committee One (of ISO)
NMF	Network Management Forum
OSI	Open Systems Interconnection
PICS	Protocol Implementation Conformance Statement
ROER	Remote Operation Error Report
ROIV	Remote Operation Invocation
RORS	Remote Operation Response
SG IV	Study Group 4 (of CCITT)
T1M1	A sub-group of the Exchange Carries Standards Association of USA
TMN	Telecommunications Management Network

References

Barber, D.L. (1976). The European Informatics Network – achievements and prospects. *Proc ICCC 76 Conf. Toronto*

ISO 8571 (1987). *Information processing systems – Open Systems Interconnection – File Transfer, Access and Management.*

ISO 8650 (1987). *Information processing systems – Open Systems Interconnection – Protocol Specification for the Association Control Service Element.*

ISO/IEC 7498-4 (1989). *Information processing systems– Open Systems Interconnection – Basic Reference Model – Part 4: Management Framework.*

ISO/IEC 9072-2 (1989). *Information processing systems – Text communications – Remote Operations – Part 2: Protocol Specification.*

ISO/IEC JTC1/SC21 N4971 (1990). *Accounting Management Working Document – Fourth Version.*

ISO/IEC 9804 (1990). *Information technology – Open Systems Interconnection – Service definition for the commitment, concurrency and recovery service element.*

ISO/IEC 9595 (1991). *Information technology – Open Systems Interconnection – Common Management Information Service.*

ISO/IEC 9596-1 (1991). *Information technology – Open Systems Interconnection – Common Management Information Protocol – Part 1: Specification.*

ISO/IEC 9596-2 (1991). *Information technology – Open Systems Interconnection – Common Management Information Protocol – Part 2: Protocol Implementation Conformance Statement (PICS) Proforma.*

ISO/IEC IS 10026, *Information technology – Open Systems Interconnection – Distributed transaction processing.*

ISO/IEC IS 10733, *Information technology – Telecommunications and information exchange between systems – Elements of Management Information Related to OSI Network Layer Standards.*

ISO/IEC DIS 10737, *Information technology – Telecommunications and information exchange between systems – Elements of Management Information Related to OSI Transport Layer Standards.*

Kahn R.E. (1972). Resource sharing computer networks. *Proc IEEE* **20**, 1397

Chapter 5

OSI Structure of Management Information

Jeremy Tucker

Logica,
68 Newman Street,
London W1A 4SE, UK
Email: tuckerj@logica.co.uk

The power, generality and efficiency of OSI Systems Management are largely due to the use of a common Management Information Model to define how resources of any kind can be managed. The model is based on the concept of managed objects, and adopts the principle of inheritance to enable specifications to be reused and extended in a controlled way. This makes it possible to take advantage of commonality between resources where it exists, as well as to provide tools for creating proprietary extensions to the standards. This chapter explains the concepts of management information and managed objects, with reference to the international standards that define them.

5.1   Introduction

5.1.1   What is management information?

The term "management information" comes from the early days of OSI Systems Management, when the communications service and protocol, CMIS and CMIP, were being standardized. CMIS defines a number of general-purpose primitives that convey requests for management operations and unsolicited event reports from one system to another, and the term management information was used to mean the particular information conveyed by them. The important distinction being made was that CMIS and CMIP provided a general-purpose communications service that could be used to manage anything, whereas the management information conveyed by them related to the particular resources that were being managed at the time. Since those days, it has been recognized that standards are needed for this kind of resource-specific management information, and such definitions are now called *managed object definitions*.

Take as an example of a resource an X.25 protocol machine in a system attached to a packet-switched network. One facet of management standardization is to specify such things as:

- what statistics are available to external managers;

- the level of control over the protocol machine state given to external managers;

- which exception conditions are reported externally.

These are specific to X.25 in this example, and are therefore part of the managed object definition.

Another quite separate facet is to standardize the formats (as opposed to the contents) of:

- the data units that convey requests to read particular data items that are sent from the manager to the switch;

- unsolicited reports that are sent from the switch to the manager.

These aspects are not specific to X.25, but are part of the general communications support; they are defined in CMIS and CMIP.

Managed object definitions thus act as a kind of bridge between the general communications protocols and the particular characteristics of resources. For compatibility with CMIS they have to use the limited repertoire of management operations and notifications that the CMIS service can convey between systems, but they apply them in ways specific to the types of resource in question.

The division in Systems Management standards between the general and the particular continues to this day, though in a more complicated form. In addition to the basic communications service provided by CMIS and CMIP, it has been realized that there are many advantages to be gained by encouraging the use of common formats and procedures at a higher level. CMIS, for instance, defines a notification service that conveys event reports between systems, and allows different types of event report to be distinguished. The alarm-reporting systems management function (ISO/IEC 10164-4) additionally defines the parameters that should be present in an alarm report, as opposed to other types of event report, and thus encourages a greater degree of consistency than CMIS alone. This is done by defining *generic* management information for alarm management (and for other functions) that can be used by managed object definers: so, for example, the X.25 managed object definers have used generic definitions of alarm notifications in their managed object definitions, but have tied the conditions for emitting them and the parameters they contain to events and data specific to the X.25 resource.

Thus management information means the information that is used to define how to manage particular types of resources: it consists of managed object definitions together with any generic definitions that have been produced in order to encourage consistency between different types of managed object when performing the same function. The term *Management Information Base* (or MIB) is defined in the OSI Management Framework (ISO 7498-4) to mean the set of managed objects in a given system. It is now rarely used in OSI.

People had some kind of object model in mind when CMIS and CMIP were being developed during the mid-1980s, but the model was never written down. It subsequently became apparent that managed object definers needed to know the "rules" for objects, and that these rules were far from obvious; and so the model had to be documented. That was the purpose of the first Structure of Management Information (SMI) standard, the Management Information Model (ISO/IEC 10165-1). It turned out to be much more complicated than had been expected, and led to the development of further SMI standards.

The complication was due to a number of technical requirements that the management community wished to meet. These included the need to:

- make managed object definitions extensible both by the standards communities (for example, to support new versions with enhanced facilities) and by suppliers (for example, to document proprietary extensions);

- promote maximum consistency between definitions and encourage the reuse of pieces of specification in different managed object definitions;

- define some common management functions to handle state variables, alarms, event reports and diagnostic testing in a resource-independent way;

- support configurations with multiple managers in various configurations;

- manage the documentation of the specifications.

These are not all met by the SMI standards alone: for example, the third requirement is largely met by the systems management function standards in the ISO/IEC 10164 series, though some of the relevant management information is in DMI (see below).

5.1.2 The SMI standards

The Structure of Management Information (SMI) standards form the multi-part standard ISO/IEC 10165. The parts that are full international standards are:

- Management Information Model (MIM), (ISO/IEC 10165-1);

- Definition of Management Information (DMI), (ISO/IEC 10165-2);

- Guidelines for the Definition of Managed Objects (GDMO), (ISO/IEC 10165-4).

- Generic Management Information (GMI), (ISO/IEC 10165-5);

There is no 10165-3 as the number was allocated in a document structure that has since been superseded. The following is still under development:

- Requirements and Guidelines for Implementation Conformance Statement Proformas associated with Management Information (MOCS), (ISO/IEC DIS 10165-6).

The *Management Information Model* sets out the fundamental concepts of managed objects, and is therefore the basis for all the other standards in the SMI series. All managed object definitions must comply with it.

The *Definition of Management Information* standard (DMI) collects together all the definitions of management information needed by the systems management standards in a single document, as a single point of reference for managed object definers. So, while state management is defined in (ISO/IEC 10164-2) and alarm reporting in (ISO/IEC 10164-4), for example, the formal GDMO definitions of the generic management information they specify are in DMI. Since most of the definitions in DMI are derived from the function standards (in the 10164 series), they are not discussed in this chapter. DMI became an international standard in 1991. To avoid continual updates to DMI, the GDMO definitions for subsequent functions are being published as annexes to the function standards.

The *Guidelines for the Definition of Managed Objects* (GDMO) provides practical assistance to those who need to define management information in the form of comprehensive specification techniques for managed objects, attributes, notifications, and so on. To be sure of completeness and compatibility with the rest of systems management, all definitions of management information should comply with GDMO. (Note that compliance with GDMO does not of itself ensure compliance with all aspects of the *Management Information Model*, though it helps considerably. Thus, managed object definers need to refer to both standards.) GDMO is the subject of Chapter 6.

The *Generic Management Information* (GMI) standard specifies generic information which is common across OSI layers. It includes definitions for SAP objects, CO and CL protocol machine objects, and so on, and is intended to encourage consistency between the managed objects for the different OSI layers. It is therefore primarily relevant to those defining managed objects for OSI layer protocols.

The *MOCS* standard (10165-6) sets out the rules and formats for the production of Managed Object Conformance Statement Proformas, which are required for all managed object definitions. They are the analog for managed objects of the protocol implementation conformance statement (PICS) proformas needed for OSI protocols.

5.2   The management information model

5.2.1   The purpose of the information model

OSI Systems Management is intended to be general-purpose enough to manage an enormously wide range of resources. Some of them will be standardized as part of OSI, such as layer protocol machines, but the majority will not be – they will include such resources as ISDN/telephone exchanges, multiplexors, communications concentrators, modems, peripheral devices, hardware components, and so on. Even though these resources will differ greatly, it is very important to be able to manage them all using the standard CMIS communications service, supported by the CMIP protocol, and highly desirable for them to share a number of fundamental concepts. Purely from the point of view of human usability, it is important for them to be documented in the same style.

It is therefore a requirement that:

- definitions of how to manage resources must be compatible with CMIS;

- there must be a common global naming structure, so that the management of different resources can be combined in a system and be referred to without ambiguity;

- similar kinds of information should be defined in similar ways;

- similar operations should be defined in similar ways; and

- there should be standard ways of extending definitions of how to manage resources and of "borrowing" pieces of specification from elsewhere and re-using them.

The *Management Information Model* tackles this by defining the concept of a *managed object*, which has various defined properties that embody means of meeting the requirements set out above. When the definition of how a particular resource is to be managed is expressed in terms of managed objects, with the properties defined in the Information Model, it is then guaranteed that the management communications between systems can be supported by CMIS and CMIP, that there is an appropriate naming structure, and so on. Hence, compliance with the Information Model enforces compatibility between those defining how to manage particular resources and those defining other aspects of management, such as how to control the distribution of event reports, exchange management knowledge or manage states generically.

5.3 Managed objects

5.3.1 Managed objects in context

Managed objects are defined as the "management view" of the resources they represent. It is important not to interpret this definition too passively. When one looks at a resource that is to be managed, it is clear that not all of the details of its operation are of interest to management. Some of them can simply be ignored for management purposes; others are of interest, but only in some summarized or statistical form. On the other hand, some information, such as accounting information, fault reports and performance statistics, has to be provided to meet management needs specifically. Hence the management view of a resource is not simply a natural consequence of its implementation; it is something that needs to be deliberately and carefully specified. Indeed, it is an important part of the specification of management to decide just which aspects of each resource a manager is to be allowed to monitor and control. Thus a *managed object* is not just another word for a managed resource: instead, a managed object *defines the capability of management of a resource*, as opposed to its normal operation, whatever that may be.

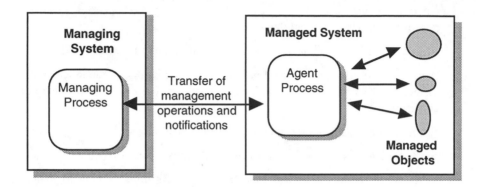

Figure 5.1 Systems management architecture.

The relationship between managed objects and the other elements of systems management, as defined in the standards, is shown in Figures 5.1 to 5.4. Figure 5.1 shows a *managing process* in a *managing system* communicating with a *managed system* concerning one or more managed objects. The managed system contains an agent process, which is responsible for mediating between what is communicated in protocol and what happens in or to the managed object(s). As explained above, the managed object definition relates what happens to the managed object to the actual effect on the resource being managed. The managing system is always the one containing the managing process and the managed system is always the one that contains the managed objects: "manager" and "agent" are roles adopted for individual communications. Systems can be implemented to act in either or both roles.

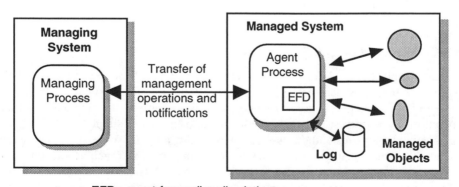

EFD= event-forwarding discriminator

Figure 5.2 Example agent functions.

The agent process is so called because it can be thought of as the "local representative" or *agent* for the remote manager in the managed system. One of the things it does is control access to the managed objects; another is to look after local logging and the distribution of event reports transmitted when various events occur in the managed system. These are illustrated in Figure 5.2.

The model places the managed objects in the managed system, but this does not necessarily mean that the resource represented by a particular managed object is in the managed system, or even necessarily controlled by it; it simply means that a view of the resource is available at the managed system. Other systems might have different views of the same resource, which would then be represented by other managed objects, regarded as lying in those systems. The following examples illustrate the point.

- A circuit joining two systems is likely to be represented by a managed object in each system. The two managed objects may have different values of some of their attributes (see later), representing the fact that the two systems may not have the same view of the circuit. For example, instantaneously, one system may regard the circuit as up and the other as down.

- Management information may be required about a network as a whole. One system (or more) may be responsible for holding or organizing a compendium of such information and be a point of inquiry for the managing system concerning it. Each such system will be regarded as containing a managed object representing the network as a whole.

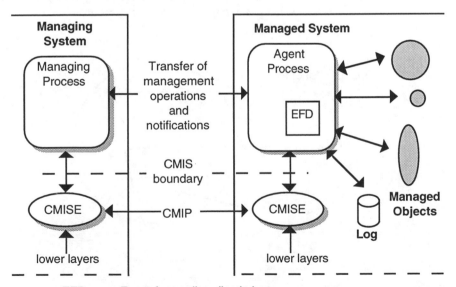

EFD   = Event-forwarding discriminator
CMIS(E) = Common management information service (element)
CMIP   = Common management information protocol

Figure 5.3 Management information transfer protocols.

The transfer of information is achieved using a stack of protocols, which are added in Figure 5.3. The figure shows the *Common Management Information Protocol*, CMIP, an application layer protocol that has been developed specifically for the purpose of transferring information concerning managed objects. It provides the CMIS service. Put briefly, it conveys:

- operation requests from managing system to managed system;

- notifications, in the form of *event reports*, from managed system to managing system;

- results and confirmations as appropriate.

5.3.2   The concept of a managed object

Figure 5.4 illustrates the idea of a managed object as the management view of a resource. The managed object is depicted as a sort of opaque sphere surrounding the real underlying resource, with a "window" through which management information may pass. The information crossing the boundary consists of:

- *management operations* on the managed object;

- the *results* of the operations that come back; and

- *notifications* that may be generated spontaneously by the managed object when something of significance (an *event*) happens to or in the resource.

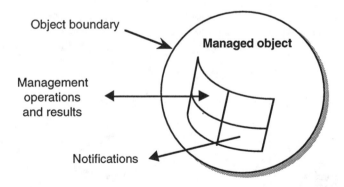

Figure 5.4 Concept of a managed object.

It is only through operations, results and notifications crossing the *managed object boundary*, coupled with means of communicating them to or from managing systems, that managing systems can have knowledge of, or control over, the managed resources. Of course, they also need the communications support of CMIS and

CMIP. The types of information that cross the managed object boundary correspond to the elements of the CMIS service, as can be seen from comparison of the two lists above.

In general, therefore, there will be two distinct specifications of the behavior of a resource. One will specify the "operational behavior" of the resource, i.e. what it does independently of any management; this might define a protocol such as OSI transport protocol, or state how a modem behaves, or define the operation of a relay. The other specification, the *managed object definition*, will define how the resource can be managed and how management operations relate to its operational behavior. It is the managed object definition that must be written in accordance with the *Management Information Model*.

5.3.3 More general object models

This is a deliberately limited use of the "object" concept. The managed object is a representation of how the resource can be managed, no more; it is not concerned with any other behavior of the resource except insofar as it is visible to management. The limitation may seem odd, but it is a consequence of the limited scope of the OSI management group; it was not and is not the task of that group to define general-purpose object models. However, general object models are being used in the *Open Distributed Processing* (ODP) activity under development in ISO/IEC JTC1 SC21 WG7 and ITU-TS Study Group 7 (where it is called DAF –*Distributed Applications Framework*).

In ODP (or any other general object model), all the components of the management architecture would be regarded as objects – the managing process, the agent process, the resources, discriminators, logs and so on; and what in Management is termed a managed object would in ODP be a "management interface to a resource object". Where the management model sees a discriminator sometimes as part of the agent process, when it is actually discriminating, and sometimes as a managed object, when it is being managed, in ODP it would be seen as a single object with several interfaces, only one of which is used to manage it. This more general object model is illustrated in Figure 5.5.

To put an object model for a managed resource in the context of a complete management system requires a general object model for systems elements other than managed resources. No such model has been standardized; it is seen as beyond the scope of OSI Management standardization. However, an example of what it might look like is shown in Figure 5.6, which is a model developed within the Regional Workshops for Open Systems to assist in the consideration of conformance testing of management profiles. The dual roles of the event-forwarding discriminator and log can be clearly seen: the lower parts correspond to the operation of discriminating and logging of potential event reports, while the upper parts correspond to the "managed object" interfaces through which the discrimination or logging behavior can be changed by management operation.

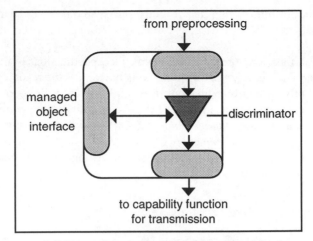

(a) Event-forwarding discriminator object

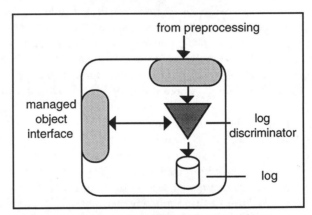

(b) Log and log discriminator object

Figure 5.5 Management control objects.

Because this type of modeling was seen as beyond the scope of OSI, not all the OSI Management standards adequately make the distinction between the normal "operational" behavior of the resource itself (that is, what it does when it is not in the process of being managed) and the managed object that represents the capability of managing it. There has been a tendency to define the managed object and assume that is all that has to be said. The *Event Report Management Function*, for example, concentrates on the managed objects – the event-forwarding discriminators – and does not define the process of event-forwarding itself.

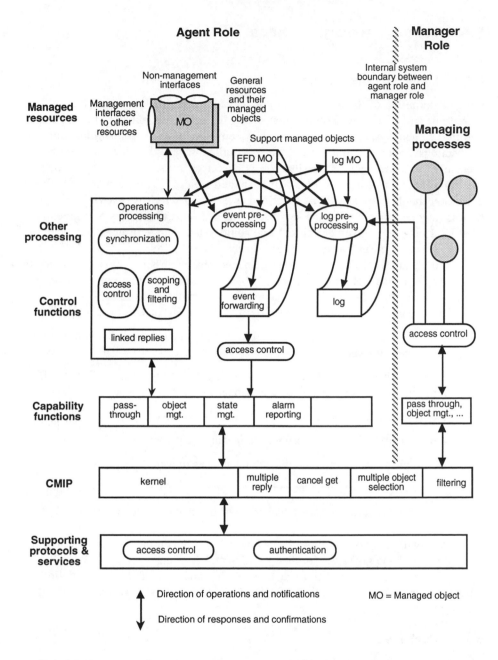

Figure 5.6 Model of a management system (combined agent and manager roles).

5.4   Defining managed objects

5.4.1   Managed object classes

Given a definition of the properties of a managed object, it is in general possible for there to be several managed objects that satisfy the definition, and possibly more than one in the same system. For example, a system may have several similar transport connections, or several similar logs, where "similar" means that they are managed in precisely the same way. This situation is described by saying that there may be several *instances* of a given *class* of managed object. Thus a managed object definition should more strictly be described as a *managed object class definition*; and a class may be thought of as the set of all managed object instances of a given type (that is, satisfying a given definition) that could exist. The term managed object on its own is used to mean managed object instance.

To be strictly accurate, the term managed object class is not used completely generally for any sets of similar managed objects, but only for those sets of managed objects that satisfy a class definition that has been documented as such.

A managed object class definition defines, for an instance of the class:

- the properties or characteristics visible at the managed object boundary – these are termed *attributes*, and each attribute has a *value*;

- the *management operations* that may be applied to it – some of these affect attributes and others operate on the managed object as a whole;

- the *matching rules* that govern the applicability of CMIS filters;

- the *behavior* it exhibits in response to management operations;

- the *notifications* it emits, and the circumstances in which it emits them;

- the *packages* it may include; and

- its position in the *inheritance hierarchy* of managed object classes.

Associated with it are one or more *name bindings*, which define how instances of the class are named and give rules for their creation and deletion.

These concepts are discussed later in this chapter. The precise definition techniques, which are the subject of GDMO (ISO/IEC 10165-4), are described in Chapter 6.

5.4.2   Packages

Allowing options in specifications is always dangerous, since it can dramatically increase the risk that two conforming systems can fail to interwork because they have chosen incompatible sets of options. However, it is recognized that there will be cases where the resources that are to be managed exist in significantly different versions that will have to be managed differently in some respects. An example is an ISO 8473 connectionless network protocol machine, which exists in two versions: an end-system version and a relay-system version. These have to be recognized as different as far as management is concerned, yet the extent of optionality must be controlled. This is done by defining conditional packages.

A *conditional package* is a collection of attributes, notifications, operations and behavior that is either present as a whole or not part of the specification of a managed object. It is not possible to have just a part of a package, except when packages overlap and one is included and one is not. Note that a package is simply a definition technique: it is not something that can be introduced and removed, or turned on and off, dynamically.

In the example above, the end-system specification is the basic one, while the relay-system version is specified as the basic one plus a defined conditional package. The term "conditional" is used since the presence of the package is conditional upon the configuration of the resource being managed, namely (in the example) whether it is in an end system or a relay system. In this example, the choice is related to the operational capability of the resource that is to be managed. It is also possible for packages to be defined to correspond to elements of management function, such as performance monitoring or accounting.

In order to prevent proliferation of managed object classes, the original intention was that the conditions associated with conditional packages should correspond to conformance claims to standards, not just implementor options. That is to say, conditional packages should represent major system differences. In practice, however, this ideal cannot be adhered to everywhere. Some organizations are doing their best to apply it as a rigid criterion – as ISO/IEC JTC1/SC6 is doing in the case of managed objects for the lower layers; others find they cannot. There are also some efficiency considerations to be taken into account when defining attributes for generic managed objects – for example **Top**, which has two packages for attributes that need not be present in absolutely all managed objects (see Section 5.4.4 below).

For consistency of definition technique, the mandatory elements of a managed object class definition are also grouped into one or more packages, called *mandatory packages*. These are just like conditional packages, except that they are always present in instances of the class.

The reader may wonder why packages were invented when it would seem perfectly possible to define new (sub)classes for the different cases of optionality. What is the advantage of the new mechanism? The reason is that it helps to restrict the number of things that need to be defined and named by ASN.1 object identifiers (for the detail see Chapter 6), particularly in the face of a possible combinatorial explosion of different cases. For example, a class with N independent optional sets of elements can be defined with N+1 packages, one mandatory and N conditional; this will need names for at most N+1 packages, plus one for the class itself. If conditional packages were not used, the number of different managed object classes needed to represent all possible cases would be 2^N, each of which would need an object identifier. And any requirements for further subclassing would make the combinatorial explosion even worse! To give an example, all the *performance* managed objects are subclasses of **Scanner**, which has scheduling and notification packages that are inherited by all metric and summarization managed objects.

5.4.3 Inheritance

There is a widespread requirement to be able to define managed objects that are extensions of other managed objects or to import pieces of specification of management information from elsewhere. For example:

- a managed object that controls diagnostic tests may need to extend the standard definition of such managed objects to include features specific to its environment;

- a new version of a managed object for a particular resource may, for reasons of backwards compatibility, need to contain all the elements of the preceding version; and

- a supplier of manageable products may wish to add proprietary features to those laid down in standards.

To do this, it is essential to be able to define one object class as an extension of another, so that it has not only all the attributes, operations and notifications of the former class, together with the behavior associated with them, but also some further attributes, operations and/or notifications. This may be done within the standards community, perhaps to define a new version of a managed object, or outside it, as when suppliers define their own proprietary extensions of the standard definition. This process is termed *specialization*. In such a case, the new class is said to be a *subclass* of the old class and the old class is said to be a *superclass* of the new class; the subclass is also said to *inherit* the characteristics of the superclass. Subclass and superclass are relative terms; thus a given class can be a subclass of one class and a superclass of another.

The resulting relationship between classes is termed *inheritance*. In fact, it is largely because of the need for inheritance that object-oriented techniques are used for the specification of management information. Inheritance provides a simple and consistent way of documenting related managed object definitions and encouraging the controlled reuse of pieces of specification.

The model allows for *multiple inheritance*; that is to say, a managed object class may inherit pieces of specification from several parent superclasses. Hence managed object classes form an *inheritance hierarchy*, (partially) ordered by the subclass-superclass relationship. A single class is defined to be at the top of the hierarchy and so to be the superclass of all other classes. It is called **Top**, and is defined in DMI (ISO/IEC 10165-2).

In management, inheritance is *strict*; that is, all the attributes, operations and notifications of a given class are present automatically in all of its subclasses and none are omitted. Within limits, the ranges of attribute values may be altered, additional parameters may be added to notifications and actions, the ranges of existing parameters may be altered and constraints across attribute values may be added, removed or changed. The limits to this kind of modification are defined precisely in the *Management Information Model*, and are designed to make extended managed objects compatible with the unextended parent ones so as to permit interworking in migration or multi-vendor environments. This concept of compatibility is discussed in Section 5.10 below.

Rules are defined in GDMO to deal with cases where there are conflicting definitions in multiple parent classes from which an element is to be inherited.

5.4.4   Generic managed object definitions

Inheritance can also be used not so much to extend standards as to define a subset of capability that is intended to be common to a number of managed object definitions, and thus impose some consistency upon them. One way of doing this is to define the subset as a superclass definition, and to define other managed objects as subclasses of that superclass. Then all the common elements are specified automatically, and the relationship between the specifications is visible in the specifications themselves. For example, the class definition of **Top** is used to define properties that all managed objects shall have. These include the attributes designed to enable managing systems to discover important properties of managed objects by interrogation, as discussed in Section 5.9.

In fact, **Top** has a mandatory package containing two attributes, which identify its managed object class and the name binding used to instantiate it. It has two more attributes each in its own conditional package, one of which is used to identify the packages that have been instantiated, the other to identify any allomorphic classes if the managed object supports allomorphism (allomorphism is discussed later, in Section 5.10.5).

As noted above, this technique is used in defining performance managed objects as subclasses of **Scanner**, and it is the rationale for defining the generic managed objects for various components of OSI layers in GMI.

Another technique is to define generic attributes, operations or notifications that can be imported into managed object definitions as appropriate. This is the approach adopted by many of the system management function standards, for items of management information such as alarm reports, state attributes, and so on.

5.5   Managed object attributes

5.5.1   Single attributes

An *attribute* is a property of a managed object that is visible at the managed object boundary and has a value. This value may have a simple or a complex data type. (That is to say, the value may have a complicated structure, such as a sequence of integers, but, except in the special case of set-valued attributes discussed below, the value may be operated on only in its entirety.) It may reflect or determine the behavior of the managed object, and its precise relationship to the underlying resource is an essential part of its definition.

There is no necessary implication that the value of an attribute is always stored somewhere in the system containing the managed object: the meaning of the definition that a given attribute can be read is simply that, if a manager asks for the value, the value is supplied. It might be stored locally, but it might equally well be calculated on request, or obtained as the result of an inquiry to another system.

Part of the definition of an attribute is the set of values it may take. Allowance has to be made for different instances of the same managed object class to operate with different sets of values for their attributes, yet some bounds have to be given in the class definition. For example, an attribute that represented the packet size used on a given X.25 virtual circuit could theoretically take any value in the set {16, 32, 64, 128, 256, 512, 1024, 2048, 4096}, yet not all systems will support all those values. In fact, many will support only the value 128.

This situation is handled by defining two sets of values for each attribute in the class definition: the *permitted value set* and the *required value set*. Then, any instance of the managed object class must support all the required values, and may support any further values from the permitted set, but must not allow values outside the permitted set. The idea here is that a manager will expect a managed system to set an attribute to any of its required values, and will not expect to read values outside the permitted set; but requests to set attributes to values outside their required sets may legitimately be refused.

Each attribute is identified by means of an *attribute identifier* (sometimes called attribute id), which is a globally unambiguous ASN.1 object[1] identifier.

5.5.2   Attribute groups

Attributes within a given managed object may be grouped into attribute groups, which have identifiers just as attributes do. Each attribute group is given a name so that its attributes may be operated on (for example, read) as a whole.

Attribute groups may be fixed or extensible. As the name implies, a fixed attribute group always has the same members, but an extensible attribute group can have attributes added (though not removed) when it is inherited from a superclass or imported. This makes it possible to use the same *attribute group identifier* for (say) the set of counter attributes in several managed objects; one first defines an empty extensible attribute group with the desired attribute group id, and then each of the managed object definitions extends it by adding its own set of counters.

5.6   Management operations

Two kinds of management operations are defined: those which are sent to a managed object to be applied to its attributes, and those which are applied to the managed object as a whole (and may also affect the values of its attributes, amongst other things).

The managed object definition may specify constraints that have to be satisfied in order for operations to be performed (for example, that the value of one attribute may not exceed that of another). If the constraint is not satisfied for a particular

---

[1]   The term "object" as used here does not mean a managed object; an ASN.1 *object identifier* is a name produced by a standardized procedure that guarantees that the name cannot be given to anything else.

request, the operation will be refused. Also, the originator of an operation request may use a CMIS filter to place conditions on the values of the attributes of the managed object that must be satisfied before the operation can be performed.

5.6.1   General-purpose operations on attributes

A number of operations on attributes are defined in the Information Model. These operations have the property of completing (or failing) immediately, in the sense that no other management operation or process internal to the object can intervene.

The value of an attribute may be observed or modified by an operation upon the object. The operations defined for attributes in general are:

*   **Get** reads the value of the attribute;

*   **Replace** sets the value of the attribute; and

*   **Replace with default** resets its value to a value known by the managed object in accordance with a specification in the managed object definition.

Such operations are defined to be performed on the managed object rather than on the attributes directly, so as to allow the object (in ways to be specified in its definition) to impose constraints on the values of attributes, singly or in combination, and also to allow filtering on the values of other attributes.

Two of these operations are available for use with attribute groups. These are the operations that do not supply new attribute values, namely **Get** and **Replace with default**.

Two additional operations, **Add** and **Remove**, are defined for a special type of attribute – the *set-valued attribute*. The value of a set-valued attribute is an unordered set of members of the same data type. This value may be read or modified as a whole by the operations described in the previous paragraph, and the additional operations may be used to add or remove members. The parameter supplied with these operations is another set of members of the same data type, and the operations performed are set-union (for **Add**) and set-difference (for **Remove**).

Part of the definition of a managed object class is the set of operations that may be performed on each of its attributes.

5.6.2   Operations on managed objects as a whole

In addition to the operations described above, other operations may be defined to operate on the managed object "as a whole". The only specific operations of this kind defined in the Information Model are those that **Create** and **Delete** managed objects. All others are regarded as particular instances of a general **Action** operation whose precise effect is to be specified in the relevant managed object definitions. These parallel the three CMIS primitives with the same names.

As its name suggests, the **Create** operation creates an instance of a managed object. This is intended to be used to initiate the operation of a resource through management action, though exactly what it will mean in practice will depend on the particular managed object definition in question and its name binding (see Section 5.8

below). It could have a significant effect on normal system operation, for example bringing a system component into live operation; or its effect could be limited to enhancement of management capability. In fact, managed object designers have a number of "initiation" mechanisms to choose from: **Create** operations, use of administrative state attributes and specially defined **Actions**. Not surprisingly, **Create** operations can be quite complicated.

When managed objects are created, attribute values are obtained, in order of precedence:

i)   from mandatory values given in the managed object definition;

ii)   from information explicitly supplied in the **Create** request;

iii) from a reference managed object cited in the **Create** request;

iv)   from an **Initial Value Managed Object** (IVMO) referenced in the managed object class definition;

v)   from defaults given in the managed object (or name binding) definition;

vi)   using local rules.

Similar rules apply to the choice of conditional packages to be instantiated. How names are assigned is discussed below, as part of the general discussion on managed object naming.

A system that supports allomorphism is permitted to create a managed object that is not actually an instance of the class requested in the **Create** operation, but one that can act allomorphically to the requested class. Exactly what the true class of the managed object created will be is a local system matter, but it must be reported in the response to the **Create** request. Allomorphism is discussed in Section 5.10.5.

The **Delete** operation is the opposite of **Create**. It is intended to stop the operation of a resource through management action, and again its precise effect on the resource is part of the definition of the managed object concerned. If a managed object contains other managed objects (see Section 5.8), it may not be deleted without deleting all the managed objects it contains, and they may not be deleted without deleting all the managed objects they contain, and so on. The rules governing deletion in such cases are specified in name bindings.

The name binding under which a managed object is instantiated may specify that the managed object can be deleted only if it contains no other managed objects. In general, a **Delete** operation on a managed object (and its subtree) will succeed only if there is no managed object in the entire containment subtree consisting of the managed object and all those beneath it that:

i)   has been created such that it can be deleted only if it has no contained managed objects, and

ii)   has one or more contained managed objects.

The **Action** operation is a generic operation that can be defined to suit the requirements of individual managed objects. That is to say, it is a vehicle for defining a special-purpose operation on a managed object, and its definition is part of the definition of the managed object to which it applies. It is possible for the result of an **Action** to be defined as a sequence of replies – for example, this facility is used in the *Test Management Function*; if so, the multiple reply functional unit of CMIS is needed to convey it in CMIP.

5.6.3   Multiple operations and synchronization

The CMIS service allows requests for management operations to be combined in the following ways, which may themselves be combined:

• an operation may be defined to operate on a collection of managed objects, to be selected by the scoping and filtering mechanisms; and

• an operation on a single managed object may specify a list of attributes to which it applies, rather than just a single one and, as a special case of this, "all attributes" may be asked for.

Although these are defined in CMIS, all CMIS and CMIP do is convey such combined requests from manager to agent: actually performing the right operations with the right synchronization is part of agent processing and managed object behavior.

The selection of managed objects by filtering works by evaluating a potentially complex logical condition on the attributes of the managed objects within the chosen scope. This condition is expressed as a *CMIS filter*. Its semantics are defined in the *Management Information Model* and its syntax in CMIP. The definition of each attribute includes the matching rules that may legitimately be used in filters.

Where a number of managed objects are selected, it is possible for the managing system to request either:

• *best-efforts synchronization*, in which case the operation is attempted on each managed object selected independently of the outcome of the attempts on the other managed objects selected; or

• *atomic synchronization*, in which case either all of the operations must be performed successfully, or none of them.

Support for cross-object atomic synchronization can be a local matter for the implementation; requirements for support of synchronization may also be specified in managed object definitions.

The general case of a CMIP operation on attributes is an operation on a list of attributes in a managed object. When more than one attribute is specified in such a list in conjunction with a request for atomic synchronization across more than one managed object, a definition of "success" for each individual managed object is needed. The rule is that an attribute operation on an individual managed object is regarded as successful if and only if all of the component operations on the individual attributes in the list are performed. However, the managed object definition may override this normal rule by specifying some other criterion for success, if necessary.

5.7   Notifications

Managed objects emit *notifications* when certain events occur. The parameters that the notifications contain and the events that trigger them are specified in the definition of the managed object concerned.

Although it is possible for managed object definers to invent their own notifications, many generally useful ones have been defined generically in the systems management function standards and specified in detail in DMI. These include notifications for managed object creation and deletion, state change, general attribute change, alarm report, security alarm report, and so on. They contain optional parameters, the use of which is to be determined by the managed object definer when they are imported into the managed object definition (see the next paragraph). Notifications defined in function standards also come with their own functional units, so that the capability of sending them can be negotiated individually at association establishment time; this is not the case with special-purpose ones.

The specification of a notification can be written to allow extension so that additional parameters may be supplied. Only if this is done can more parameters be added when a notification is inherited.

Whether a notification results in the external transmission of one or more CMIP event reports or an entry in a log (or both) is not part of the definition of the managed object that generates the notification. Management control of this transmission and/or logging uses the event forwarding and log control discriminators defined in the function standards (ISO/IEC 10164-5 & 6).

If it is desired to retrieve logged notifications selectively on the basis of values of their parameters, it will be necessary to define a corresponding **log record** managed object with the appropriate attributes.

There are some problems with defining notifications. One is a gray area called "event processing" in the architecture of the agent, which leaves it unclear where various parameters can be set. For instance, the alarm reporting function defines a number of 'optional' parameters in its generic alarm notification. For many of these, for example *probable cause*, it is obvious that it is up to the managed object definitions that import the notification to choose whether and how to use them. For others, for example *system time* and *correlated event*, it seems more reasonable that the choice should be made elsewhere. However, there is no obvious standard where such a specification could be written, and if it is not written the content of the event report is not fully defined. It is hoped that the PICS proformas being defined for the Systems Management Functions will allow the necessary statements to be made.

The same difficulty can arise with defining the content of logs, since they will contain potential event reports.

5.8   Names and containment

5.8.1   Names of properties of managed objects

Before dealing with names of managed objects, it is important to note that many definitions of properties of managed objects have names, such as managed object class, packages, attributes, name bindings and so on. These are named at definition time using standard ASN.1 object identifiers, which are globally unambiguous. Attribute-id and object class-id are examples of such names.

The remainder of this section deals with managed object instance names.

5.8.2   Containment

The naming of managed objects is based on the idea that managed objects are *contained* within other managed objects. For example, a connection is operated by a particular protocol machine in a layer in a system, and in order to refer to the **connection** managed object corresponding to the connection it is natural to say that it is contained in a **protocol machine** managed object contained in a **subsystem** managed object contained in a **system** managed object. The main purpose of containment relationships is to give a naming structure, and so they may be set up in whatever way is most natural and convenient. The only consequence of the containment structure other than on names is that there is an *existence* relationship such that a contained managed object cannot continue to exist if the managed object containing it disappears. This relationship affects the performance of the **Delete** operation, as explained earlier.

Specifically, the *containment structure* does not affect the performance of operations on managed objects, unless the definition of the managed object or its name binding explicitly defines a behavior that involves containing or contained managed objects. In object theory terms, therefore, containment is not encapsulation.

A managed object cannot be directly contained in more than one containing object, and so the containment structures of managed objects are a tree. Note that different instances of managed objects of a given class may be immediately contained in instances of managed objects of different classes.

Note also that containment is a relationship between managed object instances, not classes (cf. inheritance, which is a relationship between classes).

In the early days of development of the Management Information Model, it was intended that the highest level container in any managed system would be a **system** managed object (as defined in DMI) or a subclass of it. The managed objects in a system would then form a single containment tree, under **system**. However, it was later recognized that there were advantages to be gained in allowing other managed objects to act in this role, and even for managed systems to have managed objects arranged in more than one containment tree.

Suppose, for example, that a particular system acts as a regional manager for a network within a complex of networks. It will then contain managed objects corresponding to that regional network, as well as managed objects representing the local resources of in a tree under **system**, and the managed objects representing the regional network in a tree under a **network** managed object. The latter arrangement allows the managed objects for the network components to be named independently of the regional manager, which will facilitate distributed implementation of managing systems.

5.8.3   Name structure and usage

Each managed object (instance) has to have a name, so that it can be referred to in protocol. There are two forms of managed object names – a *local form* that just identifies the managed object relative to the highest-level managed object that contains it (often a **system** managed object); and a *global form* that adds a global identification of the system that it is in to the local form. For convenience, this identification of the higher-level container is termed the "global part" in this chapter; the standards have no special term for it. Thus the global form consists of a global part together with the local form.

The local form name is assigned when the managed object is created , whether by local action or as the result of a management **Create** operation.

When communicating with a managed system, the local form may be used as follows. If the managed system has only one containment tree within it, then the local form name will identify managed objects in that tree. If the managed system has more than one containment tree, then a local form name will identify managed objects in the containment tree headed by a **system** managed object or a subclass of it; and to identify the other managed objects, the global form will be needed.

5.8.4   The local form

The local form of the name of a managed object is constructed by going step-by-step down the containment tree, starting from the highest-level managed object. A single step, from containing object to contained object, gives a component of the name termed a *relative distinguished name* (RDN). The full local form is constructed by concatenating the relative distinguished names, starting with the one that identifies the managed object immediately contained within highest-level managed object, and going on down.

Within a given containing managed object, a contained managed object is identified by quoting the value of an attribute that is used to name it – by saying that it is the one that has a particular attribute with a particular value. Thus the relative distinguished name consists of an *attribute value assertion* (or AVA) that names an attribute and quotes the value it must have. For this to provide unambiguous names, the pair

        attribute-id, attribute value

must be unambiguous within the scope of the containing managed object. (This is because the attribute value assertion is interpreted only in the context of a known container.) There is considerable flexibility in how this may be achieved; one way is to use a different attribute (with a different attribute-id) in each managed object class; this is simple, but does not allow the identifying attribute to be inherited. The alternative is to use the same attribute to identify instances of many different classes;

in that case, control of the values assigned to the identifying attribute needs to extend over all the relevant classes.

Note also that different instances of managed objects of a given class may be identified by different attributes when contained in containing objects of different classes.

Those familiar with OSI X.500 Directory standards (ISO/IEC 9594) will recognize much of the terminology, which was, indeed, imported from the Directory work. However, while the terms are similar, there are some significant differences: for example, it is a restriction in Management that an RDN may have only one attribute value assertion.

5.8.5   The global part

For consistency of structure, the global part also has the form of an attribute value assertion, even though the highest-level managed object is not contained in any other managed object. Two ways of doing this are defined in the *Management Information Model*, and two attributes are defined in the **system** managed object class (in DMI) to support them, namely *systemTitle* and *systemId*.

The systemTitle attribute is intended to contain a particular type of registered name for the managed system, the *system-title*, which (because it is registered) names it completely unambiguously in a global context. The system-title is defined in the *Naming and Addressing* part of the OSI Reference Model (ISO 7498-3). When this attribute is used, the global part consists of a single AVA.

The other naming attribute, systemId, is intended to be used to link the managed object name into some other naming hierarchy, such as that of the OSI Directory. For example, a sequence of RDNs in the Directory Information Tree may identify some Directory entry that contains an identifier of a **system** managed object. So long as that identifier is unambiguous within that Directory entry, it can be used to form an RDN which can be concatenated with the sequence that identifies the Directory entry to form the necessary global part.

In either case, the full global form of a managed object name is a *Distinguished Name* (DN) that consists of a sequence of attribute value assertions: a global part followed by a local form.

The effect of all this is that, in order to construct global names, the naming structure (based on containment within the **system** or other highest-level managed object) is extended upwards in a consistent manner, each step being based on AVAs, to link into the global naming tree. In the *Management Information Model*, an object (in this context not necessarily a managed object) in a naming tree is said to be *subordinate* to the objects nearer the root that are used to name it; they in turn are said to be *superior* to the objects they help to name.

5.8.6   A naming example

The managed objects defined for the OSI network layer are used to illustrate the naming of managed objects. This collection of managed objects is illustrated in Figure 5.7, which shows the containment structure as a tree. The network subsystem managed object is contained in the system managed object.

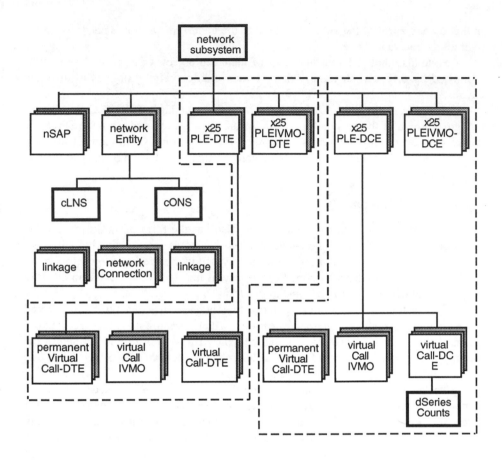

cLNS   = connectionless-mode network service
cONS   = connection-mode network service
dSeries   relates to CCITT recommendation D series tariffs
DCE   = data circuit terminating equipment (the network side of the X.25 interface)
DTE   = data terminal equipment (the terminal side of the X.25 interface)
IVMO   = initial value managed object (used to hold initial values for dynamically
            created managed objects such as connections)
nSAP   = network service access point
PLE   = packet-level entity

Figure 5.7 Network layer managed objects (from ISO/IEC 10733).

Figure 5.8 shows how the RDNs of the managed objects in one branch of the tree are constructed. The local form of the name of the managed object at the leaf of the tree is constructed by concatenating these RDNs; the global form puts the name of the **system** managed object in front.

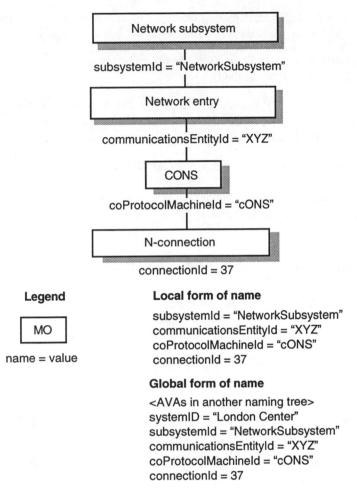

Figure 5.8 The name of a network connection managed object.

5.8.7 Name bindings

The specification that a particular managed object is contained within another managed object and is identified by a particular attribute is made by using a **name binding**. More formally, a name binding is a relation between object classes which specifies that an object of one identified class may contain an object of another identified class, using a particular attribute for naming.

Name bindings may also contain other information, such as:

- rules to be applied when creating and deleting managed objects, which may differ depending on their location in the containment tree; and

- behavior specific to the particular containment relationship.

The rules to be applied when creating managed objects include the specification of which of the following methods of naming a created object may apply:

- the manager may supply the name as part of the Create operation (there are two minor variants of this method);

- the manager may identify the managed object that is to contain the new one in the Create operation, and leave it to the managed system to complete the name by providing an additional RDN; and

- the manager may leave the entire name to the managed system.

Many of the properties of name bindings, such as inheritance, are specified in GDMO, not the Management Information Model.

5.9   Support for management knowledge

A number of attributes are defined to be present in all managed objects in order to enable managing systems to discover the capabilities of the systems that they wish to manage. This is done by defining them as attributes of **Top**. They are:

- **managed object class** – its true class name;

- **name binding** – the name binding that was used to instantiate it;

- **packages**[2] – the collection of registered packages that is present in this managed object instance; and

- **allomorphic classes**[2] – the classes that the managed object can act as allomorphically.

The values of all these attributes are ASN.1 object-ids, or sets of them.

A managing system may read some or all of these (and other) attributes of the managed objects in a system, in conjunction with scoping and filtering, to discover:

- what managed objects the system contains and with what packages they are instantiated;

- what their true classes are;

- what their allomorphic capabilities are; and

- what their names are.

---

[2]   These attributes are specified as conditional packages and hence are present only if applicable.

5.10   Compatibility and allomorphism

5.10.1   Requirements and approach

There are a number of circumstances in which a managing system that was designed to manage a particular set of managed objects may need to manage systems that actually contain managed objects that are slightly different. Suppose, for example, that an upgraded product is installed that implements a new version of a particular managed object that is an extension of a previous one, but for some interim period the managing system has not been upgraded. Then there is a need for the old manager to be able to manage the new version, which certainly ought be possible given that it is an extension of the previous version. Or suppose that in a multi-vendor network there are products from supplier A and supplier B, each of which adds different proprietary features to a standard managed object definition. There will then be a need to manage supplier A products from a supplier B manager, at least to the extent of the standard features that are common to both, even though the proprietary extensions may not be manageable in this way.

This idea leads to the concept of *compatible* managed object definitions, where one is a kind of subset of the other (this is defined precisely below). One way of achieving compatibility is to derive a new managed object from an old one by inheritance, but so long as the subset properties hold, whether or not inheritance was actually used is irrelevant.

The problem can then be stated as follows. How does one arrange for a managing system to manage other systems that contain managed objects that are compatible with, but not of the same class as, those known by the managing system?

There are two ways in which this problem can be tackled. The first, often termed *best-efforts management*, is essentially to make no special provision except that the manager must be prepared to ignore extra unexpected information it may receive. For example, if it requests the values of all the attributes of a managed object, it must be prepared to receive the values of any extra attributes that the extended managed object may have. Depending on the flexibility of the managed system, it may be possible to set its event forwarding discriminators to transmit only the notifications known to the managed system. If not, the managing system will have to be prepared to ignore extra notifications.

The other alternative is for the extended managed object to appear as if it were the unextended managed object. In this case, the managed system has to respond to a request to read all the attributes of a managed object by returning the values of just those attributes that the manager knows. This second method, in which the managed system contains knowledge of managed object classes that it can imitate, is termed *allomorphism*. (This term was chosen specifically for systems management and is not part of the general object literature. Originally the term *polymorphism* was used, but there are at least two different senses of that term in object theory literature, neither of which is exactly what was wanted for management; hence the new term.)

Broadly, the difference between these two techniques is that best-efforts management puts the responsibility for dealing with migration on the managing system, which has to be able to cope with unexpected information, whereas allomorphism puts the onus on the managed system to ensure that the manager has "no surprises".

We now look at the problem and the solutions in more detail.

5.10.2   Variation within managed object classes

First, it should be noted that even when the conditions that govern the instantiation of conditional packages are fixed, there can be many different managed objects that satisfy a given class definition. They must all have all the properties and exhibit all the behavior defined in the class definition, but that still leaves some room for variation.

Different instances of the same class may operate with different sets of values for their attributes. Firstly, variation is allowed so long as the set of values taken by an attribute is a subset of the permitted value set and a superset of the required value set (with equality allowed); secondly, the default values used with the **Replace with default** operation may be different in different managed objects.

Notifications and action results may be defined to contain information whose presence is optional (but whose syntax is defined). Managers have to be prepared to cope with the consequent variation. Moreover, the "same" notification may be defined with different information in different conditional packages.

So managing instances of just a single managed object class is not completely straightforward; and when there are many conditional packages to be taken into account, a managing system may have to be able to deal with a significant degree of variation. (The managing system can determine which packages are present in a managed system by reading the **packages** attribute defined in **Top**.)

5.10.3   Compatibility

The concept of compatibility goes beyond the level of variation found within a single managed object class and tries to capture the relationship between a managed object and a class definition that it extends in some way.

Certainly, compatibility has to include the variation within a managed object class described in the previous section. But it goes beyond that, to allow the addition of attributes and notifications. Specifically, a managed object is defined to be compatible with a class C so long as the following conditions hold:

- it has all the attributes defined in C, with the operations defined in C upon them – it may have further attributes;

- it supports all the actions defined in C – it may support further actions;

- it has all the notifications defined in C – it may have further notifications;

- it extends the action or notification parameters of actions or notifications defined in C only where the definition in C permits management extensions;

- for each of the attributes that are defined in C, the values taken include the required value set defined in C and do not go outside the permitted value set defined in C; and

- the behavior defined for attributes, actions and notifications does not conflict with that defined in C.

When a subclass S is derived from a superclass C by specialization, the inheritance rules ensure that instances of S are compatible with class C. The rules ensure that parameters may be added to inherited actions or notifications only if the original definitions explicitly provide for such extension and, for each attribute, they ensure that:

the permitted value set in C includes
the permitted value set in S, which includes
the required value set in S, which includes
the required value set in C.

However, it is not *necessary* for compatibility that one managed object class should be a subclass of the other – though it will no doubt be so in the majority of cases. All that is required is that the above conditions should apply.

We can now restate the problem. There is a managing system M that can manage objects of class C, but no more; however, it needs to manage a target system T, which contains a managed object O that is compatible with class C, but not an instance of C.

5.10.4 Best-efforts management

The idea behind best-efforts management is essentially to do nothing, to take no special action at all. If the manager M restricts itself to the operations valid for the managed objects it knows about, that is, managed objects of class C, then operations will all work correctly (within reasonable limits) as a consequence of the compatibility constraints. It may be possible to set the event forwarding discriminators in T to transmit only the notifications that M can understand, that is, those in C; if not, M will have to be prepared to ignore them. So a lot can be achieved automatically, so to speak, within the level of variation expected within a managed object class. However, there are exceptions; because O may have attributes not defined in C, the result of a "Get all attributes" operation may include attributes unknown to M; and similarly the result of an operation on an attribute group may affect attributes defined in O but not in C. And some event reports may have to be ignored.

In many circumstances it is not unreasonable to implement a managing system that is capable of dealing with the occasional surprise attribute in this way, and the benefit is much greater flexibility to deal with migration and multi-vendor environments.

On the other hand, there is no mechanism defined by which a manager can discover whether best-efforts management is appropriate or not in any given case –

unless the allomorphic classes attribute is set in the extended managed object instance. One would expect best-efforts management to be used where there is prior knowledge of the names of managed object instances, together with expectations that they are compatible with a set of known classes.

When best-efforts management is used, the managing system will typically not know the class of O. But the manager does not always have to know the class of a managed object it wants to manage: there is a general-purpose value that can be used for the object class in CMIP in such cases, whose meaning is "the class you are". When an object is created, its class is returned in the response; and object class is always available as an attribute inherited from **Top**.

Note that best-efforts management could be used even when the compatibility conditions did not hold, though then the managing system would have be able to deal with a greater variety of surprising responses from the target system. These might include refusals to set attributes to what the manager regards as required values and responses containing attribute values beyond the supposed legal limits, as well as strange notifications and action responses.

5.10.5   Allomorphism

The other approach to the problem is for the managed system T to act as if managed object O were an instance of class C. This is called *allomorphism*. More generally, allomorphism is the ability of a system containing a managed object to act as if the managed object were a member of another managed object class, at least as far as can be seen externally in management protocol. This class does not have to be a superclass of the managed object's own class. The managed system must be aware of the managed object class a particular managed object is expected to appear to be. Mechanisms in the managed system are required to restrict the capability of a given managed object to the capability defined in another class definition (the *allomorphic class*) in order to allow it to be managed effectively by a managing system that has been designed to manage instances of the allomorphic class but cannot manage the given managed object directly. The differences from best-efforts management are that:

- operations on "all attributes" are performed just on the attributes defined in C;

- operations on extended attribute groups are performed on the attributes defined to be in those groups in C; and

- notifications defined in O are transmitted or logged only if they are defined in C.

In other cases, the managed object acts as "itself". For example, when allomorphic behavior is requested in conjunction with **Replace with default**, the rules for setting to default that will be used are those defined for the true class, not those defined for the allomorphic class. This is necessary in order to avoid possible inconsistencies.

Allomorphism is an optional system capability in the sense that managed object class definitions cannot require any form of allomorphic behavior for conformance.

For each managed object in a system, whether it can act allomorphically and, if so, to what classes, are implementation choices.

The mechanisms by which the target system comes to know what allomorphic behavior is required of it, that is, which managed objects are supposed to behave as instances of which classes, are not yet fully standardized. Currently, a manager can use CMIP to request the creation of a particular class, in response to which the managed system can create a compatible managed object. If it does, the managed system must return the value of the actual class created and put the value of the requested class in the allomorphs attribute inherited from **Top**. Subsequent requests for management operations using the allomorphic class (the class originally requested) require the managed object to behave allomorphically to that class. However, no mechanisms are yet defined to constrain notifications to those for the allomorphic class, and hence best-efforts management has to be used for notifications, whether in event reports or logs. Enhancements to the Systems Management standards are now being worked on to extend the support for allomorphism.

5.10.6 Remarks

Currently neither "best-efforts" management nor allomorphism is fully supported by the standards, though both techniques are supported as far as managed object definition is concerned by the *Management Information Model* and GDMO. But in neither case is there a mechanism for establishing the appropriate regime: for "best-efforts" the deficiency lies in discovering when it could be used, for allomorphism it lies in setting up the appropriate treatment of notifications. Which of these is more significant will no doubt depend on the specific practical requirement.

Neither technique is actually required for conformance to the standards, but in practice something has to be done. It would be unwise to implement a management regime that did not permit interworking with systems containing extended or "other" proprietary managed objects. Whatever the longer-term goal, today it would seem reasonable to design into managing systems the ability to accept and ignore unexpected event reports or logged information. Additional mechanisms can be added as requirements dictate and the necessary standards are developed.

5.11   Relationship with Directory standards

Because of the similarity of terminology and the fact that both Management and Directory involve stored information, it is worth making some remarks about the relationship between them. They have in common some terminology, an object-oriented approach and the idea of naming things with attribute value assertions (though with minor differences). In addition, as has been explained in Section 5.8.

However, an unfortunate side effect of the adoption of Directory concepts in Management has led some readers to believe that there are other, much stronger structural similarities. So it is perhaps useful to point out that managed objects have no structural similarity with Directory entries, managed object classes are not Directory classes, managed object attributes are not Directory attributes (though they play the same role in naming), the definition techniques are entirely different, and so on. In fact, there is no necessary relationship between them at all.

In practice, relationships can and no doubt will be constructed. Indeed, it is likely that the Directory will be used to provide location information about managing and managed systems and managed objects themselves. The Directory naming structure will no doubt be used in some circumstances to provide part of the global names of managed objects, as explained in the section on naming above. There are other possibilities; the GDMO of a managed object class definition can be placed in a Directory entry, and so on.

5.12   Documentation of management information

The documentation of management information, which comprises a variety of different pieces of specification from a variety of sources, is a huge and complicated task. The standards committees, ISO/IEC and ITU-TS, have given some thought to the problem and have recognized that the ideal would be to organize the documentation of standardized management information so that:

- it forms a coherent structure;

- individual items can be found without difficulty and compared with related items; and

- users can discover what has already been specified and are encouraged to use existing elements of specification rather than reinventing them differently.

This is not just a problem for the standards organizations. Industry groupings such as the NM Forum have the same need to organize their own specifications, which come from an even wider variety of sources.

The items range in scale from complete managed object class definitions with their associated name bindings down to single attributes (such as state attributes, counters, etc.) that are intended to be imported into a wide variety of managed objects. They range in "specificity" from the most generic, such as **Top**, to the most specific, such as **NSAP-MO** (Network Service Access Point MO).

Typically, the specific managed object definitions for the management of resources within OSI layers are being developed by the groups responsible for those layers, and published either as separate standards, or as components or parts of the standards for the resources being managed. In the network layer, for example, the standards for the management of X.25 are published with other elements of network layer management in a separate standard, (ISO 10733), whereas the management of routing is an integral part of the routing standards. In addition, various ITU-TS Study Groups are defining the management information they need to support the management of public networks. This is a large and rapidly growing body of documentation.

The groups responsible for OSI Management (ISO/IEC JTC1/SC21/WG4 and ITU-TS Study Group 7) have produced two standards that document the management information they standardize, so that the groups developing specific managed object definitions (for example, for the network layer) can refer to them readily and use them as sources for generic and reusable elements of specification. These two standards are:

- Definition of Management Information (DMI)

- Generic Managed Information (GMI).

5.12.1 The Definition of Management Information (DMI)

The Definition of Management Information (ISO/IEC10165-2) began its life as a modest standard which was to contain some generic definitions of attributes, actions and notifications of general use that could be imported and made specific in particular managed object definitions. It was intended to supplement the systems management function standards, and included definitions of counters, thresholds, tidemarks and the like, so as to avoid a large number of different and incompatible definitions of such things in different managed object definitions.

Subsequently, the function definers decided to use DMI to collect together in a single standard the detailed definitions of the attributes, actions and notifications required to support the functions. So, for example, the *State Management Function* ISO/IEC 10164-2 defines the concepts of state and the semantics and behavior of a number of types of state attribute; but the detailed definitions of the attributes and their syntax are in DMI. The published DMI contains all the GDMO and ASN.1 definitions of management information needed to support the functions ISO/IEC 10164-1 to 7, including managed object class definitions for discriminators, logs, log records and other things needed by the functions. It also contains the definition of **Top** and a generic definition of the **system** managed object.

Being a standard, DMI had to be finalized and published in a stable form. Yet systems management functions are still being defined. Rather than continually update DMI to add further definitions of management information every six months or so – standards are expected to be more stable – it has been decided to publish the GDMO definitions of the management information required by new Systems Management Functions as normative annexes to the individual function standards.

Working out new procedures that will enable management information to be centrally documented after DMI has turned out to be more of a problem than expected, and at the time of writing there is still no agreement on exactly what should be done. The ITU-TS has been considering the development of a "catalog" of management information that would reference standard managed object definitions from a variety of sources.

5.12.2 Generic Management Information (GMI)

The objective of GMI (ISO 10165-5) is to align the definitions of managed objects for the various OSI layers as far as is reasonable. Since the layers are all based on the OSI reference model, their components are to some extent similar; they have service access points (SAPs), addresses, entities, protocol machines, connections and so on. The idea of GMI is to define generic managed objects for such components, including attributes and other properties that are common to them all, independent of the particular OSI layer; then the specific layer standards can define their managed objects as specializations of the generic ones. Thus there are generic **protocol machine** managed objects from which specific protocol machine managed objects such as **X.25 PLE** (packet layer entity) managed objects will be specialized (by inheritance), a generic **connection** managed object, and so on.

GMI was developed in close collaboration with the groups in SC6 developing the standards for management of OSI protocols in the data-link, network and transport layers (the upper layer groups were not working on management at the time). It proved possible to make a number of generic definitions, though there are significant differences between OSI layers that sometimes require different representations in management. The current managed object standards for the lower layers do indeed derive layer-specific managed objects from the generic ones in GMI. GMI has generic definitions of the following managed object classes:

- application process
- communications entity
- communications information record
- connectionless-mode protocol machine
- connection-mode protocol machine
- sap1 and sap2 (two different varieties of a SAP managed object)
- single peer connection
- subsystem.

It defines a generic communications information notification and some activate and deactivate actions. It also defines several attributes, including a number of names, counters and a timer, and it provides a number of useful name bindings.

Acknowledgments

Some material for this work was developed with support from the UK Department of Trade and Industry's Open Systems Technology Transfer programme. In collaboration with DISC, one result of the programme was the publication of the *Technical Guide for OSI Management,* and its companion *Practical Guide* for OSI Management, NCC Blackwell, 1992, ISBN 1-85554-187-4 and 1-85554-195-5

Abbreviations

ASN.1	Abstract Syntax Notation 1
AVA	Attribute value assertion
CL	Connectionless

CMIP	Common Management Information Protocol
CMIS	Common Management Information Service
CO	Connection(-oriented)
DAF	Distributed Applications Framework
DMI	Definition of Management Information
DN	Distinguished name
GDMO	Guidelines for the Definition of Managed Objects
GMI	Generic Management Information
ISDN	Integrated Services Digital Network
IVMO	Initial value managed object
MIB	Management information base
MO	Managed object
PICS	Protocol implementation conformance statement
NSAP	Network service access point
ODP	Open Distributed Processing
OSI	Open Systems Interconnection
RDN	Relative distinguished name
SAP	Service access point
SMI	Structure of Management Information

References

Architecture

ISO 7498-4. *Basic Reference Model —Part 4: Management Framework.*

ISO/IEC 10040. *Systems Management Overview.*

Management Communications

ISO/IEC 9595 (1991). *Common Management Information Service Definition.*

ISO/IEC 9596-1 (1991). *Common Management Information Protocol Specification.*

Systems Management Functions

ISO/IEC 10164-1. *Object Management Function.*

ISO/IEC 10164-2. *State Management Function.*

ISO/IEC 10164-3. *Objects and Attributes for Representing Relationships.*

ISO/IEC 10164-4. *Alarm Reporting Function.*

ISO/IEC 10164-5. *Event Report Management Function.*

ISO/IEC 10164-6. *Log Control Function.*

ISO/IEC 10164-7. *Security Alarm Reporting Function.*

Management Information

ISO/IEC 10165-1. *Management Information Model.*

ISO/IEC 10165-2. *Definition of Management Information.*

ISO/IEC 10165-4. *Guidelines for the Definition of Managed Objects.*

ISO/IEC 10165-5. *Generic Management Information.*

ISO/IEC DIS 10165-6. *Requirements and Guidelines for Implementation Conformance Statement Proformas Associated with Management Information.*

ISO/IEC 10733. *Elements of Management Information Related to OSI Network Layer Standards.*

Other standards

ISO 7498-3. *Basic Reference Model - Part 3: Naming and Addressing.*

ISO/IEC 9594. *The Directory.*

ISO 8473. *Protocol for Providing the Connectionless-mode Network Service.*

Chapter 6

Guidelines for the Definition of Managed Objects

Tony Jeffree

Sema Group Consulting Ltd,
Norcliffe House, Station Road,
Wilmslow, Cheshire, SK9 1BU, UK
Email: 100271.522@compuserve.com

The Guidelines for the Definition of Managed Objects (GDMO) is the international standard that defines the notation used to specify managed object classes that permit management of resources in the OSI environment. The standard also provides the managed object definer with the background information and guidance that will assist in the process of definition.

This chapter introduces the aspects of GDMO that give general advice to managed object definers, the concept of templates and the notation used, describing each of the templates defined in GDMO and identifying the purpose of each component. The chapter continues with a discussion of the relationship between the Managed Object Class Definition and the OSI management communications protocols, and concludes with an example of the application of the GDMO notation.

6.1 The purpose of the guidelines

The *Management Information Model*, described in Chapter 5, provides the modeling concepts and terminology that are used within Open Systems Interconnection (OSI) management to model managed objects and management information. However, the model in isolation is insufficient to allow the development of managed object definitions that are consistent with the OSI management approach. The *Guidelines for the Definition of Managed Objects*, commonly known as GDMO, provides the link between the abstract modeling concepts contained in the Management Information Model and the concrete requirements for specifying particular managed object classes that permit the management of particular resources in the OSI environment. In order to achieve this aim, GDMO contains material which is purely for the guidance of the managed object definer. GDMO also includes definitions of the syntax and semantics of the notation that the managed object definer must use when specifying managed object classes and their components. The overall intent of the standard is to provide the managed object definer with the background information and notational tools that will allow the required management functionality of a resource to be converted into a formal description of a managed object class that realizes that functionality.

6.2   Guidance to managed object definers

After setting its scope, giving references and defining terms, GDMO:

- establishes general principles that should underpin the development of managed object classes;

- identifies global issues that the managed object definer must address; and

- encourages consistency of approach between independent managed object class definitions.

6.2.1   General principles

When embarking on the process of defining managed object classes, it is relatively easy to get caught up in the process itself and to lose sight of the objective, which is to provide a set of management tools with which to manage a particular resource. Thus, the general principles stress the importance of keeping a clear view of the requirements against which the managed object class is being developed. Part of this process involves applying the structuring mechanisms (subclasses, multiple inheritance, packages, containment, and attribute grouping) in an appropriate manner. Appropriate choices of structuring techniques can reduce the complexity of the definition process by permitting reuse of specifications in different contexts.

It is also important to keep the level of complexity of the management functionality within a managed system consistent with the complexity of the resource being managed. If the resource itself is simple, keeping the management functionality correspondingly simple will minimize the impact of management on the overall complexity of the resultant products. It may, however, be the case that complex management techniques and procedures are required in order to manage devices whose management functionality is simple; in such cases, the burden of any additional complexity involved in managing such devices must be borne by the managing system. In some cases, it may be appropriate to employ hierarchical management structures for managing simple resources, where a high-level manager deals with a "proxy" manager which in turn manages the resource. This arrangement has the advantage of allowing preprocessing of information to be performed by the proxy manager, which can mediate between the complex commands generated by the manager and the simple management capabilities of the target resource.

6.2.2   Global issues

The global issues identified include advice related to registration, naming, optionality and consistency.

Registration

GDMO describes the registration tree structure that has been adopted in OSI management standards for allocating globally unique identifiers (*object identifiers*) to components of managed object definitions that appear in those standards. This is intended to give an example of an allocation scheme that may be used as a model for similar allocation schemes in other situations where it is necessary to define managed object classes; for example, a company may wish to define its own nonstandard managed object classes for proprietary use.

An object identifier value consists of a sequence of integer values, known as arcs, which define the structure of the registration tree. The first (leftmost) arc defines the initial branch of the tree, and identifies the *registration authority* responsible for allocating the second arc, and so on for subsequent arcs. Three first-level arcs are defined: one for ISO use, one for CCITT use and one for joint ISO-CCITT use. The allocation scheme described in GDMO, because it relates to standards developed jointly by ISO and CCITT, is based on the registration scheme that has been established for joint ISO-CCITT use; the joint ISO-CCITT arc has been allocated the integer value 2. Under this scheme, the second level arcs are allocated jointly by ISO and CCITT to particular topic areas or families of standards; the arc labeled as "ms", which has the integer value 9, has been reserved for use by the systems management standards, and arcs below "ms" are defined and allocated in the text of GDMO.

The third-level arc is used to identify groups of standards; at present, four arcs are allocated at this level, corresponding to the *Systems Management Overview*, the *Common Management Information Protocol (CMIP)* standards, the *Systems Management Function* standards and the *Structure of Management Information (SMI)* standards.

The fourth-level arcs identify particular standards in the group concerned; the allocation of arcs below this level is then the responsibility of the individual standard.

In the case of the SMI and systems management function standards, a common scheme exists for the allocation of the fifth-level arcs; these values are used to identify categories of registered information objects, such as Abstract Syntax Notation One (ASN.1) modules, managed object classes, and attribute types. The sixth-level arcs in these cases are used to identify instances of that particular category of information object. Thus, an object identifier value allocated in GDMO to the 49th attribute type definition would have arcs allocated as follows:

```
{joint-iso-ccitt ms(9) smi(3) part4(4) attribute(7) type-49(49)}
```

A prerequisite for defining managed object classes and their components is for the organization concerned to be able to allocate object identifier values, either by obtaining an object identifier arc for its own use and thereby becoming a registration authority for its own information objects, or by making use of the services of an existing registration authority that is prepared to allocate object identifier values for use by third parties. The usual route for establishing a private registration authority is via the relevant national standards organizations. For example, in the UK, procedures have been established by the British Standards Institute (BSI) whereby organizations may obtain an arc for their own use, under which they can allocate object identifiers to information objects that they wish to register; in the US, similar procedures are administered by the American National Standards Institute (ANSI).

Naming

It is necessary to make an appropriate choice of data type for the attribute that will be used to form the relative distinguished name of a managed object. Generally it is desirable to choose a data type that will allow the name to be represented in human readable form; the choice of *Graphic String*, which permits the use of any standardized character set, fulfills this requirement and allows the use of any natural language for which a standardized alphabet exists.

Options

Generally speaking, options in standards lead to problems with interworking, so the philosophy proposed by GDMO is that optionality *per se* is not permitted in managed object definitions unless it is related to some standardized optional feature of the resource being managed, or some standardized subset of the functionality provided by OSI management. For example, if a protocol standard includes a number of optional conformance classes, the corresponding managed object class might be defined in such a way that its functionality varies according to the conformance classes that are implemented in a given system.

Consistency

GDMO contains a number of items of advice related to maintaining consistency across the various standards in which managed object classes will be developed. The objective is to reduce the burden upon the managed object definer by encouraging re-use of existing definitions of components of managed object classes, and to reduce the burden on the eventual user of management facilities by reducing the number of different approaches taken to solve similar problems. For this purpose, the reader is referred to other standards that are sources of generic definitions (such as the Definition of Management Information (DMI), Generic Management Information (GMI) and systems management functions). Managed object definers are encouraged to make re-usable definitions available to other developers and to make use of particular, commonly applicable techniques such as non-resettable counters, initial value managed objects and definitions in the function standards.

6.2.3 A concrete realization of the Management Information Model

The remainder of GDMO is concerned with the practicalities of defining managed object classes, and in particular, with the language that managed object definers are required to use in order to document their managed object class definitions. This language can be viewed as the mechanism whereby the modeling techniques identified in the information model are converted into concrete form as managed object class definitions from which managed objects can be instantiated.

In addition to providing a syntactic definition of the notation, GDMO defines how that notation is to be interpreted; in particular, it defines the precedence rules that apply where the notation is used to extend existing definitions or to combine existing definitions. The notation also provides the necessary links that provide the binding between managed object classes and the services/protocols (the Common Management Information Service (CMIS), CMIP and the services/protocols defined in systems management function standards) that will be used to convey management information related to instances of the classes. In effect, the notation provides the means of specifying how the "holes" in the CMIP protocol and in any extensible syntaxes associated with generic management information definitions are filled in with meaningful information related to managed objects.

6.3   Introduction to the notation

6.3.1   Templates

The notation used for defining managed object classes is based on the concept of **templates**. A template is a proforma for the specification of some aspect of a managed object class, such as an attribute; the definition of the attribute template identifies what items may or shall be specified in order to produce a valid attribute definition. The definition of the template defines the overall syntax of the piece of specification including the order in which components of the specification may appear, which components may be omitted, which may be repeated, and what each component may consist of.

The templates can, therefore, be regarded as a set of standard forms, with spaces that the user (the managed object definer) is required to fill in particular ways; each template can be combined with other templates in order to construct the complete definition of a managed object class. Some elements of the templates, the keywords, are predefined; other elements require the managed object definer to determine what is inserted into the template at that point, such as the labels of other referenced templates. Each time a template is used, the resultant piece of specification (the filled-in form) is given a label which can be used to refer to it from other templates. This labeling and referencing mechanism provides the means whereby the individual components of a managed object class definition are combined to form the whole.

6.3.2   References between templates

The majority of the templates defined in GDMO permit references to be made to other templates of defined types. For example, the *MANAGED OBJECT CLASS* template may reference one or more *PACKAGE* templates. The effect of such references is that the piece of specification embodied in the referenced template is imported into the template that makes the reference. The meaning of such references is as defined for a particular template.

Template labels are the means by which such references are made; if the referenced template is in the same document as the referencing template, the template label itself is sufficient to identify the reference. However, where the referenced template is in a different document, the template label is preceded by the unique identifier of the document, either its name or its ASN.1 object identifier value notation.

This referencing mechanism provides the means whereby modular definitions can be developed, and is the mechanism that permits reuse of generic definitions of, or components of, managed object class definitions. Any piece of template-based specification can be referenced by this mechanism, regardless of which document it resides in, provided that a globally unambiguous identifier for the document can be constructed. In particular, this mechanism permits managed object class definers to make use of the information types and managed object classes defined in other standards, such as DMI and GMI, and to refine them for their own purposes. The most obvious use of referencing as a means of refining managed object class definitions is that all managed object classes are refinements of **top** ; if the chain of class definitions in the inheritance hierarchy is traced back, sooner or later a reference will be found to the definition of the managed object class **top** which is defined in the DMI standard. Examples of the use of the referencing mechanism, to refer to templates defined in this document and in the DMI standard, are to be found below.

6.3.3   In-line templates

Wherever a template label appears in the body of a template definition, it can be replaced by the entire text of the referenced template. It is therefore possible to document an entire managed object class definition with all referenced templates included "in line", if so desired. Generally this is only feasible where the complexity of the definition is not great; with complex definitions, the nesting involved in producing an in-line definition can rapidly render the definition unreadable. This feature of the language is therefore generally used sparingly.

6.3.4   References to ASN.1 modules

Some of the templates defined in GDMO include references to ASN.1 data types or data values, in order to specify aspects of the managed object class definition that relate to data items that will be carried in management protocol. This is achieved by means of a reference to an ASN.1 type or value definition contained in an ASN.1 module that is part of the same document as the referencing template. Where it is necessary to refer to ASN.1 constructs defined in other documents, the ASN.1 IMPORTS and EXPORTS mechanisms are employed in order to create local names for the remote definitions. As with template references, a reference to an ASN.1 type or value definition includes that definition in the piece of specification that the template describes.

6.4   The templates

6.4.1   Elements of a managed object class definition

As identified in the description of the *Management Information Model* in Chapter 5, the process of defining a managed object class involves the specification of the following elements:

- attributes and their value ranges
- operations on attributes
- other operations on the managed object
- notifications that may be emitted
- behavior definitions
- attribute groups
- packages
- naming.

In order to specify these elements, nine separate templates have been defined. These are:

- managed object class template
- package template
- parameter template
- attribute template
- attribute group template
- behavior template
- action template
- notification template
- name binding template.

The content of each of these templates, and the way that they achieve the required elements of specification, are described in detail below.

6.4.2   Managed object class template

The *MANAGED OBJECT CLASS* template forms the "core" of a managed object class definition. With the exception of the *NAME BINDING* template, all other templates that form part of the definition of a managed object class are referenced, either directly or indirectly, from this template, as shown in Figure 6.1.

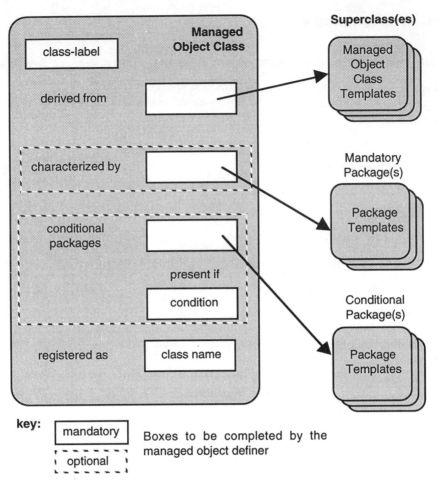

Figure 6.1 Managed object class template.

All managed object classes inherit characteristics from one or more superclasses; ultimately, all classes are derived from a special managed object class, called **top**, which forms the apex of the inheritance hierarchy. The DERIVED FROM construct in the *MANAGED OBJECT CLASS* template provides the means to specify the superclass(es) from which a managed object class has been derived, and whose characteristics it inherits. Although marked as optional in the formal template definition, this construct may not be absent from any managed object class definition other than **top**; hence it is shown as a mandatory element of the template in Figure 6.1. The precedence rules that govern how inherited specification and additional specification are combined to form the whole of the managed object class definition are described in the *Management Information Model*; the text of GDMO shows how these rules are interpreted in the context of the templates.

The remainder of the template is concerned with the specification of refinements to the superclass(es) named in the DERIVED FROM construct. This involves the addition of *packages* of specification to the inherited specification, by referencing one or more PACKAGE templates. Packages permit a collection of attributes, operations, notifications, parameters and behavior to be defined. A package may contain elements that augment the specification inherited from superclasses, or which further specify the value ranges of inherited attributes.

The CHARACTERIZED BY construct lists any mandatory packages which are to be included in all instances of the class; the CONDITIONAL PACKAGES construct lists any packages whose inclusion in an instance of the class is dependent upon a condition which is evaluated at instantiation time. These constructs may be used to modify conditions that were applied to inherited packages; for example, a conditional package that appears in a superclass can be converted to a mandatory package in the subclass by including it in the CHARACTERIZED BY construct.

The REGISTERED AS construct is used to allocate a globally unique identifier as the managed object class name corresponding to a managed object class definition. This identifier is carried in the parameters of CMIS service primitives when it is necessary to identify the managed object class.

Inheritance and the use of packages provide two powerful mechanisms for structuring managed object definitions, and for reuse of specification that may apply to more than one managed object class.

Inheritance forms a natural mechanism for defining enhanced versions of existing managed object classes. This might occur as a result of revision of a standard managed object class, where the revised standard introduces additional functionality but maintains backwards compatibility. Equally, it might be desirable to define an enhanced version of an existing managed object class for proprietary use.

Conditional packages form a natural mechanism for defining managed object classes that have a "core" of functionality to which additional capabilities may be added under defined circumstances. For instance, conditional packages that add accounting, diagnostic or performance measurement facilities might be defined for a managed object class whose "core" functionality was concerned with the management of an X.25 protocol machine. The use of packages can therefore allow the desired flexibility without the necessity of defining distinct managed object classes for each combination of core plus additional functionality.

Both inheritance and packages provide a means of reusing existing specification, in circumstances where there is a common subset of functionality that exists across a number of managed object classes.

6.4.3 Package template

The PACKAGE template permits a logically related set of characteristics of a managed object class to be grouped together. The PACKAGE template brings together elements defined in BEHAVIOUR[1], ATTRIBUTE, NOTIFICATION, ACTION and PARAMETER templates, as shown in Figure 6.2. As indicated in the description of the MANAGED OBJECT CLASS template, the package so defined is incorporated into the class definition as either a mandatory or a conditional package.

---

[1]   Note that GDMO uses the spelling "behaviour" and not the US spelling "behavior".

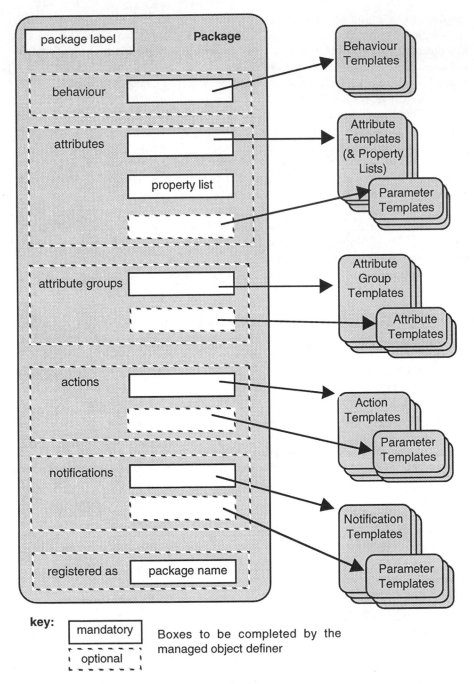

Figure 6.2 Package template.

The BEHAVIOUR DEFINITIONS construct allows the package to specify aspects of the behavior of a managed object class that are specific to the package.

Such behavior might include interrelationships between the values of attributes; relationships between the behavior of elements of the package and the underlying resource that the managed object will model; and the relationship between the behavior of the managed object and the operations and notifications that it recognizes.

The ATTRIBUTES construct lists any attributes that are included in the package, along with a property list for each attribute that defines:

- operations available on the attribute (GET, REPLACE, ADD, REMOVE);

- default, initial, permitted and required values for the attribute;

- parameters that specify any extensions to the vocabulary of the CMIS error reporting mechanism that apply to the operations available on the attribute.

The default value specified for an attribute is used in the **Replace with default** operation, and may also be used at managed object creation time. The value itself can be specified as a fixed value, by means of an ASN.1 value specification, or as a derived value, by means of a textual description of the derivation rules to be used. These rules enable the managed object definer to allow for dynamic considerations in setting default values; for example, the default value might be defined in a manner that makes it dependent upon the value of attributes of another managed object. If no default value is specified, the determination of default values is not restricted.

A mandatory initial value can be defined for use when creating a managed object. As with default values, the initial value may be a static value, or a value derived from a derivation rule. If the initial value specification is omitted, initial values for the attribute are determined at creation time either by values specified in the **Create** operation, or by local means.

The permitted value specification allows the definer to constrain the set of values that an attribute may take to some subset of the values that are possible for the data type of the attribute. For example, the base data type may be integer, but if the attribute models a number of degrees of angular rotation, the permitted value set might legitimately be constrained to the range 0–359. It is advisable to avoid specification of a permitted value set unless the semantics of the attribute are such that it is inconceivable that the excluded values will ever become relevant in a subclass. If no permitted value specification is included, there are no restrictions placed on the values that the attribute can take other than those inherent in the base data type of the attribute.

The required value specification allows the definer to state particular values that the attribute is required to support in order to conform to the managed object class definition. For example, a data rate attribute might have an unconstrained permitted value range, allowing any positive integer value; however, in a conformant implementation of a 300/1200 BPS modem, it might be a requirement for this attribute to support at least the values 300 and 1200. If no required value specification is included, there are no particular values that an implementation is required to support.

The ATTRIBUTE GROUPS construct permits the inclusion of attribute groups in the definition of the package. Attribute groups provide a shorthand for accessing groups of logically related attributes; performing a **Get** operation on an attribute group has the same effect as performing individual **Get** operations on each group member. When a **Get** operation is performed using a group attribute name, the response is identical to the response that would be returned for a **Get** operation that individually identified the members of the group. Attribute groups may be of fixed composition as defined by the ATTRIBUTE GROUP template, or may be extended by the inclusion of additional attribute references in the construct; the intention here is to permit named groupings of attributes that express the semantic "all attributes of type X" where X might be state attributes, counter attributes, and so on.

The ACTIONS and NOTIFICATIONS constructs permit the inclusion of actions and notifications in the definition of a package, along with any parameters that may be associated with them. The parameters are used in this context for two purposes:

• to define any necessary extensions to the CMIS error reporting vocabulary that are required by the use of the operation or notification;

• to define any package-specific extensions to the syntaxes of the operation or notification.

The latter use of parameters applies in cases where a generically defined operation or notification is to be used (as defined in a systems management function, for example) and the original definition of the syntaxes associated with the operation or notification was designed to be extensible in order to cater for more specific requirements.

The REGISTERED AS construct allows a globally unique identifier to be allocated as the name of a package definition. If a package is referenced by a CONDITIONAL PACKAGES construct, it must have a global identifier; this identifier is used to identify the package in the Packages attribute that is inherited by all managed object classes from **top**. Reading the contents of the Packages attribute therefore allows the manager to determine which conditional packages have been instantiated in a given managed object.

6.4.4   Parameter template

The PARAMETER template, whose structure appears in Figure 6.3, is a general-purpose extension mechanism, designed to cater for the fact that CMIP contains fields whose definition has to be completed by the managed object class definition. Some of those fields, and in particular those used to carry CMIS error information, operation syntaxes and notification syntaxes, are structured in CMIP in a manner that makes them inherently extensible. Other fields, particularly fields in notification and action syntaxes defined in DMI, have a defined syntactic structure, but it is desirable to further define the values that may appear in the fields.

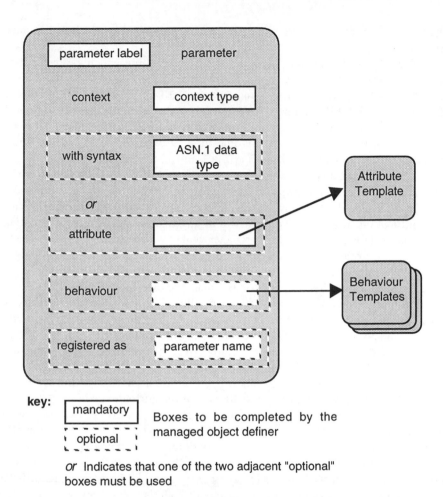

Figure 6.3 Parameter template.

The syntactic definition that leads to extensible syntactic structures is of the general form:

```
Datatype ::= SEQUENCE {
    ......
    label      OBJECT IDENTIFIER,
    .....
    extension  ANY DEFINED BY label
    .....
                    }
```

The PARAMETER template permits the specification of the syntax to be used to replace the ANY DEFINED BY in a given identified context, along with any behavior that is necessary in order to define the circumstances in which the parameter is used.

The CONTEXT construct identifies the context within which the parameter is used. A number of possible contexts are specified. The ACTION-INFO, ACTION-REPLY, EVENT-INFO and EVENT-REPLY contexts indicate that the parameter is used to fill in an ANY DEFINED BY that is part of the structure of the information or reply syntax defined for an action or a notification. This allows the definition of actions and notifications that may be extended to include additional information that was not envisaged at the time of the original definition. The SPECIFIC-ERROR context permits the use of the CMIS processing failure error to carry managed object class-specific error information that cannot be expressed by means of the standard CMIS error values. The context-keyword context permits the identification of a particular field within any management Protocol Data Unit (PDU) that is the site at which the parameter syntax will be carried. This is used in cases where the other defined contexts are not sufficient to define unambiguously where the parameter is to be used. For example, an action reply syntax might be defined in such a way that it includes more than one extensible field. Alternatively, an action reply syntax might be of fixed structure, but it is desired to specify the values carried by one of its fields. In such cases, the context-keyword provides the means of specifying which field is used to carry the parameter.

PARAMETER templates may be referenced from a number of other templates, with a variety of contexts and for a variety of purposes.

Parameters may be attached to attributes, either in the ATTRIBUTE template itself (if the parameter is applicable to all uses of the attribute) or in the PACKAGE template (if the parameter is specific to the use of the attribute within a given package). The context type that applies to this use is SPECIFIC-ERROR; in other words, the parameter is used to define error conditions for **Get** or **Replace** operations on the attribute that cannot be represented using the existing CMIS error codes. It would be technically feasible to use the context-keyword context with attributes, either to define the attribute syntax or to specify value ranges; however, this is not recommended, as explicit mechanisms exist in the templates to do these jobs. The use of parameters to extend the error reporting capability of CMIS also applies to the NAME BINDING template, where it is used in conjunction with **Create** and **Delete** operations, and to actions and notifications, where, as with attributes, the parameters may be attached either in the ACTION and NOTIFICATION templates, or where they are referenced from within a package.

Parameters may be used with the context-keyword, ACTION-INFO, ACTION-REPLY, EVENT-INFO and EVENT-REPLY contexts in order to define elements of the syntax associated with action and notification information and reply syntaxes. The context-keyword context is used in cases where the only unambiguous way of defining how the parameter is used is to point explicitly at a labeled field of the PDU; the other contexts apply where the parameter is to be used to fill in an extensible field in the PDU. These contexts may be used either in the NOTIFICATION or ACTION templates themselves, or in the PACKAGE templates where actions and notifications are referenced. The former use generally only applies where it is desired to associate an attribute type with an action or notification field, as most other uses of parameters within the ACTION and NOTIFICATION templates simply duplicate the explicit mechanisms that exist in those templates for defining the action and notification information and reply syntaxes.

The syntax-or-attribute-choice construct defines the ASN.1 syntax that is used to 'fill in' the field identified by the CONTEXT. This may be done either by making direct reference to an ASN.1 type definition, or by referencing an ATTRIBUTE template whose syntax is to be used for this purpose. In the latter case, the reference to the ATTRIBUTE template is simply a means of defining the syntax to be used; it does not necessarily mean that the values carried in protocol in such a parameter are actually derived from attributes of that type. The behavior definition(s) attached to the parameter determine how the parameter is actually used.

The globally unique identifier allocated by the REGISTERED AS construct is used as the parameter name. This identifier establishes the context that permits the ANY DEFINED BY in the ASN.1 construct shown above to be correctly interpreted. In other words, the object identifier value is carried in the OBJECT IDENTIFIER field referenced by the ANY DEFINED BY construct.

6.4.5   Attribute template

The ATTRIBUTE template is used to define the syntax of an attribute type and its behavior. Its structure is shown in Figure 6.4.

Provision is made for derivation of an attribute type from an existing, generic, attribute definition; for example, a generic definition for Counters might define the general behavior and syntax that applies to all counters, and this could be refined to produce definitions of error counters, PDU counters, and so on. Where an attribute definition is refined in this way, the new definition inherits the entire specification contained in the generic attribute definition, consisting of its syntax, matching rules, behavior and parameters.

The syntax of the attribute defines how values of the attribute are to be conveyed in management protocol, and, as a side effect, whether the attribute is set-valued or single-valued. Attributes whose data type is based on the ASN.1 SET OF type are set-valued; all others are single-valued.

The MATCHES FOR construct permits the specification of legitimate matching rules that may be applied to the attribute value; for example, in the case of a set-valued attribute, it might be legitimate to test values of the attribute for equality, but not legitimate to test for ordering. These matching rules determine which filter operators are legitimate when a CMIS filter is applied to the attribute. For example, a filter operator that tests the current value of an attribute to determine whether it is equal to a specified value is only valid if the MATCHES FOR construct of the attribute definition specifies EQUALITY.

The BEHAVIOUR construct permits the specification of the attribute behavior. This particular use of behavior should be limited to those aspects of the behavior of the attribute that apply to all packages (and hence managed object classes) in which the attribute may appear; it is therefore not appropriate to include aspects of the behavior here that are specific to a particular package, unless it is certain that the attribute will be used only in that package. Where it is not obvious how a given matching rule is applied to an attribute value, it is necessary for the behavior definition to resolve any ambiguity that may arise.

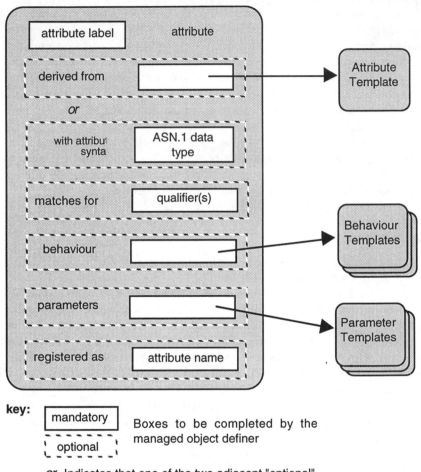

Figure 6.4 Attribute template.

The PARAMETERS construct permits parameters specific to the attribute type to be included in its definition. In this context, the parameters are generally used only to extend CMIS's error reporting vocabulary to express error conditions specific to the attribute.

It would technically be possible to define an attribute whose syntax was:

```
AttributeSyntax ::= SEQUENCE {
    label    OBJECT IDENTIFIER,
             ANY DEFINED BY label }
```

and to use a parameter to resolve the ANY DEFINED BY, in order to define a generic attribute whose behavior is fixed but whose syntax is user-definable; however, this sort of use of the parameter mechanism is likely to be confusing, as there can be no common understanding of the syntax of the attribute; this technique is therefore not recommended unless absolutely necessary.

The globally unique identifier allocated by the REGISTERED AS construct is used as the attribute type name. This identifier is carried in the parameters of CMIS service primitives when it is necessary to identify the attribute type. In particular, it is used in the construction of the components of managed object instance names, known as relative distinguished names, and to identify the attribute in **Get** and **Replace** operations.

6.4.6   Attribute group template

Attribute groups permit sets of attributes to be grouped together in order to permit operations to be performed on them as a group. The operations available are **Get** and **Replace with default** value; the attribute grouping provides a group name that can be used with these operations and that is interpreted as if it is directly equivalent to the set of individual attribute names of its member attributes. In other words, if Group G in managed object O consists of attributes A, B and C, the operation "Get O; G" is interpreted as being exactly equivalent to the operation "Get O; A, B, C". This equivalence is true both of the effect of the operation on the managed object and of the protocol exchanges that convey the operation in CMIP; the M-GET confirmation is identical in both cases.

The ATTRIBUTE GROUP template defines the membership of an attribute group, whether the group is fixed or extensible, and describes the purpose of the grouping. Figure 6.5 shows the structure of the template.

The GROUP ELEMENTS construct defines all the attributes that are mandatory members of the group.

If the attribute group is defined to be extensible (by omitting the FIXED construct), the GROUP ELEMENTS construct may be omitted altogether, or may be used to define the "core" membership of the group. The extension of the group is achieved by adding attributes to the group when it is referenced in PACKAGE templates.

If the attribute group is defined to be of fixed membership (by including the FIXED construct), the attributes listed in the GROUP ELEMENTS construct completely define the group membership.

When a managed object is instantiated, the definition of any attribute groups that it contains must be consistent with the attributes that the managed object contains; that is, the attribute group shall not include attributes that are not instantiated in the managed object. In order to ensure that this is the case, it is a requirement that any attributes defined to be members of a group must be referenced in the ATTRIBUTES construct of the package that references the group or in the ATTRIBUTES construct of one or more of the mandatory packages of the managed object class.

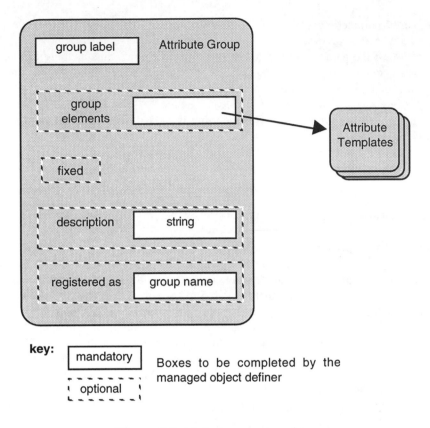

Figure 6.5 Attribute group template.

The DESCRIPTION construct permits a textual description of the purpose of the grouping to be included. For example, it might be desirable to define a group consisting of all counter attributes, in which case the description would indicate that membership of the group was open to attributes of type Counter. Such a group could be defined as extensible and have no fixed membership, the membership being defined on a per-managed object class basis. Alternatively, it might be desirable to define a group consisting of the set of attributes that are used in a particular managed object class to control and operate performance measurement mechanisms. Such a group could be defined as of fixed membership, containing as its mandatory membership the list of attributes concerned.

The group identifier allocated in the REGISTERED AS construct provides a shorthand identifier which may be used in the parameters of CMIS service primitives that define operations on attributes, in particular in **Get** and **Replace** operations. When used in this way, the operation is performed as if the group identifier had been replaced by the identifiers of the set of attributes that are members of the group in the target managed object.

6.4.7   Behaviour template

The BEHAVIOUR template, illustrated in Figure 6.6, is used to define an element of the behavior of a managed object or a component thereof. The behavior definition is currently not constrained in any way, and may be achieved by means of human readable text, formal description techniques, high level languages, references to clauses in a standard, other techniques that involve a textual description, or combinations of the above. Future development of the GDMO syntax may result in the provision of standardized mechanisms for including formal descriptions in this template.

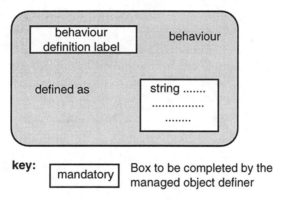

key:

<table>
<tr><td>mandatory</td><td>Box to be completed by the managed object definer</td></tr>
</table>

Figure 6.6 Behaviour template.

6.4.8   Action template

The ACTION template is used to define operations upon a managed object that cannot be modeled by means of the predefined operation types such as **Get** or **Replace**. The structure of this template is as shown in Figure 6.7.

The BEHAVIOUR construct is used to define the behavior specific to the **Action** operation. Elements that are appropriate here are:

- the effect upon the managed object of an **Action**;

- the effect upon the resource of an **Action**;

- constraints that may apply to an **Action**, for example, conditions under which the **Action** would be rejected.

The presence or absence of the MODE CONFIRMED construct defines the operation mode(s) that may apply to the **Action**. If MODE CONFIRMED is present, the **Action** may only operate in confirmed mode, that is, a response will always be generated. If absent, the **Action** may operate in either confirmed or unconfirmed mode, at the discretion of the requesting CMIS service user.

The PARAMETERS construct permits the specification of action-specific parameters applicable across all uses of the **Action**. In this context, the parameters are used only for the purpose of specifying extensions to the error reporting vocabulary of

CMIS in order to cater for the specific needs of the **Action**. It is technically possible to use parameters within the ACTION template that define the contents of the Action information and/or reply syntaxes; however, this is inappropriate, as the WITH INFORMATION SYNTAX and WITH REPLY SYNTAX constructs are provided specifically for that purpose.

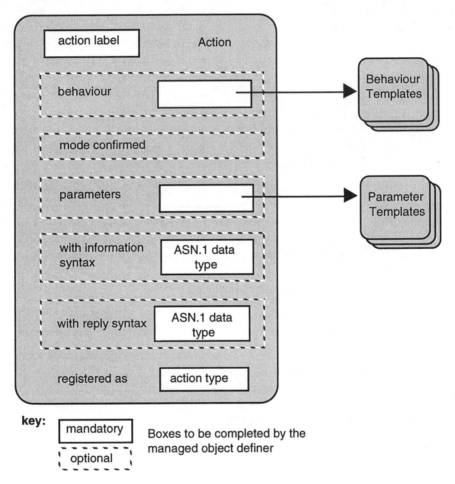

Figure 6.7 Action template.

The WITH INFORMATION SYNTAX and WITH REPLY SYNTAX constructs are used to specify the syntaxes to be carried by CMIP in an **Action** invocation, and in the corresponding **Action** reply if confirmed mode is used. Either construct may be absent, independently of the mode of operation of the **Action**. On the **Action** invocation, there may be no necessity to provide any additional arguments other than the Action type, and in confirmed mode, there is no need to specify a reply syntax unless there is specific information to be passed in the confirmation other than simply to indicate that the operation completed.

The REGISTERED AS construct allocates a globally unique identifier to be used as the Action type name. This identifier is used in the parameters of CMIS service primitives when it is necessary to identify the Action type. Its value establishes the context in which the structure of the Action information and reply syntaxes may be understood.

6.4.9   Notification template

The NOTIFICATION template is used to define notifications that may be emitted by managed objects. The structure of the template is shown in Figure 6.8.

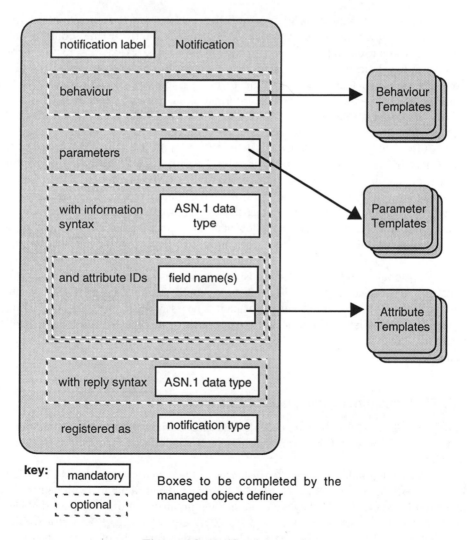

Figure 6.8 Notification template.

The BEHAVIOUR construct is used to define the behavior specific to the notification. Elements that are appropriate here are:

- whether the notification is generated as a direct result of some resource-related event(s), or as a result of some derived event such as a threshold on a counter being exceeded;

- the sequence of events in a resource that would trigger a notification.

There is no ability to define the operation modes that apply to a notification; all notifications may operate in confirmed mode or unconfirmed mode, at the discretion of the CMIS service user.

The PARAMETERS construct permits the specification of notification-specific parameters applicable across all uses of the notification. In this context, the parameters are used only for the purpose of specifying extensions to the error reporting vocabulary of CMIS in order to cater for the specific needs of the notification. It is technically possible to use parameters, as with the ACTION template, to define the contents of the information and/or reply syntaxes; however, this is inappropriate, as the WITH INFORMATION SYNTAX and WITH REPLY SYNTAX constructs are provided specifically for that purpose.

The WITH INFORMATION SYNTAX and WITH REPLY SYNTAX constructs are used to specify the syntaxes to be carried by CMIP in a notification invocation, and in the corresponding action reply if confirmed mode is used. Either construct may be absent; on the notification invocation, there may be no necessity to provide any additional information other than the notification type, and in confirmed mode, there is no need to specify a reply syntax unless there is specific information to be passed in the confirmation other than simply to indicate that the notification was received.

A globally unique identifier is allocated, using the REGISTERED AS construct, to be used as the notification type name. This identifier is used in the parameters of CMIS service primitives when it is necessary to identify the notification type. Its value distinguishes a particular notification type from all others and therefore allows the structure of the notification information and reply syntaxes to be understood.

6.4.10   Name binding template

The NAME BINDING template provides the means whereby the legal containment and instantiation possibilities for managed objects are defined. Its structure is shown in Figure 6.9.

The name binding defines, for instances of the managed object class identified by the SUBORDINATE OBJECT CLASS construct, the attribute that will be used to name those instances when they are contained within instances of the managed object class identified by the NAMED BY SUPERIOR OBJECT CLASS construct. The qualifier AND SUBCLASSES can be added to either (or both) of these constructs. This qualifier permits the name binding to be used not only with the base managed object class named in the construct but also with any subclass(es) of that class, at any depth in the inheritance hierarchy. The AND SUBCLASSES feature is useful in circumstances where it is anticipated that a given managed object class will be further refined at some future date, as it permits this to be done without the need for re-defining the name bindings at the same time.

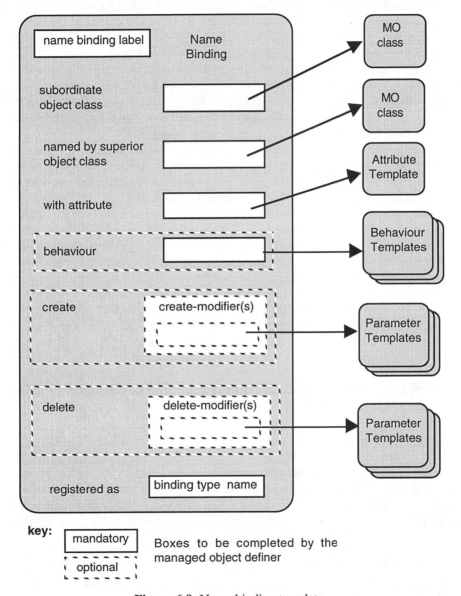

Figure 6.9 Name binding template.

Under some circumstances, there may be special conditions that apply to the containment relationship. For example, there might be a limit placed upon the number of managed objects of managed object class X that are permitted to exist at any time contained within an instance of managed object class Y. Constraints such as these that are specific to the containment relationship are represented in the NAME BINDING template by means of the BEHAVIOUR construct.

The template also defines whether or not a managed object of a given class may be created within or deleted from a given superior object by means of remote management activity using CMIS. The CREATE and DELETE constructs permit this specification to be made, along with parameters which are used to define extensions to the CMIS error reporting vocabulary, if necessary.

The CREATE construct allows the definer to specify whether the options of using reference objects or automatic instance naming are to be made available when creating instances of the subordinate managed object class. If the CREATE construct is absent from the template, creation of managed objects of the subordinate object class by means of remote management action is not permitted.

The DELETE construct allows the definer to specify whether all contained objects must be deleted before deleting a superior object, or whether deletion of the superior object destroys all contained objects. The rules defined by this construct are applied recursively from the point of deletion down through the containment hierarchy. If managed object A contains managed object B which in turn contains managed object C which is at the bottom of the containment hierarchy, A may only be deleted (and thus B and C deleted) if the name bindings under which both A and B were created allow the DELETES-CONTAINED-OBJECTS qualifier. If the DELETE construct is absent from the template, deletion of managed objects of the subordinate object class by means of remote management action is not permitted.

As with most of the other templates, the REGISTERED AS construct is used to assign a globally unique identifier to each name binding. This identifier enables a manager to tell an agent which name binding should be used in a Create operation.

6.5 Relationship between managed object class definition and CMIS/CMIP

As can be seen from the description of the templates, there are elements of the managed object definition that relate to the use of CMIS (and hence CMIP) and the services/protocols defined by the systems management functions, and hence complete the definition of systems management protocol in the context of operations on managed objects. In particular, the managed object class definition includes the definition of:

- object identifier values, used to identify managed object classes, attribute types, action types, notification types, packages, group attributes, and name bindings;

- attribute value syntaxes, and allowable matching rules that may be applied in CMIS filters;

- Action and Notification information and reply syntaxes;

- allowable operation modes for Actions;

- extensions to "partially defined" syntaxes (by means of the PARAMETER template);

- error syntaxes (by means of the PARAMETER template);

- which operations/notifications apply to a managed object class as a whole; and

- which operations (**Get** or **Replace**) apply to attributes of a managed object class.

6.6   Using the templates

The general structure of a template is as follows:

```
<template-label> TEMPLATE-NAME
    CONSTRUCT-NAME (<construct-argument>);
    (CONSTRUCT-NAME (<construct-argument>);)*
(REGISTERED AS <object-identifier>);
(supporting productions
(<definition-label> -> <syntactic definition>)*)
```

The meaning of the various brackets and asterisks is described below, but translated into English, this means that a template always commences with a template-label, which is a user-defined string that serves as an identifier for the template within a particular document, and a TEMPLATE-NAME, which identifies the type of template, such as ATTRIBUTE in the case of the ATTRIBUTE template.

The body of the template consists of one or more *constructs*. Each construct has a CONSTRUCT-NAME which identifies the type of construct and may have a construct argument whose structure and meaning is dependent upon the construct type. Each construct is terminated by a semicolon. The type of constructs that may be used and the order in which they appear are dependent upon the template type.

Templates may, depending upon the template type, require or allow the allocation of a globally unique identifier, an ASN.1 object identifier value, to the piece of specification that is documented by the template. This allocation is achieved by means of the REGISTERED AS construct which appears as the last construct of a template. If the REGISTERED AS is omitted, the trailing semicolon is retained in order to mark the end of the template. The one exception to this generalized structure is the BEHAVIOUR template, which never has the REGISTERED AS construct or its trailing semicolon.

Where the structure of the construct argument(s) is complex, the template definition may include some *supporting productions* which further define the structure of the arguments. In these cases, the name of a supporting production is included in the construct argument, and this is used as a pointer to the definition of the supporting production which follows the end of the template definition.

6.6.1   The template "meta-language"

The templates themselves are specified by means of a simple syntax definition language which is somewhat similar to BNF (Backus-Naur Form). It should be noted that although the language specified by GDMO bears some resemblance to ASN.1, which itself is defined using BNF, it must be emphasized that the notation defined in GDMO is a distinct language from ASN.1; neither is it written in ASN.1. However, there is a connection between GDMO and ASN.1 in so far as some GDMO templates include ASN.1 type and value definitions by reference. Descriptions of the main elements of the meta-language follow:

Semicolons are used to *terminate constructs* that form part of the body of the template, and to *terminate the template as a whole*.

Spaces, blank lines, comments and end-of-line are significant only as *delimiters*, and are generally ignored from the point of view of the semantics of the template. They are used wherever it is necessary to determine where one element of the template ends and the next one starts.

Comments, which are introduced by a double hyphen (--) and terminated by the next end-of-line or double hyphen encountered, may appear in any place where a valid delimiter may appear. The exception to this rule is that comments may not replace spaces that are included in construct names or template names.

Square brackets, [ ] , are used to enclose *optional elements* of a template definition, that is, elements that may be omitted in a use of the template.

An *asterisk* following a closing square bracket indicates that the optional element may be *repeated* 0 or more times at the definer's discretion.

Choices are separated by vertical bars, | . This symbol is used only in the definition of supporting productions, to define two or more choices that are available. The interpretation of this symbol is that exactly one of the N choices provided must be taken.

Strings that are to be replaced by the user of the template in a defined way are surrounded by angle brackets, <<>>. The manner in which these strings are to be replaced is defined in the textual description of the template concerned.

Supporting productions consist of a definition label, which is used to reference the supporting production, followed by the symbol "->>" which acts as a delimiter, followed by a syntactic definition which is constructed using text strings and the symbols identified above.

Delimited strings appear in the template definitions in places where natural language text or formal specification text is to be included. They consist of an arbitrary string of characters which may optionally be surrounded by a pair of string delimiter characters, chosen from the following:

$$ "\ \$\ \%\ \^\ \&\ *\ '\ \grave{}\ \sim\ ?\ @\ \backslash $$

If the first character of the delimited string is one of this set of punctuation characters, the delimited string is defined to include all text up to and including the next single occurrence of that character in the template. If the character is one that appears naturally in the body of the text, it is replaced by a pair of characters. If the first character of the string is not chosen from this set, the delimited string is terminated by the next occurrence of a valid punctuation character (comma or semicolon) that is called for by the definition of the template.

6.7   Example of a managed object class definition

The following example illustrates how a managed object class definition is built up, using the template notation defined in GDMO. The resource modeled by the managed object class defined below is fictitious, and has deliberately been kept to a simple structure in order that the example is clear and understandable. Comments included in the template definitions (preceded by --) and text following the template definitions are used to describe the features of the managed object class and how they are built up.

A name binding definition is also included, in order to illustrate how the containment relationship is expressed between an instance of this managed object class and its superior object. For the purposes of this example, it is assumed that all instances of this class will be contained within instances of the system managed object class defined in DMI.

Figure 6.10 shows the overall structure of this managed object class and the relationships between its component templates. It should be noted that in some cases, particularly with package and behavior definitions, the examples make use of the option of including templates in-line at the point where another template makes reference to them.

The pduCounterObject definition gives the overall structure of the managed object class. It is derived directly from the definition of top, contained in ISO/IEC 10165-2, so it inherits all the characteristics of top as a starting point.

```
pduCounterObject MANAGED OBJECT CLASS
     DERIVED FROM "CCITT REC.X.721(1992)|ISO/IEC 10165-2: 1992":top ;
     CHARACTERIZED BY
          basePackage PACKAGE   -- in-line PACKAGE definition
                    ATTRIBUTES    pduCounterName
                                        GET ;
                         pduCounter
                                   INITIAL VALUE syntax.initialZero
                                   GET;
          ; -- End of in-line PACKAGE definition
     ; -- End of CHARACTERIZED BY construct
     CONDITIONAL PACKAGES additionalPackage
          PRESENT IF  *enable/disable control is required*;
REGISTERED AS {object-identifier 1} ;
```

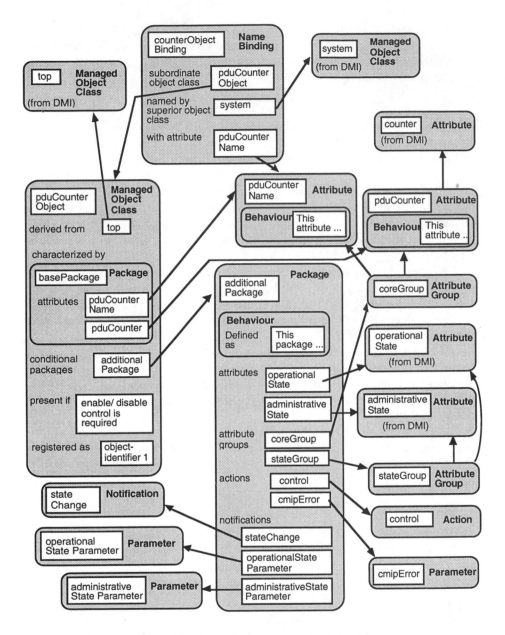

Figure 6.10 Structure of managed object class.

The class has two additional attributes, defined as part of the mandatory package contained in the CHARACTERIZED BY construct. The first attribute, pduCounterName, will be used as the naming attribute for the managed object class; the second, pduCounter, performs the main function of the managed object class, which is to provide a mechanism for counting PDUs. Both attributes are read-only, and the counter attribute is defined to have an initial value of zero on creation. No additional behavior is introduced by the package; the behavior defined for the individual attributes is sufficient (in this case) to describe the operation of the managed object class for the case where only the mandatory package is present. Although the package has been documented "in-line" with the MANAGED OBJECT CLASS template, the in-line documentation technique still requires the package to have a distinct label, so the package is available to be referenced by other MANAGED OBJECT CLASS templates if so desired. As it is not being used as a conditional package, it has no REGISTERED AS construct.

The CONDITIONAL PACKAGES construct introduces a second package, additionalPackage, which is instantiated only if enable/disable control is required. The package is introduced by a reference. The function of the package is described below. The REGISTERED AS construct for the managed object class makes use of a dummy value for the Object Identifier value, as it is not the intention of this document to register information objects.

```
pduCounterName ATTRIBUTE

     WITH ATTRIBUTE SYNTAX syntax.CounterName ;
     MATCHES FOR EQUALITY;
     BEHAVIOUR
          counterNameBehavior BEHAVIOUR
              DEFINED AS
                   *This attribute is the naming attribute for the
                   pduCounterObject managed object class.  It has no
                   function other than to provide a unique identifier for
                   instances of the class contained within a given
                   superior object class.*
          ; -- End of embedded BEHAVIOUR template
       ; -- End of BEHAVIOUR construct
REGISTERED AS {object-identifier 2} ;
```

The pduCounter attribute is an enhanced version of the **counter** attribute defined by ISO/IEC 10165-2, DMI. The enhancement is simply a behavior statement that indicates the purpose and range of the counter.

```
pduCounter ATTRIBUTE
         DERIVED FROM    "CCITT REC. X.721 (1992) | ISO/IEC 10165-2 :
                         1992":counter ;
         BEHAVIOUR
             pduCounterBehavior BEHAVIOUR
                 DEFINED AS
                      *This counter counts the number of PDUs received by
                      the underlying resource modeled by the
                      pduCounterObject managed object class.  Its value
                      is unbounded.*
             ; -- End of embedded BEHAVIOUR template
          ; -- End of BEHAVIOUR construct
REGISTERED AS {object-identifier 3} ;
```

```
additionalPackage PACKAGE
    BEHAVIOUR
        additionalPackageBehavior BEHAVIOUR
            DEFINED AS
                    *This package adds operational control to the
                    pduCounterObject managed object class. The
                    operationalState attribute indicates whether or not
                    the pduCounterObject is operational.  If the value
                    is enabled, the counter will count PDUs received.
                    If disabled, the counter stops counting.  The
                    administrativeState attribute reflects the
                    availability of the counter to external managers.
                    If the value is locked, attempts to read the
                    counter will fail.  If the value is unlocked, the
                    counter will be readable.*

            ;
    ;
    ATTRIBUTES
        "CCITT REC. X.721 (1992) |
                ISO/IEC 101652:1992":operationalState GET,
        "CCITT REC. X.721 (1992) | ISO/IEC 10165-2
                :1992":administrativeState GET,
        pduCounter cmipErrorParameter GET;
        -- The pduCounter attribute is repeated here in order to
        -- associate a parameter with it, which reflects the
        -- additional error condition that occurs if a read attempt
        -- is made on this attribute when the administrative state
        -- is locked.
    ATTRIBUTE GROUPS
        stateGroup
        "CCITT REC. X.721 (1992) | ISO/IEC 10165-2 :
                1992":operationalState
        "CCITT REC. X.721 (1992) | ISO/IEC 10165-
                :1992":administrativeState,
        -- The membership of this attribute group is defined
        -- entirely by this construct.
        coreGroup;
    ACTIONS
        control ;
    NOTIFICATIONS
        stateChange
            operationalStateParameter
            administrativeStateParameter;
        -- Two parameters have been attached to the stateChange
        -- notification in this construct.
REGISTERED AS {object-identifier 4} ;


stateGroup ATTRIBUTE GROUP
    DESCRIPTION
                *Extensible group with no mandatory members.  Includes
                all state attributes in the managed object class.* ;
REGISTERED AS {object-identifier 5} ;
```

```
coreGroup   ATTRIBUTE GROUP
    GROUP ELEMENTS      pduCounterName, pduCounter ;
    FIXED ;
    DESCRIPTION
              *Fixed group, includes the attributes defined as part
              of the mandatory package.* ;
REGISTERED AS {object-identifier 6} ;


control ACTION
    BEHAVIOUR
        controlBehavior BEHAVIOUR
            DEFINED AS
                *The control action provides the means of
                controlling the state of the two state attributes
                of the pduCounterObject.  Values of the action
                argument, enable, disable, lock and unlock have
                corresponding effects upon the state attributes;
                however, the enable/disable values are inoperative
                when administrative state is locked.*
            ;
        ;
    -- The MODE CONFIRMED construct is missing, so this action may be
    -- confirmed or unconfirmed.
    PARAMETERS     cmipErrorParameter ;
    -- This parameter extends the CMIP error reporting to permit an
    -- error response indicating that the managed object is in the
    -- LOCKED state.
    WITH INFORMATION SYNTAX syntax.ControlSyntax ;
REGISTERED AS {object-identifier 7} ;


stateChange NOTIFICATION
    BEHAVIOUR
        stateChangeBehavior BEHAVIOUR
            DEFINED AS
                *Provides a generic mechanism for notification of
                changes of state of state attribute values.  The
                attributes to be carried are specified by use of
                Parameters added when the notification is included
                in a Package.*
            ;
        ;
    WITH INFORMATION SYNTAX syntax.StateChangeSyntax ;
REGISTERED AS {object-identifier 8} ;


operationalStateParameter PARAMETER
    CONTEXT EVENT-INFO
    -- This parameter is used to complete the definition of the event
    -- info syntax
    ATTRIBUTE  "CCITT REC. X.721 (1992) | ISO/IEC 10165-2 :
              1992":operationalState ;
    -- The ATTRIBUTE construct defines the syntax of the parameter to
    -- match that of the operationalState attribute.
```

```
    BEHAVIOUR
        operationalStateParamBehavior BEHAVIOUR
            DEFINED AS
                *This parameter causes the current value of the
                operational state attribute to be inserted into the
                notification's information syntax.*
        ;
    ;
REGISTERED AS {object-identifier 9} ;


administrativeStateParameter PARAMETER
    CONTEXT EVENT-INFO
    -- This parameter is used to complete the definition of the event
    -- info syntax
    ATTRIBUTE   "CCITT REC. X.721 (1992) | ISO/IEC 10165-2 :
                1992":administrativeState ;
    -- The ATTRIBUTE construct defines the syntax of the parameter to
    -- match that of the administrativeState attribute.
    BEHAVIOUR
        administrativeStateParamBehavior BEHAVIOUR
            DEFINED AS
                *This parameter causes the current value of the
                administrative state attribute to be inserted into
                the notification's information syntax.*
        ;
    ;
REGISTERED AS {object-identifier 10} ;


cmipErrorParameter PARAMETER
    CONTEXT SPECIFIC-ERROR ;
    WITH SYNTAX syntax.CMIPErrorSyntax ;
    BEHAVIOUR
        cmipErrorBehavior BEHAVIOUR
            DEFINED AS
                *This error parameter is returned when a manager
                attempts to perform a prohibited operation and the
                administrative state is locked.*
        ;
    ;
REGISTERED AS {object-identifier 11} ;
```

The following name binding establishes the naming structure for the
pduCounterObject managed object class. Instances of the class may be
contained within instances of the system managed object class, and the
pduCounterName attribute is used to form the relative distinguished name in this
case. The use of AND SUBCLASSES makes the name binding applicable not just to
the two named classes, but also to subclasses of those base classes. The CREATE and
DELETE constructs indicate that the subordinate object class may be dynamically
instantiated, and that instances may be deleted, by means of the **Create** and **Delete**
operations.

```
counterObjectBinding NAME BINDING
     SUBORDINATE OBJECT CLASS pduCounterObject AND SUBCLASSES;
     NAMED BY SUPERIOR OBJECT CLASS
          "CCITT Rec. X.722 (1992) | ISO/IEC 10165-2 : 1992":system
          AND SUBCLASSES;
     WITH ATTRIBUTE pduCounterName;
     CREATE;
     DELETE DELETES-CONTAINED-OBJECTS;
REGISTERED AS {object-identifier 12} ;
```

The ASN.1 definitions required by the templates are contained in the following module:

```
syntax {asn1-module-identifier} DEFINITIONS ::=
BEGIN
CounterName ::= GRAPHIC STRING
initialZero ::= INTEGER {0}
StateChangeSyntax ::= SET OF SEQUENCE {
     attributeID      OBJECT IDENTIFIER,
     attributeValue   ANY DEFINED BY attributeID }
ControlSyntax ::= INTEGER {
     enable (0),
     disable (1),
     lock (2),
     unlock (3) }
CMIPErrorSyntax ::= IA5STRING {"Operation rejected as
          Administrative State is locked"}
END
```

Acknowledgments

Some material for this work was developed with support from the UK Department of Trade and Industry's Open Systems Technology Transfer programme.   In collaboration with DISC, one result of the programme was the publication of the Technical Guide for OSI Management, and its companion Practical Guide for OSI Management, NCC Blackwell, 1992, ISBN 1-85554-187-4 and 1-85554-195-5.

Abbreviations

ANSI	American National Standards Institute
ASN.1	Abstract Syntax Notation One
BSI	British Standards Institute
BPS	Bits Per Second
CMIP	Common Management Information Protocol

CMIS	Common Management Information Service
DMI	Definition of Management Information
GDMO	Guidelines for the Definition of Managed Objects
GMI	Generic Management Information
OSI	Open Systems Interconnection
PDU	Protocol Data Unit
SMI	Structure of Management Information

References

CCITT Recommendation X.720 (1992) | ISO/IEC 10165-1 (1992). *Information Technology – Open Systems Interconnection – Structure of Management Information : Management Information Model*

CCITT Recommendation X.721 (1992) | ISO/IEC 10165–2 (1992). *Information Technology – Open Systems Interconnection – Structure of Management Information : Generic Management Information*

CCITT Recommendation X.722 (1992) | ISO/IEC 10165–4 (1992). Information Technology – Open Systems Interconnection – Structure of Management information : Guidelines for the Definition of Managed Objects

ISO/IEC 18824 (1990). *Information Technology – Open Systems Interconnection – Specification of Abstract Notation One (ASN.1)*

Jeffree T., Langsford A., Sluman C., Tucker J. and Westgate J. (1992). *Technical Guide for OSI Management.* NCC Blackwell.

Chapter 7

Simple Network Management Protocol

William Stallings

Comp-Comm Consulting,
P. O. Box 2405,
Brewster, MA 02631, USA
Email: 72500.3562@compuserve.com

This chapter provides a survey of the Simple Network Management Protocol (SNMP) and the recently-standardized version 2 of the protocol (SNMPv2). The chapter discusses the way in which management information is represented in the SNMP framework, the protocol functionality of SNMP and SNMPv2, and the security features of SNMPv2.

7.1   Background

SNMP was developed for use as part of the TCP/IP (transmission control protocol/internet protocol) suite. To understand the motivation for both SNMP and SNMPv2, it is useful to look at the history of this development.

7.1.1   The origins of TCP/IP network management

As TCP/IP was being developed, little thought was given to network management. Initially, virtually all of the hosts and subnetworks attached to ARPANET were based in an environment that included systems programmers and protocol designers working on some aspect or another of the ARPANET research. Therefore, management problems could be left to protocol experts who could tweak the network with the use of some basic tools.

Up through the late 1970s, there were no management protocols as such. The one tool that was effectively used for management was the Internet Control Message

Protocol (ICMP). ICMP provides a means for transferring control messages from routers and other hosts to a host, to provide feedback about problems in the environment. ICMP is available on all devices that support IP. From a network management point of view, the most useful feature of ICMP is the echo/echo-reply message pair. These messages provide a mechanism for testing that communication is possible between entities. The recipient of an echo message is obligated to return the contents of that message in an echo–reply message. Another useful pair of messages are timestamp and timestamp reply, which provide a mechanism for sampling the delay characteristics of the network.

These ICMP messages can be used, along with various IP header options such as source routing and record route, to develop simple but powerful management tools. The most notable example of this is the widely used PING (Packet Internet Groper) program. Using ICMP, plus some additional options such as the interval between requests and the number of times to send a request, PING can perform a variety of functions. Examples include determining if a physical network device can be addressed, verifying that a network can be addressed, and verifying the operation of a server on a host. The PING capability can be used to observe variations in round-trip times and in datagram loss rates, which can help to isolate areas of congestion and points of failure.

With some supplemental tools, the PING capability was a satisfactory solution to the network management requirement for many years. It was only in the late 1980s, when the growth of the internet became exponential that attention was focused on the development of a more powerful network management capability.

With the number of hosts on the network in the hundreds of thousands, and the number of individual networks in the thousands, it is no longer possible to rely on a small cadre of network experts to solve management problems. What was required was a standardized protocol with far more functionality than PING and yet one that could be easily learned and used by a wide variety of people with network management responsibilities.

The starting point in providing specific network management tools was the Simple Gateway Monitoring Protocol (SGMP) issued in November 1987. The SGMP provided a straightforward means for monitoring gateways. As the need for a more general-purpose network management tool grew, three promising approaches emerged:

- *High-Level Entity Management System (HEMS)*: This was a generalization of perhaps the first network management protocol used in the internet, the Host Monitoring Protocol (HMP).

- *Simple Network Management Protocol (SNMP)*: This was an enhanced version of SGMP.

- *CMIP over TCP/IP (CMOT)*: This was an attempt to incorporate, to the maximum extent possible, the protocol (common management information protocol), services, and database structure being standardized by ISO for network management.

In early 1988, the Internet Activities Board (IAB) reviewed these proposals and approved further development of SNMP as a short-term solution and CMOT as the long-range solution. At the time the line of reasoning was as follows. It was felt that within a reasonable period of time, TCP/IP installations would transition to OSI-based protocols. Thus, there was a reluctance to invest substantial effort in application-level protocols and services on TCP/IP that might soon have to be abandoned. In order to meet immediate needs, SNMP could be quickly developed and provide some basic management tools and support the development of an experience base for doing network management. HEMS was more capable than SNMP, but the extra effort on a dead end seemed unwarranted. Meanwhile, if CMIP could be implemented to run on top of TCP, then it might be possible to deploy CMOT even before the transition to OSI. Then, when the time came to move to OSI, the network management aspect of the move would require minimal effort.

To further solidify this strategy, the IAB dictated that both SNMP and CMOT use the same database of managed objects. That is, both protocols were to use the same set of monitoring and control variables, in the same formats, within any host, router, bridge, or other managed device. Thus, only a single structure of management information (SMI: the basic format conventions for objects) and a single management information base (MIB: the actual structure, or schema, of the database) would be defined for both protocols. These common databases would greatly facilitate transition: only the protocol and supporting software would need to be changed; the actual database would be the same in format and content at the time of transition.

It soon became apparent that this binding of the two protocols at the object level was impractical. In OSI network management, managed objects are seen as sophisticated entities with attributes, associated procedures and notification capabilities, and other complex characteristics associated with object-oriented technology. To keep SNMP simple, it is not designed to work with such sophisticated concepts. In fact, the objects in SNMP are not really objects at all from the point of view of object-oriented technology; rather, objects in SNMP are simply variables with a few basic characteristics, such as data type and whether the variable is read-only or read-write. Accordingly, the IAB relaxed its condition of a common SMI/MIB and allowed SNMP and CMOT development to proceed independently and in parallel.

7.1.2   The evolution of SNMP

With the SNMP developers freed from the constraint of OSI compatibility, progress was rapid and mirrors the history of TCP/IP. SNMP soon became widely available on vendor equipment and flourished within the Internet. In addition, SNMP soon became the standardized management protocol of choice for the general user. Just as TCP/IP has outlasted all predictions of its useful lifetime, so SNMP appears to be around for the long haul, and widespread deployment of OSI network management continues to be delayed. Meanwhile, the CMOT effort languishes.

The "basic" SNMP is now in widespread use. Virtually all major vendors of host computers, workstations, bridges, routers, and hubs offer basic SNMP. Work is even progressing on the use of SNMP over OSI and other non-TCP/IP protocol suites.

In addition, there have been a number of directions in which enhancements to SNMP have been pursued.

Perhaps the most important of these initiatives, so far, is the development of a remote monitoring capability for SNMP. The remote monitoring (RMON) specification defines additions to the basic SNMP MIB as well as the functions that exploit the RMON MIB. RMON gives the network manager the ability to monitor subnetworks as a whole, rather than just individual devices on the subnetwork. Both vendors and users view RMON as an essential extension to SNMP, and RMON, though relatively new, is already widely deployed.

In addition to RMON, other extensions to the basic SNMP MIB have been developed. Some of these are vendor-independent, and have to do with standardized network interfaces, such as token ring and fiber distributed data interface (FDDI). Others are vendor-specific, private extensions to the MIB. In general, these extensions do not add any new technology or concepts to SNMP.

There is a limit to how far SNMP can be extended by simply defining new and more elaborate MIBs. RMON perhaps represents as far as one would want to go in trying to enhance the functionality of SNMP by adding to the semantics of the MIB. However, as SNMP is applied to larger and more sophisticated networks, its deficiencies become more apparent. These deficiencies are in the areas of security and functionality.

Much has been done to remedy these deficiencies. As a first step, a set of three documents defining a security enhancement to SNMP were published in July 1992 as proposed standards. This enhancement is not compatible with the original SNMP: it requires a change to the outer message header and to a number of the message-handling procedures. However, the format of the protocol data units (PDUs) carried inside an SNMP message that define the actual protocol operation remained the same, and no new PDUs were added. The intent was to make the transition to a secure version of SNMP as painless as possible.

Unfortunately, the security enhancement was overtaken by events. In the very same month, July 1992, a proposal for a new version of SNMP, referred to as the Simple Management Protocol (SMP), was submitted by four key contributors to the SNMP effort. At the same time, four interoperable implementations were made available. Two of these implementations are commercial products; the other two are public-domain software. SMP provides both functional and security enhancements to SNMP; in particular SMP adds several new PDUs. The overall message header and security functionality are similar to that of the proposed security enhancement standard.

SMP was accepted as the baseline for defining a second generation of SNMP, known as SNMP version 2 (SNMPv2); no other proposals were submitted. In addition, a consensus emerged within the Internet Engineering Task Force that a single transition from SNMP to SNMPv2 was desirable. Therefore, the just-completed security enhancements were tabled.

Two working groups were formed to develop the specifications for SNMPv2. One group concentrated on all of the aspects of SNMPv2 other than security, while the other worked on the security features of SNMPv2. The result was a set of 12 documents that were published as proposed standards in early 1993. The documents must progress from proposed standards to draft standards to final standards. It is not unknown for technical changes to be made during this process, but it is not particularly common, and it is likely that the proposed standards will pass through this process with virtually no technical changes. This is certainly the hope of the many vendors who have already begun product development.

7.1.3   SNMP-related standards

The set of specifications that define SNMP and its related functions and databases is comprehensive and growing. The three foundation specifications are:

- Structure and Identification of Management Information for TCP/IP-based networks (RFC 1155): Describes how managed objects contained in the MIB are defined.

- Management Information Base for Network Management of TCP/IP-based Internets: MIB-II (RFC 1213): Describes the managed objects contained in the MIB.

- Simple Network Management Protocol (RFC 1157): Defines the protocol used to manage these objects.

The remaining RFCs developed under version 1 of SNMP define various extensions to the SMI or MIB. The following list of RFC documents define SNMPv2.

- Introduction to SNMPv2 (RFC 1441): Provides an overview of version 2 of the Internet-standard Network Management Framework, termed the SNMP version 2 framework (SNMPv2). This framework is derived from the original Internet-standard Network Management Framework (SNMPv1).

- Structure of Management Information (RFC 1442): Defines the subset of Abstract Syntax Notation One (ASN.1) used to define the SNMPv2 MIB. The document also defines the module types and ASN.1 macros used to define the MIB.

- Textual Conventions (RFC 1443): Defines the initial set of textual conventions available to all MIB modules.

- Protocol Operations (RFC 1448): Defines the protocol data units (PDUs) for SNMPv2, and the protocol operations for those PDUs.

- Transport Mappings (RFC 1449): Defines how SNMPv2 maps onto an initial set of transport domains. The mapping onto UDP is the preferred mapping.

- Management Information Base (RFC 1450): Defines managed objects that describe the behavior of an SNMPv2 entity.

- Manager to Manager MIB (RFC 1451): Defines managed objects that describe the behavior of an SNMPv2 entity acting in both a manager and an agent role.

- Conformance Statements (RFC 1444): Defines the acceptable lower bounds of implementation, and the notation to be used to specify the actual level of implementation achieved.

- SNMPv1/SNMPv2 Coexistence (RFC 1452): Describes coexistence between SNMPv2 and SNMPv1. The document covers management information and protocol operations.

- SNMPv2 Administrative Model (RFC 1445): Presents an elaboration of the SNMP administrative model. This model provides a unified conceptual basis for administering SNMP protocol entities to support authentication and integrity, privacy, access control, and the cooperation of multiple protocol entities.

- SNMPv2 Security Protocols (RFC 1446): Defines protocols to support three data security services: (1) data integrity, (2) data origin authentication, and (3) data confidentiality.

- SNMPv2 Party MIB (RFC 1447): Defines a portion of the Management Information Base (MIB) for use with network management protocols in TCP/IP-based internets. It describes a representation of the SNMP parties as objects, consistent with the SNMP security protocols.

7.2   Basic concepts

This section provides an overview of the basic framework for SNMP. The details of SNMP itself are not addressed separately. Rather, they will be summarized as part of the discussion of SNMPv2.

7.2.1   Network management architecture

The model of network management that is used for SNMP includes the following key elements:

- Management station,

- Management agent,

- Management information base,

- Network management protocol.

The **management station** is typically a stand-alone device, but may be a capability implemented on a shared system. In either case, the management station serves as the interface for the human network manager into the network management system. The management station will have, at minimum:

- A set of management applications for data analysis, fault recovery, and so on;

- An interface by which the network manager may monitor and control the network;

- The capability of translating the network manager's requirements into the actual monitoring and control of remote elements in the network;

- A database of information extracted from the MIBs of all the managed entities in the network.

Only the last two elements are the subject of SNMP standardization.

The other active element in the network management system is the **management agent**. Key platforms, such as hosts, bridges, routers, and hubs, may be equipped with SNMP so that they may be managed from a management station. The management agent responds to requests for information from a management station, responds to requests for actions from the management station, and may asynchronously provide the management station with important but unsolicited information.

The means by which resources in the network may be managed is to represent these resources as objects. Each object is, essentially, a data variable that represents one aspect of the managed agent. The collection of objects is referred to as a **management information base** (MIB). The MIB functions as a collection of access points at the agent for the management station. These objects are standardized across systems of a particular class (for example, bridges all support the same management objects). A management station performs the monitoring function by retrieving the value of MIB objects. A management station can cause an action to take place at an agent or can change the configuration settings of an agent by modifying the value of specific variables.

The management station and agents are linked by a **network management protocol**. The protocol used for the management of TCP/IP networks is the simple network management protocol (SNMP). This protocol includes the following key capabilities:

- Get: enables the management station to retrieve the value of objects at the agent;

- Set: enables the management station to set the value of objects at the agent;

- Trap: enables an agent to notify the management station of significant events.

There are no specific guidelines in the standards as to the number of management stations or the ratio of management stations to agents. In general, it is prudent to have at least two systems capable of performing the management station function, to provide redundancy in case of failure. The other issue is the practical one of how many agents a single management station can handle. As long as SNMP remains relatively "simple", that number can be quite high, certainly in the hundreds.

7.2.2   Network management protocol architecture

SNMP was designed to be an application-level protocol that is part of the TCP/IP protocol suite. It is intended to operate over the user datagram protocol (UDP). Figure 2.15 in Chapter 2 suggests the typical configuration of protocols for SNMP. For a stand alone management station, a manager process controls access to the central MIB at the management station and provides an interface to the network manager. The manager process achieves network management by using SNMP, which is implemented on top of UDP, IP, and the relevant network-dependent protocols (for example, Ethernet, FDDI, X.25).

Each agent must also implement SNMP, UDP, and IP. In addition, there is an agent process that interprets the SNMP messages and controls the agent's MIB. For an agent device that supports other applications, such as the file transfer protocol, TCP as well as UDP is required.

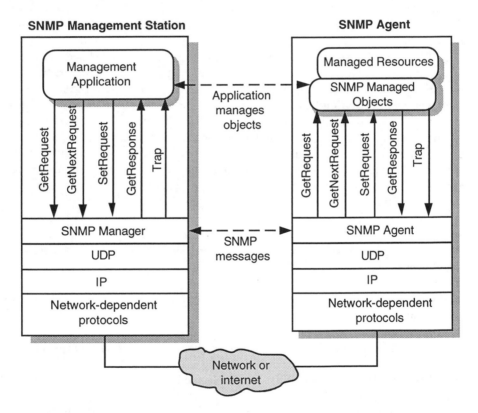

Figure 7.1 The role of SNMP.

Figure 7.1 provides a somewhat closer look at the protocol context of SNMP. From a management station, three types of SNMP message are issued on behalf of management applications: GetRequest, GetNextRequest, and SetRequest. The first two are variations of the get function. All three messages are acknowledged by the agent in the form of a GetResponse message, which is passed up to the management application. In addition, an agent may issue a trap message in response to an event that affects the MIB and the underlying managed resources.

Because SNMP relies on UDP, which is a connectionless protocol, SNMP is itself connectionless. No ongoing connections are maintained between a management station and its agents. Instead, each exchange is a separate transaction between a management station and an agent.

7.2.3   Trap-directed polling

If a management station is responsible for a large number of agents, and if each agent maintains a large number of objects, then it becomes impractical for the management station to regularly poll all agents for all of their readable object data. Instead, SNMP and the associated MIB are designed to encourage the manager to use a technique referred to as trap-directed polling.

The recommended strategy is as follows. At initialization time, and perhaps at infrequent intervals, such as once a day, a management station can poll all of the agents it knows of for some key information, such as interface characteristics, and perhaps some baseline performance statistics, such as average number of packets sent and received over each interface over a given period of time. Once this baseline is established, the management station refrains from polling. Instead, each agent is responsible for notifying the management station of any unusual event. Examples are the agent crashes and is rebooted, the failure of a link, or an overload condition as defined by the packet load crossing some threshold. These events are communicated in SNMP messages known as traps.

Once a management station is alerted to an exception condition, it may choose to take some action. At this point, the management station may direct polls to the agent reporting the event and perhaps to some nearby agents in order to diagnose any problem and to gain more specific information about the exception condition.

Trap-directed polling can result in substantial savings of network capacity and agent processing time. In essence, the network is not made to carry management information that the management station does not need, and agents are not made to respond to frequent requests for uninteresting information.

7.2.4   Proxies

The use of SNMP requires that all agents, as well as management stations, must support UDP and IP. This limits direct management to such devices and excludes other devices, such as some bridges and modems, that do not support any part of the TCP/IP protocol suite. Further, there may be numerous small systems (personal computers, workstations, programmable controllers) that do implement TCP/IP to support their applications, but for which it is not desirable to add the additional burden of SNMP, agent logic, and MIB maintenance.

To accommodate devices that do not implement SNMP, the concept of proxy was developed. In this scheme an SNMP agent acts as a proxy for one or more other devices; that is, the SNMP agent acts on behalf of the proxied devices.

Figure 7.2 indicates the type of protocol architecture that is often involved. The management station sends queries concerning a device to its proxy agent. The proxy agent converts each query into the management protocol that is used by the device. When a reply to a query is received by the agent, it passes that reply back to the management station. Similarly, if an event notification of some sort from the device is transmitted to the proxy, the proxy sends it on to the management station in the form of a trap message.

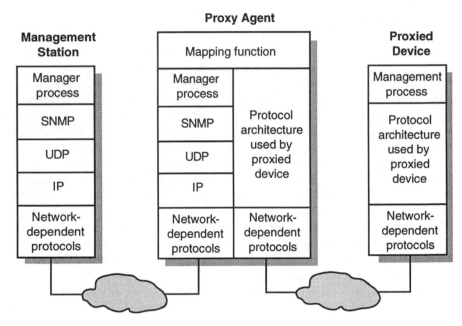

Figure 7.2 Proxy configuration.

7.3   SNMPv2 functions

In a traditional centralized network management scheme, one host in the configuration has the role of a network management station; there may be possibly one or two other management stations in a backup role. The remainder of the devices on the network contain agent software and a MIB, to allow monitoring and control from the management station. As networks grow in size and traffic load, such a centralized system is unworkable. Too great a burden is placed on the management station, and there is too much traffic, with reports from every single agent having to wend their way across the entire network to headquarters. In such circumstances, a decentralized, distributed approach works best (for example, Figure 7.3). In a decentralized network management scheme, there may be multiple top-level management stations, which might be referred to as management servers. Each such server might directly manage a portion of the total pool of agents. However, for many of the agents, the management server delegates responsibility to an intermediate manager. The intermediate manager plays the role of manager to monitor and control the agents under its responsibility. It also plays an agent role to provide information and accept control from a higher-level management server. This type of architecture spreads the processing burden and reduces total network traffic.

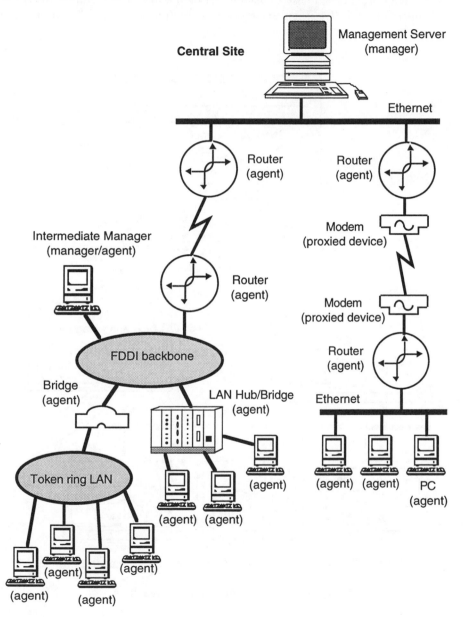

Figure 7.3 Example distributed network management configuration.

7.3.1   The elements of SNMPv2

As with SNMP, SNMPv2 provides a framework on which network management applications can be built. Those applications, such as fault management, performance monitoring, accounting, and so on, are outside the scope of the standard. What SNMPv2 does provide is, to use a contemporary term, the infrastructure for network management. Figure 7.4 is an example of a configuration that illustrates that infrastructure.

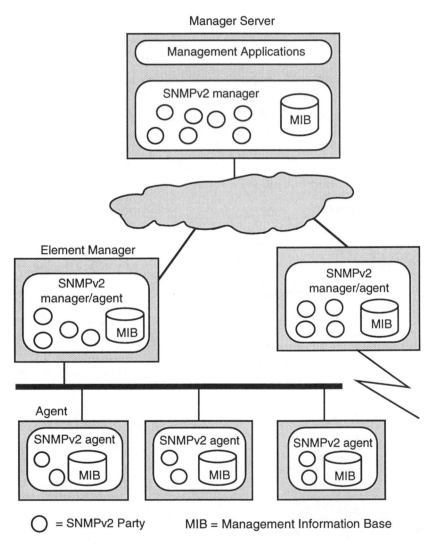

Figure 7.4 SNMPv2-managed configuration.

The essence of SNMPv2 is a protocol that is used to exchange management information. Each "player" in the network management system maintains a local database of information relevant to network management, known as the management information base (MIB). The SNMPv2 standard defines the structure of this information and the allowable data types; this definition is known as the structure of management information (SMI). We can think of this as the language for defining management information. The standard also supplies a number of MIBs that are generally useful for network management.[1] In addition, new MIBs may be defined by vendors and user groups.

At least one system in the configuration must be responsible for network management. It is here that any network management applications are housed. There may be more than one of these management stations, to provide redundancy or simply to split up the duties in a large network. Most other systems act in the role of agent. An agent collects information locally and stores it for later access by a manager. The information includes data about the system itself and may also include traffic information for the network or networks to which the agent attaches.

SNMPv2 will support either a highly centralized network management strategy or a distributed one. In the latter case, some systems operate in the role of both manager and agent. In its agent role, such a system will accept commands from a superior management system. Some of those commands relate to the local MIB at the agent. Other commands require the agent to act as a proxy for remote devices. In this case, the proxy agent assumes the role of manager to access information at a remote agent, and then assumes the role of an agent to pass that information on to a superior manager.

All of these exchanges take place using the SNMPv2 protocol, which is a simple request/response type of protocol. Typically, SNMPv2 is implemented on top of the user datagram protocol (UDP), which is part of the TCP/IP protocol suite. It can also be implemented on top of the ISO transport protocol.

The final ingredient illustrated in Figure 7.4 is that of party. The actual exchange of information takes place between two parties. The use of parties allows systems to define access control and security policies that differ depending on the combination of manager, agent, and desired information. This gives the user considerable flexibility in setting up a network management system and assigning various levels of authorization to different persons.

7.3.2   Structure of management information

The structure of management information (SMI) defines the general framework within which a MIB can be defined and constructed. The SMI identifies the data types that can be used in the MIB, and how resources within the MIB are represented and named. The philosophy behind SMI is to encourage simplicity and extensibility

---

[1]   There is a slight fuzziness about the term MIB. In its singular form, the term MIB can be used to refer to the entire database of management information at a manager or an agent. It can also be used in singular or plural form to refer to a specific defined collection of management information that is part of an overall MIB. Thus, the SNMPv2 standard includes the definition of three MIBs and incorporates, by reference, a MIB defined in SNMP.

within the MIB. Thus, the MIB can store only simple data types: scalars and two-dimensional arrays of scalars, called tables. The SMI does not support the creation or retrieval of complex data structures. This philosophy is in contrast to that used with OSI systems management, which provides for complex data structures and retrieval modes to support greater functionality. SMI avoids complex data types and structures to simplify the task of implementation and to enhance interoperability. MIBs will inevitably contain vendor-created data types and, unless tight restrictions are placed on the definition of such data types, interoperability will suffer.

There are actually three key elements in the SMI specification. At the lowest level, the SMI specifies the data types that may be stored. Then, the SMI specifies a formal technique for defining objects and tables of objects. Finally, the SMI provides a scheme for associating a unique identifier with each actual object in a system, so that data at an agent can be referenced by a manager.

Table 7.1 Allowable data types.

Data Type	Description	SNMP v1	SNMP v2
INTEGER	Integers in the range of -2^{31} to $2^{31} - 1$,	X	X
UInteger32	Integers in the range of 0 to $2^{32} - 1$,		X
Counter32	A non-negative integer which may be incremented modulo 2^{32}.	X	X
Counter64	A non-negative integer which may be incremented modulo 2^{64}.		X
Gauge32	A non-negative integer which may increase or decrease, but shall not exceed a maximum value. The maximum value cannot be greater than $2^{32} - 1$.	X	X
TimeTicks	A non-negative integer which represents the time, modulo 2^{32}, in hundredths of a second.	X	X
OCTET STRING	Octet strings for arbitrary binary or textual data; may be limited to 255 octets.	X	X
IpAddress	A 32-bit internet address.	X	X
NsapAddress	An OSI address. The first octet contains a binary value in the range 0–20 that indicates the length of the address. The remaining octets contain the actual address.		X
BIT STRING	An enumeration of named bits.		X
OBJECT IDENTIFIER	Administratively assigned name to object or other standardized element. Value is a sequence of up to 128 non-negative integers.	X	X

Table 7.1 shows the data types that are allowed by the SMI in both versions of SNMP. This is a fairly restricted set of types. For example, real numbers are not supported. However, it is rich enough to support most network management requirements.

The SNMPv2 specification includes a template, known as an ASN.1 (Abstract Syntax Notation One) macro, which provides the formal model for defining objects. Figure 7.5 is an example of how this template is used to define objects and tables of objects.

```
grokTable  OBJECT-TYPE
    SYNTAX    SEQUENCE OF GrokEntry
    MAX-ACCESS     not-accessible
    STATUS         current
    DESCRIPTION
      "The (conceptual) grok
      table."
    ::=  { adhocGroup 2 }


grokEntry  OBJECT-TYPE
    SYNTAX         GrokEntry
    MAX-ACCESS     not-accessible
    STATUS         current
    DESCRIPTION
      "An entry (conceptual row)
      in the grok table."
    INDEX          { grokIndex }
    ::=  { grokTable 1 }


GrokEntry ::=  SEQUENCE {
    grokIndex      INTEGER,
    grokIPAddress  IpAddress,
    grokCount      Counter32,
    grokStatus     RowStatus }


grokIndex  OBJECT-TYPE
    SYNTAX         INTEGER
    MAX-ACCESS     not-accessible
    STATUS         current
    DESCRIPTION
      "The auxiliary variable
      used for identifying
      instances of the columnar
      objects in the grok table."
    ::=  { grokEntry  1 }
```

```
grokIPAddress  OBJECT-TYPE
    SYNTAX         IpAddress
    MAX-ACCESS     read-create
    STATUS         current
    DESCRIPTION
      "The Ip address to send
      grok packets to."
    ::=  { grokEntry  2 }


grokCount  OBJECT-TYPE
    SYNTAX         Counter32
    MAX-ACCESS     read-only
    STATUS         current
    DESCRIPTION
      "The total number of grok
      packets sent so far."
    DEFVAL { 0 }
    ::=  { grokEntry  3 }


grokStatus  OBJECT-TYPE
    SYNTAX         RowStatus
    MAX-ACCESS     read-create
    STATUS         current
    DESCRIPTION
      "The status object used for
      creating, modifying, and
      deleting a conceptual row
      instance in the grok
      table."
    DEFVAL { active }
    ::=  { grokEntry  4 }
```

Figure 7.5 An example of an SNMPv2 table.

The first three productions serve to define a table, grokTable, stored at an agent. As with all SNMPv2 tables, grokTable is organized as a sequence of rows, or entries, each of which has the same sequence of objects; in this case, each row consists of four objects. The INDEX clause specifies that the object grokIndex serves as an index into the table; each row of the table will have a unique value of grokIndex.

The access type of grokIPAddress is read-create, which means that the object is read-write and that the object may be assigned a value by a manager at the time that the row containing this object is created by a manager. Each row of the table maintains a counter for the number of grok packets sent to the grokIPAddress specified for that row. The grokCount object is read-only; its value cannot be altered by a manager but is maintained by the agent within which this table resides. The grokStatus object is used in the process of row creation and deletion. The algorithm for row creation and deletion is rather complex. In essence, a RowStatus type of object is used to keep track of the state of a row during the process of creation and deletion.

Each object definition includes a value, which is a unique identifier for that object. For example, the value for grokEntry is {grokTable 1}, which means that the identifier for grokEntry is the concatenation of the identifier for grokTable and 1. The objects in a MIB are organized in a tree structure, and the identifier of an object is found by walking the tree from its root to the position of the object in the tree structure. For scalar objects, this scheme provides a unique identifier for any given object instance. For objects in tables, there is one instance of each object for each row of the table, so a further qualification is needed. What is done is to concatenate the value of the INDEX object to the identifier of each object in the table.

7.3.3   Protocol operation

The heart of the SNMPv2 framework is the protocol itself. The protocol provides a straightforward, basic mechanism for the exchange of management information between manager and agent.

Table 7.2 SNMP Protocol Data Units (PDUs).

PDU	Description	Direction	SNMP v1	SNMP v2
Get	Return value for each object.	Manager to agent	X	X
GetNext	Return next value for each object.	Manager to agent	X	X
GetBulk	Return N values for each object.	Manager to agent		X
Set	Set value for each object.	Manager to agent	X	X
Trap	Transmit unsolicited information.	Agent to manager	X	X
Inform	Transmit unsolicited information.	Manager to agent		X
Response	Respond to manager request.	Agent to manager	X	X

The basic unit of exchange is the message, which consists of an outer message wrapper and an inner protocol data unit (PDU). The outer message header deals with security, and is discussed later in this section.

Seven types of PDUs may be carried in an SNMPv2 message. Table 7.2 lists these PDUs and indicates which are the ones that are valid for SNMPv1 as well. The general formats for these are illustrated in Figure 7.6. Several fields are common to a number of PDUs. The request-id field is an integer assigned such that each outstanding request can be uniquely identified. This enables a manager to correlate incoming responses with outstanding requests. It also enables an agent to cope with duplicate PDUs generated by an unreliable transport service. The variable-bindings field contains a list of object identifiers; depending on the PDU, the list may also include a value for each object.

PDU type	request-id	0	0	variable-bindings

(a) GetRequest-PDU, GetNextRequest-PDU, SetRequest-PDU, SNMPv2-Trap-PDU, InformRequest-PDU

PDU type	request-id	error-status	error-index	variable-bindings

(b) Response-PDU

PDU type	request-id	non-repeaters	max-repetitions	variable-bindings

(c) GetBulkRequest-PDU

$name_1$	$value_1$	$name_2$	$value_2$	• • •	$name_n$	$value_n$

(d) Variable-bindings

Figure 7.6 SNMPv2 PDU formats.

The GetRequest PDU, issued by a manager, includes a list of one or more object names for which values are requested. If the get operation is successful, the responding agent will send a Response PDU. The variable-bindings list will contain the identifier and value of all retrieved objects. For any variables that are not in the relevant MIB view, its identifier and an error code are returned in the variable-bindings list. Thus, SNMPv2 permits partial responses to a GetRequest, which is a significant improvement over SNMP. In SNMP, if one or more of the variables in a GetRequest is not supported, the agent returns an error message with a status of noSuchName. In order to cope with such an error, the SNMP manager must either return no values to the requesting application, or it must include an algorithm that responds to an error by removing the missing variables, resending the request, and then sending a partial result to the application.

The GetNextRequest PDU also is issued by a manager and includes a list of one or more objects. In this case, for each object named in the variable-bindings field, a value is to be returned for the object that is next in lexicographic order, which is equivalent to saying next in the MIB in terms of its position in the tree structure of object identifiers. As with the GetRequest-PDU, the agent will return values for as many variables as possible. One of the strengths of the GetNextRequest-PDU is that it enables a manager entity to discover the structure of a MIB view dynamically. This is useful if the manager does not know *a priori* the set of objects that are supported by an agent or that are in a particular MIB view.

One of the major enhancements provided in SNMPv2 is the GetBulkRequest PDU. The purpose of this PDU is to minimize the number of protocol exchanges required to retrieve a large amount of management information. The GetBulkRequest PDU allows an SNMPv2 manager to request that the response be as large as possible given the constraints on message size.

The GetBulkRequest operation uses the same selection principle as the GetNextRequest operation; that is, selection is always of the next object instance in lexicographic order. The difference is that, with GetBulkRequest, it is possible to specify that multiple lexicographic successors be selected.

In essence, the GetBulkRequest operation works in the following way. The GetBulkRequest includes a list of (N + R) variable names in the variable-bindings list. For each of the first N names, retrieval is done in the same fashion as for GetNextRequest. That is, for each variable in the list, the next variable in lexicographic order plus its value is returned; if there is no lexicographic successor, then the named variable and a value of endOfMibView are returned. For each of the last R names, multiple lexicographic successors are returned.

The GetBulkRequest PDU has two fields not found in the other PDUs: non-repeaters and max-repetitions. The non-repeaters field specifies the number of variables in the variable-binding list for which a single lexicographic successor is to be returned. The max-repetitions field specifies the number of lexicographic successors to be returned for the remaining variables in the variable binding list. To explain the algorithm, let us define the following:

L = number of variable names in the variable-bindings field of the GetBulkRequest PDU

N = the number of variables, starting with the first variable in the variable-bindings field, for which a single lexicographic successor is requested

R = the number of variables, following the first N variables, for which multiple lexicographic successors are requested

M = the number of lexicographic successors requested for each of the last R variables

The following relationships hold:

N = MAX [MIN (non-repeaters, L), 0]

M = MAX [max-repetitions, 0]

R = L − N

The effect of the MAX operator is that if the value of either non-repeaters or max-repetitions is less than 0, a value of 0 is substituted.

If N is greater than 0, then the first N variables are processed as for GetNextRequest. If R is greater than 0 and M is greater than 0, then for each of the last R variables in the variable bindings list, the M lexicographic successors are retrieved. That is, for each variable:

- Obtain the value of the lexicographic successor of the named variable;

- Obtain the value of the lexicographic successor to the object instance retrieved in the previous step;

- Obtain the value of the lexicographic successor to the object instance retrieved in the previous step;

- And so on, until M object instances have been retrieved.

If, at any point in this process, there is no lexicographic successor, then the endOfMibView value is returned, paired with the name of the last lexicographic successor or, if there were no successors, with the name of the variable in the request.

Using these rules, the total number of variable-binding pairs that can be produced is $N + (M \times R)$. The order in which the last $(M \times R)$ of these variable-binding pairs are placed in the Response PDU can be expressed as follows:

```
for i := 1 to M do
     for r := 1 to R do
         retrieve i-th successor of (N+r)-th variable;
```

The effect of this definition is that the successors to the last R variables are retrieved row by row, rather than retrieving all of the successors to the first variable, followed by all of the successors to the second variable, and so on. This matches with the way in which conceptual tables are lexicographically ordered, so that if the last R values in the GetBulkRequest are columnar objects of the same table, the Response will return conceptual rows of the table.

The GetBulkRequest operation removes one of the major limitations of SNMP, which is its inability to efficiently retrieve large blocks of data. Moreover, the use of this operator can actually enable reducing the size of management applications that are supported by the management protocol, realizing further efficiencies. There is no need for the management application to concern itself with some of the details of packaging requests. It need not perform a trial-and-error procedure to determine the optimal number of variable bindings to put in a request PDU. Also, if a request is too big, even for GetBulkRequest, the agent will send back as much data as it can, rather than simply sending a tooBig error message. Thus, the manager simply has to retransmit the request for the missing data; it does not have to figure out how to repackage the original request into a series of smaller requests.

The SetRequest PDU is issued by a manager to request that the values of one or more objects be altered. The receiving SNMPv2 entity responds with a Response PDU containing the same request-id. The SetRequest operation is atomic: either all of the variables are updated or none are. If the responding entity can set values for all of the variables listed in the incoming variable-bindings list, then the Response PDU includes the variable-binding field, with a value supplied for each variable. If at least one of the variable values cannot be supplied, then no values are returned, and no values are updated. In the latter case, the error-status code indicates the reason for the failure, and the error-index field indicates the variable in the variable-bindings list that caused the failure.

The SNMPv2-Trap PDU is generated and transmitted by an SNMPv2 entity acting in an agent role when an unusual event occurs. It is used to provide the management station with an asynchronous notification of some significant event. The variable-bindings list is used to contain the information associated with the trap message. Unlike the GetRequest, GetNextRequest, GetBulkRequest, SetRequest, and InformRequest PDUs, the SNMPv2-Trap PDU does not elicit a response from the receiving entity; it is an unconfirmed message.

The InformRequest PDU is sent by an SNMPv2 entity acting in a manager role, on behalf of an application, to another SNMPv2 entity acting in a manager role, to provide management information to an application using the latter entity. As with the SNMPv2-Trap PDU, the variable-binding field is used to convey the associated information. The manager receiving an InformRequest acknowledges receipt with a Response PDU.

For both the SNMPv2-Trap and the InformRequest, various conditions can be defined that indicate when the notification is generated; and the information to be sent is also specified.

7.3.4   SNMPv2 management information base

The objects defined as part of SNMPv2 are organized into three MIBs: the SNMPv2 MIB, the manager-to-manager MIB, and the party MIB. Each MIB is in turn organized into a number of groups. A group is simply a related collection of objects. Typically, implementations are characterized in terms of which groups they implement. An implementation is said to include a group if all of the objects in that group are supported. This provides a concise way for vendors and customers to gain a mutual understanding of what management information is supported by the vendor's product.

The **SNMPv2 MIB** defines objects that describe the behavior of an SNMPv2 entity. This information enables a manager to monitor the amount of SNMPv2-related activity at an agent and the amount of dedicated SNMPv2-related resources at the agent. This MIB contains five groups: SNMPv2 statistics, SNMPv1 statistics, object resource, traps, and set.

The SNMPv2 statistics group provides basic instrumentation of the SNMPv2 entity. It consists of counters used to record the number of incoming and outgoing SNMPv2 messages, broken down into successful messages plus those that suffered various error conditions. The SNMPv1 statistics group includes several objects that are useful if an SNMPv2 entity also implements SNMPv1. The object resources group enables an SNMPv2 entity acting in an agent role to describe its dynamically configurable object resources; essentially, this group consists of a table with one entry for each resource, with a text description of the resource. The trap group consists of objects that allow the SNMPv2 entity, when acting in an agent role, to be configured to generate SNMPv2-Trap PDUs. Finally, the set group consists of a single object, snmpSetSerialNo, that is used to solve two problems that can occur with the use of the set operation. First, multiple set operations on the same MIB object may be issued by a manager, and it may be essential that these operations be performed in the order that they were issued, even if they are reordered in transmission. And second, concurrent use of set operations by multiple managers may result in an inconsistent or inaccurate database. The snmpSetSerialNo is an integer-valued object that obeys the following rules. If the value of the object is K and a set operation is received that attempts to assign K to this object, then the object is incremented to $(K + 1)$ mod 2^{31}, and the operation succeeds. If any other value is used, the operation fails.

The snmpSet object can be used in the following way: when a manager wishes to set one or more object values in an agent, it first retrieves the value of the snmpSet object. It then issues a SetRequest PDU whose variable-binding list includes the snmpSet object with its current value. If two or more managers issue SetRequests using the same value of snmpSet, the first to arrive at the agent will succeed (assuming no other problems exist), resulting in an increment of snmpSet; the remaining set operations will fail owing to an inconsistent snmpSet value.

The **manager-to-manager MIB** is specifically provided to support the distributed management architecture. It enables a superior manager to define events that a subordinate manager will use as triggers for sending alert-type messages to the superior manager. The manager-to-manager MIB may be used to allow an intermediate manager to function as a remote monitor of network media traffic. It may also be used to allow an intermediate manager to report on activities at the intermediate manager or at subordinate agents. This MIB consists of two groups: the alarm group and the event group. The alarm group is used to define a set of threshold alarms. Each threshold alarm specifies some object in the local MIB that is to be monitored. When the value of that object crosses a threshold, an event is triggered. Typically, the triggered event is an InformRequest PDU that is to be sent to a superior manager. Each alarm in the alarm group points to an entry in the event group, which in turn defines the information that is to be sent with that InformRequest PDU.

The **Party MIB** relates to security, which is discussed next.

7.4   SNMPv2 security

The security features of SNMPv2 are designed to provide, in essence, three security-related services: privacy, authentication, and access control.

Privacy is the protection of transmitted data from eavesdropping or wiretapping. Privacy requires that the contents of any message be disguised in such a way that only the intended recipient can recover the original message.

A message, file, document, or other collection of data is said to be authentic when it is genuine and came from its alleged source. Message authentication is a procedure that allows communicating parties to verify that received messages are authentic. The two important aspects are to verify that the contents of the message have not been altered and that the source is authentic. We may also wish to verify a message's timeliness (it has not been artificially delayed and replayed) and sequence relative to other messages flowing between two parties.

In the context of network management, the purpose of access control is to ensure that only authorized users have access to a particular management information base and that access to and modification of a particular portion of data are limited to authorized individuals and programs.

Before examining these three services, we need to introduce the concept of party and look at the message structure for SNMPv2.

7.4.1   SNMPv2 parties

It is essential for secure communication to identify specifically a source and a destination for any exchange. Authentication depends on the source: it is the responsibility of the source to include in any message information that assures that the origin is authentic, and it is the responsibility of the source to perform the required functions to ensure message integrity. However, message privacy, which is achieved by encryption, depends on the destination. That is, encryption must be done in such a way that only the intended destination can perform the decryption. Finally, access control depends on both source and destination. That is, each destination may have an distinct access policy for each potential source.

Thus, each message must identify both the source and destination. Furthermore, it is insufficient to equate the source with a sending SNMPv2 entity and the destination with a receiving SNMPv2 entity. Each SNMPv2 entity may behave differently, from a security point of view, depending on the identity of the other SNMPv2 entity involved in an exchange. Put another way, the role of an SNMPv2 entity depends on the context of its operation. The concept of role is captured in SNMPv2 as the SNMPv2 **party**. A party is defined as an execution context of an SNMPv2 protocol entity. Any protocol entity may include multiple party identities.

The way in which parties are handled is as follows. Each SNMPv2 entity maintains a database with information that represents all SNMPv2 parties known to it. This includes:

- *Local parties:* The set of parties whose operation is realized by the local SNMPv2 entity; that is, the set of "roles" for this SNMPv2 entity.

- *Proxied parties:* The set of parties for proxied entities that this SNMPv2 entity represents.

- *Remote parties:* The set of parties whose operation is realized by other SNMPv2 entities with which this SNMPv2 entity is capable of interacting.

7.4.2   Message format

In SNMPv2, information is exchanged between a management station and an agent in the form of a message. Each message includes a message header, which contains security-related information, and one of a number of types of protocol data units. The message structure is depicted in Figure 7.7.

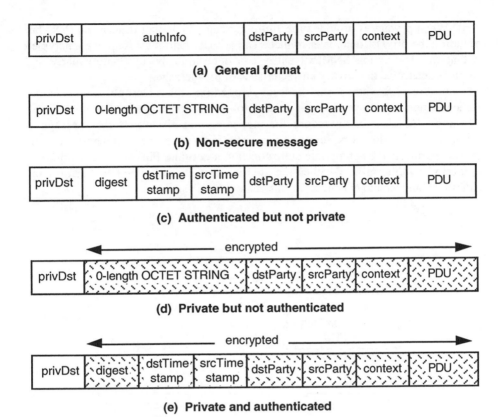

Figure 7.7 SNMPv2 message formats.

The header consists of five fields. The **srcParty** identifies the party at a manager or agent that is sending this message. The **dstParty** identifies the party at a manager or agent to whom the message is sent. The **context** may indicate that this exchange relates to an access to a MIB local to the agent; in this case, the context value serves to identify a portion of the agent's MIB, known as a MIB view. A MIB view is simply a subset of the MIB at the agent, which is the subject of this protocol exchange. Otherwise, the context value indicates that this exchange involves access to a third system by means of a proxy relationship; in this case, the context value serves to identify the proxied device and the access control privileges associated with accessing that proxied device. In either case, the combination of source party, destination party, and context value are used to determine the access control privileges for this exchange. The **authInfo** field contains information relevant to the authentication protocol. The **privDst** field repeats the object identifier of the destination party.

If the message is non-secure (not authenticated and not private), the authInfo field consists of an ASN.1 (Abstract Syntax Notation One) encoding of an octet string of zero length. If the message is authenticated but not private, the authInfo field contains information needed for authentication.

When privacy is provided the entire message, including header and PDU but excluding the privDst field, is encrypted. The privDst field must remain unencrypted so that the destination SNMPv2 entity can determine the destination party and therefore determine the privacy characteristics of the message.

Figure 7.8 shows the general procedure for message transmission. Authentication is performed first, if needed, followed by encryption, if needed. Figure 7.9 shows the general procedure for message transmission. If the message is encrypted, decryption is performed first. Then, if the message is authenticated, the receiver performs the appropriate authentication algorithm. Finally, access control is performed to determine whether the source party is authorized to perform the requested management operation for this context and destination party.

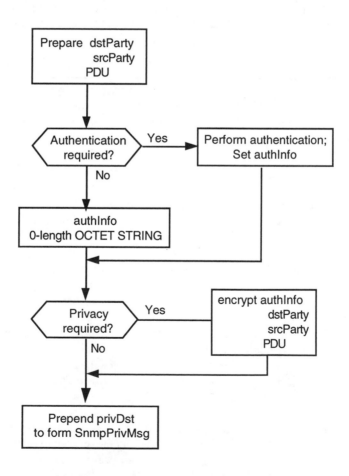

Figure 7.8 Transmission of SNMPv2 messages.

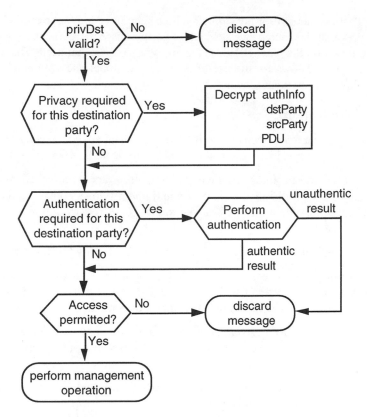

Figure 7.9 Reception of SNMPv2 messages.

7.4.3   Privacy

For each party known to an SNMPv2 entity, the party database contains three variables whose significance is specific to the privacy protocol:

- partyPrivProtocol: Indicates the privacy protocol and mechanism by which all messages received by this party are protected from disclosure. The value noPriv indicates that messages received by this party are not protected from disclosure.

- partyPrivPrivate: A secret value needed to support the privacy protocol. It may be a conventional-encryption key or the private key in a public-key encryption scheme.

- partyPrivPublic: Represents any public value that may be needed to support the privacy protocol. It may be a public key in a public-key encryption scheme.

The specific privacy mechanism chosen for the current version of secure SNMPv2 is the symmetric privacy protocol. It provides for protection from disclosure of a received message (that is, only the intended recipient, and the sender, can read the message). The mechanism for providing such protection is conventional encryption, which requires that the source and destination parties share the same encryption key. The Data Encryption Standard (DES) is the encryption algorithm used. The database structure, however, allows for the use of other conventional encryption schemes as well as public-key encryption schemes.

7.4.4   Authentication

For each party known to an SNMPv2 entity, the party database contains five variables whose significance is specific to the authentication protocol:

- partyAuthProtocol: Indicates the authentication protocol and mechanism used by this party to authenticate the origin and integrity of its outgoing messages. The value noAuth indicates that messages generated by this party are not authenticated.

- partyAuthClock: Represents a current time as kept locally for this party.

- partyAuthPrivate: A secret value needed to support the authentication protocol. It may be a secret value used in a message digest, a conventional encryption key, or the private key in a public-key encryption scheme.

- partyAuthPublic: Represents any public value that may be needed to support the authentication protocol. It may be a public key in a public-key encryption scheme.

- partyAuthLifetime: An administrative upper bound on acceptable delivery delay for messages generated by this party.

The specific authentication mechanism chosen for the current version of secure SNMPv2 is the MD5 digest authentication protocol. It provides for the verification of the integrity of a received message (that is, the message received is the message sent), for authentication of the origin of the message, and for the timeliness of message delivery.

In essence, the authentication procedure is as follows. A message digest is computed over the message to be sent prefixed by a secret value, using the MD5 message digest algorithm. The message, plus the message digest (but not the secret value), is transmitted. On reception, the message digest is recomputed using the incoming message and a local copy of the secret value. If the incoming message digest matches the calculated message digest, the received message is declared authentic. The use of the message digest guarantees integrity, and the use of a secret value guarantees origin authentication.

We now turn to the details of the authentication protocol, considering first transmission and then reception. To support authentication, the message header in a transmitted SNMPv2 message includes an authentication-information field, which consists of three components:

- authDigest: Represents the digest computed over an appropriate portion of the message, plus the secret value (partyAuthPrivate).

- authSrcTimestamp: Represents the time of generation of this message according to the partyAuthClock of the SNMPv2 party that is the source party. The granularity of the clock and therefore of this timestamp is one second.

- authDstTimestamp: Represents the time of generation of this message according to the partyAuthClock of the SNMPv2 party that is the destination party. Note that this is the value of the destination party clock stored at the source SNMPv2 entity.

The procedure to be followed for authentication upon reception is somewhat more complex to describe than that for message generation, since various error-checking functions must be taken into account. Suppose that a message is sent from party A on one system to party B on another system. The message authentication process consists of the following steps:

i)   If the authSrcTimestamp value does not satisfy the criterion for timeliness the message is rejected. The timeliness criterion states that the message must be received within a reasonable period of time that does not exceed an administratively set value. This criterion can be expressed as follows. A message is timely if:

$$partyAuthClock.A - authTimestamp \leq partyAuthLifetime.A$$

Put another way, the age of the message at the time of receipt must be less than the maximum allowable lifetime.

ii) The authDigest value is extracted and temporarily stored. The authDigest value is temporarily set to the secret value. The message digest is computed over an appropriate portion of the message, plus the secret value (partyAuthPrivate), and compared to the value that was stored (the value that arrived in the incoming message). If the two values match, the message is accepted as authentic.

The relationship between partyAuthClock, partyAuthLifetime, and authSrcTimestamp is illustrated in Figure 7.10. Part (a) of the figure shows the relationship that exists for a message that is authentic in terms of timeliness. Part (b) shows the case of an unauthentic message. Part (c) illustrates the fact that the timestamp of the incoming message may actually exceed the current value of partyAuthClock for the sending party as maintained at the destination. From a logical point of view this indicates that a message arrives "before" it is sent. Of course, this logical impossibility is due to a mismatch in clocks. When this condition occurs the clock at the destination is advanced to equal the incoming timestamp. Similarly, to keep the clocks synchronized in the other direction, the partyAuthClock of the receiving party is compared to authDstTimestamp and advanced if necessary to equal the incoming timestamp.

The lifetime value for a party should be chosen to be as small as possible given the accuracy of the clocks involved, round-trip communication delays, and the frequency with which clocks are synchronized. If the lifetime value is set too small, authentic messages will be rejected as unauthentic. On the other hand, a large lifetime increases the vulnerability of messages to malicious delays.

It is important to note that the generation of the message depends on the values of the source party that are stored by the sending SNMPv2 entity, where the source party resides, while the authentication of the message at the destination depends on the party values *for the source party* that are stored at the receiving SNMPv2 entity, where the destination party resides. The values in the two instances may differ.

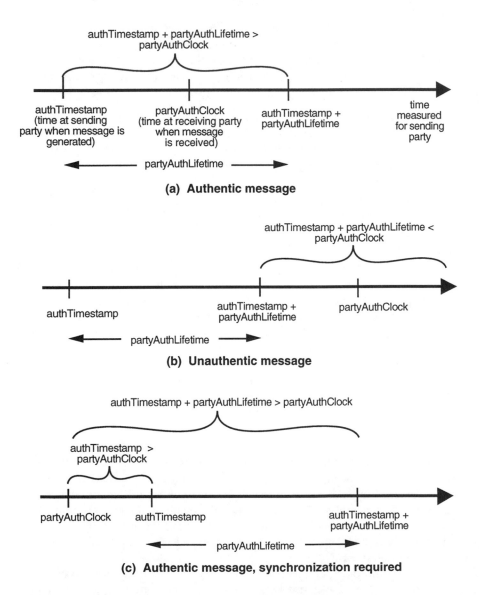

Figure 7.10 Authentication timeliness requirement.

7.4.5   Clock synchronization

When a message is transmitted, it includes the value of both the sending and receiving party clocks. Upon message reception, authentication depends on the timeliness of the message with reference to the source timestamp.

When a party is first configured, its clock is set to zero. The clock then increments once per second. There are, however, two versions of a party's clock: one stored with the party information at the management station and one stored with the party information at the agent. Thus there is the potential for drift between the two versions, which could adversely affect authentication.

For any pair of parties, four possible conditions can occur that require correction:

i)   The manager's version of the agent's clock is greater than the agent's version of the agent's clock. This creates the risk of a false rejection of a message from the agent to the manager.

ii)   The manager's version of the manager's clock is greater than the agent's version of the manager's clock. This creates the risk of a false acceptance of a message from the manager to the agent.

iii) The agent's version of the agent's clock is greater than the manager's version of the agent's clock. This creates the risk of a false acceptance of a message from the agent to the manager.

iv)   The agent's version of the manager's clock is greater than the manager's version of the manager's clock. This creates the risk of a false rejection of a message from the manager to the agent.

Now, let us consider the case in which an agent receives a message from a manager. If the authSrcTimestamp in the message exceeds the agent's value of partyAuthClock for the sending manager party, that clock is advanced and condition 2 is corrected. If the authDstTimestamp in the message exceeds the agent's value of partyAuthClock for the receiving agent party, the clock is advanced and condition 1 is corrected. To complete this line of reasoning, consider the case in which a manager receives a message from an agent. If the authSrcTimestamp in the message exceeds the agent's value of partyAuthClock for the sending agent party, the clock is advanced and condition 3 is corrected. If the authDstTimestamp in the message exceeds the agent's value of partyAuthClock for the receiving manager party, the clock is advanced and condition 4 is corrected.

At first glance, the effects of these clock updates would appear to eliminate the need for explicit, manager-directed clock synchronization, since all four clock skew conditions are corrected when messages are exchanged. However, in most cases of manager–agent interaction, the interaction is in the form of a manager request and an agent response. It is intended that a trap message, which originates at the agent, is to be used sparingly. If there has been a considerable lapse of time between requests from a particular manager party to a particular agent party, then clock drift may have created condition 4 with a substantial difference in the two clock values. The result is that any request by the manager will be rejected. Accordingly, it remains necessary for the manager to perform clock synchronization on all manager party clocks, but it is not necessary to synchronize agent party clocks. For this purpose, the manager periodically retrieves the manager party clock values from agents and advances its clocks as necessary.

7.4.6   Access control

Management information at a system is stored as a collection of objects that represent manageable resources. These objects are arranged in a tree structure to form the management information base (MIB) at the system.

For purposes of access control, the concepts of MIB view and view subtree are used. A view subtree consists of a node in the MIB tree plus all of its subordinate elements. Each view subtree in the MIB view is specified as being included or excluded. That is, the MIB view either includes or excludes all objects contained in that subtree. This specification technique provides a flexible but concise means of defining a MIB view.

Access control is determined by information in the Party MIB. This MIB consists of four groups: party database, contexts, access privileges, and MIB view. The best way to describe the purpose of each of these groups is to consider their use during message transmission.

Consider that a message is sent from a manager to an agent. The message header includes the fields srcParty, dstParty, and context. The party database group at the agent contains information about each local and remote party known to the agent. The party information includes authentication parameters that need to be applied to srcParty, and privacy parameters that need to be applied to dstParty. The context group consists of a table with one entry for each context known to the agent. Each entry specifies whether the context is local, in which case the appropriate MIB view must be used, or remote, in which case the proxied device is indicated. The MIB view group is referenced by the contexts group. The appropriate entry defines a subset of the local MIB that is accessible through this context. Finally, the access privileges database group contains the aclTable. Each entry in the table has a unique combination of srcParty, dstParty, and context, and indicates which management operations (which PDUs) are allowed for this combination.

7.5   SNMPv1, SNMPv2, and CMIP

Many network installations already make use of SNMPv1. Thus, there is the issue of transition from SNMPv1 to SNMPv2. Fortunately, in this area, techniques have been developed. SNMPv2 includes specifications for the coexistence of SNMPv2 managers with SNMPv1 agents. In essence, one or more SNMPv2 managers must act as proxies to translate SNMPv2 manager commands into SNMPv1 commands to be issued to agents. Alternatively, all SNMPv2 managers can be configured to "speak" SNMPv1. Thus, a user can begin the transition by replacing all management stations and only gradually upgrade/replace agent software.

For those users who do not yet employ SNMPv1, or are using SNMPv1 and have been contemplating a move to OSI, SNMPv2 complicates the SNMP versus OSI choice. A massive collection of standards is being developed under the general umbrella of OSI systems management, which is OSI-speak for network management. The bad news about OSI systems management is that it is complex and a resource hog. The good news is that it does include both application-level utilities and actual network management applications. With a choice between SNMPv1 and OSI systems management, there was a clear pressure on users to eventually migrate to the more powerful and flexible OSI systems management. SNMPv2 partially bridges that gap, giving the users three choices instead of two. Muddy waters become muddier.

7.6   What have we gained?

SNMPv2 is a substantial improvement over SNMPv1, while retaining its essential character of ease of understanding and ease of implementation. SNMPv2 fixes the most obvious failings of version 1: lack of security. It also provides better support for a decentralized network management architecture. Finally, it enhances performance and provides a few other bells and whistles of interest to application developers. These improvements over SNMPv1 should make SNMPv2 a clear winner in the marketplace. Vendors will be quick to adopt the new version to provide more features and more efficient operation to their users, so we can expect additional MIBs to be defined within the SNMPv2 framework to extend its scope to support various network management applications.

Abbreviations

CMIP	Common Management Information Protocol
CMOT	CMIP Over TCP/IP
FDDI	Fiber Distributed Data Interface
HEMS	High-Level Entity Management System
IAB	Internet Activities Board
ICMP	Internet Control Message Protocol
IP	Internet Protocol
MD5	Message Digest Algorithm Number 5
MIB	Management Information Base
OSI	Open Systems Interconnection
PDU	Protocol Data Unit
PING	Packet Internet Groper
RMON	Remote Network Monitoring
SMI	Structure of Management Information
SMP	Simple Management Protocol
SNMP	Simple Network Management Protocol
SNMPv2	Simple Network Management Protocol Version 2
TCP	Transmission Control Protocol

UDP   User Datagram Protocol

References

The material in this chapter is based on:

Stallings W. (1993). *SNMP, SNMPv2, and CMIP: The Practical Guide to Network Management Standards*. Addison-Wesley

Chapter 8

Comparison of SNMP and CMIP Management Architectures

Michael Gering

IBM Corporation, PO Box 12195,
Research Triangle Park, NC 27709, USA
Email: gering@vnet.ibm.com

This chapter compares and contrasts the management schemes defined for the TCP/IP and OSI environments, taking into account customer requirements, functional capabilities, and implementation considerations.

8.1   Introduction

Today's environment for systems and network management is characterized by the following factors:

- multi-vendor,

- multi-enterprise,

- diversity of types and numbers of resources.

Most, if not all, customers have installed systems and network equipment and software from more than one vendor. Usually, each vendor supplies a unique management system, or set of unique applications, on one or more management platforms to manage the vendor's gear. Some vendors develop multiple, unique applications and platforms to manage specific types of resources, which usually implies that integration of the end-user interfaces, application data, and application function is very low. Consequently, both vendors and customers pay high costs associated with low levels of integration. From the customer's perspective each management application requires additional operator training to cope with different end-user interfaces, additional equipment to interface to the resources being managed, a different set of applications to provide for automation, and redundant sets of data to represent the same information to different applications. From a vendor's perspective, the application code to manage new resources is relatively unique, and is more complex if it needs to communicate information to or obtain information from other management applications.

Information exchange between enterprises is a business requirement increasingly satisfied by data communications. The data communications services may themselves be supplied by one or more other organizations, such as common carriers and value-added service providers. In all these cases, the data communications path between the end users and applications is likely to cross multiple organizational boundaries. Each enterprise typically has an autonomous management system, consisting of equipment, software, and humans, for its own systems and network resources. Management scenarios involving related resources belonging to different enterprises arise naturally. For example, when problems occur in a data communications path, the autonomous management systems must cooperate to isolate, bypass and repair the problem. Unfortunately, the maximum level of information exchange between the management systems today is likely to be people talking over telephones. To improve this situation, the management systems should be able exchange relevant and appropriate information electronically.

The important implications of the multi-enterprise environment derive from what is meant by "relevant and appropriate". Not all the management information within an enterprise is relevant to another enterprise. Only some of the management information about resources which are used in some way by another enterprise are relevant to management tasks shared between the enterprises. For example, the complex configuration of telephone equipment supporting a leased circuit is not generally relevant to the customer leasing the circuit. However, the identity of the circuit, its capabilities, performance, and operational status are relevant to the customer. Of the relevant management information, only a subset may be considered appropriate for business, legal, or ethical reasons.

Customers increasingly require integration of their network and systems management tasks over a broader range of resource types. One direct implication is the requirement for management systems that provide high levels of integration for different resource types. For example, many asset management tasks do not depend on differences between physical resource types. Serial numbers, depreciation schedules, and so on, are example concepts needed by asset management tasks that do not change in any important way when applied to different resource types such as modems and computers. An indirect implication of this requirement is that the complexity and cost of building and operating an integrated management system is related to the diversity of the types of resources it must manage. Consequently, the most cost-effective solutions will recognize and exploit inherent similarities[1] between resource types. The extent to which existing management applications can adapt to the appearance of a new resource type reflects decreasing cost and increasing value of a management system. A necessary enabler for achieving these economies is an

---

[1]   From a system and network management perspective.

information model for describing resources that has enough expressive power to make explicit the inherent similarities between different resource types.

As the number (instances, not types) of resources brought under an integrated management umbrella increases, physical limitations of the management systems themselves create the need to distribute and coordinate management tasks between management systems.

In summary, the strongest requirements arising from these factors include:

- integrated management systems with consistent end-user and application interfaces;

- common data definitions and the ability to share data between applications;

- reuse of code to support similar equipment from different vendors;

- communications mechanisms to distribute and coordinate management tasks between different management systems;

- security mechanisms to control the exchange of management information.

Consistency is the key to reducing cost and complexity of network and systems management and is the goal for integration of any aspect of a general system.

CMIP and SNMP represent the two most widely discussed non-proprietary approaches for distributed management. In the remainder of this chapter, the term *SNMP* will refer, for the most part, to the collection of protocols and services used in managing TCP/IP networks, including SNMP, SMI (Rose and McCloghrie, 1990), UDP, and the MIBs. Similarly, the term *CMIP* will refer collectively to CMIP (ISO/IEC 9596, 1990), ROSE, ACSE, system management functions, SMI (ISO/IEC 10165-1, 1991), and OSI managed objects. This chapter compares the similarities and differences between the two.

8.2   Comparison criteria

The CMIP and SNMP approaches are compared according to these criteria:

- information structure;

- management functions;

- underlying communications.

A management system must model the resources that it manages. Most of the modeling requirements are to represent information about resources. The information- structuring mechanisms offered by a management approach determine the ease or difficulty which it copes with:

- the diversity and complexity of managed resources,

- presenting that information in a consistent way to end users, and

- sharing data between applications.

Management functions represent the task-oriented aspects of systems management, that is, the functions that managers perform on managed resources. Commonly defined management functions that apply to many different resource types promote consistency and reduce the costs and complexities of building and operating a management system.

In a distributed management environment, the management applications and managed resources rely on underlying communications capabilities to exchange information and perform management functions. The complexity and scalability of management applications depends to a great extent on the underlying communications services available to them.

8.3 Information structure

This section discusses the differences between the information structures provided for by SNMP and CMIP. Information-structuring mechanisms are needed to represent management information about the resources being managed. For example, what information is needed to represent the properties associated with modems, how is that information packaged, how does it relate to other packages, how do we identify them, and how are they communicated between managers and agents? The following sections discuss information-structuring methodology, naming, and data representation.

8.3.1 Information-structuring methodology

Network and systems management is a problem of mastering an immense and open-ended amount of diversity and complexity. The motivation behind an information-structuring methodology is to bring order to this chaos in ways that:

- provide tools to model objects in the real world;
- reduce complexity by exploiting natural similarities in the real world;
- provide a clean boundary between the implementation of information and the way it is accessed or used;
- promote reuse of specification and implementation.

CMIP and SNMP use the term "object" to represent something that can be manipulated with their management protocols. Object-oriented methodologies provide these mechanisms to accomplish the above goals: encapsulation, classes, inheritance, and polymorphism. The following sections describe how these object-oriented methodology concepts apply in the CMIP and SNMP worlds.

8.3.1.1 SNMP object-oriented features

The SNMP SMI specifies the rules and guidelines for names, data syntax, and notation for managed objects. The various MIBs are defined according to the SMI. The term *variable* is often used interchangeably with object in this model because each object represents a single, atomic data element. Example variables are:

- *ifAdminStatus* represents the up/down/testing status of a physical interface;

- *ifSpeed* represents the nominal bandwidth of a physical interface;

- *ifInOctets* represents the number of octets received over a physical interface.

Encapsulation

SNMP does not provide a formal mechanism for encapsulating related variables. The most serious drawback is that implementers have no formal guidance for how consistency between variables should be maintained. Variables are separately accessible and modifiable. Although the SNMP protocol allows multiple *GET* or *SET* requests to be conveyed in one protocol data unit, it does not require that the requests be processed in order or that they have any relationship with each other.

SMI allows variables to be aggregated in lists and tables. This is not a suitable encapsulation mechanism since the SNMP protocol has no list- or table-oriented operations, that is, a manager cannot operate on a list or table as a whole. SMI provides no formal mechanism for specifying that the variables in a list or table are related in any special way, for example, that they together represent information about a single managed resource.

The SNMP *SET* operation allows side effects. For example, setting a variable *powerStatus* to zero might have the effect of causing a piece of equipment to power down. This enables a variable to encapsulate behavior. However, the utility of this feature is significantly reduced because the variables are limited to unstructured syntaxes (see Section 8.3.3); there is no structured way to set a variable to a list of parameters. An alternative might be to define one variable per parameter and use multiple *SET* operations to effect the desired behavior. However, this introduces problems of consistency, integrity, and synchronization, which are contrary to encapsulation. Another approach is to design a parameter switch to flip between different sets of parameters (variables); the agent sets the switch to indicate which parameter set is currently available to a manager. This approach, however, introduces the problem of mutual exclusion when multiple managers have access to the parameter switch, that is, the problem of how to prevent two managers from simultaneously attempting to use the same parameter set.

Classes

The object class concept analog in SNMP is the MIB variable or object type. The SMI defines the rules and guidelines for MIB variable types and a formal notation for specifying them. A MIB variable type includes:

- a unique identifier for the type (an ASN.1 *OBJECT IDENTIFIER*);

- a syntax for the type (see Section 8.3.3);

- access – read-only, read-write, not-accessible;

- status – mandatory, optional, obsolete.

One of the principle advantages of the class concept in object-orientation is its recognition and expression of similarities between instances of things being modeled. This advantage is negated by SNMP because it intertwines class and instance identification; every MIB variable instance name includes its class name, and the structure of instance names depends on how the data are aggregated in the MIB. This implies that a variable type definition cannot be reused in different parts of the MIB to represent similar things. For example, if we define a MIB variable that keeps count of the number of protocol errors, we might want to use different instances of that variable type to count token ring protocol errors, session protocol errors, and so on. Unless all these protocol error counters are structured in the same list or table, they cannot share the same class definition. Instead, we would have to specify separate MIB variable types for each of the protocol error counters. The fact that they share many semantics is not formally specified, and the similarities are lost to any managing user or application.

Inheritance

SNMP does not support inheritance. The principle advantages of inheritance are specification reuse, and by extension, code reuse. SNMP MIB variable specifications are not reused for other MIB variables. An implementation consequence is that manager application logic depends uniquely on each MIB variable type. The manager application must be changed to specifically accommodate each new MIB variable.

Polymorphism

SNMP defines only these polymorphic operations on variables:

- *GET* to retrieve the value(s) for one or more variables,

- *GET-NEXT* to retrieve the next value(s) for one or more variables,

- *SET* to set the value(s) for one or more variables.

SNMP defines another message, *TRAP*, which is not related to any variable, but to the system as a whole. SNMP handles migration by obsoleting old variable types and defining new ones. SMI provides no specification mechanism for relating a new variable type to one it obsoletes, nor does SNMP provide a protocol mechanism to carry such information.

8.3.1.2   CMIP object-oriented features

OSI management defines an object-oriented paradigm in the Management Information Model standard. The following sections describe the object-oriented concepts as they pertain to OSI management, and contrast them with the SNMP counterparts.

Encapsulation

OSI management provides a formal means of encapsulation. OSI managed objects encapsulate behaviors, attributes, operations and notifications at an object boundary. The object boundary is a formal model for specifying aspects of the managed resource that are visible to management processes. Aspects of a managed resource that are inside the object boundary are invisible to the management process. A managed object class specification defines the encapsulated behaviors, attributes, operations, notifications, and integrity and consistency constraints for instances of that class.

One key difference between CMIP and SNMP objects is that a single CMIP object may model a complex resource. For example, CMIP objects may contain attributes to model properties of that resource, whereas an SNMP object models only one property of a resource. From this perspective, SNMP objects are like CMIP attributes, and the CMIP object has no counterpart in SNMP.

It might seem that CMIP attributes violate the orthodox definition of encapsulation because their values are visible and changeable from outside the object boundary. However, this view is based on the incorrect assumption that attributes correspond to object instance variables. An instance variable is a property of an object's implementation that is hidden (encapsulated) inside the object boundary. OSI management specifically excludes implementation aspects of objects and therefore has no concept of instance variables. Attributes, on the other hand, are properties of an object that are specifically intended to be visible outside the object boundary using the CMIP operations GET and SET. The same properties could be modeled without using attributes, in which case the CMIP ACTION operation would be used to manipulate them.

A complex operation may be defined for an OSI managed object with the ACTION operation, which may take any number of parameters.

Classes

OSI management provides for object classes. Each object instance is a member of one class. The specification for an object class uses a formal notation, GDMO (ISO/IEC 10165-4, 1991), as described in Chapter 6.

Both SNMP MIB variable types and OSI managed object classes are assigned globally unique identifiers. However, because OSI managed object instance identification is independent of OSI managed object class identification, instances of the same class may occur in different places of the naming schema.

Class component specifications for attributes, actions, and notifications are assigned unique identifiers which are independent of each other and of the class identifier. This permits reuse of attribute, action and notification specifications in many object classes. For example, an attribute to represent operational status (enabled or disabled) can be used for many different classes including printer, modem or processor. Similarly, a single notification may be defined to signal a change in the operational state of the example resources. A manager application can take advantage of the fact that these identifiers are global and that CMIP carries them in the protocol by building a knowledge base of attributes, etc. Presented with an object class it does not understand, the manager may still understand much about the class's behavior because it already knows about the class's parts. In the above example, if the manager understands operational state change notifications, it can interpret such a notification from an object class about which it knows nothing else.

Inheritance

OSI management permits inheritance as a means for defining object classes that are extensions or refinements of other object classes. A subclass inherits the properties (attributes, actions, notifications, and behaviors) of its superclasses and may add additional properties. OSI management requires strict inheritance, which means no inherited properties may be suppressed or redefined. OSI management permits multiple inheritance, which allows a subclass to have more than one superclass. Because these properties are assigned global identifiers and strict inheritance is required, multiple inheritance does not introduce ambiguity for properties that are inherited from more than one superclass.

Object class inheritance can be used to exploit similarities between managed resources. Implementations may take advantage of inheritance relationships with code reuse and by promoting consistency in application design and end-user interfaces.

Polymorphism

OSI management includes provisions for a restricted form of polymorphism, called *allomorphism*, which permits an object instance of one class to be managed as though it were an instance of another class. Usually, allomorphic classes of an object are also superclasses of that object; however, this is not a requirement. Allomorphic relationships are modeled in OSI managed objects and may be negotiated and exchanged with CMIP[2]. The primary benefit of allomorphism is to aid migration and co-existence for managers and agents of different versions and capabilities.

8.3.1.3   Summary of SNMP and CMIP information structuring methodologies

Table 8.1 summarizes the features of SNMP and CMIP.

Table 8.1 CMIP and SNMP object-oriented features.

Feature	SNMP	CMIP
Encapsulation	single, atomic data only	attributes, actions, notifications
Classes	not reusable	reusable
Inheritance	none	multiple, strict
Polymorphism	GET, GET-NEXT, SET defined by SNMP	GET, SET, ACTION, EVENT and as specified by the object class

8.3.1.4   Reusability example

Reuse of specification and code is a key benefit offered by object-oriented design and implementation models. To illustrate how SNMP and CMIP differ in this respect, consider that we must model two similar, but different, kinds of resources: modems and LAN stations. Assume the following properties of modems and LANs:

i)   There exist standard definitions for both modems and LAN stations that share a status property. The status value may be either *enabled* or *disabled.*

ii)   The standard modem definition has a *speed* property with one or more of these values: 300, 600, 1200, 2400, 4800, 9600, 14400.

iii)   IBM modems have all the standard modem properties, and also a nonstandard ability to initiate and report link problem determination aid (LPDA) tests.

---

[2]   The object class *Top* has a conditional package with the *allomorphs* attribute which, when instantiated, indicates the allomorphic classes for the object instance.

With the above assumptions, we would like to achieve these reuse objectives:

i)   A manager should understand *status* information even if it does not know every other property of either resource type.

ii) A manager that understands IBM modems can reuse code for standard modems. That is, once a manager has support for standard modems, adding support for IBM modems should only require new logic for the features unique to IBM modems.

iii) A manager that understands only that the IBM modem is like a standard modem can manage it like a standard modem. This is useful for a customer who has installed a manager product that understands standard modems, but not IBM modems. Rather than requiring the customer to upgrade the manager product, we should allow the customer to configure the manager product to understand that IBM modems are like standard modems. The manager product will not be able to initiate LPDA tests, but it will be able to monitor the *status* and *speed* properties.

iv) An agent that knows the manager only supports standard modems may behave as if it has only standard modems when it in fact also has IBM modems. This case allows agents to interoperate with managers that only understand standard modems that do not have the ability to be configured to treat IBM modems like standard modems.

With these objectives in mind, SNMP and CMIP solutions are shown below.

SNMP reuse solution

A possible MIB structure for representing standard modems, IBM modems, and LAN stations is shown in Figure 8.1. It shows the standard modem and LAN station variables that are contained in a standard MIB *mib-x*. Since we may have multiple modems in a system, we model modems as a table (*modemTable*) with each modem as a row (*modemEntry*) and the status and speed as columns. The LAN stations are modeled as rows (*lanEntry*) in a table (*lanTable*) with columns for the status. Because IBM modems are not standard, their variables must be modeled in a private MIB. We have chosen to model the IBM modems in a structure like that for standard modems, but with an additional column to represent the *lpdaTest* property.

Although the modems and LAN stations are modeled as tables, only the individual table entries (the leaves in the tree) are settable or gettable. SNMP does not provide operations for aggregations of data. Also, the *speed* property must be single-valued in SNMP even though the modems may be able to support more than one speed. If we wish to represent *speed* as a multivalued attribute, we would have to design another table for it and somehow relate the modem and speed table rows.

The first reuse objective is not met because the *status* property is modeled as three different variables: standard modem status, standard LAN station status, and IBM modem status. All three have different type identifiers, and there is no formal technique to relate all of them. An alternative design would be to not duplicate the status variable in the IBM modem part of the MIB. This alternative suffers from the requirement for managers and agents to relate one entry in the standard *modemTable* with a corresponding entry in the IBM *modemTable*. There is no standard or guideline for representing such a relationship.

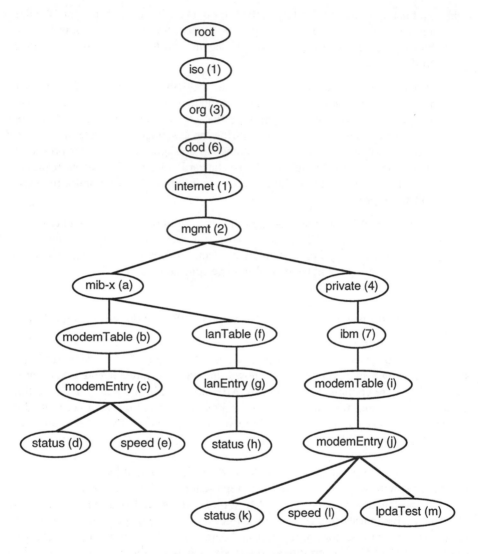

Figure 8.1 SNMP MIB example.

The second reuse objective is not met because the IBM modem variables are duplicated from the standard modem and must have different names. A manager application must learn about these new variables as all being unique to IBM modems.

The third reuse objective is not met because there is no way for a manager to know that the IBM modem is an extension of a standard modem.

The fourth objective may be met if the agent implementation can map one set of MIB variables onto another. However, SNMP provides no mechanism for a manager to request or understand such a mapping.

CMIP reuse solution

An OSI management solution uses object classes to represent the three kinds of resources: *modem*, *ibmModem*, and *lanStation*, as shown in Figure 8.2.

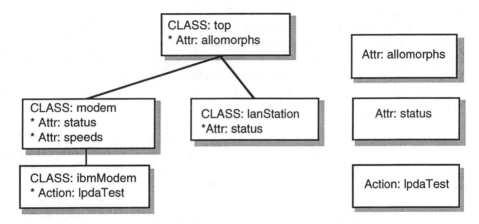

Figure 8.2 OSI classes for reuse example.

Each of these object classes has a unique identifier. The attributes, actions, and notifications also have unique identifiers which are independent of the classes that use them. This example shows single inheritance; a more elaborate example would demonstrate multiple inheritance. The object class *top* is standard and includes an attribute, *allomorphs,* which every other object inherits. The allomorphs attribute identifies the object classes to which an instance of an object is allomorphic. Using CMIP, a manager can retrieve these values for any object to aid it in identifying mutually compatible classes with its agents.

The object class *modem* derives from *top* and inherits the allomorphs attribute. It includes the additional attributes *status* and *speeds*. We model speeds as a multivalued attribute to enable modems to indicate more than one supported speed. The object class *ibmModem* derives from *modem* and inherits the *allomorphs*, *status* and *speeds* attributes. It also adds an action, *lpdaTest*, to enable a manager to initiate an LPDA test.   The object class *lanStation* derives from top and inherits the *allomorphs*. It adds the *status* attribute.

This model achieves the reuse objectives as follows. The first objective is achieved because the *status* attribute is defined once and given a globally unique identifier. In all the classes where it is used directly or inherited, it retains the same definition and identity. The CMIP protocol includes its id in operations that refer to it. If a manager receives an attribute change notification referring to this attribute, it will understand that this is a status change even if it knows nothing else about the class which emitted the notification. Using CMIP, the manager can obtain other information to understand the class.

The second objective is achieved because *ibmModem* is a subclass of *modem*. A manager that implements support for a standard modem should reuse this code for supporting IBM modems because the inheritance relationship is formally and explicitly represented in the model.

The third objective is achieved because the manager may learn or be told that *ibmModem* is a subclass of *modem*. With only that knowledge, it can manage IBM modems like standard modems. Agent systems require no changes to support this mode of operation.

The fourth objective is achieved because the agent may support allomorphism and thereby behave as if its IBM modems were actually just standard modems. A manager may query an object to learn its allomorphic classes, and CMIP allows each operation on an object instance to indicate which allomorphic class to use.

8.3.2   Object naming

Object instance names identify the targets and sources of management operations and notifications. CMIP and SNMP differ markedly in the way they name object instances. The naming techniques are described below, but the most important differences are scope of uniqueness and flexibility.

The scope of name uniqueness is important because it determines where names may be used without the possibility of misinterpretation owing to ambiguity. A name is ambiguous if it refers to more than one object instance in a context where the name is used. Note that this does not preclude the possibility of an object possessing more than one name. In management, a manager and agent both must understand and agree on the naming context where ambiguity is not allowed. For enterprise management, global naming is a requirement since the resources to be managed generally cannot be restricted to a predetermined set of contexts. For example, it is unreasonable for an enterprise manager to understand only SNA names and require that all managed resources in the enterprise be assigned SNA names. It is even more unreasonable to require that other enterprises assign SNA names to the resources about which they communicate to the enterprise manager.

8.3.2.1   SNMP variable naming

The structure of SNMP variable names is defined in the SMI standard for TCP/IP. SNMP variable names are hierarchical, untyped, and based on the ASN.1 (ISO/IEC 8824, 1990) object identifier. Each variable name uses the ASN.1 object identifier syntax of the form $\{x\ y\}$, where x and y are sequences of ASN.1 object identifier components. The first part x (the prefix) is assigned and fixed at the time the variable type is defined. The second part y (the suffix) is assigned and fixed when the variable is instantiated in the MIB.

SNMP variable names are only unique within a system; the same variable name is reused to instantiate variables in different systems. To provide for global naming, variable names must be qualified with globally unique system names. However, SNMP makes no provision for carrying this additional information. One limitation this imposes is that one SNMP manager has no defined way to direct a request to another SNMP manager to perform an operation on a MIB variable in an agent.

The structure of the name for an SNMP variable is fixed when the variable is architected. The only means for a customer to change this structure is to define a new variable type, with a unique name. Because the class of the variable is incorporated into its name and SNMP does not carry the class information separately, a customer who does this must also change the managing applications to recognize the new variable class.

The X.500 directory standards (CCITT, 1988) do not permit directory objects to be named with ASN.1 object identifiers. Therefore, the management system is prevented from accessing a standard directory with SNMP variable names to obtain information about a variable.

8.3.2.2 CMIP object naming

The OSI management information model defines the naming mechanism for managed object instances based on the X.500 distinguished name. The names are hierarchical, typed, and global. Because they are compatible with the X.500 Directory, management applications may, but are not required to, use a standard directory service to obtain other useful information about resources. The hierarchical nature of OSI managed object names is defined by a naming tree where each node represents an object instance. The name of each instance is relative to its superior's name. The global name for an instance is formed by concatenating the relative names of each of the object instances in the path from Root to the instance.

OSI management uses typed names because the relative distinguished name for an object instance is formed by the combination of one of its attribute types and the associated attribute value. Typed names permit greater flexibility than untyped names for vendors and customers. Because attribute types have global identifiers, vendors can define naming structures for their managed object classes without worrying about ambiguous names for object instances. At the same time, customers are provided flexibility in being allowed to assign attribute values for each instance.

Because object names are typed, hierarchical and allow different ASN.1 syntaxes, they require more octets than SNMP for their encodings.

Table 8.2 summarizes the important differences between SNMP and CMIP naming.

Table 8.2 CMIP and SNMP naming differences.

SNMP	CMIP
Unique only within a single system	Globally unique
Based on class name at specification time	Independent of class name, set at instantiation
Untyped	Typed
Incompatible with X.500	Compatible with X.500
Compact encoding	Lengthy encoding

8.3.3   Data representation

Distributed management requires exchanging data between managers and agents to perform operations on and to convey information about managed resources. Both CMIP and SNMP use a standard notation, Abstract Syntax Notation One, for specifying management data, and a related standard, Basic Encoding Rules, for encoding the data for transmission.

CMIP places no restrictions on which ASN.1 data types may be used to represent the syntax of object attributes, notifications, and actions. The designer of an object class may choose any of the 26 appropriate data types; an implementation must accommodate only the data types needed for the object classes it supports.

However, SNMP purposefully limits the ASN.1 data types that a MIB designer may use to four: *INTEGER, OCTET STRING, NULL*, and *OBJECT IDENTIFIER*. On the positive side, an SNMP agent need only provide the allowed subset of ASN.1 data types. On the negative side, overloading these data types with semantics for more complicated data implies the manager and agent must agree on the encoding; they cannot take advantage of the self-describing data characteristics provided by ASN.1 and BER. This trade-off between simplicity and flexibility is mostly subjective. However, SNMP does not provide for some common requirements.

Some ASN.1 data types are particularly useful in addressing international and inter-enterprise management requirements:

- Character strings

- Time

- *SEQUENCE*

- *SEQUENCE OF*

- *SET*

- *SET OF*

ASN.1 provides for a variety of character sets, ranging from a minimal set, *PrintableString*, to most general set, *GeneralString*. In SNMP, character strings would be encoded as *OCTET STRING*. Since OCTET STRING carries no explicit identification of the character set it conveys, the manager and agent must understand it a priori on a variable by variable basis. Similarly, ASN.1 defines two representations for time, *GeneralizedTime* and *UTCTime*. SNMP does not have a standard method of encoding time values. ASN.1 provides data types to structure data. The *SEQUENCE* data type is used to aggregate data that are fixed in number and perhaps of different types. *SEQUENCE OF* is a variation that allows a variable number of elements, each element being of the same type. The *SET* and *SET OF* data types are like their counterparts *SEQUENCE* and *SEQUENCE OF*, except the ordering of the elements is unimportant.

SNMP allows data to be aggregated in the form of tables. In fact, every table is defined as a *SEQUENCE OF Entry*, and *Entry* is defined as a *SEQUENCE*. However, the SNMP protocol does not allow tables or table entries to be transferred as single units. Instead, the manager application must operate on each column or entry separately. Although this limitation simplifies the agent's task of collecting and packaging data, it complicates the manager's logic because the manager must combine multiple, related variables in different operations. In practice, this also prevents the manager and agent from synchronizing the data and ensuring their consistency.

8.3.4   Relationship representation

Many relationships between managed resources are useful to the management process. It follows that the models that represent managed resources should also be able to represent relationships between resources, and management operations should be able to query and modify relationships. This important requirement is evidenced by the role that database management systems play for integrated management applications. Typically, relationships are modeled at the conceptual level with entity-attribute and entity-attribute-relationship paradigms, and implemented at the logical level with relational, hierarchical, and network database systems. CMIP and SNMP provide enough raw material to model relationships, though the means and details differ considerably.

Since OSI management provides objects with attributes as a basic modeling tool, these are used to model relationships. The participants in a relationship are object instances. Two basic techniques are used to model relationships, and the choice of which technique is most appropriate depends on whether the relationship has attributes of its own.

If a relationship has no attributes, it may be modeled as attributes in the participant object classes. These attributes have values that identify the other participants, that is, they contain object instance names. If the cardinality of the relationship is greater than one, the attribute is set-valued. Because object instances have global names, this technique allows relationships that span systems. Also, since attributes have their own global identifiers which are independent of the object classes where they are used, relationships can be reused in different object classes and their names do not change. Managing applications may take advantage of this feature to provide generic functions. For example, a managing application that only understands attributes for topology relationships need not understand any other object class details to build a map. This technique and a number of useful relationships have been standardized.

If a relationship has attributes, it may be modeled as an object class that has attributes to identify the participants in the relationship and other attributes to model the attributes of relationship. The relationship has a global name since the object representing the relationship has a global name.

Work is underway in OSI management to provide formal specification tools to model concepts familiar in the database world today, for example, cardinality.

The table is the basic SNMP structuring tool. Variable names, and therefore table entry names, are ASN.1 *OBJECT IDENTIFIERs*. One of the allowed syntaxes for a variable is also *OBJECT IDENTIFIER*, permitting table entries to point to other tables and table entries. This allows the relationships to be modeled as variables and tables, very much as CMIP allows them to be modeled as attributes and objects, but with two differences. First, variables have only local names, restricting the participants of a relationship to a single MIB instance. Second, the name of a relationship depends on the name of the table in which it is defined, restricting the possibility of defining generic relationships. This last limitation partly explains why SNMP has no standard for defining relationships.

8.4   Management functions

A crucial aspect of developing integrated management applications is the creation of functions common to managing a wide range of resource types. CMIP and SNMP differ considerably in the extent to which they enable and provide common management functions.

The only functions that SNMP defines as common to different resource types are the primitive management operations *GET, GET-NEXT, SET*, and *TRAP*. In addition to the primitive management operations defined by CMIP, *GET, SET, ACTION/NOTIFICATION, ADD, REMOVE*, and *CANCEL-GET*, a number of common functions have been defined and more are in development. These common functions build on CMIS and define attributes, actions and notifications that can be incorporated into resource-specific object class definitions.

The common functions, called system management functions, are defined as separate parts to ISO/IEC 10164. Currently, the following system management functions have been completed or are in the process of being standardized:

- Object management

- State management

- Attributes for representing relationships

- Alarm reporting

- Event reporting

- Logging

- Security alarm reporting

- Security audit trail

- Objects and attributes for access control

- Accounting meter function

- Workload monitoring

- Test management

- Measurement summarization

8.5   Underlying communications

CMIP and SNMP make minimal demands on underlying communications services. One key difference between the two is that CMIP requires a connection-oriented service and SNMP requires a connectionless service. Another key difference is that SNMP assumes a polling paradigm, whereas CMIP assumes an event-driven paradigm. The implications of these differences are discussed below.

8.5.1   SNMP communications

The SNMP protocol operates over a connectionless service provided by the user datagram protocol (UDP) and the internet protocol (IP).

The size of a UDP packet is limited by the operational characteristics of the underlying internet routing network. The IP standard requires implementations to be able to relay, under normal conditions, packets of 484 octets or larger. Therefore, a sending system may assume, under normal conditions, packets of 484 or fewer octets will be received by the destination system. As a connectionless service, IP and, by extension, UDP provide no indication to either the sender or receiver of packets lost or discarded by the network. Packets may be lost or discarded for a variety of reasons, including:

- Receiver unavailable

- Packet too large to be relayed by an intermediate system

- Network congestion

- Loss of connectivity.

Because traps are unconfirmed events and are sent as datagrams, an agent has no indication that the manager is unavailable and that it should switch to sending its traps to another manager.

The connectionless model provides no way to control the flow of data between a manager and agent. Managers that are unable to process large volumes of incoming traps have no recourse but to discard them. SNMP partially solves this problem by using traps judiciously to let a manager know that some event has occurred. It is then up to the manager to request more information about the event with subsequent *GET* and *GET-NEXT* operations. The connectionless model does not provide an opportunity for a manager and agent to exchange and negotiate information such as capabilities, security parameters, and other operational parameters.

Event-based management is not feasible because the SNMP model relies on polling. Applications that require periodic samples, such as those for performance management, must periodically poll each agent to collect the samples.

SNMP makes so few demands on underlying services that it easily adapts to operate over other protocols, including connection-oriented protocols.

8.5.2   CMIP communications

The CMIP protocol is defined to operate over the connection-oriented OSI presentation service, and it refers to two other protocols: association control service element (ACSE) and remote operations (ROSE). The OSI presentation layer service provides data representation services, including encoding and decoding ASN.1 and BER. The presentation service relies on connection-oriented OSI session services.

Although the OSI session layer is functionally very rich, CMIP, ROSE and ACSE use only a few functions: segmentation/reassembly and connection establishment/termination procedures. They have no defined maximum data unit size; the session, transport and network layers provide segmentation/reassembly for large data units. CMIP is also readily adaptable to other communications services. CMIP has only one procedure, the multiple reply functional unit, that requires connection-oriented services. CMIP has been adapted to operate over layer two logical link control for Heterogeneous LAN Management and over SNA sessions.

ACSE is used by the manager and agent applications during the connection establishment phase to exchange and negotiate mutually agreeable parameters, including application contexts and functional units. It is also used during the connection termination phase to release the allocated resources in both manager and agent systems. ROSE is a simple protocol machine which is used to structure requests and responses for the CMIP protocol.

Table 8.3 summarizes the differences in the underlying communications.

Table 8.3 Summary of underlying communications.

Feature	SNMP	CMIP
Signaled data loss	no	yes
Signaled data corruption	yes	yes
Negotiation	none	allowed and extensible
Multiple application contexts	not allowed	allowed
Length limitations	484 octets	unlimited
Paradigm	connectionless	connection-oriented
Interaction model	polling	event driven
Adaptable to other stacks	yes	yes

8.6   Conclusion

CMIP and SNMP are quite different in their scope, complexity, and approaches to solving network management problems. SNMP was designed to be simple in order to make it ubiquitous in TCP/IP networks, and it has achieved that goal with outstanding success. However, the same characteristics that make it simple to implement also make it unsuitable for environments consisting of large, diverse, multi-enterprise networks. On the other hand, CMIP was designed to be more general and flexible, but at the expense of additional complexity and implementation cost. Whether CMIP will eventually achieve the same success as SNMP remains to be seen.

Abbreviations

ACSE   Association Control Service Element
ASN.1 Abstract Syntax Notation One
BER   Basic Encoding Rules
CMIP   Common Management Information Protocol
GDMO   Guidelines for the Definition of Managed Objects
IP   Internet Protocol
MIB   Management Information Base
ROSE   Remote Operation Service Element
SMF   Systems Management Function
SMI   Structure of Management Information
SNA   Systems Network Architecture
SNMP   Simple Network Management Protocol
TCP   Transmission Control Protocol
UDP   User Datagram Protocol

Acknowledgment

This is an extended version of a paper published in Integrated Network Management III, Proc. of IFIP WG6.6 Third International Symposium on Integrated Network Management, eds. Hegering H.G. and Yemini Y., North Holland, 1993.

References

Rose M. and McCloghrie K. (1990). Structure and identification of management information for TCP/IP-based internets. *Internet Working Group Request for Comments 1155,* Network Information Center, SRI International, Menlo Park, California, May 1990

ISO/IEC 9596. (1990). *Common management information protocol specification.*

ISO/IEC 10165-1 (1991). *Management Information Services – Structure of Management Information – Part 1: Management Information Model.*

ISO/IEC 10165-4. (1991). *Management Information Services – Structure of Management Information – Part 4: Guidelines for the Definition of Managed Objects.*

ISO/IEC 8824. (1990). *Specification of Abstract Syntax Notation One (ASN.1).*

CCITT Recommendation. (1988). The Directory – overview of concepts, models, and services. *BLUE Book, Vol. VIII.8 Rec. X.500,* ITU, Geneva

Chapter 9

The Telecommunications Management Network (TMN)

Roberta S. Cohen

AT&T Paradyne, Room IP-250,
200 Laurel Avenue,
Middletown, NJ 07748, USA
Email: rcohen@attmail.com

The Telecommunications Management Network defines standard architectures for the management of telecommunications services. CCITT, the international body that sets telecommunications standards, has developed TMN to achieve interconnection among the operations systems and telecommunications systems that must exchange management information to assure the smooth and continuous operation of the telecommunications services provided. This chapter describes these architectural standards and discusses the progress seen to date in implementations of TMN.

9.1   Introduction

In 1979, when I joined what was then Bell Telephone Laboratories, Incorporated, Issue 3 of the handbook *Bell System Information and Operations Systems* was published listing some 380 operations and information systems in use at that time supporting what was then the primary US telephone company. The handbook provided brief descriptions of systems performing functions as varied as the near real-time transmission of call data in support of billing and the curve generation systems used by outside plant engineering to develop feeder cable sizing curves. These 380 systems supported local as well as long-distance telephone operations and planning, supported what little distinct data communications was offered by the "phone company" at that time, and supported the business operations of one of the largest companies in the world. Today, AT&T has divested the local telephone operating businesses from its corporation, spinning off the seven regional Bell operating companies and Bellcore into entirely separate companies, each sizable in its own right. Yet, were we to prepare a catalog of systems similar to the 1979 handbook, we would list, just for what remains of the AT&T company, several hundred more systems than in 1979. Automation is a key aspect of telecommunications.

The systems in the handbook, and those in use today to operate the telecommunications networks of service providers, include:

- those supporting the business functions of a telephone company;

- those supporting the engineering and planning of the network and its subsystems;

- those supporting the real-time operations, monitoring and control, of the existing network and its subsystems.

This array of operations capabilities, coupled with the service offerings of telecommunications service providers, results in four levels of operations and management:

i)   the network element level;

ii) the network level;

iii) the service level; and

iv) the business level.

Each level can be considered with regard to the functions and capabilities of management and operations needed to conduct that aspect of the enterprise, with somewhat more sophisticated capabilities applied to each more complex level of telecommunications. All levels are generic with regard to technology and implementation, and it is believed that numerous capabilities (and probably, therefore, numerous systems) are needed to achieve full management at each and every level.

The systems that provide management and operations capabilities tend to be separate from the network itself, often communicating with the parts of the network (network elements) that they support through carefully constructed interfaces. In particular, the systems that support the ongoing monitoring and control of in-service networks, including functions such as fault monitoring, performance measurement, routing and configuration control, billing and access control, are the focus of activities within the international telecommunications standards community known as **Telecommunications Management Network** (TMN). Indeed, the management scope of TMN is broadly defined as the capabilities to exchange and process management information to assist network operators in conducting their business efficiently at all four levels of management.

The TMN efforts have arisen within the community of public telephony administrations, which are the telephone companies that provide public networks, often as monopolies, within a defined geographic area. This community concerns itself with telecommunications **services**, defined as telecommunications capabilities offered to a customer base external to the network provider, often under publicly agreed-upon tariffs. Networks that provide such telecommunications services contain large numbers of interdependent devices and applications, which continue to provide services at the levels expected by their users through continuous monitoring and control on the part of the service providers. The telecommunications networks of service providers worldwide are increasingly monitored and controlled by a large number of operations systems that provide administration, monitoring, maintenance, provisioning and other operations tasks, in support of telecommunications service providers offering the highest quality services.

The explosion in operations systems is, in part, the result of a trend toward multi-vendor networks. Few telecommunications service providers can offer up-to-date network technologies by utilizing only a single vendor of networking hardware, and fewer still rely on a single source for the wide variety of logical elements needed within the network, including networking applications, protocols, translations and other software. With network elements supplied by an ever-increasing set of different vendors, and with the number and variety of network technologies and network services on the increase as well, telecommunications service providers have been presented with a dramatically increasing diversity of management needs and solutions, and a proliferation of unique interfaces between physical and logical network elements and operations systems.

9.2   TMN objectives

TMN has been developed to manage heterogeneous networks, services and equipment. TMN is defined to operate across multiple vendors and multiple technologies with rich management functionality. It allows for inter working among the multiple management and operations systems supporting the multi-vendor network, and it allows for management inter working among separately managed networks, known as network domains, so that inter-networked and cross-domain services can be managed on an end-to-end basis. Without an effective TMN, providing services that span multiple networks is a difficult, and often unreliable business.

The concept of the Telecommunications Management Network has been developed within CCITT, the International Telegraph and Telephone Consultative Committee. This organization, historically a community of common carriers and telephone administrations, although now a much broader consortium of telephone service providers and vendors, has sought to provide a common framework under which telecommunications management can be conducted, worldwide. Basically, TMN provides

'an organized architecture to achieve interconnection between various type of Operations Systems and/or telecommunications equipment for the exchange of management information using an agreed architecture with standardized interfaces including protocols and messages.'[1]

---

[1]   From section 1 of CCIT Recommendation M.3010.

The TMN can be thought of as an overlay network with regard to the telecommunications service provider's network. This is shown graphically in Figure 9.1 where the TMN is seen to represent the communications among operations systems and to represent communications between operations systems and the telecommunications network. This overlay is, at times, logical with regard to the actual communications systems, as will be seen in subsequent discussion.

Moreover, while the TMN shown in Figure 9.1 and discussed above has been that of the telecommunications service provider, the TMN can be extended in special cases to manage customer premises equipment such as matrix or private branch exchange switches, multiplexors, modems and even telephone sets. The extent of the TMN, whether solely within the service provider's realm or extending onto the customer's premises, is determined by the boundary of the management domain, and the assignment of the domain is not a technical decision but one steeped in the vagaries of historical practice. Regardless of the management domain to which it applies, a TMN provides the management capabilities for a telecommunications network and the services that are provided on that network. It also defines the communications between itself and the telecommunications network and services.

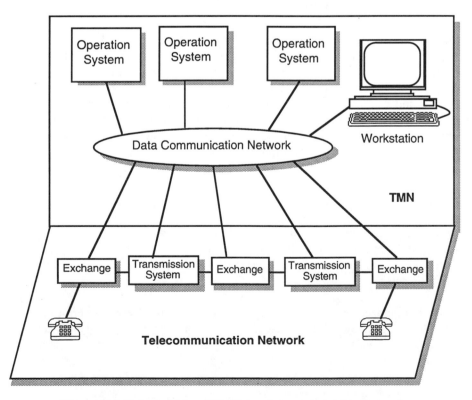

Figure 9.1 Relationship of TMN to telecommunication network.

9.3   TMN activities

The activities to create and define what we know as TMN have involved and continue to involve a significant number of different Study Groups within CCITT. Table 9.1 lists the CCITT Study Groups that have projects during the next plenary (four-year) period that are either a part of the TMN effort or directly relate to it.

Table 9.1 CCITT Study Group responsibilities for TMN.

Study Group	Study Topic
SG II	Traffic management
SG IV	TMN architecture definition
	Generic network model
	F-interface
SG VII	OSI base management standards
	Data network management and MHS
	Customer network management
SG X	User-interfaces
	Specification languages
SG XI	Q3-interface protocols
	Switching and signaling system management
	ISDN management
	Intelligent network management
	UPT management
SG XV	Transmission system management
	Transmission system modeling
	SDH, PDH, ATM management
SG XVIII	Broadband management requirements
JRM (JCG)	Overall coordination of TMN

To date, Study Group IV has been the key provider of TMN specifications, having had responsibility for all of the TMN architectural specifications. They have relied on Study Group VII, through its joint activities with ISO, the International Organization for Standardization, to provide the essential OSI Systems Management framework and specifications, but Study Group IV has provided us with the TMN principles, methodology, generic information model and general listing of services and functions for TMN. Their series of Recommendations, the CCITT term for standards, known as the M. series (pronounced M dot series), is shown in Figure 9.2 along with key contributions from several other Study Groups.

In Figure 9.2, each rectangle represents a document; the shaded rectangles represent documents that are in progress and not completed at this time. In addition to a number of M. series documents providing basic definition for TMN, several key documents produced in the Q. series and G. series are shown. The Q. series of documents comes from CCITT Study Group XI and covers switching and signaling systems and their management. The G. series of documents convey recommendations associated with transmission systems and in particular the system called Synchronous Digital Hierarchy (also known as Synchronous Optical Network or SONET) and originate in CCITT Study Group XV.

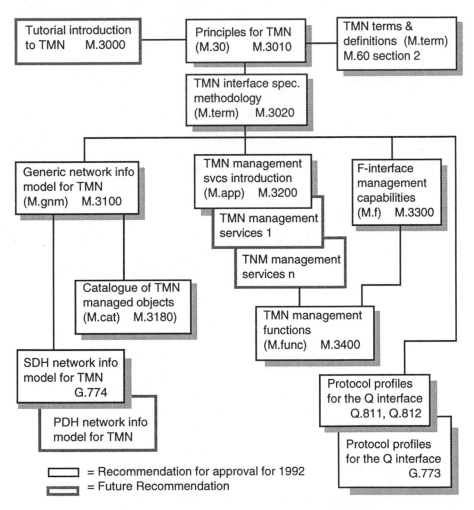

Figure 9.2 TMN document relations.

Not shown in Figure 9.2 are the X. series documents relating to OSI management. These documents, jointly produced by CCITT Study Group VII and ISO's Joint Technical Committee 1, Study Committee 21 (JTC1/SC21), provide the underlying systems management foundation for Open Systems Interconnection as well as the standards for common and specific management functions. These documents are specifically known as the X.700 series of documents.

At the bottom of Table 9.1, we show a group called the Joint Rapporteurs Meeting (Joint Coordination Group), shown in the table as JRM (JCG). This group has recently formed to coordinate all of the TMN activities spread throughout CCITT. Originally called the Joint Rapporteurs Meeting (JRM), the group formed by having the convenors of the various study efforts meet together to discuss work activities and progress. In the fall of 1992, this group agreed to formally organize within CCITT as a Joint Coordination Group (JCG) and work to disseminate and coordinate the interdependent TMN-related work plans of the CCITT study groups.

9.4   TMN applications

A key aspect of TMN is the acknowledgment of the need for reliable and secure transport of management information across three types of boundaries: jurisdictional boundaries of telecommunication service providers, the boundaries between the service providers and their customers and the boundaries that separate any one system from another. The transfer of management information at these boundaries must involve, in two of the three cases, capabilities for granting controlled access to management information for other service providers, administrations and customers. To achieve this, the TMN recognizes two types of management applications:

- interactive;

- file-oriented.

The interactive category is supported by the transaction-like processing of ISO's Open Systems Interconnection (OSI) Systems Management services using Common Management Information Service Element (CMISE), running over ROSE, the Remote Operations Service Element. These TMN application services use the object-oriented approach of OSI to represent the TMN resources, described more fully below in the section on the TMN management information model.

The file-oriented category of applications use ISO's OSI FTAM (File Transfer, Access and Management). For both the interactive and file-oriented services, ISO has defined detailed implementation directives called A-profiles[2] that may be used for TMN applications: the Application profile for Object Management AOM-11 (ISP 11183-1,3) or AOM-12 (ISP 11183-1,2) are available for interactive applications and the Application profile for File Transfer AFT-11 (ISP 10607-1,3) is available for file-oriented applications.

Both types of applications require the Association Control Services Element (ACSE) to establish, release and abort associations. In addition, each application type requires its own application context, which, in the case of the interactive applications, is identified as

{ccitt recommendation m(13) gnm(3100) protocolsupport (1)
applicationContext (0) tmnApplicationContextOne (1)}.

---

[2]   A-profiles are explained in ISO TR 10000, Framework and Taxonomy of International Standardized Profiles.

File-oriented applications can make use of generic application contexts since the context of the data is specified as one of several defined FTAM abstract-syntax-definitions.[3]

The Common Management Information Services have been defined in OSI Systems Management for remote access to systems management services when near real-time, transaction-like processing is appropriate. However, within Study Group VII, discussions on Customer Network Management have resulted in requirements for a store-and-forward service that could be used to forward reports and status information from telecommunications service providers to end customer control systems. Requirements of this sort can be addressed by the Message Handling System (MHS) described in the CCITT X.400 standard. There are three management requirements for store-and-forward service:

- In many end-customer management applications, the majority of management information is not thought to be time critical. Having a store-and-forward alternative to CMIS allows the non-time critical management information to flow in a background activity while synchronous application connections are available for the time critical management flow.

- Some management information must flow between infrequently connected systems. The cost of setting up additional application contexts for the transfer of management information may be, at times, out of proportion to the value of the management traffic. If an MHS connection is already available in such cases, it may be appropriate to use it for management traffic, as well.

- MHS can provide a secure message path through intermediate third parties. When two systems that need to exchange management information are not directly inter-networked, MHS can be used as a third-party relay.

At present, Customer Network Management deliberations in CCITT have not resulted in a formal Recommendation. But the case for providing a third transfer mechanism, that of a store-and-forward service, to the interactive and file transfer services already prescribed in the standards is a compelling one. Work in the coming study period is needed to understand how information transfers in this way should be represented and whether restrictions need to be applied to the permitted functionality on such links.

Regardless of the protocol used, the basic TMN concept provides an architecture for achieving interconnection between various types of operations systems and/or telecommunications equipment for the exchange of management information. There are three distinct architectures defined within the general TMN architecture:

- Functional architecture describes the appropriate distribution of functionality within the TMN. Function blocks and reference points between function blocks defined here lead to the requirements for the TMN recommended interface specifications.

---

3   See CCITT Recommendation X.208 for a description of the FTAM abstract syntax names.

- Physical architecture describes realizable interfaces and examples of physical components that make up the TMN.

- Information architecture rationalizes the application of OSI systems management principles to the TMN by providing an object-oriented view of management and managed resources.

We will discuss each in turn.

9.5   TMN functional architecture

For the TMN to effectively interlink operations systems, it must provide the following functionality, as described in Recommendation M.3010, principles of the TMN:

- the ability to exchange management information between the telecommunications network environment and the TMN environment;

- the ability to convert management information from one format to another so that information flowing within the TMN environment has a consistent format;

- the ability to transfer management information between locations within the TMN environment;

- the ability to manipulate management information into a form which is useful or meaningful to the management information user;

- the ability to deliver management information to the management information user and to present it with the appropriate representation;

- the ability to ensure secure access to management information by authorized management information users.

To realize these objectives, the TMN functional architecture is comprised of six components called function blocks. Function blocks provide the general capabilities of Operations, Administration, Maintenance and Provisioning (OAM&P) within the TMN. Included are the following function blocks:

- *Operations System Function (OSF)* – The operations system function block processes information related to telecommunications management to support and/or control the instantiation of various telecommunication management functions.

- *Mediation Function (MF)* – The mediation function block acts on the contents of information passing between network elements and operations systems, performing such functions as converting object representations and/or providing upper layer protocol interworking functions. Mediation function blocks may store, adapt, filter, determine thresholds and condense information, and they may also include decision-making capabilities. Within the physical architecture, mediation functions can be shared among network elements and/or mediation devices.

- *Data Communications Function (DCF)* – The data communications function block provides the means for data communication to transport information related to telecommunication management between function blocks.

- *Network Element Function (NEF)* – The network element function block represents the manageability of the network element to the TMN by supporting communications with a TMN over one or more standard interfaces for the purpose of being monitored or controlled or both.

- *Work Station Function (WSF)* – The work station function block provides the means of communication between TMN function blocks and the user.

- *Q Adapter Functions (QAF)* – The Q adapter function block acts on the content of information passing between TMN function blocks and non-TMN equivalents of OSF and NEF function blocks to perform mediation functions.

Relative to the TMN as a bounded functional environment, the latter three function blocks represent edge functions found at the boundaries of the logical management network. The TMN functional architecture describes and assigns management functions to architectural blocks and specifies the relationships between pairs of function blocks. TMNs of various complexity can be implemented using these function blocks. By specifying the function block pairs that may exchange

Table 9.2 Simplified relationship of function blocks to functional components.

Function Block	Functional Components
Operations system function	Management information base, OSF-management application function (agent or manager), Human machine adaptation
Work station function	Presentation function
Network element function	Management information base, NEF-management application function (agent)
Mediation function	Management information base, MF-management application function (agent or manager), Information conversion function, Human machine adaptation
Q-adapter function	Management information base, QAF-management application function (agent or manager), Information conversion function

information, the TMN identifies architectural reference points with associated requirements for the interfaces at each reference point. The physical architecture (see the section below) describes these interfaces and provides examples of the physical components that make up the TMN.

The function blocks are themselves made up of functional components. Table 9.2 shows the relationship of function blocks to functional components in so far as the allowable combinations permit. The key functional components are as follows:

Management Application Functions actually implement TMN management services. The management services found within the TMN are listed in M.3200, *TMN Management Services: Overview*, and their supporting functions are found in M.3400, *TMN Management Functions*. Management services are described within the Management Applications Template shown here as Table 9.3. Over time, we expect CCITT to fill in the Management Applications Template completely, standardizing how each service is provided with regard to needed functions and supporting managed objects.

Table 9.3 Management applications services template.

Layer	Functional Areas					
	Fault	Configuration	Performance	Security	Accounting	Others
Business Mgmt						
Service Mgmt						
Network Mgmt						
Element Mgmt						

Services such as customer administration, service order management, alarm surveillance, fault localization, testing, routing administration, traffic measurement and analysis administration, tariff and charging administration, management of the security of the TMN, performance management, management of customer access, and others are included among those services supported within the TMN at the reference points surrounding the Operations System Function Block.

A function is the smallest part of a TMN service, as perceived by the service user. It usually consists of a sequence of actions on a defined managed object or objects. Functions can be generic or specialized to the telecommunications management tasks, and like services, they can be categorized (at least roughly) into functional areas. M.3400 discusses functions in detail, but some examples of TMN functions, drawn from M.3400, include:

- Generic functions for performance management control such as "set performance management attributes", "schedule Quality of Service test calls" and "schedule performance management data report";

- Traffic Administration (specific) functions for performance management control such as "establish/change/remove a measurement schedule", "establish/change/remove thresholds for status and data reporting" and "report routing table information on demand".

Management Application functions, whether generic or specific, are found within the Operations System function block, the Network Element function block, the Mediation function block and the Q-Adapter function block. While the mediation and Q-adapter blocks are not routinely associated with management applications, both function blocks are permitted to select and condense information on the basis of decision criteria that must be implemented in management applications.

Management Information Base (MIB) is the conceptual repository of management information. All of the managed objects within a managed system are represented in the MIB. It can be implemented in many different ways which are not subject to standardization under TMN, but the information architecture of TMN specifies the information models to which the MIB must correspond.

Information Conversion Function is used in intermediate systems to translate information from one model into another. This translation effectively converts object representations either syntactically or semantically. Most often, the information conversion function is associated with the Mediation or Q-Adapter Function Blocks, although in layered implementations of Operations System Function Blocks information conversion can occur in the subordinate layers of operations systems.

Presentation Function translates the information held in the TMN information model to a displayable format for human beings, and vice versa. The presentation function is relied upon to make user interfaces friendly for information entry, display and modification.

Human Machine Adaptation translates between the information held in the management application function and that presented to the Presentation Function by the TMN (and vice versa). While the presentation function is found at the Work Station Function block, the Human Machine Adaptation function is found at the Operations System Function block (or the Mediation Function block). In addition, this function supports authentication and authorization of the user.

Finally, there is a function that is associated with all of the function blocks that have a physical interface. This is the **Message Communication Function** (MCF) whose capability is limited to exchanging management information contained in information transmissions called messages with other Message Communication Functions. It is the MCF that comprises a protocol stack that can connect function blocks to Data Communication functions. Different protocol stacks may result in different types of MCF, and multiple Message Communication Functions may be implemented within the same system.

At the service boundaries of TMN function blocks are TMN **reference points**. A reference point is a conceptual point of information exchange between non-overlapping function blocks. Reference points identify the information that passes between function blocks and are classified as either:

q-class reference points found between function blocks within the TMN that can contain a management application function;

f-class reference points found where a Work Station Function Block "attaches" to the TMN; or

x-class reference points found between the Operations System Function Blocks of two TMNs or the Operations System Function Block of a TMN and the equivalent functionality of another network.

Reference points are a significant part of the TMN functional architecture because of the requirements they place on interface technologies. Each reference point represents a significant form of interface capability. In actual implementations of the TMN, reference points may fall within systems or equipment and are then realized as physical **interfaces**.

9.6   TMN physical architecture

The TMN Physical Architecture specifies the realization of TMN functions into network-related systems. A physical entity is defined corresponding to each of the six TMN function blocks:

- Operations System which optionally implements mediation functions, q-adaptation functions and work station functions in addition to the operations system functionality;

- Mediation Device which optionally implements q-adaptation functions, operations system functions and work station functions, in addition to the mediation functionality;

- Data Communications Network[4] implementing the data communications functionality;

- Work Station implementing the work station functionality;

---

[4]   The physical realization of the data communications network may be thought of as restricted to the media of the network. Within the TMN, however, the DCN within the physical architecture should be regarded as layers 1–3, physical, link and network layers.

- Network Element which optionally implements mediation functions, q-adaptation functions, operations system functions and work station functions in addition to the network element functionality;

- Q Adapter implementing the q-adaptation functionality.

These six entities can be configured into a variety of implementations to produce the TMN. Moreover, each TMN physical entity may contain the additional functionality that allows it to be managed, over and above the functionality that it brings to the TMN. In this sense, every TMN physical entity may be a Telecommunications Management Network Element (TMN Element).

Within the TMN architectural framework, the TMN physical entities are referred to as TMN building blocks to contrast them with TMN functional blocks representing functionality without physical implementation.

A key aspect of the physical architecture of the TMN is the information interfaces that form the common boundary between associated building blocks. Interfaces (designated with capital letters F, Q3, Qx, and X) are found at the TMN-defined reference points (designated with lower-case letters f, q3, qx, and x). A reference point is a conceptual point of information exchange between non-overlapping function blocks. When the connected function blocks are embodied in separate pieces of equipment, the reference point becomes an interface.[5]

A representation of the physical architecture of the TMN is shown in Figure 9.3, including the reference points at which different physical elements interface to one another. Three key reference points are shown as interfaces:

- the F interface between workstations and the TMN;

- the Q3 interface between TMN devices (devices within the TMN);

- the X interface linking the TMN devices of one TMN with those of another TMN via the data communications network (DCN).

The physical view of the TMN and the interfaces shown in Figure 9.3 is somewhat of a signature view of TMN, if there can be said to be one. Early implementations of TMN will, most likely, implement a Q3 interface between a Network Element and an Operations System or will implement a Q3 interface between two operations systems, over a Data Communications Network. The details of the Q3 interface are the best understood of any of the TMN defined interfaces, having been detailed in Study Group XI's Q.811, Q.812 and Q.821 recommendations and also defined in Study Group XV's G.773 recommendation.

---

[5]   The TMN architecture also includes G and M interfaces for g and m reference points. These reference points are used to exchange information between TMN and non-TMN functions, with g lying between the work station function and the human user and m lying between q-adaption functions and non-TMN functionality. Other than recognizing that they exist, this chapter does not deal with these reference points.

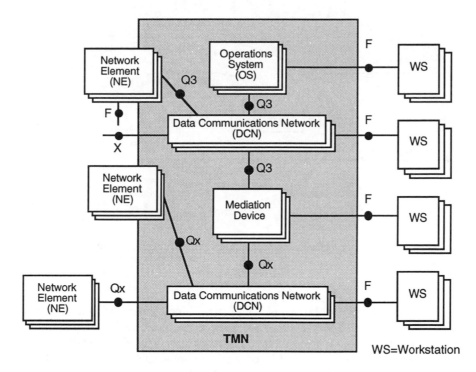

Figure 9.3 TMN architecture depiction.

Architecturally, multiple Q interfaces have been defined to provide flexibility for future implementations. In particular, the Qx interface (applied at the qx reference point) is reserved for the connection between network elements and mediation devices, while the Q3 interface (applied at the q3 reference point) is used to connect network elements to operations systems. For an interface to operate effectively, the entities connected over the interface must share a common view of the management tasks and managed resources. For this to occur, the third component of TMN architecture, that of Information, comes into play.

9.7   TMN management information model

The TMN interfaces that support transaction-oriented protocol utilize an object-oriented approach to information exchange. In this approach, worked out jointly between CCITT and ISO, resources are represented as classes of managed objects whose informational content is created, exchanged and modified across TMN interfaces. The rules of OSI Systems Management Information construction and representation are used to define object classes, capturing for each class the behavior, attributes, controls and notifications applicable to each class of managed resource. Figure 9.4 reproduces the concept of managed objects from ISO's OSI Systems Management Information Model (see Chapter 5).

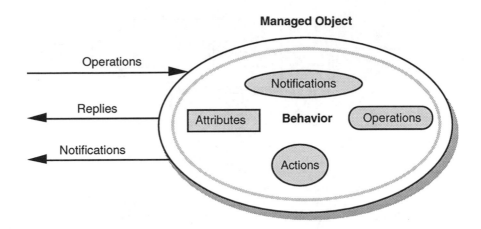

Figure 9.4 OSI systems management information model.

The object-oriented approach of the Systems Management Information model calls for interfaces to TMN entities to share a common understanding of the manageability of a resource or combination of resources. This shared understanding is an aspect of the information models used at the communications interfaces and need not constrain the internal implementation of the elements and systems providing telecommunications management. Indeed, the TMN information model explicitly notes that:

- there is not necessarily a one-to-one mapping between managed objects and resources;

- a resource may be represented by one or more managed objects. When multiple managed objects are used to represent the same resource, each object provides a different abstract view of the resource;

- managed objects may exist to represent logical resources of the TMN in addition to those of the telecommunications network. These objects are known as support objects;

- if a resource is not represented by a managed object, it is not visible to a managing system and it cannot be managed across the TMN interface;

- managed objects may be embedded within other managed objects.

The TMN Interface Specification Methodology (M.3020) defines procedures for understanding the management tasks in object-oriented terms and modeling resources into usable managed objects. M.3100 is an outgrowth of this activity, providing a set of managed objects that are generally applicable to all managed networks. This set is known as the TMN Generic Network Information Model.

9.8   Generic network information model

TMN defines management interoperability between services, networks, network elements and operation systems by offering uniform definitions of management functions and management information. Examples of the equipment, networks and services that may be managed by the TMN include public and private networks, integrated services networks, mobile networks, private voice networks, virtual private networks and intelligent networks, computers, front-end processors, cluster controllers, file servers, private branch exchanges, and software running in computers. TMN offers its management framework for the management of services as well as equipment. Indeed, the TMN may be used to manage the TMN.

At a generic level, TMN defines classes of managed objects that are intended to apply across different telecommunications technologies, services, and architectures. These managed objects are defined to serve as the superclasses of technology-specific managed objects. Taken together, they form a model of any telecommunication network. The following classes of resources are defined in the TMN Generic Network Information Model (M.3100).

i)   *Network Fragment*: Describes a network, or sub-network, as a manageable object. For example, a network is defined as a cluster of telecommunication entities which together provide communication services.

ii) *Managed Element Fragment*: Describes as element within the network, its equipment and its software as manageable objects.

iii) *Termination Point Fragment*: Describes communication accesses as manageable objects. For instance, a trail termination point sink object class is defined to represent the point where a trail is terminated. It represents the access point in a layer network.

iv) *Transmission Fragment:* Describes communication mechanisms between elements in the network as manageable objects. For instance, a trail represents a layer network which is responsible for the integrity of transfer of characteristic information between two trail termination points. A trail is composed of two or more trail termination points and one or more connections.

v)   *Cross-Connection Fragment*: Represents as manageable objects communication relationships existing within elements of the network. For example, a fabric is defined as the function of managing the establishment and release of cross-connection functions.

vi) *Functional Area Fragment*: Describes OSI Systems Management support mechanisms as manageable objects.

The Generic Network Information Model includes managed object and attribute definitions, object inheritance relationships, and name bindings to containment relationships for the generic managed objects. At present, the Generic Network Information Model is biased toward transmission technology, with the most detailed definitions descriptive of the capabilities of advanced, electronic transmission gear. But this model is expected to expand in the future, and other CCITT Study Groups are expected to use the GNIM as a guide for developing Network Information Models for their specific technologies and equipment.

For example, Recommendation G.774, developed in Study Group XV, defines managed objects specific to the Synchronous Digital Hierarchy (SDH) transmission technology. SDH, similar to what is known in North America as Synchronous Optical Network (SONET), takes the seven Termination Point Fragment object classes defined in the Generic Network Information Model and defines 81 subclasses of these objects to represent the manageable capabilities of specific end points used in SDH.

A catalog of TMN management information is provided in M.3180. This catalog lists managed object classes found in the Generic Management Information Model, as well as those defined by the various Study Groups in support of specific management efforts. In addition to listing the defined managed objects, the catalog provides a listing of the inheritance relationships of the managed objects so that one can readily see derivation relationships between object classes.

9.9   TMN management implementations

The TMN architecture, defined in CCITT Study Group IV, is only the framework for creating interoperable management. Implementations of TMN depend upon the efforts of technology-specific study groups to apply the principles of TMN in the management of their specific technology. The first protocol profiles for TMN have been produced in the Switching Systems area, CCITT Study Group XI, specifically for the Q3 interface. Q3 is the interface of the q3 reference point found between the Operations System Function block and any of the function blocks with which it exchanges information (the network element function blocks, the Q-adapter function blocks, the mediation function blocks and other operations systems function blocks). In the case of the specific profiles from Study Group XI, the interface between a central office switch, implementing a network element function, and an operations system is being specified.

An implementation specification of TMN must specify several things:

i)   the selection of protocols over which information exchange applications will be conducted;

ii) the selection of information exchange services and functions specifically addressing the needs of the implementation;

iii) the resources to be managed and the managed object definitions that represent those resources.

The first of these is referred to as protocol profiling which is thought to be a key part of functional standardization. In functional standardization, a generic standard is applied to a specific functional need. Since the specific functional need can be expressed in terms of reasonably precise requirements, optionality in the generic standard can be reduced or eliminated so that interoperability for the specific purpose can be more easily achieved. One could think of the second and third items above as other forms of profiling, but in the cases of selecting services and functions and selecting managed objects, the repertoire of standard specifications and definitions is meager. More often than not, the creation of an implementable selection in these areas requires extending the existing standards to embrace the specification of new capabilities and the definitions of new managed objects.

The work within CCITT Study Groups XI and XV has progressed in this way. Each has defined protocol profiles for their respective implementations. Study Group XI has issued Recommendations Q.811 and Q.812 and Study Group XV has issued G.773 to specify the protocol over which they will exchange information. Both sets of profiles are for the Q3 interface.

The alignment of the lower and upper layer profiles specified for these applications with the protocol profiling of ISO is very close. ISO profiles are produced as part of ISO's functional standards efforts, recognizing that protocol profiles will often be specific to the functionality conducted using the profile. Q.811 provides a high-level, lower layer Q3 profile for the switching system management applications. The sub-profiles included in Q.811 correspond to the International Standardized Profiles for connection-oriented and connectionless transport. In general, TMN requires that the lower layers be able to carry the upper layers of the protocol, noting that several network types are able to provide such suitable transport.

Q.812 provides a high-level, upper layer Q3 profile calling for the use of CMIS/CMIP and ROSE for management transactions. Optionality in the CMIP functional units is maintained in this profile, but it requires the use of transport-expedited service at the session layer if it is available. The upper layer ISP 11183-1 from ISO makes transport-expedited data usage out-of-scope. (An ISP-compliant initiator would not be tested for its use of transport-expedited data, even if it is available, but as a responder, it would be required to be able to negotiate away its proposed use when not available.)

For TMN Q3 and ISO-compliant systems to interoperate, any protocol profile differences must be mitigated. But more importantly, the functionality implemented through services and functions at the interface must be complementary and the managed objects used must be shared. CCITT service definitions and managed object definitions extend well beyond the ISO functional standards and ISO managed objects. For instance, Q.821 defines a Q3 interface for alarm surveillance that uses the ISO OSI Specific Management Functions for alarm reporting and event logging plus defines actions for audible and visual alarms, a reset audible alarm operation and a alarm summary report service.

Implementations that wish to comply with both ISO and CCITT capabilities must either implement considerable functionality that is specific to the TMN world or must constrain the implementation to basic capabilities on which others may build functionally specific applications. For some implementors, the choice between implementing ISO Systems Management and implementing TMN has been sufficiently daunting to stall implementation altogether.

But while implementors may be concerned with leveraging their developments into multiple markets, many telecommunications administrations, especially those whose experts have actively participated in the CCITT TMN definitional work, claim readiness to build and procure against TMN specifications. The *Telecommunication Journal of Australia* published a series of TMN-related articles in 1991 noting the Telecom Australia early experiences in TMN implementation. Similarly, a 1990 issue of the *CSELT Technical Reports* (Italy) focusing on network management and operations discusses CSELT's first TMN prototyping efforts. Other telecommunications administrations have been including TMN in their requests for proposals, and the equipment providers to the world's Telecoms have been among the most active proponents of additional functional specifications in TMN. Most are thought to have TMN Q3 interface implementations under way. There is little doubt that TMN is being widely embraced, if not deployed, within the public network communities of the world, such that it is only a matter of time before implementations catch up to the fervor.

Private networks, however, continue to rely on proprietary or *de facto* architectures and standards for their primary management philosophy and capabilities. The widespread deployment of Q3 interfaces within the TMN over the coming years may make such interfaces available to private network management systems which in turn may stimulate the use of OSI systems management in those environments.

9.10   Future TMN activities

Over the course of the next several years, CCITT study groups will work to expand the management services and functions of the TMN and to define an enlarged set of managed objects to which the services and functions apply. Alarm surveillance is really the only management function specific to TMN that is described in detail as a Recommendation at this time. There are 18 other functions listed in M.3200 that require specifications similar to that provided in Q.821 for alarm surveillance. Work is under way on traffic management and common channel signaling systems management.

Along with the efforts to extend the functionality of the TMN, work to define additional managed objects will progress in a number of CCITT Study Groups. This work presents a significant challenge to the generic management information model since the Study Groups needing specific managed object definitions should be able to use the generic model provided by the Generic Network Information Model as the basis from which their specific object classes are defined. Reusability of object fragments depends on common underlying modeling of resources and their overall relationships. The current model will come under great scrutiny in these efforts.

Putting aside the more routine extensions and expansions of TMN, there remain a number of difficult issues that TMN architects will need to address in the coming study periods if TMN is to be successful in the long run. These issues include:

- Synchronization of data maintained in different managed resources is a firm requirement for many TMN functions. For instance, modifications to routing control tables must occur simultaneously and with assurance that each table is modified. The mechanisms for achieving this is TMN are yet to be specified.

- Some areas of telecommunications management activity generate considerable amounts of data. For instance, traffic management is often implemented by collecting resource utilization counts every five minutes. TMN needs to be specific as to whether such voluminous data should be transferred between systems as an interactive application, using CMISE, as one or more files, using FTAM, or on a store-and-forward, send when ready, basis using MHS.

- The telecommunications networks that TMN is designed to manage are exceedingly large and complex. The operations infrastructures already in place for these networks is also large and complex in many parts of the world. As TMN systems appear, they will require mechanisms for :

  - ascertaining the management knowledge and scope they share at each interoperable interface;

  - authenticating and authorizing each information exchange association; and

  - locating and addressing each interoperating building block.

- These needs are not unique to the TMN environment. OSI Systems Management, in general, needs mechanisms for shared management knowledge, security of management and directory services. But the potential size and complexity of the TMN environment increases the need.

9.11   Closing comment

Furthering the objectives and deployment of TMN in the coming years will require considerable expenditures on the part of organizations working in the CCITT standards arena, building telecommunications networks and services and providing telecommunications services to customers. These expenditures will include engineering and development dollars, documentation and training dollars and marketing expenses associated with new management technologies, new management practices and new management offerings. The payback for this effort comes in the increased manageability of multi-vendor, multi-domain networks, ultimately at less cost, and in the long run with greater functionality. As with all new developments, the learning curve is steep and hard to climb. But TMN holds great promise to the telecommunications service provider, and many consider it an essential part of their future networks.

Abbreviations

CCITT   Consultative Committee for International Telegraph and Telephone
CMISE   Common Management Information Service Element
FTAM   File Transfer and Management
MHS   Message Handling Service

MIB   Management Information Base
ROSE   Remote Operations Service Element
TMN   Telecommunications Management Network

References

CCITT Recommendation G.773. (1990). *Protocol Suites for Q-Interfaces for Management of Transmission Systems*. Geneva

CCITT Recommendation G.774. *SDH Management Information Model for the Network Element View*. Geneva, to be published

CCITT Recommendation M.3010. *Principles for a Telecommunications Management Network (TMN)*. Geneva, to be published

CCITT Recommendation M.3020. *TMN Interface Specification Methodology*. Geneva, to be published

CCITT Recommendation M.3100. *Generic Network Information Model*. Geneva, to be published

CCITT Recommendation M.3180. *Catalogue of TMN Managed Objects*. Geneva, to be published

CCITT Recommendation M.3200. *TMN Management Services: Overview*. Geneva, to be published

CCITT Recommendation M.3300. *F-Interface Management Capabilities*. Geneva, to be published

CCITT Recommendation M.3400. *TMN Management Functions*. Geneva, to be published

CCITT Recommendation M.60. *Terms and Definitions*. Geneva, to be published

CCITT Recommendation Q.811. *Lower Layer Protocol Profiles for the Q3 Interface*. Geneva, to be published

CCITT Recommendation Q.812. *Upper Layer Protocol Profiles for the Q3 Interface*. Geneva, to be published

CCITT Recommendation Q.821. *Stage 2 and Stage 3 Description for the Q3 Interface*. Geneva, to be published

CCITT Recommendation X.208. (1988). *Specification of Abstract Syntax Notation One*. Geneva

CCITT Recommendation X.217 I ISO/IEC 8649: 1988 (E). *Information Processing Systems – Open Systems Interconnection – Service Definition for the Association Control Service Element*

CCITT Recommendation X.219 I ISO/IEC 9072-1: *Information Processing Systems – Text Communications – Remote Operations Part 1: Model, Notation and Service Definition*, 19 September 1989

CCITT Recommendation X.227 I ISO/IEC 8650: *Information Processing Systems – Open Systems Interconnection – Protocol Specification for the Association Control Service Element*

CCITT Recommendation X.229 I ISO/IEC 9072-2: *Information Processing Systems –- Text Communications – Remote Operations Part 2: Protocol Specification*, 19 September 1989

CCITT Recommendation X.700 (to be published). *Management Framework Definition for Open Systems Interconnection (OSI)*

CCITT Recommendation X.701 I ISO/IEC 10040: 1992. *Information Technology – Open Systems Interconnection – Systems Management Overview*

CCITT Recommendation X.710. (1991). *Common Management Information Service Definition for CCITT Applications*

CCITT Recommendation X.711 I ISO/IEC 9596-1: 1991 (E). *Information Technology – Open Systems Interconnection – Common Management Information Protocol Specification – Part 1: Specification*, Edition 2

CCITT Recommendation X.712 I ISO/IEC 9596-2: 1992 (E). *Information Technology – Open Systems Interconnection – Common Management Information Protocol – Part 2: Protocol Implementation Conformance Statement (PICs) Proforma*

CCITT Recommendation X.720 I ISO/IEC 10165-1: 1992. *Information Technology – Open Systems Interconnection – Structure of Management Information: Management Information Model*

CCITT Recommendation X.721 I ISO/IEC 10165-2: 1992. *Information Technology –- Open Systems Interconnection – Structure of Management Information: Definition of Management Information*

CCITT Recommendation X.722 I ISO/IEC 10165-4: 1992. *Information Technology – Open Systems Interconnection – Structure of Management Information: Guidelines for the Definition of Managed Objects*

CCITT Recommendation X.723 I ISO/IEC DIS 10165-6: 1992. *Information Technology –- Open Systems Interconnection - Structure of Management Information – Part 6: Requirements and Guidelines for Implementation Conformance Statement Proformas Associated with Management Information*

CCITT Recommendation X.724 I ISO/IEC DIS 10165-5: *Information Technology – Open Systems Interconnection –- Structure of Management Information – Part 5: Generic Managed Information*, ISO/IEC JTC1/SC21 N6572, February 20,1992

CCITT Recommendation X.730 I ISO/IEC 10164-1: *Information Technology – Open Systems Interconnection – Systems Management – Part 1: Object Management Function*, ISO/IEC JTC1/SC21 N6355, October 15,1991

CCITT Recommendation X.731 I ISO/IEC 10164-2: *Information Technology - Open Systems Interconnection - Systems Management - Part 2: State Management Function*, ISO/IEC JTC1/SC21 N6356, October 15,1991

CCITT Recommendation X.732 I ISO/IEC 10164-3: *Information Technology – Open Systems Interconnection – Systems Management – Part 3: Attributes for Representing Relationships*, ISO/IEC JTC1/SC21 N6357, October 15,1991

CCITT Recommendation X.733 (1992) I ISO/IEC 10164-4: 1992. *Information Technology – Open Systems Interconnection - Systems Management: Alarm Reporting Function*

CCITT Recommendation X.734 I ISO/IEC 10164-5: 1992. *Information Technology – Open Systems Interconnection – Systems Management: Event Report Management Function*

CCITT Recommendation X.735 I ISO/IEC 10164-6: 1992. *Information Technology – Open Systems Interconnection – Systems Management: Log Control Function*

CCITT Recommendation X.736 I ISO/IEC 10164-7: *Information Technology – Open Systems Interconnection – Systems Management – Part 7: Security Alarm Reporting Function*, ISO/IEC JTC1/SC21 N6367, October 15, 1991

CCITT Recommendation X.737 I ISO/IEC CD 10164-14: *Information Technology – Open Systems Interconnection – Systems Management – Part 14: Confidence and Diagnostic Test Categories*, ISO/IEC JTC1/SC21 N6769, March 10, 1992

CCITT Recommendation X.738 I ISO/IEC CD 10164-13: *Information Technology – Open Systems Interconnection – Systems Management – Part 13: Summarization Function*

CCITT Recommendation X.739 I ISO/IEC CD 10164-11: *Information Technology – Open Systems Interconnection – Systems Management – Part 11: Workload Monitoring Function*

CCITT Recommendation X.740 I ISO/IEC 10164-8: *Information Technology – Open Systems Interconnection – Systems Management – Part 8: Security Audit Trail Function*, ISO/IEC JTC1/SC21 N7039, June 2,1992

CCITT Recommendation X.741 I ISO/IEC CD 10164-9: *Information Technology – Open Systems Interconnection – Systems Management – Part 9: Objects and Attributes for Access Control*, ISO/IEC JTC1/SC21 N7227, June 5, 1992

CCITT Recommendation X.742 I ISO/IEC CD 10164-10: *Information Technology – Open Systems Interconnection – Systems Management – Part 10: Accounting Meter Function*

CCITT Recommendation X.745 I ISO/IEC CD 10164-12: *Information Technology – Open Systems Interconnection – Systems Management – Part 12: Test Management Function*, ISO/IEC JTC1/SC21

CCITT Recommendation X.746 I ISO/IEC NWI 10164-15: *Information Technology– Open Systems Interconnection – Systems Management – Part 15: Scheduling Function,* ISO/IEC JTC1/SC21

CCITT Recommendation X.400 I ISO/IEC 10021-1: *Message Handling System and Service Overview*, Geneva, 1989

CSELT Technical Reports Volume XVIII, August 1990. Issue on Management

ISO/IEC 7498-2: 1988 (E). *Information Processing Systems – Open Systems Interconnection – Basic Reference Model - Part 2: Security Architecture*

ISO/IEC 7498-3: 1992 (E). *Information Processing Systems – Open Systems Interconnection – Basic Reference Model - Part 3: Naming and Addressing*

ISO/IEC 7498-4: 1989. *Information Processing Systems – Open Systems Interconnection – Basic Reference Model - Part 4: Management Framework*

ISO/IEC 7498: 1984. *Information Processing Systems – Open Systems Interconnection – Basic Reference Model*

ISO/IEC 8649/AM1: 1988 (E). *Information Processing Systems – Open Systems Interconnection – ACSE Service Amendment 1: Authentication During Association Establishment*, ISO/IEC JTC1/SC21 N2326

ISO/IEC 8650/AM1: 1988 (E). *Information Processing Systems – Open Systems Interconnection – Protocol Specification for the Association Control Service Element – Amendment 1: Authentication During Association Establishment,* ISO/IEC JTC1/SC21 N2327

ISO/IEC 9595: 1991. *Information Technology – Open Systems Interconnection – Common Management Information Service Definition*

ISO/IEC DISP 10609-5: 1990. *Information Technology –- International Standardized Profile TB, TC, TD, and TE – Connection-mode Transport Service over Connection-mode Network Service – Part 5: Definition of Profiles.* TB1111/TB1121

ISO/IEC DISP 10609-6: 1990. *Information Technology - International Standardized Profile TB, TC, TD, and TE – Connection-mode Transport Service over Connection-mode Network Service – Part 6: Definition of Profiles* TC1111/TC1121

ISO/IEC ISP 10608-2: 1992 (E). *Information Technology – International Standardized Profile TA – Connection-mode Transport Service over Connectionless-mode Network Service, Part 2: TA51 Profile including subnetwork-type dependent requirements for CSMA/CD Local Area Networks (LANs)*

ISO/IEC ISP 10608-5: 1992 (E). *Information Technology – International Standardized Profile TA – Connection-mode Transport Service over Connectionless-mode Network Service, Part 5: TA1111/TA1121 Profiles including subnetwork-type dependent requirements for X.25 Packet Switched Data Networks using switched virtual calls*

ISO/IEC ISP 11183-1. *Information Technology – International Standardized Profiles AOM1n OSI Management – Management Communications Protocols – Part 1: Specification of ACSE, Presentation and Session Protocols for the use by ROSE and CMISE*, May 1992

ISO/IEC ISP 11183-2, *Information Technology – International Standardized Profiles AOM1n OSI Management - Management Communications Protocols – Part 2: AOM12 –- Enhanced Management Communications*, June 1992

ISO/IEC ISP 11183-3, *Information Technology - International Standardized Profiles AOM1n OSI Management – Management Communications Protocols –- Part 3: AOM11 – Basic Management Communications*, May 1992

ISO/IEC pDISP 12059-0, *Information Technology - International Standardized Profiles - OSI Management – Common Information for Management Functions –- Part 0: Common definitions for management function profiles*, July 1992

ISO/IEC pDISP 12059-1, *Information Technology – International Standardized Profiles – OSI Management – Common Information for Management Functions – Part 1: Object Management*, July 1992

ISO/IEC pDISP 12059-2, *Information Technology – International Standardized Profiles – OSI Management – Common Information for Management Functions – Part 2: State Management*, July 1992

ISO/IEC pDISP 12059-3, *Information Technology - International Standardized Profiles – OSI Management – Common Information for Management Functions – Part 3: Attributes for Representing Relationships*, July 1992

ISO/IEC pDISP 12059-4, *Information Technology – International Standardized Profiles - OSI Management – Common Information for Management Functions – Part 4: Alarm Reporting*, July 1992

ISO/IEC pDISP 12059-5, *Information Technology - International Standardized Profiles – OSI Management – Common Information for Management Functions – Part 5: Event Report Management*, July 1992

ISO/IEC pDISP 12059-6, *Information Technology – International Standardized Profiles – OSI Management – Common Information for Management Functions - Part 6: Log Control*, July 1992

ISO/IEC pDISP 12060-1, *Information Technology – International Standardized Profiles AOM2n OSI Management – Management Functions – Part 1: AOM211 – General Management Capabilities*, July 1992

ISO/IEC pDISP 12060-2, *Information Technology –   International Standardized Profiles AOM2n OSI Management – Management Functions – Part 2: AOM212 – Alarm Reporting and State Management Capabilities,* July 1992

ISO/IEC pDISP 12060-3, *Information Technology– International Standardized Profiles AOM2n OSI Management -– Management Functions – Part 3: AOM213 - Alarm Reporting Capabilities,* July 1992

ISO/IEC pDISP 12060-4, *Information Technology – International Standardized Profiles AOM2n OSI Management – Management Functions – Part 4: AOM221 – General Event Report Management,* July 1992

ISO/IEC pDISP 12060-5, *Information Technology – International Standardized Profiles AOM2n OSI Management – Management Functions – Part 5: AOM231 - General Log Control,* July 1992

ISO/IEC TR 10000-1, *Information Technology – Framework and Taxonomy of International Standardized Profiles – Part 1: Framework*

Telecommunications Journal of Australia Volume 41 (1991). Issue on Management

Part IV

Management Functions

Chapter 10

Name Management and Directory Services

Stefano Zatti

IBM Zurich Laboratory,
Säumerstrasse 4,
8803 Rüschlikon, Zurich, Switzerland
Email: zat@zurich.ibm.com

Naming and directories are tightly bound to distributed systems management – all objects must be identified by the manager in order to be operated upon. In addition, a directory service is a fundamental component in support of a naming scheme and is a suitable repository for many types of management information. This chapter first deals with the evolution of name spaces, from a historical point of view, then focuses on particular types of names defined by the X.500 standard. It shows how a global naming strategy can be based on such names and analyzes the conditions and the practical implications for the deployment of this name space in the complex global internetwork which is being shaped today. Finally, it discusses the problems and challenges connected with managing increasingly complex name spaces, specifically as they relate to the management of network objects.

10.1   Introduction: the problem of object identification

In a computing environment, users and programs acting for them require a means to identify the objects on which they want to operate. The fundamental property of a good naming scheme is that there must be no confusion or ambiguity about what a particular name is referring to. Objects of a computing system normally bear low-level identifiers whereby the system (software or hardware) can refer to them and perform operations on them. However, these identifiers are unappealing to humans, hard to remember and to spell out; hence the requirement for humans to be able to identify objects via high-level identifiers soon arises. This reflects the way object identification happens in the real world, that is, by means of *names* rather than numeric identifiers or addresses following computationally efficient numbering schemes.

The conflicting requirements of user-friendliness and machine time-and-space efficiency contributed to the name–address duality that is universal today. Mapping mechanisms had to be devised to translate user-level identifiers to machine-level ones. A great advantage of using these mechanisms is that lower-level information can be modified at a frequent rate without changing the human perception of an object, making it easier for computer systems to evolve and undergo major changes. Examples of such dual identification are file systems, where files are named by humans with high-level names semantically related to the file contents, while special mechanisms (like UNIX i-tables) are used to map the filename to internal identifiers, and these to the real data at a particular location on the disk. Processes in operating systems are identified to users by the name of the file containing the executable code, whereas they are known to the operating system by a process identifier (PID). The process table performs the mapping in this case. Managing such identifiers in the stand-alone case is rather simple – it is sufficient for a system administrator to make sure that any newly created object within the system is not assigned a name that is already being used, and that each name is uniquely mapped.

The identification problem assumes a new, complex dimension when systems are connected to other systems by networks whose range increasingly approaches that of the world itself. Naming schemes must be devised to be powerful and flexible enough that they can cope with scaling and distribution without requiring continuous redesign of name spaces (with consequent renaming costs) and mapping functions. Mapping functions in support of human-oriented naming also are complex as they have to associate names to useful information, but also have to cope with the distributed nature of such information. In this respect all name management functions such as name assignment, shaping the naming space, distributing management information among different naming spaces and naming functions, are likely to be distributed among numerous individuals. They therefore become much harder to design and to operate.

10.2   The evolution of naming schemes

10.2.1   Terminology

The term *Name* will be used hereafter to mean any identifier seen or used by humans to refer to objects that they seek, or wish to have access to, or communicate with; in other words, a name conveys a sense of "what" we are talking about. This definition is consistent with the one given by Hauzeur (1986). Naming and addressing concepts are formally introduced in (Comer and Peterson, 1989). Such names are used and supported by computer systems through *mapping functions* which associate the name of a particular object to a set of related attributes. They are therefore a major element of the interface between humans and computers. The information content of the name itself does not necessarily (but of course may) denote the nature of the object it refers to, or its location; nor will a name normally enable direct access to the object. For human users, the binding between the name and its meaning can be intuitively obvious from the value, or it can be more subtle, requiring some form of disambiguation, which normally happens by looking at the context the name is used in. For example, a human user expects "San Francisco" to identify a city in California, but the same name may also identify in Spanish a 13th-century saint from Assisi. This topic is however beyond the scope of this chapter. For computing systems, the binding takes the form of a specific *directory* function associating to the name a set of attributes of the named object in some sort of data record, called a directory entry.

Typically, among those attributes are one or more *addresses*, whereby the named object can be located and operated upon. Several (that is, not necessarily only one) levels of addressing may be hidden behind a name, each supported by a particular function. Addresses are normally not seen by humans, and do not normally have a very *human-friendly* look, but in case they do they can be considered names as well, subject to the same kind of rules that apply to high-level names. Whatever its form, an address conveys a sense of "where" the object resides or can be found. This definition tries to circumvent a name–address duality which has generated much confusion in the past. The directory functions needed to support use of names are described in Section 10.3.

10.2.2 Historical perspectives in naming

At the dawn of computing, name spaces were *flat*, managed by a single administrator who was responsible for ensuring name uniqueness and for setting up mappings. In a single system that was easy to achieve. When systems were first interconnected, the management function was still kept centralized at a specific site. The US Department of Defense network *Arpanet,* for example, maintained a flat naming space of host names, supported by a centralized host table at a Network Information Center (NIC), from where all sites could remotely retrieve addressing information about other hosts of the network. IBM's Systems Network Architecture also originally supported a name space where each node, called *Logical Unit* (LU), was named by a flat, eight-character LU name. LUs were located through a global search in the network, and their uniqueness was ensured through administrative registration procedures.

Predictably, such a level of simplicity could not cope for long with the growth and the progressive interconnection of existing networks. The burden on the administrator to ensure name uniqueness and to keep the mapping information up to date soon became unbearable and it was increasingly hard to perform these functions in a centralized fashion. In addition, whenever existing networks were interconnected, no mechanism other than massive renaming could be used to avoid conflict of existing names. The natural answer to this evolution was to allow names to be *structured* in components reflecting the configuration of the existing networks or of the administrative authorities managing them. Beyond being structured, names can be *hierarchical* when the name components are ordered according to some particular relationship. The Grapevine system developed at Xerox PARC, providing general facilities for electronic mail, naming, authentication, and resource location, pioneered the concept of structured hierarchical names in networks, also featuring distributed mapping functions (Birrel *et al.*, 1982). The two-level hierarchy suggested by Grapevine soon turned out to be insufficient (Schroeder *et al.*, 1984), and a third level appeared in a related commercial product, the Xerox Clearinghouse (Oppen and Dalal, 1983). This product featured three-level names of the form *ObjectName:Domain:Organization*, reflecting the administrative hierarchy up to the level of a commercial organization that networks were covering at the time. The Arpanet grew beyond the critical threshold, with the NIC being unable to provide real-time naming functions at reasonable performance. The flat host-naming scheme was thus modified into the structured, open-ended scheme of *Arpa Domain Names*, where host names consist of components each representing a *domain* of administrative responsibility. For example, the highest-level domains reflect subdivisions like *mil* (military), *gov* (government), *com* (commercial companies), or *edu* (educational). These domains are further subdivided into individual components like IBM within *com* or NIST within *gov*, giving rise to names like *watson.ibm.com* or *nist.gov* or *ernie.berkeley.edu* (Mockapetris 1987). Domain Names are supported by a set of interconnected naming functions called Domain Names Servers (DNS), described in Section 10.3. SNA also evolved into more structured names, qualifying LU names with Network Identifiers (NetIDs) somehow reflecting the physical structure of the internetwork.

The trend towards global interconnection of networks requires an extensible hierarchical naming structure with the flexibility to permit names to reflect any real-world organizational structures. This is essential for the ambitious goal of a global name space providing the basis for global connectivity. This goal can be achieved through the naming scheme proposed within the ever-increasingly important X.500 standard, on which we will focus next.

10.2.3   Distinguished names and X.500

The concept of *Distinguished Name* has been developed in parallel with the architecture and information framework of the X.500 directory standard (CCITT X.500, 1989). We will first describe the syntax of this kind of names, and discuss their advantages and their power, finally relating them to the supporting X.500 directory in Section 10.3.

A *Distinguished Name* (DN) is composed of an ordered sequence of *Relative Distinguished Names* (RDN), where each RDN is an unordered set of one or more *Attribute-Value Assertions* (AVA) each containing an attribute type and a purported attribute value. No assumption is made on what kind of objects can be named within this scheme. The attribute type denotes a particular syntactic space from which the attribute value is taken. The insertion of the types in the name components accomplishes a level of power and flexibility unmatched by other naming schemes. Any particular matching rules and character sets may be encompassed, in order to support a wide range of natural languages, and parsing of a name and identification of its components are facilitated. For example, names of countries are taken from the small set of two-character country codes standardized by ISO 3166 (to avoid conflicts between country names in different languages); names of people can be taken either from the Latin alphabet, or optionally from the larger T.61 character set that includes Kanji for Japanese or Chinese names. Different attribute types will trigger different matching rules when names have to be compared. Attribute types are assigned within the scope of the particular standards where the attributes and their syntaxes are defined and follow the special syntax of *Object Identifiers* described in the next subsection.

DNs in the world can be organized in a Global Naming Tree. The tree is supported by the X.500 directory as described in Section 10.3, but there is no requirement that all objects named by DNs be contained in the directory. Each RDN is assigned by a specific naming authority. A naming authority can delegate its naming responsibility to another authority, hierarchically inferior. At any level, an authority will make sure that the RDNs it assigns are not ambiguous. For example, when assigning a naming attribute to a computer object representing a new employee named "John A. Smith", the local naming authority (most likely a system administrator in connection with personnel) will make sure no other individual at the same level will have that name. Disambiguating mechanisms (like use of middle names for humans) must be used in case of conflicts.

Table 10.1 Distinguished and relative distinguished names.

RDN	DN	Object Class
CountryName = IT	CountryName = IT	Country
OrgName = IBM	CountryName = IT OrgName = IBM	Organization
LocName = Rome	CountryName = IT OrgName = IBM LocName = Rome	Location
CommonName = Gino	CountryName = IT OrgName = IBM LocName = Rome CommonName = Gino	Residential person

The hierarchical naming scheme guarantees uniqueness of names across a global network, and at the same time allows an unlimited number of variations. For example, Table 10.1 shows the DNs of several hypothetical hierarchically related objects, each one of which has a DN. In the above example:

- the DN for the country "Italy" is simply C=IT, "IT" being an internationally standardized code, from ISO 3166;

- the DN for IBM within Italy is C=IT/O=IBM;

- the DN for the particular IBM location in Rome is C=IT/O=IBM/L=Rome;

- the DN of the Residential Person "Gino" at this location is C=IT/O=IBM/L=Rome/CN=Gino.

Often, for human readability, attribute types are represented as short mnemonic codes, like "C" for "country name", "O" for "organization name", "OU" for "organizational unit name", and "CN" for "common name"; in reality, they actually have numeric values, as explained in the next section.

DNs are globally unique, because at any given level the uniqueness of the RDN component at that level is guaranteed by the responsible naming authority; they are flexible, because the individual components have to comply only with syntaxes dictated by requirements specific to the responsible naming authority; and they are open-ended, because the components are determined level-by-level in a decentralized fashion, up to any depth. They provide the flexibility and the power to name any entity anywhere in the world, at the cost of having a potentially large number of name components.

The flexibility and power of the DN naming scheme is such that other standards use DNs to name their objects. The 1988 version of the CCITT X.400 Message Handling System, for example, chose to identify mail originators and recipients with DNs, thus folding into the DN space a very similar pre-existing naming scheme based on so-called O/R names (CCITT X.400, 1988). The ISO CMIP/CMIS Network Management standards use DNs to identify managed objects, as well as object managers and agents themselves (OSI CMIP 1990). Computer manufacturers and users too are taking a similar decision for their own objects.

10.2.4   Distinguished names at the user interface

DNs are successful in providing a convenient and powerful universal representation for structured names with different syntaxes in each component; on the other hand, paradoxically, although they were conceived to the advantage of human users, DNs fall short of their original goals for several reasons:

- attribute types in their internal numeric form are cumbersome and totally meaningless to the user;

- components are inflexibly ordered;

- with all the variants of spelling and abbreviations, and the exotic character sets allowed by the utterly flexible scheme, it is hard to guess a DN without previously knowing many details about it.

Therefore, in order for DNs to be used in practice, two major requirements must be satisfied at the human–computer interface:

- mechanisms must be provided to support entering DNs at the user interface, and DN presentation to the users on the screen and on paper;

- fancier systems must be provided to support descriptive or attribute-based naming, allowing users to build names by guessing their structure and the value of their components.

Catering to the first requirement, sophisticated user interfaces can help to simplify DN usage by locally providing an additional level of naming where types can be implied by their position or automatically presented to the users by means of pre-fixed formats. For example in the OSI-DS directory pilot a format for *User Friendly Names* has been proposed by Kille (1991b). This format leaves out attribute types when they are sufficiently obvious and is oriented mostly to names of humans. A complex DN like C=GB/O=UCL/OU=ComputerScience/ CN=SteveKille would be more attractive to the user if it looked like *GB,UCL,CS,Steve Kille*. Mechanisms at the user interface are provided to ensure that the construct that actually goes on the wire is the correct DN. Visual syntaxes to represent DNs on paper or on terminal screens (with types and values) are also being proposed, in order to facilitate exchange of DNs by external means (for example, to allow printing of DNs on business cards as mailing addresses). There is no need though for these conventions to be standardized or even globally advertised as the issue of name entry is totally independent of name exchange, and typically confined to local decisions and local cultures. The name of a country or the choice of the character set can depend on location, but as far as the computer is concerned, a common unambiguous representation is already defined.

Catering to the second requirement, an extremely fertile area of research has been dealing with *Descriptive name servers*, which let users specify names in incomplete, unordered, and even incorrect fashion. Suppose we have met a person at a conference and all we can remember is her name and the country of origin, and that her organization was a university. This information is clearly not sufficient to build a DN, and even if it were, the inflexibility of the DN syntax would make the DN building procedure so error-prone that a directory search would have an extremely small likelihood of success. But this information is sufficient to be given as input to descriptive name servers like Profile (Peterson, 1988) or Nomenclator (Ordille and Miller, 1991), which feature intelligent mechanisms to exploit the underlying directories (for example the X.500 information base) and find out what is the real DN of an object (with possibly more than one outcome) and, if desired, the related information.

10.2.5   Other forms of "names": object and universal identifiers

We mentioned that the attribute types contained in DNs follow the syntax of *Object Identifiers* (OI). OIs are themselves sequences of *integers* representing nodes of another global tree, the Registration Authority tree. This tree, different and *a priori* unrelated to the DIT, is designed to allow independent identification by Registration Authorities throughout the world of the different standards they control and object types defined within those standards. Countries, organizations, standard bodies, and PTTs, appear as nodes in the tree in their capacity of Registration Authorities as well as Standard-specific classes of objects like countries, persons and common names, telephone numbers, and so on. New entries in the tree can be registered in a decentralized fashion according to a specific procedure defined in the ISO 9834 standard (OSI REG, 1990). It is important to observe that the OI tree is not a *directory* tree, that is, its nodes do not correspond to physical entries in some existing directory, storing information (attributes) about the objects. It just reflects a convenient mechanism for assigning world-unique identifiers to standard-related objects. Figure 10.1 shows an example of a small fraction of the OI tree. In this example, the OI for the *mhs-motis* standard (X.400) is (2 6); in the context of the directory standard (2 5), the OI for the *Country Name* attribute type is (2 5 4 6), which is the actual value of the attribute type used in Table 10.1.

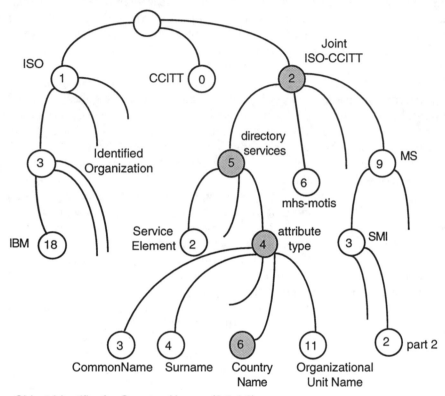

Object identifier for Country Name : (2 5 4 6)
Object identifier for Common Name : (2 5 4 3)

Figure 10.1 Object identifiers and the registration tree.

In object-oriented systems the concept of class of objects is distinct from that of instance of such an object. Classes are typically defined by Registration Authorities as they introduce new standards and new types of objects within those. Then, when vendor organizations decide to implement those standards, they instantiate a number of those objects of the defined types. Finally, customers and end users finalize the object definition and instantiation by installing them at specific locations in their networks. At this point the "position" of those object instances in the world does not depend on their registration, but on their administrative situation. An X.400 Message Transfer Agent (MTA), for example, may be located with a particular company in some country, even though the concept of MTA was originally defined by ISO and CCITT within the X.400 standard. Such object instances are then named by DNs.

A major problem with high-level names in general is the definition and enforcement of their lifetime, to avoid their reuse for circumventing name-based security mechanisms. When a user leaves a company or disappears, for example, his name could be later reassigned to a newly hired namesake. If no counter-measures are taken, this newcomer may inherit privileges belonging to the old user, thereby gaining unauthorized access to objects. This highly undesirable security loophole can be plugged by assigning to each named object a unique identifier that never gets reassigned, and then basing any security mechanism protecting the object on such identifiers and not on object names (refer to Chapter 15 for a discussion of security mechanisms). Such an identifier is called a Universal User IDentifier (UUID), and is ideally unique in space and in time. Typically, a UUID is based on an unbounded, monotonically increasing function, which could be a very large counter or just the absolute time. In the case of interconnected systems, the UUID can be obtained in a decentralized fashion by concatenating an absolute timestamp to a world-unique machine ID (assigned according to some global host numbering scheme such as a unique network address), identifying the host where an object is created. The UUID is forever bound to the object and bears no intrinsic meaning. The object can move and even be destroyed, but the ID remains its own forever. However, UUIDs do not have any of the user-friendly features of high-level names and they cannot constitute a naming level by themselves. A directory function must still be used to obtain the UUID from the high-level name (for example, a DN) used by humans. Directory functions accomplishing this kind of mapping are described in the next section.

10.3   Support mechanisms for naming: directory services

10.3.1   Definition of centralized and distributed directory

The need for directory functions to support user-friendly naming clearly emerges from the past discussion. We now review some of these services and describe in some depth the functions provided by the X.500 directory.

Formally, a directory is a function d that maps a name into a set of attributes (or properties):

$$d: \text{Name} \rightarrow \{<\text{Attribute}>^*\}$$

The most immediate way to implement this function is through a table. A protocol for remote query can then be provided for remote sites to interrogate the directory function. This is the service originally provided by the Arpanet NIC and by the CSNET Name Server (Solomon *et al.*, 1982). But this centralized solution does not scale up well with size and runs into insurmountable administrative difficulties when large amounts of information have to be entered and maintained up to date. Hence comes the fundamental idea of partitioning the directory information into different servers, providing to the user a distributed service to retrieve the information through an additional step of locating the server where the information is kept. The problem resembles that of a distributed database, but with the more limited scope of a specific kind of mapping for a particular set of data structures, which allows a greater degree of optimization.

The directory function in a distributed directory is decomposed into more steps:

d: name → <ServerName>

d: ServerName → {attribute: <Server_address>}

d: name → {<attribute>*}

where ServerName is the name of the server where the information for the named object is stored. The search function to locate such a server is called *Navigation*, and can actually require several steps when the connectivity among servers is complex. The complexity of the navigation process is related to the complexity of the server connectivity, and in particular to their hierarchical organization. Grapevine had only one level of servers, corresponding to the upper level of the names, and navigation took place just in two steps. All servers would go to a logically centralized but fully replicated Grapevine directory (called GV registry, corresponding to the root of the name space), which contained references to all other directories. So the address of a specific directory server could be retrieved by querying the GV registry, and the relevant information could successively be obtained by querying the appropriate server. The Clearinghouse had a similar structure, but with one more level of indirection corresponding to an extra level of naming. The fundamental contribution of these early systems was to take advantage of the information contained in the name structure to help suggest the search path to the mapping, which is the basis of the X.500 navigation mechanism. A similar search mechanism is applied by the Arpanet Domain Names Server, which distributed the function of the NIC while still maintaining a centralized knowledge base for the highest level of names.

Whatever the structure of the name and the number of components, there must be in all cases a minimal level of initial *knowledge* available to all servers, either through full replication (like for Grapevine or Clearinghouse registration servers) or through centralization (like the new version of the Arpanet NIC). The two basic ideas of name-based navigation and initial knowledge, with the additional flexibility of the naming structure pushed to the extreme, are the basis of the X.500 architecture that we describe next.

10.3.2   The X.500 directory standard

The X.500 directory standard is the offspring of a joint effort of the International Standard Organization (ISO) and the International Consultative Committee for Telephony and Telegraphy (CCITT), and culminates at least 10 years of research and development in the area of naming and directory services (CCITT X.500 1989). The architecture of the directory is intimately bound to the structure of the names it supports – DNs, described in Section 10.2. Normally a DN refers to an entry in the directory containing the object's attributes. The directory information framework is object-oriented as an entry in the directory is a set of *attributes* of an *object* belonging to a specific *object class*. One or more of the attributes of an object can be tagged as *Distinguished* and used to uniquely identify the entry (and the corresponding object). All entries can be organized hierarchically in a gigantic, worldwide tree reflecting the administrative hierarchies of the real world. Because of this hierarchical nature, the information in the directory is also referred to as the *Directory Information Tree* (DIT).

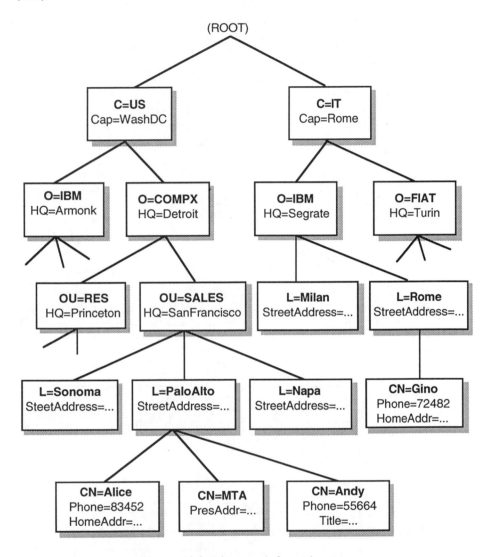

Figure 10.2 Directory information tree.

Figure 10.2 shows a hypothetical example of a fraction of the DIT, with two countries (the USA and Italy) containing two organizations each. Within the USA, the internal structure of the hypothetical company COMPX is also shown. Both leaves and nodes of the tree are directory entries containing attributes describing information about the corresponding object, in addition to distinguished naming attributes. The validity of a DN (that is, whether it names an object or not) is assessed through a directory lookup. An AVA evaluates to *True* when a directory entry does have a distinguished attribute of the given type with the purported value. A DN uniquely names an entry if and only if all its component AVAs evaluate to True.

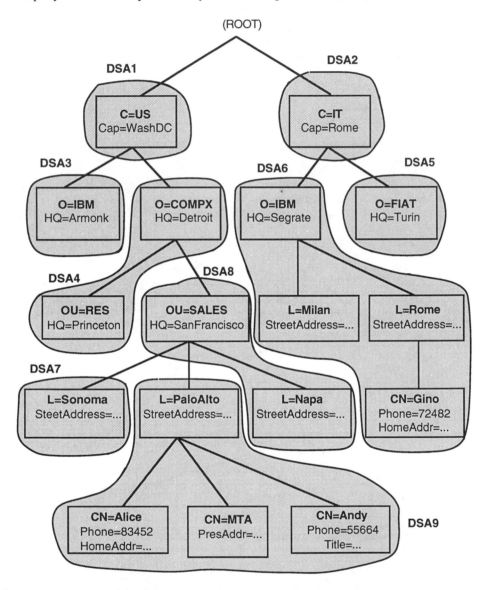

Figure 10.3 Directory structure and navigation.

The directory is a distributed service whose components are called Directory System Agents (DSA) and communicate with each other by means of a standardized application-layer protocol called Directory System Protocol (DSP). Each DSA is responsible for the administration of a particular portion of the DIT, and stores the information related to the objects contained in that portion. Figure 10.3 shows an example of a DIT partitioned into nine *domains* each covered by a separate DSA. The information of the DIT can be replicated, but the replication granularity is that of a whole DSA domain. DSAs are bound to each other in a hierarchical structure that mirrors the DIT portions they are responsible for and their relationships, the *Knowledge Information Tree* (KIT). In practice, this means that the database of each DSA contains specific *knowledge references* binding each DSA with the one responsible for the superior domain (*superior references*) and with all those responsible for any inferior domains (*subordinate references*). In addition, all DSAs at the topmost level must know about all others at that level; as in Grapevine or Clearinghouse, the root knowledge must be fully replicated. Figure 10.5 shows the KIT for the DIT partition of Figure 10.3, and shows within each DSA the knowledge references they are required to have. In addition, *cross-references* can be maintained to other peer domains in order to speed up some searches on frequently used paths. This information is part of the directory configuration, and must be exchanged by the various system managers via administrative procedures as explained in Section 10.4. The knowledge information is the key to the navigation mechanism.

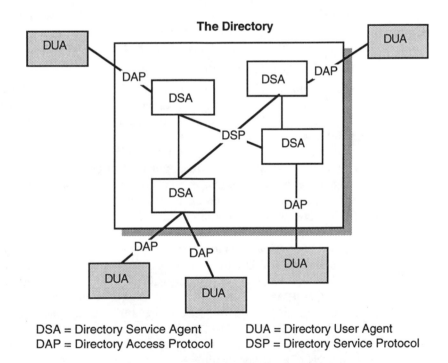

DSA = Directory Service Agent   DUA = Directory User Agent
DAP = Directory Access Protocol   DSP = Directory Service Protocol

Figure 10.4 Directory architecture.

Users have access to the directory via a service interface provided by a user stub called Directory User Agent (DUA), running locally on their machine. The DUA requests the services from the DSA by means of another standardized application-layer protocol, the Directory Access Protocol (DAP). The architecture of X.500 is portrayed in Figure 10.4. When a DSA is queried about a particular object, it is given the name of the object as an argument to the query. If the object is contained in the domain covered by the DSA, the information is retrieved and returned to the caller. If the object is not local, the DSA must locate the other DSA where the object is contained, so it starts a navigation procedure, passing the initial request to another DSA. The order in which DSAs are contacted depends on the structure of the naming space, and can be derived directly from the name of the requested object and the knowledge information possessed by each DSA. DSAs need to communicate with each other by means of the DSP protocol, in order to resolve a particular name into the address of the particular DSA that contains the information for that object. This navigational procedure is particularly complex in X.500 because there is no limit to the depth of the DIT. We will explain it through an example in the next subsection.

10.3.3   Distributed directory operation: an example

Let us assume that the DIT of Figure 10.2 has been partitioned among nine DSAs as shown in Figure 10.3. Each DSA knows about the parent DSA and its children DSAs through preconfigured references that include the DSA name and address, as shown in Figure 10.5. Let us also assume that the user Andy, whose DN is

C=US/O=COMPX/OU=Sales/L=PaloAlto/CN=Andy,

wants to find out some information like the phone number of his friend Gino, whose DN is C=IT/O=IBM/L=Rome/CN=Gino. Andy will contact his local DSA9 through the DUA on his own station, via the DAP protocol, requesting a directory *Read* on the destination DN. DSA9 does not know Gino, nor does it know any of the upper domains forming Gino's administrative hierarchy. But DSA9 knows how to reach its own parent, DSA8. So it will forward the request via DSP to DSA8, which will forward the request up the tree to the parent DSA4, which in turn will forward it to the parent, DSA1. In this case, a request can go all the way up to a first-level DSA, usually corresponding to a country or some international organization. At this level, the DSA knowledge is fully replicated, as it was in Grapevine or Clearinghouse. So the DSA1 for the US will know how to contact the DSA2 for Italy, forwarding the request that always contains the full DN of the object being searched. DSA2 will know all the DSA children to which it has yielded authority, and will be able to resolve the component ON=IBM into the address of DSA6, responsible for it. Finally, DSA6 will locate the directory entry, retrieve the attribute, and return it to Andy via the reverse path in a DSP reply. The search is guaranteed to terminate, if all the knowledge information is correct, in m+n steps, where m is the length (in terms of number of RDNs) of the DN of the caller (intuitively: the steps necessary to go *up* the tree), and n is the length of the DN the search is keyed upon (to go *down* the tree at the other end).

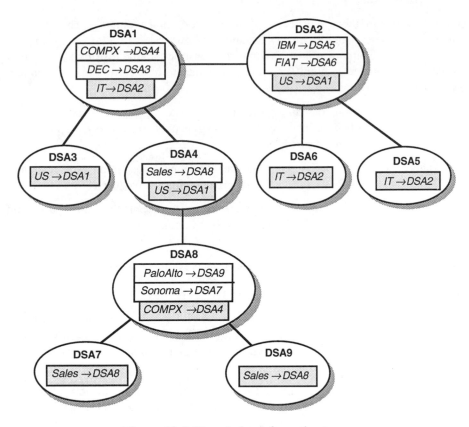

Figure 10.5 Knowledge information tree.

10.4   Operational aspects of naming

The previous discussion has tried to clarify the intimate relationship existing in computing systems between object names and the directory services supporting them. The directory in its name server function plays such a major role in a distributed system that it can be considered as the *glue* holding all different services and applications together, enabling them to share their basic information framework. The various components in fact take advantage of the directory to find out about each other and to find the names of the managers of the objects they do not directly manage. The centrality of the directory in a distributed system was again pioneered by Grapevine, which provided a host of services that used the Grapevine name service to identify each other and interoperate.

Once a name space and a supporting directory service have been architected, the time comes to actually deploy them in the real world through a sequence of operational steps that require coordinated actions on behalf of system managers. Reflecting the intimacy of naming and directory support, the management of a name space is effected though procedures of directory management. The practical implementation of a naming strategy is addressed now.

From the operational point of view, the construction of a distributed system of global scope centered in a unified naming scheme and in uniform directory support hinges on the following steps:

- name unification (or name federation at the least), whereby existing name spaces are unified, or interoperation among them is afforded in case unification is impossible or not desired;

- global worldwide definition of the structured name space through delegation of naming responsibilities reflecting external administrative hierarchies;

- construction of a distributed directory service to support the name space, with distribution of knowledge information to ensure full connectivity.

Each of these fundamental steps is separately discussed in the following.

10.4.1   Unification of naming spaces

In today's multi-connected computer world we have to cope, as we have seen in the previous discussion, with a large number of different naming schemes, each supported by a different directory. However, we detect a trend towards unification of many naming spaces, for the following reasons:

- to avoid the proliferation of different directory services, all doing the same thing, and the need for interfacing them through complex mechanisms;

- to uniquely and uniformly identify objects that can be accessed and operated upon by different protocols with different semantics. In the same way that a human being can perform different operations and cover different roles in life (father, employee, sportsman, cook) by using always the same name, it is desirable that a computer-related object like a printer or a modem can be used, operated upon, managed, and described via the same name, contrary to what has been the case in the past. A common naming framework can contribute to efficient system and network management.

The DN scheme is the most promising candidate for name unification. It is in fact sufficiently open and flexible to gracefully encompass existing naming schemes, both flat and already structured, in a process of gradual migration. To this end, either one of two tree-merging techniques can be utilized: encapsulation or grafting.

Encapsulation: An existing name is wholly inserted into one single RDN, with an appropriately selected attribute type. For example, the name of a UNIX file such as "/etc/bin/service" could be inserted under the DN

C=CH/O=SwissBank/CN=FileServer

of the file server managing it as:

C=CH/O=SwissBank/CN=FileServer/FILE=(/etc/bin/service).

The advantage of this solution is that the existing structure is perfectly preserved and the impact on existing programs can be minimized. The components of the encapsulated name are not burdened with any extra meanings that their original designers had not foreseen. The disadvantage is that the hierarchical structure of the old name ends up being totally hidden within the RDN, and is therefore unavailable to standard services for purposes such as name navigation.

Grafting: The structure of an existing name is exploded into its components, each of which becomes an RDN with appropriately selected attribute types. For example, the UNIX file "/etc/bin/service", inserted under the DN of the managing file server, becomes:

C=CH/O=SwissBank/CN=FileServer/DIR=etc/DIR=bin/FILE=service.

Even names perceived to be "untyped" can be inserted in this scheme, by imposing an appropriately registered attribute type on each of their name components. The main advantage of this solution is the elegant uniformity of name spaces it generates: all services using these names can see and exploit all components without the need for any further decoding. The disadvantage is that each RDN-level name component must conform to the possibly conflicting requirements of all pertinent standards. A mechanism to insert OIs into the DIT, thus allowing OI-based directory searches, is described by the author of this chapter (Zatti, 1991). Kille describes instead a possible way of inserting Arpa Domain names into the DIT (Kille, 1991c). In both cases appropriate new attribute types are defined for the naming attributes of the new name spaces, and the existing names are broken into their individual components, each of which, typed with the new attribute types, becomes the RDN of a DIT entry. The X.500 directory can thus be exploited to store and retrieve information about objects named with names other than DNs (basically OIs and Domain Names *become* DN by applying these mechanisms, but do not have to *look like* DNs to the users or programs accustomed to them).

This form of unification of name spaces, though, does not necessarily imply that all the objects named by DNs have to be directory objects, contained in the Directory Information Base. The directory services may in fact apply only to the portion of the DN tree closest to the root, which plays the crucial role of interconnector of naming spaces. Existing naming spaces such as those used by file systems or e-mail servers, or name spaces from other standards, can be hooked to the global tree without requiring that each object they name becomes a directory object. Network Management, for example, uses DNs to name managed objects (OSI CMIP 1990).

The techniques of encapsulation or grafting can both be used for tree merging, depending on the circumstances. In both cases, though, the fundamental step to hook a foreign name space to the DIT is that a point in the global DN tree be selected, or created, to be the root of the existing name space's subtree. The subtree root points through its directory entry to an *object manager* application responsible for all the objects contained in the subtree. The resulting DN for a non-directory object will be made up of a portion contained in the directory, up to the subtree root, the object manager at the junction point of the two name spaces, and a portion reflecting the foreign naming space. In the example above, all file names of a global worldwide file system would be made up of a portion

(like: C=CH/O=SwissBank/CN=FileServer)

identifying a particular file server, and another portion

(like: DIR=etc/DIR=bin/FILE=service)

identifying the file within that server. In many cases, an object manager will be aware of the existence of other peer managers, and explicitly query the directory to locate them, using their own DNs, that is, the upper portion of the object's DN. In our example, each file server would be aware of the existence of other file servers, use the directory to locate them, and set up connections with them, exchanging files through the file system protocol. In some other cases, the manager may not know this and query the directory with the complete name. Even if this query fails, the failure report does describe how much of the DN was matched, and may even, as a desirable optimization, return the address of the right manager. Otherwise, more generally, a follow-up query with the truncated DN will locate the peer manager. As a concrete example, in OSI network management, which as we said earlier uses DNs to identify managed objects, the DN of an object would contain a portion leading to the management application entity responsible for the object, which could be located using the directory.

The unification of name spaces is useful and attractive but not always necessary, if the visibility of an object is limited and there is no need for multiple kinds of operations on the same object. In many cases name spaces can and will be kept segregated, but even then appropriate mechanisms can be provided to make it possible to switch from one naming system to another whenever necessary. A loosely interconnected collection of independent name spaces, with independent objects, is often called a *federated space*; (Comer and Peterson, 1989) formally describes such a federated space, showing how different name spaces can be composed into one another. A unified directory can play a significant role also in this case, to retrieve alternate name forms for particular objects, or to store information about servers that themselves independently manage sub-name spaces. For example, one may use the directory to translate a DN into a UUID or, more rarely, even vice versa.

10.4.2   Design of a structured name space

The X.500 standard defines the structure of DNs and mechanisms for a distributed directory, but does not mandate the way names will actually look, that is, it does not specify the shape of the DIT. Some sort of naming guidelines are required in order for the global naming structure to be actually realized and deployed. At the very end of the standard document, however, Annex B to X.521 informally suggests a tree shape that is being taken as the basis for deployment by many organizations and consortia of X.500 developers, like the OSI Implementors' Workshop (OIW), sponsored by the US National Institute for Standards and Technology (NIST), and its European equivalent the European Workshop for OSI (EWOS). This annex suggests a *Directory Schema*, that is, a set of *order* relationships between various object classes, that would correspondingly determine the structure of DNs.

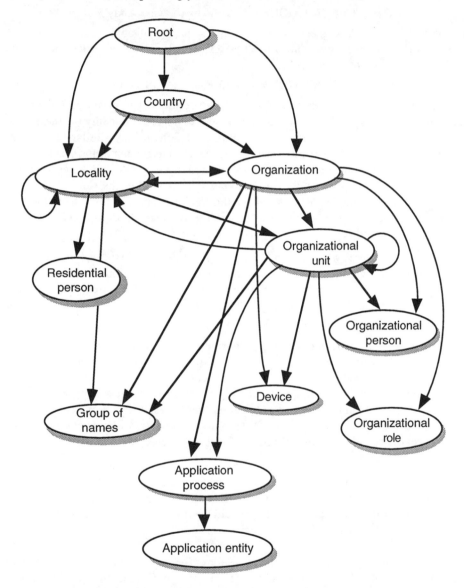

Figure 10.6 Suggested DIT structure (from X.521).

The suggested directory schema is portrayed in Figure 10.6, which is taken from page 224 of the CCITT X.521 standard (1988 version). Each oval in the figure represents an object class, a member of which can be administratively dependent on a member of the immediately superior class (connected by an incoming arrow) and can be responsible for a member of the immediate subordinate class (outgoing arrow).

The concepts suggested by this figure should be put into practice with common sense, trying to avoid the pitfalls of the loops. For example, a name like

C=US/O=COMPX/OU=Sales/L=PaloAlto/CN=Andy

is compliant with the suggestion, because the sequence of object classes Country-Organization-Organizational_unit-Locality-Residential_person describes a legal path in the portrayed graph. A name like

C=US/O=COMPX/OU=Sales/L=PaloAlto/CN=MTA

for an object of class *Application Entity*, on the contrary, would not be acceptable, because an Application Entity should not be subordinate to a Locality (as there is no arrow joining the two classes). Such recommendations or any similar future ones constitute the commonly accepted basis on which a universal name space can be built and any DNs can be recognized and operated upon. We can expect that a corresponding naming tree will progressively take shape "in the field". An ideal scenario for such a deployment would see the tree growing *top-down* from the root through branches down to the leaves. Using the recommendations of Figure 10.6 as a guideline, we would see the following steps happening:

- Countries agree on their own names, and admit to the first level also a certain number of international organizations like the United Nations or the Red Cross. This restricted elite will constitute the first level of the tree, and only the generally agreed-upon names of its members will be allowed as first RDN of each DN.

- Each country delegates naming authority to organizations within its own legal responsibility, registering each one with specific names according to the various national rules. To be determined case by case is whether a country will want to further subdivide its naming responsibility on a geographic base, establishing subdomains for political entities like states or provinces using the State_or_Province or the Locality object class, or will the country allow organizational levels directly below the country level.

- Each legitimate organization will exert its own naming authority by further subdividing into organizational units as requested by its administrative structure, eventually assigning names to all the objects under its jurisdiction. Residential users and services would be assigned their names by public authorities like the PTTs or the registry offices.

Each naming authority is responsible for enforcing name uniqueness, but only within a particular level, global uniqueness being guaranteed by the hierarchical structure of the naming tree. An additional naming step is to properly register the naming information in the directory database, as explained in the next subsection.

All of the above would happen in an ideally disciplined world. In reality, the process is actually taking place in a bottom-up fashion, with a two-tiered process. At one level various consortia of pilot implementors (in most cases, computer manufacturers and software houses) define their own subtrees first, reflecting their internal structures, and figure out some interim ways to get interconnected with each other. Examples of this process are the OSI-DS effort (Kille, 1991a) to deploy an X.500 directory in the DARPA internet, and the PARADISE pilot within RARE WG3 (PARADISE, 1991). These processes can also start encompassing existing name spaces like the Arpa Domain Names for OSI-DS. At another level, with a similar, parallel effort, institutional organizations like national PTTs and some telecommunications carriers and information service providers like AT&T, MCI Communications Corp., Sprint International, or IBM Information Networks are also defining, deploying, and maintaining their own naming trees, in joint efforts e.g., the North American Directory Forum (NADF) (Blum, 1991) and the related Expert Group on Directories (EGDIR) in Europe. It is to be expected that at some point all these efforts will want to come together and unify their name spaces. Hopefully it will be possible to hook each one of the organizational trees under some existing level of the institutional hierarchy. Otherwise, a less elegant but equally operational solution would be to put the trees next to each other like a forest, with mechanisms in place to allow jumping from one tree to the other. In this case the same real object (possibly an organization or even a country) could appear in different trees, maybe with different names, encoding, or spellings, generating quite some confusion for users.

The nature of the information and mechanisms required to connect and graft trees to each other are related to the way the supporting directories are configured and used, and are discussed in the next subsection.

10.4.3   Construction and operation of the distributed directory

Building a name space amounts in practice to constructing a distributed directory to support the name space, which in turn amounts to installing a set of separate DSAs interconnected through knowledge information. This is by no means a centralized process, and must take place through a number of independent actions on behalf of individual network managers responsible for the various subdomains. Each sub-domain of the tree (a shaded area in Figure 10.3) stores in the database of its DSA a portion of the Directory Information Base and information necessary to link the portions to one another.

The procedure for the construction of a global name space can be summarized in a set of management actions taking place at three different times:

i)   at the time of installation of a new DSA, when the new database must be populated with new entries;

ii)   when naming responsibility is yielded from one authority down to another one of lesser scope;

iii) at run time, when new objects are created and when directory searches traverse the DSA domain.

The various operational steps are described in the following.

At installation time:

- Define the portion of the tree which falls under the domain of a particular DSA. In particular, be aware of the name of the subtree root, which is assigned by the parent domain.

- Create an instance of a DSA (a running program, in OSI terms an Application Process). Define for it a presentation address and register it with the network (global procedure for each network address) and the system (local OS procedure). Provide this information, making up a subordinate knowledge reference, to the parent DSA via external administrative procedures. The parent DSA associates this reference with the name of the particular object from which the subtree depends. All searches targeted to that subtree will then be rerouted to the DSA specified by the reference.

- Create a superior knowledge reference within the database managed by the new DSA pointing to the parent DSA, using information obtained through external administrative procedures; all searches targeted outside the subtree covered by this DSA will then be rerouted to the parent DSA specified by the reference.

- Register in the database entries for all the objects contained in the domain of the DSA.

- Handle replication of the information if the DSA is replicated in more than one site, providing all references (as a group address) to the parent DSA. When yielding naming responsibilities to a subdomain, for which possibly a DSA is already up and running, recursively:

  - assign the name to the subdomain for which responsibility is being given (the name is always assigned by the parent);

  - make sure to provide superior references to the child, and to receive subordinate references from the child, through external administrative procedures.

At run time:

- Whenever a new object is created, add a new database entry for it, with all the attributes, making sure the naming attribute is marked as distinguished. There is no need to notify individual object creation to other DSAs.

- Cache the cross-references traversed by or resulting from a search, for optimization of future searches. This step is clearly automated, and does not require human intervention. It is fundamental to improve performance, as discussed in Section 10.5.

It is important to remark that each knowledge reference must contain not only the *name* of the superior, subordinate, or cross-DSA, but also its presentation address, to allow setting up of a communication connection without any further directory lookup. Otherwise, at run time a DSA would have to query the directory to locate another DSA, giving rise to a condition of circularity that could possibly prevent the success of the operation.

10.5 The challenges of future global naming

Throughout this chapter we have tried to describe general trends in the highly complex and changing field of network operations. The tactical details of the evolution of name spaces are still changing at a high rate, but a general tendency towards a unified, uniformly supported name space is visible, and stands a good chance of success. However, some technical and administrative issues are still open and require more work. Without satisfactory solutions to these issues the emerging trend will not become a reality. In conclusion to the chapter, we will now analyze some of the points where more work needs to be done before a fully operational global naming strategy can be put in place.

From the architectural point of view, since it is almost hopeless to foresee a totally uniform and harmoniously managed directory information base, it must be accepted that a particular object may be seen under more than one *view*, that is to say, more than one directory entry. Different views of an object would cover its different (possibly, but not necessarily, disjoint) operational aspects. However, it is still desirable to have an object maintain a single name across all its views, for the reasons described in Section 10.4.1. The current X.500 is inflexible and does not allow separate directory entries to be identified by the same name, forcing the administrator to create disjoint entries with different names. In addition, when these objects must contain the same attribute, consistency problems could possibly arise and, what is worse, users could end up with inconsistent views. A design effort is therefore required to allow *distributed entries*, whereby objects would get different sets of attributes possibly under different authorities (that is, even on different DSAs) while still being identified by the same DN.

An apparently contrasting requirement, but equally important, is to let one particular directory entry be identified by more than one DN. This is already achieved today through *aliasing*, which requires construction of a full-fledged entry containing just the alternative DN as attribute, but can be more cheaply achieved by supporting *synonyms*, which are alternative naming labels for the same entry. This is particularly important to accommodate national character sets and spellings side by side with language-neutral ones, thus facilitating inter-cultural lookups. In this case, for example, a Japanese user would register with the directory with two synonym distinguished attributes, one with the Latin and one with the Kanji representation of his name. So anybody in the world could look him up even without recourse to a Kanji keyboard – under the assumption that Latin characters can be entered from any keyboard in the world. Synonyms are equally useful for allowing other kinds of alternative name forms, like calling "Andy" a user with a much longer full name. A global directory must allow synonym-naming attributes.

From the point of view of system management, we have seen in Section 10.4.3. the importance of dissemination of knowledge information to hold the directory structure together. An administrative procedure has been outlined for DSAs to exchange knowledge references at the moment of their creation or when yielding naming authority. It is desirable to automate the procedures of knowledge distribution through a specific network configuration protocol that can take advantage of existing network management tools to disseminate and retrieve the information.

No directory service will have any chance of success unless its contents are secured against unauthorized access. X.509, a component of the X.500 set of standards, specifies public-key based procedures for secure authentication of directory accessors, and new extensions to X.500 (still due for acceptance) deal with access controls at the entry and attribute level. The management issues related to the distribution of this security information are similar to those described in Chapter 15.

Another key issue on which much work is still required is performance management, the ability to deliver responses in "acceptable" time, depending on different classes of service: for real-time naming queries in support of connection establishment, immediate response is fundamental; for wide-reaching searches, routing through cheaper links may be preferred. An architecture for *shadowing* of whole domains, that is, for replicating the database of a particular DSA into another one, was added to the X.500 family of standards in 1992 (ISO 9594, soon to be realized as a standard in 1994). Shadowing would reduce response time by making some frequently accessed information available locally, based on appropriate statistical analysis of traffic patterns. More work is required on behalf of implementors' consortia to devise strategies for the definition of classes of service and their dynamic selection depending on types of requests.

Finally, the key to the success of global directory services will be their commercial exploitation and their economical reward. Private and public service providers will both compete and cooperate to share this potentially huge market for added value. The boundaries among their service domains will have to be clearly defined, and accurate accounting and settlement procedures devised to handle billing and charging, similarly to what happens today in the worldwide telephone network.

All the issues above are objects of continuing extensive research and define today's boundaries of naming technology.

10.6   Summary

This chapter has reviewed the evolution and current trends of naming in distributed systems. Directory services to support global naming have been described. The X.500 directory standards have been identified as the potential basis for a unifying naming strategy that can provide a convenient and open-ended identification solution for today's and tomorrow's global networks. The requirements and the practical implications for the deployment and management of such a naming space have been analyzed, including the relationships and potential synergy of directory and network management services.

Abbreviations

AVA   Attribute-Value Assertion
CCITT   International Telegraph and Telephone Consultative Committee

DAP	Directory Access Protocol
DIT	Directory Information Tree
DN	Distinguished Name
DNS	Domain Names Server
DSA	Directory System Agent
DSP	Directory System Protocol
DUA	Directory User Agent
EGDIR	Expert Group on Directories
EWOS	European Workshop on Open Systems
ISO	International Standardization Organization
KIT	Knowledge Information Tree
LU	Logical Unit
MTA	Message Transfer Agent
NADF	North American Directory Forum
NIC	Network Information Center
NIST	National Institute for Standards and Technology
OI	Object Identifier
OIW	OSI Implementors' Workshop
PID	Process Identifier
UUID	Universal User IDentifier

References

Birrel A., Levin R., Needham R. and Schroeder M. (1982). Grapevine: an exercise in distributed computing, *CACM,* **25**(4), 260–74.

Blum D. (1991). Plotting a direction for X.500. *Network World Magazine,* 4 Nov.

Comer D. and Peterson L. (1989). Understanding naming in distributed systems. *Distributed Computing* **3**, 51–60

Hauzeur, B. M. (1986). A model for naming, addressing, and routing. *ACM Transactions on Office Information Systems*, **4**(4), 293–311

ISO 9594 1-8 / CCITT X.500–X.521 (1989). *The Directory*. Available electronically by anonymous FTP from ties.itu.ch

ISO 9596 (1990). *Information Processing Systems – Open Systems Interconnection – Common Management Information Protocol.*

ISO 9834 (1990). *Information Processing Systems – Open Systems Interconnection – Procedures for the operation of OSI Registration Authorities.*

ISO 10021/CCITT X.400 (1988). *Message Handling Systems: Information* Processing *Systems – Text Communications – MOTIS.*

Kille S. (1991a). *IETF Working Group on OSI Directories (OSI-DS) to build an Internet directory using X.500.* Internet Draft, Feb. 1991.

Kille S. (1991b). *User Friendly Names*. Internet Draft, March 1991.

Kille S. (1991c). *X.500 and Domains.* Internet Draft, March 1991.

Mockapetris,P. (1987). *Domain names – Concepts and Facilities,* RFC 1034, DDN Network Information Center, SRI International, Nov. 1987.

Oppen D. and Dalal Y. (1983). The Clearinghouse: A decentralized agent for locating named objects in a distributed environment, *ACM TOIS,* **1**(3), 230–53

Ordille J. and Miller B. (1991). Nomenclator descriptive query optimization for large X.500 environments. *Proceedings of ACM Sigcomm*, Zurich 1991, 185–96

Paradise International Report No. 2: *Piloting an International Directory Service.* Paradise Project, University College London, Nov. 1991.

Peterson L. (1988). The profile name server. *ACM TOCS* **6**(4), 341–64

Schroeder M., Birrel A. and Needham,R. (1984). Experience with Grapevine: the growth of a distributed system. *ACM TOCS*, **2**(1), 3–23.

Solomon M., Landweber L. and Neuhengen D. (1982). The CSNET name server. *Computer Networks*, North Holland, **6**, 161–72

Zatti S. (1991). Naming in OSI: distinguished names or object identifiers?, *Proceedings of IEEE CompEuro 91,* Bologna, 258–62

Chapter 11

Quality of Service Management in Distributed Systems

David Hutchison, Geoff Coulson, Andrew Campbell and Gordon S. Blair

Computing Department,
Lancaster University,
Lancaster, LA1 4YR, UK
Email: mpg@comp.lancs.ac.uk

The integration of distributed multimedia systems support into a communications architecture including the new multiservice networks is important for realizing the next generation of open systems standards; it is also a significant technical challenge. A key observation is that Quality of Service (QoS) provides a unifying theme on which the functions and facilities of the new integrated standards can be constructed. For future applications, especially highly interactive applications and those relying on the transfer of multimedia information, it is essential that QoS is guaranteed system-wide, including the distributed system platform, the transport protocol and the multiservice network. Enhanced communications protocol support such as end-to-end QoS negotiation, renegotiation, indication of QoS degradations and coordination over multiple related connections are required. This chapter examines the state of the art in QoS provision in current distributed systems architectures and standards, reviews the layer-specific work that has been done, and highlights the need for the definition of a coherent framework that incorporates QoS interfaces, mechanisms and management across all the communications layers.

11.1   Introduction

Recent years have seen dramatic advances in computer communications technology. At the network level, new high-speed technologies such as Fiber Distributed Data Interface, Distributed-queue, Dual-bus and, most recently, Asynchronous Transfer

Mode (ATM) networks are becoming available. These networks not only have the capability to transmit information at high speed, but also offer a range of properties including bounded delay, guarantees on throughput and isochronous communications.

Multimedia workstation technology for generating, compressing and displaying streams of digital video and audio is available in the marketplace in a range of price/performance categories, along with very high capacity storage systems such as compact disk.

These technological developments are complemented by new user perspectives. New classes of distributed application are being developed, such as distance learning, desktop video-conferencing and remote multimedia database access. These applications are characterized by their highly interactive nature and their significant use of multimedia information transfer. In these applications, communication requirements are extremely diverse, and demand varying levels of service in terms of parameters such as latency, bandwidth and jitter. Furthermore, for digital video and audio communications it is often a requirement that levels of service are *guaranteed*.

Other time-critical distributed applications such as distributed real-time control systems are also growing in prominence; these may or may not involve multimedia information transfer, but also have stringent requirements for both reliability and guaranteed bounds on message latency.

These various applications share the need for *Quality of Service (QoS) management* in order to ensure that the requirements of the users are met. Until recently, the notion of QoS has been dealt with in a haphazard and inconsistent way in international standards, and barely at all in commercial systems or de facto standards.

This chapter examines QoS concepts and QoS management, considers the current state of the art and examines the impact of the new technological and application environment on QoS management in distributed systems. The approach of the chapter is, first, to set out a framework and terminology for thinking about QoS; second, to review and evaluate current research on QoS and, third, to highlight the need for a more integrated approach to QoS provision in system architectures. QoS in standards is covered briefly – this is not because it is unimportant (on the contrary, we argue that it will be highly significant), but rather because little work has yet been done. In fact, the research described in this chapter is intended to be fed into the work in progress on QoS standardization.

11.2   Fundamental concepts

11.2.1   Activities, dimensions and categories

As a first step in our analysis of QoS provision in distributed systems, we introduce the term *activity* to refer to those aspects of a system to which it is useful to ascribe quality of service characteristics. Examples of activities are processes, communications, or complete computer systems. One particularly important type of activity in the context of multimedia and real-time distributed applications is the notion of a *flow* which is defined as the production, transmission and eventual consumption of a single media stream as an integrated activity governed by a single statement of QoS (Partridge, 1990; Topolcic, 1990; Campbell *et al.*, 1993). Flows are always simplex but can be either unicast or multicast. They may carry a range of data types including both continuous media and control data such as RPC packets.

In characterizing the QoS of activities, it is necessary to identify *dimensions* along which QoS can be measured and quantified. To take a familiar example, it is common to measure the QoS of a timesharing computer system along the dimensions of system throughput and user response time. It is also useful to group sets of QoS dimensions into QoS *categories* where each category contains dimensions pertaining to some logically identifiable aspect of QoS. As an example, we may define a "system reliability" category which contains system-related reliability dimensions such as mean time between failure (MTBF) or mean time to repair (MTTR). Another reliability category relating more particularly to the field of multimedia and real-time distributed systems may contain dimensions relating to, for example, the permitted percentage of loss of media frames in a flow or the permitted bit error rate in ATM cells.

Other important QoS categories of relevance to the distributed multimedia application area are *timeliness* and *volume*. The timeliness category contains dimensions relating to the end-to-end delay of control and media packets in a flow. Examples of such dimensions are *latency*, measured in milliseconds and defined as the time taken from the generation of a media frame to its eventual display, and *jitter*, also measured in milliseconds and defined as the variation in overall nominal latency suffered by individual packets on the same flow. The volume category contains dimensions that refer to the throughput of data in a flow. At the level of end-to-end flows, an appropriate QoS dimension may be video frames delivered per second. Alternatively, at the ATM layer, a typical volume QoS dimension would quantify throughput in terms of *peak-rate* throughput and *statistical* throughput measured in cells per second. These examples illustrate that certain dimensions are often only applicable at certain system layers and imply that a complete category should contain dimensions for each system layer involved in the support of that category.

The above list of categories and dimensions is far from exhaustive. Other categories worthy of mention are *criticality* which relates to the assignment of relative priority levels between activities, *quality of perception* which is concerned with dimensions such as screen resolution or sound quality, and *logical time* which is concerned with the degree to which all nodes in a distributed system see the same events in an identical order. *Cost* is another important category. This may contain dimensions such as the rental cost of a network link per month, the cost of transmitting a single media frame in a flow, or the cost of a multiparty, multimedia conference call. Cost considerations are also typically applied to the level of QoS provided in the various other QoS categories. A more complete selection of QoS categories can be found in (ISO, 1992c).

11.2.2 QoS management

Having established a framework for the measurement and quantification of QoS we now consider the extension of our conceptual framework to cover the *management* of

QoS along the various dimensions. QoS dimensions are abstract characterizations of QoS requirements whereas QoS management is the concrete realization of required levels of QoS in a real system. It is useful to consider the management of QoS under the headings of specification, mapping between layers, negotiation, resource allocation, admission control, performance maintenance, performance monitoring, and policing and renegotiation.

QoS specification and mapping

QoS specification is concerned with defining required levels of QoS which are interpretable by a system. QoS specifications are different at each system layer, but each layer is similar in consisting largely of a list of relevant QoS dimensions together with required values for those dimensions. Required values may be expressed in terms of advisory values, mandatory values, upper and lower limits or a variety of other forms. In addition to values of dimensions, a QoS specification may also contain information on actions to take if the requested QoS levels are violated (Campbell *et al.*, 1993). Often, particularly in the case of throughput QoS categories, a QoS specification is interpreted as a two-way *service contract* whereby the QoS provider undertakes to support a given level of QoS if and only if the traffic generator undertakes to supply its data at the agreed QoS.

QoS mapping performs the function of automatic translation between representations of QoS at different system levels and thus relieves the user of the necessity of thinking in terms of low-level dimensions. For example, a user at the flow level may express a jitter dimension in terms of a statistical variance in arrival times of video frames and this could be translated at the lower layers into a requirement for an absolute bound on ATM cell jitter and a jitter smoothing buffer of a certain size. Note that QoS mapping is concerned simply with translating between representations: the resource allocation function (discussed next) is responsible for the actual instantiation of the ATM connection and buffers.

QoS negotiation, resource allocation and admission control

The QoS negotiation function is responsible for analyzing an activity onto components and finding a composite of the individual QoS levels supportable by those components which is necessary and sufficient to realize the QoS of the complete activity. In a continuous media flow, the system entities concerned would typically be media devices such as video codecs and frame buffers, operating system threads, transport protocol entities and network links. At the network layer *QoS based routing*, whereby a network route is chosen in accordance with the QoS supportable at each node, is an important consideration. When an activity is initiated, the negotiation function asks each component to state the level of QoS it is able to provide. Then, depending on the results, it assigns particular QoS levels to each component (or reports back to the initiator that the activity cannot be supported).

In order to support a given level of QoS it is usually necessary for the system components comprising an activity to dedicate certain resources to the activity. For example, an operating system thread acting as a component of a flow may require a certain number of processor cycles per second to process video frames at a rate compatible with the flow's throughput requirement. In addition, buffer space and network bandwidth will have to be allocated. In practice, resource allocation is often closely associated with QoS negotiation because it is often the case that low-level system components can only determine whether or not they are capable of supporting a given level of QoS by actually requesting the necessary resources and noting the outcome of the request.

The admission control function is also intimately tied into the negotiation function. Admission control is responsible for comparing the resource requirement arising from the QoS levels associated with a new activity with the available resources in the system. The decision as to whether a new activity can be created depends on system policies as well as simple resource availability. For example, if the new activity has a high priority it may preempt resources currently dedicated to another activity.

QoS maintenance, monitoring and policing

To maintain an agreed level of QoS it is often not sufficient to *statically* dedicate resources to an activity at QoS negotiation time as described above. Instead, *dynamic* QoS maintenance is frequently required to ensure that the required performance of individual system components is kept within bounds. The QoS maintenance function is particularly important in cases where resources must be statistically multiplexed among activities. Prime examples are processor schedulers and ATM switch schedulers which must simultaneously meet the targets of QoS-controlled activities while dealing with transient overloads and avoiding starvation of low-priority activities.

QoS monitoring is used to allow each level of the system to track the ongoing QoS levels achieved by the lower layers and compare them with the initial requirement. It often takes the form of a feedback loop which monitors the QoS being achieved by the monitored component, compares it against the target and then performs fine-grained resource adjustments if necessary. At the interface of the top-level activity the QoS monitoring function issues a *degradation indication* to the user when it determines that the lower layers have failed to maintain the QoS of the activity and nothing further can be done by the maintenance function. In response to such an indication the user can choose either to adapt to the reduced level of QoS, terminate the activity or attempt to *renegotiate* (see next section) the QoS of the activity.

QoS policing is used when a symmetrical service contract is in force. Policing can be viewed as the dual of monitoring: the latter observes whether QoS contracted by a provider is being maintained whereas the former observes whether the QoS contracted by a user is being adhered to. Policing is often only appropriate where administrative and charging boundaries are being crossed, for example at a user-to-network interface. The action taken by the policing function can range from accepting violations and merely notifying the user, through to shaping the incoming traffic to an acceptable QoS level terminating the activity.

QoS renegotiation

Renegotiation is distinguished from the component level "adjustment" referred to above in that the latter involves tuning the local QoS of an individual component whereas the former involves a global reconfiguration of all components of an activity through reinvocation of the QoS specification and negotiation functions. Note, however, that it is not necessarily the case that renegotiation can only be initiated by the top-level user of an activity; activities themselves may form components of a hierarchically structured top-level activity.

Although renegotiation is commonly initiated in response to the receipt of a degradation indication, it is also requested in a number of other situations. For example, a user may simply wish to conserve global system resources by downgrading a low-priority activity. Alternatively, the user may wish to use the same communication channel successively for different purposes at different times. As an example of this latter possibility, a flow activity may be used for the transmission of full motion video interspersed with intervals of slow motion, or it may be upgraded from monochrome to color video, or telephone quality to CD quality audio.

11.3   QoS in standards

Because the effects of the new technological and application environment discussed in Section 11.1 are only just making themselves felt, it is not surprising that current network architectures fail to comprehensively address the need for QoS support of distributed multimedia applications over high-speed networks. To give an impression of the degree of QoS support in present-day systems, this section reviews the ISO's Reference Model for Open Systems Interconnection (OSI-RM) and the CCITT's I-Series recommendations for ATM networking with regard to their support of QoS. The OSI reference model and the I-series recommendations are highlighted as the most prominent of the currently standardized network architectures.

11.3.1   ISO's reference model for Open Systems Interconnection

The International Standards Organization (ISO) has developed a set of standards for computer communications in the form of the seven-layer OSI-RM, and these standards are now mature and widely implemented. However, the OSI-RM evolved in an environment of data-only applications running over low-speed networks, and the QoS support provided by the OSI-RM reflects the limited QoS requirements of this class of applications. QoS support in the OSI-RM is limited to statically defined parameters intended to be supported at the session and transport layers. To enable applications to access QoS facilities, the OSI upper layers (application and presentation layers) simply map QoS dimensions (parameters) through to the lower layers unchanged. At the transport layer, QoS parameters relate to each of the phases of the session; that is, connection establishment, data transfer and connection release. The parameters are also classified as either *performance-oriented* or *non-performance-oriented* (Henshall and Shaw, 1988). Non-performance-oriented parameters do not directly affect the performance of the communications but are concerned with protection, priority and cost QoS categories. The complete set of parameters together with their interpretations is given in Table 11.1 which lists the performance-oriented parameters and Table 11.2 which lists the non-performance-oriented parameters.

Table 11.1 OSI performance-oriented QoS parameters.

Parameter	Description
Throughput	The maximum number of bytes, contained in Service Data Units (SDUs), that may be successfully transferred in unit time by the service provider over the connection, on a sustained basis.
Transit delay	The time delay between the issuing of a *data.request* and the corresponding *data.indication*. The parameter is usually specified as a pair of values, a statistical average and a maximum. Those data transfers where a receiving service user exercises flow control are excluded. The computations are all based on SDUs of a fixed size.
Residual error rate	The probability that an SDU is transferred with error, or that it is lost, or that a duplicate copy is transferred.
Establishment delay	The delay between the issuing *connect.request* and the corresponding *connect.confirm*.
Establishment failure probability	The probability that a requested connection is not established within the specified maximum acceptable establishment delay as a consequence of actions that are solely attributable to the service provider.
Transfer failure probability	The probability that the observed performance with respect to transit delay, residual error rate or throughput will be worse than the specified level of performance. The failure probability is, as such, specified for each measure of performance of data transfer, discussed above.
Resilience	The probability that a service provider will, on its own, release the connection, or reset it, within a specified interval of time.
Release delay	The maximum delay between the issuing of a *disconnect.request* primitive by the service user and a corresponding *disconnect.indication* primitive issued by the service provider.
Release Failure Probability	The probability that the service provider is unable to release the connection within a specified maximum release delay.

Table 11.2 OSI non-performance-oriented QoS parameters.

Parameter	Description
Protection	The extent to which a service provider attempts to prevent unauthorized monitoring or manipulation of user data. The level of protection is specified qualitatively by selecting either *(i)* no protection; *(ii)* protection against passive monitoring; *(iii)* protection against modification, addition or deletion, or *(iv)* a combination of *(i)* and *(ii)*.
Priority	High-priority connections are serviced before lower ones. Lower-priority connection packets will be dropped before high-priority packets, should the network become congested.
Cost determinants	A parameter to define the maximum acceptable cost for a network connection. It may be stated in relative or absolute terms. Final actions on this parameter are left to the specific network providers.

11.3.2   CCITT I-series recommendations

The CCITT have recognized the need for QoS configurability in the emerging standards for broadband integrated services digital networks (B-ISDN) which are to be based on asynchronous transfer mode (ATM) networking technology. As a result of this recognition they have issued a series of draft recommendations known as the I-series recommendations which define a fairly comprehensive set of QoS dimensions at the ATM layer. QoS characterization in ATM networks is applicable at three different levels. The *call control* and *connection levels* are concerned with the establishment and release of calls and the allocation of resources along a path of ATM switch nodes. The *cell control* level is concerned with the data transfer phase itself.

At the call control level, the available parameters are similar to those defined in OSI for analogous purposes: that is, establishment delay, establishment failure probability or release delay. At the connection level the parameters outlined in Table 11.3 are applicable.

The first four parameters are intended to allow traffic to be characterized in advance so that the network can both allocate resources to support the desired traffic patterns and police the traffic inserted at the network by the user to ensure that the user does not attempt to inject data into the network at a higher QoS than that agreed to. It is also intended to use these parameters to support QoS renegotiation (known as *in-call renegotiation*). The remaining parameters control the degree of reliability expected by the user from the network.

As an example of traffic characterization using the CCITT parameters, a characterization of variable bit rate encoded video could be: peak rate = 50 Mbps, average cell arrival rate = 25 Mpbs, burstiness = 2 and the peak duration = 10 ms.

Table 11.3 CCITT QoS parameters.

Parameter	Description
Peak arrival rate of cells	The maximum resources required by the application at peak load.
Peak duration	The average duration of the maximum load.
Average cell arrival rate	The average amount of network resources requested by the source. This is the number of cells measured during the duration of the connection divided by the duration.
Burstiness	The ratio between the peak cell rate and the average cell rate.
Cell loss ratio (CLR)	The ratio of the number of lost cells to transmitted cells. This type of error usually occurs because of congestion in switches.
Cell insertion ratio (CIR)	This type of error occurs when the address field in the header is corrupted to another valid network address.
Bit error rate (BER)	Defined as the number of bits which are delivered erroneously divided by the total number transmitted. These sorts of errors are mainly caused by the transmission system.

11.3.3   Evaluation

It is clear that QoS support in the OSI standards is severely limited when related to the generality of the discussion in Section 11.2. The current OSI service definitions do not provide for the specification of a full range of QoS dimensions such as jitter, criticality and cost. In addition, there is no support for QoS monitoring and no interface for renegotiation, and the precise semantics of responsibilities and guarantees are not clear. Even more limiting is the fact that at the protocol level there is no notion of QoS management in terms of QoS negotiation, mapping, resource allocation, and QoS maintenance. It is simply assumed that the underlying network provider will support the requested QoS levels.

Another important observation is that the OSI upper layers are not QoS-aware. QoS parameters are simply mapped unchanged through to the transport layer. If users want to specify QoS they are forced to drop below the level of abstraction provided by the upper layer architecture and interact with layers that are intended to be hidden from applications.

The CCITT's ATM recommendations are more comprehensive and include a fairly detailed traffic characterization model. The major service-related limitation here is the lack of consideration of how traffic characterization at the ATM layer can be derived from user QoS needs at the transport layer and above. Below the service interface, the current state of ATM standardization suffers from a comparable lack of QoS management support to that found in the OSI field. There is currently no consensus on how resources will be allocated and how requested QoS levels will be maintained, policed and renegotiated in both networks and end-systems.

The essential characteristics of the current state of QoS provision in the major standards may therefore be summarized as follows:

- *Incompleteness*: current service interfaces typically provide only a small subset of the facilities outlined in Section 11.2;

- *Lack of mechanisms to support QoS guarantees*: research is needed in basic protocol and monitoring mechanisms so that contracted QoS levels can, in fact, be maintained;

- *Lack of overall framework*: it is necessary to evolve an overall architectural framework to build on and reconcile the existing notions of QoS at different systems levels and among different network architectures.

11.4   Layer-specific QoS

Most of the developments in QoS provision have occurred in the context of individual architectural layers. Much less progress has been made in addressing the large-scale architectural QoS requirements implied in the section above. This section reviews some of the layer-specific work and attempts to extract some recurrent issues which have arisen in the research. We leave the question of large-scale architectural issues until Section 11.5 in which the progress achieved so far in this area is assessed.

The layers considered in this section are the ATM network, transport, operating system and distributed system platform. The scope of the network, transport and operating system layers is self-explanatory. By distributed systems platform we have in mind operating-system-independent application support layers such as the computational model of the ISO's Open Distributed Processing (ODP) standards (ISO, 1992b), the ANSA computational model (APM Ltd., 1993), the OSF's Distributed Computing Environment (Open Software Foundation, 1992).

11.4.1   Network layer

Unlike some existing telecommunications networks which dedicate a physical path (and thus a guaranteed QoS) to each connection, ATM networks operate by multiplexing fixed-sized packets (known as cells) from different *virtual connections* over the same physical link. This multiplexing technique has the potential advantage of "statistical gain" whereby network capacity can be over-committed because of the unlikelihood that all connections will use their maximum bandwidth allocation at any one time. At the present time, significant research is being undertaken in the ATM arena to design networks which are consistent with QoS provision in the face of such statistical behavior. In outline, research in this area is concerned with the following topics.

QoS categorization

Several different ways of categorizing QoS guarantees in packet switched networks have been identified. In (Clark, 1992) a distinction is made between three different service commitments: *(i)* guaranteed service for hard real-time applications; *(ii)* predicted service, which utilizes the measured performance of delays and is targeted towards continuous media applications; and *(iii)* best-effort service, where no QoS guarantees are provided. A unified traffic scheduling mechanism based on a combination of weighted fair queuing and static priority algorithms is also discussed. In the Lancaster QoS-A project (see Section 11.5.2 below), commitment is supported both at the end-systems and in the network. The idea of QoS commitment introduced by Clark *et al.* is extended; that is, each individual QoS dimension can be configured to meet a specific level of service commitment (Campbell *et al.*, 1993).

Service discipline

Means of providing QoS guarantees in high-performance networks have been widely covered in the literature. For example, in (Lazar *et al.*, 1990), an Asynchronous Time-Sharing network which provides a QoS capability is proposed. The switching provided by the network is novel in that the concept of QoS explicitly appears in the design specification at both the edge (at call level) and the core (at cell level) of the network. The network supports four well-defined traffic classes which support circuit emulation, voice and video, file transfer and network management flows. Following on from this work (Hyman *et al.*, 1992) describes a joint scheduling and admission control mechanism used to guarantee the QoS of each traffic class.

Reservation and admission algorithms

The area of resource reservation is fundamental in providing end-to-end QoS guarantees. There have been a number of significant contributions to resource allocation in communication networks which have emerged over the past few years. For example, ST-II (Topolcic, 1990) is a network layer resource reservation protocol designed specifically for packetized audio and video communications across the Internet. In contrast to ST-II which provides source-initiated point-to-multipoint flows, RSVP (Zhang *et al.*, 1993) provides receiver-initiated reservation and multipoint-to-multipoint support. SRP (Anderson *et al.*, 1992), also designed for the Internet, supports end-system and networks resource allocation. The Lancaster QoS-A flow reservation protocol (Campbell *et al.*, 1993) is tailored for the local ATM environment and borrows heavily from ST-II and SRP. The QoS-A flow reservation service differs from ST-II, SRP and RSVP in that it supports a fast connect and a forward reservation service.

11.4.2 Transport layer

A large number of research teams have investigated the provision of QoS at the transport layer. As a significant example of such work, the recent Esprit OSI 95 project has proposed an enhanced transport service and protocol collectively described as TPX (Danthine *et al.*, 1992). TPX provides support for connection-oriented services with sequenced delivery, configurable and renegotiable QoS, and error notification. It also provides connectionless, multicast, and request-reply services. The enhanced connection-oriented service takes QoS parameters relating to throughput, delay, delay jitter, error selection policy and relative priority. Three transport-level QoS semantics in addition to "best effort" are proposed for this service: *compulsory*, *threshold* and *maximal* QoS. When a *compulsory* semantic is selected, the transport protocol commits to monitor the connection and will abort the service should the QoS drop below the requested value. The *threshold* QoS semantic, which is motivated by the needs of a multimedia service (Leopold, 1992b), commits the service provider to monitor the ongoing performance of the connection. In this case, however, a QoS indication informs the user should the QoS degrade below the requested value. The *maximal* QoS value deals with limiting the over-utilization of communications resources on a connection. In (Danthine *et.al.*, 1992) a number of negotiation rules are laid out for each of the QoS values. The threshold semantic is suitable for multimedia communications where applications may accommodate service fluctuations. The compulsory value, however, is not a suitable semantic for the multimedia communications as many applications prefer degraded service to no service. The OSI 95 transport service provides a set of QoS features which are suitable for a range of transport service users' needs; however, QoS maintenance, commitment and adaptation have not been addressed in any detail.

The QoS-A project (Campbell *et al.*, 1993) has also defined a QoS enhanced transport service interface. In this design, the QoS requirements of the user and the potential degree of service commitment of the network provider are unified and formalized in a *service contract* agreed by both parties. The service contract subsumes the well-accepted performance parameters of jitter, error, delay and throughput, but also allows the specification of a wider range of options. These are characterized in terms of the following clauses:

- *Flow spec* characterizes the user's QoS in terms of a set of values for a range of QoS dimensions;

- *Commitment* clause specifies the degree of resource commitment required from the lower layers (see below);

- *Adaptation* clause identifies actions to be taken in the event of violations to the contracted service;

- *Maintenance* clause selects the degree of monitoring and active QoS maintenance required of the QoS-A;

- *Connection type* clause selects from on-demand, fast reservation, and forward reservation connection services;

- *Cost* clause specifies the costs the user is willing to incur for the services requested.

While the flow spec permits the user to express the required performance parameters in a quantitative manner, the commitment clause of the service contract allows these requirements to be refined in a qualitative way so as to allow a distinction to be made between hard and soft network performance guarantees. The commitment clause permits the selection of one of three possible commitment types (Ferrari *et al.*, 1992): *(i) deterministic*, which is typically used for hard real-time performance applications; *(ii) statistical*, which allows for a certain percentage of violations in the requested flow spec and is particularly suitable for continuous media applications; and *(iii) best effort*, the lowest priority commitment and synonymous with a datagram service. Once a flow has been established the transport protocol actively monitors and maintains the flow based on the user-supplied flow spec and service commitment identified in the service contract.

García (1993) reports on the development of a transport service tailored for the support of continuous media communications. Multimedia synchronization support is a novel feature of the transport service interface (Campbell *et al.*, 1992c). Connections are represented as QoS-configurable simplex streams which can be unicast or multicast. The protocol, which uses rate-based flow control, can detect lost or corrupt data. When this happens, the transport service user is informed via an error announcement.

The HeiTS project (Hehmann *et al.*, 1991) has concentrated on the integration of transport QoS and resource management (primarily processor scheduling). HeiTS puts considerable emphasis on an optimized buffer pool which minimizes copying and also allows efficient data transfer between local devices. The scheduling policy used in the supporting operating system is a rate-monotonic scheme whereby the priority of an operating system thread performing protocol processing is proportional to the message rate accepted. However, QoS monitoring, maintenance and commitment are not addressed in this work.

Other significant work on QoS provision at the transport layer has come from The Tenet Group at the University of California at Berkeley. This group have developed a family of protocols (Wolfinger and Moran, 1991) which run over an experimental wide area ATM network known as Aurora (Clark, 1991). The protocol family includes the Real Time Internet Protocol (RTIP), the Continuous Media Transport Protocol (CMTP) and the Real Time Channel Administration Protocol (RCAP). The latter provides generic connection establishment, resource reservation, and signaling functions for the rest of the protocol family. CMTP is explicitly designed for continuous media support. It is a lightweight protocol which runs on top of RTIP and provides sequenced and periodic delivery of continuous media samples with QoS control over throughput, delays and error bounds. Notification of all undelivered and/or corrupted data can be provided if the client selects this option. The client interface to CMTP includes facilities to specify traffic characteristics in terms of burstiness, which is useful for variable bit rate encoding techniques, and workahead, which allows the protocol to deliver faster than the nominal rate if data is available. CMTP also permits dynamic QoS renegotiation by sending a special *on* Transport Protocol Data Unit which contains the new QoS parameters at the start of a new "stream", and an *off* Transport Protocol Data Unit to signal the onset of a silent period.

11.4.3 Operating system layer

The need for QoS in operating systems

Traditionally, work on QoS has concentrated on the network and communications infrastructure. Recently, however, the topic has become increasingly important in an end-system context because of the interest in operating system support for multimedia applications. It is becoming recognized in the multimedia community that classes of application exist which must actively manipulate real-time continuous media data in an operating system environment (as opposed to merely controlling and supervising the flow of media in specialized hardware). In order to support multimedia applications, operating systems must provide a degree of QoS support to uphold the real-time isochronous nature of continuous media data types such as audio and video.

There has already been considerable research in operating systems support for more traditional real-time applications (Stankovic and Ramamritham, 1988). However, such real-time operating systems tend to be tailored towards specific application areas such as factory automation or robotics. Consequently, they tend to assume a *static* environment where the number of processes and their resource requirements are fixed and known in advance. Unfortunately, this assumption of static resource needs is not valid in the multimedia field where it is important that real-time applications coexist with existing applications and run on general-purpose workstations. What is required are QoS driven operating systems which can support existing applications and simultaneously offer predictable performance in a dynamic and unpredictable environment.

One solution to this problem is to provide adequate resources to comfortably meet all anticipated demand for processing capacity, disk bandwidth, and so on. In practice, however, this is unlikely to be achievable given the heavy resource needs of continuous media data (Davies and Nicol, 1991). Instead, it is important that *resource management strategies* are developed to more effectively exploit limited resources and provide some guarantees of predictability. This task, although challenging, is eased by the inherently "soft" real-time nature of many multimedia applications – for example, it is often acceptable to downgrade picture quality in a videophone application if insufficient resources are available to provide adequate audio quality. Resource management strategies are required for all areas of operating system management including processor scheduling, communications, device management and memory management. There is also a need for new abstractions and interfaces which capture the notion of QoS driven resources.

State of the art

To date, most of the work on QoS in the operating system community has focused on *processor scheduling*. It is now recognized that currently used scheduling policies, primarily priority-based scheduling, are too static and coarse-grained for the support of multiple isochronous sessions in a dynamic environment. In such sessions, each information unit has an implicit deadline and, hence, it is natural to schedule the processes handling these units on the basis of such deadlines. This has led to the adoption of *earliest deadline first* scheduling (Liu and Layland, 1973) as an attractive policy for multimedia. Recent research has proposed the use of *split-level scheduling* for the processing of continuous media (Govindan and Anderson, 1991). In such schemes, the application programmer is presented with the abstraction of multiple user-level threads in a single address space (the use of user-level threads has the advantage of minimizing context switches in a multi-threaded application). Responsibility for scheduling of user-level threads is split between a user-level scheduler and a kernel-level scheduler. The two schedulers communicate through the use of shared memory, to ensure that scheduling decisions are globally valid.

The issue of QoS-driven *communication protocols* has already been dealt with in some detail in the previous section. However, the *implementation* of protocols in an operating system environment remains to be discussed. Protocol implementation involves predictability issues such as the need for correct scheduling of protocol activities, and efficiency issues such as the minimization of data copying, system calls and context switches. Efficiency considerations have increased in importance as the communications bottleneck has shifted from the network to the end-system in the new communications environment. The current situation is that a number of widely agreed principles for QoS-driven protocol implementation are beginning to emerge, including the avoidance of multiplexing (Tennenhouse, 1990), the use of hardware assists for protocol processing and the importance of executing protocol code in a schedulable process rather than as an interrupt service routine.

In the area of *device management*, most of the research has concentrated on the development of storage techniques for continuous media. Examples of research in this area are the Video-on-Demand service designed at the University of California at San Diego (Vin and Rangan, 1993), the Continuous Media File System developed at the University of California at Berkeley (Anderson *et al.*, 1992), and the Lancaster Continuous Media Storage Server (Lougher and Shepherd, 1993). Most of this research has concentrated on disk layout and disk head scheduling. The aim is to optimize the layout of continuous media data on the disk to minimize disk head movements and guarantee transfer rates. The technique of *disk striping* is commonly used whereby successive segments of a continuous media stream are stored on separate disks arranged in an array. This technique enables N disks to provide a throughput approaching N times that of a single disk. So far, however, these techniques have failed to produce fully scalable solutions for the simultaneous retrieval of large numbers of continuous media streams.

Finally, there has been some work carried out on the overall architecture of QoS-driven operating systems. Most of this work has attempted to maintain a level of compatibility with the de facto standard UNIX interface. Two main approaches can be identified: (i) modifying existing UNIX implementations, and (ii) completely re-implementing UNIX. In the first approach, alterations are made to the existing UNIX kernel to provide more predictable behavior. For example, a range of projects is currently under way at SUN Microsystems in this area. Their proposal is for *time-driven resource management* (Hanko *et al.*, 1991) which allows applications to signal their likely forthcoming resource requirements in terms of QoS dimensions such as quantity, deadline and priority. The second approach is to preserve the standard UNIX interface, but reimplement it in terms of the *micro-kernel* model. Examples of micro-kernels capable of supporting UNIX interfaces are Chorus (Bricker *et al.*, 1991), Mach (Accetta *et al.*, 1986) and Amoeba (Tanenbaum *et al.*, 1988). Work has been undertaken at CWI, Amsterdam to support continuous media in an Amoeba-based UNIX environment (Bulterman and van Liere, 1991). Work is also being carried out at Lancaster University using Chorus as the basis of a distributed system with end-to-end QoS support (Coulson *et al.*, 1993a). Finally, work has been carried out in a Mach environment to provide processor scheduling appropriate to continuous media (Govindan and Anderson, 1991; Tokuda and Kitayama, 1993).

Outstanding issues

There has been considerable progress in operating system support for QoS with most progress having been made in the specific areas of communications and scheduling. There has been considerably less work on *integration* of the various components into an overall operating system design. Most significantly, work is required to integrate techniques for communications and scheduling. For example, to implement an audio connection with a given quality of service, it is necessary to achieve the desired quality of service in the transport protocol *and* to schedule threads at the desired rate to deal with the arrival of audio data. Such integration should also eventually extend to areas such as device management and memory management.

In addition, work is required on the integration of the abstract quality of service management functions described in Section 11.2.2 into the operating system environment. Functions such as negotiation protocols, admission control, and graceful degradation have a wider scope than individual resource managers and are important for the correct operation of the system as a whole. However, as yet almost no work has been carried out in this area.

A number of other outstanding issues remain:

i)   It is not clear where protocol processing should be performed in future operating systems: some researchers still advocate traditional kernel implementations; others advocate the use of specialized hardware to implement protocol processing (Arnould *et al.*, 1989); a third group suggest that protocols should be implemented in user space (Forin *et al.*, 1990) (this is consistent with trends in micro-kernel design to move functionality out of the kernel and into user space).

ii)   It is recognized that earliest deadline first policies do not operate well in overload situations. Some researchers therefore propose extensions to earliest deadline first policies either by adding resource reservation or by aborting certain threads (Tokuda and Kitayama, 1993). It is not clear at this stage whether such extensions are required in a generalized QoS support environment.

iii) The real-time synchronization of related continuous media streams in the operating system environment remains an unsolved problem. Multimedia applications need related streams to be tied together for such purposes as maintaining "lip-sync" between audio and video streams without, at the same time, violating the temporal integrity of the individual streams. This problem has been addressed at a specification level – for example, (Little and Ghafoor, 1990), but there has been little work on realizing the specified behavior in the operating system environment.

iv)   More work is required on abstractions for QoS-driven operating systems. For example, many application platforms are structured in terms of objects, but it is not yet clear what level of support at the operating system level is needed to support objects with real-time behavior. In addition, multimedia applications typically use the concept of structured objects to represent multimedia documents. It is not clear how much support is required for such abstractions in multimedia file servers. Most experimental file servers in existence today deal only with individual streams.

v)   As discussed above, it is necessary in the emerging application environment for applications with varying needs and assumptions to coexist in an operating system environment able to simultaneously satisfy all their various requirements. For example, few real systems have been built with the ability to effectively run batch mode applications, interactive applications and continuous media applications.

11.4.4   Distributed systems platform

The need for QoS in distributed systems

The role of the distributed systems platform is to provide a network- and computer-independent programming environment for the development of distributed applications. There has been considerable research in this area over the past ten years (Mullender, 1993). However, until recently, there has been very little work on quality of service support in such platforms. With the emergence of distributed multimedia applications, however, quality of service has become a major issue in distributed systems research. There has also been some relevant research in the more specialist area of distributed real-time systems (Stankovic and Ramamritham, 1988).

Quality of service in distributed systems platforms is fundamentally an *end-to-end* issue, that is, from application to application. For example, consider remote access to a storage sequence of video. In the distributed systems platform, QoS specification should apply to the complete flow of information from the remote server, across the network to the point of application. This requires careful coordination of disk scheduling, thread scheduling and the various layers of communications protocols. QoS specification at this level should also be *user-oriented* rather than system-oriented. In other words, the QoS dimensions provided should be meaningful to the end-user, and lower-level considerations such as the rate and burst size of a transport connection should be hidden. Finally, it is important that QoS specifications are *declarative*, that is, users should be specifying what is required rather than how this is to be achieved.

In a distributed system, there are three areas where QoS might apply.

i)   *Message passing services*: these allow a programmer to explicitly send a message between two processes in a distributed system. Normally, message passing in distributed systems is asynchronous, that is, there is a delay between the sending and the receiving of the message. Such message passing services are provided in, for example, distributed operating systems such as Chorus (Bricker *et al.*, 1991) and Mach (Accetta *et al.*, 1986). QoS support in this context is concerned with bounding the latency of the message. It is also desirable to specify whether delivery should be reliable or unreliable. Finally, if facilities are offered to multicast messages to a group of processes, it is important to be able to specify the constraints on the ordering of message arrivals (Birman *et al.*, 1991).

ii) *Remote invocation*: this allows operations in a server process to be invoked by a client process. The results of this invocation are then returned directly to the client. This style of interaction is often referred to as the remote procedure call paradigm and can be found in platforms such as ANSAware (APM Ltd, 1993) and the Distributed Computing Environment (Open Software Foundation, 1992). QoS specification on remote invocations is more abstract than with message passing and is defined over the whole interaction between client and server (involving a number of message exchanges). Crucial QoS dimensions in this category include the round-trip latency and the semantics of the remote operation (for example, at least once, at most once, or exactly once).

iii) *Stream services*: these are connections which support the transmission of continuous media data such as audio or video. Such services have only recently been developed and are not yet available in commercial distributed systems. Quality of service in this context is concerned with managing the ongoing flow of data between a continuous media source and sink and is therefore defined in terms of parameters such as required throughput, latency, jitter and error characteristics (Hehmann *et al.*, 1990).

State of the art

A number of experimental QoS-driven distributed systems platforms are now beginning to emerge. For example, researchers at Lancaster University have developed an extended version of ANSAware (APM Ltd, 1993) featuring bounded invocations and QoS-controlled streams (Coulson *et al.*, 1992). Similar work has also been undertaken at Cambridge University (Nicolaou, 1990).

More recently, research on quality of service has centered on Open Distributed Processing (ODP) standardization. ODP is an ISO-sponsored activity to develop international standards for distributed computing in potentially heterogeneous environments. The ODP community have now recognized the importance of quality of service and have proposed extensions to the ODP Computational Language to support QoS specification.

The ODP Computational Language defines the basic concepts necessary to develop computer- and network-independent designs of distributed applications. The language is object-based and features concepts such as computational objects, operational interfaces, stream interfaces and operation invocation (ISO, 1992b). QoS specification is included in the form of annotations on ODP interfaces. In addition, extensions have recently been proposed to enable the creation of explicit *bindings* between interfaces. Bindings are abstractions over communication between objects and can only be established if both type and QoS specifications match. Bindings are themselves objects; this provides a placeholder and access point for the management of QoS of the binding.

Ongoing research in this area is being carried out at CNET in France (Stefani, 1993). The aim of this research is to develop a more complete Computational

Language for both real-time and multimedia applications. In the CNET approach, quality of service annotations are written in a real-time logic called QL. The logic statements are then used to generate quality of service monitors written in the real-time control language Esterel. This work is also being extended, in a collaboration with Lancaster University, to include engineering support for the enhanced Computational Language (Coulson and Blair, 1993a).

In summary, there has historically been little work on QoS support in the distributed systems community. Recently, though, there have been some significant developments particularly in the context of ODP standardization. However, it is clear that further research is needed to provide a complete framework for QoS management incorporating the various functions identified in Section 11.2.2. Furthermore, work is required to integrate the distributed system view of quality of service with the other layers discussed in this section.

11.5   Towards an integrated view of QoS

In recognition of the QoS limitations of current systems a number of research teams have recently proposed a *systems architectural* approach to QoS provision in distributed systems. The intention is to extend current systems by defining a set of service interfaces which generalize and formalize the existing OSI and CCITT QoS services and also provide a framework for the integration of new QoS management mechanisms. It is hoped that a systems approach can help avoid duplication of functions across layers and maximize efficient QoS management by providing a global framework for QoS specification and management extending from the distributed application platform through the transport subsystem and the network.

One significant pioneering contribution to the provision of QoS in the OSI domain is being made by the "Quality of Service Framework" New Work Item project, the aim of which is to enable the future extension of OSI standards in the direction of QoS provision by defining a reference architecture and standard terminology. The intention of this project at this stage is *not* actually to develop new standards for QoS in the OSI-RM.

Another project which is attempting to build a framework for QoS provision in distributed systems is the UK SERC-funded Quality of Service Architecture (QoS-A) project at Lancaster University. This project is more pragmatically biased than the OSI initiative. It is the aim of the QoS-A project to design and implement a QoS framework in a specific distributed systems environment consisting of multimedia applications running over an ODP platform which, in turn, is supported by newly developed QoS configurable transport services running over a local, campus-wide, ATM network.

The remainder of this section describes the above two projects in more detail.

11.5.1   SC21 QoS framework

The SC21 QoS Framework project was initiated by the ISO to address many of the QoS inconsistencies and deficiencies inherent in the current suite of OSI protocols and services: incompleteness, lack of mechanisms to support QoS guarantees, and lack of an overall framework.

The QoS framework represents a progression in the development of QoS for OSI by describing a set of concepts, services and mechanisms that can be applied to all OSI layers and to OSI management. The key QoS framework concepts (which are related to but not identical with the concepts introduced in Section 11.2) include:

- QoS requirements, which are realized through QoS management and maintenance entities;

- QoS characteristics, which are a description of the fundamental aspects of QoS that have to be managed;

- QoS categories, which represent a policy governing a group of QoS requirements specific to a particular environment such as time-critical communications; and

- QoS management functions, which can be combined in various ways and applied to various QoS characteristics in order to meet QoS requirements.

The framework, which is illustrated in Figure 11.1, is made up of two types of management entities that attempt to meet the QoS requirements by monitoring, maintaining and controlling QoS dimensions:

- Layer-specific entities: The task of the policy control function is to determine the policy which applies at a specific layer of the open system. The policy control function models any priority actions that must be performed to control the operation of the layer. The definition of a particular policy is layer-specific and therefore cannot be generalized. Policy may, however, include aspects of security, time-critical communications and resource control. The role of the QoS control function is to determine, select and configure the appropriate protocol entities to meet layer-specific QoS goals.

- System-wide entities: The system management agent is used in conjunction with OSI systems management protocols to enable system resources to be remotely managed. The local resource manager represents end-system control of resources. The system QoS control function combines two system-wide capabilities: to tune performance of protocol entities and to modify the capability of remote systems via OSI systems management. The OSI systems management interface is supported by the systems management manager which provides a standard interface to monitor, control and manage end-systems. The system policy control function interacts with each layer-specific policy control function to provide an overall selection of QoS functions and facilities.

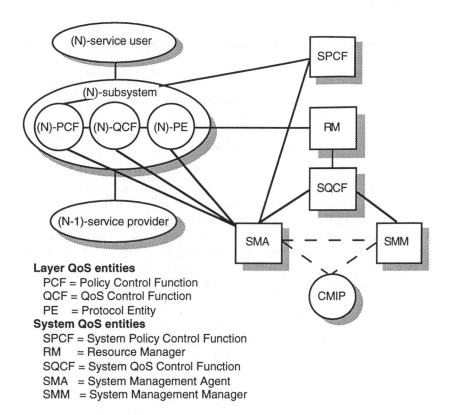

Layer QoS entities
  PCF = Policy Control Function
  QCF = QoS Control Function
  PE   = Protocol Entity
System QoS entities
  SPCF = System Policy Control Function
  RM   = Resource Manager
  SQCF = System QoS Control Function
  SMA   = System Management Agent
  SMM   = System Management Manager

Figure 11.1 QoS framework model.

11.5.2   Quality of Service Architecture

The Lancaster Quality of Service Architecture (QoS-A) (Campbell *et al.*, 1993) is a layered architecture of services and mechanisms for QoS management in an environment based on the ISO's Open Distributed Processing standards and ATM networks. The architecture is geared mainly to the support of continuous media applications and uses the concept of a flow described in Section 11.2.1 above.

In functional terms, the QoS-A illustrated in Figure 11.2 is broadly divided into a number of layers and planes. The upper layer consists of a *distributed applications platform* provided by an ODP-compatible distributed systems platform with services to provide multimedia communications and QoS configuration in an object-based environment (Coulson *et al.*, 1993b). Supporting this is a *transport layer* which contains a range of QoS-configurable protocols. For example, separate protocols are provided for continuous media and constrained latency message protocols. The three vertical planes in the QoS-A are as follows:

- The Protocol Plane: this consists of a *user plane* and a *control plane*. Separate protocol profiles are used for the control and data components of flows because of the essentially different QoS requirements of control and data.

Control generally requires a low-latency, full-duplex assured service whereas multimedia data generally requires a range of non-assured, high-throughput simplex services.

- The QoS Maintenance Plane: this contains a number of layer-specific QoS managers. These are each responsible for the fine-grained monitoring and maintenance of their associated protocol entities. Based on flow monitoring information and a user-supplied service contract, QoS managers maintain the level of QoS in the managed flow by means of fine-grained resource tuning strategies.

- The Flow Management Plane: this is responsible for *flow establishment* (including flow admission control, resource reservation and QoS-based routing), *QoS renegotiation*, *QoS mapping* (which translates QoS representations between layers) and *QoS adaptation*. The latter is a facility whereby users can pre-specify actions to be taken in the event of QoS degradations. For example, users can choose to take no action, to be informed via a degradation indication, or to transparently renegotiate.

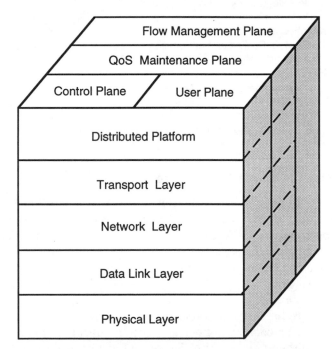

Figure 11.2 Lancaster Quality of Service Architecture.

11.5.3   Other QoS research

Work carried out at the University of Pennsylvania (Nahrstedt an Smith, 1993) describes a *brokerage* model which incorporates QoS translation, and QoS negotiation and renegotiation. The notion of *eras* is introduced to describe variations in QoS parameters for complex, long-lived applications. Negotiation and renegotiation provide a mechanism to signal variations in QOS performance parameters at the user–network interface. They are invoked at era boundaries, and can aid resource allocation. In the model, application requirements and network resource allocation are expressed in fundamentally different terms and languages. A key part of the model, called a *broker,* is responsible for the translation of QoS at the user–network interface.

In addition, several projects in the European funded RACE program are concerned with QoS for integrated broadband networks. A significant contribution has been made by the QOSMIC (R.1082) project which studied QoS concepts in broadband networks, focusing on the user–network interface in particular. The major goal of the project was the specification of a QoS model for service life-cycle management which maps the user communication requirements to network performance parameters in a methodical manner. The model takes into account the life cycle of service from both the user and network provider viewpoints, and QOS performance mapping between the viewpoints based on the decomposition of end-to-end services into elements. The service life cycle covers conception, planning, provision and operation of multimedia services in an integrated broadband environment. In some related work Jung and Seret (Jung and Seret, 1993) propose a framework for the translation of the performance parameters between the ATM Adaptation Layer (AAL) and ATM layers. They extend the QOSMIC model to include QoS verification. In this case the user can verify whether the achieved bearer QoS provided by the ATM network meets the contracted requirements expressed in terms of performance parameters.

11.6 Conclusion

In this chapter we aimed to indicate the importance of Quality of Service management in distributed systems, and to show how this could be built into the framework of the OSI communications standards.

We summarized and evaluated key research in QoS support and ended the chapter by describing work that has the aim of integrating and extending some of the layer-specific research into a broader architecture. The notion of a flow and a service contract were introduced as key concepts in capturing, requesting and negotiating end-to-end QoS. We also introduced the idea of flow management which provides for the monitoring and maintenance of the contracted QoS. These QoS concepts emerged from work carried out at Lancaster University and are motivated by the widely accepted communication needs of distributed multimedia applications.

The Quality of Service architecture (QoS-A) promotes the idea of *integrated* QoS, spanning the end-systems and the network, and takes the support of QoS for a wide range of applications as its primary goal. Many researchers to date have concentrated on either the network or the end-system in isolation. In contrast, in the QoS-A work, QoS concepts are coherently applied across all architectural layers, resulting in a complete framework for the specification and implementation of the multimedia flows in the local ATM environment.

The area of network support for flows remains an important aspect of the QoS architecture which is yet to be addressed. This future work will draw heavily from the recent literature on providing QoS guarantees in packet switched networks. In particular, the investigation of suitable switch scheduling disciplines and resource management strategies for the QoS-A is required, given the types of service commitment proposed in the QoS-A at the transport service interface.

Acknowledgments

The QoS-A project is funded as part of the UK Science and Engineering Research Council specially promoted program in Integrated Multiservice Communication Networks (GR/H77194) in cooperation with Netcomm Ltd. The authors would like to thank Frank Ball and Francisco García, as this paper builds on their earlier work in the area of communication services for distributed multimedia applications.

Abbreviations

ANSA	Advanced Networked Systems Architecture
ATM	Asynchronous Transfer Mode
B-ISDN	Broadband Integrated Services Digital Network
CCITT	Consultative Committee for International Telegraph and Telephone
CMTP	Continuous Media Transport Protocol
MTBF	Mean Time Between Failures
MTTR	Mean Time to Repair
ODP	Open Distributed Processing
OSI-RM	Open Systems Interconnection Reference Model
QoS	Quality of Service
RTIP	Real Time Internet Protocol
SDU	Service Data Unit

References

Accetta M., Baron R., Golub D., Rashid R., Tevanian A. and Young M. (1986). Mach: A new kernel foundation for UNIX development. *Technical Report*, Department of Computer Science, Carnegie Mellon University

Anagnostou, M. E. *et al.* (1991). Quality of service requirements in ATM-based B-ISDNs. *Computer Networks and ISDN Systems*, **14**(4), 197–204

Anderson D. P., Herrtwich R. G. and Schaefer C. (1991). SRP: a resource reservation protocol for guaranteed performance communication in the internet. *Internal Report*, University of California at Berkeley

Anderson D. P., Osawa Y. and Govindan R. (1992). A file system for continuous media. *ACM Transactions on Computer Systems*, **10**(4), 311–37

ANSI (1991). High speed transport protocol (HSTP) specification *X3S3.3/91-264*, American National Standards Institute

APM Ltd (1989). *The ANSA Reference Manual Release 01.01* Architecture Projects Management Ltd, Poseidon House, Castle Park, Cambridge CB3 0RD, UK

APM Ltd (1991). *ANSAware 3.0 Implementation Manual* APM Ltd, Poseidon House, Castle Park, Cambridge CB3 0RD, UK

APM Ltd (1993). *The ANSA Application Programmer's Guide, Release 4.1* APM Ltd, Poseidon House, Castle Park, Cambridge CB3 0RD, UK

Arnould E. A., Bitz F. J., Cooper E. C., Kung H. T., Sansom R. D. and Steenkiste P. A. (1989). The design of Nectar: a network backplane for heterogeneous multicomputers. *ACM Computer Architecture News*, **17**(2), 205–16

Ball F., Hutchison D., Scott A. C. and Shepherd W. D. (1990). A multimedia network interface. *3rd IEEE COMSOC International Multimedia Workshop (Multimedia '90)*, Bordeaux, France

Birman K. P. and Joseph T. A. (1982). Exploiting virtual synchrony in distributed systems. *ACM Operating System Review,* **21**(5), 123–38

Birman K. P., Schiper A. and Stephenson P. (1991). Lightweight causal and atomic group multicast. *ACM Transactions on Computer Systems*, **9**(3), 272–314

Boerjan J., Campbell A., Coulson G., García F., Hutchison D., Leopold H. and Singer N. (1992). The OSI 95 transport service and the new environment. *ISO/IEC JTC1/SC6/WG4 N824*, International Standards Organization, UK, December, (1992), and *Internal Report No. MPG-92-38* Department of Computing, Lancaster University, Lancaster LA1 4YR

Bricker A., Gien M., Guillemont M., Lipkis J., Orr D. and Rozier M. (1991). Architectural issues in microkernel-based operating systems: the CHORUS experience. *Computer Communications*, **14**(6), 347–57

Bulterman D. C. and van Liere R. (1991). Multimedia synchronization and UNIX. *Proc. Second International Workshop on Network and Operating System Support for Digital Audio and Video*, Heidelberg, Springer Verlag

Campbell A. and Hutchison D. (1992a). Contribution to the new ISO work item: key issues in distributed multimedia communications. *Draft BSI/IST6/-/2/738*, British Standards Institute, UK

Campbell A., Coulson G. and Hutchison D. (1992b). A suggested QoS architecture for multimedia communications. *ISO/IEC JTC1/SC21/WG1 N1201*, International Standards Organization, UK, November, (1992) and *Internal Report No. MPG-92-37,* Dept. of Computing, Lancaster University, Lancaster LA1 4YR

Campbell A., Coulson G., Garcia F. and Hutchison D. (1992c). A continuous media transport and orchestration service. *Proc. ACM SIGCOMM '92,* Baltimore, Maryland, USA, 99–110

Campbell A., Coulson G., García F., Hutchison D. and Leopold H. (1993). Integrated quality of service for multimedia communications. *Proc. IEEE INFOCOM'93,* Vol. 3, San Francisco, USA, 732-9

CCITT. (1990). Draft recommendations I.*, CCITT, Geneva, Switzerland

Cidon I., Gopal I., Gopal P. M., Janniello and Kaplan M. (1992). The plaNET/ORBIT high speed network. *Internal Report No. 18270*, IBM T. J. Watson Research Center

Clark D.D., Davie B.S., Farber D.J., Gopal I.S., Kadaba B.K., Sincoskie W.D., Smith, J.M. and Tennenhouse D.L. (1991). The AURORA gigabit testbed, *Internal Report,* Bellcore, New Jersey, US

Clark D. D., Shenker S. and Zhang L. (1992). Supporting real-time applications in an integrated services packet network: architecture and mechanism. *Proc. ACM SIGCOMM'92*, Baltimore, USA, 14–26

Cocchi R., Estin D, Shenker S. and Zhang L. (1991). A study of priority pricing in multiple service class networks. *Proc. ACM SIGCOMM '91*, 123–130

Coulson G., Blair G. S., Davies N. and Williams N. (1992). Extensions to ANSA for multimedia computing. *Computer Networks and ISDN Systems*, **25**(11), 305–23

Coulson G. and Blair G. S. (1993a). Micro-kernel support for continuous media in distributed systems. To appear in *Computer Networks and ISDN Systems, Special Issue on Multimedia*; also available as *Internal Report MPG-93-04*, Department of Computing, Lancaster University, Bailrigg, Lancaster, U.K

Coulson G., Blair G. S., Stefani J. B., Horn F. and Hazard L. (1993b). Supporting the real-time requirements of continuous media in open distributed processing. *Internal Report MPG-93-10*, Department of Computing, Lancaster University, Lancaster LA1 4YR, UK

Crosby S., (1993). MSNL connection management. *ATM Document Collection 2, Technical Notes*, 12-1, 12-11, Systems Research Group, Computer Laboratory, University of Cambridge, UK

Danthine A., Baguette Y., Leduc G. and Leonard L. (1992). The OSI 95 connection-mode transport service – Enhanced QoS. *Proc. 4th IFIP Conference on High Performance Networking*, University of Liege, Liege, Belgium

Davies N. A. and Nicol J. R. (1991). A technological perspective on multimedia computing. *Computer Communications*, **14**(5), 260–72

Davies N., Coulson G., Williams N. and Blair G.S. (1991). Experiences of handling multimedia in distributed open systems. *Proc. SEDMS '92, Usenix Symposium on Distributed and Multiprocessor Systems,* Newport Beach, CA, USA

DEC (1991). *Digital Network Architecture, Naming Service Functional Specification,* Version V2.0.0. Order No. EK-DDNANS-FS-002

DePrycker M. (1991). *Asynchronous Transfer Mode: Solution for Broadband ISDN.* ISBN 0-13-053513-3, Ellis Horwood

Feldmeier D. (1992). Architectural concepts for high speed communications systems. *Internal Report,* Bellcore, Morristown, NJ, USA

Ferrari D. and Verma D. C. (1990). A scheme for real-time channel establishment in wide-area networks. *IEEE JSAC,* **8**(3), 368–77

Ferrari D., Ramaekers J. and Ventre G. (1992). Client-network interactions in quality of service communication environments. *Proc. 4th IFIP Conference on High Performance Networking,* University of Liege, Liege, Belgium

Floyd S. (1993). Link-sharing and resource management models for packet networks. Draft available via anonymous ftp from ftp.ee.lbl.gov: link.ps.Z

Forin A., Golub D. and Bershad B. (1990). An I/O system for Mach 3.0. *Internal Report,* Carnegie Mellon University, Pittsburg, USA

García F. (1993). A continuous media transport and orchestration service. *Ph.D Thesis,* Department of Computing, Lancaster University, Lancaster LA1 4YR, UK

Govindan R. and Anderson D. P. (1991). Scheduling and IPC mechanisms for continuous media. *Thirteenth ACM Symposium on Operating Systems Principles,* Asilomar Conference Center, Pacific Grove, California, USA, ACM SIGOPS, **25**(5), 68–80

Hanko J. G., Keurner E. M., Northcutt J. D. and Wall G. A. (1991). Workstation support for time critical applications. *Proc. Second International Workshop on Network and Operating System Support for Digital Audio and Video,* Heidelberg, Springer Verlag

Hehmann D. B., Salmony M. G. and Stüttgen H. J. (1990). Transport services for multimedia applications on broadband networks. *Computer Communications,* **13**(4), 197–203

Hehmann D. B., Herrtwich R. G., Schulz W., Schuett T. and Steinmetz R. (1991). Implementing HeiTS: architecture and implementation strategy of the Heidelberg high speed transport system. *Second International Workshop on Network and Operating System Support for Digital Audio and Video,* IBM ENC, Heidelberg, Germany

Henshall J. and Shaw S. (1988). *OSI Explained: End-to-end Computer Communication Standards.* ISBN 07458-0253-2, Ellis Horwood

Hutchison D., Campbell A. and Leopold H. (1992). Key issues in multimedia dommunications. *ISO/IEC JTC1/SC6/WG4 SD/14,* International Standards

Organisation, UK, November, (1992) and *Internal Report No. MPG-92-39* Department of Computing, Lancaster University, Lancaster LA1 4YR

Hyman J., Lazar A.A. andPacifici G. (1992) Joint scheduling and admission control for ATS-based switch networks. *ACM SIGCOMM'92*, Baltimore, Maryland, USA, 223–234

ISO (1992a). Draft guidelines for enhanced communication function and facilities for the lower layers. *ISO/IEC JTC1/SC6/WG4 N7309* International Standards Organisation

ISO (1992b). Draft recommendations X.903: basic reference model of open distributed processing. *ISO/IEC JTC1/SC21/WG7*, International Standards Organisation

ISO (1992c). Quality of service framework – outline. *ISO/IEC JTC1/SC21/WG1 N1145,* International Standards Organisation

ISO (1992d). User requirements for quality of service. *ISO/IEC JTC1/SC21/WG1 N1146,* International Standards Organisation

Jung J. and Seret D. (1993). Translation of QoS parameters into ATM performance parameters in B-ISDN, *Proc. IEEE Infocom'93*, Vol. 3, San Francisco, USA 748–55

Lazar A.A., Temple A.T. and Gidron R. (1990). MAGNET II: A metropolitan area network based on asynchronous time sharing. *IEEE Journal on Selected Areas in Communications*, **8**(1), 1582–94

Leopold H., Blair G., Campbell A., Coulson G., Dark P., García F., Hutchison D., Singer N. and Williams N. (1992a). Distributed multimedia communications system requirements. *OSI95/ Deliverable ELIN-1/C/V3,* Alcatel ELIN Research, A-1210 Vienna, Ruthnergasse 1-7, Austria

Leopold H., Campbell A., Hutchison D. and Singer N. (1992b). Towards an integrated quality of service architecture (QoS-A) for distributed multimedia communications. *Proc. 4th IFIP Conference on High Performance Networking*, University of Liege, Liege, Belgium

Little T. D. C. and Ghafoor A. (1990). Synchronisation properties and storage models for multimedia objects. *IEEE Journal On Selected Areas in Communications*, **8**(3), 413–27

Liu C. L. and Layland J. W. (1973). Scheduling algorithms for multiprogramming in a hard real-time environment. *Journal of the Association for Computing Machinery*, **20**(1), 46–61

Lougher P. Shepherd D. (1993). The design of a storage server for continuous media. *The Computer Journal*, **36**(1), 32–42

Mullender S., ed. (1993). *Distributed Systems*, 2nd edn., Addison-Wesley

Nahrstedt K. and Smith J. (1993). Revision of QoS guarantees at the application/network interface, *Technical Report,* Distributed Systems Laboratory, University of Pennsylvania

Nicolaou C. (1990). An architecture for real-time multimedia communication systems. *IEEE Journal on Selected Areas in Communications*, **8**, (3), 391–400

Nicolaou C. (1991). A distributed architecture for multimedia communication systems, *Ph.D Thesis*, University of Cambridge, Computer Laboratory, UK

Open Software Foundation (1992). *Distributed Computing Environment*, 11 Cambridge Center, Cambridge, MA 02142, USA

Parekh A. (1993). A generalised processor sharing approach to flow control in integrated service networks – the multiple node case. *Proc. IEEE INFOCOM'93*, San Francisco, USA, 521–30

Partridge C. (1990). A proposed flow specification; RFC-1363. *Internet Request for Comments No. 1363*, Network Information Center, SRI International, Menlo Park, CA, USA

Pasquale G., Polyzos E., Anderson E. and Kompella V. (1992). The multimedia multicast channel. *Proc. Third International Workshop on Network and Operating System Support for Digital Audio and Video,* San Diego, USA

Shenker S., Clark D. and Zhang L. (1993). A scheduling service model and a scheduling architecture for an integrated service packet network. Draft available via anonymous ftp from parcftp.xerox.com:/transient/service-model.ps.Z

Shepherd W. D., Hutchison D., García F. and Coulson G. (1991). Protocol support for distributed multimedia applications. *Second International Workshop on Network and Operating System Support for Digital Audio and Video,* IBM ENC, Heidelberg, Germany

Sluman C. (1991). Quality of service in distributed systems. *BSI/IST21/-/1/5:33,* British Standards Institute, UK

Stankovic J. A. and Ramamritham K. (1988). Tutorial on hard real-time systems. *IEEE Computer Society Order Number 819*, ISBN 0-8186-0819-6

Stefani J. B. (1992). Sur les proprietes temporelles d'une machine d'execution ESTEREL. *Internal Report,* Centre National d'Etudes Telecommunications, 38-40 rue du General Leclerc, 92131 Issy-les-Moulineaux, Paris, France

Stefani J. B. (1993). Some computational aspects of QoS in ANSA. *Technical Report* available from: Centre National d'Etudes des Télécommunications (CNET), 38-40 rue du Général Leclerc, 92131 Issy-les-Moulineaux, France

Tanenbaum A. S., van Renesse R., van Staveren H. and Mullender S. J. (1988). A retrospective and evaluation of the Amoeba distributed operating system. *Technical Report*, Vrije Universiteit, CWI, Amsterdam

Tennenhouse D.L. (1990). *Layered Multiplexing Considered Harmful, Protocols for High-Speed Networks*. Elsevier Science Publishers B.V. (North-Holland)

Tokuda H. and Kitayama T. (1993). Dynamic QOS control based on real-time threads. *Proc. Fourth International Workshop on Network and Operating System Support for Digital Audio and Video*, Lancaster University, Lancaster LA1 4YR, UK

Topolcic C. (1990). Experimental internet stream protocol, version 2 (ST-II). *Internet RFC-1190*

Vin H. M., and Rangan, P. V. (1993). Designing a multi-user HSTV storage server. *IEEE Journal on Selected Areas in Communications*, **11**(1), 153–64

Williams N. and Blair G. S. (1991). Distributed multimedia application survey. *Internal Report N. MPG-91-11*. Department of Computing, Lancaster University, Bailrigg, Lancaster LA1 4YR, UK

Wolfinger B. and Moran M. (1991). A continuous media data transport service and protocol for real-time communication in high speed networks. *Second International Workshop on Network and Operating System Support for Digital Audio and Video,* IBM ENC, Heidelberg, Germany

Zhang L. and Ferrari D. (1993). Rate-controlled static-priority queueing. *Proc. IEEE INFOCOM'93*, San Francisco, USA, 227–37

Zhang H. and Keshav S. (1991). Comparison of rate-based service disciplines. *Proc. SIGCOMM'91*, Zurich, September, 113–21

Zhang L., Deering S., Estin D, Shenker S. and Zappala D. (1993). RSVP: a new resource ReSerVation Protocol. Draft available via anonymous ftp from parcftp.xerox.com:/transient/ rsvp.ps.Z

Chapter 12

Monitoring Distributed Systems

Masoud Mansouri-Samani, Morris Sloman

Imperial College of Science Technology and Medicine,
Department of Computing,
180 Queen's Gate, London SW7 2BZ, UK
Email: m.mansouri-samani@doc.ic.ac.uk, m.sloman@doc.ic.ac.uk

Monitoring is an essential means for obtaining the information required about the components of a distributed system in order to make management decisions and subsequently control their behavior. Monitoring is also used to obtain information about component execution and interaction when debugging distributed or parallel systems. This chapter presents a functional model of monitoring in terms of generation, processing, dissemination and presentation of information. Based on the model a general survey of the area is presented. This model can provide a framework for deriving the facilities required for the design and construction of a generalized monitoring service for distributed systems. A number of approaches to monitoring of distributed systems are compared in the chapter.

12.1   Introduction

12.1.1   What is monitoring?

Monitoring can be defined as the process of dynamic collection, interpretation and presentation of information concerning objects or software processes under scrutiny (Joyce *et al.*, 1987). It is needed for program debugging, testing, visualization and animation. It may also be used for general management activities which have a more permanent and continuous nature such as, performance management, configuration management, fault management or security management (Sloman, 1987). In this case the behavior of the system is observed and monitoring information is gathered. This information is used to make management decisions and perform the appropriate control actions on the system as shown in Figure 12.1. Unlike monitoring which is generally a passive process, control actively changes the behavior of the managed system and in our opinion it should be considered and modeled separately. In this chapter we are only concerned with monitoring of object-based distributed systems and particularly its use for management purposes. Note that the generic model of management shown below can be recursively applied to the components of the model itself. As a result, a monitoring system itself would have to be managed.

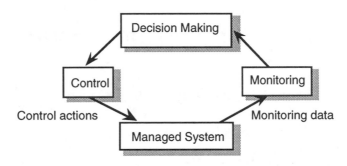

Figure 12.1 Management model.

There are a number of fundamental problems associated with monitoring of distributed systems. Delays in transferring information from the place it is generated to the place it is used means that it may be out of date. This means that it is very difficult to obtain a global, consistent view of all components in a distributed system. Variable delays in reporting events may result in recording events as having occurred in the incorrect order and so some form of clock synchronization is necessary to provide a means of determining causal ordering. The number of objects generating monitoring information in a large system can easily swamp managers, thus necessitating the filtering and processing of information. Another problem is that the monitoring system may itself compete for resources with the system being observed and so modify its behavior.

In order to overcome these problems, it is necessary to design a monitoring system in terms of a set of general functions relating to generation, processing, dissemination and presentation of monitoring information. Before we describe this model of monitoring in terms of these activities, we shall introduce some necessary terms and concepts in Section 12.1.2.

12.1.2   Concepts and terminology

A *managed object* is defined as any hardware or software component whose behavior can be controlled by a management system (from now on we refer to a managed object just as an object unless explicitly specified). The object encapsulates its behavior behind an interface that hides the internal details which may be vital for monitoring purposes. For this reason, the concept of encapsulation in object-based distributed systems causes a problem as far as monitoring is concerned. The interface of a managed object can be divided into two parts (Sloman, 1987), shown in Figure 12.2:

i)   An *operational interface* which supports the normal information processing operations, fulfilling the main purpose of the service provided by the object.

ii)   A *management interface* which supports monitoring and control interactions with the management system.

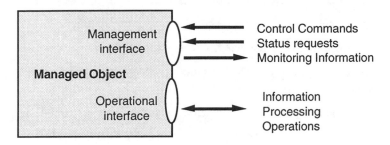

Figure 12.2 A managed object.

The management interface allows three types of operations:

(1)   Control commands (stop, halt, and so on)

(2)   Requests for status information

(3)   Monitoring information generated by the object.

An object may be *passive* or *active*. A passive object (or server) encapsulates some permanent resource, such as a data structure, and a set of routines and operations that can be performed on the resource (cf. monitors). It provides services which are used by one or more active objects or clients. An active object performs some function and may also encapsulate some shared resource and the operations for accessing it, but it may invoke operations on other objects. It should be possible to monitor both active and passive objects.

Monitoring can be performed on an object or a group of related objects (a *monitoring domain*). Each object has associated with it a *status* and a set of *events* (that is, status changes). The behavior of an object can be defined and observed in terms of its status and events. The status of an object is a measure of its behavior at a discrete point in time and is represented by a set of *status variables* contained within a *status vector* (Feldkuhn and Erickson, 1989). These variables or attributes may be *static* (for example, machine type) or *time-varying* (for example, load). A static attribute may further be subdivided into those associated with a *permanent* object or a *temporary* object.

An *event* is defined as an atomic entity that reflects a *change* in the status of an object. The status of an object has a duration in time, for example, "process is idle" or "process running", whereas an event occurs instantaneously, for example, "message sent" or "process started". Usually, the status of an object is changing continually and therefore the behavior of the object is normally observed in terms of a distinguished subset of events, called *events of interest*. These reflect changes that are of significance to the management and therefore are generated when a predefined set of conditions is satisfied. In a distributed system three kinds of events can be identified (Bemmerl *et al.*, 1990):

i) A *control flow event* represents a control activity and is associated with a control thread. Such an event occurs when a process or the operating system reaches a previously defined statement. For example:

- process P1 enters/leaves procedure Fred for the nth time;

- the operating system enters the scheduler.

ii) A *data flow event* occurs when a status variable is changed or accessed. For example:

- variable a of process P1 is assigned value X;

- variable b in the third invocation of procedure Fred is read by process P2.

Although such an event is caused by a specific control flow event, it is not associated with any particular control thread.

iii) *Process-level events* show the creation and deletion of processes and the interactions and data flow between them. For example:

- process P1 started;

- process P1 sends message m to process P2;

- the number of waiting processes in queue w is incremented by one.

Control flow and data flow events can be referred to as *internal events* which are related to the local state of a component or object and are not visible outside it, unless explicitly made visible at the management or debugging interface. Such events are particularly useful for debugging purposes. Note that debug tools often create a new "interface" to make visible internal events and state which are not normally visible at either the operational or management interface to an object. Internal events thus violate the encapsulation of objects and are more appropriate for analyzing the behavior of a single component.

Process-level events can be considered as *external events*, which represent the external behavior of an object and its interactions with other objects. These events are of particular interest to management. A generalized monitoring system should allow us to observe a combination of these events. Many monitoring tools enable the users to specify and detect only process-level events such as interprocess communication, as these events do not violate the encapsulation of objects and are at the correct level of abstraction for analyzing the behavior of distributed systems (Bates, 1988; Joyce *et al.*, 1987; LeBlanc and Robbins, 1985).

Events can also be classified, according to their level of abstraction, into *primitive* and *combined* (or *correlated*) events.

i)   A primitive event signifies a simple change in the state of an object.

ii) A combined event is defined as a combination or grouping of other primitive and combined events.

This classification is useful for describing the global behavior of a group of objects in terms of the local behavior of every object in the group[1]. Various languages are used for specifying combined events and states. This is described in more detail in Section 12.3.4, on combination of monitoring information.

Monitoring information describes the status and events associated with an object or a group of objects under scrutiny. Such information can be represented by individual status and event reports, or a sequence of such reports in the form of logs or histories, as described later.

Time-driven monitoring is based on acquiring periodic status information to provide an instantaneous view of the behavior of an object or a group of objects. There is a direct relationship between the sampling rate and the amount of information generated. *Event-driven monitoring* is based on obtaining information about occurrence of events of interest, which provide a dynamic view of system activity as only information about the changes in the system are collected. Most monitoring approaches use event-driven monitoring but a generalized monitoring system must provide both of these complementary techniques to suit various monitoring requirements and constraints.

12.1.3 Monitoring model

This survey is based on a general functional model which is derived from the Event Management Model of (Feldkuhn and Erickson, 1989), with some changes and enhancements. This model identifies the following four monitoring activities performed in a loosely coupled, object-based distributed system:

i)   *Generation*: Important events are detected and event and status reports are generated. These monitoring reports are used to construct monitoring traces, which represent historical views of system activity.

ii) *Processing*: A generalized monitoring service provides common processing functionalities such as merging of traces, validation, database updating, combinationm, correlation and filtering of monitoring information. They convert the raw and low-level monitoring data to the required format and level of detail.

iii) *Dissemination*: Monitoring reports are disseminated to users, managers or processing agents who require them.

iv) *Presentation*: Gathered and processed information is displayed to the users in an appropriate form.

Implementation issues relating to the intrusiveness of the monitoring system, which depends on whether it is implemented in hardware or software and how clock synchronization is achieved for event ordering, provide a fifth dimension for comparing monitoring systems. Figure 12.3 summarizes the elements of the monitoring reference model presented in this chapter.

---

[1]   Holden *et al.* (1988) use the terms *object set states* and *object set events* to describe the overall behavior.

Generation of monitoring information
- Status reporting
- Event detection and reporting
- Trace generation

Processing of monitoring information
- Merging and multiple trace generation
- Validation
- Database updating
- Combination
- Filtering
- Analysis

Dissemination of monitoring information
- Registration of subscribers to dissemination service
- Specification of information selection criteria

Presentation
- Textual displays
- Time process diagrams
- Animation of events and status
- User control of levels of abstraction
- User control of information placement and time frame for updates
- Multiple simultaneous views
- Visibility of interaction message contents

Implementation issues
- Special purpose hardware
- Software probes
- Time synchronization for event ordering

Figure 12.3 Elements of a monitoring reference model.

Many models have been developed in order to describe the monitoring process. One approach has been to identify a set of layers such as the model proposed in (Marinescu *et al.*, 1990). At first sight, the above four activities appear to be a layered model with generation as the lowest layer and presentation using the services of the lower layers. However a generalized monitoring system may need to perform these activities in various places and in different orders to meet specific monitoring requirements. For example, generated information may be directly displayed by an object without processing or dissemination. Events and reports which are distributed to particular managers could be reprocessed to generate new monitoring information or events. Presentation of information may occur at many intermediate stages. For these reasons we present the monitoring model as a set of activities which can be combined as required in a generic monitoring service.

We shall describe these activities of the monitoring model in detail in Sections 12.2 to 12.5. Section 12.6 discusses some issues related to implementation of a monitoring service, such as intrusiveness of monitoring and ordering of events. A brief summary of some of the existing approaches is presented in Section 12.7 and the relevant Open Systems Interconnection Management standards are described in Section 12.8.

12.2   Generation of monitoring information

Monitoring data is generated in the form of *status* and *event report*s (Figure 12.4). A sequence of such reports is used to generate a *monitoring trace*. Status reporting, event detection and reporting, and trace generation are described below.

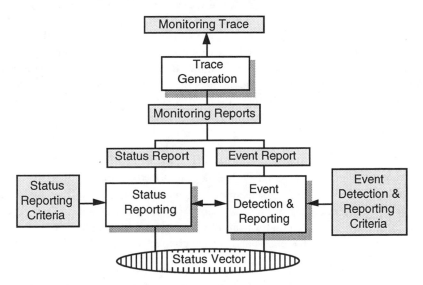

Figure 12.4 Generation of monitoring reports and traces.

12.2.1   Status reporting

A status report contains a subset of values from the status vector and may include other related information for example, timestamp and object identity. It represents the status at a specific instance in time and can be generated as described below.

i)   *Periodic*: Reports are generated based on a predetermined schedule.

ii)   *On request*: A report is generated upon receiving a request (*solicited* reporting). Note that the request may itself be periodic (that is, polling) or on a random basis.

One example of periodic status reporting can be found in the Conic environment (Magee *et al.*, 1989) where each node sends a configuration status report to a name server every five seconds. The OSI event management permits scheduling of event reports on both daily and weekly basis (ISO 10164-5, 1990).

The Clouds operating system (Dasgupta, 1986) uses an on-demand status reporting scheme. Requests are called *probes* and every object or process has a predefined or user-defined probe procedure which is executed whenever a probe is received. The probe handler sends a message back to the originator of the request, reporting the status condition of the process.

Status reporting criteria will define which reporting scheme to use, what the sampling period is and the contents of each report.

12.2.2   Event detection and reporting

Significant changes in the status of an object or a group of objects (that is, events of interest) would have to be detected. An event is said to have occurred when conditions, defined by *event detection criteria*, are satisfied. Software or hardware *probes* or *sensors* have to be inserted in the object to detect events – this is called *instrumentation*. Where, how and when event detection is carried out depends on the resources available for detection (for example, dedicated hardware, communication channels) and the *intrusiveness* of the monitoring system. This intrusiveness or *probe effect* is the degree to which the observed system is perturbed by the act of monitoring[2] and is discussed further in Section 12.6.1 on intrusiveness of monitoring systems.

Location of event detection

Event detection may be internal within the object and typically performed as a function of the object itself. For example, a function that updates the status vector may check the event detection criteria when it performs the update. Event detection may also be performed externally from the object itself for example, by an external agent which receives status reports and detects changes in the state of the object.

Time of event detection

Detection of event occurrences may be *immediate* (real-time), or *delayed*, detected some time after the occurrence. For example, signals on the internal bus of a node may be monitored, using a hardware monitor, to detect any changes in the status of the node as and when they occur. This is particularly used for detection of events in time frames of milliseconds. Alternatively, status reports may be generated, stored and used to detect events at some later time.

Event report format

Once the occurrence of an event is detected an event report is generated. It contains *attributes* such as the event identifier, type, priority, time of occurrence, the state of

---

[2]   Here we only consider *detection intrusion*, associated with the recognition of events, and not *action intrusion*, associated with performing control actions on the system.

the object immediately before and after the occurrence of the event and other application-specific status variables.

Event and status reports may be generated in one or more stages. A preliminary report may be generated by an object, containing a minimum amount of monitoring information (for example, object and event id). Such a report could then be sent to a different object which can generate a more complete report by adding further attributes such as time stamps, event type or text messages.

Obviously, the amount of information contained in a monitoring report depends on the requirements of users or clients who need them. The attributes assigned to each event or status may be of two kinds *Independent* or *Dependent* (Mohr, 1990). Independent attributes are those primitive attributes which are assigned to all events and status, such as the timestamp and identity of the object. Dependent attributes are assigned depending on the type of the event or status. For example, a configuration event report, representing a "create process" event, may contain the identity of the created process. Event and status reporting criteria are used to determine what information to include within each report.

The format and structure of a report may be *fixed* or *variable*. Obviously with a variable report structure some amount of filtering can be performed implicitly, where only the necessary information is included within a report, as explained in Section 12.3.5 on filtering.

12.2.3 Trace generation

In order to describe the dynamic behavior of an object or a group of objects over a period of time, event and status reports are recorded in time order as monitoring traces.

A *complete* trace contains all the monitoring reports generated by the system since the beginning of the monitoring session. A *segmented* trace is a sequence of reports collected during a certain period of time. It describes "a completely observed time interval" of the behavior of the monitored object or system. A trace may be segmented owing to overflow of a trace buffer or deliberate halting of trace generation which results in the loss or absence of reports over a period of time.

A trace may have a header giving general information such as the start and end timestamps, the identity of the monitored object, its size, and the identity of the program. Monitoring traces may be generated for various reasons:

- *Archiving purposes and post-mortem analysis*: Monitoring reports may be needed at some later stage for further processing, analysis and usage. They are stored as monitoring traces and examined by the user at a later time, possibly after the completion of the program. This is particularly important for debugging purposes (McDowell and Helmbold, 1989).

- *Availability of resources:* Other reasons for forming these traces may be lack of processing power to analyze and interpret the monitoring reports "on the fly"; or limited communication resources to send reports to an external processing agent, as and when they are generated. This is particularly true for real-time monitoring.

- *Speed of visualization*: Trace generation might be necessary when the rate at which monitoring information is received and displayed is too quick for the observer to follow. This is especially true for real-time observation and display of system activity. Special display tools can be used to control the speed at which information is presented to the user.

- *Transformation of the logical view of the system activity:* This enables the construction of a global monitoring trace from local traces, which describe the behavior of the system as a whole. Also multiple traces can be generated from a single trace, to reflect specialized or restricted views of the system activity (see Section 12.3.1 on merging and multiple trace generation). Lower-level histories can be used to generate more meaningful higher-level monitoring information (McDowell and Helmbold, 1989), by using combination and filtering (see Sections 12.3.4 and 12.3.5 respectively).

The design alternatives relating to trace generation include:

- *Location of trace generation*: Traces could be formed by the objects which generate the monitoring reports, by intermediate monitoring objects when processing monitored information, or by the final user of such information.

- *Temporary vs. long-term traces*: Temporary storage involves placing the monitoring reports in a temporary buffer before they are processed or transferred to another object for use. Long-term storage involves recording the reports in persistent log or history files by making use of a logging service.

- *Storage capacity:* Obviously there is a limit to the available storage space and therefore the size of a monitoring trace. Overwriting older records when the maximum storage size is reached can be appropriate if we are interested in the most recent behavior of the system. Alternatively, trace generation is halted until more space is available (LaBarre, 1991). Both these strategies may result in a segmented trace as some of the reports may be discarded. A capacity threshold event should be generated to indicate storage overflow.

- *Sophistication of trace generation*: A simple scheme would store all the reports, in the arrival order, in a local trace buffer of a monitoring object, without changing the contents of the stored information. This is usually used for temporary storage of monitoring data.

   A sophisticated scheme might use a logging service (which can be modeled as a managed object (LaBarre, 1991)) for the long-term storage of reports together with some extra information, in a variety of formats, representations and orderings. It may allow the generation of multiple traces or logs, representing different logical views of system activity (see Section 12.3.1). Special log records could be generated containing a log record identifier, logging time, information contained in the report to be logged, and other related data. Various implicit or explicit filtering activities can be performed when such records are generated and stored in log files.

A sophisticated trace generation mechanism may allow reports to be stored in occurrence order if an occurrence timestamp is available. This overcomes the problems of ordering according to arrival order, which may lead to incorrect interleavings of monitoring reports and invalid observations owing to communication delays. Determining the order of monitoring reports is discussed in Section 12.6.2.

* *Access to the trace reports* may be *on demand* by issuing an explicit request to the storage entity, or according to predetermined conditions. On-demand access enables the processing agent to receive the reports when it has the necessary resources to deal with them, or when the communication traffic is low. By using a scanning and selection service the user may be able to specify the particular reports required (for example, generated by a particular object), the trace file from which they may be read or the number of reports needed.

Predetermined conditions may be used to transfer reports from a trace buffer to a remote processing agent when the buffer is full, contains n elements, the communication load is below a certain threshold or the processing load is low (Van Riek and Tourancheau, 1991). These strategies are particularly useful for reducing the communication overheads by sending reports in blocks and therefore economizing on channel set-up time.

12.3 Processing of monitoring information

In previous sections we discussed the steps necessary for generation of monitoring information. In this section we will consider some common processing activities that can be performed on this information. A monitoring service could provide certain functional units, as building blocks, that can be combined in different ways to suit the monitoring requirements. Figure 12.5 shows one possible combination. Note that these processing functionalities are often integrated and are performed in different places and at various stages.

12.3.1 Merging and multiple trace generation

In order to provide different logical views of system activity over a period of time, monitoring traces may be constructed and ordered in various ways. The attributes of a report which can be used as selection criteria in determining how monitoring traces are processed include:

* Generation or arrival timestamp, priority or type of the report
* Identity, priority or type of the reporting entity
* Identity or type of the managed object to which the report refers
* Identity or type of the destination of the report.

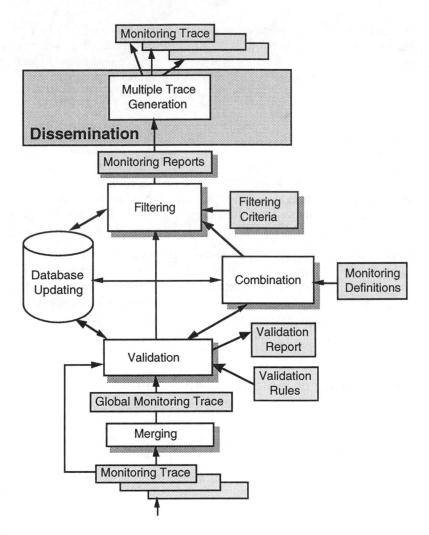

Figure 12.5 Processing of monitoring reports.

Construction of monitoring traces is performed according to a *trace specification*, based on these factors. It specifies how the final traces are formed and what they will contain. Obviously, not including a report in a trace is equivalent to filtering out that report from the point of view of the users who access that trace.

Monitoring traces may be generated from event or status reports as they arrive or from one or more already existing traces, as described in the following sections.

Merging of monitoring traces

A trace segment containing all the reports related only to one object is called a *local trace segment*. A set of all the local trace segments from all the objects under scrutiny, over the same period of time, can form a *global trace segment*.

One of the important activities in a monitoring system is merging of several monitoring traces into one trace. Local trace segments from different objects can be merged to generate a global trace segment, representing the global behavior of the system in a particular interval. The resulting trace can then be used by various processing agents.

Merging may be an iterative operation. A trace generated in this way could itself be merged with others to generate a more general trace. The original traces may be discarded once merging is complete. Generating one global monitoring trace from several local traces is in effect imposing a linear (total) ordering on the event and status occurrences within the system. An ordered trace is simpler to understand and can be easier to work with, but a linear stream may be misleading since it implies an ordering between every pair of event or status reports, even when they are completely unrelated. A partial ordering can more accurately reflect the behavior of a distributed system (McDowell and Helmbold, 1989). A general technique for obtaining the required partial ordering is described in (Fidge, 1988). To achieve this a vector of logical timestamps is associated with each event. By comparing the vectors the ordering of events can be determined. This is described in more detail in Section 12.6.2.

Generating multiple traces

A monitoring trace can be used to generate several other traces, representing various logical views of object or system activity. Selection of reports from a trace segment may be based on a combination of destination, priority, report type or other factors. For example, a trace could be generated with all high-priority security events, so that they can be processed first, then another trace with all the accounting events destined for a particular process. A trace generated in this way may be used to generate other traces. Obviously some duplication may be necessary because some reports may have to appear in several traces. For example, an event report may be of interest to two processing agents and therefore it is stored in each of their trace buffers.

12.3.2   Validation of monitoring information

Another important monitoring activity is performing validation and plausibility tests on monitoring information, to make sure that the system has been monitored correctly. This may be performed at different levels. When an individual report is received, its contents may be checked to see if they are valid, for example, whether the event-id represents one of the expected events, or the value of the timestamp is valid. Invalid reports are discarded. Monitoring reports may also be validated in relation to one another, for example, to see whether two event reports in a trace satisfy an expected temporal ordering, or to check the validity of an event report against the current system status before applying the status change to the model (see database updating). The detection of invalid orderings may be followed by reordering or filtering of the reports. Validation is done according to certain validation rules, and a validation report may be generated. The SIMPLE monitoring system (Hofmann *et al.*, 1992) performs some validation and plausibility tests on selected event reports and event traces (Section 12.7.1).

12.3.3   Database updating

Valid monitoring information may be used to maintain and update a representation or model of the current status of the system. In OSI terminology it is called the *Management Information Base* (MIB). This representation could be used by other users, managers or processing agents (for example, by the configuration manager to detect component failures). Section 12.7.3 describes a data-oriented approach to monitoring communication networks in which a conceptual database model of the network is constructed and continuously updated to represent the current status of the network (Wolfson *et al.*, 1991). Some approaches use temporal and historical databases in order to maintain both the current and also the historical behavior of the system (Shim and Ramamoorthy, 1990; Snodgrass, 1988).

There are two general approaches to collecting MIB data:

i)   The *dynamic* approach collects only the information requested by the user (Snodgrass, 1988). User queries result in the automatic activation of relevant sensors in monitored objects and the collection of the required data. The advantage of this approach is that only the requested data is collected. This is particularly important when monitoring resources (processors, memory, and so on) are limited and/or there are many sensors present. The disadvantage is that the queries must be specified *before* the data is collected. The user, however, may not know in advance exactly what information is required.

ii) The *static* approach collects data independent of its use – all possible monitoring data must be collected and stored for potential access by users. This is done by permanently enabling all the sensors, or forcing each sensor to be enabled manually. This solves the problem associated with the previous approach but results in the collection of large amounts of information that may not be used.

In a distributed system, owing to various factors such as communication delays and component failures, it is usually impossible to construct a model which could provide a truly up-to-date and consistent snapshot of the system status. This is further discussed in Section 12.6.2.

12.3.4   Combination of monitoring information

Combination (also referred to as correlation or clustering) of monitoring information is the process of increasing the level of abstraction of monitoring data. In conjunction with filtering, it prevents the users of such information from being overwhelmed by the considerable volume of details present in all of the system's activity, so that they can observe the behavior of the system at a desired level of detail. To do this, low-level primitive events and states can be processed and interpreted to give a higher-level view of the complex states and events that occur in the system. The ability to combine monitoring information is particularly important in distributed systems that implement fault tolerance.

Combination is performed by defining higher-level, more abstract events and states in terms of lower-level, primitive ones. In a distributed system the task of combining monitoring data is more difficult and complicated when the components of a definition are events and states associated with objects that are distributed across several nodes. In this case, local monitoring agents at each node cooperate with one another in order to detect a global event or state. Each local agent must be told what events and states it should monitor and which other agents have to be informed after their occurrence (see Section 12.4 on dissemination of monitoring information). This will inevitably increase the communication overheads.

Various languages have been developed that enable the user to define new events and states and combine monitoring information. In the State and Event Specification Language (SESL) (Holden, 1989), a user can define two declarative statements:

    e WHEN elist   event e occurs when elist occurs

    s EQUALS expr   state s will have the value of expr

An event list (elist) defines a pattern of occurrence of events, which is specified in terms of other event lists, events, low-level events (represented by an event notification message), and state changes. These are related by temporal operators => and –>, and the logical operators | and ! (see Table 12.1). Each time a sequence of events occurs which matches the pattern, the event list also occurs.

Table 12.1 Example SESL operators for creating event lists.

Event List	Meaning
elist1 =>elist2	matches when elist2 occurs immediately after elist1
elist1 > elist2	matches every time elist2 occurs after elist1 has once occurred
elist1 –> elist2	matches when elist2 occurs sometime after elist1
elist1 | elist2	matches when either of the event lists occurs
!elist	matches only if elist did not occur
elist PROVIDED condition	matches if condition is true at the time elist occurs

Various conditions and expressions can be defined using the operators listed in Table 12.2. A condition is also an expression with a zero value representing true and a non-zero value representing false.

As an example, to check the availability of a service consisting of two servers, the user can write the following SESL script:

```
busy       WHEN  EVENT ("received request")

free       WHEN  EVENT ("sending reply")

non_busy   WHEN  one_busy => free

one_busy   WHEN  non_busy => busy | two_busy => free

two_busy   WHEN  one_busy => busy
```

Table 12.2 SESL operators for creating expressions and conditions.

Operator	Meaning
$state	value of state defined by EQUALS
#event	number of times event occurred
State("string")	value of state string of monitoring activity
constant	a numerical constant
!expr −expr	unary operators
* / + −	binary arithmetic operators
< > ≤ ≥ == !=	binary relational operators
& I	binary logical operators

The first two SESL statements can be used to show when the server is busy and when it is free. Internal events free and busy are defined in terms of external events "received request" and "sending reply", respectively. The next three statements define *non_busy*, *one_busy*, and *two_busy* events. For example, non_busy is the internal event associated with the state transition where no server is being used, and is triggered by the event of one server becoming busy followed (without any other events) by the detection of a server becoming free. More details about SESL can be found in Holden (1991).

A specification language for defining process-level events that can be used for debugging and performance monitoring is described in Lumpp *et al.* (1990). The user or programmer includes, with the application, a monitoring section that defines primitive and combined events. This is similar to the declaration of data structures and procedures for the application program. Examples of some event definitions are shown below:

```
e1 ::=    (xmitregister == 1)            on node 0;

e2 ::=    (rcvregister == 2)             on node 0;

e3 ::=    e1 && (waitregister == 1)      on node 0;

e4 ::=    e2 && (waitregister == 1)      on node 0;

e5 ::=    e3 && e4;

e6 ::=    (ptr > 0xE4000)                on node 2

e7 ::=    (touch(flag))                  on node 1;

e8 ::=    (reach(label_1))               on any node;

e9 ::=    (done_flag == TRUE)            on all nodes;
```

Events *e1–e6* are self-explanatory. They are defined in terms of counters such as *rcvregister*, *xmitregister* and *waitregister*, a pointer *ptr* and other events on specific nodes. In the definition of *e7*, the *touch()* operator is used which specifies events that correspond to any change of a specified variable regardless of the value stored (for example, *flag*). In the definition of *e8*, the operator *reach()* is used for tracing the flow of control of a thread. The user can place labels in appropriate sections of the application and define events that correspond to the program counter reaching those points (in this case *label_1*) during execution. The definition of an event can span more than one node in the target system (for example, any node, all nodes, five nodes). The user can specify various temporal, relational and logical relationships between events.

In another approach, Wolfson *et al.* (1991) use a data manipulation language based on SQL, with some enhancements to specify primitive and combined events (Section 12.7.3). Also, the Event Definition Language (EDL) (Bates, 1988) allows the user to define primitive and higher-level events with various filtering constraints.

12.3.5   Filtering of monitoring information

A typical distributed system may generate large amounts of monitoring information. This results in heavy usage of resources such as CPU and communication bandwidth for generation, collection, processing, and presentation of monitoring information. In addition, the users of the monitoring information may be overwhelmed with vast amounts of data which they are unable to comprehend. Filtering is the process of minimizing the amount of monitoring data, so that users only receive desired data at a suitable level of detail relevant to their purposes. It is also needed for security, where certain users should not have access to particular monitoring information.

Filtering functionality must be considered separately from the process of combination of monitoring information. Filtering discards information, but combining information permits both high-level and low-level views of the information, that is, the information is not discarded. Filtering may be performed, explicitly or implicitly, in different places and at various stages:

*   *Global filtering*: Performed by discarding the monitoring reports or traces which do not satisfy global filtering criteria. This includes validation failures.

*   *Reducing report contents*: With a variable report structure and the use of a selection facility, a monitoring object could receive a report and generate a new one with only a subset of monitoring information contained in the old report. The old report could be discarded and the new one used or stored by the object itself or forwarded to another object.

Obviously the best policy is to avoid generating unwanted or unnecessary information. For example this could be done by:

*   *Controlling report contents*: by using event and status reporting criteria at the generation stage so that only the required information is included in each report.

- *Conditional generation*: A monitoring report or trace is generated when certain predefined conditions are satisfied. For example, in periodic status report generation, the frequency and number of generated reports can be reduced, by increasing the sampling period. Also, report generation mechanisms can be *activated* or *deactivated*. This could be done at various levels of granularity. For example, the reporting mechanisms for all or individual events associated with a component may be deactivated.

- *Dissemination filtering*: Disseminating monitoring reports based on a subscriber/provider principle performs an implicit filtering function, as selected reports are forwarded only to those subscribers who have requested them (as explained in Section 12.4). A monitoring trace may be generated for each destination object. A report may not be discarded, but simply placed in one trace buffer and not the others. Obviously, not including a report in a trace would be equivalent to filtering it out from the point of view of the users who have access only to that trace.

Clearly, it is better to perform the necessary filtering at an early stage in order to reduce the resource usage in subsequent stages. In all the above cases, implicit or explicit filtering criteria may be based on the information contained within the reports (for example, event type, time, priority, type) or external information such as previous status or events and the capacity to process each report. Some approaches provide a language in which various filtering criteria can be defined (for example, FDL in the SIMPLE environment – Section 12.7.1). Users of monitoring reports should be able to define their own filtering criteria.

12.3.6   Analysis of monitoring information

Monitoring information can be analyzed to determine average or mean variance values of particular status variables (see Section 12.8.5). Trend analysis is important for forecasting faults in components. Diagnosis of faults requires correlation of event reports. Some aspects of analysis are considered part of the presentation of information for example, displaying information as histograms or graphs. In general, analysis is application-specific so is not really considered part of a generalized monitoring service. It can range from very simple gathering of statistics to very sophisticated model-based analysis.

Some monitoring tools collect various statistics such as total CPU usage, ready, blocked, idle and busy times, number of messages or bytes sent. (TMP (Wybranietz and Haban, 1990)). In the SIMPLE environment (Mohr, 1990), a commercial data analysis and graphics package S, from AT&T, has been integrated for interactive and complex analysis of monitoring data. A more complex approach has been adopted in the Event Based Behavioral Abstraction approach (EBBA), which is a paradigm for high-level debugging of distributed systems (Bates, 1988). The EBBA toolset allows the user to construct models of system behavior in a top-down manner. These models reflect user understanding of the expected system behavior, and are compared to the actual system activity represented by the monitoring information.

12.4   Dissemination of monitoring information

Monitoring reports generated by the objects would have to be forwarded to different users of such information. The destination of such reports may be human users, managers, other monitoring objects or processing entities. Dissemination schemes range from very simple and fixed to very complex and specialized. An example of a fixed scheme is the broadcasting of reports to all the users. In this case the monitoring server will forward all the reports to all the users. A complex and specialized dissemination scheme could be based on the subscription principle (Feldkuhn and Erickson, 1989) as shown in Figure 12.6.

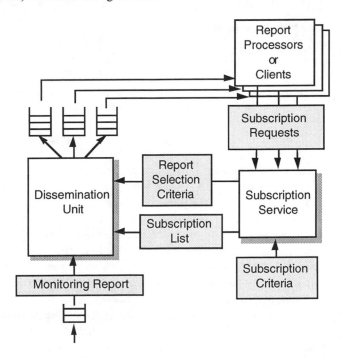

Figure 12.6 Dissemination of monitoring reports.

Clients of a monitoring service subscribe to receive the required status or event reports from the dissemination unit by registering themselves with the subscription service. Each client sends a subscription request indicating its identity, the list of reports and the frequency of the reports required. Subscription authorization information, held by the service, is used to determine whether the client is an authorized user and what reports it is permitted to receive. Only authorized users are permitted to subscribe and are entered in the *Subscription List* maintained by the dissemination unit. *Selection Criteria* contained within the subscription request are used by the dissemination system to determine which reports and their contents should be sent to the clients. This provides implicit filtering as only the requested reports are forwarded.

12.5   Presentation of monitoring information

Generated, collected, and processed monitoring information has to be presented to clients in a format that meets their specific application requirements. A suitable user interface should enable the user to specify how to display information as well as cope with:

- large amounts of monitoring data generated by the system,

- various levels of abstraction of such information,

- the inherent parallelism in the system activity, represented by monitoring data,

- the rate at which this information is produced and presented.

Various presentation techniques have been used for displaying debugging data in parallel debugging systems (McDowell and Helmbold, 1989). Similar techniques can be used in a generalized monitoring system to display different types of monitoring information relating to configuration, performance, security, accounting, etc. These approaches include the following:

Textual data presentation is the most common type of display with a simple text presentation of the monitoring information, which may involve highlighting or color (for example, the Jade monitoring system (Joyce *et al.*, 1987)). Events may be displayed in their *causal* rather than *temporal* order (for example, Traveler (Manning, 1987)). Appropriate indentation, highlighting and coloring can be used to increase the expressive power of visualization and also to distinguish monitoring information at various levels of abstraction. Advantages of this technique are that no special devices are necessary to present monitoring data and that it is simple to convert such information to textual form. However, this technique is not enough to present parallel system activities. Nowadays, simple textual presentation is often used in combination with other more expressive techniques as outlined below.

Time process diagrams shows the state of the parallel system as a two-dimensional diagram, with one axis representing the objects and the other representing time. It shows the current status of the system and the sequence of events that led to that status, and therefore can display patterns of behavior over time. The unit of time may be the occurrence of an event or a period of real time. One or two characters can be used to represent each of the possible events associated with an object or group of objects. The advantage of using a time-process diagram is that monitoring information can be presented on a simple text screen, as in Jade (Joyce *et al.*, 1987). Time-process display tools may use graphics. For example, in IDD (Harter *et al.*, 1985) two points in the display are connected by a line to indicate the exchange of a message, instead of placing one character at each point in the display. The user can magnify or scroll to see only a selected portion of the display. Various filters may be selected by the user to limit the information displayed on the screen.

Time-process diagrams usually require a global clock. However, in one approach using a concurrency map (Stone, 1988), events are arranged to show only the order in which they occurred, based on causal ordering of a logical clock, instead of showing the exact times of event occurrences based on a global clock.

Animation allows the observation of the instantaneous state of the system. A representation of every object or selected portions of monitoring data, can be placed at a different point in a two-dimensional display. The entire display represents a snapshot of system activity. Such a representation may be in the form of icons, boxes, Kiviat diagrams, bar charts, dials, X-Y plots, matrix views, curves, pie graphs, meters, and so on. Subsequent changes in the display, over a period of time, could provide an animated view of the evolution of the system state. For animation purposes, heavier use of graphics provides the user with more expressive and easily understood views of system activity. Examples of approaches that use animation are SMART and VISIMON tools (Mohr, 1991), the Radar (LeBlanc and Robbins, 1985) and TMP (Haban and Wybranietz, 1990).

Often a combination of various presentation techniques may have to be used to provide different views of system activity, because no single view may be sufficient for monitoring purposes. Based on the studied monitoring display tools, we can mention some desirable features which a general-purpose user interface must possess. They include:

- *Visualization at different abstraction levels*: A general-purpose user interface must enable the user to observe system behavior at a desired level of abstraction. The stepwise refinement, usually used in software engineering, should also be applied to monitoring (Klar *et al.*, 1992). The user should be able to start the observation at a coarse level such as the entire system and progressively focus on lower levels – subsystems, processes or procedures. This can be achieved by using the combination and filtering techniques discussed previously. Some of the tools which provide this feature are TMP (Haban and Wybranietz, 1990) and ConicDraw (Kramer *et al.*, 1989). Observation of system activities need not be restricted to exactly one level of abstraction at a time, and it would be useful to enable the user to observe an activity at several levels simultaneously.

- *Placement of monitoring information*: The ability to place a portion of monitoring data on a selected part of the screen can greatly enhance the visibility of the information and aid in comprehension of potentially very cluttered display. In the time-process diagrams of IDD (Harter *et al.*, 1985) the user can move the rows so that information about the related processes can be placed close together. ConicDraw (Kramer *et al.*, 1989) provides various facilities expected of a diagram editor. It allows the user to interact with the tool to improve the visual layout of the display by moving or resizing the boxes representing components and moving the ports so that the lines representing port bindings do not cross.

- *Controlling the time of display*: Some display tools provide a history function, permitting the user to scroll the display forward or backward in time and to control the speed at which the behavior of the system is observed. The display options include start, stop, interrupt, restart, step-by-step display, continuous display (real-time or slow-motion). Some of the tools that provide this feature are SIMPLE (Mohr, 1991) and Radar (LeBlanc and Robbins, 1985).

- *Use of multiple views*: As mentioned before, one single view of system activity may not be enough and multiple complementary views may be needed to enable the user to obtain a more comprehensive picture of system behavior. This can be achieved by using multiple windows presenting the system activities from different points of view, as in Voyeur (Socha *et al.*, 1988).

- *Visibility of interactions*: Some tools enable the user to display the contents of a particular message as in Radar (LeBlanc and Robbins, 1985). More specifically, it would be useful to be able to choose an event or status report and display its contents (for example, its timestamp, object identifier, and so on). In TMP, The width or color of the lines representing component interconnections can represent the volume of communication between them (Haban and Wybranietz, 1990).

12.6   Implementation issues

12.6.1   Intrusiveness of monitoring systems

Intrusiveness is the effect that monitoring may have on the behavior of the monitored system, and results from the monitoring system sharing resources with the observed system (e.g., processing power, communication channels, storage space). Intrusive monitors may alter the timing of events in the system in an arbitrary manner and can lead to:

- degradation of system performance,

- a change of global ordering of these events,

- incorrect results,

- an increase in the execution time of the application,

- masking or creating deadlock situations.

This means that the results of monitoring with an intrusive monitor can only be taken as an approximation of what happens in an unmonitored system (Lump *et al.*, 1990). The way that a monitoring system identifies the occurrence of events is an important parameter by which its intrusiveness can be measured. Various detection mechanisms are available and, according to which mechanism is used, monitoring systems can be categorized into three types: hardware monitors, software monitors and hybrid monitors.

Hardware monitors

In this class of monitoring systems a separate object (a hardware monitor) is used to detect events associated with an object or group of objects. It performs the detection by observation of system buses or using physical probes connected to the processors, memory ports, or I/O channels (Marinescu *et al.*, 1990; Tsai *et al.*, 1990).

Hardware monitors have the advantage of being nonintrusive – this is achieved by separating the resources used by the monitoring system from those used by the monitored system, so that the monitoring system has minimal or no effect on the observed system. This is particularly important for monitoring real-time systems. Hardware monitors have been successfully used for monitoring communication networks, where a lot of information is generated and processed very rapidly. The disadvantages are that:

- They require additional hardware, and therefore are more expensive.

- Generally, they provide very low-level data and do not meet the requirements of application programmers in parallel environments. Usually considerable processing and complicated mechanisms are required to provide application-level monitoring information, from low machine-level data.

- Hardware monitors form the least portable class of monitoring mechanisms. Their installation requires great expertise and thorough knowledge of the system, as they often use specific and sophisticated features of the hardware (Wybranietz and Haban, 1990). Nowadays, the design of hardware monitors is greatly complicated by the use of pipelining and on-chip cache to increase the throughput of microprocessors and also an increase in the integration of various functional units (for example, floating point units and memory management units) which makes monitoring difficult. In the future, this will lead to integration of monitors on the chip (Bemmerl *et al.*, 1990).

Software monitors

Software monitors usually share the necessary resources with the monitored system. The program is instrumented by inserting *software probes* in the code to gather information of interest. The source code, library routines, the object code and the kernel may be instrumented, manually or automatically, to obtain the required data (Van Riek and Tourancheau, 1991). Use of software monitors has the following advantages:

- Monitoring information is presented in an application-oriented manner which is easy to understand and use, compared with the low-level information generated by hardware monitors.

- Software monitors are portable and can easily be replicated.

- Compared with hardware monitors they are easier to design and construct and are more flexible.

- No additional and dedicated hardware resources are required. This makes them much cheaper than hardware monitors.

The disadvantage of software monitors is that they use the same resources as the monitored system and therefore interfere in both the timing and space of the observed system, which impacts on its behavior. This impact increases if monitored data is processed and displayed on-line. For this reason, pure software monitors are not adequate for on-line, real-time monitoring. To limit the effect of intrusion, instrumentation must be limited to those events whose observation is considered essential.

In Meta (Marzullo *et al.*, 1991) the source code is instrumented in a manual fashion (see Section 12.7.2). Lumpp *et al.* (1990) use an event specification language to include a monitoring segment with the source code. This segment is used by the compiler to automatically perform the instrumentation. In the SIMPLE environment (Klar *et al.*, 1992) source code instrumentation is done automatically by using a tool called AICOS (see Section 12.7.1). In Jade (Joyce *et al.*, 1987) instrumented library routines are used to monitor the system. An example of kernel instrumentation technique can be found in TOPSYS (Bemmerl and Bode, 1991).

Hybrid monitors.i.monitor:hybrid;

Hybrid monitors are designed to benefit from the advantages of both hardware and software monitors, while overcoming their inefficiencies. They have their own independent resources but also share some of the resources with the monitored system. Typically such a system consists of an independent hardware device that receives monitoring information generated by software probes inserted into monitored software objects. The event reports generated are processed and displayed by dedicated hardware.

The main advantage of hybrid monitors is that they introduce less intrusion into the monitored system compared with pure software monitors. Like software monitors, they generate high-level application-oriented monitoring information, compared with the low-level data generated in a purely hardware monitor. It gives them the same flexibility as software monitors. They are also cheaper than hardware monitors as they share their resources with the monitored system and therefore use fewer dedicated facilities. Because of this sharing of resources, they are more intrusive than hardware monitors. Hybrid monitors are less portable than software monitors because of their use of dedicated hardware.

Many monitoring systems prefer the hybrid approach. An example is the Test and Measurement Processor (TMP) which allows measuring, monitoring, testing and debugging of distributed applications (Wybranietz and Haban, 1990). The designers of TMP claim that the degradation in the performance of the monitored system is less than 0.1%. The TOPSYS environment (Bemmerl and Bode, 1991) supports software, hardware and hybrid monitoring. ZM4 (Hofmann *et al.*, 1992) supports both hybrid and hardware monitoring (see Section 12.7.1).

12.6.2   Global state, time and ordering of events

A typical loosely coupled distributed system consists of a number of independent and cooperating nodes that communicate through message passing, with no shared memory or common clock. Every node has its own local clock, which can be used to timestamp events occurring at that site. Distributed systems are more difficult to design, construct and monitor than centralized systems because of parallelism among processors, random and non-negligible communication delays, partial failures and no global synchronized time.

These features can affect both the behavior of the system and the way it is monitored. Several executions of the same distributed algorithm may result in different interleavings of events and therefore various outcomes. This makes the behavior of the system non-deterministic and unpredictable. Furthermore, arbitrary message delays make it impossible to obtain an instantaneous and consistent "snapshot" view of the system. Also, the same execution of a distributed program may be observed differently by various observers because of different interleavings of monitoring reports. Lack of global time makes it difficult to determine causal relationships between events by analyzing monitoring traces.

We shall briefly describe a number of approaches used to overcome these problems.

Physical clock synchronization

The aim is to obtain a unique physical time frame within a system, where each processor maintains its own local physical clock. Physical clock synchronization is based on the exchange of messages containing timestamps. These may contain an external timestamp received from an accurate radio time signal or local time-stamps and the nodes try to maintain processor clocks within some maximum deviation of each other.

For example Lamport (1978) proposed an algorithm which assumes that both a lower bound (min) and an upper bound (max) are known for message delays. Every T seconds each process sends a *synch* message on all of its channels to other processes. This protocol is deterministic but cannot guarantee a precision better than (max-min)(1-1/n), where n is the number of clocks that have to be synchronized. Deterministic protocols offer a high probability of successful synchronization with a small number of messages, at the expense of low precision.

Cristian (1989) proposed a probabilistic approach for reading remote clocks subject to unbounded message delays, which offers a higher precision than the best achieved by the deterministic protocols, but which carries with it a certain risk of not achieving synchronization.

One disadvantage of keeping clocks synchronized is the additional overhead that it introduces into the monitored system. Duda *et al.* (1987) described an off-line approach which records local traces of external events, using (unsynchronized) local clocks, and analyzes the traces after the execution of a distributed program to deduce global properties or global performance indices. The global time is estimated from local traces with a desired precision. A least-square regression analysis is used to estimate the time offset and the time offset rate between two local clocks.

Logical clocks

A system of logical clocks, based on the *causality relation*, can be used to establish a partial ordering of events in the system (Lamport, 1978). The system of logical clocks can be represented by a function LC which assigns to any event e a locally maintained timestamp LC(e), such that the following condition is satisfied:

For any events a and b, if $a \rightarrow b \Rightarrow LC(a) < LC(b)$

where $a \rightarrow b$ means a precedes b.

To satisfy this condition each process must increment its clock between any two events. Also, upon receiving a message, a process must advance its clock to be later than the timestamp of the message.

This scheme has several advantages. It imposes small overheads on the monitored system. The quantity of information contained in messages and maintained by each process is minimal – an integer. The system can easily accommodate dynamic changes in that a component can be added to the monitoring domain with no changes to the ordering scheme or other components.

A problem with the logical clock approach is that it lacks what is called *density*. Given e_1 and e_2 where $LC(e_1) < LC(e_2)$, it is not possible to determine if there is another event e_3 such that $LC(e_1) < LC(e_3) < LC(e_2)$. This is particularly important for run-time reordering of events where we want to detect message loss or delays. Another problem with both logical and physical time is that although they are consistent with causality, they do not characterize it (Schwarz and Mattern, 1992). It is not always possible to determine whether two events are causally related or concurrent by looking at their timestamps.

Vector clocks

Fidge (1988) has proposed an approach based on *a vector of logical timestamps*. Rather than one clock value, each process P_i maintains a vector of logical timestamps VC_i, where every element of the vector corresponds to one interacting process. Intuitively, element j of P_i's logical vector for event e is the number of events that P_i knows P_j has executed up to e. This vector is maintained by a process and included in outgoing messages. The vector is updated whenever a message is received from a process. Although vector clocks can overcome the problems outlined above the overheads could be very high. A logical clock has to be maintained by every process for all other processes with which it communicates. The vectors of timestamps included in messages can be quite long, thus increasing the communication overhead. Also, dynamic changes to the monitoring domain becomes much more difficult.

Global snapshots

In contrast to the approaches described above, Chandy and Lamport (1985) proposed a technique which concentrates on constructing a global snapshot of system activity. This technique encompasses the entire system in the gathering and grouping of state information. This snapshot is constructed through the transmission of *marker messages* over every communication link in the system (FIFO channels are assumed). Any process can initiate such a snapshot by saving its local state and transmitting marker messages over each of its outgoing links. Upon receiving its first marker, a node is incorporated into the snapshot, saves its local state, begins recording messages on its incoming links and transmits a marker over each of its outgoing links. A node stops recording the information received on a link when a marker is received over it. The dissemination of these marker messages throughout the system serves to create a timeslice, which demarcates the edge of a snapshot. The global snapshot can then be calculated from all of the local states (snapshots) of the nodes and all of the channel information recorded. Partial ordering is not violated by the system view captured.

The major disadvantage of this technique is that all the processes and communication links are involved in the formation of a snapshot. This is a highly inefficient means of gathering state information to recognize an event whose scope is limited to only a small subset of the system processors (Spezialetti and Kearns, 1989).

For general monitoring purposes, we are interested in the time intervals between occurrences of different events in addition to the ordering of events. Using a combination of logical vector clocks and synchronized clocks may be preferable for this purpose, but the overheads involved have to be considered.

12.7   Some existing monitoring systems

In this section we describe three of the existing monitoring systems in more detail.

12.7.1   ZM4/SIMPLE

A monitoring system which allows the observation and analysis of the functional behavior and the performance of programs in distributed systems is described in (Hofmann *et al.*, 1992; Mohr, 1990, 1991). This system is used for performance evaluation, tuning and debugging. Their approach is based on what they call model-driven monitoring. An event-based formal model of the program behavior using graphs, petri-nets, or queuing models is used, with the help of certain tools, for systematic program instrumentation (*model-driven instrumentation*), event recognition, event trace validation, and for creating a performance model. The tool AICOS has been developed to allow Automatic Instrumentation of C Object Software. Arbitrary statements in the program under investigation can be instrumented. The instrumented program is executed and it generates an event trace. The model is systematically checked against this linearly ordered trace and program errors are detected (*model-driven validation*). If the trace is valid, it is evaluated.

ZM4

Instrumented objects write event tokens to the hardware interface of ZM4 (Figure 12.7), which is a distributed hybrid monitoring system. It is structured as a master/slave system with a *control and evaluation computer* (CEC) as the master and an arbitrary number of *monitor agents* (MA) as slaves. The master controls the measurement activities of the MAs, stores the measured data and supports the user with a powerful toolset for evaluation of the measured data. Each MA has up to four *dedicated probe units* (DPUs) which are printed circuit boards and link it to the nodes of the object system. The MAs control the DPUs and buffer the measured event traces on their local disk. Event traces are transferred to the CEC for evaluation. The DPUs are responsible for event recognition, timestamping, event recording, and for high-speed buffering of event traces. Event recording is independent of the object system.

A local clock with a resolution of 100 ns and a timestamping mechanism are integrated into the DPU. The *tick channel* is used to synchronize the local clocks of the DPUs to the master clock on the *measure tick generator* (MTG). The data channel (Ethernet with TCP/IP) forms the communication subsystem of the ZM4 and is used to distribute control information and measured data.

ZM4 is scalable by adding more DPUs and MAs and can record events of arbitrary objects with arbitrary physical event representation and format.

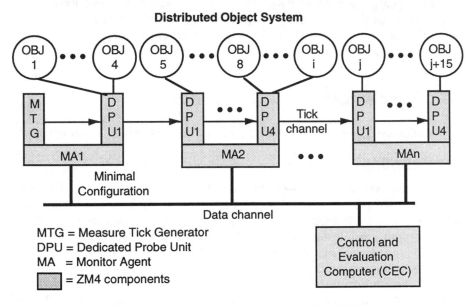

Figure 12.7 Distributed architecture of the ZM4.

SIMPLE

SIMPLE is a tool environment designed and implemented for performance evaluation of arbitrarily formatted event traces and runs on UNIX and MS-DOS systems. The measured data is considered as an abstract data structure or object which can only be accessed via a standard set of generic procedures. This enables the user of such reports to abstract away from different data formats, structures, representations and meanings and thus become independent of the monitored system and monitor devices used. Events can be identified by application-oriented names to give reference to the source.

The formats, structures and properties of monitored data are described in a trace description language (TDL) which clearly reflects the fundamental structure of an event trace (see Figure 12.8). The TDL description is compiled and an access key file is generated (Figure 12.9). This file is used by a standardized Problem Oriented Interface (POET) which enables the user or evaluation tools to access monitored data stored in event trace files in a user-defined, problem-oriented manner. A language called Filter Description Language (FDL), similar to TDL, has also been developed to specify rules for filtering event reports depending on their contents. The problem-oriented identifiers of the TDL file are also used for filtering. By using TDL/POET/FDL, all tools of SIMPLE are independent of the properties of a monitored system, especially its operating system and programming languages.

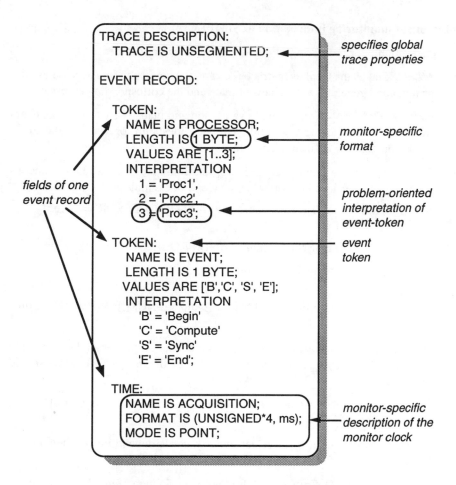

Figure 12.8 Event trace description in TDL.

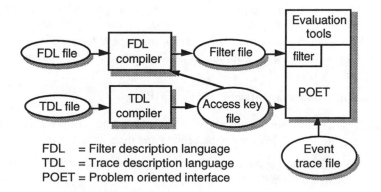

FDL = Filter description language
TDL = Trace description language
POET = Problem oriented interface

Figure 12.9 Event trace access with TDL/POET/FDL.

Processing of monitoring information in SIMPLE

The tools available for processing of monitored information include:

- *MERGE*: takes the local event trace files and the corresponding access key files as input and generates a global event trace and the corresponding access key.

- *CHECK TRACE:* performs simple validation and plausibility tests on an event trace, such as checking the validity of the timestamp, or whether the token fields contain only defined token values.

- *VARUS:* performs more detailed, application-specific, validation checks specified as assertions in a formal language. For example:

  i) ASSERT   (EVENT == 'Compute' AND PROCESSOR == 'Proc1')
      ALTERNATING

      WITH   (EVENT == 'Sync' AND PROCESSOR == 'Proc1')

      ELSE   "sequence error on processor 1";

  ii) ASSERT

              NUMBER(EVENT=='Begin')==NUMBER(EVENT=='End')

  Rule (i) states that the Compute and Sync events on processor Proc1 should alternate. Rule (ii) specifies that the number of Begin and End events should be the same.

  Both CHECK TRACE and VARUS generate a report containing all errors detected.

- *FILTER*: allows the user to select event records depending on their record fields.

- *ADAR* (Activity Definition and Recognition System): enables the user to combine lower-level events to form higher-level events called activities, and assign new attributes to them.

- *TRCSTAT*: performs simple statistical computations on an event trace. It computes frequencies, durations, and other performance indices. For more complex computations the data analysis package S from AT&T is used. It provides a high-level programming language for data manipulation and graphics.

Presentation of monitoring information in SIMPLE

- *LIST:* generates a simple textual list of events and permits the specification of which event record fields are to be printed and their format.

- *SMART* (Slow Motion Animated Review of Traces): is used for simple display on any ASCII terminal.

- *VISMON*: permits graphical display and animation of monitoring information. It is based on X-Windows.

12.7.2 Meta

The Meta system is a collection of tools for constructing distributed application management software (Marzullo *et al.*, 1991). It enables the management functions to monitor and control the behavior of the underlying application. It runs on UNIX and uses the ISIS distributed programming toolkit.

In the Meta model of a distributed application (Figure 12.10), the management and functional aspects are separated by a well-defined interface. The management layer is called the *control program* and is programmed in a rule-based control language called *Lomita*.

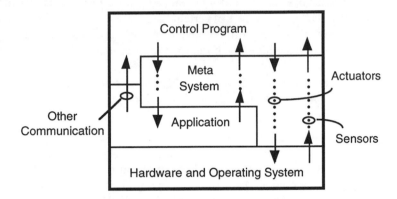

Figure 12.10 Meta application structure.

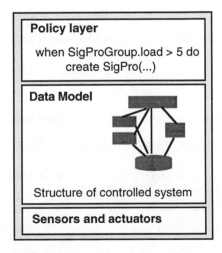

Figure 12.11 Meta function layers.

The Meta system presents the control program with an abstract view of the application and the environment in which it is run. Figure 12.11 shows the functional layering in the Meta system. Using Meta to manage a distributed application takes three steps: instrumenting the application, structure description and expressing policy rules.

Instrumenting the application

The programmer uses a set of sensors and actuators to instrument the application and its environment. Sensors are functions that return values of the application's state and its environment. A sensor can be polled, at intervals defined by the programmer, to obtain its current value or a *watch* can be set up that alerts the client when the sensor value satisfies some predicate. Built-in sensors obtain information directly from the run-time environment for example, CPU and memory utilization. Meta provides the *read-var sensor* for reading the values of certain kinds of global variables in an active process. There are also user-defined sensors which are implemented by the programmer and registered with Meta at run time to measure application throughput, or a queue length.

Built-in actuators can be used to change a process's priority; a global variable (using *write-var* actuator) and user-defined actuators can be used to change the application's behavior.

Structure description

The programmer describes the structure of the application using Lomita's object-oriented data modeling facilities. Meta provides an object-oriented temporal database in which the application and environment provide the data values. Components in the application and the environment are modeled by entities, following entity-relationship database terminology. The resulting model is used by the control program at the Policy Layer.

To provide higher-level views of the behavior of the program Meta allows the combination of multiple sensors, or values of one sensor over a period of time in the form of *derived sensors*. Lomita provides simple arithmetic operations, and also functions for min., max., size, median and so on. that operate over sets of values, for example:

> **sensor** load_ratio: **real**:= SigPro.load / Machine.load
>
> **sensor** high_load: **integer** := max(history(load, 600))

where load_ratio is the derived sensor calculated from primitive sensors SigPro.load and Machine.load and high_load is a derived sensor representing the maximum load over the last 10 minutes (600 seconds).

Expressing policy rules

Using the data model, the programmer defines a set of Lomita policy rules which describes the intended behavior of the system and can make direct calls on sensors and actuators and other functions in the data model, for example:

> **when** condition **do** action

where condition is a predicate expressed on the underlying data model and the action component is a sequence of actuator invocations and data model operations (e.g., create or delete). The condition may contain interval temporal logic expressions, in which case they are converted to finite state automata. The following temporal operators are used in Lomita:

During I **always** P: true if and only if predicate P is true throughout time interval I.

During I **occurs** P: true if and only if predicate P is true at some point within time interval I.

P **until** Q: Expresses the time interval beginning when predicate P next becomes true, and ending when predicate Q subsequently becomes true.

P **for** T: Expresses the time interval beginning when predicate P next becomes true, and ending when T seconds have passed.

12.7.3   Monitoring databases

A data-oriented approach to network management in which monitoring and control are specified as data manipulation statements on a network database is presented in (Wolfson *et al.* (1991)). In their approach a conceptual database model of the network is constructed and continuously updated to represent the current status of the network. Monitoring is done by "watching" for certain important events to occur. An event is represented by a data pattern, and watching for it means the continuous retrieval of this data pattern from the database.

They have extended the SQL data manipulation language to include new features which allow real-time and temporal monitoring of database changes. Two types of data are stored in the network database. The configuration data gives the current status of the network and history data consists of trace information about the evolution of the network and its status over time.

Events

For a primitive or correlated event to occur it has to be *specified* and then *activated*. After the occurrence the specification has to be reactivated in order for the event to occur again. There are three types of basic event:

i) *Data-pattern events* occur when a certain data pattern appears in the data-base. This is equivalent to the data flow events in our model. Such an event is specified using a data-retrieval operation which is executed if only one of the retrieved objects changes. One of the parameters of such an event is PERSISTENCE. If PERSISTENCE >= "time-interval" is associated with an event it indicates that the event is to occur only if the data-pattern persists in the database at least for the specified time interval. Therefore transient events can be ignored.

ii) *Data manipulation events* occur when a data manipulation operation is invoked in the system (for example, a retrieve, add, delete, replace or update). This is equivalent to the control flow events in our model. Such an event is specified by a data manipulation operation. For example, the following defines an event that occurs when a tuple is deleted from the relation LINKS which has a DELAY > 5.

DELETE LINKS DELAY > 5

iii) *Calendar-time events* are specified using a date and time. For example, "12 A.M. January 8" says the event occurs every year on January 8th at 12 A.M.

Trace collection service

The trace parameters which can be specified include trace identifier, the class of objects being monitored, the attribute whose change is being tracked, the event to activate a collection and the duration. A selection predicate for an attribute can be specified which results in the attribute's old value being appended to the trace after a change, or a separate trace for one or more objects can be requested (for example, all objects with COLOR = "yellow").

Combination

Combined or correlated events are specified using correlation rule such as

OVERLOAD-AT-12 :- OVERLOAD, 12 A.M.

means that the combined event OVERLOAD-AT-12 occurs if the data-pattern event OVERLOAD occurs at the same time as the calendar-time event 12 A.M. The operator "~" is used to denote negation, for example, ~EV1 means that event EV1 did not occur. The definition of a combined event could also consist of a disjunction of two events. For example:

OVERLOAD-OR-12 :- OVERLOAD.

OVERLOAD-OR-12 :- 12am.

specifies that the event OVERLOAD-OR-12 will occur when OVERLOAD occurs or at 12 A.M., whichever is first.

For each rule it is also possible to specify a temporal order for events (for example, E1 →E2), and temporal constraints (for example, {OVERLOAD, 12 A.M.} = 5 s says that OVERLOAD-AT-12 will occur only if OVERLOAD and 12 A.M. are at most 5 s apart).

Table 12.3 presents a brief comparison between the approaches described in Sections 12.7.1 to 12.7.3, against the functionalities identified in the model.

Table 12.3 Comparison of features of example systems.

	ZM4/Simple	Meta	Monitoring Database
Purpose of monitoring	Debugging and performance tuning	Management of distributed applications	Managing communication systems
Status reporting	No. Event-driven monitoring used.	Yes. Polling object state. Sampling period set at instrumentation time	No. Event-driven monitoring used
Event detection and reporting	H/w and hybrid monitoring. Automatic S/W instrumentation supported. Internal and external detection of process level and control flow events	S/W Monitoring. Manual instrumentation. External detection of data flow events	S/W monitoring. Changes to data in network database detected (external detection)
Trace generation	Yes. Trace format specified using TDL language	No.	Yes. User-specified trace generation – part of a history database
Merging and multiple trace generation	Yes. Merging supported using the tool MERGE	No.	Yes. User-specified merging and multiple traces
Validation	Yes. Supported using CHECK TRACE and VARUS tools	Valid event orderings guaranteed by ISIS OS	No.
Database updating	No	Yes. A system data model is maintained and referenced.	Yes. A network database is continuously updated and referenced
Combination	Supported using ADAR tool	Supported using LOMITA language.	Supported using an SQL-like language
Filtering	Explicit filtering supported using FILTER tool based on event attributes. FDL language used	Implicitly by setting polling periods or guards at instrumentation time	Done explicitly by specifying conditions at event recognition and implicitly through activation and deactivation
Dissemination	Monitoring information sent to a fixed central station.	Using a subscription mechanism status data is distributed to other monitoring agents	Not specified
Presentation	Textual, time-process and animation display tools with user-specified display rate. Graphical display	Not specified	Not specified

12.8   OSI management standards

12.8.1   OSI Management Approach

The International Standards Organization (ISO) has defined a series of standards for the management of the communication system for Open Systems Interconnection

(OSI). These define managed objects as a representation of a managed resource, but managers do not directly invoke operations on managed objects as we have assumed in Figure 12.2. Instead, managers interact with a management agent which is local to the managed objects, using the Common Management Information Protocol (CMIP) as shown in Figure 12.12. CMIP provides the primitives for supporting management operations to permit the managers to control remote managed objects and query state; notifications can be used by the agent to send status and event reports from the managed objects to the manager.

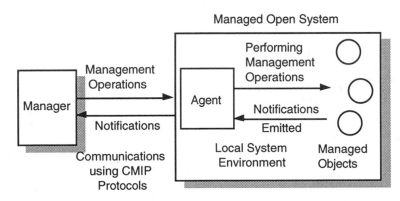

Figure 12.12 OSI interaction model.

Managed objects may also be used to implement elements within a monitoring system to perform processing or dissemination functions as explained below. Managed objects may be created and deleted dynamically, in response to changes in the managed system or to change the monitoring system. Managed objects constitute the Management Information Base (MIB).

The OSI standards define a set of management functions relating to configuration management, fault management, performance management, accounting and security management for communications systems, but there is no monitoring as a specific management function. However, the specifications relating to the above five functions, and in particular fault and performance management, define elements which could be used as a generic monitoring service for distributed systems. A summary of monitoring and event reporting in OSI can be found in LaBarre (1991). The OSI Guidelines for the Definition of Managed Objects (GDMO) define a set of techniques and a notation for specifying managed objects (ISO 10165-4 (1992)).

12.8.2   Generation of monitoring information

The state variables which are made visible by objects are called *attributes*. A generic set of states and the changes which can take place between those states are defined in (ISO 10164-2, 1990). These states are reflected in a set of attributes which are common to all managed objects. Additional attributes may be provided to represent the application-specific status vector of the object. The typical information which would be generated in a state change event report sent to a manager includes:

- Managed object class and instance identifiers

- Event time

- Old and new values for all state attributes

- Application-specific status attributes

Objects often generate notifications to their local agent as event or status reports. The agent performs filtering and dissemination of this monitoring information using event discriminator objects as explained in Section 12.8.3 below. An alternative, for very simple objects, is to use a *metric object* to periodically poll the managed object to read the attributes and then generate the notifications (ISO 10164-11, 1992).

The predefined event reports include the following:

i) *Object Management* reports are generated whenever a managed object is created/ deleted, an operational/administrative state change occurs, or changes occur in non-state attributes for example, names or important operational parameters (ISO 10164-2, 1990).

ii) *Alarm Reports* have been defined for the following alarm classes (ISO 10164-4, 1990):

- communication faults such as call set-up errors or signal distortion

- quality of service degradation for example, problems with throughput or response time

- processing errors for example, buffer overflow, file access error, memory violation.

- equipment alarms for example, cable cut detected, locked ports or power problems

- environment problems for example, high/low temperature, smoke detection or excess humidity.

An alarm message can include probable cause, specific problem code, additional problem data, perceived severity, severity trend, backup status, backup object instance, threshold information, proposed repair, and additional textual information actions as well as state attribute values.

12.8.3 Event reporting service

The OSI event reporting service performs both the processing and dissemination functions of our monitoring model in that it is responsible for both filtering of event reports and dissemination of the selected reports to chosen destinations (ISO 10164-5, 1990). The components which constitute the service are shown in Figure 12.13.

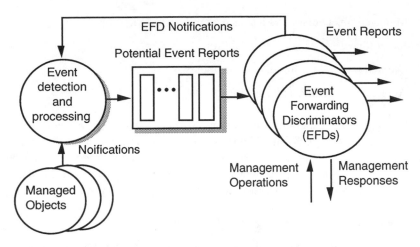

Figure 12.13 OSI event reporting service.

Notifications are received by a local event detection and processing component which adds the event time, originating object class and instance to the notification message to form a potential event report. These are conceptually sent to all local *Event Forwarding Discriminators (EFDs)*. An EFD holds a discriminator construct which defines the criteria used to select which of the potential event reports are forwarded to the destination address stored in the EFD. An EFD sends reports to a single destination at any time. The EFD is a managed object and so itself can generate notifications which are forwarded by another local EFD. The EFDs specify the following information:

EFD identifier: unique identifier for the EFD.

Discriminator construct: A logical expression on attributes within the potential event reports, for example:

$$\{\{(dest=fred) \text{ and } (count >50)\} \text{ or } \{(source=xyz) \text{ and } (size <100)\}\}$$

Only those potential reports which meet the criteria specified are forwarded.

Administrative, operational, and availability state information which indicates whether or not it is actually forwarding events.

Destination: primary destination to which events should be forwarded.

Backup destination: a list of alternative destinations to which events reports are to be sent if the primary is unavailable.

The scheduling of event reports can be achieved by internal or external scheduling packages.

Daily schedule: a list of times within a 24-hour period when forwarding is enabled

Weekly schedule: start/stop operating date and time, and periodic weekly schedule for enabling the event forwarding.

EFDs can be created and deleted dynamically to accomplish the registration of subscribers to a dissemination service, as described in section 12.4. A manager can also enable/disable the operation of an EFD and so override the predefined scheduling. It is not clear whether EFDs can be used to combine lower-level events to form higher-level events as described in Section 12.3.4

12.8.4   Log service

Trace generation is by means of log records which can be stored in log managed objects (ISO 10164-6, 1990). The structure of the Log service is shown in Figure 12.14. The collection process receives event reports from local or remote managed objects and formats them into potential log records by adding a log record identifier and logging timestamp. A set of criteria for selecting which of these potential records are actually stored can be specified in terms of comparison operations on data within the event reports, daily or weekly time schedules and so on.

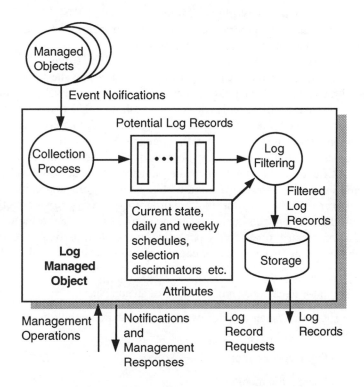

Figure 12.14 OSI Log Service.

Two options are available if the log reaches maximum capacity. Either the log activity is halted, with new records being discarded, or the log wraps, with the oldest records being discarded. An event report must be generated for a log halt condition and optionally to indicate a wrap condition. A capacity threshold event may be generated to warn a manager before the log is actually full. Every log must support the halt behavior, but support of the wrap behavior is optional.

Logs are themselves managed objects and can have their state controlled by managers for enabling/disabling the logging function. Internally defined time schedules may also change their operational state. Log attributes specify the logID, maximum number of log records, current size in bytes, number of records, log full action, the threshold for generating nearly full warning events and attributes to control the log record selection criteria. This logging service is very flexible in that managers can change the filtering criteria by changing the relevant log attributes.

12.8.4   Processing of monitoring information

There are a number of OSI standards that specify managed objects that can be used for performing the monitoring information processing functions defined in Section 12.3.

The OSI standard on Workload Monitoring (ISO 10164-11, 1992) defines metric objects as a means of processing monitoring information with the emphasis on statistical measurement of the performance of resources.

The simplest metric objects are counters and gauges. *Counters* increase until they reach a maximum value then wrap to zero. There may be three thresholds, associated with a counter. When the counter reaches a threshold value, a notification is emitted, the second notification is emitted at threshold value + offset and the third notification at threshold value + 2 × offset. *Gauges* can both increase and decrease in value. Two thresholds are associated with a gauge. A notification is emitted when the gauge crosses the high-level threshold (when the gauge is increasing) and similarly a notification is emitted when the gauge crosses the low-level threshold (when decreasing). Only one notification will be emitted from a particular threshold until the gauge crosses the other threshold in order to give a hysteresis effect and stop multiple notifications being emitted if the gauge oscillates about a threshold level. As mentioned above, metric objects may periodically sample a particular attribute in a managed object in order to implement a counter or gauge with threshold notifications.

Other metric objects which have been defined include:

*   Mean monitor to calculate a mean value of an attribute;

*   Moving Average mean monitor which uses an exponentially weighted moving average algorithm;

*   Mean and variance monitor;

*   Mean and percentile monitor;

*   Mean and min-max monitor;

*   Scanner Summarization Objects which provide a report on a list of attributes, values of the same or different types that have been read as a single scan;

*   Buffered Scanner provides a report of a list on different types of attribute values over multiple scans.

12.8.5 Discussion

Considerable international effort is being put into defining the comprehensive set of OSI management standards. These will support a very sophisticated monitoring service, but very few products that comply with these standards are available as yet. In addition, the number of options available and the sophistication of the service leads to some doubts as to the cost and performance capabilities of an OSI-based monitoring service. The OSI standards do not define anything about the presentation of management information as this is considered an implementation issue.

12.9 Summary

There is a need for a generic service for monitoring distributed systems as an underlying service to support all aspects of management. A monitoring service is also essential for debugging during system development and it may be needed as part of applications such as process control or factory automation.

This chapter has defined a monitoring model in terms of a set of monitoring functions. This has been used as a reference model for explaining the alternative approaches to monitoring distributed systems described in the literature. The main monitoring functions described are:

- *Generation* of monitored information which includes status and event reports and traces;

- *Processing* of monitored information to validate, combine and filter so that only relevant information is provided to clients;

- The required information must be *disseminated* to those clients who have subscribed to the service and specified the particular information they require;

- Flexible graphical facilities are needed for the *presentation* of monitored information to human users in a form which aids comprehension and meets specific application requirements.

The emphasis of the chapter has been on a survey of the current approaches to monitoring of parallel and distributed systems. However, the monitoring model could be used as a framework for specifying and designing a generalized monitoring service. This is work that we intend to undertake in the future as part of a European collaborative project.

Acknowledgments

We gratefully acknowledge the support of the SERC and HP Laboratories, Bristol for a CASE studentship. We also acknowledge the support of our colleagues in the Distributed Software Engineering Section at Imperial College for comments on the concepts described in this chapter.

Abbreviations

AICOS	Automatic Instrumentation of C Object Software
CEC	Control and Evaluation Center
CMIP	Common Management Information Protocol
DPU	Dedicated Probe Unit
EBBA	Event Based Behavioral Abstraction
EDL	Event Definition Language
EFD	Event Forwarding Discriminator
FDL	Filter Description Language
FIFO	First In First Out
GDMO	Guidelines for the Definition of Managed Objects
IP	Internet Protocol
ISO	International Standards Organization
MA	Monitoring Agent
MIB	Management Information Base
OSI	Open Systems Interconnection
POET	Problem Oriented Interface
SESL	State and Event Specification Language
TCP	Transport Control Protocol
TDL	Trace Description Language
TMP	Test and Measurement Processor

References

Bates P. (1988). Distributed debugging tools for heterogeneous distributed systems. In *Proc. IEEE 8th Int. Conf. on Distributed Computing Systems*, June, 308–16.

Bemmerl T., Lindhof R. and Treml T. (1990). The distributed monitor system of TOPSYS. In *Proc. CONPAR 1990 - VAPP IV*, September, 756–65, Springer-Verlag

Bemmerl T. and Bode A. (1991). An integrated environment for programming distributed memory multiprocessors. In *Proc. 2nd European Dist. Memory Comp. Conf.*, April, 130–42.

Chandy K. M. and Lamport L. (1985). Distributed snapshots: determining global states of distributed systems. *ACM Trans. on Comp. Syst.*, 3(7), 63–75

Cristian F. (1989). Probabilistic clock synchronisation. *Distributed Computing*, 3, 146-58

Dasgupta P. (1986). A probe-based monitoring scheme for an object-oriented, distributed operating system. In *ACM Proc. of the Conf. on Object Oriented Programming Systems, Languages and Applications*, 57–66

Duda A., Harrus H., Haddad Y. and Bernard G. (1987). *Estimating Global Time in Distibuted Systems*. ISEM Université de Paris-Sud, 91405 Orsey, France, 299–306

Feldkuhn L. and Erickson J. (1989). Event management as a common functional area of open systems management. In *Proc. IFIP 6.6 Symp. on Integrated Network Management*, Boston, 365–76, North-Holland

Fidge C. J. (1988). Partial orders for parallel debugging. In *Proc. of ACM Workshop on Parallel and Distributed Debugging*, 183–94

Haban D. & Wybranietz D. (1990). A hybrid monitor for behaviour and performance analysis of distributed systems. *IEEE Trans. on Software Eng.*, **16**(2), 197–211

Harter P. K., Heimbigner D. M. and King R. (1985). IDD: An interactive distributed debugger. In *Proc. IEEE 5th Int. Conf. on Distributed Computing Systems*, Denver, May, 498–506.

Hofmann R., Klar R., Mohr B., Quick A. and Siegle M. (1992). *Distributed Performance Monitoring: Methods, Tools, and Applications*. University of Erlangen-Nurnberg, IMMD VII, Martensstrabe 3, D-8520 Erlangen, Germany

Holden D. *et al.* (1988). An approach to monitoring in distributed systems. In *Proc. Eur. Teleinformatics Conf.*, Vienna, 811–23, North-Holland

Holden D. (1989). Predictive languages for management, In *Proc. IFIP Symposium on Integrated Network Management*, Boston, 585–96, North-Holland

Holden D. B. (1991). A Tutorial to Writing Programs in SESL. *Internal Report DMP/55*, Sys. & Software Eng. Grp., AEA Industrial Technology, Harwell, Jan. 1991

ISO 10164-1 (1990). *Information Technology - Open Systems Interconnection - Systems Management Part 1: Object Management Function*.

ISO 10164-2 (1990). *Information Technology - Open Systems Interconnection - Systems Management Part 2: State Management Function.*

ISO 10164-4 (1990). *Information Technology - Open Systems Interconnection - Systems Management Part 4: Alarm Reporting Function.*

ISO 10164-5 (1990). *Information Technology - Open Systems Interconnection - Systems Management Part 5: Event Report Management Function.*

ISO 10164-6 (1990). I*nformation Technology - Open Systems Interconnection - Systems Management Part 6: Log Control Function*,.

ISO 10164-11 (1992). *Information Technology - Open Systems Interconnection - Systems Management Part 11: Workload Monitoring Function.*

ISO 10165-4 (1992). *Information Technology - Open Systems Interconnection - Structure of Management Information: Guidelines for the Definition of Managed Objects.*

Joyce J., Lomow G., Slind K. and Unger B. (1887). Monitoring distributed systems. *ACM Trans. Comput. Syst.*, **5**(2), 121–50

Klar R., Quick A. and Soetz F. (1992). Tools for a model-driven instrumentation for monitoring. In *Proc. of the 5th Int. Conf. on Modelling Techniques and Tools for Computer Performance Evaluation* (Balbo G., ed.), Torino, Italy, 165–80. Elsevier Science Publisher B.V.

Kramer J., Magee J. and Ng K. (1989). Graphical configuration programming. *IEEE Computing*, Oct., 53–65

LaBarre L. (1991). Management by exception: OSI event generation, reporting, and logging. The MITRE Corporation, *2nd IFIP Symposium on Integrated Network Management*, Washington, April, 227–44

LeBlanc R. J. and Robbins A. D. (1985). Event-driven monitoring of distributed programs. In *Proc. 5th Int. Conf. on Distributed Computing Systems,* May, 515–22

Lamport L. (1978). Time, clocks and the ordering of events in distributed systems, *Communications of the ACM*, **21**(7), 558–64

Lumpp J. E., Jr., Casavant T. L., Seigle H. J. and Marinescu, D. C. (1990). Specification and identification of events for debugging and performance monitoring of distributed multiprocessor systems. In *Proc. IEEE 10th Int. Conf. on Dist. Sys.*, June, 476–83

Magee J., Kramer J. and Sloman M. (1989). Constructing distributed systems in Conic. *IEEE Trans. on Software Eng.*, **15**(6), 663–75

Manning C. R. (1987). Traveler: The apiary observatory. In *Proc. European Conference on Object Oriented Programming*, 97–105

Marinescu D. C., Lump J. E., Casavant T. L. and Siegel H. J. (1990). Models for monitoring and debugging tools for parallel and distributed software. *Journal of Parallel Distributed Computing*, **9**(2), 171–84

Marzullo K., Cooper R., Wood M. D. and Birman K. P. (1991). Tools for distributed application management. *IEEE Computer*, August, 42–51

McDowell C. E. and Helmbold D. P. (1989). Debugging concurrent programs. *ACM Computing Surveys*, **21**(4), 593–621

Mohr B. (1990). Performance evaluation of parallel programs in parallel and distributed systems. In *Proc. CONPAR 1990 - VAPP IV*, Sep., 176–87, Springer-Verlag

Mohr B. (1991). SIMPLE: A performance evaluation tool environment for parallel and distributed systems. In *Proc. of the 2nd European Distributed Memory Computing Conference*, EDMCC2 (Bode A., ed.), 80–9, Munich, Germany, April 1991. Berlin, Springer-Verlag, LNCS 487

Schwarz R. and Mattern F. (1992). *Detecting Causal Relationships in Distributed Computations: In Search of the Holy Grail.* Department of Computer Science, University of Kaiserslautern, D-6750 Kaiserslautern, Germany, 1992

Shim Y. C. and Ramamoorthy C. V. (1990). Monitoring and control of distributed systems. In *Proc. of First Int. Conf. on Sys. Integration,* Morristown, NJ, IEEE Computing Press, April 23–26, 672–81

Sloman M. (1987). Distributed Systems Management. *Imperial College Research Report, DOC 87/6*, 1 April 1987

Snodgrass R. (1988). A relational approach to monitoring complex systems. *ACM Trans. on Comp. Sys.*, **6**(2), 157–96

Socha D., Bailey M. L. and Notkin D. (1988). Voyeur: Graphical views of parallel programs, In *Proc. of Workshop on Parallel and Distributed Debugging*, May 5–6, *SIGPLAN NOTICES*, **24**(1), 206–15

Spezialetti M. and Kearns J. P. (1989). Simultaneous regions: A framework for consistent monitoring of distributed systems. In *Proc. 9th IEEE Intl. Conf. on Dist. Comp. Sys.*, 61–8

Stone J. M. (1988). A graphical representation of concurrent processes. In Proc. of Workshop on Parallel and Distributed Debugging, ACM Published as *SIGPLAN Notices,* **24**(1), January, 226-35

Tsai J. J.-P., Fang K.-Y. and Chen H.-Y. (1990). A non-invasive architecture to monitor real-time distributed systems. *IEEE Computer*, **23**(3), 11-23

Van Riek M. and Tourancheau B. (1991). *A General Approach to the Monitoring of Distributed Memory Machines – A Survey.* Laboratoire de l'Informatique du Parallelisme, Ecole Normale Superieure de Lyon, Institut des Sciences de la Matiere de l'Universite Claude Bernard de Lyon, Institut IMAG, Unite de Recherche Associee au CNRS No. 1398, Research Report No. 91/28, September 1991

Wybranietz D. and Haban D. (1990). Monitoring and measuring distributed systems. In *Performance Instrumentation and Visualization* (Simmons M. and Koskela R., eds.), 27–45, ACM Press

Wolfson O., Sengupta S. and Yemini Y. (1991). Managing communication Networks by monitoring databases. *IEEE Trans. on Software Eng.*, **17**(9), 944–53

Chapter 13

Network Planning and Performance Engineering

Ulrich Herzog

Computer Science Department (IMMD VII),
University of Erlangen–Nürnberg,
Martensstr. 3, D-91058 Erlangen, Germany
Email: herzog@informatik.uni-erlangen.de

This chapter first elaborates the major steps of the process of planning a network and then focuses on performance engineering. It covers the definition of service criteria, measurement techniques, modeling and analysis and configuration and capacity planning. The various solutions to these problems which are presented in the literature are surveyed giving a detailed insight into both theoretical and practical issues.

13.1   Introduction

Planning entails the preparation of all future steps of network development. Most important is to acquire and evaluate information on the current situation and trends. This is true for both workload characteristics and network components. Therefore, planning is a continual task starting with the first ideas on network design and accompanying the whole life cycle of a system.

Network management comprises monitoring, evaluation and control during network installation and its operation. Consequently, there is a strong relationship between both the planning process and network management.

We put emphasis on different issues, depending on the purpose and the overall objectives of a network. For example, when designing and managing wide area networks, we have to study how the workload, different topologies and routing strategies impact response times, resource utilization and throughput; the ever-changing tariff rates also play a major role. It is important to guarantee a uniform and fair grade of service for all customers. When planning the information subsystem of a manufacturing plant, the network topology should closely follow the organizational hierarchy of the enterprise. At each level of the network hierarchy we have to consider different performance requirements for management purposes, for example, large files have to be moved (via broadband networks) within hours or even minutes. At the same time we have to provide for protocol architectures guaranteeing real-time requirements on the factory floor, that is, response times ranging from milliseconds to seconds for messages with a few bits.

Any planning process comprises the following typical phases (Moulton, 1980; Gupta, 1985) to cater for a variety of scenarios, despite having special requirements and particular constraints:

- problem identification;

- conceptual design phase;

- detailed design including configuration, installation strategy, test and management;

- realization (installation and test);

- operation including network analysis and tuning;

- network analysis and enlargement;

- upgrading.

In almost all stages of the planning process we are faced with the problems of:

- identifying the characteristics of the workload;

- determining the quality of the system behavior;

- detecting and removing critical bottlenecks;

- developing optimal (hardware and software) modules, components and overall strategies.

A systematic approach and formal techniques are mandatory for mastering this rather complex task. We therefore regard and formulate the entire planning process as a mathematical optimization problem. Three examples may illustrate this view:

Example 1: Suppose we are given a banking system with one main processing location, all traffic going back and forth between remote terminals and the central CPU (see Figure 13.1). The overall objective is to minimize the total cost of the network configuration which is a function of:

- terminal locations,

- traffic characteristics and volume,

- line tariff, and

- communication components,

subject to constraints such as:

- the response time should be less than one second for 95% of transactions;
- a specific number of transactions per second should be guaranteed.

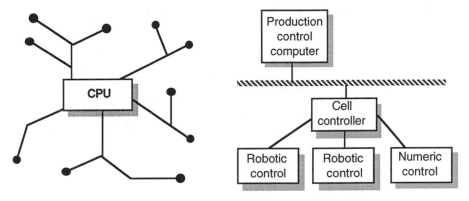

Figure 13.1 Centralized network configuration.

Figure 13.2 Hierarchical network configuration.

Example 2: On the manufacturing floor we have to download programs from the production control machine via a cell controller to a robot or numerical control system (Figure 13.2). Using standard protocols (for example, MAP – manufacturing automation protocols, EPA – enhanced performance architecture) we are faced with the problem of minimizing the program transfer time which is a function of:

- the computation power of the components, and
- the protocol architecture MAP and/or EPA

and subject to constraints such as:

- prescribed network structure, and
- given traffic characteristics.

Example 3: Suppose we are given a nationwide distributed airline reservation network (such as SITA or LUFTHANSA) with data processing capabilities and data terminal equipment at various locations, as shown in Figure 13.3. Such data networks have been built since the 1960s. However, traffic increases year by year and new terminals, hosts or switching centers have to be added from time to time to expand it regionally. So rather than planning the network from scratch we have to take into consideration both the configuration and operation mode of the existing network. Therefore, the planning task may be viewed as a local or partial optimization problem. So the overall objective might be to minimize the message transfer time, which is a function of:

- traffic,

- network topology,
- line capacity,
- routing strategy,
- processing power of the switches,

and subject to:

- a given overall cost, and
- constraints owing to the existing network.

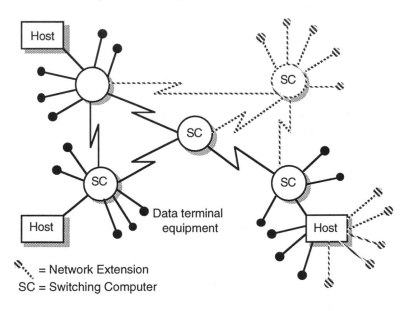

Figure 13.3 Distributed system configuration.

This rather difficult optimization problem is usually split into several subproblems such as capacity assignment or flow assignment, and then solved iteratively, as explained in Section 13.7.4.

These three examples show the complexity of our task as well as the intermixed technical and mathematical problems.

Performance engineering has to be an integral part of network and distributed system design (Harvey, 1986; Reiser, 1991; Herzog, 1992). Even at the highest architectural level one should attempt to quantify the important performance parameters. Then, as the design proceeds, decisions can be made to eliminate competing approaches and to dimension the selected components properly. Traditionally, such unified, concerted actions are often not the case. Redesign, additional cost and considerable delay are the consequence, and therefore W. Chou's statement may still be true (Chou, 1974):

`In most data communication networks currently in operation, costs can easily be reduced by fifteen percent or more with only minor alterations in the network. The cost savings can often reach thirty percent or more if reoptimization of the whole network is allowed'.*

The implication of the above statement is that the existing networks are not properly planned and designed.

13.2 Communication networks – fundamental problems and performance measures

Independent of the network size, operating strategy, services and its application we are always faced with the following three fundamental problems:

i) Preparation of the messages in the source system, for example:

   • formatting and encoding of data or programs in computers and terminals,

   • handling and coordination of control information in a cell controller,

   • buffering for output processing and transmission.

ii) Transfer and message switching

   • transmission on the individual links of the network,

   • routing and switching towards the correct destination,

   • overall control of the source-to-destination path.

iii) Message handling in the receiving system

   • buffering and transport-oriented preprocessing,

   • end-to-end control,

   • application-oriented preprocessing.

Each step may significantly contribute to the overall delay of messages. Of course, nowadays we have a selection of standardized communication services, protocols and products supporting various scenarios. However, it is also known that communication processing (in the end systems and switches) significantly slows down the actual transfer rate. Hence, when determining performance measures for a system we clearly have to distinguish between "gross" and "net" values. We first define some general measures:

i) *Capacity and throughput* measured in units of work (bits, messages, tasks) per time unit (seconds, minutes) serviced by a resource. Typical examples are:

   • Transmission rate of lines, trunks and channels ("capacity" measured in kbps or Mbps – kilobits or megabits per second),

- Number of messages to be handled and transferred by the end systems, individual communication links and switches ("throughput" measured in messages per second), or

- Number of messages to be handled by the communication subsystem in total ("throughput" in messages per second).

ii) *Response time and transfer time* – overall message delay in both end systems and the communication subsystem, from the point of departure until the arrival time, measured in seconds. Of interest are the maximum and mean values as well as percentiles. Typical examples are the host response time or message transfer time.

iii) *Utilization* – ratio between the time a component is used during a given interval of observation and the duration of that interval.

The utilization of the various components, for example, CPU utilization, channel activity, link occupancy, shows whether a system is well balanced or not. A more detailed description of the system behavior is possible by means of the following measures:

i) *Traffic request rate* – number of requests per second for transportation or processing offered by some traffic sources (source system). Typical examples are packet transfer rates, request rates for the installation of virtual circuits or call rates in telephone networks.

ii) *Traffic intensity* – the mean number of requests per second multiplied by their mean duration (transfer, processing, or holding time) in seconds. Traffic intensity is measured by the dimensionless unit "Erlang" in honor of the principal founder of traffic theory. We distinguish between the original "offered traffic", the successful "carried traffic" and the rejected "lost traffic".

iii) *Probability of loss or overflow* – number of rejected requests related to the total number of offered requests. Typical examples are the probability of buffer overflow or the loss probability in circuit-switching networks.

iv) *Delay* – because there are multiple requests competing for a limited number of resources, we may buffer them in queues. Queuing delays requests until service is granted. Delay-related measures of interest are mean, percentiles and maximum as well as the probability of delay.

All of these measures are important in order to:

- determine and represent the current state of network performance,

- find out bottlenecks in the individual components and in the overall design, and

- prepare for configuration changes with varying traffic volume, service demands and performance requirements.

When evaluating the overall grade of service of a network we do have to include, of course, reliability aspects (for example, distributed control, redundancy) as well as technical issues (for example, maximum number of DTEs to be attached to a network, maximum spatial extension, mechanical and electrical protection, on-line repair and extensions). In this survey, we put emphasis on performance engineering.

13.3   The planning process

In Section 13.1, we mentioned the typical phases of any planning process. The subtasks, their chronological sequence and interdependencies are summarized in Figure 13.4. It is self-explanatory and therefore we only stress some main points:

- The *conceptual phase* starts with a problem analysis and the comprehensive formulation of the communication problem. The master plan is laid down after some principal decisions concerning the overall strategy and disposition.

- The *design phase* starts with a second detailed analysis, classification and elaboration of all aspects related to both the workload description and system alternatives.

- Mapping the workload into the system alternatives, we analyze and compare the various solutions with respect to the quality of service and cost. By direct comparison or, more often, by a multiphase decision process the optimal solution is synthesized.

- All details of the chosen design are summarized in the configuration plan: communication channels, switching nodes, data terminal equipment. This includes the hardware specification, system and communication software as well as user relations. It also contains the network management plan as well as the installation and test strategy.

- The configuration plan *is realized* step by step. We order hardware and software, special application and system programs have to be implemented, and all these components are tested in pilot projects. Thus the new components gradually replace the former configuration.

- Once we start *to operate* the complete installation we systematically have to monitor, analyze and evaluate the grade of service in order to tune the individual components and the overall behavior of the system.

- In the course of time *extensions* are necessary owing to traffic increase, enhanced services or geographic expansions. Finally, the upgrading process leads to a new network generation.

It is obvious that network planning is a rather complex and demanding process. It is also clear from the above that performance engineering has to be an integral part of this continual task. Usually we distinguish between long-range planning, medium-term and short-term design periods. Table 13.1 summarizes related time intervals and objectives from the point of view of telecommunication system engineering (Freeman, 1989; Bergmann, 1986;Woehlbier, 1990).

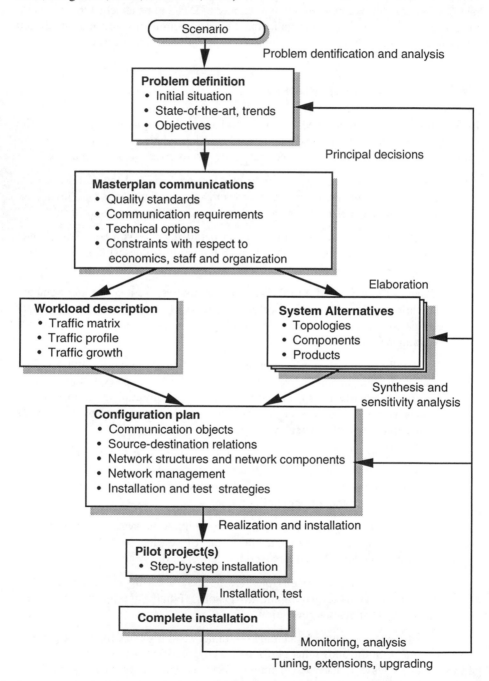

Figure 13.4 The planning process.

Table 13.1 Planning stages.

Planning stage	Planning period in years (frequency)	Planning objectives and underlying planning information
Long-range	20–25 (5 years)	Initial guidelines to satisfy future demands; mostly driven by economics and service demand forecast.
Medium-term	5–8 (yearly)	Timely preparation of network extensions (topology, capacity, routing, etc.) based on long-range planning results
Short-term	1–2 (on demand)	Topological optimization, capacity assignment, dimensioning of routes, concentrators, switches etc. driven by short-term traffic demand.

Network planning draws on scientific tools such as monitoring, statistics, mathematical modeling and simulation as well as mathematical optimization. These tools are indispensable, but the final result will always depend on human judgment, policy and other constraints difficult to formulate mathematically (Purser, 1987). We shall, therefore, concentrate on the formal methods, but skip traffic forecasting and related statistical methods since they are well documented in the textbooks on statistics and performance modeling (Trivedi, 1982; Kobayashi, 1978; Jain, 1991) or network planning (Freeman, 1989; Terplan, 1987; Storck, 1990; Bergmann, 1986).

13.4 Monitoring

Performance monitoring requires measurement of the performance of a network and critical observation of its dynamic behavior and interdependencies. In other words, there are two main objectives:

i) Measured standard performance values give information about source traffic, the effective transmission rates, the utilization of hardware and software components and other global performance characteristics discussed in Section 13.2. Long-term measurements are necessary to predict traffic trends and grade of service changes.

ii) The idea of observing the dynamic behavior is to uncover in detail the timely cooperation of hardware and/or software components, and to investigate interactions between distributed components. Therefore, the objective is now to find explanations for the standard performance values mentioned above (Klar, 1981)

The special objectives of performance monitoring for communication networks and distributed systems are:

- the correct recording of concurrent hardware and software events at all levels of the communication architecture as well as application processing;

- the analysis and evaluation of these events to find bottlenecks in the user or communication subsystem, to evaluate protocol design and its implementation, to check process cooperation and end-to-end delays, to investigate load distribution and routing strategies and to determine the efficiency of local scheduling and priorities for the support of the network management decisions and activities;

- the visualization of the results for system management and application programmers;

- the validation of performance models and performance predictions.

Both types of monitoring – measurement and observation – may be carried out at various locations:

- on the communication lines of the network (network monitoring),

- in the application and switching machines (system monitoring).

Moreover, we may distinguish how the monitoring is done:

- electronically (hardware monitoring),

- by special system programs (software monitoring), or

- by combining both (firmware and hybrid monitoring).

Efficient data compaction tools and data analysis packages are most important. (McKerrow, 1988; Hofmann *et al.*, 1990).

13.4.1   Network monitoring

Network monitors are independent instruments directly connected to the transmission media. The network traffic is monitored, filtered and recorded on buffer and background storage facilities. Network monitors may also actively put packets onto the network in order to simulate a specific workload or to test protocols.

Depending on the functionality and price, network monitors may be dedicated to the evaluation of a specific class of transmission protocols and one medium or – as more recently – universal in their application. Specific data representation languages such as ASN.1 (Gora, 1989) allow for efficient and flexible traffic analysis at various levels of any protocol architecture.

Network monitors are well suited to determining global performance characteristics at different protocol layers. Typical examples are:

- the number of frames per second at the data link layer or packets at the network layer, and

- the delay distribution between connect-request-PDUs (protocol data units) and the corresponding connect-confirm-PDUs of an ISO-transport protocol.

They are also well suited to supervising line characteristics and the protocol behavior. This includes:

- the measurement of bit-error rates, data distortion and synchronization timing,

- the selective monitoring and interpretation of characteristic protocol sequences,

- the systematic detection, analysis and display of protocol errors.

However, network monitors are less convenient for detecting and interpreting causal dependencies and they are inappropriate when we are interested in:

- analyzing and tuning complete protocol stacks, or

- precisely investigating the temporal relations between cooperating processes at the same site or at different locations.

Then, network monitoring has to be combined with system monitoring in the end systems and switching processors, respectively, as shown in Figure 13.5.

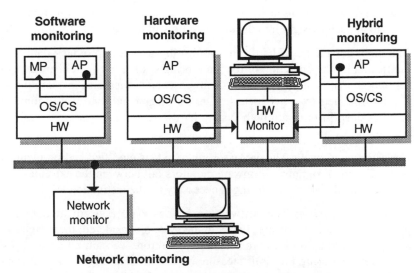

MP= monitoring programs,   AP = application program,   HW = hardware
OS/CS = operating system and communication software.

Figure 13.5 Monitoring techniques.

13.4.2   System monitoring

System monitors are dedicated to the observation of all activities within the end systems, communication controllers or switching centers.   There are several techniques:

i) *Software monitoring*: Data are gathered by special programs which are added and run upon the examined system. The common method is to embed within the operating system some data collection programs which selectively monitor events of interest.

The main advantage of this user-oriented approach is that it can directly refer to the software load and problem-oriented names; operations are traced at a macro level in synchronization with major events of the software observed. Hence the interpretation of results is also possible for the application programs. Software measurement packages are often included in the standard system software.

This approach, however, has a disadvantage in that it corrupts the statistics it is attempting to measure; therefore we have to be aware that the measurement procedure itself uses a considerable percentage of system resources (Shemer and Robertson, 1972; Rafii, 1981; Jain, 1991). This drawback is eliminated by the second method.

ii) *Hardware monitoring*: Typically, a separate piece of equipment is attached to the monitored system via hardware probes; binary information is gathered and transferred to event counters or to automatic comparators. The data records may incidentally be used for utilization statistics, but the main objective is often to get deep insight into the dynamic flow of data and control information.

The main advantage of hardware monitoring is that it provides data that is unaffected by the operation of the monitoring system itself. It also has a high resolution, that is, it provides data at microsecond timescales that could not be readily obtained by other means. On the other hand, hardware monitoring requires deep insight into both system hardware and software. Specialists in both are necessary.

iii) *Firmware monitoring*: The processor microcode is modified and supplemented by monitoring programs. Firmware monitors fall between the extremes above and are suitable when monitoring is necessary on the instruction level.

iv) *Hybrid monitoring*: The software to be observed (system or application program) activates hardware signals in the system considered; these signals are then monitored by a hardware monitor. Therefore we gain all advantages of software monitoring but limit measurement overhead. Hybrid monitoring is particularly important for the observation of modern microprocessors which do not allow sensing of internal signals.

13.5   Modeling techniques

13.5.1   Performance modeling methodology

The aim of performance modeling is to describe, analyze and optimize the dynamic time-dependent behavior of systems. Therefore, we have to model and investigate the processing, buffering and transfer of data and control information within the endsystems as well as the communication subsystem. Performance modeling has a long tradition. Fundamental results came out of teletraffic theory, operations research, and, more recently, from computer science.

Features of influence

The dynamic behavior of a system is influenced by many parameters which may be classified in two groups:

i)   Characteristics of the service demands ("workload parameters")

- arrival process, describing the timely sequence of arriving service requirements;

- service process, describing the duration of processing or transportation times for the individual demands;

- additional characteristics, for example, priority, storage requirements, or dependencies between subtasks,

ii)   Characteristics of the servicing system ("machine parameters")

- system components: hardware and software features of the individual components influence processing and transportation times;

- system structure, describing the location of components as well as the topology of the connecting network between them;

- service strategies, that is, the order in which demands are processed or transferred.

Depending on the purpose of our performance investigations, all these characteristics have to be captured more or less precisely by our modeling technique.

Classical and advanced modeling techniques

When developing performance models in the classical way, one usually assumes that:

- requests competing at the same time for resource access are independent of each other, and

- requests dependent on previous requests occur in sequence, rather than overlap.

All load and system features are incorporated in an informal pictorial representation as a unique (queuing) system model in which only a few parameters may be varied, as shown in Figure 13.6. The advantage of this classical approach is that it is standard. Many theoretical results are available as well as engineering tables and program packages. The main disadvantages are the high modeling costs – for each combination of load, machine configuration and load distribution the corresponding overall model has to be developed from scratch and there is not much automatic support.

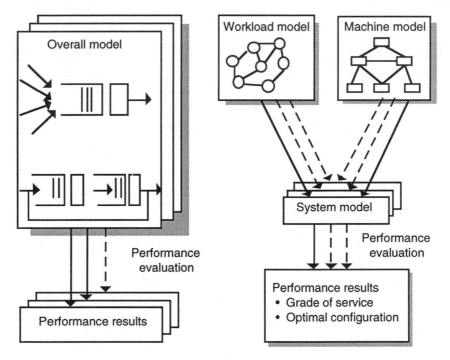

Figure 13.6 Comparison between the classical modeling technique (left) and the three-step methodology (right).

This modeling technique was reasonable and successful in the past. It was mainly applied to investigate hardware configurations and operating strategies for standard computer systems and networks.

Totally different, however, is the situation when we investigate distributed systems – application and system programs are decomposed into well-defined cooperating subtasks, that is:

- there are strict dependencies between subtasks,

- subtasks may be processed sequentially or simultaneously, and

- subtasks may compete at the same time for the same resources.

There is a great variety of strategies to distribute code and data segments to processors and memories, or to schedule tasks and subtasks. Obviously the classical technique is no longer reasonable because for each variant we need to develop a completely new model.

The costs of modeling may be reduced significantly if we use a three-step methodology instead (Woo and Herzog, 1980; Fromm, 1982; Kleinrock, 1982; Kleinöder, 1983; Beilner, 1985; Herzog, 1986; Tripathi *et al.*, 1986):

i)   Develop the workload model independent of the implementation constraints and separately develop the machine model.

ii) Deduce the system model by mapping the workload model into the machine model. Therefore, the system model describes the real dynamic behavior and shows how service requirements are influenced by the concrete implementation.

iii) Analyze the system model by means of simulation and/or analytic methods in order to predict characteristic performance values.

Hence the most demanding and time-consuming parts, workload and machine modeling have to be elaborated only once, and different mappings may be supported by software tools. This new methodology has proven true in many cases, in analytic modeling (Herzog 1989; 1990) as well as in simulation (Beilner *et al.*, 1988).

13.5.2   Modeling and evaluation techniques

There are various possibilities for describing, analyzing and optimizing the dynamic behavior within and between the components of a network. The two most successful techniques with respect to network modeling and evaluation have been graph or network flow models and stochastic service-and-traffic models.

Graph or network flow models

According to the terminology of the theory of graphs these models consist of a set of junction points called *nodes* with certain pairs of the nodes being connected by lines called *branches*. Goods of some type, called *flow*, are carried via branches; the flow *capacity* shows the upper limit of the flow rate. A node may also have a limited flow capacity. A branch of a graph is said to be *directed* if one node is considered the point of origin and the other node the point of destination.

Graph theory is well established and many results are available (Gallager and Bertsekas, 1987; Girard, 1990). The models are well suited to representing structural properties and functional dependencies. Their main advantage is that there are efficient algorithms available not only to analyze the performance but also to optimize model parameters. Typical examples are algorithms for bottleneck analysis, maximum flow between two network nodes, optimal routing strategies and optimal flow control schemes. These results, however, are often just first estimates, since the time-dependent dynamic behavior is usually described by a continuous network flow (see Figure 13.7).

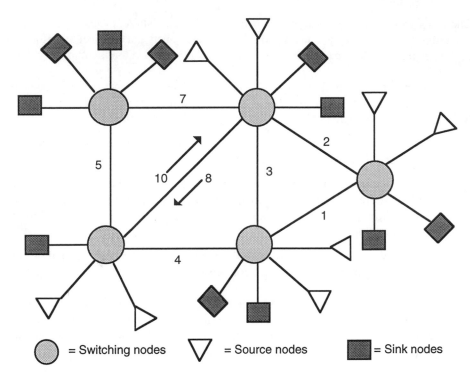

Figure 13.7 Graph representing a communication network.

Stochastic service-and-traffic models

Fundamental to this wide class of models are *service stations* and *stochastic processes*.

Service stations consist of *servers* which may be interpreted as processing locations or as communication channels. If all servers are busy, arriving requests may be allowed to queue until service is granted (*queuing models or delay models*), they may be rejected by the station (*loss models*), or there may be a compromise between both extremes (*combined delay-loss models*). Arrows between different service stations show the flow of service requests within the overall model as shown in Figure 13.8.

Stochastic processes allow random time variations of both the arrival instant and service time of requests to be characterized. They also allow many real-world situations where we cannot predict future events exactly (Kobayashi, 1978) to be modeled very efficiently.

The stochastic service-and-traffic theory is well established (Kleinrock, 1976; Gallager and Bertsekas, 1987; Girard, 1990; Jain, 1991). Its main advantage is a more detailed modeling of the dynamic system behavior; all characteristic performance values of interest may be investigated and mean values as well as percentiles may be determined. These probabilistic models may be evaluated either by mathematical methods, or, if they are very sophisticated, by means of simulation.

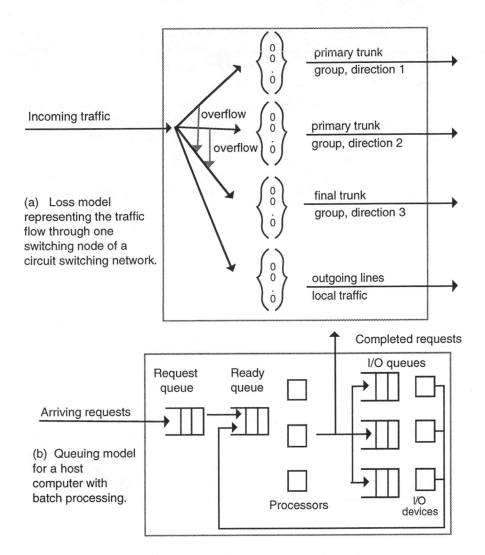

Figure 13.8 Stochastic service and traffic models.

Many standard situations have been investigated and numerous analytic results are available and applicable. However, there are only a few general results for optimization. So, usually, we have to embed these analytic results into mathematical optimization techniques. In the case of simulation such a combination is impossible; we therefore have to systematically vary model parameters in order to find a good solution.

There are other successful modeling styles in addition to these two classical techniques. Considering the evolution of performance modeling, including recent activities, it is quite interesting that these techniques follow the approach of functional program specifications (Herzog, 1991).

- Specification techniques for simulation models employ general-purpose programming languages or languages especially designed for this purpose. More recently, grammars have been used to algorithmically generate workload models from data measured (Dulz and Hofmann, 1991).

- Stochastic graph models are used to capture the functional dependencies between cooperating subtasks (workload model), and to express functional or structural dependencies between the system components (machine model).

- Finite state machines, especially some extended models, have been applied most successfully to specify protocols between communicating subsystems. However, relatively little has been done to include time and to support performance evaluation (Liu, 1989; Rudin, 1985).

- Performance evaluation has been a central aspect of Petri Net models for many years. These methods are most advanced, capturing both the functional dependencies as well as the timing behavior (Ajmone Marsan *et al.*, 1986). For larger applications, however, the models grow disorderly.

- Several extensions have been proposed to represent time in process algebras. A careful review shows, however, that the major aspects of performance evaluation are not taken into account (Herzog, 1990). But this is the challenging topic of ongoing research (Herzog *et al.*, 1992).

In the classical planning methodology, functional specifications and performance models have been developed and investigated separately from each other. Relative simplicity of the description techniques and evaluation tools is the result. However, there is a clear trend observable and supported by the listings above. Specification techniques are being extended by time attributes and performance evaluation techniques capture functional dependencies (Herzog, 1991). The future will be a homogeneous technique combining both functional and temporal specification and allowing for both functional verification and performance evaluation to be fully integrated into the planning process. This trend is irresistible because of the following:

i)   The functional system behavior is directly influenced by temporal features. For example, in specifying communication protocols we often need timeout mechanisms; depending on the selected time value the protocol may deadlock or not.

ii) The timing behavior is directly influenced by functional dependencies. For example, in analyzing the performance of distributed systems we definitely have to consider the synchronization of communicating subtasks. Program execution times and resource utilization significantly depend on these functional properties.

iii) An integrated design is necessary to cut down development periods and to avoid redesign of components and complete network installations.

13.6   Selection of techniques and tools

We have seen that there are three different techniques available for performance evaluation: monitoring, mathematical modeling and simulation. We also discussed briefly that all three techniques do have their advantages and their disadvantages. It is not reasonable to pose questions like "which one is best?"! Recalling the phases of the network life cycle, we immediately realize that there are different preconditions, requirements and objectives at each individual step of the planning process. All three techniques do have their place and supplement each other.

Which one is best in what situation? This question is important and will be discussed below. Of course, there is no universal answer possible. Depending on our business environment, our position and our personal interest, the judgment may vary. We may also value criteria for selecting an evaluation technique differently, such as:

- usability at each planning step,

- time required,

- tools,

- trade-off evaluation,

- cost, and

- scalability.

They do, however, support an effective discussion. Jain (1991) presents such a table and compares the different techniques accordingly. With kind permission of Reinhard Bordewisch, Siemens Nixdorf, I present two survey tables summarizing his long industrial experience in performance evaluation of computer systems (Bordewisch 1987; 1991).

Table 13.2 Usability of mathematical modeling, simulation and monitoring (Bordewisch, 1991).

Phase	Activities	Technique
Design	Gross performance predictions to value the system architecture	Mathematical modeling
Realization	Detailed trade-off evaluation	Combined use of simulation/ modeling and monitoring
System integration	Validation of the overall system performance	Load simulation and monitoring
Trading	Performance predictions supporting configuration planning	Mathematical modeling and load simulation
Maintenance	Tuning	Monitoring (and modeling)

Table 13.3 Comparison of evaluation techniques (Bordewisch, 1991)
(++ very good, + good, o satisfactory, – deficient, —poor).

Criterion	Modeling		Monitoring
	simulation	mathematical	
Width of usability	+	+	o
Depth of system study	+	o	+
Expenditure (time, cost)			
• Construction or preparation without tool support	—	–	—
• Construction or preparation with tool support	o	+	o
• Execution of experiments	o	+	+
• Evaluation and interpretation of results	+	++	+
Clearness and understandability			
• without tool support	+	o	o
• with tool support	++	+	++
Accuracy	+	o	+
Acceptance and Confidence	+	o	++

In total, the rating of simulation and monitoring seems to be somewhat better than that of mathematical modeling. Note, however, that the weights of the criteria may not be equal and dependent on the situation considered. Remember also that modeling and monitoring supplement each other rather than compete. Moreover, in many situations, mathematical modeling has considerable advantages over simulation. This statement is confirmed by the observation that nowadays mathematical modeling is being applied more frequently (Bordewisch, 1991).

Many companies and institutes do have their own tools and packages. However, there is also a considerable market of commercially available modeling tools supporting various subtasks during the entire planning process (van Norman, 1990).

13.7   Synthesis of optimal structures

13.7.1   Overview

In the introductory section we demonstrated in general and by examples that the entire planning process may be viewed and formulated as a mathematical optimization problem. This is true whether we plan a new network (global optimization) or we want to partially extend an existing installation (local or partial optimization). In each case, however, the optimization task is so complex that the mathematical techniques and tools of today do not allow an overall optimization in a single step. Rather, it is convenient to decompose the problem and to determine the overall solution in a multiphase process iteratively. Of course, mutual dependencies between different subproblems and their solutions have to be considered very carefully.

Next, we introduce the standard notation for any optimization problem and classify specific subclasses. Depending on the kind and problem size, we may apply, and therefore further discuss, exact and heuristic optimization methods.

13.7.2   Mathematical formulation and classification

The general problem is to minimize or maximize some objective function

$$Z = f(x_1, x_2, ..., x_n)$$

over all variables x_i ($i = 1, 2,...n$) subject to constraints

$$
\begin{aligned}
g_c(x_1, x_2,..., x_n) &\leq b_c & c &= 1, 2,..., m_1 \\
g_c(x_1, x_2,..., x_n) &= b_c & c &= m_1 + 1,..., m_2 \\
g_c(x_1, x_2,..., x_n) &\geq b_c & c &= m_2 + 1,..., m
\end{aligned}
$$

The objective function may be of general type including arbitrary cost functions, analytic functions from classical mathematical models (for example, the $M|D|1-$ queue, cf. Section 13.7.3.(b)) or determined functions of advanced modeling styles, mentioned before (Section 13.5.2). The constraint functions are assumed to be well defined and all b_c are given constants. Any number of constraints are allowed ($m>n$, $m<n$ or $m=n$); there are no restrictions if m is equal to zero.

If both objective and constraint functions are of the following type:

$$Z = \sum_{i=1}^{n} k_i \cdot x_i$$

$$g_c(x_1, ..., x_n) \begin{array}{c} \leq \\ = \\ > \end{array} \sum_{i=1}^{n} a_{ci} \cdot x_i \qquad c = 1, 2, ..., m$$

and all k and a values are given constants, the problem is called a "linear optimization problem". All other problems are called "nonlinear optimization problems".

Often the values of (some or) all variables are discrete or integer. We then call the task a "(mixed) discrete or integer optimization" problem.

13.7.3   Exact methods

There are a large number and considerable variety of exact methods available. We just survey them briefly and refer to the specific literature. In each case, however, such algorithms are expected to be:

- exact, in the sense that the optimal solution must be found or approximated with any prescribed accuracy;

- universal, in that they allow for a particular class of optimization problems to be solved rather than just a specific one;

- finite, that is, convergence of the algorithms must be guaranteed and the optimal solution found within a finite number of steps.

Linear optimization (LO)

LO plays an important role in mathematical optimization theory and is one of its fundamentals. Nowadays there are several efficient algorithms available; the most prominent is the "simplex method" by George Dantzig, 1947. It is an algebraic procedure which progressively approaches the optimal solution through a well-defined iterative process until optimality is finally reached. The procedure is straightforward and well suited for computers ("linear programming") (Hillier and Liebermann 1973). Rather than going into details of the algorithm we show by example how to apply it for network design.

Suppose we are given a distributed system with several computers for application processing and DTEs (terminals, PCs, workstations) requiring service from the hosts, see Figure 13.9.

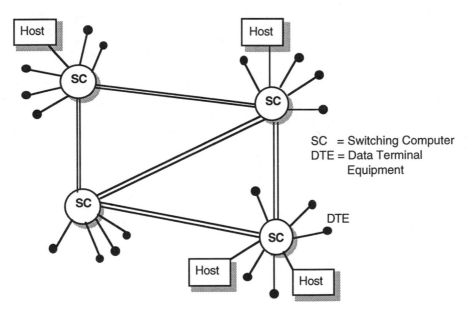

Figure 13.9 Workload distribution problem.

We introduce the following notation:

n_D number of DTEs,

b_{Dj} computer power (per unit time) needed for DTE_j, $j \in \{1,2,...n_D\}$,

n_H number of host computers,

b_{Hi} maximum computer power of $host_i$, $i \in \{1,2,...n_H\}$,

k_{ij} flat-rate for compute service of $host_i$ for DTE_j (sum of all costs including processing data transfer etc. per computer service unit),

x_{ij} computer service from $host_i$ for DTE_j (requests per minute, processor time per second etc.)

Then the optimization problem can be formulated as follows. Minimize the objective function (overall cost):

$$K = \sum_{i=1}^{n_H} \sum_{j=1}^{n_D} k_{ij} \cdot x_{ij}$$

subject to constraints:

$\sum\limits_{i=1}^{n_H} x_{ij} = b_{Dj}$ indicating that the total service requirements of DTE_j have to be fulfilled,

$\sum\limits_{j=1}^{n_D} x_{ij} \leq b_{Hj}$ meaning that the computer power of $host_i$ is limited,

$x_{ij} \geq 0$ capturing the fact that all DTEs require service than producing computer power.

Until recently, the algorithms used in commercial optimization packages had hardly changed from the original algorithms developed in the late 1950s and in the 1960s. Although we still rely on the simplex method, in the past five years major advances have taken place in its computational aspects. In addition, so-called interior-point methods now offer serious competition to simplex methods (Johnson and Nemhauser, 1992).

Nonlinear optimization

We demonstrated above how to apply linear optimization to formulate an important class of planning problems. However, most often planning problems are of nonlinear type. Two crucial examples are the following ones:

- the functional dependency between traffic parameters and performance characteristics is usually nonlinear;

- the tariffs in public and commercial telecommunication networks partially depend on the distance, the volume and the hour of the day.

Figure 13.10 shows a concentrator configuration with a central host site. Each concentrator subsystem maybe modeled by a so-called M|D|1--queuing model: interarrival times are assumed to be exponential, transmission times considered constant. The typical curve shows that the expected queuing-plus-transmission time is a nonlinear function of the arrival rate. So, in order to optimize the number of concentrators (and their locations) and transmission lines subject to some capacity and response-time constraints, we have to solve a nonlinear optimization problem.

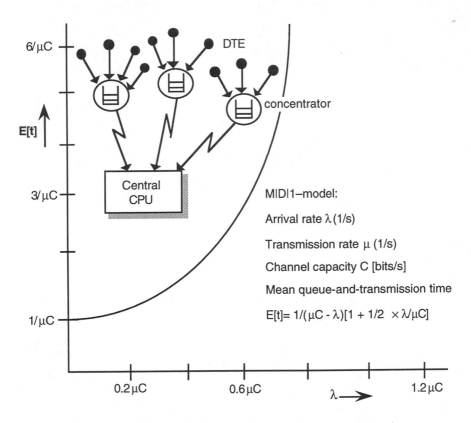

Figure 13.10 Example showing the typical nonlinear behavior.

The same is true if we take into consideration the ever-changing tariff rates. Depending on the type of lines (leased or dial-up), traffic volume (number of requests and their duration), line speed, transmission quality, and so on, various types of non-linear cost functions occur, see Figure 13.11.

We are still far away from the solution of a general nonlinear optimization problem capturing all essentials of network design. However, for special situations (for example, convex cost functions and constraints) there are several exact methods available, including:

- classical methods (Lagrangian multiplier method, Kuhn-Tucker conditions);

- mathematical approximations (separable objective functions and piecewise linearization);

- gradient projection (hill climbing, steepest ascent).

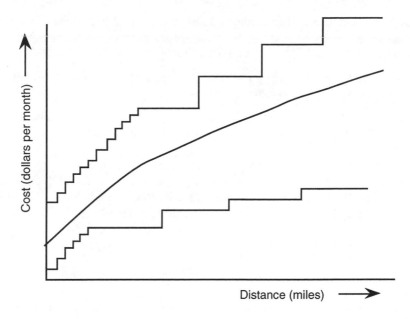

Figure 13.11 Typical examples of line tariffs.

Of particular interest are solution techniques for discrete (integer) optimization since we are often faced with the fact that a technical solution is feasible only for integer values (number of concentrators or trunks). Again, there are various methods available, for example:

- cutting planes (integer restriction by additional constraints),

- stochastic search (random selection of feasible solutions, systematic search for local optima),

- combinatorial methods of different types, (dynamic programming, branch-and-bound).

In conclusion, there are a large variety of methods available for the exact treatment of nonlinear problems; depending on the structure and parameter range of the optimization task their efficiency may vary considerably (Girard, 1990; Hillier and Liebermann, 1973; Neumann, 1975). In general, these methods are well suited for the solution of subproblems with some restricted search space. However, in planning complex network configurations the amount of processing time and storage requirements are often exorbitant, forcing the design engineer to search for heuristic methods.

13.7.4   Heuristic methods

Heuristic methods are intuitively designed procedures that do not guarantee an optimal solution but promise to find a good "suboptimal" approximation. There are several reasons making them particularly attractive:

- The corresponding exact methods are too complicated with respect to cost (see above) and implementation if we are interested in problems of realistic size (for example, terminal networks with some ten thousand sites).

- The significance of an exact solution is questionable, as often data material is incomplete and traffic predictions vague.

- In many situations the design problems do have a specific structure, allowing us to develop simple, accurate and efficient heuristic solution techniques.

There is an immense fund of heuristic techniques for the solution of many problems and new proposals regularly appear in the relevant journals and conference proceedings (Lada, 1989). We just survey, the two areas of main interest, the design of centralized and decentralized mesh networks, respectively.

Optimization of the communication subsystem for centralized networks

Assume we are given the locations of the central site and the terminals, traffic rates, and some constraints with respect to the expected grade of service. Then, the following formulation of the optimization problem is standard – to minimize the overall cost:

$$K = \sum_{i=1}^{n_D} k_i \cdot x_i$$

subject to some (nonlinear) constraints, for example:

- expected response time,

- maximum line capacity,

- reliability constraints.

The cost factor k_i includes the relative cost for servicing station i (i=1,2,...n_D), and x_i represents directly (or with some weight factor) the distance between station i and the central site.

There are many procedures available for the heuristic solution of this class of problem, including the classical idea of Esau and Williams and many successful siblings (Esau and Williams, 1966; Green and Tang, 1973; Woo and Tang, 1973). Two fundamental features are typical of this and other successful classes of algorithm:

- The basis is an exact solution technique; it is used until some constraints are violated. Thereafter, a heuristic continuation still related to the initial procedure is chosen.

- Trying to improve the actual solution, a hill-climbing strategy is used, that is, we proceed in the direction of the maximum gradient of the objective function.

Following these lines, the optimization procedures produces solutions, which are mostly within five to ten percent of the objective function, even for very large networks.

Synthesis of mesh networks

Suppose we are given some matrices specifying the internode traffic requirement, the cost of links between all pairs of nodes and the cost for switching within the nodes. Then the optimization problem may be stated as follows. Minimize the overall cost:

$$K = \sum_{ij} L_{ij}(\lambda_{ij}, C_{ij}) \cdot k_{ij}(\lambda_{ij}) + \sum_{i} S_i(\lambda_i, C_i)$$

where:

L_{ij} = Line speed between node i and j, dependent on the traffic rate and some constraints C_{ij}

λ_{ij} = Traffic routed on the link between nodes i and j (requests per second)

k_{ij} = Relative cost-dependent on the related traffic rate

S_i = Cost for switching within node i dependent on the corresponding traffic rate and C_i represents some constraints

and where the various constraints take into account requirements concerning:

- performance, for example, prescribed average packet delay or connection set-up time;

- reliability, for example, for each source-destination pair at least two different routes are required;

- technology, for example, terrestrial and/or satellite links, coaxial cables or fiber optics;

- operating mode, for example, packet versus circuit switching, or different routing and flow control strategies.

Again, the solution of such complex optimization problems is usually a multistep procedure, even in the case of heuristic algorithms. Several subproblems have been identified, in particular (Kleinrock, 1976):

- topological design

- capacity assignment

- flow assignment

- combinations of these subproblems.

Many systematic results are available, starting as early as 1964 (Kleinrock, 1976) and then continuously being a research area of great importance (Frank *et al.* , 1970; Green and Tary, 1973; Kershenbaum *et al.* ,1989; Cahn *et al.* , 1991). It is quite interesting to observe that nowadays all efficient heuristics include more or less the following design concepts:

- Use time-sensitive dynamic routing to take advantage of traffic non-coincidence.

- Route traffic along the least cost (direct) path.

- Utilize the links heavily.

- Favor long, high capacity links whenever possible.

- Ensure efficient overflow strategies.

- Minimize incremental network cost .

A detailed justification for these design steps, illustrating examples and experiments and experiences with implemented tools, may be found in the above-mentioned literature. Moreover, it is interesting to observe the following trend: people try to develop general architectures for network design tools (Cahn *et al.,* 1991) in order to keep up to date with the rapidly changing network design environment, rather than just developing (efficient) algorithms and designing programs for network design, or integrating several design tools into a specific design environment.

Acknowledgment

I would like to express my thanks to Mrs Kerstin Weikert and Mrs Gabriele Blank, both of whom attentively read the manuscript, checked the writing style and spent many hours carefully typing it. I also owe thanks to Dr Martin Paterok who helped to find adequate references. Moreover, two referees contributed with their valuable comments and suggestions.

Abbreviations

ASN.1	Abstract Syntax Notation One
DTE	Data Teminal Equipment
EPA	Enhanced Performance architecture
FAN.1	Frame Analyzing Notation One
ISO	International Standards Organization
LO	Linear Optimization
MAP	Manufacturing Automation Protocol
M|D|1	Standard Single Server Queuing Model with constant service times
PDU	Protocol Data Unit
SITA	Société International des Télécommunication Aéronautique

References

Ajmone Marsan M., Balbo G. and Conte G. (1986). *Performance Models of Multiprocessor Systems*, MIT Press, Computer System Series

Ash G. R., Cardwell R. H. and Murray R. P. (1981). Design and optimization of networks with dynamic routing, *BST J* , **60**(8), 1787–821

Beilner H. (1985). Measurement, modeling and evaluation of computing systems (in German). *University of Dortmund and Computer Science and Information Techniques Society (GI)*.

Beilner H., Mäter J., and Weissenberg N. (1988). Towards a performance modeling environment. News on HIT. In *Modeling Techniques and Tools for Computer Performance Evaluation*., (Puigjamer R. and Potier R., eds.), Plenum Press

Bergmann K. (1986). *Lehrbuch der Fernmeldetechnik*. 5th Edn. Berlin: Schiele and Schön

Bordewisch R. (1987). Das Verbundprojekt GESINE. *Informatik—Forschung und Entwicklung,* **2** (3)

Bordewisch R. (1991). Fallbeispiele aus industrieller Praxis (Case studies out of industirl practice). GI-ITG Tutorial on Measurement, Modeling and Performance Analysis of Computing Systems, September

Cahn R. S, Chang P.-C. Kermani, P. and Kershenbaum, A. (1991). Intrepid: an integrated network tool for routing, evaluation of performance and interactive design. RC 16455, IBM Research Division Report, January.

Chou W. (1974). Planning and design of data communications networks. In *Proc 1974 National Computer Conf., Chicago*, 553–9

Dulz W. and Hofmann S. (1991). Grammar-based workload modeling of communication systems. In *Proc. 5th International Conf. on Modeling Techniques and Tools for Computer Performance Evaluation*, Turin, 16–30

Esau L. R. and Williams K. C. (1966). On teleprocessing system design, part II. *IBM System Journal*, **5**(3), 142–7

Frank H., Frisch I. and Chou W. (1970). Topological considerations in the design of the ARPA Network. In *AFIPS Conf. Proc. 1970, Spring Joint Computer Conference 36*, 381–87

Freeman R. L. (1989). *Telecommunication System Engineering*. 2nd Edn. Wiley

Fromm H. J. (1982). *Multiporzessor-Rechenanlagen: Programmstrukturen, Maschinenstrukturen und Zuordnungsprobleme*. Dissertation, Universität Erlangen-Nürnberg

Gallager R. and Bertsekas D. (1987). *Data Networks*. Prentice Hall.

Girard A. (1990). *Routing and Dimensioning in Circuit-Switched Networks.* Addison-Wesley

Gora W. (1989). *Konzept, Methoden und Werkzeuge für ein universelles Netzmanagement.* Dissertation, Universität Erlangen-Nürnberg

Green P. E. and Tang D. T. (1973). Some recent developments in teleprocessing system optimization. In *IEEE Intern. Convention*, 1–6

Gupta V. P. (1985). What is network planning. *IEEE Communications Magazine*, **23**(10), 10–16

Harvey C. (1986). Performance engineering as in integral part of system design. *British Telecom Technology Journal*, **4**(3), 142–7

Herzog U. (1986). Flexible Networks of tightly and loosely coupled processors. In *Proc. Int. Seminar on Teletraffic Analysis and Computer Performance Evaluation*, 439–46. North Holland.

Herzog U. (1989). Leistungbewertung und modellbildung für Parallelrechner. *Informationstechnik (it)*, **31**(1), 31–8

Herzog, U., 1990. Formal description, time and performance analysis. In *Entwurf und Betrieb Verteilter Systeme*, Härder T., Wedekind H. and Zimmermann G. eds, IFB 264, Berlin, Springer Verlag

Herzog U. (1991). Perfornace evaluation and formal description. In *Proc.IEEE CompEuro 91: Advanced Computer Technology, Reliable Systems and Applications,* Bologna, May, Monaco V. A. and Negrini R. eds, 750–5

Herzog U. (1992). Performance evaluation as an integral part of system design in *Proc. of Transputer '92*, Amsterdam, IOS Press

Herzog U., Götz N. and Rettelbach M. (1992). TIPP – A language for timed processes and performance evaluation. *Technical Report* 4/92, Universität Erlangen-Nürnberg

Hofmann R., Klar R., Luttenberger N., Mohr B., Quick A. and Sötz F. (1990). Integrating monitoring and modeling to a performance evaluation methodology. In *Entwurf und Betrieb verteilter Systeme,*, Härder T., Wedekind H. and Zimmermann G. eds, 122–49, IFB 264, Berlin: Springer Verlag

Hillier F. S. and Liebermann G. J. (1973). *Introduction to Operations Research.* San Francisco: Holden Day Inc.

Jain R. (1991). *The Art of computer ssytems Performance Analysis.* I: Overview, II: Measurement, III: Probability, IV: Experimental Design, V: Simulation, VI: Queuing Models. New York: J. Wiley

Johnson E. L. and Nemhauser G. L. (1992). Recent developments and future directions in mathematical programming. *IBM Systems Journal*, **31**(1), 79–92

Kershenbaum. A. Kermani P. and Grover G. (1989). Mentor – An algorithm for mesh network topological optimization and routing. *Technical Report RC14764*, IBM Research Division Report, June

Klar R. (1981). Hardware measurements and their application on perforamnce evaluation in a processor array. *Computing*, Suppl **3**, 65–88

Kleinöder W. (1982). *Stochastische Bewertung von Aufgabenstrukturen für hierarchische Mehrrechnersysteme*. Dissertation, Universität Erlangen-Nürnberg.

Kleinöder W. (1983). Evaluation of task structures for a hierarchical multiprocessor. In *Proc. Int. Conf. on Modeling Techniques and Tools for Performance Evalaution*. North Holland

Kleinrock L. (1976). *Queueing Systems*, Vol. 2: Applications. John Wiley & Sons.

Kobayashi H. (1978). *Modeling and Analysis – An Introduction to System Performance Evaluation Methodology*. Addison-Wesley

Lada L. ed. (1989). *Networked Planning in the 1990s*. Fourth International Network Planning Symposium, North Holland

Liu M. T. (1989). Protocol engineering. *Advances in Computers*, **29**, 79–195

McKerrow P. (1988). *Performance Measurement of Computer Sytems*. Sydney: Addison Wesley

Moulton P. D. (1980). Data communication system planning. In *Advances in Data Communications Management*, Vol. 1. (Rullo T.A. ed.) 1–53. Heyden and Son:

Neumann K. (1975). *Operations Research Verfahren, Vol. 1, 2*. München: Hanser Verlag

Purser M. (1987). *Computers and Telecommunications Networks*. Blackwell Scientific Publications

Rafii A. (1981). Structure and application of a measurement tool – SAMPLER/3000.. ACM/SIGMETRICS Conf. on Measurement and Modeling of Computer Systems, Sep. 14 - 16 1981, *ACM Perf. Eval. Review,* **10**(3), 110–20

Reiser M. (1991). A quarter century of performance evaluation – impact on science and engineering. In *Proceedings of the IEEE CompEuro '91*, 885–7

Rudin H. (1985). An improved algorithm for estimating protocol performance. In *Proc IFIP Int Workship on Protocol Specification, Testing and Verification IV*, Yemini, Strom and Yemini, eds, 515–25, North Holland.

Shemer J. and Robertson J. (1972.) Instrumentation of time-shared systems. *Computer*, July/August, 39–48

Storck G. K. (1990). Prognosen für den Bedarf an Fernmeldedienstleistungen. In *Planung von Telekommunikationsnetzen.*, Wöhlbier G. ed., R. v. Deker's Verlag, G Schenk, Heidelberg

Terplan K. (1987). *Communication Network Management*. Prentice Hall

Tripathi S., Kaisler S., Chandran S. and Agrawala A., eds. (1986). *Report on the Workshop on Design and Performance Issues in Parallel Architectures*. Inst. for Advanced Computer Studies, University of Maryland, College Park, MD

Trivedi K. S. (1982). *Probability and Statistics with Reliability, Queuing and Computer Science Applications*. Prentice Hall

van Norman H. J. (1990). WAN-Design tools: the new generation. In *Data Communications International,* October, 105–12

Woehlbier G., ed. (1990). *Planung von Telekommunikationsnetzen,* Vol. 1 and 2. R V Deker's Verlag, G Schenk, Heidelberg.

Woo L. and Herzog U. (1980). Design and Performance Analysis for Multi-Microprocessor Communication Controller Models. Unpublished Memo, Yorktown Heights, October

Woo L. S. and Tang D. (1973). Optimization of teleprocessing networks with concentrators. In *Proc. Nat .Telecomm. Conf.,* 37C1–5

Chapter 14

User Administration and Accounting

Barry Varley

Sema Group Consulting,
Regal House,
14 James Street,
London, WC2E 8BT
UK
Email: b.varley@semalc.co.uk

An important part of running any distributed system is managing the users of the system. This activity includes registering the users and their service entitlement, controlling and recording their usage of the services, issuing bills, and handling payments. In systems that offer commercial services, many of these administration and accounting functions are essential. This chapter concentrates on commercial distributed systems, and in particular on the pan-European digital cellular telecommunications system. Non-commercial systems, such as in-house or academic systems, also have administration requirements and these are contrasted with the commercial requirements.

The chapter describes each of the major functions and the type of information required for administration, then looks at policies for accounting and draws the distinction between service usage accounting and resource usage accounting. Mechanisms for usage accounting, based loosely on the OSI accounting management standard, are discussed, followed by billing and charge generation, with emphasis on charging for services that involve many service providers. The chapter outlines the service provider's motivations for controlling who has access to their services and how they try to minimize the risk of debt. Finally, the requirements for reconciliation of usage between service providers is described.

14.1   Administration overview

14.1.1   Services

Most of this chapter is based upon services provided by distributed systems so it is natural to start by examining what we mean by a **service**. Distributed systems provide two types of services: those offered by the operating system, which are generally similar to those of centralized operating systems, and those offered by applications running on the distributed system. Examples of system services are processing, information storage and retrieval, user access, and communications; examples of application services are electronic mail, directory service, document transfer, and Electronic Data Interchange.

A service provider uses the resources of the distributed system to provide a service to users. **Resources** have generally been thought of as the system hardware, such as disks, CPUs and communications lines. Nowadays, it is increasingly taken to include the applications on the system and the raw information in the system. The distinction between hardware and software is becoming increasingly blurred, as hardware manufactures bring out ever more sophisticated applications embedded in the silicon. Data is also being recognized as a valuable resource that can be traded in its own right.

A service provider may use other services, as well as resources, to provide a service and this type of service is known as a **complex service**. Traditionally, all the services used in the provision of a complex service belonged to the same service provider. In distributed systems, however, the services may be supplied by different organizations and one instance of complex service usage may involve many services from many different service providers. There are two ways to handle such services: each service provider may have a separate agreement with the user (the **individual approach**); or one of the service providers may deal with the user, as a main contractor, and the other service providers deal with this service provider, as subcontractors (the **group approach**). Section 14.4 discusses both these approaches.

An example of a complex service is international telephony. A single call uses services provided by two or more telephone companies. This spans more than one organizational domain, as well as more than one geographic domain, and its administration must allow the independent telephone companies to cooperate as equals. An introduction to the concept of domains in systems management is presented in Chapter 16.

14.1.2   Users

It is useful to make a distinction between subscribers and users. A **subscriber** is an organization or person that has a contract with the service provider for use of the service. A **user** is the person or entity that uses the service on behalf of the subscriber. In a system offering commercial services a subscriber might be a company that contracts for the services, and users might be the authorized representatives of that company. A similar setup can exist in an academic environment, where the subscribers might be the different departments and the users the students and staff.

There are many different types of user of a distributed system but no attempt is made here to classify them. One important point is that users interact with a distributed system only through the services it offers. Therefore their interest is only in services provided by the system, not the system itself.

14.1.3   Administrative functions

In most organizations the administration system is some combination of sales processing, contract processing, user support, service registration, payment processing, debt collection, financial accounting, management reporting, usage accounting, charge generation and billing. Figure 14.1 is a simplified representation of an administration system. The arrows show the flow of data between functional areas. These data flows are complicated and in the interests of simplicity have not been labeled.

The administrative requirements for commercial services are more exacting than for non-commercial services, so the emphasis will be placed on the former throughout this chapter. Specific examples are drawn from the pan-European digital cellular telecommunications system, which is a very large, multinational, multi-organizational, distributed system. We will now look briefly at the administrative functions and data shown in Figure 14.1.

Sales processing includes functions such as managing sales leads, enquiring on service availability and prices, and placing orders. Non-commercial systems do not have sales forces. Nevertheless, they do need to handle requests from users for services and this can be thought of as a minimal sales processing function.

Contract processing covers the creation of new contracts, and the amendment and deletion of existing contracts. A contract is an agreement between the service provider and the subscriber specifying the services that shall be provided, the users entitled to use the services, the cost of the services, how payment shall be made, the period the contract covers, and the action to be taken if either party breaks the contract. Many distributed systems do not include all of this concept of a contract. For example, an academic institute does not usually grant a student compensation if the system is unavailable for an afternoon. Distributed systems must be able to relate users to their service entitlements, hence all systems have some form of contract processing.

User support covers functions such as answering user enquiries, registering users and resolving user complaints. It is possible to automate many of these functions and offer them as services to the users. For example, an enquiry service could allow a user to examine their usage details and their billing records by using a remote terminal to call up the service.

Payment processing and debt collection are the control and entry of subscriber payments, and the monitoring of debt positions and initiation of actions to recover debts. Payments and debts may be expressed in terms of quotas and budgets rather then money (see Section 14.5).

Financial accounting, management reporting and marketing all depend upon information from the administration system. Examples of the types of information are billing records, which are needed for the general ledger, and service usage patterns, which may be needed to review the impact of a marketing campaign. Managers also feed information into the administrative system, such as defining the service offerings and the tariffs.

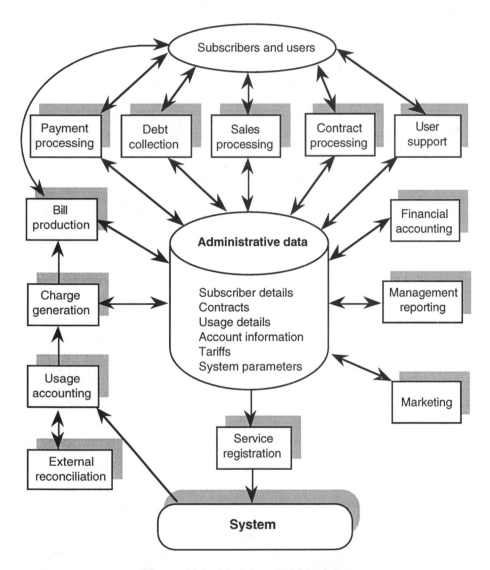

Figure 14.1 Administrative functions.

Service registration is the process of notifying the distributed system of a subscriber's service entitlement. This service entitlement may change at the subscriber's request (the subscriber may ask for a new service) or at the service provider's request (a service may be suspended if the subscriber's usage budget is exhausted).

Service registers may be distributed and this can lead to conflicting entitlements – a situation that can arise in the pan-European cellular system. Imagine a customer who subscribes to national and international voice services. These services will be registered on the cellular system as the subscriber's service entitlement. The customer's mobile terminal also offers a number of services, in particular a call-barring service to prevent certain numbers being dialed. These services are registered on the mobile terminal, so service entitlement can be registered in two places. Suppose the customer lends the mobile terminal to a devious colleague and before doing so bars international calls on the handset. Being devious, the colleague then calls the operator to make an international call, bypassing the local bar. The operator checks the service entitlement on the network, finds it is permitted and allows the call.

Although this a fairly trivial example it does show that different components of the distributed system may have potentially conflicting service registers. Rather than attempt to outlaw all such conflicts, it is better to devise a policy to resolve situations where conflicts exist. In the example above, the handset bar should take precedence over the network entitlement. To resolve this the operator would need information on all service entitlements on the distributed system and instructions on the course to take in cases of conflict. The issues surrounding policy conflict and resolution are discussed in (Moffett and Sloman, 1991).

To provide some types of complex service the service entitlement of one service provider's subscribers may have to be accessible to other, cooperating service providers. The roaming service in the pan-European cellular system raises this requirement. Roaming service allows customers to subscribe to service from one service provider (the home service) in one country, and be able to use their mobile terminals on other pan-European cellular networks in other countries. When a subscriber roams to another country and attempts to make a call, the service provider in that country must check that the subscriber is entitled to this service and this can only be done by asking the subscriber's home service provider.

Usage accounting is the monitoring and logging of the service usage on the system. This is discussed in detail in the next two sections. External reconciliation is the process by which cooperating service providers account for instances of complex service that involve more than one service provider. This has already been touched upon and is discussed in more detail in Section 14.6.

Charge generation handles two types of charges: access charges and utilization charges, and is described in Section 14.4. Bill production covers the production of statements or invoices. In many commercial systems billing has assumed more responsibility than just informing the subscriber of the amount of money they have been charged. Billing subscribers is discussed in Section 14.4.

14.1.4 Administrative data

Subscriber details include: demographic data, such as name and address; contract identifiers; credit information, such as credit card details or credit worthiness status; subscriber history, such as a record of the enquiries made by a subscriber; billing and payment details, although these may be overridden by contract details; marketing information, such as how the subscriber learnt of the service, and administrative identifiers, such as an account number.

In many countries subscriber details are subject to a Data Protection Act (DPA) if they relate to individuals rather than companies. The purpose of a DPA is to protect the rights of an individual. It requires service providers to register all the types of personal data they hold, and the purposes they hold it for, and restricts them to using this data for these specified, lawful purposes. Different countries have different DPAs and this can cause problems in multinational, distributed systems. How a service provider handles personal data (such as a customer's credit status) and how long they are permitted to hold this data may be different in each country and place conflicting demands on the administration system.

Contract details include: services covered by the contract, the contract start and end date, the users that are eligible for service under the contract, the subscriber who signed the contract, the tariff plan that will be used for the contract, any discount arrangements, and details of the consequences should either party break the contract.

Tariff information covers how access to a service and usage of a service are charged. Usage details identify who used a service and how much service they used. Account information includes the users' billing records and payment records. In a commercial system this may be a complete accounts receivable ledger, while in a non-commercial system it may be details of the quantity of budget the user has and the period of time it covers.

Administration system parameters include operational control data, such as the frequency of billing, and management data, such as the definition of service offerings, the advertising messages on bills and the criteria for selecting which subscribers' bills include these messages.

The categories of information listed here are by no means the only ones that may exist in an administration system. For example, if use of a service is tied to a specific resource then information about the resource may also be held. The imaginative reader could undoubtedly think of many other categories.

14.2   Usage accounting overview

Usage accounting is a management process that collects, collates and logs usage information that is pertinent to the cost of using a service or to the cost of providing a service. As in the previous section, the emphasis is on service usage rather than resource usage. In the traditional, centralized system usage tended to be measured in terms of hardware resource consumption. Many different methods, of varying complexity and fairness, were employed to measure resource usage and charge for it (McKell et al.,1979).

One such method (Synderman and Kline, 1969) based charges for system usage upon a user's effective processing time, which was calculated as a function of the sum of individual job times and the total operating time required by the system. This was simple to implement but had some serious disadvantages, including no allowance for non-uniformity of demand. Other methods were fairer but all had the fundamental flaw that they accounted only for hardware resources and did not take into consideration other elements of the service, such as the software. For example, a slow compiler that produced poor code would cost more to use than a quick compiler that produced efficient code (Mullender, 1989). Nevertheless, there are uses for resource usage accounting in a distributed system.

14.2.1 Resource usage accounting

Resource usage accounting can be used to determine the cost of a providing a service, or to determine the cost efficiency of the system. A service provider may wish to identify the cost of providing a service to help determine the cost of the service to users. Services consume resources, therefore it is necessary to determine the amount of resource consumed by a particular quantity of service usage. This may be an average quantity of resource usage, as the same quantity of service usage may not always require the same quantity of resource usage. This application would normally be an *ad hoc* management function, and not a daily process.

Measuring how the resources are used also makes it possible to plan for efficient resource usage. For example, resources that are reserved for an infrequently used service may be redeployed, or unused resources may be removed from the system. Service demand may fluctuate with time, so this form of usage accounting should be run regularly. This application could equally well be categorized as a performance management application and is included here only because it involves cost.

To aid this process of determining cost effectiveness, resources can be divided into two types: durable resources and non-durable resources. Durable resources remain in existence until they are explicitly consumed by usage, for example listing paper. Non-durable resources will be consumed after a period of time regardless of whether or not they are explicitly consumed by usage, for example available processor time.

An easy method of differentiating between these two types of resource is to examine the metrics used in accounting for them. Durable resources are measured in purely quantitative metrics, for example listing paper is measured in the number of sheets of paper used. Non-durable resources are measured in a combination of quantitative and temporal metrics, for example available processor time is measured in the number of seconds on each processor and the number of processors. In performance terms the aim should be to maximize the use of non-durable resources.

14.2.2 Service usage accounting

The activities that are included in service usage accounting depend upon the **accounting policy** of the organization. Because usage accounting is a management process that supports costing and charging, the policies in these areas largely determine the accounting policy. However, there are other factors that will influence the policy, for example legislation imposed by government or recommendations and guidelines from regulatory bodies.

At its highest level the usage accounting policy consists of abstract objectives. These are refined into more detailed functional objectives and then implemented as the usage accounting system. In implementing a usage accounting policy the service provider must stipulate what constitutes an instance of service usage and how the quantity of service usage will be measured. The definition of an instance of service will determine when usage accounting takes place. For example, in telephony service if the caller receives no reply he or she is not deemed to have used any service, so the usage accounting system would not record this type of call.

The definition of how service usage will be measured determines the information that is gathered. It is hard to envisage a way of measuring service usage that is not, in some way, related to the resources used in the provision of the service. But the metric may be affected by other factors, such as the service provider's tariff policy, cross-service subsidies and the costs of obtaining usage information. These additional factors can lead to the use of service metrics that are not directly related to all the resources used (for example, accounting for usage of a print service by the number of pages printed, while ignoring the amount of processing time it took to print the pages) or that are not directly proportional to the resources used (for example, accounting for the invocation of a service but not for the quantity of service used in the invocation).

The granularity of accounting information gathered is always a trade-off between the benefits that can be derived from the information and the costs of obtaining and analyzing the information. The cost includes the cost of the distributed system's resources and services consumed in providing the service, and the cost of researching, developing, maintaining, and improving the accounting service.

If the identified costs outweigh the perceived value then the service provider will be loath to implement usage accounting. Many distributed systems, including commercial systems, currently have little or no usage accounting for this very reason. There are even systems where the users account for their own usage and relate this information to the service provider, who does no accounting. Since this requires a very high level of trust it is quite rare.

The decision of whether or not to implement usage accounting needs to be periodically reviewed as factors on each side of the equation change. The balance of this equation can be seen to be swinging towards more detailed usage accounting. This is due to:

i)   The managers – there are more service providers offering more services. This has led to both increased competition and increased cooperation between service providers, changing the ways in which they interact with the consequential increase in the importance of administration management. Managers are also recognizing the need to control access (see Section 15.5.3) to ensure efficient use of the system, and this requires usage accounting.

ii) The users – power has shifted from the supplier to the customer. Now the users are in a stronger position to negotiate the tariff structure and the detail of information provided with their bills.

iii) The technology – miniaturization, improvements in performance, and reductions in price are having a considerable impact on distributed systems. It is becoming increasingly economical to implement accounting management applications because of these advances.

There is also evidence to suggest that tariffs for using services in distributed systems are becoming more usage-related. An example is British Telecom's decision to charge for each call to directory service instead of including this cost in the subscriber's access charges. Obviously this would also increase the importance of usage accounting.

Finally, it is important to stress that there are boundaries to usage accounting. By way of an illustration, imagine a service provider that decides that reading and writing to a database are two services it offers (the service definition) and that the service usage recorded includes the information written or read each time a service is used, together with the user identifier and the date and time of the service usage (the service metrics). The resulting audit trail can be used to hold users responsible for their actions, which is clearly an objective of security management and not accounting management. Accounting management collects information that relates to the *cost* of usage and this is the criterion used to decide if an application is a usage accounting application.

14.3   Usage accounting mechanisms

14.3.1   Basic model

Information on the activities of the managed system is required to perform management tasks in a functional area (see ISO 10040, 1991). This is obtained by monitoring specific parts of the system, shown as monitored objects in Figure 14.2 (Varley, 1991). Monitoring information is collected by meter objects, which may then process it in some way. The information produced by the meter is logged and can be used by applications. There are other basic functions that are common to all the functional areas (for example, filtering of management information to prevent the system and the managers from becoming overloaded) and these are described in (Langsford and Moffett, 1993).

Figure 14.2 Monitoring information flow.

Accounting management is a management service that collects, collates and logs cost-related usage information. The monitored objects are abstractions of services or resources from which usage information can be derived. The meter objects are **accounting meters** that collect, and may process, usage information from the monitored objects. The log objects are **accounting logs** that are repositories of information obtained from accounting meters, covering many instances of service or resource usage. The application objects are applications that require usage information, as well as other types of information.

14.3.2   Monitoring and metering

An accounting meter is 'an abstraction which represents the managed properties associated with provision of accounting for resource utilization' (ISO 10164-10). This definition appears to limit a meter to resource usage accounting, but the standard defines resource to encompass services as well. The definition of an accounting meter object must include the data it records and reports, and when and how it is recorded and reported. Most accounting meters will record the following basic set of information: the user of the service, the subscriber to the service, the provider of the service, the service provided, the units of usage, the quantity of usage and tariff-related information.

The service provided will identify the service used and may also identify the quality of service, if the service has different qualities. An example of this is an electronic mail service where the user is allowed to specify the speed with which the mail is delivered (first or second class mail) or specify that they wish to be notified when the mail is delivered (registered mail). If first class service costs more than second class it is insufficient for charging purposes to record that electronic mail was sent – the quality of service is also needed. Some accounting meters will also record the service requested, in situations where this may differ from the service provided. In our electronic mail example, the user may request first class mail service but receive only second class service and this may lead to the user being granted some form of compensation for poor service. Therefore there is a need to record the service requested.

Units of usage identify a suitable measure for quantifying the service or resource usage. Examples are service data units, protocol data units, units of time, bits, bytes, octets, characters or blocks. There are also units of usage that are closely related to the service being accounted. Examples are records read in an information service, where a "record" will be defined by the service provider, or pulses in a telephony service. In telephony, pulses are continually sent down the telephone line, with the interval between pulses being governed by the time of day and date. An accounting meter may use more than one type of unit of usage to measure service or resource usage. Therefore there needs to be a quantity-of-usage attribute for each unit-of-usage attribute.

Tariff information may be needed if the service is chargeable and this varies greatly between accounting meters. For example, the time of day and the called party's directory number are also needed to calculate the tariff that will be used in fixed-wire telephony services.

This list is not exhaustive. Examples of other types of information are the start and stop times of service usage or an instance-of-usage identifier. An instance-of-usage identifier is helpful in resolving disputes about a particular charge. It may be something the meter is already recording (such as the time of day), it may be a computer-generated identifier (such as a sequential number), or it may be something provided by the user (such as a service order number). Another use of this is to relate together components of a complex service (see Section 14.4.2).

In response to certain events an accounting meter will update its usage accounting information. Similarly, an accounting meter will generate accounting meter records in response to predefined events occurring. The events that cause these actions are known as **recording triggers** and **reporting triggers** respectively.

Recording triggers determine when the meter will record information, for example a recording trigger may cause the meter to be updated every 60 seconds. Reporting triggers determine the conditions under which a meter will generate an accounting notification, for example a reporting trigger may cause an accounting notification to be generated for each instance of usage.

14.3.3 Logging

An accounting log is a repository of accounting meter information, which may be retrieved in the form of accounting records. These records are a combination of information supplied by an accounting meter and standard log attributes (ISO 10164-6), namely a log record identifier and a logging time. There is also little to differentiate an accounting log, or the processes used to control logs, from any other type of log and its log support services. Readers with an interest in logging are referred to (LaBarre, 1991).

14.4 Billing and charging

14.4.1 Commercial billing

For commercial systems, the provision of information with which to bill customers is unquestionably the main reason for accounting management applications. A bill is the comprehensive set of information supplied to the subscriber to elicit payment for services used. A subscriber's bill can be broken down into a number of parts, including: subscriber details, bill details, charges and credits, usage details, account details, bill messages, and management reports. Many of these parts are self-explanatory and are not discussed any further.

Charges can be subdivided into access charges, usage charges, and miscellaneous charges such as a late payment charge. The subscriber may also earn credits, such as a discount for volume usage or compensation for poor service. The vast majority of commercial service providers will bill for access but the same is not true for usage charges. In the Sultanate of Brunei, subscribers are charged for the right to access the electricity system but not for the electricity they use. This is because in this oil-rich state, electricity is cheap to produce and the cost of accounting for its usage is more than the cost of the electricity.

If usage is charged the bill may include usage details, depending upon the granularity of the usage information collected. Some service providers will simply record a subscriber's usage on a meter, which is periodically read to generate the usage charge. Individual instances of usage cannot be identified and this approach is used when the charge for an instance of usage is low, such as for natural gas usage.

The usage accounting system may generate information on instances of usage and this approach is becoming increasingly common. As well as a charge for the total usage in a period, the service provider may also supply details of each instance of usage and the charge it incurred. Instances of usage require unique identifiers to make them meaningful, and this may be supplied by the subscriber or the service provider. It allows subscribers to record their usage independently and then check it against the usage charged. This approach is taken for services where the charge for an instance of usage is appreciable, for example in cellular telephony.

Bill messages may be one way for a service provider to gain competitive advantage, but a more effective method is to provide comprehensive management breakdowns of the bill. The subscriber may wish to have the same billing information presented in many different ways, for example, broken down by departments and by regions. This can be difficult to achieve. The service provider may have distributed billing, with regional billing centers handling different groups of subscribers. A company may have subscribers in each region, and request a management report showing the company-wide charges. This will require coordination between the regional billing centers, which can be viewed as autonomous domains, and can be just as demanding as coordinating different service providers.

Yet another way to gain competitive advantage is to allow the subscriber some degree of control over the criteria that will be used to determine when they will be billed. The subscriber may want to be billed periodically, or whenever a certain level of charges has been incurred, or when a threshold level of usage has been passed, or on an *ad hoc* basis. To meet the many permutations for billing service the billing system must be highly flexible.

14.4.2   Charge generation

This section concentrates on complex service usage charges. In Section 14.1.1, the two approaches to charging for services involving many service providers were introduced: the group approach and the individual approach. With the group approach the subscriber views the service provider as the supplier of all the service and may not be aware that a number of service providers are involved. Furthermore, the metrics used to account for the complex service may not indicate that there are a number of component services involved. In international telephony, the amount of service used in a call is measured in pulses. The call charge depends on the number of pulses, time of day and the country called. The call itself is not broken down into a number of components of usage from different service providers with a related charge for each leg of the call.

Situations exist where the user is shown that an instance of complex service usage is composed of a number of components. Imagine an information service where you are charged for the time you are connected to the service and the amount of information you retrieve. The bill for this service may be broken down into instances of service usage, each with an identifier such as the time of the session and each with a charge. Each instance-of-usage charge may be further subdivided into a component for the connect time and a component for the information retrieval. The components may be related to the instance of complex service in which they were used, as in the example above, by an instance-of-usage identifier. The main contractor bills the subscriber for all component services used in an instance of complex service and is billed, in turn, by the subcontractors (see Section 14.6).

With the individual approach, the subscriber has contracts with each of the service providers involved in providing the service. The subscribers are billed by each service provider separately so service providers must be able to identify every subscriber. It is not customary for the different service providers to relate the instance of usage of their service to any other services used. This method has the advantage, to the service providers, of removing the need for inter-service provider reconciliation. This is weighed against the cost to each service provider of having to bill users directly, which may be especially onerous for small service providers.

These two different approaches are both common, and can be illustrated with examples from British Telecom (BT) services. The first example is a derived service where users can obtain voice information over the telephone network, for example a weather forecast. There are two services involved, the telephone service and the information service. BT bills the subscriber for all instances of derived service usage and pays the information provider for providing the information service. An instance-of-usage identifier is provided, namely the dialed number in combination with the time and date, but components are not shown. This is an example of the group approach.

The second example is British Telecom's Videotex service (Prestel), which is a data information service that can be accessed over the public communications networks. The information is provided by third parties who rent Videotex pages from BT. The users perceive two services: the communications service and the Prestel service. In fact the Prestel service is composed of two components: the Videotex service and the information provider's service. This is billed using the group approach. The subscriber receives a communications bill and a Prestel bill separately and no attempt is made to relate the charge for an instance of communications service with the charge for the Prestel service. This is an example of the individual approach.

Usage charging has traditionally been a back-office application and usage accounting a distributed application but there are requirements for on-line charging in some commercial systems. In the pan-European cellular system, subscribers can request advice of charge on completion of a call. The tariffs normally used for a call are determined by the subscriber's contract and the amount of usage already accumulated in the billing period. If a subscriber uses advice of charge then the call will be charged at standard rates and any special charging arrangements in the subscriber's contract will be ignored. This is due to the difficulty of distributing usage charging details.

Some subscribers prefer the idea of stipulating what they will pay for a service before the service is used, in the form of a quality of service parameter included with their service invocation. This cost parameter could be used as a guideline. For example, the service will be invoked only if the service provider can meet the price parameter. It can also be used in conjunction with other quality of service parameters, such as timeliness or confidentiality. For example, the user may want an electronic message delivered for under $x, and within y hours but be unconcerned with its confidentiality.

It is important to stress that the charges for a particular instance of service may not be consistently related to the cost of providing each instance of service. When the service provider creates the tariff structure the cost of service provision is only one ingredient, others being market demand and profit margins. Once subscribers are apprised of the tariff structure they can often predetermine what an instance of usage will cost them, which might not be the case if the charge was more cost-related.

Tariffs also offer service providers the means to influence user behavior. The service provider would like to have a uniform demand for service throughout the service provision period (whereas users would like to have timely service when they need it). Therefore the service provider may use different tariff rates for peak time usage and off-peak time usage, to encourage users to move to off-peak periods and hence create a more uniform demand. This can be counter-productive if it results in too many users moving to off-peak periods. In the UK, the electricity suppliers offered cheap-rate electricity in the early hours of the morning. This has led to a power surge at 12.30 a.m., so instead of smoothing out demand the policy has created a new peak. To avoid this problem, many service providers are targeting groups of subscribers with tailored tariff packages.

14.5   Payment and quotas

In commercial systems, there is a risk that subscribers will renege on their payment obligations. Service providers want to minimize this risk, so new prospects are assessed on their ability and intention to repay debts. This can lead to the subscriber being assigned a credit rating and a credit limit, the latter representing a subscriber's maximum permitted debt. When a subscriber reaches this credit limit the service provider may wish to take some action to encourage the subscriber to settle the debt. A subscriber's credit rating and limit may change, depending upon how promptly they settle debts and the trust the service provider places in them.

To manage debt effectively a service provider requires accurate, up-to-date account information on each subscriber, including usage charges. The service provider would ideally like usage charges calculated as soon after the instance of usage as possible, a topic discussed in the previous section. In a distributed system usage can take place in many parts of the system and it is usually accounted for locally. This accounting information needs to be collected and conveyed to the service provider's charging applications, which takes time and therefore increases risk. In the pan-European cellular system, subscribers may use their mobile stations on any of the cooperating networks. Usage information is periodically exchanged between the service providers so that subscribers can be billed. This information is exchanged monthly, which gives a subscriber time to amass a large debt on other networks without the home service provider's knowledge.

One way of reducing the risk would be for service providers to exchange usage information more frequently. The usage records still need to be charged and these charges included in the subscriber's outstanding balance, which also takes time and leaves the service provider vulnerable. A safer method is to use usage budgets combined with access controls, which works as follows. For each service that will be controlled, users are allocated a limited quantity of service that they may use in a given period. Each time they use the service the quantity of service used will be recorded. When the quantity of service used in the period becomes equal to the quantity allocated, they may be prohibited from using the service until they are next allocated a budget.

In the pan-European example the subscriber's credit limit would be converted into a usage budget. When a subscriber wishes to make a call on a visited network, not only could the service entitlement be checked (access), but the amount of usage budget would also be checked (budget). Different types of usage, for example local and overseas usage, could be allocated different budgets. When the subscriber has made a call, the usage budget will be reduced. When the subscriber pays a bill, the usage budget will be increased. An alternative approach is to restore the usage budget periodically. If the subscriber has no usage budget left he will be prohibited from making a call. This greatly simplifies the process, as the on-line charging requirement is removed.

The Amoeba bank service (Mullender, 1989) implements many of these ideas in a distributed system. Different types of usage are measured in different virtual currencies. Instead of using credit limits as budgets, the system uses the concept of bank accounts. Subscribers are first required to deposit a sum of virtual money in the service business account. When the subscriber makes a request for service this bank account is checked to ensure there are sufficient funds to cover the request. If so, the request is granted, the service used and charged, and the appropriate sum transferred from the service business account to the service provider's private account.

The principles of the Amoeba bank service are equally applicable to non-commercial systems, where the need to be fair to all users is important (Estrin and Zhang, 1991). If they are uncontrolled, users may keep increasing their demands for services until the system resources are consumed in managing the demands rather than providing service. A step towards influencing user behavior would be to provide users with feedback on their usage and its impact on the system, and trust that this will encourage them to behave in a manner that would benefit the whole user community. A more effective method is to implement access controls combined with usage budgets. This is along the general lines described above, which can be enhanced in many ways, for example, charging more of a user's budget for provision of service during peak periods than off-peak periods. Users may also be rewarded for dependable usage patterns by having their budgets increased. This allows the service providers to predict the demand for usage accurately and thereby run their services more efficiently.

14.6 Usage reconciliation

The situation where a complex service uses services from a number of service providers has already been discussed. This section looks at how the service providers charge each other for this type of service when the group approach is used. As a vehicle for explaining the issues surrounding this form of reconciliation, we shall begin by looking at international telephony service and move on to examine roaming service in the pan-European cellular system.

14.6.1   International telephone reconciliation

In an international call, each service provider involved in the call will want to receive some payment for the use of their services. The current methods of international inter-administration settlement originated when the telephony services of a country were provided by a single organization. These are set out in the CCITT recommendation D.150 on accounting procedures in international traffic (CCITT, 1989). In the simplest case, two countries are directly connected, with no transit carriers. Call traffic would flow both ways and at regular intervals the two organizations would settle their accounts according to their bilateral agreement. The CCITT recommends that they use one of three different procedures for settlement:

i)   **Accounting revenue division procedure**. This is the simplest method and is widely practiced. The two countries pool the revenue generated from international calls between them, and then divide it in two, usually on a 50/50 basis. Other proportions are negotiated between the countries if 50/50 is not deemed equitable.

ii) **Flat-rate procedure**. This method works on the principle that the call-originating network operator pays for the facilities they use on the call-terminating network. The terminating network charges a flat rate per incoming circuit that takes into account the international circuits and exchange, and the national network extensions. The settlement will be the difference in charges between outgoing and incoming circuits' cost. This is an access charge method.

iii) **Traffic-unit price procedure**. This method works on the principle that the terminating network operator will be paid a price per traffic unit they receive. The traffic-unit price will be related to the facilities made available to the originating network operator. This is a usage charge method.

If two countries are not directly connected then calls between them will have to be routed via intermediary networks, owned by transit carriers. In international calls the simple rule is that a carrier receives payment from the network that passed it the call, and pays the network it passed the call to. This means that a network operator does not have to know where a call originated, only the network that passed it the call. It also means that network operators need bilateral agreements with only those network operators with which they directly interconnect.

Figure 14.3 shows a call that is passing through a number of networks (NN = National Network, ISC = International Switching Center). If the inter-administration costs of this call are settled using the traffic-unit price procedure, the settlement would work as follows:

NN1 charges ISC1 x for terminating the call.

The ISC1 operator charges y for using its facilities,
  so the charge to ISC2 is $x + y$.
The ISC2 operator charges z for using its facilities,
  so the charge to NN2 is $x + y + z$.
The NN2 operator charges the subscriber for the call, based upon NN2's tariffs.

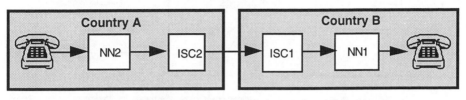

NN = National Network   ISC = International Switching Center

Figure 14.3 A call traversing multiple networks.

A different way of settling this call would be for each network operator to identify where the call originated. The charge for using their services would then be sent to the originating network operator. In the above example, the cost to the NN operator in country A would still be $x + y + z$, but the NN operator would know what using each network cost and the accounting procedure for all but the originating operator is greatly simplified. Instead of having to pay one operator and get paid by another, each network operator is paid by the originating operator alone. There would be a great increase in the number of bilateral agreements for each network operator and these would need to be far simpler than those currently in use.

14.6.2 Pan-European reconciliation

The pan-European cellular system was developed to allow Public Land Mobile Network (PLMN) operators to run compatible networks across Europe, thereby enabling a subscriber to use the same mobile station on all the networks. This was achieved by all the PLMNs conforming to Groupe Speciale Mobile (GSM) technical and administrative recommendations, and agreeing commercial practices through a memorandum of understanding.

A subscriber will contract for service with one Groupe Speciale Mobile PLMN (GPLMN) and this will be designated as their Home PLMN (HPLMN). Subscribers may request service on other PLMNs (ETSI/GSM recommendation 2.13) through their HPLMN. The practice of using cellular service on another network is known as **roaming**. In the pan-European cellular system all charges a subscriber incurs through using GSM services will be billed by the subscriber's HPLMN, including any charges for roamed calls. This is a group approach, raising the requirement for inter-administration service reconciliation.

Figure 14.4 shows a call from a roamed mobile station to another roamed mobile station. The calling subscriber (M1) will first request service from the Visited PLMN (VPLMN), which identifies the subscriber's HPLMN and checks the subscriber's service entitlement. If the request is cleared the next step is to locate the called mobile station (M2) by interrogating its HPLMN. In our example, M2 has roamed to the same GPLMN as M1.

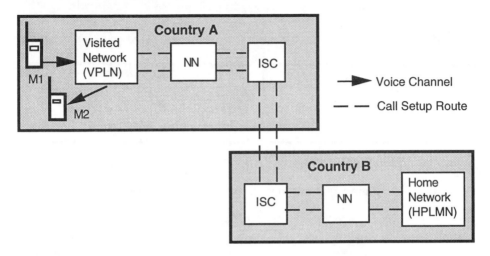

Figure 14.4 Roamed caller and callee.

This is quite a complex call if the voice channel follows the route of the call setup (the dotted line). The CCITT have made the following recommendation (Rec D.93) on how this call may be charged: M1 is charged for an international call to country B based on the tariffs of the VPLMN and M2 is charged for the forwarded element to country A based on the tariffs of its HPLMN. Both the caller and called party will therefore be charged for this call.

However, under Signaling System No. 7 (to which all GPLMNs conform) the voice channel does not have to follow the route of the call setup. In the example all the information about M2's location will be fed back to the VPLMN, on a control channel, before a voice channel is allocated. Therefore the VPLMN could set up a voice channel that did not use any international legs. In this example, the service providers' usage costs bear little resemblance to the service users' usage charges.

14.6.3 The clearing house concept

For each roamed mobile receiving a call or making a call, a usage record will have to be sent from the VPLMN to the HPLMN. There are many GPLMNs, so if roaming service becomes popular the amount of usage information they exchange could be colossal.

One problem, already mentioned, is that rogue users could move between GPLMNs and run up large bills in the process. The HPLMN is contracted to pay the VPLMNs for this usage, but may have difficulties in recovering the debt from the user. So the service provider would ideally like usage charges to be exchanged frequently: at least daily. Each service provider would potentially need to maintain an account with every other service provider and run this process daily for each GPLMN.

A simpler method would be for service providers to identify roaming calls and cost them, then send them to a central clearing house. The clearing house would handle the exchange of usage information between the service providers. It would also handle the exchange rates between the European currencies, using Standard Drawing Rights, and apply the appropriate credits and debits to the service providers' accounts. This concept is partly met by the CEPT clearing house, but it does not yet handle the exchange of usage data. The clearing house concept can equally well apply to other distributed services which involve many service providers and are billed using the group approach.

14.6.4   Roaming while a call is in progress

A common fallacy is that a call will continue when a user moves between the areas covered by two GPLMNs. In theory this is possible, but in practice it is banned (ETSI/GSM recommendation 2.11). As the mobile station leaves the GPLMN where the call was initiated the signal will grow weaker until the call is eventually dropped. The user will then have to redial and connect with the new GPLMN. This is an inconvenience for the user and it is possible that this call type will be permitted in the future.

This type of call does raise a number of problems for the administrations involved. Figure 14.5(a) shows the route of a call in progress from a mobile station to a station on the Public Switched Telephone Network (PSTN). Figure 14.5(b) shows how the call could now be routed if the call could be handed over between GPLMNs, in this example from Base Station 3 (BS3) to BS4.

The call now has an additional leg between the two gateway Mobile Switching Centers (MSCs). (This assumes that interconnection between adjoining GPLMNs will be permitted by European regulators; it is currently forbidden). It is highly unlikely that the circuits used in the fixed line portion of the call can be changed. Therefore the GPLMN to PSTN interconnection point that was set up when the call was initiated would remain throughout the call's duration.

This is the most complex of the situations involving many network operators in a single instance of service provision, because the organizations will not be involved in the service provision throughout the entire instance. The limitations of the CCITT model are shown if we consider how to account for this type of call. The CCITT traffic-unit price procedure would fail to account accurately for this call, because it tacitly assumes that all the service providers involved in a call are involved for the entire duration of the call. The alternative accounting method described in Section 14.6.1 could be used to handle this call. Let us suppose that the call lasted x units before hand-over (Figure 14.5(a)) and y units after hand-over (Figure 14.5(b)). The cost of the call might therefore be:

PSTN unit charge $\times (x + y)$

\+ GPLMN A unit charge $\times (x + y)$

\+ GPLMN B unit charge $\times y$.

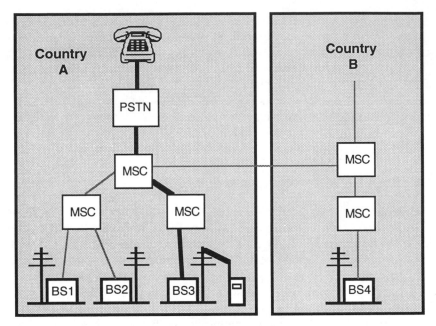

PSTN = Public Switched Telephone Network
MSC = Mobile Switching Center   BS = Base Station

(a) Initial call setup

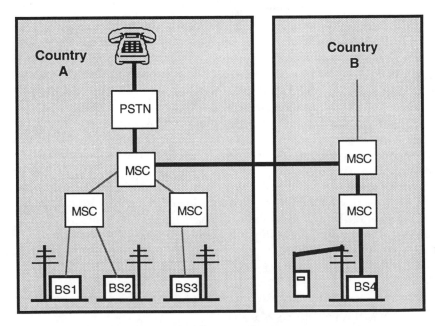

(b) After roaming

Figure 14.5 Call routing.

Both the PSTN and GPLMN B would identify that the subscriber was from GPLMN A and send that GPLMN the bill for their service. GPLMN A would bill the subscriber. The algorithm above might be different if the PLMN that initially handled the call charged differently for the first x units and the last y units.

This approach could be extended to all roamed calls (Sloman *et al.*, 1993). The subscriber's HPLMN could be identified by all the parties involved and they could send the bill to the HPLMN, rather than the VPLMN. If this concept is used in conjunction with the clearing house concept, the subcontracting service providers have only to send usage and charge information, for each component service they supplied, to the clearing house and the clearing house would handle the redistribution of this information to the HPLMN and the settlement of inter-administration accounts.

14.7 Summary

This chapter has presented an overview of a distributed system's administration requirements and has focused, in particular, on usage accounting and the applications that require usage accounting information. In summary, two points about usage accounting are worth repeating.

The first is that *usage accounting serves more purposes than just supporting usage charging*. It underpins a number of other activities, such as controlling access to ensure users have a fair share of the system services, and measuring the system cost efficiency.

The other is that *usage accounting services need to be cost-justified in the same way as any other service*. The granularity of accounting information gathered is always a trade-off between the benefits that can be derived from the information and the costs of obtaining and analyzing it. The cost includes the cost of the distributed system's resources and services consumed in providing the service, and the cost of researching, developing, maintaining, and improving the accounting service. If the costs outweigh the value, there will be no net benefit from implementing usage accounting.

Abbreviations

BT	British Telecom
DPA	Data Protection Act
GPLMN	Groupe Speciale Mobile Public Land Mobile Network
GSM	Groupe Speciale Mobile
HPLMN	Home Public Land Mobile Network
PLMN	Public Land Mobile Network
VPLMN	Visited Public Land Mobile Network

References

CCITT 1989 CCITT Blue Book (1989). Volume II – Fascicle II.1 – General tariff principles – *Charging and accounting in international telecommunications services*. Series D Recommendations

Estrin D. and Zhang L. (1991). Design considerations for usage accounting and feedback in internetworks. In *Integrated Network Management II* (Krishnan I. and Zimmer W., eds.), pp. 719–33, North Holland

ETSI/GSM 2.11 *Service Accessibility* – version 3.4.0. March 1990.

ETSI/GSM 2.13 *Subscription to the Service of a GSM PLMN* – version 3.1.0. January 1990

ISO 10040 (1991). Information Technology – Open Systems Interconnection – *Systems Management Overview*

ISO 10164-6 Information Technology – Open Systems Interconnection – Systems Management – *Part 6: Log Control Function*

ISO 10164-10 Information Technology – Open Systems Interconnection – Systems Management – *Part 10: Accounting Meter Function*

LaBarre L. (1991). Management by exception: OSI event generation, reporting and logging. In *Integrated Network Management II* (Krishnan I. and Zimmer W., eds.), 227–34. North Holland

Langsford A. and Moffett J.D. (1993). Distributed Systems Management. Addison Wesley

McKell L.J., Hansen J.V. and Heitger L.E. (1979). Charging for eomputing resources. *Computing Surveys* , **11**(2), 106–19

Moffett J.D. and Sloman M.S. (1991). *The Representation of Policies as System Objects*. Conference on Organizational Computer Systems, Atlanta, Georgia

Mullender S.J. (1989). Accounting and resource dontrol. *Distributed Systems,* (Mullender S.J. ed.), 133–45. ACM Press

Sloman M.S. (1990). Management for open distributed processing, *Second IEEE Computer Society Workshop on Future Trends in Distributed Computing Systems,* 533–39

Sloman M.S., Varley B.J., Moffett J.D. and Twidle K.P. (1993). Domain management and accounting in an international cellular network. In *IFIP Transactions C12 Integrated Network Management III*. (Hegering H-G. and Yemini Y., eds.), pp. 193–206, North Holland

Synderman M. and Kline R.A. (1969). Job costing a multiprogramming computer. *Data Management,* **7**(1), January

Varley B.J. (1991). Usage accounting in distributed systems, *IEE Colloquium on Network Management,* London

Chapter 15

Security for Management and Management of Security

Philippe A. Janson

IBM Zurich Research Laboratory,
Säumerstrasse 4,
8803 Rüschlikon, Zurich, Switzerland
pj @zurich.ibm.com

In this chapter, we discuss security issues in computer networks and distributed systems with emphasis on security management aspects. First, we review the main services required to ensure the security of objects and resources in networks and distributed systems, and also mechanisms used to implement these services. Then we discuss requirements and directions for managing network security, and how security management relates to system management in general. Given the state of the art, this second part of the chapter is, of necessity, more speculative than descriptive.

The chapter is addressed to readers with a background in networks and distributed systems but little or no understanding of security issues in general, and security issues in networking and distributed environments in particular.

15.1 Introduction

With the ever-increasing pervasiveness of computer networks, information accessible through or transported by networks, as well as network components and resources themselves, are often at risk (Neumann, 1991). Information and network security are thus becoming the focus of intense concern on the part of network users and operators. Techniques for implementing network security are being standardized and products have started appearing on the market. However, just as operating a network takes more than stacking a few layers of protocols, securing it takes more than providing basic security mechanisms. Network operation and network security both require *management*. In fact, besides network configuration, fault, performance, and accounting functions, network security is the fifth aspect that has been recognized explicitly by the Open Systems Interconnection (OSI) architecture as requiring management functions (ISO 7498-1 and ISO 7498-2, 1988).

The primary focus of this chapter is a review of the state of the art in management of network security. However, before talking about the *management* of security, it is necessary to review the *mechanisms* of security for two reasons: first, it is necessary to understand what kind of security objects and functions need to be managed; second, it is necessary to understand how these can be used to secure the management functions themselves. More specifically, it is necessary to understand what sort of managed objects are needed to administer security, and what can be expected from security services and mechanisms to secure the management functions. This discussion raises the question of where to draw the line between basic mechanisms and their associated management functions.

For the purpose of this chapter, we have chosen to use the OSI Reference Model (ISO 7498-1, 1988), described in Chapter 2, as a guideline to separate security functions themselves from security management functions. Figure 15.1 represents a system including the seven OSI layers together with their respective Layer Management Entities (LME) and the associated System Management Application Entity (SMAE). Within this context, we have chosen to regard as a security function any security service or mechanism entirely implemented within one of the seven layers. By contrast, we regard any function requiring services or mechanisms provided by the LMEs or the SMAE as belonging to security management.

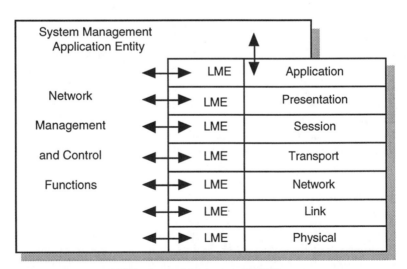

LME = Layer Management Entity

Figure 15.1 OSI layers and management functions.

Before we start discussing security functions and their management, it is useful to review some basic concepts relevant to the topic.

(Target) objects and (user) subjects

A first important concept is the distinction between objects and subjects. The information, network components and resources to be protected are referred to as objects, while the active entities, end users and applications operating on objects on their behalf are called user subjects. Clearly, applications or processes can be at the same time objects and subjects. Subjects are also sometimes referred to as *principals*, a principal being an end user or a network-internal (electronic) subject acting on a user's behalf, for instance a process or application. In the present context of security management, the term "object" refers to both protected objects (targets of subject access requests) and managed objects; but to avoid overusing the term, the word "target" will be used instead to refer to protected objects. Use of the unqualified word "object" will be restricted to managed objects from now on.

Threats and attacks

A second point concerns what threats subjects pose to targets, and what attacks need to be protected against:

- *Disclosure* – a first threat is unauthorized release of information, for instance to intruders carrying out passive attacks such as wire-tapping. Such attacks can be prevented by cryptographic means.

- *Modification* – a second threat is unauthorized alteration of information, for instance by intruders carrying out active attacks such as message modification on the fly. Such attacks are harder to prevent: indeed, unless a network link is protected physically over its entire length, an intruder may be able to cut the link, insert a computer at the cut and modify messages as they pass through. However, such attacks can always be detected and in that sense defeated.

- *Denial of use, misuse, abuse* – a third kind of threat is denial of network use *to* legitimate users. This can result from several different attacks: other legitimate users making abusive use of network resources or intruders perturbing the network (for instance cutting links or physically disabling switching nodes). Such attacks can be either prevented or detected depending on their nature.

- *Repudiation* – a fourth, and more rarely noted, type of threat is in a sense the dual of the above: denial of network usage *by* a legitimate user refusing to admit that he sent or received some information, or that he used some resource. Such attacks can be prevented by suitable measures.

Domains and policies

A last important notion before we review security functions and their management is the concept of a security domain and its associated security policy. A definition of the notion of management domain is given in Chapter 16. For the purpose of this chapter it is sufficient to view a domain as a set of targets and subjects whose security is governed by a set of rules, called the domain policy, defined by one administrative authority.

With the above definitions we are now in a position to review security functions and discuss their management. In Section 15.2 we will describe briefly the main security services required to counter the threats and attacks seen above. In Section 15.3 we will give a short overview of the techniques and mechanisms used to implement those services. Then, in Section 15.4 we will discuss functions necessary to the management of security mechanisms. Finally, in Section 15.5 we will relate security management to the broader topic of network management.

15.2   Network security services

The first problem that arises when trying to understand what security management is about consists of defining what security services are to be managed. Many studies, surveys, and tutorials on network security have been published in the past, each proposing its own definitions of the different security services (Popek and Kline, 1979; DeMillo and Merritt, 1983; Voydock and Kent, 1983; Voydock and Kent, 1984; Davies and Price, 1984; Karger, 1985; Abrams and Podell, 1987; Janson and Molva, 1991). While not all authors agree on definitions, a large consensus exists today and is best expressed in Part 2 (Security Architecture) of the OSI Reference Model (ISO 7498-2, 1988). This document defines five security services:

- Access control;

- Authentication;

- Confidentiality;

- Integrity;

- Non-repudiation.

We have added availability and accountability to this list as they are discussed in other documents on network security (for instance in the Trusted Network Interpretation (TNI) documents (TNI, 1987)), though not explicitly mentioned in ISO 7498-2 (1988):

Access control

One of the main objectives of security is the provision of access control, namely the ability for users to precisely control who should have the right to access which targets in what ways. Access control in a network environment has two aspects:

- Control of access to resources located within individual computers attached to the network. This aspect of the service relies entirely on access control mechanisms within the operating systems of the responsible computers.

- Control of access to network resources such as the attached computers themselves, switching nodes, links, or abstract resources, such as routes or connections. These resources are not protected by the operating system of any individual computer but rather by the network as a whole.

Access control policies are classified in two broad families.

i) *Discretionary Access Control (DAC)* are policies where the access rights of subjects to targets are under control (at the discretion) of the users owning or controlling the targets. For instance, Alice may be free to let her colleague Bob access her own files. Such policies are defined typically by so-called *identity-based* rules, where access control decisions are based on the identity of the subject requesting the access.

ii) *Mandatory Access Control (MAC)* are policies where the access rights of subjects to targets are mandated by obligatory rules. For instance, a company policy may forbid Alice to show Bob a confidential memo even if she wanted to, simply because Bob is not cleared to receive such classified data. Such policies are defined typically by so-called *rule-based* directives, where access control decisions are based not on the identity of the subjects requesting access but on fixed rules beyond the control of normal subjects. Subjects are labeled with clearances defining their privileges, while targets are labeled with classifications defining their sensitivity. Access decisions are based on comparing subject clearances to classifications.

Authentication

Given that access control is meant to control who may access which targets, an essential service must be the ability for the system to correlate the identity of end users and other subjects (processes, applications, network entities) with the requests they make to access targets inside the system. This entails being able to precisely identify (authenticate) end users and subjects. This authentication requirement exhibits two aspects:

i) *Origin authentication* – the ability to identify the sender of a message or originator of a communication, sometimes referred to as one-way authentication.

ii) *Peer authentication* – the ability for two communicating parties to mutually authenticate one another, sometimes referred to as two-way authentication.

Confidentiality

Next, the system must provide confidentiality services to protect information against the threat of disclosure to unauthorized users. This confidentiality requirement also comes in two flavors:

i) *Data confidentiality* – the ability to protect against disclosure of the content of data traveling through the network (or stored within attached computers).

ii) *Traffic confidentiality* – the ability to protect against disclosure of the origin, destination, volume and indeed the very existence of data traveling through the network (or by extension stored within attached computers).

Integrity

Similarly, the system must provide integrity services to protect information against the threat of modification by unauthorized users.

Non-repudiation

Finally, to counter repudiation threats, the system must provide so-called non-repudiation services. This requirement also comes in two flavors.

i) *Non-repudiation of origin* is a stronger form of origin authentication. Origin authentication means that the recipient of a message or communication must be able to convince himself of the identity of the sender or originator. Non-repudiation of origin means that the recipient must in addition be able to convince a third party of the origin's identity thus preventing the origin from denying that he or she ever sent the information.

ii) *Non-repudiation of destination or receipt* is in a sense the dual of the previous one. It gives the originator of a message or communication the ability to prove to a third party that the message or communication was indeed received by an identifiable recipient, thus preventing the recipient from denying that he or she ever received the information.

Availability

This service represents what users expect from a normally operating network in the absence of accidental or, more specifically in the present security context, malicious disruptions, perturbations, abuses or misuses of network components and resources.

Accountability

This service is at the border between security and accounting. It goes beyond authentication in that it requires the system to hold some user or principal accountable for every action or event occurring in the system. It is essential in fending off network abuse and repudiation, as well as in billing users for actual resource usage through proper accounting procedures.

15.3   Network security mechanisms

It is clearly necessary to understand security services in order to discuss security management – however, it is not sufficient. Security services correspond to abstract network user or operator requirements; they do not directly define the objects that security management must deal with. Identifying these objects requires a deeper understanding of how security services are implemented. Security services are realized by what OSI calls mechanisms (ISO 7498-2, 1988) or what the ECMA Security Framework calls facilities (ECMA, 1988). Neither the OSI nor the ECMA document explicitly distinguishes layer mechanisms from management mechanisms. In the present section we briefly review layer security mechanisms, while in the next section we address management mechanisms proper. Throughout, we try to correlate the OSI and ECMA terminologies.

15.3.1 Cryptography

Both OSI and ECMA recognize explicitly the techniques that are the foundation of all network security: *cryptography*. Cryptographic mechanisms are the basis for implementing all confidentiality, integrity, authentication, and non-repudiation services, which in turn support the ultimate access control objective. Many surveys and tutorials on modern cryptography have been published (Popek and Kline, 1979; Diffie and Hellman, 1979; IEEE Computer, 1983; IEEE Proceedings, 1988; Diffie, 1988; Massey, 1988). Cryptographic mechanisms come in two flavors.

i) *Symmetric or secret-key systems* are characterized by the fact that two (or more) parties wanting to protect their communications need to share a common secret cryptographic key that must remain known only to them. Encryption and decryption functions are the inverse of one another and use the same key.

   The main problem posed by such systems is that common secret keys must somehow be distributed to communicating parties, which poses a challenge since the parties do not trust the network (otherwise they would not need keys in the first place). The main advantage of symmetric systems is that there are readily available, relatively efficient, and reasonably affordable hardware implementations on the market.

   The most notable symmetric system today is the internationally standardized system referred to as *Data Encryption Standard (DES)* or *Data Encryption Algorithm (DEA)* (NBS, 1977), for which hardware as well as software implementations are widely available from many manufacturers.

ii) *Asymmetric or public-key systems* are characterized by the fact that each party wanting to use cryptography must define for itself a pair of mathematically related keys, one of which, used for encryption and integrity verification, is made public (for instance listed in an open directory), while the other one, used for decryption and integrity enforcement, is kept a private secret by its owner. While the two keys are related, it is not possible to retrieve the private key from the public-key. Encryption and decryption functions are of course also related but they are not strictly the mathematical inverse of one another.

   The main problem of asymmetric systems is that they call upon relatively sophisticated computations, thus making hardware implementations less efficient and more costly than for symmetric systems. While the hardware cost and performance ratios for symmetric and asymmetric systems is not likely to change very much in the future, technology will certainly move performance up and cost down to more appealing levels for asymmetric system implementations.

   The main advantage of asymmetric systems is that key distribution is somewhat less of a problem since the keys that must be distributed are public knowledge by definition. It should however be noted that their authenticity, namely the identity of their owner, must still be guaranteed. Indeed if an intruder could substitute his or her own public key for that of other legitimate users in the public key directory listing, he or she could impersonate those users and read confidential traffic destined for them.

While the idea of asymmetric cryptographic systems was originally proposed by Diffie and Hellman (1976), the system most broadly used and discussed today is the *Rivest-Shamir-Adleman (RSA) algorithm* (Rivest *et al.*, 1978), for which hardware and software implementations are available from a number of licensed manufacturers.

The issue of key distribution is a management problem to be addressed later.

15.3.2   Confidentiality

Data confidentiality

DES is the currently preferred mechanism for enciphering "large" amounts of data to provide message confidentiality, connection confidentiality, or complete bit stream confidentiality between two or more parties.   There are several possible and standardized ways to use DES for this end (ISO 8372, 1987). As suggested above, asymmetric systems can also be used to provide data confidentiality by using the public key of the intended recipient as the encryption key, since that recipient is the only one possessing the matching private key needed for decryption. However, given the relatively low performance of these systems, their use is typically limited to what is called selected-field confidentiality, meaning the encipherment of only short fields within larger messages.

Traffic confidentiality

Data confidentiality hides from potential intruders the content of data being transmitted between end users. However, packet headers remain in clear text so that the network can properly route traffic, which implies that potential intruders could still figure out the volume of traffic between communicating parties. To protect the confidentiality of traffic the network must support either traffic padding or route control. Traffic padding means that the network should fill transmission blanks with bogus traffic and encipher all resulting link or sub-network traffic, so that it becomes impossible for an intruder to tell how much traffic is exchanged between whom, or in fact that any traffic is exchanged at all between any parties. Route control allows users to specify routes across links that they know cannot be easily tapped by potential intruders – for instance enciphered instead of regular links, underground cables rather than satellite or radio links, optical links rather than electrical ones (because tapping light is hard without cutting the fiber, which is detectable).

15.3.3   Integrity

Providing integrity of network data can be achieved by appending to the transmitted data an integrity-checking field called Integrity Check Vector (ICV), Modification Detection Code (MDC), Message Integrity Code (MIC), or Message Authentication Code (MAC, abbreviation not to be confused with Mandatory Access Control) whose validity can be verified by the receiver. Such integrity-checking fields are merely digests of the transmitted data in which a shared secret or a private key is factored according to some cryptographic or other technique. ICVs, MDCs, MICs, and MACs differ from one another simply in the technique used for producing and verifying the digest field. An increasingly popular MDC is for instance the MD4 algorithm (Rivest, 1990). The International Standards Organization (ISO) has specified several algorithms for computing MICs – see for instance ISO 9797 (1990); or ISO 8731 (1987), where the MIC is computed as the leftmost 32 bits of the last block resulting from the encryption of the transmitted data using DES in Cipher-Block-Chaining (CBC) mode). As in the case of confidentiality, one can protect the integrity of only selected message fields, entire messages, all traffic, or even complete bit streams exchanged between communicating partners.

15.3.4 Authentication

Authentication classes

Authenticating an end user, subject, or entity in the network entails requiring that the user or subject demonstrate access to some unique identification information: biometric information (for end users only) such as handwritten signature, finger-print, or voice sample; secret information such as a password or a cryptographic key; or personalized information (again for end users only) such as an identification badge (magnetic or smart card). We will refer to the subject being identified as the *claimer*, while the subject verifying the claimed identity will be referred to as the *verifier*.

The OSI Authentication Framework (ISO 10181-2, 1990) defines five classes of authentication mechanisms that differ in the way in which they use the identification information:

- **Class 0 – Direct disclosure**

  With these mechanisms, the claimer is directly prompted for identification information, typically a password, which is disclosed and transmitted in the clear over the network to the verifier. This is a very weak identification technique: an intruder tapping the network lines can see the password being transmitted in the clear and subsequently type it on any terminal to masquerade as the legitimate password owner. In fact, since the identification information is transmitted in the clear, the scheme assumes that the claimer trusts the verifier: if such trust did not exist the claimer might be sending a secret straight to an intruder!

- **Class 1 – One-way functions**

  With these mechanisms, the claimer does not transmit the secret (password) in the clear over the network. Instead a one-way function of this secret is sent, so that a potential intruder could not simply tap the password and replay it on a terminal. However, an intruder could still record the bit string representing the one-way function of the password and play it back on some communication line (rather than some keyboard). This demands more than passively tapping a line but remains a threat in many cases.

- **Class 2 – One-way functions with verifier identification**

These mechanisms are identical to Class 1 mechanisms, except for the fact that the one-way function includes information about the identity of the verifier, so that the one-way function sent to one verifier can never be used for another verifier even if the claimer uses the same password with all verifiers in the system. Replay of recorded bit strings to the same verifier is, however, still possible.

- **Class 3 – Cryptographic functions**

With these mechanisms, rather than being sent over the network, the secret identification information is used as a cryptographic key to encipher some known message to the verifier. In case the claimer's secret consists of a private key for asymmetric cryptography, decryption is performed using the claimer's public key: the authentication message is thus no secret since anybody knowing the public key can decipher the message; however, anyone doing so will know immediately that the message came from the claimer, since only that claimer has the private key that must have been used to encipher the message. This usage of asymmetric cryptography for authentication represents a particularly strong kind of authentication, called *digital signature* (see for instance El-Gamal, 1985), which provides the answer to the problem of non-repudiation of origin. Once a claimer has sent a message authenticated by a Class 3 mechanism using asymmetric cryptography, he or she has effectively digitally signed that message and cannot later deny having sent it. Given the relative inefficiency of asymmetric systems, digital signature is used in practice to sign a digest of the message (ICV or MDC) rather than the whole message (ISO 9796, 1990). This limits the amount of data to be processed.

   To prevent replay of Class 3 authentication messages, the claimer includes in the enciphered message some unique stamping information that will allow the verifier to assert that the received message is not a recording of an earlier one. Such stamping information may consist of a sequence number that is incremented with every execution of the authentication protocol, a timestamp indicating the real time for which the authentication message is valid, or some other unique number distinguishing each authentication message from all others. Sequence numbers and timestamps have the drawback that both parties must keep synchronized counters or clocks. Unique numbers, if generated by the claimer, require that the verifier keep track of all numbers used in the past (or of some upper bound to these if they are always increasing). Alternatively, the unique number, then called a *challenge* or *nonce*, could be assigned by the verifier, using a good random number generator, but then it takes an extra message to be transmitted to the subject being authenticated, as illustrated in Figure 15.2.

- **Class 4 – Cryptographic functions with verifier identification**

  These mechanisms are identical to Class 3 mechanisms, except for the fact that the authentication message includes information about the identity of the verifier, so that it can never be used for another verifier even if the subject being authenticated uses the same identification information and same stamping scheme with all verifiers in the system. This is the strongest possible type of authentication.

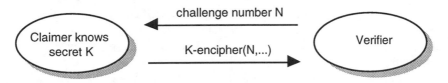

Figure 15.2 Class 3 authentication with replay detection through challenge-response.

New techniques based on the concept of *zero-knowledge protocols* may provide even more powerful authentication mechanisms in the future. These techniques demand rather intensive mathematical computations but they present several attractive features for authentication. First of all they allow the claimer to prove that he or she knows the right identification secret without actually transferring any knowledge about that secret to the verifier, as the qualifier "zero-knowledge" suggests. Second, some of the zero-knowledge schemes that have been proposed are such that verification of the authentication messages of any claimer all require the same well-known "public key", which avoids altogether the problem of key distribution exhibited by DES- or RSA-based authentication mechanisms.

Many different mechanisms providing either one-way, origin or two-way peer authentication have been designed (for instance Needham and Schroeder, 1978; Needham and Schroeder, 1987; Otway and Rees, 1987) or even standardized (ISO 9798-1, 1990; ISO 9798-2, 1990; ISO 9798-3, 1990; ISO 9799, 1988; ISO 8649, 1989; ISO 8650, 1989). These designs differ in strength, depending not only on the class of protocol they use but also on the time granularity with which the protocol is exercised. In the weakest case, authentication might be performed only on initial contact messages (sign-on or logon), in which case it is assumed that no intruder will try to capture or otherwise interfere with ongoing work-sessions or network connections. At the other extreme, authentication may be performed on every single message. Many intermediate solutions can be envisaged, for instance authentication of every new request message or the first message of every new unit of work.

As an example, the Kerberos system (Steiner *et al.*, 1988) includes Class 4 mechanisms for origin and peer authentication, using timestamps (or sometimes nonces) and DES technology. The X.509 Directory Authentication Framework (ISO 9594-8, 1988) includes a weak Class 0 one-way authentication scheme based on passwords in the clear, a somewhat stronger Class 1 scheme based on password hashing, and a strong Class 4 peer authentication scheme using asymmetric cryptography on timestamps and nonces.

Designing proper authentication mechanisms appears to be hard. Many existing designs suffer from various drawbacks (Bellovin and Merritt, 1990) or even present weaknesses (I'Anson and Mitchell, 1990) and it is very hard to prove their properties such as correctness (Burrows *et al.*, 1989; Nessett, 1990; Gong *et al.*, 1990).

15.3.5   Access control

As suggested in the definition of access control, this service relies partly on mechanisms built into the operating systems of attached computers to protect local targets, and partly on network-wide mechanisms to protect physical targets like computers, switching nodes, and links or distributed logical targets like routes, connections, buffer pools, and so on.

Within the realm of local operating system mechanisms, one finds traditional concepts of access control lists and capabilities (see for instance Saltzer and Schroeder, 1975). Access control list systems allow users to attach to each target they control a list of subjects authorized to access that target, together with the ways in which these subjects are allowed to use the target. By contrast, capability systems, which are less frequent, attach to each subject a list of the targets it is authorized to access, together with the ways in which it can use that target. In either case, access control lists as well as capabilities need to be protected by the operating system to prevent subjects from tampering with them.

In the broader realm of network access controls, the concepts of access control lists and capabilities are also found, albeit under different names and in a somewhat generalized form. ECMA (ECMA, 1988) distinguishes two facilities as essential to the implementation of network access control: the *Attribute Facility* and the *Authorization Facility*. The former is the repository for network access control information, so-called *Privilege Attributes*, which are network-wide forms of capabilities specifying the privileges attached to individual subjects or groups of subjects, and so-called *Control Attributes*, which are network-wide forms of access control list entries specifying the sensitivity attached to individual targets or groups of targets. The Authorization Facility, which OSI calls the *Access Control Decision Facility (ACDF)* (ISO 7498-2, 1988), is the mechanism that implements the applicable security policy and is invoked to compare a subject's Privilege Attributes with a target's Control Attributes to decide whether to accept or reject an access request. OSI also defines the *Access Control Enforcement Facility (ACEF)* as the entity responsible for implementing the policy decision made above.

The ACEF facility is typically located next to the target being protected. When the ACEF, ACDF and Attribute Facility are all located in the same computer, the network is really not involved in the access control process: the process involves only local operating system access control list or capability mechanisms. However, if the protected target, the Attribute Facility, and/or the ACDF and ACEF are located on different computers, then access control takes on a network dimension: the secure transmission of attributes, network capabilities or access control list entries between the three facilities requires the involvement of secure, integrity-protected (tamper-proof) system management flows to collect or distribute the necessary information;

furthermore, the network-wide dimension of subjects, targets, and attributes starts demanding network-wide identification schemes for them. One trend for global subject and target identification in attribute lists is apparent in the OSF Distributed Computing Environment (DCE), where entities are referred to using the Universal Unique Identifier (UUID) under which they are registered in the OSI Directory. An interesting issue that will arise in porting the DCE (or any network-wide security mechanism) onto an existing operating system is how to map global subject/target identifiers and security attributes onto (pre-existing) local ones.

A related mechanism needed for network access control is what the ECMA Framework (ECMA, 1988) calls the *Inter-Domain Facility*. Its main role is to translate attributes at the boundary between different protection domains that may be using different security policies and different attributes.

A last set of access control mechanisms, which are barely addressed in standards work but involve the network most directly, are the mechanisms needed to control access to "pure" network resources, such as physical links, sub-networks, logical connections, routes, and so on, for which the ACEF is distributed in the network in the sense that these targets do not "belong" to any single computer in the network. A fair amount of work has been done and products even exist in the area of packet filters that control the flow of data between networks, sub-networks, and links based on origin and destination addresses in packet headers (see for instance Mogul, 1989). Such mechanisms are very useful, though determined intruders can potentially get around them because the packet headers are assumed to be trusted: their integrity is not protected so that an intruder could "get a free ride" across a bridge or gateway if he or she tampered with the address fields of packets on either side of the gateway. More importantly perhaps, bridges and gateway packet filters can only check layer 2 or 3 addresses. A fine grain of access control based on application-layer addresses would require application-layer mechanisms that require more protocol processing and thus impact performance. Estrin and her colleagues (Estrin, 1986; Estrin, 1987a; Estrin, 1987b; Estrin *et al.*, 1989) have done some interesting work on enhancing address filters with cryptographic means involving integrity checks of inter-network packets using *visas*, essentially privilege attributes allowing given network boundaries to be crossed. Unfortunately, retrofitting these mechanisms into existing network protocols would require altering network software in all gateways. Furthermore, the cryptographic computations involved would impact gateway performance. Much work remains to be done in this area.

15.3.6 Positioning of security mechanisms within layers

Having reviewed the main categories of security mechanisms, it is interesting to discuss which mechanism should be implemented at which layer of the OSI model. OSI (ISO 7498-2, 1988) specifies the following:

- Link layer – the OSI link layer provides only a confidentiality service. This is somewhat contradicted by the IEEE 802.10 Standard for Inter-operable LAN Security (SILS) effort (IEEE 802.10, 1989, 1990), which provides also integrity, authentication, and access control functions at that layer.

- Network and Transport layers – these two layers may provide confidentiality, integrity, authentication and access control functions. Emerging standards in this area are the SP3 and SP4 secure network and transport protocols originally developed as part of the Secure Data Network System (SDNS) effort and now being considered for inclusion in OSI (SDNS-SP3 and SDNS-SP4, 1989).

- Session layer does not provide any security function.

- Presentation layer may provide only confidentiality.

- Application layer may provide any security service. The ECMA work (ECMA, 1988, 1989) has gone a long way to define a detailed architecture for security functions at this level. The X.400 Mail Handling System standard (Mitchell *et al.*, 1989) and the Internet Privacy-Enhanced Mail (PEM) architecture (Linn, 1989a; Linn and Kent, 1989; Linn, 1989b) now include mechanisms for enforcing integrity, confidentiality, authentication and non-repudiation of electronic mail, using the public-key-based X.509 mechanisms (ISO 9594-8, 1988).

Availability and accountability are different from other services in the sense that they do not rely primarily on cryptography and layer mechanisms. They do of course depend to some extent on layer protocol features such as, for instance, flow control mechanisms to prevent excessive traffic or authentication and metering of traffic to account for usage. However, the provision of availability and accountability rests primarily with network management and monitoring mechanisms discussed in the next section.

15.4   Network security management

At this point, we have reviewed in some detail the different security facilities that need to be managed in each layer. This allows us to understand the sort of security objects that need to be managed: user and resource registration records, cryptographic keys, privilege or control attributes, and consequently to discuss the mechanisms needed to manipulate these managed security objects. The main objective of security management is to create, delete, activate, suspend, query, update or otherwise maintain the status of managed security objects through continuous gathering or distribution of information about ongoing security-relevant activities, using proper management services and protocols, such as CMIS and CMIP (ISO 9595 and ISO 9596, 1990) in OSI networks, SNMP (Case *et al.*, 1990) in the Internet, or, in the future, the protocols based on remote procedure calls being defined by OSF as part of the Distributed Management Environment (DME) effort. We explore further some of the main security management functions.

15.4.1   Key management

Given the central role played by cryptography in a secure network, it is no surprise that one of the main types of security object to be managed is cryptographic keys.

Many mechanisms for key management have already been defined (see for instance Matyas and Meyer, 1978; Denning and Sacco, 1981; Bauer *et al.*, 1983; Okamoto and Tanaka, 1989). Cryptographic key management includes essentially six main functions:

i) *Key generation*: The generation of good cryptographic keys should not be left to unchecked software or hardware. Instead it must be controlled by approved and secured management mechanisms. In the case of DES, good cryptographic keys must be produced by proven random number generators. The whole power of DES would be defeated if generated keys were in any way predictable by an intruder. In the case of RSA, the generation of suitable keys requires searching for large prime numbers that must remain secret, which requires time-consuming and delicate computations with large integers that are best left to specialized and secure hardware.

ii) *Key distribution*: Given that key generation is best left to approved and secured devices, the function may not be available on every station in the network. Subjects requiring keys must thus get them over the network from suitable *key distribution centers (KDC)*. However, since DES keys are confidential and RSA public keys must be authenticated (digitally signed to be accurate), every subject in the network must share a DES key with, or know the public key of, some KDC so it can get additional keys from that KDC under suitable cryptographic protection.

    With any cryptographic system, if a subject A requests (DES or RSA) keys to communicate with a subject B, the KDC needs to issue two key *certificates* or *tickets*, one for A and one for B. Key certificates are authenticated and timestamped messages linking the issued keys to the partner names. With DES, the certificate for A would have the form Ka(B, Kab, time), where Kab is the distributed DES key and Ka(..) indicates encryption under the DES key initially shared by A and the KDC. With RSA, the certificate for A would have the form K*(B, Kb, time), where Kb is B's public key and K*(..) indicates digital signature under the KDC's private key K*. One difference between DES key certificates and RSA key certificates is that DES ones are confidential while RSA ones are not (since anybody has the KDC's public key). Another difference is that DES key certificates have a "connection-oriented" flavor (since DES keys such as Kab are associated with pairs/groups of communicating entities) while RSA certificates have an "entity-oriented" flavor (since RSA keys such as Kb are attached to an individual subject rather than communicating subjects). As a result, new "connection-oriented" DES keys need to be generated typically whenever a new pair/group of entities needs to communicate, whereas individual RSA key pairs are generated typically when entities are created. Since the frequency with which entities set up and take down communication is typically higher than the frequency with which entities are created and destroyed, RSA keys tend to have a more static existence than DES keys. By the same token, a DES KDC should be available to handle requests for new keys essentially at any time, whereas an RSA KDC may typically generate new certificates off-line and leave them in a relatively static directory where any entity can retrieve the public key certificate of any other entity.

Exactly where and how the party names and timestamps appear in the syntax of certificates varies from one design to another, but all designs implement variations of the semantics suggested above. The key distribution schemes sketched for DES and RSA environments correspond closely to the specifications of the Kerberos design (Steiner *et al.*, 1988) or the ISO 8732/ANSI X9.17 standard (ISO 8732, 1988) for DES key distribution, and to the RSA-based key distribution of the X.509 OSI Directory Authentication Framework (ISO 9594-8, 1988). Beyond syntactic variations between these schemes, their main difference resides in the connectivity that is required between the KDC and its clients. If a subject A wants to initiate communication with a subject B, in Kerberos A first obtains the necessary certificates from the KDC and then contacts B. X9.17 defines several possible cases: the KDC may be located in the same computer as A, in the same computer as B, or in a third machine, in which case A contacts B first, and lets B get the necessary certificates from the KDC. X.509 leaves it to each subject to get the peer's public key certificate from the directory.

An interesting inter-domain security management issue arises when A and B reside in different security domains so that no KDC can build key certificates for both. Several designs have been developed to deal with such situations (Birrell *et al.*, 1986; Lu and Sundareshan, 1989). Whether in DES or RSA environments, these designs all rely on hierarchies of trust between KDCs, where each KDC shares DES keys with or knows the public RSA keys of its parent KDC and all its descendent KDCs in the trust hierarchy. This way, the KDCs of two subjects A and B in different domains can always propagate key certificates up and then down the hierarchy of KDCs between A's domain and B's domain, so that the certificates may be properly counter-signed (with RSA) or "key translated" (deciphered and re-enciphered with DES).

iii) *Key storage*: As was just said, RSA public key certificates may be stored simply in public directories. However, RSA private keys and DES keys, being secret, must be kept in well-protected storage. The maintenance of that storage is an important security management issue. As an example, the IBM Transaction Security System (TSS, see Abraham *et al.*, 1991), a sealed plug-in card for PCs or PS/2s which provides full DES-based confidentiality, integrity, authentication and key management services, is such that the keys it manipulates never appear in the clear outside the sealed module. When stored in main memory or on peripheral devices, the keys are kept encrypted in their certificate form. Only the sealed module can decipher the certificates under the station master key, which must be entered by the end user at initialization.

iv) *Key update*: Since it is not advisable to use keys for very long periods, they must be replaced from time to time. The proper synchronized update of RSA key pairs or pair-wise DES keys must also be coordinated by key management.

v)   *Key archival*: Even after a key has been replaced and is no longer in active use, it may be necessary to keep it for several years. For instance if the key was used to digitally sign documents with legal value, it may have to be archived for years in case a legal proof is required.

vi) *Key destruction*: Finally, when a key is no longer needed, it must be properly disposed of so that it is not used or exposed by mistake, thereby compromising information it was used to protect in the past.

15.4.2   Authentication management

Class 3 and 4 authentication mechanisms, being based on cryptographic mechanisms, depend heavily on key management. Certificates used to distribute keys for authentication purposes are sometimes called *credentials*. Beyond the basic key management issues addressed above, authentication presents an additional key management challenge. When a subject A requests some service from a target B, B will most likely want to authenticate A, which requires some key distribution. Now it may happen that in the course of handling A's request, B needs to invoke a service C on behalf of A. B's right to invoke C may or may not be dependent on the identity of A. In case it is, C will want to authenticate A. However, A may not be aware that C is involved and certainly is not prepared to interact directly with C. Thus there is a need for B to be able to prove that it is acting for A. This calls for what Kerberos refers to as *proxy certificates,* namely certificates that contain keys that will enable B to contact servers such as C on A's behalf. In certain cases, C may even have to contact further servers. In that case it also would need proxy certificates. However, A may not know in advance how many servers and which servers need proxy certificates. In such a case A may ask for what Kerberos has called *"forwardable" certificates,* namely certificates that allow A to give a mandate to B allowing B to get additional certificates on A's behalf.

Kerberos also addresses the initial authentication key distribution problem known as *single sign-on* (Steiner *et al.*, 1988). Remember that to get any certificate, a subject must either share a DES key with, or know the public key of, the KDC and his or her own private key. Now, human end users are not good at remembering (and typing!) random-looking binary bit strings like keys. Thus when a user sits down at a workstation, he or she may not have any initial key that could be used to contact the KDC – only a password or biometric information.

If the system supports smart card technology, a user's secret key may be stored on his card and he can recover it by signing onto the card with his handwritten signature or password to activate the stored secret. If the user has a secure personal workstation, his secret may be kept stored on the workstation disk and he can use his password to sign onto the workstation and activate the secret. However, if the user has neither a smart card nor a personal workstation, as assumed in the Kerberos environment, the question arises of what secret key he can use to communicate with the KDC. Deriving a key from biometric information is delicate as such information tends to be fuzzy (thus hard to convert into a deterministic key), static (as a user's biometrics remain in principle the same throughout his life), and hardly secret (as it is easy for an intruder to collect a biometric sample and derive the key). Deriving a key from a password is easier and somewhat safer as passwords are deterministic and changeable. However, they are still poor secrets as they are not really random and can often be guessed (Morris and Thompson, 1979). Yet this is the only solution left and the one used by Kerberos with the resulting weakness that it is possible to crack a message enciphered under a password by trying all likely or possible passwords exhaustively. The problem seems to be inherent in the context of public workstations without smart cards, and not a flaw in the Kerberos design. Lomas *et al.*, (1989) have suggested a way to avoid the exposure but it requires using public keys. Simple and safe solutions can be imagined using simplified smart cards with limited intelligence and a timer or keypad rather than an electrical interface.

Besides key distribution, the main management issue in authentication is maintenance of the list of registered users and subjects acting for them. There exist *ad hoc* implementations of such mechanisms in today's Kerberos and OSF DCE products. However, no international standards for user registration in an open system is defined yet.

15.4.3   Access control management

Similarly, the main access control management problem is the maintenance of privilege and control attribute lists, as well as their distribution or centralization across the network. Work to standardize access control attributes has only recently begun (ISO 10164-9, 1990). Being critical to security, it is clear that such attributes must be protected at least against tampering and possibly even against disclosure when traveling through the network between an Attribute Facility, an Authorization Facility, and possibly a network management focal point. Thus such attributes must be transported in messages called *Privilege Attribute Certificates (PAC)* that are at least timestamped and authenticated, like key certificates or credentials, and possibly even enciphered (ECMA, 1989).

15.4.4   Notarization

The concept of *notarization* refers to providing on the network a trusted management application, sometimes called an electronic notary, that can be invoked to certify that given messages have been sent or received by given subjects at given times, thus supporting non-repudiation of origin and destination.

In an RSA environment, digital signature of timestamped messages is sufficient to provide non-repudiation of origin. However, in a plain DES environment, an authenticated message proves its origin only to the recipient, not to a third party, since the recipient could have faked the message. Thus, non-repudiation of origin in a plain DES environment normally requires a trusted notary to certify that a given party has sent a given message. An alternative is to use secure cryptographic devices such as IBM's TSS product, which, through the use of asymmetric control vectors associated with DES keys, precisely prevent the recipient of a message from computing an integrity check of that message using a key defined only for verifying such a check.

Though advanced algorithms are being investigated to provide non-repudiation of delivery without a notary, this technology is not yet mature. In practice, it remains necessary to resort to a trusted notary. The problem is that the recipient of a message may receive it ten times and never send an acknowledgment. Thus non-repudiation of delivery takes a trusted notary to guarantee the delivery process and demand an acknowledgment of receipt or file a complaint against the recipient if it persistently denies receipt.

15.4.5 Auditing

Last but not least, a very important aspect of security management is the set of functions necessary to support auditing and accountability. Security audits are necessary to regularly review and reassess the list of authorized users (deleting stale registrations), the rights and privileges of each user, especially privileged ones, the proper compliance with applicable security policies, and the level and adequacy of implemented controls.

These objectives are achieved through constant monitoring of security-related events at every system in the network. Registrations of new users, changes to user access rights by security administrators, login attempts, especially failed ones, access requests to critical resources, especially rejected ones, any suspicious or unusual activities are monitored and reported to security management focal points, where they are logged to construct an audit trail.

Subsequent analysis of this audit trail can then reveal traceable evidence of all relevant activities. It can be used to trigger alarms in the case of repeated events of a suspicious nature (such as failed logins or rejected accesses), to detect possible violations and trigger necessary recovery actions (for example, deactivation of misbehaving subjects, revocation of compromised keys and PACs). Technology and standards for providing these functions are only emerging today and will be the focus of much activity in the coming years (ISO 10164-7, 1990; ISO 10164-8, 1990).

Before leaving the subject of security functions and their management, it is worth discussing an architectural issue. The fact that several different layers and management mechanisms may implement similar functions of course does not mean that each layer must implement all possible functions. Different network architectures may specify use of different mechanisms at different layers. (Of course the definition of functional profiles is desirable to ensure interoperability.) Furthermore, even if comparable functions are provided at several layers, these layers may very well share the same internal interfaces to a common functional implementation. For instance, the IBM Common Cryptographic Architecture (CCA, see IBM, 1990) implemented in the TSS product (Abraham *et al.*, 1991) defined an extensive interface for DES-based confidentiality, integrity, authentication and key management functions. This interface can be made available to all layers and management mechanisms inside a real system. In fact, since security functions generally involve sensitive mechanisms and manipulate confidential information, they are indeed best isolated in a secure subsystem rather than spread around throughout the code of an operating system and network software. This is again a fundamental idea behind a product such as TSS.

15.5   Security management and network management

The security of a network depends not only on the basic security features it provides and suitable management functions for controlling these, but also on a number of other related network management aspects.

15.5.1   Network management security

A first management issue that is essential to overall network security is the need to protect the entire range of network management and control mechanisms and procedures.

All the network security mechanisms that were discussed in Section 15.4 are ultimately targeted at end user requirements, but the very first application that must use these mechanisms, and depends on them perhaps more than any end user application, is network management itself. Configuration, performance, and fault management are vital functions in most significant networks and must be defended against subversion by potential intruders. Accounting is another aspect of management that may not be as vital to network operation but is certainly vital to network profitability and depends directly on secure authentication, access control, and audit trail records. Proper authentication of all subjects involved in network management functions and protection of the integrity of all data and messages pertaining to network management are requirements essential to overall network security. Protecting the confidentiality of network management information may be less of an issue in most environments (except for secret information such as passwords and encryption keys) (Galvin *et al.*, 1991).

15.5.2   Supportive security applications

A second design issue directly relevant to network security is the proper integration of security mechanisms and their associated management functions into the broader context of network management. Not only are all other components of network management probably the first users of security, but network security in turn uses or depends on a number of network and management functions.

Two examples of management services that security depends upon have already been encountered: Directory functions and time server functions. Standards refer to such functions as *Security Supportive Applications* (SSA). The Directory, especially X.500 in the case of open networks, is the repository for naming information and, as seen earlier, also public key information, both of which are directly related to authentication and digital signature functions. This does not mean, however, that one can subvert the security of the whole network by subverting the Directory; indeed, public key certificates stored in the Directory are all digitally signed by the KDC and enforce an indelible binding between keys and identities of their owners (expressed as UUIDs).

The case of the time server is different. As indicated earlier, some Class 3 or 4 authentication designs (for instance Steiner *et al.*, 1988) use timestamps to prevent the replay of authentication messages. This makes them directly dependent on the existence of relatively tightly synchronized clocks; the tighter the synchronization, the more secure the authentication. This requirement in turn implies that all computers participating in such a scheme must have access to a common *trusted* time server. And here is the catch: for the time server to be trusted, it must be authenticated by its clients, but since secure authentication relies on synchronized clocks, an interesting chicken-and-egg problem arises. Clearly things are not as bad as they sound in the real world: almost anyone is willing to rely on an in-house time server, on time information delivered over the phone, radio, or TV. However, if high security is an issue, the exposure must be kept in mind. Nonce-based authentication does not suffer from this exposure.

15.5.3   Security management context

Last but not least, a network, together with its security and management mechanisms, is embedded in a context that presents non-electronic threats of its own to secure and reliable operation. Though these threats are outside the immediate technical context, they must be addressed. The means to do so are briefly reviewed here, though their exhaustive discussion is beyond the scope of this chapter.

Risk analysis and contingency planning

In any network, the cost and sophistication of security mechanisms must be in proportion to the value of assets in the network, and the possible threats posed by intruders. Thus network operators must conduct an assessment of the risks faced to decide what security mechanisms are right for their networks. Further, even in the best protected networks, disasters may always happen, if only by the fault of nature, uncontrollable political events, or deception by an otherwise legitimately authorized insider. No technical security measure can prevent such catastrophic events, but risks must be analyzed and recovery plans put in place to contain damages and be able to put as much of the network back into operation as soon as possible after an accident.

Installation and operational procedures

Of the catastrophic events alluded to above, perhaps the most insidious one is subversion by authorized insiders. If legitimate users with powerful rights decide to create havoc, there are hardly any limits to the damage they can cause. They can even defeat disaster recovery plans. The best means to reduce the probability of such events occurring and to bound the impact that any single event can have is to put in place physical barriers and stringent administrative procedures for controlling, cross-checking, surveillance, and logging of all actions pertaining to installation and daily operation of network components. This should restrict the power of any one individual and the effect that he or she can have on the entire network.

Design documentation and assurances

Finally, an aspect not to be neglected in these days of viruses and other treacherous software is getting proper documentation and assurances from the manufacturer, or even from an independent auditing and certification body, concerning the quality of the design, the design process, and the design environment of all hardware, software, and security components used in the network.

Of the above security-related aspects of a network, the last has become an important element for rating networking systems according to official security evaluation criteria, both in the US (TNI, 1987) and in Europe (ITSEC, 1991). The European ITSEC specification also factors installation and operational procedures into the rating. These norms can be expected to play a determining role in system selection in the future. They define in more or less concrete terms the standards that networks have to meet in order to deserve given labels corresponding to different levels of security.

15.6   Summary

This chapter reviewed the now well-established definitions of basic network security services as well as existing and emerging techniques for providing these services. This review served as a foundation for discussing both the objects that security management must deal with and the security mechanisms that network management can rely on. The topic of network security and its management was then put into perspective within the broader context of security-related aspects of administrative procedures for network operation, installation, planning, procurement, design, and assurance.

Abbreviations

802.10	IEEE Committee on Inter-operable LAN Security (SILS)
CBC	Cipher Block Chaining, mode of operation in DES
CCITT	Comité Consultatif International des Téléphones et Télégraphes
CMIP	The OSI Common Management Information Protocol
CMIS	The OSI Common Management Information Service
DAC	Discretionary Access Control
DCE	Distributed Computing Environment
DES	Data Encryption Standard
DEA	Data Encryption Algorithm
ECMA	European Computer Manufacturers Association
ICV	Integrity Check Vector
IEEE	Institute of Electrical and Electronics Engineers
ISO	International Organization for Standardization
ITSEC	Information Technology Security Evaluation Criteria
LME	Layer Management Entity
KDC	Key Distribution Center
MAC	(depending on context) Mandatory Access Control
MAC	(depending on context) Message Authentication Code
MDC	Modification Detection Code
MIC	Message Integrity Check
OSF	Open Software Foundation
OSI	Open Systems Interconnection

PAC   Privilege Attribute Certificate
PEM   the Internet Privacy-Enhanced Mail design
RSA   Rivest-Shamir-Adleman asymmetric cryptographic system
SDNS   Secure Data Network System Architecture of DoD/NIST
SILS   (IEEE) Standard for Inter-operable LAN Security
SMAE   System Management Application Entity
SNMP   The Internet Simple Network Management Protocol
SP3   Secure Protocol 3 (layer 3) of SDNS
SP4   Secure Protocol 4 (layer 4) of SDNS
SSA   Security Supportive Application
TNI   Trusted Network Interpretation of the Trusted Computer System Evaluation Criteria
UUID   Universal User IDentifier
X.400   The international Message Handling System standard
X.500   The joint CCITT-ISO Directory Standard
X.509   The Authentication Framework of the X.500 standard
X9.17   Financial Institution Key Management, ANSI Standard

References

Abraham D. G., Dolan G. M., Double G. P. and Stevens J. V. (1991). Transaction Security System. *IBM Syst. J.* **30**(2), 230–43

Abrams M. D. and Podell H. J. (1987). *Computer and network security*. IEEE Comp. Soc. Press No. 756

Bauer R. K., Berson T. A. and Feiertag R. J. (1983). A key distribution protocol using event markers. *ACM Trans. on Comp. Syst.*, **1**(3), 249–55

Bellovin S. M. and Merritt M. (1990). Limitations of the Kerberos authentication system. *ACM Comp. Comm. Rev.*, **20**(5), 119–32

Birrell A., Lampson B. W., Needham R. M. and Schroeder M. D. (1986). A global authentication service without global trust. In *Proc. IEEE Symp. on Security and Privacy*. April

Burrows M., Abadi M. and Needham R. (1989). A logic of authentication. In Proc. 12th ACM Symposium on Operating System Principles. December *ACM Operating Systems Review*, **23**(5), 1–13

Case J. D., Fedor, M. S., Schoffstal M. L. and Davin J. R. (1990). *A Simple Network Management Protocol (SNMP)*. RFC 1157, Network Information Center, SRI International

Davies D. and Price W. (1984). *Security for Computer Networks*. John Wiley & Sons.

DeMillo R. and Merritt M. (1983). Protocols for Data Security. *IEEE Comp.*, **16**(2), 39–51

Denning D. E. and Sacco G. M. (1981). Timestamps in key distribution protocols. *Comm. ACM*, **24** (8), 533–6

Diffie W. (1988). The first ten years of public-key cryptography. *Proc. IEEE*, **76**(5), 560–77

Diffie W. and Hellman M. E. (1976). New directions in cryptography. *IEEE Trans. on Info. Th.*, **22**(6), 644–54

Diffie W. and Hellman M. E. (1979). Privacy and authentication: an introduction to cryptography. *Proc. IEEE*, **67**(3), 397–427

ECMA (1988). *Security in open systems: A security framework*. ECMA TR/46

ECMA (1989). *Security in open systems: Data elements and service definitions.* ECMA TR/138

El-Gamal T. (1985). A public key cryptosystem and a signature scheme based on discrete logarithms. *IEEE Trans. on Info. Th.*, **31**, 469–72

Estrin D. (1986). Inter-organization networks: Implications of access control requirements for interconnection protocols. In *Proc. ACM SIGCOMM Symp. on Comm. Arch. & Prot.* August

Estrin D. (1987a). Controls for inter-organization networks. *IEEE Trans. Softw. Eng.,* **13**(2), 249–61

Estrin D. (1987b). Interconnection protocols for inter-organization networks. *IEEE J. on Select. Areas in Comm.*, **5** (9), 1480–91

Estrin D., Mogul J. C. and Tsudik G. (1989). Visa protocols for controlling inter-organization datagram flow. *IEEE J. on Select. Areas in Comm.*, **7** (4), 486–98

Galvin J. M., McCloghrie K. and Davin J. R. (1991). Secure management of SNMP networks. In *Integrated Network Management II* (Krishnan I. and Zimmer, W. eds.), North Holland, 703–14

Gong L., Needham R. and Yahalom R. (1990). Reasoning about belief in cryptographic protocols. In Proc. 1990 *IEEE Comp. Soc. Symp. on Research in Security and Privacy.* Oakland CA, May

I'Anson C. and Mitchell C. (1990). Security defects in CCITT Recommendation X.509 – The Directory Authentication Framework. *ACM Comp. Comm. Rev.,* **20**(2), 30–4

IBM (1990). *Common Cryptographic Architecture: Cryptographic Application Programming Interface Reference.* SC40-1675-1, IBM.

IEEE 802.10 (1989). *Standard for Inter-operable Local Area Network Security, Part A –The Model.* Unapproved Draft P802.10A/D1, IEEE 802.10

IEEE 802.10 (1990). *Standard for Inter-operable Local Area Network Security, Part B –Secure Data Exchange.* Unapproved Draft P802.10B/D1, IEEE 802.10

IEEE Computer (1983). Special issue on cryptography. *IEEE Comp.*, **16**(2)

IEEE Proceedings (1988). Special issue on cryptography, *IEEE Proc.*, **76**(11)

ISO 7498-1 (1988). *Information Processing Systems, Open Systems Interconnection, Reference Model, Part 1: Basic Reference Model*

ISO 7498-2 (1988). *Information Processing Systems, Open Systems Interconnection, Reference Model, Part 2: Security Architecture*

ISO 8372 (1987). *ISO Information Technology, Security Techniques, Modes of Operation for 64-bit Block Cipher Algorithms*

ISO 8649 (1989). *Information Processing Systems, Open Systems Interconnection, Association Control Service Element, Addendum 1: Authentication*

ISO 8650 (1989). *Information Processing Systems, Open Systems Interconnection, Peer Entity Authentication During Association Establishment*

ISO 8731-1 (1987). *Banking – Approved algorithms for message authentication - Part 1: DEA*

ISO 8732 (1988). *Banking –Key management (Wholesale).* ISO 8732 / ANSI X9.17

ISO 9594-8 (1988). *Information Processing Systems, Open Systems Interconnection, The Directory, Part 8: Authentication framework.* ISO 9594-8 / CCITT X.509

ISO 9595 (1990). *Information Processing Systems, Open Systems Interconnection, Common Management Information Services*

ISO 9596 (1990). *Information Processing Systems, Open Systems Interconnection, Common Management Information Protocols*

ISO 9796 (1990). *ISO Information Technology, Security Techniques, A Signature Algorithm for Short Messages*

ISO 9797 (1990). *ISO Information Technology, Security Techniques, A Data Integrity Mechanism*

ISO 9798-1 (1990). *ISO Information Technology, Security Techniques, Entity Authentication Mechanisms, Part 1: General Model for Entity Authentication Mechanisms*

ISO 9798-2 (1990). *ISO Information Technology, Security Techniques, Entity Authentication Mechanisms, Part 2: Entity Authentication Using Symmetric Key Techniques*

ISO 9798-3 (1990). *ISO Information Technology, Security Techniques, Entity Authentication Mechanisms, Part 3: Entity Authentication Using a Public Key Algorithm*

ISO 9799 (1988). *ISO Information Processing Systems, Peer Entity Authentication Using a Public Key Algorithm with a Two-Way Handshake*

ISO 10164-7 (1990). *Information Processing Systems, Open Systems Interconnection, Systems Management, Part 7: Security Alarm Reporting Function.* ISO/IEC DIS 10164-7 / CCITT X.736

ISO 10164-8 (1990). *Information Processing Systems, Open Systems Interconnection, Systems Management, Part 8: Security Audit Trail Function.* ISO/IEC DIS 10164-8 / CCITT X.740

ISO 10164-9 (1990). *Information Processing Systems, Open Systems Interconnection, Systems Management, Part 9: Objects and Attributes for Access Control.* ISO/IEC DIS 10164-9 / CCITT X.741

ISO 10181-2 (1990). *Information Technology, OSI Security Model Part 2: Authentication Framework*

ITSEC (1991). *Information Technology Security Evaluation Criteria (ITSEC), Provisional Harmonised Criteria, Version 1.2,* Office for Official Publications of the European Communities, Luxembourg

Janson P. and Molva R. (1991). Security in open networks and distributed systems. *Comp. Netw. & ISDN J.,* **22**(5), 323–46

Karger P. A. (1985). Authentication and discretionary access control in computer networks. *Comp. Netw.,* **10**(1), 27–37

Linn J. (1989a). *Privacy Enhancement for Internet Electronic Mail: Part I: Message Encipherment and Authentication Procedures.* RFC 1113, Network Information Center, SRI International

Linn J. and Kent S. (1989). *Privacy Enhancement for Internet Electronic Mail: Part II: Certificate-Based Key Management.* RFC 1114, Network Information Center, SRI International

Linn J. (1989c) *Privacy Enhancement for Internet Electronic Mail: Part III Algorithms, Modes and Identifiers.* RFC 1115, Network Information Center, SRI International

Lomas T., Gong L., Saltzer J. and Needham R. (1989). Reducing risk from poorly chosen keys. In *Proc. 12th ACM Symp. on Oper. Syst. Princ.* December. *ACM Oper. Syst. Rev.,* **23**(5), 14–18

Lu W-P. and Sundareshan M. K. (1989). Secure communication in internet environments: a hierarchical key management scheme for end-to-end encryption. *IEEE Trans. on Comm.,* **37**(10), 1014–23

Massey J. (1988). An introduction to contemporary cryptology. *Proc. IEEE,* **76**(5), 533–49

Matyas S. M. and Meyer C. H. (1978). Generation, distribution, and installation of cryptographic keys. *IBM Syst. J.,* **17**(2), 127–37

Mitchell C., Walker M. and Rush D. (1989). CCITT/ISO Standards for Secure Message Handling. *IEEE J. on Select. Areas in Comm.*, **7** (4), 517–24

Mogul J. C. (1989). *Simple and flexible datagram access controls for Unix-based gateways.* DEC West. Res. Lab.

Morris R. and Thompson K. (1979). Password security: A case history. *Comm. ACM,* **22**(11), 594–97

NBS (1977). *Data Encryption Standard.* FIPS 46, US National Bureau of Standards (now National Institute for Standards and Technology)

Needham R. M. and Schroeder M. D. (1978). Using encryption for authentication in large networks of computers. *Comm. ACM*, **21**(12), 993–8

Needham R. M. and Schroeder M. D. (1987). Authentication revisited. *ACM Oper. Syst. Rev.,* **21**(1), 7

Nessett D. (1990). A critique of the Burrows, Abadi and Needham logic. *ACM Oper. Syst. Rev.,* **24**(2), 35–8

Neumann P. G. (1991). Illustrative risks to the public in the use of computer systems and related technology. *ACM Softw. Eng. Newsletter,* **16**(1), 2–9

Okamoto E. and Tanaka K. (1989). Key distribution system based on identification information. *IEEE J. on Select. Areas in Comm.*, **7**(4), 481–5

Otway D. and Rees. O. (1987). Efficient and timely mutual authentication. *ACM Oper. Syst. Rev.*, **21** (1), 8–10

Popek G. J. and Kline C. S. (1979). Encryption and secure computer networks. *ACM Comp. Surv.*, **11** (4), 331–56

Rivest R. (1990). *The MD4 Message Digest Algorithm* (Version 2/17/90, Revised). ISO/IEC JTC1/SC 27/WG20.2 N193

Rivest R. L., Shamir A. and Adleman L. (1978). A method for obtaining digital signatures and public-key crypto-systems. *Comm. ACM,* **21** (2), 120–6 and *Comm. ACM*, **26**(1), 96–9

Saltzer J. H. and Schroeder M. D. (1975). The protection of information in computer systems. *Proc. IEEE*, **63**(9), 1278–307

SDNS-SP3 (1989). *SDNS, Secure Data Network Systems, Security Protocol 3 (SP3).* Specification SDN.301, Revision 1.4

SDNS-SP4 (1989). *SDNS, Secure Data Network Systems, Security Protocol 4 (SP4).* Specification SDN.401, Revision 1.3

Steiner J. G., Neuman C. and Schiller J. I. (1988). Kerberos: an authentication server for open network systems. In *Proc. Winter 88 Usenix Conf.*, Dallas Texas

TNI (1987).   *Trusted Network Interpretation of the Trusted Computer Systems Evaluation Criteria. NCSG-TG-005, Version 1,* National Computer Security Center, USA

Voydock V. L. and Kent S. T. (1983).   Security mechanisms in high-level network protocols. *ACM Comp. Surv.,* **15**(2), 135–71

Voydock V. L. and Kent S. T. (1984).   Security mechanisms in a transport layer protocol. *Comp. Netw.,* **8**(5,6), 433–50

Part V

Management Policy

Chapter 16

Domains: A Framework for Structuring Management Policy

Morris Sloman and Kevin Twidle

Imperial College of Science Technology and Medicine,
180 Queen's Gate,
London SW7 2BZ, UK
Email: m.sloman@doc.ic.ac.uk

This chapter and the one following discuss the work on management policy that has emerged from a research project funded by the UK Science and Engineering Research Council and the Department of Trade and Industry. The DOMINO project on Domain Management for Open Systems involved Imperial College, Sema Group and BP. Domains, as defined in the DOMINO project, are a means of grouping objects to which a common management policy applies as well as being a naming context. This chapter explains how subdomains provide the means of partitioning management responsibility and structuring the overall management of a large distributed system. The use of access rules as a flexible means of specifying relationships between managers and the objects they manage is also explained. An example of the use of domains for configuration management is described, and some of the issues relating to implementation of the domain concepts are briefly discussed.

16.1 Requirements for management of large distributed systems

A distributed system may consist of a variety of types of objects which have to be managed, for example users and the agents representing users in the system; hardware components such as workstations, mainframes, or modems; software components such as processes, threads or files; services such as databases or electronic mail and the servers that implement them. In a very large distributed system there may be millions of objects, making it impossible to specify management policy for individual objects. Instead it is necessary to specify policy for groups of objects. (Note that the term **object** is being used in this chapter as an entity that encapsulates state and processing. There is no implication about the concept of inheritance found in many object-oriented systems.)

A distributed processing application may span the computer systems belonging to a number of different organizations. In general, there is no central authority in such systems and the management of the application as well as the underlying communication and processing resources may have to operate across organizational and legislative boundaries. Peer-to-peer negotiation between independent managers is needed to define policies for managing inter-organizational interactions.

There will be multiple hardware and software vendors supplying the components for such an environment and so management has to accommodate heterogeneity of hardware and operating systems as well as software components implemented in a variety of programming languages. This heterogeneity can be found both in objects being managed and within the management system itself.

The communication system supporting this distributed processing is typically made up of multiple interconnected local area and wide area networks, which implies a variety of protocols and communication mechanisms to be supported.

The components and services being managed are physically distributed with genuine parallelism between components. This makes it difficult to obtain consistent global state information on which to base management decisions, or to synchronize management actions on different components.

The above characteristics of a large distributed system lead to the following requirements for management of such systems:

- Management cannot be centralized in a single human or automated entity but must be distributed to reflect the distribution of the system being managed.

- There is a need to automate as much as possible of the management which will thus have to cater for a mixture of both automated and human manager objects.

- Management must be structured to partition and demarcate responsibility amongst the multiple managers. This structuring could reflect physical network connectivity, structuring of the distributed application or possibly reflect the hierarchical management structure (for example, corporate headquarters, regional, site, departmental, and section management) found in many organizations.

- Management will have to be implemented as a set of distributed components, with interaction between peer managers, and hierarchical interaction between higher-level managers and lower-level managers.

- There will be a variety of managers fulfilling different roles and operating in different contexts, but having responsibilities for the same object. For example, the maintenance engineer and the user of a workstation have different management responsibilities for the same workstation. The management structure must be able to model these overlapping responsibilities.

- Flexibility in naming of objects is needed in order to permit human managers to assign aliases of their choice to the objects they manage.

Domains provide the framework for partitioning management responsibility by grouping objects for the convenience of managers. This grouping may be to apply a common management policy, or to represent organizational structure or physical structure.

16.2   Domains

16.2.1   Concepts

Domains provide a flexible and pragmatic means of specifying boundaries of management responsibility and authority. A **domain** is an object that represents a collection of objects which have been explicitly grouped together to apply a common management policy. From the user's view objects exist in a domain, but this does not imply the strict containment relationship found in OSI managed objects (see Chapter 5). Domains in fact hold references to member objects as shown in Figure 16.1. In addition, domains provide a flexible structuring of the name space for identifying objects, as explained below. Domains are a generalization of the concepts of a tree-structured directory found in many file systems.

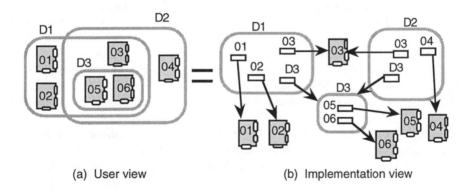

(a) User view   (b) Implementation view

Figure 16.1 User and implementation views of domains.

It is not practical to specify membership of a domain in terms of a predicate on attributes of objects in a distributed system. For example, to determine the membership of a domain based on the predicate "objects created before 1 January 1990" would require checking the creation date attribute of all distributed objects throughout the system. The only valid management domains are those where the members have been explicitly inserted into the domain or created in the domain.

Most management applications require persistent domains, and it must be possible to create an empty domain and later include objects in it. This permits first defining a management structure for a system and then populating it with managed objects. Since domains are themselves objects, they may be members of other domains.

Domains provide the means of naming and applying policy to managed objects, so all managed objects must exist within a domain. Objects should always be created within a domain.

The concept of grouping objects should not be confused with that of encapsulation. Hierarchical composition can be used to construct a composite object from several primitive or other composite objects (Magee *et al.*, 1989). The composite object is viewed as a single object for the purposes of invoking operations and the interface of the composite object hides its internal structure from the user. The component objects are then said to be encapsulated. Encapsulation is an essential concept for coping with the complexity of distributed systems as it permits subsystems containing multiple composite or primitive objects to be treated as a single object with an interface. In particular, a manager may be encapsulated with one or more managed objects to form a **self-managing** composite object. Note that although it is sometimes useful to apply a management operation to a set of objects, in many cases the external managers have to perform management operations on the individual objects, which encapsulation prevents. Domains provide grouping but not encapsulation.

16.2.2   Domain relationships

Any policy specified in terms of the domain will apply to all its members, which are the objects referenced by its **policy set**. A **subdomain** is a domain that is a member of another domain, so D3 is a subdomain of both D1 and D2 in Figure 16.1. Subdomains form the mechanism for partitioning a large group of objects and applying different policies to subsets of the original group or assigning responsibility to different managers. Note that a subdomain is not a subset, as a change of membership of the subdomain does not affect the direct membership of the **parent** domain.

Objects O1, O2, O3 and D3 in Figure 16.1 are said to be **direct members** of D1, whereas O5 and O6 are **indirect members** of both D1 and D2.

As shown in Figure 16.1, objects can be members of more than one parent domain. This fact, which is necessary from the management policy viewpoint as discussed later, makes it difficult to prevent cycles in the domain graph. We advocate a strategy of permitting cycles, and building mechanisms into domain traversal procedures for coping with cycles rather than preventing them.

Two domains **overlap** if there are objects which are members of both domains, for example D3 and O3 in Figure 16.1. Overlap arises in many situations relating to sharing of resources such as a gateway between two networks for which both networks have management responsibility or to a person who is a member of two different departments. Overlapping domains reflect the fact that multiple managers can be responsible for an object or that multiple policies apply to the object. Obviously this can lead to conflicts between policies or managers. In some applications there may be a decision to prevent overlap by creating a new domain with an independent manager and all objects from the overlapping set are moved into this new domain. This would be analogous to setting up a new management authority for a service shared by multiple organizations. However, the model should permit the overlap case as it does arise in real-life situations. There may be a policy decision to prevent overlap of a particular domain by preventing members of that domain being included in other domains or members of other domains being included in that domain.

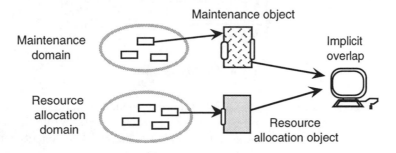

Figure 16.2 Implicit overlap.

Figure 16.2 shows two domains used for different management functions – maintenance and resource allocation. In this case an **implicit overlap** arises because both the maintenance and resource allocation objects relate to the same hardware workstation, although they are different managed objects. Further examples of the use of domains for specifying security policy are given in Chapter 17.

The labels attached to objects and references in Figure 16.1 are unique identifiers. The requirement for flexible naming of objects for management purposes was identified earlier, but a local name for an object is only unique within the context of a single domain, which can act as a naming context. Domain path names can be used to name objects in a similar manner to the naming schemes discussed in Chapter 10. Since objects can be members of multiple domains different path names can map onto the same object, and therefore path names do not provide unique identifiers for objects. Another strategy for unique identifiers is needed, as explained in Section 16.7.2.

16.3   Managers and managed objects

Managers are responsible for:

i)   obtaining information about managed objects by monitoring them;

ii) interpreting management policy and using this monitored information to make decisions about the objects they manage;

iii) performing control actions to modify the behavior of managed objects.

Managers can be human or they may be implemented as automated manager objects acting on behalf of human managers. There is a need to be able to trace responsibility for manager objects back to a human manager. This may be a legal requirement in some applications where wrong decisions could lead to loss of life.

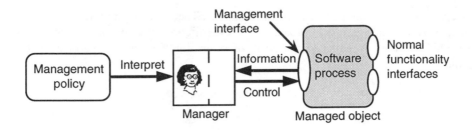

Figure 16.3 Management.

A **managed object** is an object with a management interface, as shown in Figure 16.3. An object may have other interfaces representing its normal functionality. For example, a file server would have a normal functionality interface to open, close, read and write files and a management interface to change caching strategy, modify the numbers of buffers allocated to requests or enable/disable the service. It may be necessary for a managed object to be a representation of an external resource such as a hardware entity but for many software components the managed object is the resource itself. In the OSI approach to management (ISO 10040, 1992), the managed object is modeled as a separate object from the resource it represents. This is applicable to managing hardware resources or to a database approach where there is a database object representation for resources. It is not a suitable generalized approach for managing distributed processing components as it introduces a level of indirection into interactions between managers and resources as well as problems in maintaining consistency between resource state and the managed object state. As OSI-compliant managed resources emerge, they are likely to have an OSI management interface and a normal functionality interface.

The typical management interactions indicated in Figure 16.4 indicate the need for a remote procedure call interaction mechanism for requesting information and performing control actions. In addition, an asynchronous unidirectional message primitive is need to support notification of events. The ISO Common Management Information Protocol does support the above type of interactions, although simple distributed processing interaction primitives as described in Chapter 3 would be easier and more efficient to use.

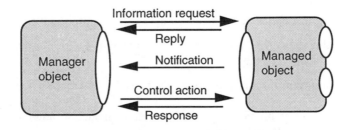

Figure 16.4 Management interactions.

Another problem about the OSI management framework is that it insists on managers interacting via a manager agent which is in the same system as the managed objects and shields them from direct interaction with managers. This arises out of the historical OSI insistence on protocols only being defined between peer entities and a manager, and managed objects are obviously not peers. Delegation of detailed management from a remote manager to local node manager, with the remote manager acting in a supervisory capacity, is a sensible hierarchical implementation approach for some applications (Yemini *et al.*, 1991). However, this is not what the OSI management framework is advocating as the management decisions are still being made by remote managers.

16.4   Management relationships

16.4.1   Access rules

Managers are normally not members of the domains they manage, as in many cases different policies apply to managers and the objects they manage. Other reasons for maintaining a separation between managers and the domains they manage is that this permits managers in one organization to be given (limited) management rights over objects in another organization and structuring a system into subdomains would require including a manager in every subdomain.

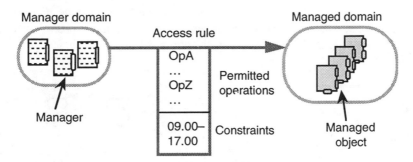

Figure 16.5 Access rules.

Access rules (Figure 16.5) provide a flexible means of specifying management authorization policy as a relationship between a manager domain and managed domain in terms of the operations managers are authorized to perform on the managed objects. A **manager domain** contains manager objects and a **managed domain** contains managed objects. Access rules can also specify constraints such as the permissible time of access or location of managers.

An access rule is a generalized means of specifying access control policy which has been applied to management (Moffett *et. al.*, 1990). It permits the specification of arbitrary management relationships as shown in Figure 16.6.

- There may be multiple managers in a domain for improved availability or performance.

- Managers may perform multiple roles and so be responsible for managing a number of different domains.

- Managers may themselves be managed objects permitting hierarchical management relationships.

- Managers can optionally be members of a domain they manage which permits a reflexive management relationship whereby managers manage themselves.

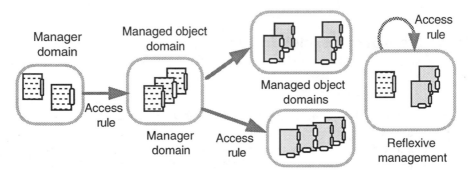

Figure 16.6 Typical management relationships.

There is a need for self-managed objects which encapsulate manager and managed objects. However, this object is not a domain but a composite object (see Chapter 18) constructed using hierarchical composition which hides its internal structure behind an interface.

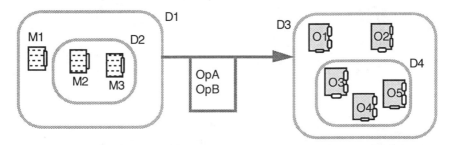

Figure 16.7 Inheritance of access rules.

Objects in a subdomain, by default, "inherit" the access rules applying to direct and indirect parents. In Figure 16.7 objects in domain D2 inherit the access rule applying to the parent domain D1, so they can perform operations (OpA and OpB) on objects in domains D3 and D4 as the latter is a subdomain of D3. There may be more than one access rule which satisfies a particular request, for example as a result of an object's membership of overlapping domains. This indicates that authority has been granted via more than one route. The implications of this inheritance is that the domain service must provide a means of determining the parent and **ancestor** (indirect parent) domains of an object to determine what policies apply to that object.

It is also necessary to control inheritance at both the domain and access rule level. A particular access rule can specify that it applies only to direct members of the source and/or target domains or a domain can specify no inheritance of any access rule by its subdomains.

16.4.2   Representing users

Two default domains shown in Figure 16.8 are needed to represent human users within the system:

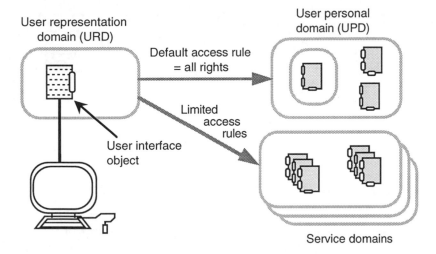

Figure 16.8 Default user domains.

i)   A **User Representation Domain (URD)** is a persistent representation of the human user or manager. When the user logs into the system a user interface object is created within the URD and inherits all access rules specified for the URD.

ii)   A **User Personal Domain (UPD)** corresponds to a user's home directory and represents the personal resources that the user "owns". In addition the user may have limited access to other service domains representing the shared resources the user can access.

16.4.3   Manager positions

It is necessary to specify the rights of a manager position independently of the human manager who occupies that position so that when the human manager is transferred to another position, the access rules pertaining to the position do not have to be changed. This can be accomplished by a creating a manager position domain and specifying all access rules with respect to this domain. Allocating a human manager to a position is accomplished by including his or her URD within the position domain, as shown in Figure 16.9. The manager automatically inherits all rights for that position and may be a member of multiple position domains if performing multiple management roles. The model permits multiple URDs to be included in a manager position domain, indicating a shared position, but obviously this would require the managers to coordinate their activities via a suitable protocol.

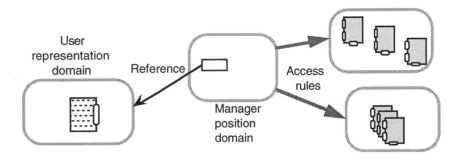

Figure 16.9 Manager positions.

16.5   Application to configuration management (CM)

In the previous sections we have explained the basic concepts of management domains and access rules. We will now discuss how these concepts can be applied to a particular management application, namely configuration management of distributed software components in a distributed programming environment such as the Conic system (Magee *et al.*, 1989). In this environment a human manager makes use of a configuration language to create software components (objects), allocate them to hardware nodes and bind interfaces between component instances. The human manager interacts with a configuration manager object (called *cman*) which executes the management operations on his or her behalf. Domains and access rules are used to control on which objects the manager can perform configuration management operations and what interfaces can be bound.

The assumption is that the managed object corresponds to a composite software component with an application-specific interface as well as a management interface. An interface type is defined, using an Interface Specification Language (ISL), in terms of *ports* which correspond to operations provided (or messages received) by a server or operations invoked (or messages sent) by a client. Port types define the data types of the operation parameters as shown in Figure 16.10.

The *interface_xyz* within the definition unit *ifdefs* defines three operations *i, j, k* together with the parameters of the operations. Note that port *k* defines a unidirectional message with no return parameters.

```
define ifdefs = {
            data    = array [512] char
            name = array [64] char
            length = int
            interface_xyz =
            {
                i:    port name –> length, data        // bidirectional
                j:    port name –> int                 // bidirectional
                k:    port name, length, data          // unidirectional
            }
}
```

Figure 16.10 Interface type definitions.

A server template would declare the interface as an *entry* and provide the code to implement the operation defined, while a client template would declare the interface as an *exit* and invoke operation on the ports (see Figure 16.11).

```
object xyzclient = exit interface_xyz {          object xyzserver = entry interface_xyz {
        use xyz_defs: interface_xyz                      use xyz_defs: interface_xyz
        /* Component is implemented in a                 /* Component is implemented in a
        suitable programming language                    suitable programming language
        – invokes operations /*                          – implements operations/*
}                                                }
```

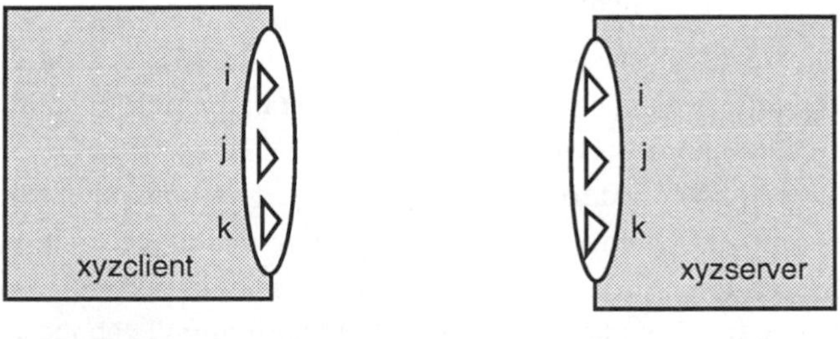

Figure 16.11 Declaring interfaces on client and server.

When an interface on a client object instance is bound to an interface on a server object instance, ports of the same type are bound together. An access rule specifies for which port types bindings are permitted. So the binding of *xyzclient* to *xyzserver* in Figure 16.12 results in ports *i* and *k* being bound as *j* is not permitted by the access rule. Note that if there is no ambiguity the interface name can be omitted from a bind statement, as in Figure 16.12.

The generic configuration management operations available include delete, stop, start, and reset components; query, bind and unbind interfaces. Binding can apply to individual ports in an interface or all the ports. Every configurable object must support a server CM interface which defines ports corresponding to each CM operation. Note that a configuration manager may also have a create port which would be linked to a factory object, as this is not part of the generic interface supported by all configurable objects.

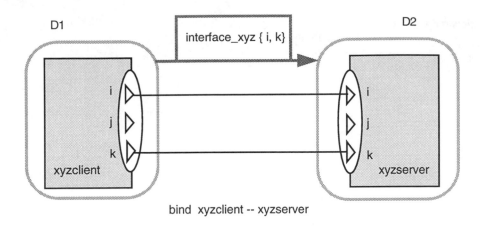

Figure 16.12 Interface binding.

In general a manager or application programmer would be responsible for initially installing the components of a distributed application or service as well as subsequently replacing components with new versions to support evolutionary change. Reconfiguration can be performed dynamically without shutting down the complete service.

In Figure 16.13, a human manager (*Fred*) responsible for configuration would have a configuration manager object, called *cman,* which supports a graphical interface and a CM client interface. This *cman* would be created in *Fred's* URD. The *cman* interface can be bound to any managed object that implements the CM server interface to permit CM operation to be performed on that object. The operations that *cman* is authorized to perform are specified as access rules between Fred's URD and the managed domain. Assume Fred decides to reconfigure the application running in Domain *D1* which consists of the objects *A* and *B,* with *B* bound to *A.* He installs a new object *C* of type *ctype* and binds it to *A* in *D1* and to *xyzserver* in domain *D2.*

Physical nodes are represented as factory objects which provide a remotely accessible interface to local operating system facilities for loading object templates and creating object instances. In Figure 16.13, an access rule gives Fred access to nodes *N1* and *N2.* Fred can perform any configuration management operation on objects in *D1*, but can only perform bind operations on objects in *D2.* The bind between *D1* and *D2* permits *C* to invoke only operations *i* and *k* on *xyzserver.* Note that if a manager has CM {all} permission on a domain he can perform arbitrary configuration management of objects in that domain including binding of any type-compatible interfaces of objects that are direct members of that domain, but configuration between that domain and any other is subject to access control.

Manage D1

use	ctype;	// Specifies required template
create	C : ctype @ loc= 'N2'	// Creates an object C at node N2
bind	C.fileio -- A.fileio	
	C.xyz -- D2/xyzserver.interface_xyz	
start	C	

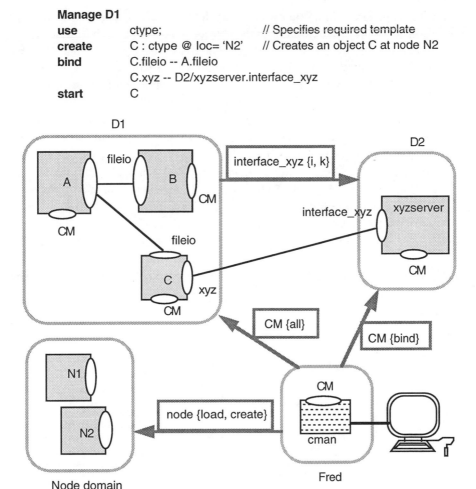

Figure 16.13 Configuration management example.

16.6   Inter-organizational domains

As explained in Section 16.1, a large distributed application may span multiple organizations. Managers in one organization may need to perform (possibly limited) operations on objects in other organizations, for instance to query state or perform diagnostic tests. The domain service must therefore be capable of supporting inter-organizational management. The domain hierarchy is also used as a means of naming objects and so it should be possible to include objects or subdomains from another organizational hierarchy into your own domain hierarchy, assign a local name to these objects and hence manage or just access the objects. However, including organization A's domain into the policy set of organization B's domain implies that A's sub-domain inherits policy applying to B's domain, which would violate the mutual independence of the two organizations. The domain permits **context references** to other objects (usually domains) that do not carry policy implications; in this case the referencing domain is not considered as a parent of the referenced domain so there is no inheritance of policy such as access rules (see Figure 16.14). A domain may hold two sets of object references, the **policy set** to which domain policy will, by default, apply, and the **context set** to which domain policy does not apply. If a member of Imperial College has access to the DOC domain, he or she can obtain an address for objects in the BP/Research domain, but cannot access those objects as access rules applying to the DOC domain do not apply to context references. A separate access rule must be set up to enable Imperial College staff to access the BP/Research domain. Once that access rule has been set up, objects in the BP/Research domain can be accessed as though they were members of the DOC/BP subdomain. The context references are analogous to context links found in many directory services.

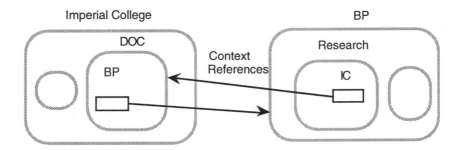

Figure 16.14 The use of inter-organization context references.

The disadvantage of this scheme is that it does not use a well-known naming convention and so cannot use any existing directory service to locate objects in remote organizations. The addresses of objects from other organizations must be inserted manually. A solution we have adopted is to set up a domain hierarchy at each organization that mirrors the structure of the well-known Internet Domain Naming system (see Figure 16.15). We could equally have used X.500 naming, but it is not yet widely used.

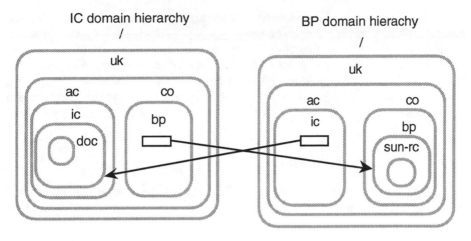

Figure 16.15 Context references plus well-known naming.

16.7   Domain service

The description of the domain service has so far been from a functional point of view. We will now take a more detailed look at the interface the domain service provides to users and how this interface is actually implemented by means of a set of servers.

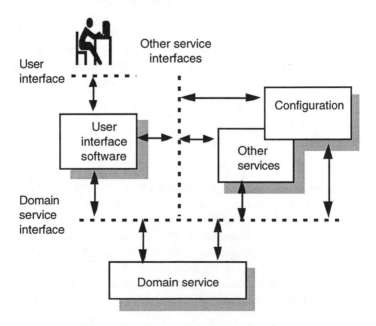

Figure 16.16 Domain service interface.

The domain service provides the underlying services required for naming and grouping objects for applying management policy. This is used by all aspects of management as well as configuration management as shown in Figure 16.16.

In this section we will describe the domain service implemented as part of the Domino project on Domain Management of Open Systems (Law *et al.*, 1990). This was a collaboration project funded by the UK Department of Trade and Industry and Science and Engineering Research Council involving Imperial College, Sema Group and BP Research.

16.7.1   User and mechanism views

There is a need to distinguish between the view of the human manager (user) managing a distributed system and the underlying mechanism(s) used within the system for implementing this view, as illustrated below.

* Management domain objects provide a means of defining sets of objects and structuring them by the use of subdomains. The user view of domains is that they contain a set of named objects. However, the system holds the local name (a text string) and an object reference for each member of a domain. Users refer to objects by names, while the system refers to them using the internal object references described below.

* Access rules specify discretionary access control policy in terms of the set of operations that any of a set of users is authorized to perform on any of a set of target objects. This also is a concept that managers find intuitively easy to deal with, but does not lead to efficient implementation. It would involve unreasonably long searches to evaluate access requests if the system had to search through all access rule objects in order to decide whether to allow the request. Therefore, for the Domino project, we are implementing the access rules by means of Access Control Lists (ACLs) attached to target object domains, as described in Chapter 17.

* The user views object creation as being an operation on a domain, but the underlying mechanism is an operation on a factory object which inserts the reference into the domain.

We believe that it is important to maintain both a distinction and a relationship between the user and mechanism views of management concepts. As with any system, the user requirements must drive the mechanism, but it must be subject to the condition that it can be implemented efficiently. In the remainder of the chapter we will concentrate on the prototype domain service implemented as part of the Domino research project. It was necessary to implement both the user and mechanism views, as human managers have to be able to work with objects which are implemented in accordance with the user view, while the underlying system has to be able to use a mechanism that provides an efficient implementation of the functions seen by the user. This distinction is similar to Ansa's (1991) five different viewpoints of a system, but we find the simple binary distinction of views adequate for our purposes.

16.7.2   Object references

Users refer to objects by local textual names which are only unique within the context of a domain. An **Object Identification Descriptor (OID)** is used internally within the system to reference objects. This OID is unique across a much broader namespace – all systems supporting a domain service. The domain service provides the means of translating between these two forms of identifier.

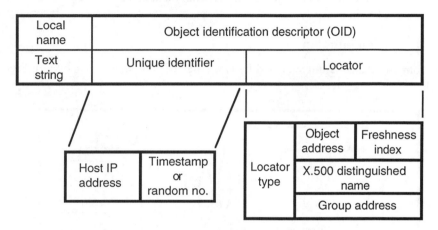

Figure 16.17 Object entry held by domain service.

Figure 16.17 shows the format of the OID. Every object is assigned a unique identifier, created from the Host IP address where it was first created plus a "uniquefier" (timestamp or random number). This does not change if the object is migrated to another host. The current implementation uses actual addresses as a means of locating objects, but the system could be extended to use an X.500 distinguished name (see Section 10.2.3) or a group address for replicated objects. The freshness index associated with the actual address is incremented when the object is migrated, so two addresses for the same object can be compared to find the most recent one.

16.7.3   Domain operations

The following set of operations is supported by our domain service implementation:

Create/destroy a subdomain;

Include/remove object in/from domain policy set;

Include/remove object in/from domain context set;

List domain – returns policy set and context set entries;

Query object's parents – returns OIDs of direct parents;

Query object's ancestors – returns list of direct and indirect parent OIDs;

Translate path name to OID and address;

Translate OID to path name, choosing an arbitrary path name where there are multiple paths through the domain tree to the object.

Note that object creation is not considered a domain service operation, but is invoked on an object factory which creates the object and includes it within a domain as an atomic action. Object deletion is performed on the object itself and the object support system attempts to remove all entries from the domain service, but this cannot be guaranteed as in a distributed system some parts of the service may be inaccessible.

16.7.4   Implementation

The domain service is implemented by two types of component as shown in Figure 16.18.

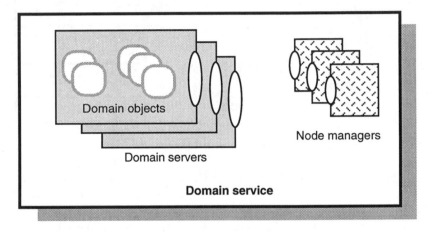

Figure 16.18 Domain service components.

i)   **Domain servers** store and maintain domain objects corresponding to a subtree in the domain hierarchy. If it does not hold the information relating to a particular part of the subtree, it will have the address of the server responsible. The current implementation caters for distributed, partitioned domain information, but we will be investigating replication of domain information for performance and availability.

ii) **Node managers** reside on every physical node that supports managed objects and maintain information about local objects, such as their parent domains. They act as local agents for interaction with the domain servers and are responsible for requesting the domain server to include a newly created object in its parent domain, maintaining a cache of addresses of domain servers, and holding forwarding addresses for objects which have migrated from their host. An advantage of having a permanent server running on a host is that it can cache some of the domain information such as where the main domain servers are and information on frequently used domains. This is available to local objects which may be dynamic and short-lived.

Another function of the node manager is that of a generic factory server. It creates object instances on the node from the object template which is passed as a parameter. The node manager inserts the created object in a domain specified by the user and also in a node domain of all objects created on that node. The node domain is used by the system administrator responsible for managing the node.

Cycles of membership, in which a domain is an indirect member of itself, may arise within the domain service. These must be catered for by all programs (such as a user interface program) which trace down the membership tree. Unbounded search for parents, possibly across remote sites, is dealt with by an arbitrary limitation on the number of ancestors which can be searched. We need implementation experience to find out how satisfactory this will be.

16.8   Related work

The OSI security framework (ISO 10181-1, 1991) defines a subdomain as a subset. If domain B is a subset of domain A then any member of domain B must also be a direct member of domain A. If an object X is inserted in domain B, then X will also be a direct member of A. Therefore any policy applying to the superset (A) must, by definition, apply to the subset (B). However, B is a subdomain of A and if X is inserted in B, it is not a direct member of A. Our definition of subdomains permits inheritance of policy as an option and permits domains to be used to partition responsibility, as the manager of a domain does not necessarily manage the member of the subdomain. The manager of a superset would by definition manage all objects in the domain and would not see subsets. Another problem with the OSI definition is that domains include both managers and managed objects. This reduces the flexibility of the domain concepts as it is impractical for inter-organizational management where managers have limited management rights over objects in another organization (that is, a different domain). It does not permit different policies to apply to managers and the objects they manage. In our opinion the OSI concept of domains has not been fully thought through, and there is no implementation experience to validate it.

The DEC Enterprise Management Architecture (Strutt, 1991) uses a domain to define a "sphere of interest of a set of managed objects for a manager" – managers are not part of the domain. Only the managers are aware of the domains and objects do not know which domains they are members of. This model is compatible with the Domino approach as it implements a subset of our concepts. There are no domains of managers and the relationship between a manager and domain is implicit in the knowledge of the domain name rather than the use of explicit access rules. Managers do not use the domains for access control. Domain membership information is held by the name service.

Domains perform a name service function and so the implementation is similar to the Digital Equipment Corporation Name Service (DECdns) (DEC, 1991) where a domain corresponds to a directory and their soft-links serve a similar function to our context references. However DECdns does not permit cycles and a sub-directory can have only one parent. DECdns makes use of globally unique names rather than names relative to a domain so names are independent of users, whereas our names are allocated by individual user and are not unique.

There was an Esprit-funded project called DOMAINS (1991) which defined an architecture for managing distributed systems. Their domains encapsulated manager and managed objects which made it difficult to support managed objects that were members of multiple domains or to support the flexible management relationships we have identified in this chapter.

16.9   Summary

Domains serve two functions:

i)   A means of grouping objects in order to specify a common policy. It is the means of grouping objects to specify a policy and the ability to partition managed objects into subdomains that cater for large inter-organizational systems.

ii) A means of allocating local names to managed objects.

These two functions of domains are reflected in that domains can hold two types of object reference: a policy reference implying that domain policy applies to the referenced object; and a context reference, used purely for convenient naming of objects, particularly those in other organizations.

Multiple domains containing the same managed object can coexist in order to reflect different viewpoints and policies with respect to a set of managed objects, corresponding to different management roles and functions.

Access rules have been used as a flexible means of defining relationships between domains of managers and managed objects by defining what operations the managers can perform on the managed domain.

The chapter has shown how domains can be used to represent individual users registered in a system and manager positions within an organization. The next chapter gives further examples of the versatility of the domain concepts as a means of specifying management policy and delegation of authority.

Abbreviations

ACL   Access Control List
CM   Configuration Management
IP   Internet Protocol
OID   Object Identification Descriptor

URD   User Representation Domain – represents a user in the system
UPD   User Personal Domain – the resources "owned" by a user

References

Ansa (1991). *ANSAware 3.0 Implementation Manual*. APM Ltd., Poseidon House, Castle Park, Cambridge CB3 0RD, UK

DEC (1991). *Digital Network Architecture, Naming Service Functional Specification,* Version V2.0.0. Order No. EK-DDNANS-FS-002

DOMAINS (1991). *Esprit Project 5165 – DOMAINS Basic Concepts,* Version 2.0. Philips Gmbh., PO Box 1980, W 5100 Aachen, Germany, Nov.ember

ISO/IEC 10040 (1992). *Information Technology – Open Systems Interconnection – Systems Management Overview.*

ISO 10181-1 (1991). *ISO Security Framework I: Overview.* ISO/IEC JTC1/SC21, May

Law A.D., Sloman M.S. and Moffett J.D. (1990). The "Domino" Project. *Data Management '90 Conference*, Egham, UK, 2–3 April 1990, BCS Data Management Specialist Group, 143–54

Magee J., Kramer J. and Sloman M.S. (1989). Constructing distributed systems in Conic. *IEEE Transactions on Software Engineering,* **15**(6), 663–75

Moffett J.D., Sloman M.S. and Twidle K.P. (1990). Specifying discretionary access control policy for distributed systems. *Computer Communications,* **13**(9), 571–80

Sloman M.S. and Moffett J.D. (1989). Domain management for distributed systems. In *Integrated Network Management I*, (Meandzija B. and Westcott J., eds.), pp. 505–16. North Holland

Strutt C. (1991). Dealing with scale in an enterprise management eirector. In *Integrated Network Management II*, (Krishnan I. and Zimmer W., eds.), 577–93. North Holland

Yemini Y., Goldszmidt G. and Yemini S. (1991). Network management by delegation. In *Integrated Network Management II*, (Krishnan I. and Zimmer W., eds.), 95–107. North Holland

Chapter 17

Specification of Management Policies and Discretionary Access Control

Jonathan D. Moffett

University of York,
Department of Computer Science,
Heslington, York, YO1 5DD, UK
Email: jdm@minster.york.ac.uk

This chapter is concerned with the specification of management policy. Its aim is to treat policies in a general manner, but discretionary access control policies are used as an example, to illustrate how they are specified and what the major issues are. It consists of four sections.

Section 17.1 gives the background and motivation for this subject and sets out a general model of management policies. It explains the need to model policies, their general characteristics, and their representation as objects so that they can be created, modified and queried. There are a number of possible relationships between policies, either hierarchical or potentially conflicting, and a brief analysis of this incompletely researched area is provided.

A well-understood example of a management policy is the access rule, used to specify discretionary access control policies. Section 17.2 introduces and explains access rules. A short example shows their practical effect, and the implementation issues are discussed.

In Section 17.3 delegation of authority, the means by which access rule administration can be carried out in a controlled manner, is introduced. The roles of Owner, Manager and Security Administrator in a typical organization are explained. The downwards flow of authority is modeled and controlled by fixed policies acting on Management Role Objects (MROs). The use of MROs in ensuring the separation of powers for Security Administrators is explained.

455

17.1   Management policies

We are concerned with large distributed processing systems which typically consist of multiple interconnected networks and span the computer systems belonging to a number of different organizations. Policies cannot be delegated or imposed from one central point, but have to be negotiated between independent managers.

Large distributed processing systems may contain hundreds of thousands of resources[1] and be used by thousands of users[2]. This implies that it is impractical to specify policies in terms of individual subjects or targets. We need to be able to specify them as relationships between groups of subjects and groups of objects. For example, the same policy may apply to all people in a department or to the set of files pertaining to an application.

All formal organizations have policies, with two related purposes: to define the goals of the organization; and to allocate the resources to achieve the goals. The policies are used to influence management, in a hierarchical fashion. A high-level policy guides a manager, who may achieve the policy goals by making lower-level policies which apply to other managers lower in the hierarchy.

Most organizations issue policy statements, intended to guide their members in particular circumstances. Policies may provide positive guidance about the goals of the organization and how they are to be achieved, or constraints limiting the way in which the goals are to be achieved. Other policy statements allocate (give access authorization to) the resources which are needed to carry out the goals. If they allocate money they are typically called budgets.

A common theme in distributed system management is the need for independent managers to be able to negotiate, establish, query and enforce policies that apply to a defined general set of situations.

An example of interaction between independent managers arises from the interconnection of two network management domains such as a Public Network (PN) and a local Imperial College (IC) network. This requires communication between the PN and IC network managers in order to exchange management information and establish access rules. Let us suppose that there are two relevant policies in force: PN policy gives the PN Manager the authority to carry out all relevant management operations on the network; and IC policy requires the IC Network Manager to report regularly on the status of the academic subset of PN nodes. We call these managers the **subjects** of the policies. In the absence of any other policies, the PN Manager has the authority to provide the regular status information, but no motivation to do so, while the IC Network Manager has the motivation to obtain the information but no authority to do so. The initial situation is shown in Figure 17.1(a).

---

[1]   Referred to as **target objects** or **targets** in this chapter.

[2]   In this chapter **user** refers to a human end user of a system. The representation of users by User Representation Domains is discussed in Chapter 16. Active entities in the system, representing or acting as agents for users, are referred to as **subjects**. Subjects act as target objects when operations are performed on them.

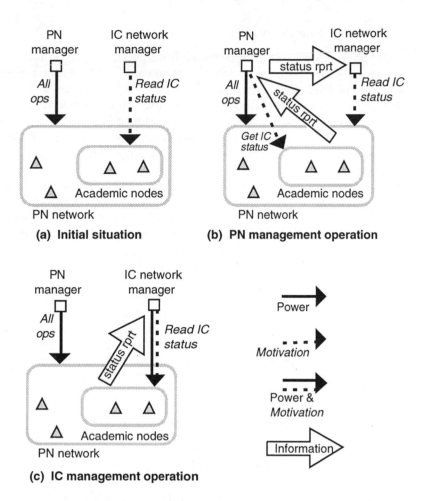

Figure 17.1 Policies for PN and IC managers.

An additional policy has to be established (created) by the PN Manager to meet IC's requirements. One approach is to create a policy that motivates the PN Manager to generate the status information and provide it to the IC Network Manager regularly, as shown in Figure 17.1(b). An alternative approach is to create a policy that gives the IC Network Manager the authority to perform the operations needed to obtain the regular status information, as shown in Figure 17.1(c).

This example brings out one of the main points in the model. Policies that motivate activities and policies giving authority to carry out activities can each exist independently of the other. However, if only one of the two kinds of policies exists in relation to an action, the action will not be performed. For management activities to be carried out, there needs to be a manager who is the subject of both kinds of policy: a policy giving authority to carry out the activity; and a policy motivating the manager to do so.

17.1.1   The need to model policies

The example above shows that there is a need for a means by which independent managers can query, negotiate, set up and change policies. It can of course be done by the well-tried method of telephone calls and the exchange of paper, but there are potential benefits in using the distributed system itself to communicate and store policies, particularly with respect to automated management. There is thus a need to be able to represent and manipulate policies within a computer system. It is important that the representation of policies and the protocols used to negotiate them should be uniform across management applications.

Storing an organization's policies in a database permits staff to search, using keywords, for policies relevant to their proposed plans. The Pythagoras project (Bedford-Roberts, 1991) was concerned with modeling policies in order to create a database of the policies of an organization. Its purpose was for users to query the database, matching textual patterns in the policy statements, in order to enable them to ascertain what policies may exist in a specified subject area. The system does not interpret or constrain the contents of policies.

With the automation of many aspects of management in distributed systems and computer networks, there is the need to represent management policies within the computer system so that they can be interpreted by automated managers in order to influence their activities. One specific class of policies, which we term **management action policies**, is particularly useful when considering distributed system management, and is discussed in detail in Sections 17.1.2–17.1.4. Other classes of policy are briefly considered in Section 17.1.5.

17.1.2   Characteristics of management action policies

We define some characteristics of the policies that we will be discussing in order to give a working definition that is more precise than simply "plans". We start from the basis that policies are intended to influence actions. However, policies are not concerned with instant decisions to perform an action, instantly carried out. If a manager specifies that something is to be done once only, and instantly, he or she does not create a policy, but simply causes the action to be carried out. Whether the policy defines a single future action to be carried out, or repeated actions, or relates to the maintenance of a condition, it needs to have *persistence*.

Policy modalities – motivation and authorization

As shown in the example above, we distinguish between policies that are intended to motivate actions to take place and policies that give or withhold power for actions to take place. **Actions** are operations that are performed by agents provided two preconditions are satisfied: motivation and power (see Figure 17.2):

- **Motivation** is the term we use to imply that the agent wishes to carry out an action, and will do so provided he or she has the power to do so.

- **Power** implies that if an agent attempts to carry out an action, he or she will succeed.

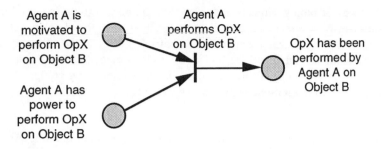

Figure 17.2 Preconditions for action.

One method of acquiring power is through delegated **authority**, which we define to be legitimately acquired power. The very concept of a policy implies a well-ordered world, and so policies are rarely concerned with unauthorized power. We take the simplifying view that all policies giving power can be viewed as giving authority, and in the rest of this chapter we categorize policies as being either authorization or motivation policies.

Agents are always humans, but it is convenient to extend the concept of "action" to include computer processes which have been commanded to carry out actions. An agent's motivation is represented by the agent submitting a command to the computer system. An agent's authorization is represented by more than one means: for an action to be carried out successfully the access control system must authorize the agent's use of named resources such as files, while his or her use of commodity resources such as file store and CPU time must also be authorized by the system, perhaps through an accounting application.

17.1.3 Policy attributes

Policies, whether concerned with motivation or with authorization, have at least the following attributes: Modality; Policy Subjects; Policy Target Objects; Policy Goals; and Policy Constraints.

Modality

A policy has one of the following modalities: **positive authorization** (permitting), **negative authorization** (prohibiting), **positive motivation** (requiring), and **negative motivation** (deterring). We do not exclude the possibility of other useful policy modalities being proposed, but these are adequate for the present analysis.

Policy subjects and target objects

Policies are about organizational goals, which need someone to achieve them. All policies in this model have subjects, the people to whom they are directed, that is, those who are authorized or motivated to carry out the policy goal within the limits defined by the policy constraints. The Policy Subjects attribute defines a set of subjects. Where a policy has been automated as a computer system command we regard the user who will input the system command as the policy subject. The Policy Target Object attribute defines the set of objects at which the policy is directed.

The sets of policy subjects and target objects may both be specified either by enumeration or by means of a predicate to be satisfied. Individual policy subjects and target objects are not normally specified, because a policy is typically expressed in terms of organizational positions and domains of objects, not individuals. One approach to specifying organizational positions and enumerating groups of objects is by using generic **management domains**; see Chapter 16.

Policy goals

The Policy Goals attribute may define either **high-level goals** or **actions**. An example of a high-level goal is "recover from media failure"; it does not prescribe the actions in detail, and we can imagine a number of different actions that could achieve the goal. On the other hand, an example of an action is "run the BackUp job on department D's disk files". Note that the distinction between high-level goals and actions may depend upon the context. In an environment in which there is one standard "back up" operation defined, a goal such as "back up department D's disk files" might be regarded as an action policy, while in other situations it might be a high-level goal in which the System Administrator has several options for action.

In order to distinguish between actions and goals, we need to have an alphabet of the operations that can be performed by objects in a system. Then any goal that is expressed purely in terms of the operations is an action, and any other goal is to be regarded as a high-level goal. **Procedures**, often found in organizations' policy manuals, can be regarded as a sequence of actions.

Actions represented by operations naturally have three components: the target object on which it is performed, the operation performed, and one or more parameters to the operation. Policies may relate not only to the operation name, but also to parameters of the operation. In the example, "Financial managers are authorized to carry out financial transactions of a value up to £1 million", the amount of the transaction is a parameter of the operation, and forms a part of the authorization policy.

Policy constraints

The Policy Constraints attribute of a policy object places constraints on its applicability. They are predicates which may be expressed in terms of general system properties, such as extent or duration, or some other condition. An example of constraints in authorization policies expressed by access rules is the limits on the terminal from which the operation may be performed, and/or limits on date or time, for example "Members of Payroll may Read Payroll Master files, from terminals in the Payroll office, between 9 a.m. and 5 p.m., Monday to Friday".

17.1.4   Representing management action policies as objects

It is useful to view management action policies as objects on which operations can be performed. For simplicity we assume the following minimal set of operations:

- Create a policy
- Destroy a policy

• Query a policy

Authorization may be required to perform operations on policy objects. If the computer system is simply a documentation aid, no restrictions may be needed. On the other hand, if the policies are actually used to influence system actions, as in the case of access control policies, restrictions on operations are required. They are discussed in detail for authorization policies in (Moffett and Sloman, 1991).

Although we regard all policies as objects, some may be altered dynamically while others are **fixed policies**, fixed for the life of the system. The following example is implicitly an example of a fixed policy: "The system coding is to ensure that it is impossible for a user to be logged on at two terminals simultaneously".

The object that expresses a fixed policy will typically be separate from the coding that implements it. On the other hand the system could use this policy object as part of its implementation; for example, the policy could be defined by an object with a Read-only attribute stating the number of terminals at which the user could be logged on, which the system queries when appropriate. The reason for recording it as an explicit policy object will be to ensure that it is recognized as deliberate, and not removed as an undesirable restriction at the next software release. Using it as part of the implementation will enable systems with differing policies to be generated more easily.

17.1.5   Relationships between management action policies

The subject of the relationships between management action policies is a complex one, which has not yet been researched completely. At this stage it is possible to identify two main sorts of relationship: policy hierarchies; and overlaps which may result in conflicts. It is also possible to throw light on the concept of responsibility by modeling it as two related policies.

Policy hierarchies

The organizations using and managing distributed processing systems are hierarchical in nature and authority is delegated downwards from senior management. It is a fundamental characteristic of policies that they are organized in a hierarchical fashion. The following example is illustrated in Figure 17.3:

(a) The Managing Director of a company is to protect its assets from loss.

(b) The Manager of Department D is to protect all files from loss owing to fire or media failure.

(c) The System Administrator is to back up Department D's disk files weekly.

(d) There is a system command (which was input by the System Administrator) to run a job which backs up Department D's disk files to tape each Thursday at 22.00. The System Administrator is to take the tapes to a safe store in a different building each Friday morning.

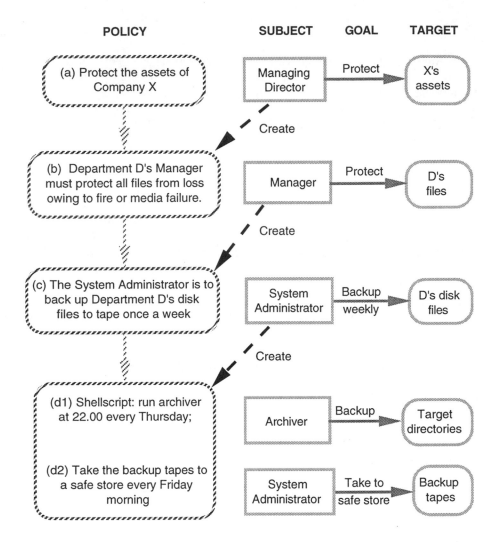

Figure 17.3 A policy hierarchy.

We may suppose that the board of a company has made policy (a) and given responsibility for carrying out the policy to the Managing Director. The Managing Director has made policy (b) and given responsibility for it to the Manager of Department D. The Manager has made policy (c) and given responsibility to the System Administrator, who has carried out that responsibility by creating policy (d). This is actually a procedure consisting of two actions, one automated and one manual.

Policies are made at a high level by senior management and responsibility for achieving their goal is assigned to other members of staff, who may in turn do one of the following:

i)   Create a lower-level policy that will achieve the policy goal they have been assigned, and assign responsibility for it to another member of staff. This is what was done in policy (b).

ii) Delegate the task not to another member of staff, but to a computer system that will carry out actions that achieve the goal. This is what the System Administrator has done in the first part of procedure (d).

iii) Achieve the specified goal themselves by carrying out actions that achieve the goal, which the System Administrator does in the second part of procedure (d).

Policy conflicts

The policy model has opened up the possibility of systematic analysis of policy conflicts. This analysis is at an early stage, but a first step has been taken by recognizing that the overlap of objects – either policy subjects or target objects or both – between policies is a necessary condition for conflict. If there are no objects in common between two policies, there is no possibility of conflict.

Conflicts of modalities can be recognized independently of any specific application. They assume overlaps between the subjects, goals and target objects of the two policies:

- There may be a direct contradiction of modalities, for example two simultaneous authorization policies, one (positive) permitting and one (negative) prohibiting the same subject to perform the same action on the same object. Some means of preventing or resolving conflicts of this kind is essential for any system, and typically this is achieved by giving policies a priority ranking.

- There may be an inconsistency between motivation and authorization. When a subject is motivated to perform an operation on an object but not authorized to do so, the organization in which this occurs will not be able to achieve its goals, and the conflict will need to be resolved.

There are also policy conflicts that are not inherent in the model, but are dependent upon the application. Several different modes of application-defined conflict emerge from the analysis of the ways in which policies may overlap:

- *Subject and target objects both overlap* – where the subject and target objects of two policies both overlap, there may be a conflict of operations, for example "The same person may not both Input and Approve a payment transaction".

- *Target objects overlap* – when the target objects of two policies overlap, there is a potential conflict arising from multiple managers of a single object. This may result in one manager reversing the operation carried out by the other, unless a coordination mechanism is introduced.

- *Subject objects overlap* – when the subject objects of two policies overlap, there is potential conflict of interests, such as the same person having management authority over two competing organizations.

- *Subject and target objects overlap in one policy* – when subject and target objects overlap in one policy, there is the situation of a manager managing himself. This is again a potential conflict which is application-dependent; it may be acceptable for an automated manager to configure itself, but not for a human manager to sign his or her own expenses.

Responsibility

The concept of responsibility is frequently associated with policies. It can be analyzed in our model in terms of the relationship between two motivation policies, for example: the Head of Department decides that the System Administrator shall be responsible to the Administration Manager for backing up the department's files. This can be modeled as two related motivation policies, each created by the Head of Department:

- One policy motivates the System Administrator to do the backup actions, and report to the Administration Manager;

- A second policy motivates the Administration Manager to supervise the System Administrator.

This analysis enables two different concerns to be separated out: responsibility *for* and responsibility *to*, which are often confused in informal discussion.

Policy analysis using deontic logic

Deontic logic, the logic of normative systems, which enables reasoning about **obligation**, corresponding roughly to motivation, and **permission**, corresponding to authorization, is potentially a useful tool in policy analysis. Conflicts of modalities have been discussed in the context of deontic logic by Alchourron (1991), among others. The analysis of the concept of responsibility into two separate policies follows Kanger (1972) who makes the distinction between responsibility *for* and responsibility *to*.

17.1.6   Other classes of policy

Although management action policies are useful for modeling several policy applications, not all policies fit easily into this framework. We discuss briefly two other classes of policy – domain membership constraints and policies about policies.

Domain membership constraints

Management domains were introduced in Chapter 16. Some policies may be expressed as constraints upon domain membership, for example:

- There must be at least two members of the domain of Security Administrators.

- Processors in a domain must be able to support the M68000 instruction set.

- Destroying an object is prohibited if the object is still a member of another domain.

There are of course two possible kinds of constraint. The first, which we favor, is a constraint upon the operations that affect domain membership, typically the create and destroy operations on any object and the include and remove operations on a domain. These add and subtract objects to and from the policy set. The predicate defined by the constraint has to be evaluated once only, when the operation is performed. Constraints on the number or type of objects in a domain, and on the values of read-only attributes, can be enforced by this means. The second kind of constraint is a general predicate, which the system is required to maintain, about the attributes of members of a domain. This is potentially very difficult to achieve, because every time any application functional operation attempts to change an object's attribute, the system is required to verify that the domain constraints, of every domain of which the object is a member, are not violated. We do not therefore envisage constraints of this kind being permitted.

Policies about policies

Some policies apply to management action policies rather than to other system objects. An example is the policies, discussed in Section 17.3, that constrain the operations that can be performed on access rules. Access rules are themselves management action policy objects, and it is necessary to place quite complex restrictions on how they can be created, altered and destroyed. These restrictions cannot themselves be expressed easily as management action policies, and we make no attempt here to model them systematically. However, there is clearly an important research task in doing so, as it is necessary to be able to reason about the relationships between all kinds of policies that may affect the actions performed upon objects.

17.2   Discretionary access control policies

Many aspects of policy modeling are still in their infancy. However, security policies have been researched quite thoroughly and we use, as an example, the management action policies for discretionary access control which are known as **access rules**.

Access control policy relates to authority, that is, power which has been legitimately obtained, and to how authority is delegated. Access control is concerned with ensuring that subjects and processes in a computer system gain access to computer-based resources in a controlled and authorized manner. Resources such as files must be protected from unauthorized access and access permission must be assigned only by subjects or managers with authority to do so. We consider only *logical* access control and not issues relating to *physical* access control such as locks and secure rooms. The USA Department of Defense Trusted Computer System Evaluation Criteria (DoD, 1985) define two kinds of logical access control. **Discretionary access control** permits managers or other subjects to specify and control the sharing of resources with other subjects. **Mandatory access control** enforces policies that are built into the design of the system and cannot be altered except by installing a new version of the system. For example, in multi-level security systems, data cannot be read by a subject with a lower security classification than has been assigned to the data. Mandatory policy is particularly applicable to military environments, whereas discretionary policy typically applies to commercial, industrial and educational environments. This chapter is concerned with the latter.

We make the assumption that there is no inherent right of access of any kind for ordinary subjects. If a person is not the owner of an object, and has not been given authority, then the computer system should refuse all access.

In general, authority is given not to a person but to a position or role within an organization. A typical policy is that "the Payroll Clerk is authorized to change the Payroll Master file". While John occupies the position of Payroll Clerk he has that authority, but when he is replaced in that position by Mary, he loses the authority and Mary gains it. An important aspect of access authority is the ability of senior management to delegate it down through an organization. We have identified distinct management roles which apply to commercial organizations, each with different authority, and in Section 17.3 we introduce the concept of **delegation of authority**, as a means of the controlled dissemination of access authority within an organization.

We use the **reference monitor** concept, as described in (Anderson, 1972 and DoD, 1985), to model an access control system. The function of a reference monitor is to enforce the authorized access relationships between subjects and targets of a system. It is a trusted component of the system. All operations requested to be carried out on an object are intercepted by the reference monitor, which only invokes the operation if the access is authorized. In this case access control is transparent to the subject, but otherwise the subject is informed by a failure message. In general, access control is carried out by the system, and not by the target object itself, although the reference monitor could be implemented by the object.

17.2.1   Access rules

Access rules were introduced in (Moffett *et al.,* 1990). They are the means for specifying access control policy and are an adaptation of Lampson's **access matrix** (Lampson, 1974) for large distributed systems. The access matrix is unsuitable for specifying policy in large distributed systems because it assumes global knowledge of the objects in the system, and specifies policy in terms of individual objects rather than groups. Access rules overcome these problems by being localized and by specifying policy in terms of sets of objects, using management domains.

An access rule object, as introduced in Chapter 16, has the attributes **subject domain**, **target domain**, **operation set** and **constraints**. It can be seen that this corresponds exactly to a policy object whose modality is positive authorization, in which the policy subjects and target objects are the objects in the subject and target domains, and the policy goals are the operation set.

Both subject and target domains can be the names of domains or more general domain expressions. The operation set defines the names of the operations, defined in the object's interface, which the access rule authorizes. There is no assumption that one operation "implies" another, for example "Write" permission implying "Read" permission. The constraints limit the applicability of the access rule.

The system authorizes a request if an access rule that matches the operation request exists. An access rule matches an operation request if the subject[3] attempting the operation is in the subject domain of the rule, the target object is in the target domain of the rule, the operation name is in the operation set of the rule, and the conditions specified in the constraints are met. See Figure 17.4. If no access rule that applies to the operation request exists, then authority for the operation does not exist and access is denied.

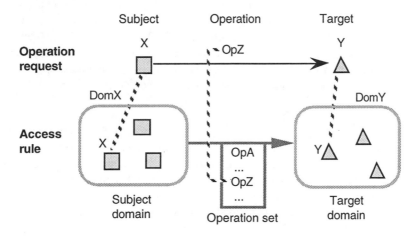

Figure 17.4 An operation request and a matching access rule.

It is possible that there are overlapping access rules – more than one access rule satisfies the requirement. No conceptual difficulty arises from this, as it indicates that authority has been granted via more than one route, but there may be practical difficulties when attempting to remove a subject's access rights; these are discussed in Section 17.2.3, below.

There is a need to modify access rules dynamically during the life of the system. We model this by treating access rules themselves as objects which are instances of an access rule type. Access permissions are given and removed by creating, destroying and modifying access rule objects. The need to control the granting and removal of permissions is achieved by imposing rules for the creation, destruction and modification of access rule objects. This is discussed in Section 17.3, Delegation of authority.

Domain expressions

The purpose of the Subject and Target Domain fields of an access rule is to enable the specification of sets of objects to which it applies. Domains and subdomains are a powerful means of doing this, but are limited in what they can achieve. Therefore the Subject and Target Domain fields are specified in terms of domain expressions which allow either a single domain name, or a more complicated expression, to be specified, in particular the standard operators on sets, **Set Difference** and **Set Intersection**.

---

[3]   We assume that the system has authenticated the identity of the user.

If domain DomA contains DomB and DomC, then an access rule applying to DomA applies to the union of the members of DomB and DomC. However, it provides no means of expressing other basic set operations such as Set Difference and Set Intersection. Set Difference can express groups of objects such as "all subjects in Payroll Dept. except the Payroll Clerks", and "all files in Payroll_Files except Payroll_Master". Set Intersection can express groups such as "all files that are in Payroll_Files and also in Personal_Data".

Domain manipulation operations could be used to create a new domain with the required membership, but in order to ensure that set operations in access rules are always evaluated at the time the rule is checked, Set Difference and Set Intersection operators are allowed in domain expressions. There is also a notation which allows the specification in a domain expression that the access rule should apply only to direct members, and not to members of subdomains also, which is the normal case.

Constraints in access rules

The constraints in an access rule permit its applicability to be limited in terms of time of day, date, and location of user. For example, it is quite common in many organizations to permit access to various objects only during normal office hours or to set up an access rule that expires after some time or only becomes valid in the future. Access to some resources may only be permitted for a particular group of terminals; for example, access to Accounts Payable data may be permitted only from the terminals in the Payments Office of an organization.

We assume that the Reference Monitor has available information about the user's environment (date and time of request, and location of user), and the parameters of the operation.

Logging switch in access rules

A Security Audit Facility requires logging of both authorized and unauthorized operation requests. It is assumed that the Reference Monitor will provide it on all unauthorized operations, but there may also be a selective need for information on authorized operations also. For example, all changes to access rules performed by a security administrator should be logged. One means of controlling this would be by a logging switch in access rules, which could be turned On in order to trigger the Reference Monitor to provide the Security Audit Facility with input. Adequate controls are required to prevent unauthorized switching Off.

17.2.2   Example of access rules

We use as an example the Payroll Department of an organization. It consists of roles for people, and a directory of payroll files; see Figure 17.5. We assume that the Payroll Manager (viewed as being outside the department he runs and not shown in the figure) can create whatever access rules he wishes.

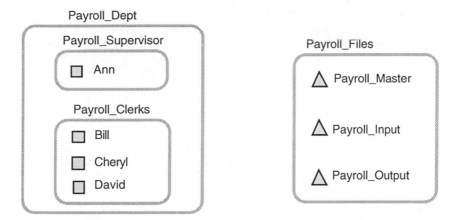

Figure 17.5 Domain structure of the payroll department.

The Payroll Manager may not know or understand the names of the files in the Payroll_Files domain or the names of the files that will be added to it in future. However, he has delegated to the Payroll Supervisor the task of maintaining the files, so an expression of this delegation policy is to give the Payroll Supervisor the ability to Create, Read and Write files in that domain. His policy is also to allow the whole Payroll Department to Read the Payroll_Files. These policies are expressed by the two access rules illustrated in Figure 17.6.

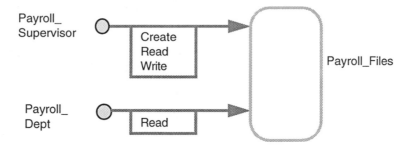

Figure 17.6 Example access rules.

The access rules do not name the subject or target objects, so we cannot tell directly from them whether access by a particular subject to a particular target will be allowed. To interpret the access rule we have to know the domain structure, as shown in Figure 17.5, in order to identify the subjects and target objects to which it applies.

17.2.3   Removal of access

The prompt removal of access authority when necessary is an essential aspect of access control. There are a number of methods of achieving this:

i)   It is simple to express the exclusion of a particular subject from accessing a target domain at the time an access rule is set up by means of a domain expression such as (Subjects_X – Subjects_Y), which excludes members of Subjects_Y from access which they would have been permitted as members of Subjects_X. Note, however, that this will not override another access rule which allows members of domain Subjects_Y to have access. Similarly, a Target domain expression may specify (Files_X – Files_Y).

ii) Negative rights, which override any positive rights, have been used in some systems as a means of rapidly and selectively revoking access to sensitive objects (Satyanarayanan, 1989). This greatly complicates the semantics of an access control system and can introduce inherent contradictions (Tygar and Wing, 1987). We therefore conclude that they should not be introduced into our model and so we only permit positive authorization.

iii) Destruction or modification of an access rule will not prevent access if there is another remaining rule that permits access. Determining which access rules permit access can be complicated because typically the subject or target object is a member of several domains which are subdomains of those specified in access rules. Tools and reporting facilities are therefore needed to permit a security administrator to determine what target domains a subject can access and what subjects can access a particular target domain. The use of these tools would be adequate for routine removal of access rules, but searching a large system for relevant access rules may be rather slow.

iv) Denying access to an individual subject in an emergency should be performed not by alteration of access rules but by suspension or deregistration of the subject. It is instant and effective and does not add complications to the system.

There are thus a number of different strategies that can be applied, depending on the circumstances.

17.2.4   Implementation issues

The above section has described access rules as a means of specifying access control policy. This is the user view of security policy, which must then be reflected in an underlying implementation that makes use of access control mechanisms to implement the policy.

The main implementation issues are:

- Granularity of access rules – what is the finest level of granularity at which a user can specify domain expressions?

- How to store access rules – should they be associated with the subjects, target objects or independent of both?

- How to implement the reference monitor in a distributed system?

- How to translate from the user view (access rule) to the implementation mechanism being used?

Mechanism requirements

It is essential that the underlying implementation should make access control decisions which are consistent with the user view of domain-based access rules. When an access rule is created, modified or destroyed, the effect of the change must be reflected in access control decisions. It may be permissible in some circumstances for the effect to be delayed (for example, until the following day, in the case of non-urgent changes), but this must be predictable. In addition, when an object is included in or removed from a domain, or a new object is created, the object's access authorizations (either as subject or target) which derive from membership of the domain must change accordingly.

The performance cost introduced for validation of authorized operation requests must be minimal if the system is not to degrade. The overhead in updating access authorizations must be tolerable for domain membership changes. It is thought that the contents of subject domains will change relatively infrequently compared to those of target domains which contain objects such as temporary files. Changing access control policy by updating access rules, or obtaining status reports, will be relatively infrequent and does not always have to take immediate effect, so higher overheads can be tolerated.

Granularity of access rules

The finer-grained the unit of specification of objects in access rules, the more detailed the access control policy can be, but the greater the problem of implementing the mechanism with acceptable performance. The two main options, both for subjects and for target objects, is to set the finest grain either at a domain or at individual objects. The Andrew project (Satyanarayanan, 1989) allows individual subjects, as well as domains, to be specified in their Access Control Lists (ACLs), but the finest granularity for the ACLs of file objects is the Directory. The problem can be simplified by representing individual human users by a specialized domain, a User Representation Domain (URD), as described in Chapter 16.

Reference monitor implementation

When considering implementation issues it is useful to refine the reference monitor into two components – an Access Control Decision Facility (ADF) and an Access Control Enforcement Facility (AEF). The ADF compares an operation request against the current access control policies and makes a decision on whether the request is to be accepted or rejected. The AEF enforces the decision made by the ADF, and we view its job as ensuring that no operation message reaches the target object unless it has been authorized by the ADF. We therefore assume that the AEF is closely associated with the target object, certainly by being in the same physical machine, and possibly by acting as a front end to the object.

This is superficially similar to the OSI Access Control Framework (ISO 10181-3, 1991). It should be noted, however, that the OSI Access Control Framework is restricted in its scope; it covers only the framework for access control *enforcement*, and not for specification of access control policy.

The ADF and access rules can be implemented as an independent authorization service, or held with the subjects or target objects.

*   *Authorization service:* An access rules database can be independent of both subject and target objects as part of an authorization service. It would have to be based on a distributed database and distributed authorization servers. There is therefore a potentially heavy performance penalty associated with it.

*   *Access rules held with subjects*: Access rules can be held as attributes of subject domain objects. The access rules (and ADFs) would thus be distributed to reflect the distribution of the subject domains and the ADF could be co-located with the domain and generate capabilities to be checked at the target object's node. The problem with holding access rules with the subject domains is that they may exist in personal workstations which cannot be trusted, and their security is therefore difficult to enforce. In addition, access rules are more likely to be generated by security administrators in the organization of a target domain rather than a subject domain.

*   *Access Control Lists (ACLs) with target domains*: An alternative approach is to hold access rules as ACLs which are attributes of the target domains. The security of the access rules can then be commensurate with the security of the objects they are protecting. Target objects are more likely to be based on servers, under the control of system managers rather than ordinary users, and their domains and access rules can be held on more secure systems.

The target object and its domain may be on different computers. If an access control decision takes place only when a session is established between a subject and target object, then the overheads of a remote access by the AEF to the ADF co-located with the target's domain would be acceptable. However, if access checking is required on every operation invocation then remote access to the ADF would be unacceptable and every target would have to hold its own ACL.

The disadvantage of a pure ACL approach is that it can lead to a breach of security in systems with nested operations. If a server object has to invoke operations on other objects on behalf of a subject it usually adopts the identity of the subject in order to obtain subject-specific authorization for the operation. It has been pointed out by Vinter (1988) (among others) that this breaches the "least privilege principle" as the server can now perform all the operations authorized for the subject, and not only the one that was requested. This only works when servers are trusted, which may not be the case if the server belongs to another organization on a remote network.

17.2.5   Domino implementation approach

The Domino project (Law *et al.*, 1990) uses the third approach, an implementation based on ACLs stored with domain objects (Twidle and Sloman, 1988). The testbed is the Conic toolkit for building distributed systems (Magee *et al.*, 1989). The access control decision is made when an interface of one object is bound to the interface of another. Each object holds information on the domains of which it is a member. When a binding takes place the list of parent domains of the subject is passed in the binding request sent to the domain of the target object. It searches its ACL for a matching rule. If none is found there will be a search upwards through the domain structure for an entry in a parent domain's ACL that will authorize the request.

User and mechanism views of access rules

The distinction between the view of the user managing a system and the underlying mechanism(s) used within the system for implementing this view was introduced in Chapter 16.

Table 17.1 User and mechanism views of access rules.

User View		Mechanism View
Access rule object	<-------->	ACLs attached to target domains
Subject domain (name-based domain expression) Object set Constraints	<-------->	Combined to form an ACL entry which is an attribute of every domain affected by the target domain expression
Target domain (name based domain expression)	<-------->	Every domain affected by the target domain expression holds an ACL entry.

In Domino the user view of access rules is an access rule object, while the mechanism view uses ACLs as described above. The relationships between the user and mechanism views of access rules are illustrated in Table 17.1. Both views are implemented; the user, typically a security administrator, specifies policy by creating and destroying access rule objects, and the system alters the ACLs to reflect these policy decisions.

There is clearly a problem of ensuring consistency between the two views of access rules. Ideally, at the design stage, we should have taken our formal specification of the user view (Moffett, 1991) and either refined it to the mechanism view while ensuring the preservation of properties, or created a formal specification of the mechanism view and proved that the properties were preserved. However, in the absence of tools to support these activities we have opted for an informal design of the mechanism view.

There is also a problem of ensuring consistency between views during operation, as the two views can become inconsistent through system errors and failures. Consistency checking and restoration tools are being implemented in order to diagnose and recover from any inconsistencies.

17.3   Delegation of authority

The model for delegation of authority must reflect the organizational management structure and policy as well as provide mechanisms for the transfer of authority from one agent to another. A resource owner should be able to delegate authority over his resources to another subject, within the mandatory constraints of the system. In addition it must be possible to delegate *the authority to delegate,* but limit the scope of this second-level delegation. For example, an owner of an organization should be able to delegate authority to a security administrator to give subjects access to objects in a defined part of it. Finally, the model should permit subjects to have personal domains where they can control the objects they create.

17.3.1   Management roles

A number of management concepts underlie our approach to authority and its delegation.

Ownership

It is assumed that humans are ultimately responsible for the actions of the system. In many situations they will use automated agents to perform operations within the system, but they will retain responsibility for the actions of the agents, and therefore require the power to control the agents. Thus we will always be able to trace responsibility back to human users, who we call the **owners** of the system (for example, managing director of a company or board of directors). Ownership in this chapter is intended to denote a concept as close as possible to normal legal ownership of goods and property. All computer systems in a country such as the UK process resources with identifiable legal owners who have legal powers over them. We regard ownership as the starting point for delegation of authority.

As a very rough approximation, ownership of an object implies the legal power to perform any feasible operation on it, together with responsibility for the operations that are performed. There are of course limitations to this power; for example, an owner of personal data may not disclose it except under the terms of data protection legislation, and the owner of petroleum spirit at a bulk distribution plant must ensure that an automated system dispensing it to tanker lorries does so in accordance with certain safety regulations. Restrictions of this kind have to be represented in computer systems as mandatory constraints, and are beyond the scope of this chapter.

Many previous authors, such as Lampson (1974), have assumed that the subject who creates an object automatically becomes its owner. We do not hold that view, but distinguish between ownership of objects and the delegated power to create them. A data processing clerk who submits a job to create a new version of a file of bank accounts is not the owner of those accounts, but is carrying out the task of creating the file as an agent of the owner of the bank.

For the purpose of discussing authority we assume that we start with an owner, who can then dispose of or share ownership or delegate a subset of his or her powers to another person. Provided that this is done legitimately we will describe this other person as having gained authority. In a computer system authority is normally represented as the ability to perform defined operations on objects through specified interfaces.

Separation of responsibilities

Separation of responsibilities is an important control concept which is familiar in the context of auditing; see, for example (Waldron, 1978). It is designed to ensure that no one has excessive authority. Clark and Wilson (1987) have pointed out that the concept should be modeled in computer systems. It requires that different aspects of certain transactions should be carried out by different users, so that no one person can carry out the transaction autonomously. An example is the authorization of payment of suppliers' invoices, where the input of invoices to a computer system must normally be carried out by a different user from the person who can trigger off the actual release of payments. Neither can carry out the other's function, so the payments cannot be made without their cooperative activity. Requirements for separation of responsibility have to be specified at an application level but support for it needs to be provided by the access control system.

This separation of authority manifests itself in the role of a security administrator, who often is responsible for granting access authority in large organizations. The security administrator should not be allowed to grant himself access to the resources under his control.

Management structures

Each organization has its own management style, which is reflected by different management structures and policies for delegation of authority. For this chapter we have identified four typical roles within an organization management structure – User, Security Administrator, Manager and Owner. Owners can share ownership with other subjects, or can delegate Manager authority. Managers can delegate authority to Security Administrators, who can create access rules which allow ordinary subjects to perform operations on target objects. Note that it is an application decision whether a subject in a management role has authority over himself, for example a Security Administrator being able to give himself access rights. We specifically allow for this case to be prevented, but we do not enforce it as part of the model.

17.3.2 Delegation of authority using management role objects

When authority is delegated, there is a need to control to whom it is delegated, the resources over which the authority applies, and how the authority can be passed on down a management chain. The existence of an access rule allowing SubjectA to create an access rule object is clearly not a sufficient control by itself. It provides no constraint on the contents of the access rule object which is created, so SubjectA would be able to create access rule objects to enable any subject to access any objects. We therefore need a means of placing controls on the contents of access rule objects.

A security administrator must be able to grant access authority which he does not possess himself, so the concepts of *having* access and *giving* access must be decoupled. Similarly owners may delegate, to managers, the authority to create security administrators. We therefore need to distinguish between the normal operations that a user can carry out, and operations that give authority.

17.3.3   Management role objects

As explained in Chapter 16, management positions can conveniently be represented by domains. However, many roles in an organization are associated with particular types and extents of authority. The concept of a management role object (MRO) extends the simple domain object in order to define the range and nature of the managerial authority of the members of a domain. Informally, it defines a type of role, which defines the nature of the authority, the subjects who occupy the role, and the scope of their authority. It is modeled as an object with three attributes:

- **Role Type**, the name of this type of role, which determines the structure of the Role Scopes attribute;

- **Role Subjects**, a domain expression defining a set of subjects who occupy the role;

- One or two **Role Scopes**, each a pair of (**authority type, domain expression**). Each domain expression defines the objects for which the role subjects have the corresponding type of authority.

In the typical management structure we are using here, there are role types of Owner, Manager and Security Administrator. The Owner and Manager role types each only have a single authority type. A Security Administrator's authority requires that the Security Administrator (SA) role type has two separate types of authority: SA Subject and SA Target, one to define the subjects and the other to define the target objects, for which he or she can make access rules. This is to achieve the separation of responsibilities for security administrators which is discussed below.

There may be multiple instances of MROs of a single type, such as a number of Managers each managing a different department. Occupation of a management role gives a subject the authority associated with that role. If a subject occupies more than one role he or she has the authority associated with each one; for example, someone may be the manager of more than one department in an organization. A subject's role in the organization changes if he or she is moved to another MRO.

We now discuss our sample management structure using MROs as the means of representation. Normal users of the system have no inherent ability at all to grant access authority, unless they are allowed to administer their own personal domains (see below).

Owner

An Owner has a set of objects (subjects and/or target objects) over which he has authority, defined by the scope of Owner authority of the role he occupies. He can give away or share ownership (create joint ownership), and delegate the Manager authority over these objects to other subjects. He does this by creating Manager MROs, with appropriate Role Subjects and scope of Manager authority. The limits of the Manager authority of an MRO that an Owner can create are set by requiring his Owner authority to be a superset of the Manager authority he is creating.

We remarked above that the creator of an object is not necessarily the owner of it. This follows automatically from our model; if a subject creates a new object in a domain, the ownership of that object, like all others in the domain, remains with the domain's owner. Indeed, the subject cannot even read the object after creation unless an access rule also allows him the Read operation.

Ownership is shared if more than one subject has Owner authority over an object. At this stage we take a simplistic view of transfer of ownership, by specifying that an Owner should be able to remove Owner authority from another Owner of the same object. This allows both for suicide and for destruction races where the first person to remove the other's ownership wins power. Further constraints on sharing and transfer of ownership will need to be considered.

Manager

A Manager similarly has a set of objects defined by the Manager authority of the role he occupies, over which he has authority. He can appoint Security Administrators and set the scope of their authority by creating SA MROs with them as Role Subjects, and appropriate scopes of SA Subject authority and SA Target authority. The limits of the SA Subject authority and SA Target authority of an MRO that a Manager can create are set by requiring his Manager authority to be a superset of the SA Subject authority and SA Target authority he is creating.

Security Administrator (SA)

A Security Administrator has two sets of objects over which he has authority, defined by the scopes of SA Subject authority and SA Target authority of the role he occupies. He can give authority to subjects to perform operations on objects by creating access rules, by virtue of his occupancy of a Security Administrator role. The limits of the access authority that a Security Administrator can create are set by requiring his SA Subject authority and SA Target authority to be supersets of the Subject Domain and Target Domain of the access rule he is creating. In our example system, no limit is placed on the operations he can permit, but a restriction of this kind could easily be added.

One of our main aims is to allow a Security Administrator to create access rules for other subjects while preventing him from giving himself access. This is done by ensuring that the membership of the Role Subjects and of the scope of the SA Subject authority of an SA MRO do not overlap. Then since the Security Administrator (an occupant of the Role Subjects of the SA MRO) cannot himself be a member of the scope of the SA Subject authority he cannot grant access authority to himself. This achieves the desired separation of responsibilities between granting access and having access.

There is of course the need for the Security Administrator himself to have access to some objects, but he cannot create the requisite access rules himself. This need is met by a second security administrator who can allocate access to the first.

We illustrate the Security Administrator's power with an example. There is a large company which employs computer security administrators (members of the SA domain) part of whose job is to set the access rules in accordance with company policy. Members of the SA domain are given the authority to make access rules relating to the subjects and files in Dept_A domain. They are given similar authority for Dept_B domain. Their powers are illustrated in Figure 17.7. Note that they are *not* authorized to make access rules that allow subjects in Dept_A to access files in Dept_B, or vice versa. SA is a member of Dept_C, and therefore its members cannot make access rules to give themselves access.

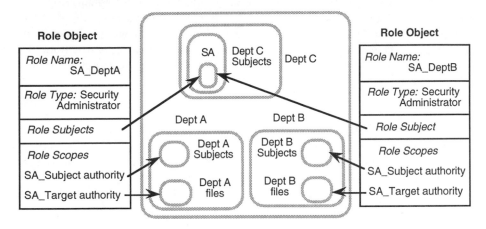

Figure 17.7 Security administrator roles for departments A and B.

Personal domains

A registered user of the system will have extensive control over a personal domain.. This can be done within this model by making each user a Security Administrator for his or her personal domain, typically with the ability to share access to that personal domain with anyone in the organization. An MRO is created for each user, with the user as sole Role Subject, SA Subject authority over all users, and SA Target authority over the personal domain. This achieves the objective, as illustrated in Figure 17.8.

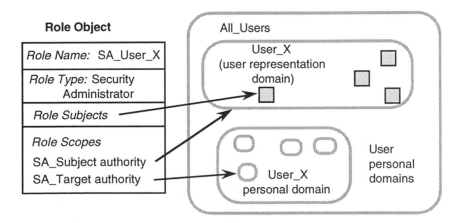

Figure 17.8 A subject acting as security administrator for his or her personal domain.

17.4 Summary

This chapter has shown how general distributed system management policies may be modeled, using discretionary access control as the main example.

Management policies are used to define the aims of an organization and to allocate the resources that are needed. They need to be modeled as objects, in order to enable the system to give support to the managers who implement them, with the aim of automating the activity where this is possible and beneficial. It is then possible to explore the relationships between policies in, for example, policy hierarchies and policy conflicts.

Discretionary access control policies, modeled as access rules, were taken as a well-developed example. Their use for security administration was illustrated. Delegation of authority was introduced as the means by which access rule administration can be carried out in a controlled manner. The downwards flow of authority from Owners through Managers to Security Administrators in a typical organization, ensuring the separation of powers for Security Administrators, was explained.

Abbreviations

ACL	Access Control Lists
ADF	Access Control Decision Facility
AEF	Access Control Enforcement Facility
MRO	Management Role Objects
SA	Security Administrator
URD	User Representation Domain

References

Alchourron C.E. (1991). Philosophical foundations of deontic logic and its practical applications in computational contexts, *Proc. First Int.Workshop on Deontic Logic in Computer Science (DEON'91)*, Amsterdam, The Netherlands, 11–13 December

Anderson J.P. (1972). *Computer Security Technology Planning Study*, ESD-TR-73-51 vol. 1, AD-758 206, ESD/AFSC Hanscom, AFB Bedford, Mass, October

Bedford-Roberts J. (1991). Concepts from Pythagoras. *Report HPL-91-22*, February, Hewlett-Packard Laboratories, Bristol, UK

Clark D.C. and Wilson D.R. (1987). A comparison of commercial and military computer security policies, *Proc. IEEE Security and Privacy Symposium*, 184–94

DoD (1985). *Department of Defense Trusted Computer System, Evaluation Criteria*, Department of Defense (USA) document DOD 5200.78 – STD, December

ISO 10181-3 (1991). *ISO Security Framework 3: Access Control.* ISO/IEC JTC1/SC21

Kanger S. (1972). Law and logic. *Theoria*, **38**, 105–32

Lampson B.W. (1974). Protection. *ACM Operating System Review*, **8**(1). 18–24

Law A.D., Sloman M.S. and Moffett J.D. (1990). The "Domino" Project. *Proc. Data Management '90 Conference*, Egham, UK, 2–3 April 1990, BCS Data Management Specialist Group, 143–54

Magee J., Kramer J. and Sloman M.S. (1989). Constructing distributed systems in Conic, *IEEE Transactions on Software Engineering*, **15**(6), 563–75

Moffett J.D., Sloman M.S. and Twidle K.P. (1990). Specifying discretionary access control policy for distributed systems, *Computer Communications*, **13**(9). 571–80

Moffett J.D. and Sloman M.S. (1991) Delegation of authority. In *Integrated Network Management II*. (Krishnan I. and Zimmer W., eds.), 595–606, North Holland

Moffett J.D. (1991). *Delegation of Authority for Access – A Formal Model.* Domino paper A2/IC/4.1 (revised May 1991), Dept. of Computing, Imperial College, London SW7 2BZ

Satyanarayanan M. (1989). Integrating security in a large distributed system, *ACM Transactions on Computer Systems*, **7**(3), 247–80

Twidle K. and Sloman M.S. (1988). Domain based configuration and name management, for distributed systems, *Proc. IEEE First Workshop on Future Trends in Distributed Computing Systems*, Hong Kong, September, 147–53

Tygar, J.D. and Wing J.M. (1987). Visual specification of security constraints, *Proc. IEEE Workshop on Visual Languages*, Linkoping, Sweden, August, 288–301

Vinter S.T. (1988). Extended discretionary access controls, *Proc. IEEE Symposium on Security and Privacy*, April 1988, Oakland, CA, IEEE Computer Society Press, 39–49

Waldron R.S. (1978). *Practical Auditing*, London: HFL (Publishers) Ltd.

Part VI

Implementing Management

Chapter 18

Configuration of Distributed Systems

Jeff Magee

Imperial College of Science Technology and Medicine,
180 Queen's Gate,
London SW7 2BZ, UK
Email: jnm@doc.ic.ac.uk

We have seen from Chapter 3 that the software of distributed systems is constructed from sets of computational components which are bound together to interact and communicate. In this chapter, we examine the nature of components and the techniques and tools available for constructing distributed applications from components. We term the activity that is concerned with system structure *configuration*. We are concerned both with the initial construction of systems – *static configuration* – and their subsequent modification. Modification is necessary to accommodate both operational and evolutionary changes. Operational changes are generally concerned with the reorganization of a system as a result of redimensioning or to accommodate failures. Evolutionary changes are those brought about by a change in requirements for the system or in the technology used to implement the system (Kramer and Magee, 1985). In both operational and evolutionary change, it is usually the case that it is uneconomic or unsafe to stop an entire distributed application or system to update part of it. Consequently, change must be performed dynamically on the running system. We term this activity of modifying a system on-line – *dynamic configuration* – since as outlined in the following, change can be accommodated by structural modification to the system. That is, by the replacement, addition and reconnection of components.

18.1 Components

We use the term component to refer to part of the software of a distributed system. A component *type* is the program code which is executed by a component *instance*.

Many instances may be created from a particular component type in the same way that many variables of a particular data type may be declared in a programming language. A component encapsulates a number of *services*[1] which it provides to other components of the distributed system. In order to implement these services, a component may require the services provided by other components (Figure 18.1). Access to the services provided by a component is achieved in a distributed system by a message passing protocol such as remote procedure call protocol (RPC). We could equally well use the term object instead of component, since components in general encapsulate data and provide operations to examine and update that data. However, in the interests of clarity, we choose not to further overload the meaning of this much-used term.

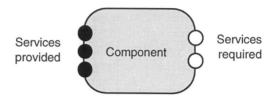

Figure 18.1 A software component.

In the following, we will see how components can be composed hierarchically from primitive components; however, at this point we are concerned with the primitive components defined in a programming language that implement the functionality of the distributed system. Primitive components may be configured by passing them initialization parameters; however, in the following we are associating the term configuration with system structure rather than parameter setting. Primitive components may have more than one thread of control (or lightweight process); however, they are located at one network node of the distributed system. Component instances may correspond at the implementation level to either heavyweight operating system processes or objects within those processes. For example, we would consider ANSA (ANSAWare, 1991) objects to be components which are then encapsulated by an operating system process termed a capsule. In our terminology, this capsule is considered to be a composite component. Similarly, in the REX system (Magee *et al.*, 1990), components correspond to lightweight processes and many REX components may be configured to form a heavyweight process – again termed a capsule.

18.2   Client-server systems

The simplest and perhaps most typical configuration of a distributed system is the client-server system in which some components only use or require the services

---

[1]   More precisely, these are service access points since a distributed service may be provided by a set of components and thus a set of service access points. In the interests of brevity, in the following, service and service access point are taken to be synonymous.

provided by components termed servers. Figure 18.2 gives the configuration of a simple mail system in which the *user* client components access a *mailserver* component to send and receive mail messages. How are the mail services required by the user components bound to the services provided by the mail server component? In the simplest case, the network address of the mail server is programmed into the user components. More typically, the user components at start-up time will look up the address[2] of the mail server using a distinguished component known as a **nameserver.** The nameserver provides a name-to-address translation service. The address of the nameserver component is well known. The mailserver component in this case would register its services with the nameserver at start-up time. ANSA allows services to be located by attribute as well as by simple name lookup. For example, one could ask for the address of the nearest printer service.

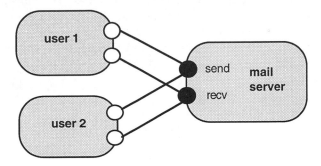

Figure 18.2 Client-server mail system.

Using a nameserver, only the name of the service required needs to be programmed into a client component. This renders component code much more portable than if it were hardwired with network addresses. However, embedding the name of services required in component code reduces the portability and reusability of components. It is advantageous for both portability and testing purposes if components can be programmed without requiring knowledge of the external service namespace. We term components that contain no knowledge of their binding to the external environment *context independent.* To achieve context independence, a component internally refers to services required by purely local names. These local names are replaced by the actual service name/address when the component is executed. Different substitutions can be made for different environments. Component parameterization is an obvious mechanism for allowing substitution. However, as we will see in the following there is a requirement to resubstitute service names during the lifetime of a component to facilitate reconfiguration.

Problems with the client-server approach arise when the systems we wish to construct have a more complex interconnection structure than the simple many-to-one interconnection pattern that the approach directly supports; in particular, where the distributed program is more sensibly viewed as a set of agents with peer-to-peer

---

2   Or more generally a location-independent reference which can be translated to an address.

connections. An example is the way applications may be constructed under UNIX from a pipeline of filter processes. Although all reasonable systems allow servers to be the client for other services, the interconnection process becomes tortuous. It is the author's view that as distributed systems mature and become more complex, and as servers themselves are realized by distributed multi-agent programs, this problem will become more acute.

18.3   Static configuration:

The configuration approach to constructing distributed systems explicitly separates the structure of a system from its constituent computational components (Magee *et al.*, 1989; Barbacci *et al.*, 1993; Hofmeister *et al.*, 1993). Components declare explicitly both the services they provide and the services they require. A configuration language is used to describe how the system is constructed from these components in terms of component instances and bindings between services required and services provided. Figure 18.3 is the configuration description of the client-server mail system of Figure 18.2.

```
component user(char *name) {
    require send, recv;
}
component mailserver {
    provide send, recv;
}
component mailsystem {
    inst
        user1:user("morris");
        user2:user("jeff");
        server:mailserver;
    bind
        user1.send -- server.send;
        user1.recv -- server.recv;
        user2.send -- server.send;
        user2.recv -- server.recv;
}
```

Figure 18.3   Configuration description of mail system.

The component descriptions for *user* and *mailserver* are merely templates that describe the interface to these components. The implementation of the component is in a conventional programming language such as C or C++. The *mailsystem* consists of the two instances *user1* and *user2* of the component type *user* and the single instance *server* of the component type *mailserver*. Components may be parameterized as in the example where components of type *user* are parameterized with the user name. The system interconnectivity is specified by the ***bind*** statement which describes the required substitution of externally provided services for locally required ones. It should be noted that while the local (required) name is the same as the external (provided) name in the example, this does not have to be so. The binding statement checks that when required services are bound to provided services they are compatible with respect to information type and invocation mechanism. The names may of course be different.

A configuration description such as that of Figure 18.3 is used to initially construct a distributed program or system. In some situations it is necessary to specify the physical location of components of the system. This mapping information can be added to a configuration language program by annotation. For example, Figure 18.4 shows an annotated form of the mail system of Figure 18.3. It specifies that instances *user1* and *server* should be located at the Internet node skid.doc.ic.ac.uk and that *user2* should be located at alfred.doc.ic.ac.uk.

```
component mailsystem {
    inst
        user1:user("morris") @ "skid.doc.ic.ac.uk" ;
        user2:user("jeff")   @ "alfred.doc.ic.ac.uk";
        server:mailserver    @ "skid.doc.ic.ac.uk";
    bind
        user1.send -- server.send
        user1.recv -- server.recv;
        user2.send -- server.send;
        user2.recv -- server.recv;
}
```

Figure 18.4 Annotated configuration description of mail system.

Using specific locations as in Figure 18.4 restricts the generality of configuration descriptions. Locations can also be specified using logical location identifiers. The correspondence of these with actual physical locations can be determined at system initialization time.

The example of Figures 18.3 and 18.4 are not the most appropriate use of a separate configuration language description since they depict a simple client-server system. Figure 18.5 depicts a pipeline configuration of filter processes together with its associated configuration description. This sort of configuration in which each component acts as both a client and a server is cumbersome to construct using the nameserver approach described in Section 18.2. The example uses an instance array of filter processes. The dimensionality of the array is predeclared by the **array** statement before individual members of the array are instantiated. It should be noted that the pipeline is itself a component which may be used in the construction of systems in the same way as primitive components. Components that are constructed from primitive components are termed *composite* components. In the configuration language we have outlined here, they have the same format for interface declaration and are used in exactly the same way as primitive components. This allows the flexibility of substituting a composite component for a primitive component (and vice versa) during design and development.

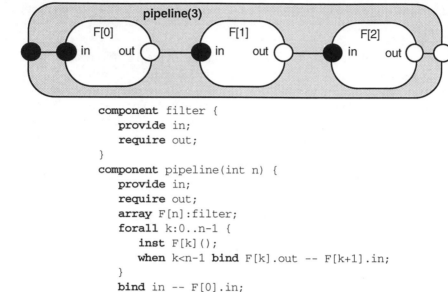

```
component filter {
    provide in;
    require out;
}
component pipeline(int n) {
    provide in;
    require out;
    array F[n]:filter;
    forall k:0..n-1 {
        inst F[k]();
        when k<n-1 bind F[k].out -- F[k+1].in;
    }
    bind in -- F[0].in;
        F[n-1].out -- out;
}
```

Figure 18.5 Configuration description of pipeline.

```
component pipeline(int n) {
    provide in;
    require out;
    when n=0 bind in -- out;
    when n>0 {
        inst head:filter;
        inst tail:pipeline(n-1);
        bind in -- head.in;
            head.out -- tail.in;
            tail.out -- out;
    }
}
```

Figure 18.6 Recursive configuration description of pipeline.

The example of Figure 18.5 illustrates the use of the conditional configuration clause **when.** In addition to allowing arrays of instances to be declared and sets of bindings on those instances to be effected using the **forall** construct, recursive configurations can be defined. Figure 18.6 gives a recursive definition of the pipeline of filters configuration. Allowing recursion permits tree-structured components and systems to be elegantly and efficiently described.

For completeness, Figure 18.7 gives a C++ implementation that satisfies the template description of the primitive *filter* component used in Figures 18.5 and 18.6. The *filter* process accepts event messages from *in* and sends them to its port reference variable *out*. The process deletes duplicates of the first event it receives. Note that *out* is a placeholder for the reference to the next filter component. This is provided when the configuration program is instantiated. *Filter* is declared as a subclass of the class *process*. *Process* implements a lightweight thread mechanism. The generic classes *port* and *portref* provide the communication methods *accept* and *send* respectively. This implementation is taken from the Regis development environment (Magee *et al.*, 1994) for distributed and parallel programming. However, components may be implemented with equal facility using the communication mechanisms provided by distributed systems platforms such as ANSAWare (1991).

```
class filter: public process {
public:
  port <Event> in;
  portref <Event> out;
  filter();
}
filter::filter(){
  Event first, tmp;
  in.accept(first);
  for(;;) {
      in.accept(tmp);
      if (tmp!=first) out.send(tmp);
  }
}
```

Figure 18.7 C++ implementation of filter component.

This section has concentrated on the initial configuration of distributed and parallel systems using a configuration language. The structure of a system is determined from the configuration description and the parameters passed to it at instantiation/initialization time. Subsequently, the structure is fixed or static.

18.4   Dynamic configuration – programmed change

In the introduction it was observed that the configuration of a distributed system does not remain static but changes as a result of operational and evolutionary requirements. In this section, we examine the techniques and tools necessary to support the dynamic configuration which results from operational change. The requirement to change for operational reasons can be programmed into a system since this requirement for operational change is present at the time the system is designed. Evolutionary changes by their nature cannot be foreseen by the designers of a system.

Figure 18.8 depicts the software components for a patient-monitoring system in the intensive care ward of a hospital. Each patient component runs on a workstation located by a patient's bed and monitors the patient via attached sensors. Periodically, the component records readings of the various factors measured (blood pressure, pulse rate and temperature) by sending them to a logger component. If the readings exceed a limit the patient component sends an alarm to the nurse component.

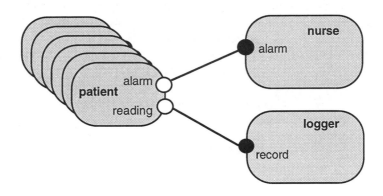

Figure 18.8 Patient-monitoring system.

18.4.1   Dynamic component instantiation

The number of patients resident in the intensive care ward will vary over time. One way of organizing the structure of the system is to create a new *patient* component instance when a new patient enters the ward and to remove it when the patient leaves. This can be described in the configuration language as shown in the configuration description of the patient-monitoring system in Figure 18.9. The operation to create a new patient component is invoked by the nurse component through the binding (N.newpatient -- **dyn** patient). This operation passes initialization parameters to the new patient instance. Note that bindings for the patient type are specified rather than for a patient instance. These type-specific bindings will be made for each patient instance created by the nurse. A patient instance is removed whenever it terminates.

Using type-specific bindings, the environment for dynamically created instances of that type can be described. The implementation of dynamically created components does not have to be concerned with making bindings to the services it requires to function correctly. This connection to the environment is described in the configuration language. Type-specific bindings have been introduced here in connection with dynamic component creation. However, they may also be used in combination with the normal static instance declaration. In this situation, they act as default bindings for a type. They may be overridden by a binding declared for a specific instance of that type.

```
component nurse
    { provide alarm; require newpatient; }
component logger
    { provide record; }
component patient(string name)
    { require alarm, reading; }

component ward {
    inst
        N:nurse;
        L:logger;
    bind                                // type-specific bindings
        patient.alarm -- N.alarm;
        patient.reading -- L.record;
    bind
        N.newpatient -- dyn patient;
}
```

Figure 18.9 Dynamically configured patient-monitoring system.

18.4.2 Lazy instantiation

In some circumstances, we may wish a component to be created dynamically only whenever the service it provides is to be used. However, we do not wish clients to be concerned with explicitly creating the service. We term this lazy instantiation. Figure 18.10 shows a lazily instantiated version of the mail system of Figures 18.3 and 18.4 in which the server component is only created when one of the users first tries to send or receive a mail message.

```
component mailsystem {
    inst
        user1:user("morris")   @ "skid.doc.ic.ac.uk" ;
        user2:user("jeff")     @ "alfred.doc.ic.ac.uk";
        dyn server:mailserver  @ "skid.doc.ic.ac.uk";
    bind
        user1.send -- server.send;
        user1.recv -- server.recv;
        user2.send -- server.send;
        user2.recv -- server.recv;
}
```

Figure 18.10 Lazily instantiated mail server.

The keyword **dyn** indicates that the instance server is not to be created at system start-up time, but only when one of its services is used. After the mailserver is instantiated, communication proceeds normally until the mailserver finds itself idle (that is, no stored messages) at which point it may terminate and allow the release of any resources it is holding. The server can be recreated by the next attempt to use it. Lazy instantiation may also be combined with recursion to permit the description of potentially infinite structures.

18.5   Dynamic configuration – evolutionary change

The configuration descriptions in the foregoing for both static and dynamic systems are essentially declarative. They describe the structure (or potential structure) of the desired system. As such, even for dynamic systems with programmed change, the configuration language description of the system is a static object which does not need to change, as the system executes, in order to maintain a descriptive relationship with that system. However, if we wish to perform changes to an executing system that were not programmed into that system, this situation no longer holds. The configuration description must be modified to reflect the modified system. The configuration description becomes a database describing the current structure of the distributed system. The configuration language description of a system is used to compute the initial state of the database. Subsequently, configuration operations must be applied in the context of this database both to change its contents and to change the executing distributed system itself. Figure 18.11 depicts this scheme.

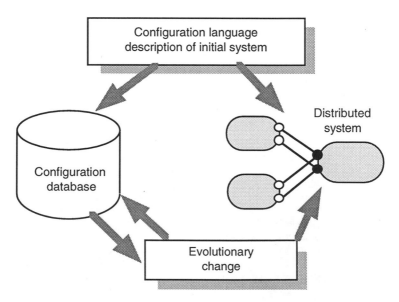

Figure 18.11 Configuration database for evolutionary change.

Change operations

Change operations describe the change we wish to make to the system that is currently executing. They may be specified in an extended form of the configuration language we have used previously. In particular, we need to add statements to remove instances and to remove bindings. The extra statements are:

```
remove instA;
replace instA : newtypeA;  // maintains instA bindings while
                           // replacing implementation.
unbind instA.X;
rebind instA.X -- instB.Y;  // equivalent to unbind..; bind... ;
```

Since a sequence of change operations may be applied over time to a system, a change operation must be specified in the context of the configuration database, *not* in the context of the initial configuration language description. The instance names and bindings formed by the original description might no longer exist in the actual system or the configuration database. This context may be found using a graphical interface to the configuration database such as ConicDraw (Kramer *et al*., 1989) or by a textual path expression of the form `instA/instB/...` which uniquely identifies the composite component instance within which the change is to be applied. Pattern matching and database search procedures are helpful in specifying changes that apply to more than one component instance or that need to find the instance to which the change applies (for example, modify all instances of type X). Prolog has been used in (Young and Magee, 1992) to implement both a configuration database and queries on that database.

A management system that supports evolutionary change must ensure that change is performed in a safe manner that results in a consistent state of the modified system. As discussed in (Kramer and Magee, 1990), it is unlikely that this consistency can be preserved without support from the application programs that form the base-level components. The conclusion is that the capability for evolution must be built into systems – it cannot simply be added as a management facility to an existing distributed system. As a simple example, consider a change that replaces a printer server implementation. We would not wish to replace the server in the middle of printing a file. It would be more satisfactory if the server indicated to the management system that it was quiescent (that is, not printing a file) and that it could thus be reconfigured safely without losing information.

For practical reasons of implementation and efficiency, it is necessary to choose an appropriate level of the system to which evolutionary change can be applied. For example, it is unlikely that we would wish to modify distributed programs at the level of an individual thread. The granularity at which we want to allow evolutionary change affects the design and implementation of the configuration database in addition to the mechanisms required to effect change in the distributed system support platform. For example, the Conic distributed system chose to accommodate evolutionary change at the level of a logical node. Logical nodes corresponded to a heavyweight process (cf. UNIX process). It was felt that the individual threads from which a logical node was composed were too tightly coupled to allow or warrant the overhead of evolutionary change. Another factor in determining what is subject to evolutionary change is the difficulty of allowing evolutionary change to coexist with operational changes. For example, if operational changes require rapid and frequent component creation and deletion, the inclusion of mechanisms to permit evolutionary change may degrade performance.

18.6   Configuration and open systems

In the foregoing, we have examined an approach to both the static and the dynamic configuration of distributed systems. We do not suggest that this configuration approach be used to structure the entire distributed open systems environment, but more reasonably, that it is a tool for controlling complexity in the initial construction and subsequent evolution of a system within a particular management domain. A system, even though subject to configuration management, must have the ability to interact with external entities. We must permit services provided by the system to be published into the external namespace and services required to be located in the external environment. The configuration notation used in the previous sections is simply extended to allow the description of these external interactions. For example, Figure 18.12 depicts a simple system which requires access to an external fileserver.

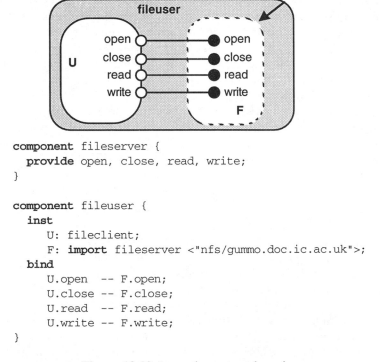

```
component fileserver {
  provide open, close, read, write;
}

component fileuser {
  inst
    U: fileclient;
    F: import fileserver <"nfs/gummo.doc.ic.ac.uk">;
  bind
    U.open  -- F.open;
    U.close -- F.close;
    U.read  -- F.read;
    U.write -- F.write;
}
```

Figure 18.12 Importing external services.

The instance *F* of Figure 18.12 is declared as being *import*. This indicates that the instance is not created locally but is located in the external namespace using the associated string name. The instance *F* is used to refer to the interface of an external service. We have used a simple Internet-style string name in the example. In general, this string name will consist of both a name identifying the context in which the required interface is to be located (for example, a domain name) and the name of the interface itself. Location can be performed dynamically by using the dynamic configuration facilities described in Section 18.4. In a similar way, a configured system can export services – Figure 18.13. In this case, the instance X is the exported interface of type *fileserver*.

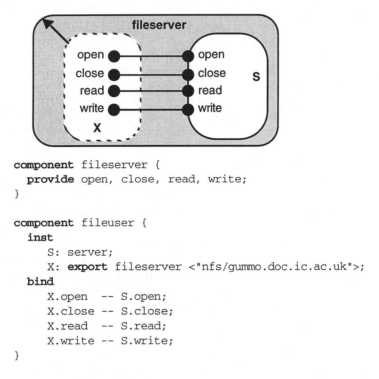

```
component fileserver {
  provide open, close, read, write;
}

component fileuser {
  inst
      S: server;
      X: export fileserver <"nfs/gummo.doc.ic.ac.uk">;
  bind
      X.open  -- S.open;
      X.close -- S.close;
      X.read  -- S.read;
      X.write -- S.write;
}
```

Figure 18.13 Exporting external services.

In this case, the instance *S* provides the *server* implementation, and an interface of type *fileserver* is exported into the external namespace with the associated string name. Typically, *export* will register the interface and associated name with a name-server such as the ANSA Trader and *import* locates the name using that nameserver. Figure 18.14 summarizes our view of how systems subject to configuration management fit into the open systems environment.

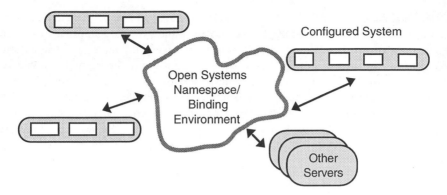

Figure 18.14 Configuration in the open systems environment.

18.7   Conclusion

This chapter has looked at the configuration of distributed systems from a set of context-independent components. A configuration language has been used to describe a set of example configurations. The notation used in this chapter is an evolution of the configuration language Darwin (Magee *et al.*, 1993) which was developed in the REX project (Magee *et al.*, 1990). It allows the concise description of complex structures. For a given system, this structural description can be found in one place rather than scattered throughout the many programs that constitute the distributed system.

The configuration language is used to construct the initial structure of the distributed system – *static* configuration. It may also describe potential changes to that structure – *dynamic* configuration. Lastly, an extended form of the configuration notation may be used to describe evolutionary changes to the system — *change* operations. Change operations are executed in the context of a configuration database which records the current structure of the system. This database is generated from the initial configuration description.

The problems of performing evolutionary change have been mentioned in Section 18.5. While there are some academic results that show how systems can be built to accommodate change and how much of a system is affected by a given change (Kramer and Magee, 1990), a practical and general management system that permits evolutionary change in a safe and controlled manner has yet to be demonstrated. However, this author is convinced that such a management tool will be based on a configuration approach in which a system is viewed as a hierarchic structure of connected instances of context-independent components.

References

ANSAWare. (1990). *ANSAware Release 3.0 Reference Manual,* Architecture Projects Management Ltd, Poseidon House, Castle Park, Cambridge, CB3 0RD

Barbacci M. R., Weinstock C. B., Doubleday D. L., Gardner M. J. and Lichota R. W. (1993). Durra: a structure description language for developing distributed applications, *Software Engineering Journal,* **8**(2), March, 83–94

Hofmeister C., White E. and Purtilo J. (1993). Surgeon: a packager for dynamically reconfigurable distributed applications, *Software Engineering Journal*, **8**(2), March, 95–101

Kramer J. and Magee J. (1985). Dynamic configuration for distributed systems. *IEEE Trans. on Software Eng.*, **11**(4), 424-36

Kramer J. and Magee J. (1990). The evolving philosophers problem: dynamic change management. *IEEE Trans. on Software Eng.*, **16**(11), 1293–306

Kramer J., Magee J., and Ng K. (1989). Graphical configuration programming, *IEEE Computer*, **22**(10), 53–65

Magee J., Kramer J. and Sloman M. S. (1989). Constructing distributed systems in Conic. *IEEE Trans. on Software Eng.*, **15**(6), 663-75

Magee J., Kramer J., Sloman M. S. and Dulay N. (1990). An overview of the REX software architecture. *Proc..IEEE International Workshop on Distributed Computing Systems in the '90s*, Cairo, 396-402

Magee J., Dulay N. and Kramer J. K. (1993). Structuring parallel and distributed programs, *Software Engineering Journal*, **8**(2), 73–83,

Magee J., Dulay N. and Kramer J. K. (1994). A constructive development environment for parallel and distributed programs. In *Proc. 2nd IEEE Int. Workshop on Configurable Distributed Systems*, Pittsburgh, USA, 21–23 March

Young A and Magee J. (1992). A flexible approach to evolution of reconfigurable systems. In *Proc. of IEE/IFIP Int. Workshop on Configurable Distributed Systems*, London, March, 152–63

Chapter 19

Application of Commercial Databases to Management

Haruo Yamaguchi† and Takeshi Tanaka*

†NTT Transmission Systems Labs.
1-2356 Take,
Yokosuka-shi, Kanagawa 238-03
Japan
Email: hy@ntttsd.ntt.jp

*NTT Information Systems Labs.
1-2356 Take,
Yokohama-shi, Kanagawa 238-03
Japan
Email: tanaka@nttvdb.ntt.jp

This chapter reviews the major types of database management system and presents a case study of database system design. First, data models which characterize the database are presented with the relevant standards. Then, a case study of database system design using a relational database in the area of telecommunications network operations and management is presented.

19.1 Review of data models

A database is defined as a logically structured collection of related data for special computer processing purposes. The general-purpose software for providing capabilities to define and manipulate a database is called a *database management system* (DBMS). Data definition is an operation on the data structure of the database which is called the *data schema*. Manipulation of a database includes such functions as retrieving specific data from the database and updating the database. A computer system implementing a database, a DBMS and the application software that uses the database is called a database system. DBMSs are classified into several different types according to the data model which consists of the data scheme and the data operations of the database. A data schema describes the structure of a database with logical concepts such as objects, their properties and relationships between objects. Data operations are defined by the *data manipulation language* (DML) and the *data definition language* (DDL). In this section, major types of DBMS are reviewed: network, relational, semantic, and object-oriented data models.

19.1.1   CODASYL data model

The CODASYL data model was originally defined by the Conference on Data Systems Languages committee (Codasyl, 1971) and uses the concepts: records, record types and set types. A *record* consists of some related data items which represent the information about an object to be managed by the DBMS. A *record type* has a name, and is a collection of records corresponding to the same kinds of object. A *set type* is a 1:N relationship between record types and is defined by its own name, an owner record type name and a member record type name. Each instance of a set type consists of one record from an owner record type and multiple records from a member record type related to it. In the schematic representation, record types and set types are depicted with rectangular boxes and arrows, respectively, as shown in Figure 19.1. Owner record instances have pointers which indicate the member record instances which are related to the owner record instance. Figure 19.1 gives an example of relationships between teachers and students.

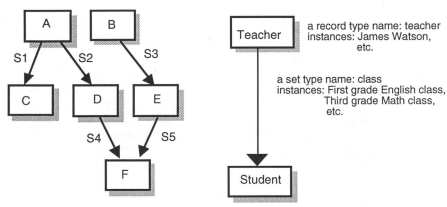

A, B, C, D, E, F : record type names
S1, S2, S3, S4, S5 : set type names

(a) Schematic representation.   **(b) Schematic relationship.**

Figure 19.1 CODASYL data model.

A CODASYL database employing the CODASYL data model is manipulated by navigating through the records stored in the database. The currency indicator is used for the navigation, and it keeps the most recently accessed record and the member record instances of it. The procedures for manipulation of a CODASYL database should be written as part of the application programs.

19.1.2   Relational data model

The relational data model was originally introduced by E.F. Codd (1970), and is defined by using the concepts relations, tuples and attributes. The relational data model is informally explained as a collection of tables. Relations, tuples and attributes respectively correspond to tables, rows of a table and columns of a table as illustrated in Figure 19.2. A relation scheme is a set of attributes. Each table has a table name and the columns have different column names. These names are used to identify relations and attributes and to help in understanding the meaning of the information. The rows and columns in the tables need not be in specific order.

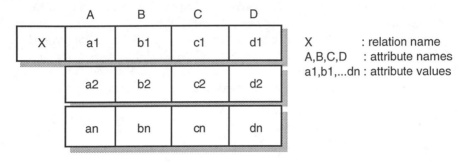

Figure 19.2 A relational data model.

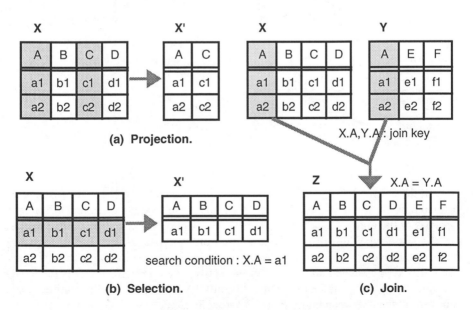

Figure 19.3 Typical data manipulation on the relational data model.

A relational database employing the relational data model is manipulated by a high-level non-procedural data manipulation language, based on set algebra.

Typical operations are:

i)   projection, where the column is fetched from the table,

ii)   selection, where the row satisfying search conditions is fetched from the tables, and

iii) join, where two or more tables are linked together (refer to Figure 19.3).

19.1.3   Semantic model

The semantic model is a high-level data model which was developed with the aim of expressing real-world data structures more directly. While researchers in this area have come up with a number of different proposals, the *Entity Relationship* (ER) model (Chen, 1973), the *functional data model* (FDM), and the *semantic data model* (SDM) are the most widely known. In this section, only the ER model is explained because it is often used for the conceptual modeling in a database design process.

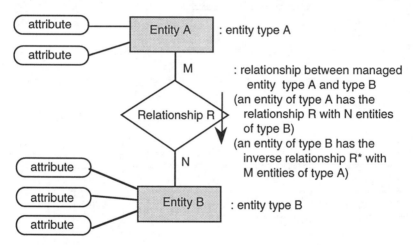

Figure 19.4 An entity-relation diagram.

In the ER model, a physical or logical "thing" which is recognized in the real world and is required to be managed by a database system is called an *entity*. Properties of the entity are called *attributes*. A collection of the entities, all of which have the same types of attribute, is called an entity type. A relationship type is defined between entity types where two entity types have a relationship. The member of an entity type is called an instance of the entity type. The ER model is depicted schematically by using an ER diagram with entity types, attributes of the entities, and relationship types between entity types as shown in Figure 19.4. In the ER diagram, an entity type is depicted by a rectangular box. A relationship type is depicted by a diamond-shaped box which combines two related entity type boxes with two participating arms. An attribute of an entity is shown as an ellipse connected to an entity type box. The ER diagram may be too complicated if the attributes are shown, in which case they may be shown in corresponding tables. The cardinality ratio of each relationship is specified by indicating a 1, M, or N on each participating arm.

The ER model was originally developed as a database design tool, particularly for data analysis and schematic design of upstream software engineering processes. There is not much work being done today on data manipulation based on this model.

19.1.4   Object-oriented model

The object-oriented model was originally derived from the programming language approach. Features of the object-oriented language can be briefly summarized as follows:

- the world is made up of objects that encapsulate data and process;

- a computing mechanism in which processing proceeds by passing messages back and forth between objects;

- a mechanism that can differentiate objects and express them in terms of class;

- specialization capability to express "A is B" by means of subclasses;

- inheritance, the capability to pass states and methods in classes to subclasses.

Object-oriented programming has much in common with the semantic model, but the former focuses on procedure while the latter is more concerned with data structure. While there are many details of object-oriented databases that are still unclear, they are nevertheless being actively researched.

19.2   Commercially available database systems

In this chapter, recent trends in the systems platforms that support commercial DBMSs are reviewed with emphasis on the distinction between centralized database systems and distributed database systems. Standardization activities on databases will also be briefly touched upon.

19.2.1   Centralized database systems

Centralized database systems are concentrated at a single physical location and are typically managed through a single computer. Until recently, most corporate database applications have been of this type.

Moreover, since the trend with centralized databases is generally towards greater capacity, high-performance CODASYL-based DBMSs have been most prevalent, particularly in the banking industry. More recently, relational DBMSs offering high-level and user-friendly interfaces have become more pervasive. This can largely be attributed to the remarkable progress of relational DBMSs in recent years, which has boosted their performance.

Recognizing the significance of the present-day migration away from mainframes to workstations and personal computers, a host of companies are offering a wide range of relational DBMS products. Commercial DBMSs based on semantic and object-oriented models are also starting to appear, but they are still largely confined to special niche applications such as CAD systems.

Two requirements that are especially crucial in implementing centralized database systems are high performance to accommodate queries converging on the database and guaranteeing the integrity of the corporate data. Commercial CODASYL-based and relational DBMSs implemented on mainframes have been around long enough to demonstrate that most of them do satisfy these requirements. In cases where centralized database systems have been implemented on workstations or where product offerings based on the latest technologies such as object-oriented DBMSs are involved, however, they should be closely scrutinized to make sure they do satisfy these minimal performance and integrity requirements.

19.2.2   Distributed database systems

In contrast to centralized database systems, distributed database systems are dispersed in different locations and the database is controlled by more than one computer. These computers, however, are not independent of one another. They are interconnected by a network such as a LAN and linked by some common control mechanism.

Distributed database systems can be configured as bottom-up or as top-down systems. *Bottom up* designates a system configured by linking together a number of database systems that were originally developed as separate, independent systems. This contrasts with a *top-down* system, which was conceived as a distributed arrangement from the very beginning, taking the distribution of system load and risk into consideration. Generally, the bottom-up approach is used to configure systems out of different vendors' hardware and software, that is, computers and DBMSs, while the top-down approach is used to configure systems with equipment and DBMSs supplied by the same vendor.

Although DBMSs with distributed database functions (especially, relational DBMSs) are becoming available, their capabilities are still somewhat deficient. On the application side, there are many instances where interconnectivity has already been achieved. In implementing a distributed database system, the fundamental concerns are mutual access among different types of database, and measures assuring that data is not corrupted in the process of updating the database. Any DBMSs hoping for commercial acceptance must offer assurance on this latter requirement that the integrity of the data will not be compromised. Mutual access is facilitated by standardizing communications protocols, database definitions (schema) and access methods.

19.2.3   Database standards

Standardization relating to databases is conducted under the auspices of the International Organization for Standardization (ISO), and work continues in the following areas:

- Database Language (DL)

- Remote Database Access (RDA)

- Information Resource Dictionary System (IRDS)

- Reference Model of Data Management (RMDM)

DL standards specify language that is used for defining and manipulating databases. RDA is a communications protocol that is used when accessing remote databases over the communications network, and is thus a necessary standard for implementing distributed databases. The IRDS provides a standard dictionary for managing so-called meta-data (definitional information) used to process information for the design, development, and operation of information systems. Finally, RMDM is concerned with the management of data in information systems, and specifies common concepts and terminology.

Next we will consider the DL and RDA in more detail.

Database languages (DL)

The structured query language (SQL) (ISO 9075, 1987) is the standard DL for the relational model and network data language (NDL) (ISO 8907, 1987) for the CODASYL model. Both languages were formalized as international standards in 1987. Standardization in DL mainly applies to the following items:

- definition language to define databases (entities and relationships between entities in the database);

- manipulation language to query and update data in the databases;

- control language to manage transactions, and

- a common concept to accommodate all of these types of language.

Many commercial DBMSs support the internationally standardized database language SQL. Work continues in an effort to expand the functionality of the language so it can be extended to even more applications.

Remote database access (RDA)

The RDA is one of the Open Systems Interconnection (OSI) standards that provides standard services and protocols for accessing databases from a remote location (ISO 9579, 1992). Its objective is to permit interconnectivity between application programs and database systems. RDA is an application service, corresponding to the seventh layer of the basic reference model for OSI (see Figure 19.5). RDA enables clients to manipulate databases on heterogeneous systems using SQL.

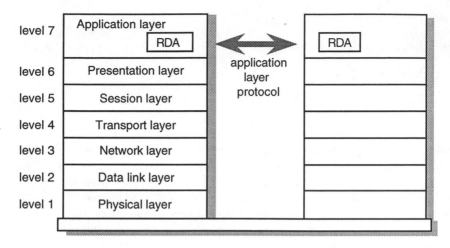

Figure 19.5 Remote data base access (RDA) and the OSI Reference Model.

19.3   Case study of database system design

In this section, a case study in the area of telecommunications network operations and management is presented as an example of a database system design (Yamaguchi *et al.*, 1992). The database system design is the key to the integrated operations and management of telecommunications networks. First, a typical database design process is presented. Next, the case study of the design process is given for understanding the process.

19.3.1   Database design process

Figure 19.6 depicts a typical database design process which includes the following four steps:

i)   requirements analysis

ii)   conceptual design

iii)   logical design

iv)   physical design

In *requirements analysis*, it is necessary to first identify the users and the application software that will access the database, then to define the requirements of those users and the application software for databases. This includes the explanation of the real world which is operated by the users and the application software. However, the description in this step is less formal because it does not employ an information modeling method such as that described in the next conceptual design step.

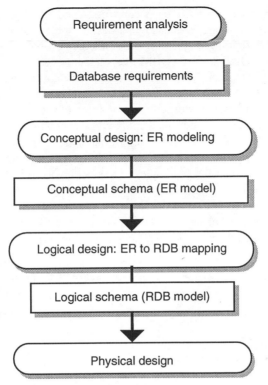

ER = Entity-relationship   RDB = Relational data base

Figure 19.6 Database design process.

Conceptual design produces an information model of the real world which is represented by data stored in the database system. The ER model explained in Section 19.1.3 is employed as a modeling method to produce a conceptual model. The ER model gives the semantic representation of the real world which is described using entities and relationships between entities.

In the design process of a telecommunications network management database, top-down design method may sometimes be appropriate. First the conceptual model of network resources is produced, then it is revised by using the requirements analysis of the applications. In this case, the designer should have enough knowledge about the real world of network resources and operations. The steps of the design process are not necessarily done in this order.

Logical design includes the choice of a database management system (DBMS) and the mapping from the conceptual model to the data model of the chosen DBMS. A DBMS is selected from various viewpoints: technical, economic, commercial, and so on. The system-independent logical design is possible by using an implementation data model before choosing a specific DBMS. In this section, we employ a relational data model as an implementation data model, but selection of a specific DBMS is left till later. The system-independent logical design is a schema mapping from an ER model to a relational data model which is conceptual and independent of a specific DBMS. After this system-independent logical design, the conceptual data model is transformed to data definition language (DDL) statements which specify the logical schema of the selected DBMS. It is a DBMS-dependent logical design.

In the mapping from an ER model to a relational data model, the entity types and relationship types of an ER model are mapped to relations which are recognized as tables in a relational data model. A row of the table is called a tuple, and it corresponds to an instance of the managed entity type. A column of the table is called an attribute. Attributes of a table in a relational data model correspond to the attributes of an entity type in an ER model. Attributes of a relation must include a primary key which is an identifier of a tuple, corresponding to an instance of an entity type in the ER model. We do not discuss the naming issues of how to choose the primary key value. An attribute which indicates the related relation is called a foreign key of the relation, and it corresponds to a relationship type in an ER model. A foreign key value is taken from the primary key value of the relevant relation.

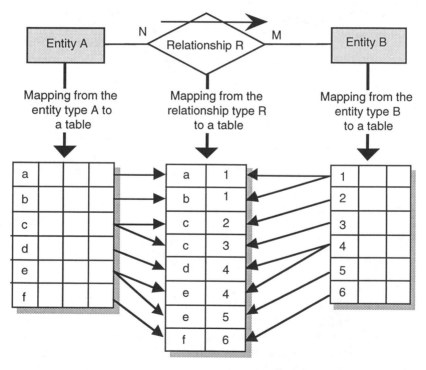

Figure 19.7 Mapping from an ER model to a relational data model using a separate relationship table.

A typical example of the mapping method from an ER model to a relational data model is illustrated in Figure 19.7. In this example, each entity type in the ER model is mapped to a corresponding relation table, and each relationship type in an ER model is mapped to the table that represents the relationship. Alternatively, the table corresponding to the binary 1:N relationship type can be deleted by adding the column to the table that corresponds to the participating entity type at the N-side of the relationship type, as shown in Figure 19.8. The added column is a foreign key attribute of the relation. In the case of a binary N:M relationship type, the relationship table is not deleted by the same method; a table corresponding to the relationship type remains as a table, as shown in Figure 19.7.

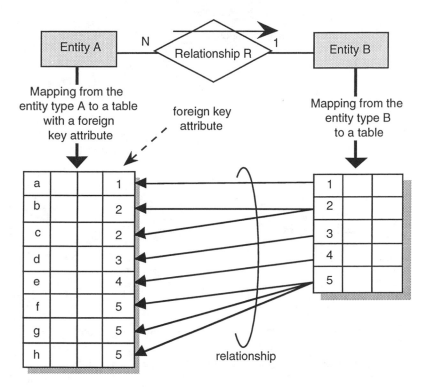

Figure 19.8 Mapping from an ER model to a relational data model by incorporating a foreign key attribute in an existing table.

In the *physical design* process, data file structures and indices for data queries are designed by considering response time and throughput with respect to the query and update of the database. The tables and index structure provided by the physical design process significantly influence the response time and throughput of the database system. For example, if applications frequently query the relationships rather than the attributes of entities, it may be better to create an extra table corresponding to a particular relationship type rather than to absorb it into the table corresponding to the relevant entity type. This is because the index of the relation-ship table gives performance improvement for relationship queries.

19.3.2   Conceptual design example

A case study in the area of telecommunications network management is presented in this section as an example of conceptual design.

The database requirements for managing the telecommunications network configuration include support for the following:

- equipment resources management including inventory management,

- transmission capability management, and

- communications capability management.

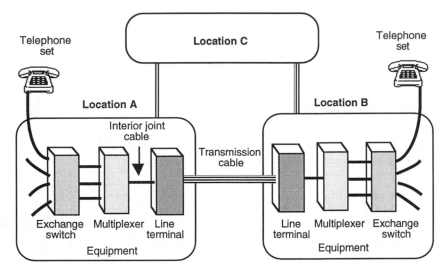

Figure 19.9 Physical construction of network equipment.

Telecommunications networks are constructed with physical network equipment which is connected by cables as shown in Figure 19.9. While equipment can be seen physically at the locations, such as the buildings of a telephone company, transmission capabilities and communications capabilities are not seen directly but recognized as functions provided by the collection of physical equipment. A conceptual model of the network is derived to meet the above requirements by analyzing the telecommunications network with respect to multiple layered views: for example, a physical layer, a transmission capability layer, and a communication capability layer.

The generic network is conceptually modeled with general nodes, links and end points of the links. Figure 19.10 depicts the logical model of the network and the corresponding ER diagram description. The generic entity types of nodes, links and end points are specialized to corresponding entity types for each layer. Physical links, transmission links and communication links respectively connect between physical nodes, transmission nodes and communication nodes. Figure 19.11 depicts the specialized layered view of the network.

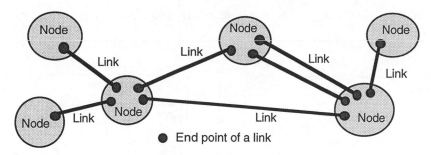

(a) Logical view of a network.

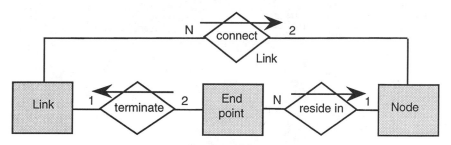

(b) Corresponding Entity-Relationship diagram.

Figure 19.10 A generic network model.

In the physical layer, physical node entities are equipment such as telephone sets, transmission terminals, transmission multiplexers, or exchange switches; and physical link entity types are transmission cables such as metallic wires, coaxial cables, or optical fiber cables. A building is included as an entity in the physical layer.

In the transmission capability layer, link entities are transmission paths that transmit multiplexed signals from a multiplexer to a de-multiplexer, and transmission node entities are locations for terminating the transmission system, such as network centers. Transmission end points include transmission multiplexers that multiplex and de-multiplex signals through transmission links.

In the communications capability layer, link entities are called communication circuits through which users of the network actually communicate, and communication node entities are circuit switch functions which switch the circuits on a call-by-call basis. The user's terminal such as a telephone set is included in the communication nodes. The circuit between two switching functions is called a trunk, and the circuit between a user's terminal and a switch is called a loop. Circuit end points are on the circuit nodes.

There exist "carry↔ carried relationships" between physical links and transmission links, and between transmission links and communication links. The ER diagram describing the conceptual model of the network for configuration management is obtained using the above case study of the conceptual design. Figure

19.12 depicts the ER diagram of the specialized layered view of the network shown in Figure 19.11.

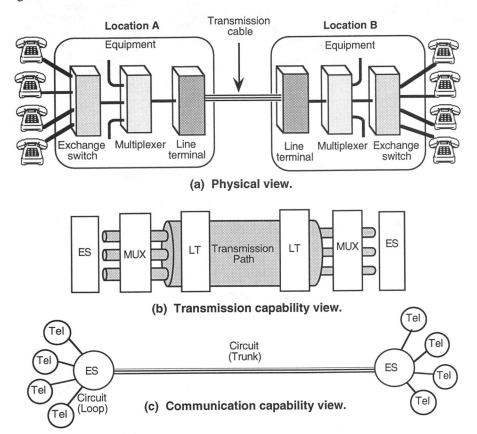

(a) Physical view.

(b) Transmission capability view.

(c) Communication capability view.

Figure 19.11 A layered view of the telecommunications network.

19.3.3   Logical design for a relational data model

A case study of a system-independent logical design is presented in this section. A relational data model is chosen as an implementation data model. The ER model which is the result of the conceptual design is transformed into the relational data model which is a collection of tables.

Figure 19.13 shows the attribute types included in the tables. Each table corresponds to an entity type of the ER model. No relationship table exists because all relationships in the ER diagram shown in Figure19.12 are absorbed into the entity type tables. Attribute types are classified using several categories for convenience: a primary key attribute, foreign key attributes, self attributes, status attributes and maintenance attributes.

A primary key attribute is the one that has the unique value that identifies a specific tuple in the table, that is, a specific instance of an entity type. The name given to the specific instance to uniquely identify it from other instances is called a distinguished name. The distinguished name is sometimes employed as a primary key attribute value.

Foreign key attributes correspond to relationships of the ER model. The value of a foreign key attribute is a primary key attribute value of a related instance.

Self attributes are the properties of an entity and these attributes have no relation to other entities. Status attributes are the conditions of an entity that has values such as operating, faulty or sustained. Maintenance attributes are the information for managing the data of the object instance, such as the update time.

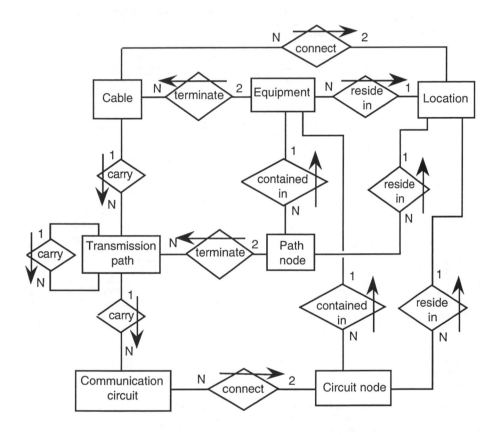

Figure 19.12 An ER diagram of the layered network view.

Cable

Primary key	Cable identifier
Foreign key	A-location identifier
	Z-location identifier
	A-equipment identifier
	Z-equipment identifier
Self attribute	Size
Status attribute	Status

Transmission path

Primary key	Path identifier
Foreign key	A-path node identifier
	Z-path node identifier
	Carried cable identifier
	Carried path identifier
Self attribute	Transmission capacity
Status attribute	Status

Path node

Primary key	Path node identifier
Foreign key	Equipment identifier
	Location identifier
Self attribute	Node name
	Node capacity
Status attribute	Status

Communication circuit

Primary key	Circuit identifier
Foreign key	A-circuit node identifier
	Z-circuit node identifier
	Carried path identifier
Self attribute	Communication capacity
Status attribute	Status

Circuit node

Primary key	Circuit node identifier
Foreign key	Equipment identifier
	Location identifier
Self attribute	Node name
	Node capacity
Status attribute	Status

Equipment

Primary key	Equipment identifier
Foreign key	Location identifier
Self attribute	System name
	Vendor name
	Construction date
Status attribute	Status

Location

Primary key	Location identifier
Foreign key	—
Self attribute	Building name
	Function name
	Construction date
Status attribute	—

Figure 19.13 Attribute examples of the entity types.

References

Chen P. (1976). The entity relationship model – toward a unified view of data. *ACM Trans. on Database Systems*, **1**(1), 9–36

Codasyl (1971). *Database Task Group Report to CODASYL Programming Language Committee.* ACM

Codd E.F. (1970). A relational model of data for large shared data banks *C.ACM*, **13**(6), 377–87

ISO 8907 (June 1987). *Information Processing system – Database Language NDL*

ISO 9075 (June 1987). *Information Processing system – Database Language SQL*

ISO 9579 (June 1992). *Information Processing system – Open Systems Interconnection – Remote Database Access*

Yamaguchi H., Isobe S., Yamaki T. and Yamanaka Y. (1992). Network information modeling for network management. In *Proc. of the IEEE/IFIP Network Operations and Management Symposium*, Santa Barbara, 57–67

Chapter 20

Graphical Management Interfaces

Thomas G. Bartz

Network and System Management Division
Hewlett-Packard Co,
3404 E Harmony Road,
Fort Collins, Colorado 80525, USA
Email: tgb@cnd.hp.com

This chapter explores pertinent and desired features of a Graphical Management Interface (GMI) framework for network and distributed systems management applications, and proposes models for implementing and integrating with such a GMI. First, requirements are discussed in order to establish a common understanding of what a GMI should provide, then human factors are taken into account to further establish a conceptual model for behavior and interaction suitable for management. Once behavioral expectations have been identified, a general model that articulates the needed components for implementing a GMI is developed. Finally, methods are proposed for integrating with such a GMI from an application perspective.

20.1   The purpose of a GMI: what should it try to achieve?

A **Graphical Management Interface, or GMI**, is a graphical user interface (GUI) for integrating resource management applications in a networked computing environment. Accordingly, the GMI provides a context – *a representation of the managed resources and their state* – from which the management applications can be launched. The GMI generates presentations that communicate the context, and give the user access to control the networks and systems in the environment.

   In order to design an effective and functional GMI, we need to understand its purpose and role in the context of the entire management system. A myriad of components make up a management system, including manageable objects, management services and applications, various protocols, the user interface, and, of course, the users (administrators) of the management system themselves and their management objectives. To understand the GMI, we must examine its role in this larger context to define its characteristics and functionality.[1]

In essence, the management GMI is the user's "bridge" to the manageable environment; it "brings" the manageable entities to him.[2] To make the user effective, there are three basic needs that the GMI must fulfill. These needs are to:

i)   provide appropriate information about the environment (that is, show the user, in the context of the user's objectives, what the environment consists of and what relevant changes are occurring in that environment worthy of the user's attention);

ii)   allow the user to control the environment accordingly (that is, give the user access to the appropriate control mechanisms for changing the behavior of the environment according to the user's management objectives);

iii) accomplish (i) and (ii) in an intuitive, highly effective manner from wherever the user is logged into the management system.

In managing the environment, the user has specific objectives to meet, such as minimizing downtime, or optimizing performance or resource utilization. Accordingly, the user is interested in seeing information pertinent to these objectives. A common failing among many GMIs today is that they show a great deal of data, but very little (relevant) information. With appropriate information available, a user can properly understand the situation at hand.

The GMI must then make available the appropriate actions, applications, and integrated tools so the user can indeed effect a desired change. Additionally, users often know what changes they need to make or what problems need to be solved, but are unsure how to go about doing so. The GMI should be sufficiently intelligent to allow the presentation of the relevant tools and guidance that users need for making changes consistent with their management objectives.

It is on the basis of the above three needs that we explore the GMI and its necessary capabilities in greater detail.

20.2   Human factors considerations: the conceptual framework and expected behaviors

20.2.1   User interaction: the object-action paradigm

The most prevalent and general user-interaction model in use today is the object-action paradigm by which a user selects an object to act on and then chooses the

---

[1]   The GMI described here is one intended for a highly functional management system, not a simple encapsulating shell for independent, minimally integrated applications.

[2]   "User" in this chapter refers to the administrator, operator, or strategic planner who manages some aspect of the distributed environment through the management system.

action to perform (Shneiderman, 1987; Hartson and Hix, 1988). This paradigm is found in windowing systems such as OSF Motif and in Microsoft Windows as well as applications that run on these windowing systems. This paradigm is well suited to management applications as well. Users naturally tend to think in terms of selecting an object they want to manage, and what they specifically want to do to that object. A given task is typically described in the context of a given object, such as: "I want to add a user (the action) to this cluster (the object)". Fault management is especially well suited to this paradigm; when an alarm is raised to indicate connectivity loss to a given system, an operator will proceed to investigate connectivity to that system.

According to this paradigm, it is important for the network and distributed systems GMI to adequately present the manageable objects that can be acted on. However, to be truly effective, the GMI must not only present the objects, it must *represent* them. A GMI for network and distributed systems management should emulate (or support the emulation of) the manageable entities it presents. Ideally, a user should be able to interact with the symbols and capabilities shown by the GMI as if he or she were interacting with the actual manageable entities themselves. This is the intent behind offering an object-oriented user interaction model; manageable "objects" in the GMI appear, behave, and are controlled like the entities they represent.

Obviously, not all manageable objects in a networked computing environment are alike. Accordingly, their expected behaviors differ, and the GMI must accommodate those behaviors. A fundamental example of this is seen in the distinction between hardware and software components. Since a software object represents a logical entity, a user expects to manipulate it in ways that would be impossible to do with a hardware object. For example, you cannot move a gateway symbol from one LAN to another through a GMI and expect the physical entity to have moved as well. However, it is perfectly reasonable to expect this type of behavior of a symbol representing a software application which has been dragged from one computer system to another. In particular, one would expect the actual software to be installed on the second system. Thus, a GMI, in conjunction with the management applications that drive it, needs to be sufficiently intelligent to match the behavior one would intuitively expect of the manipulated object; the GMI should "bring the user" to the actual resource being managed.

The following two sections discuss the two primary functions of a GMI in the context of the object-action paradigm. The two functions are: (a) providing information to the user and (b) providing control to the user. Next, usability and standards requirements are discussed before we embark on developing a model for the GMI.

20.2.2   Providing information to the GMI user

Presenting the organization of manageable objects

Objects
First and foremost, a user has to know what is in an environment in order to manage it. If a user cannot see what components make up the manageable world and how

those components are related to each other, it becomes extremely difficult to know what is happening, much less how to deal with problems that arise.

Relationships
Since the number of manageable objects in most distributed environments is a very high number, the symbols representing the objects need to be organized in some usable and navigable way. Adding hierarchy to a collection of views (or windows) is the simplest manner used to deal with this problem. Symbols are collected into groups according to properties that the objects have in common, and the group itself becomes a "higher-level" symbol representing its contained objects. The next level of hierarchy is formed by collecting group symbols and organizing them into a yet higher group.

A hierarchical organization is highly useful for breaking down a mass collection of objects into more manageable units, but is often insufficient when trying to represent the actual environment. Organization through grouping indicates only one type of relationship among objects, namely containment (or parenthood). Yet for users to grasp the essence of the environment they are managing, they often need to see additional relationships as well, such as the dependencies that one object has on others, the relative physical position among objects, or the coupling (or connectivity) that exists between objects.

For example, to manage a distributed file system or a diskless cluster, it is easier to recognize the dependencies among the client and server objects when the relationships are clearly expressed as logical, unidirectional connecting symbols. Additionally, it is effective to place background graphics, such as a floor plan or a world map, into views to establish a context for the represented objects. Views that show relationships among their contained components and allow background graphics are called **map views**. A collection of related map views forms a **map**.

Since different users of the management system typically have different responsibilities, they need to be able to view the environment from different perspectives. Thus, the GMI must support many kinds of maps. Users may desire to view the environment from a geographic perspective, from an organizational perspective, a physical perspective, or a functional perspective. For example, a user may require a map that focuses on specific services in the environment, such as printer services, or a map that shows a specific type of network connectivity in the environment, or another that emphasizes the physical layout of network elements. Some users may even require or desire map organizations that seem totally arbitrary, yet reflect the environment as they know it. Thus, regardless of the type and variety of objects to be managed, the GMI must support a wide range of representations of those objects to provide useful maps for its users.

Presenting object state and status

Representing changes
Once users have access to what is contained by the environment, the next type of information required for effective management is notification of change. A GMI must incorporate an effective way to communicate change to draw the user's attention to it. Examples include blinking an object symbol or changing its color – if the user is

viewing a map – or a simple list display of alarm conditions with color indications associated with each – if the user is monitoring alarm conditions. Not all change is relevant or noteworthy. The GMI should only expose events in which the user has indicated interest. Furthermore, while numerous events may be of interest, they vary in their importance. Critical events should never go unnoticed, whereas less important ones can probably be communicated through more subtle means, or only when necessary.

For example, when a printer runs out of toner, the print spooler administrator should be alerted right away, while the administrator of distributed file systems need not know at all (except through a warning if he or she attempts to use the impaired printer). The GMI must provide a configuration tool for denoting which events are pertinent and what their relevant importance is for a particular presentation.

Describing objects

After users are aware of a situation that demands their attention, they will often need additional information to determine how to react to it. In particular, more specific information about the objects involved will be needed. Such data is called **object description data** and includes detailed information about an object, such as its model or version numbers, its vendor, when it was installed, what it depends on, and who is responsible for it. The GMI must provide access to this type of information either by interacting directly with the objects or by accessing a datastore of object description data.

Other types of data may also be required as the users set out to determine how to respond to a given situation. They may launch applications or services to examine or gather relevant data. To comprehend the meaning of historical data which has been collected or has evolved over a period of time, dynamic charts, tables and graphs are a necessity. A sophisticated GMI should provide the ability to generate appropriate graphical views of data on demand in the most relevant form.

Additionally, since the environment and its status are continually changing, an indispensable feature is the ability to capture the current presentation in a **snapshot**, a static representation at a given point of time. These snapshots can then be retrieved at a later time to provide a context for analysis or reference. (Alternatively, the state of the environment can be captured through report generation on the underlying data through fourth-generation languages or other tools accessing a database management system.)

Locating objects

Finally, users may need to search through the object pool and filter through object properties to locate particular objects from which they need more detailed information. The simplest way to allow this is to offer a template interface with rules for combining attributes and matching values so that users can easily indicate what they are looking for. The "locate" capability should scan the object database and return the results in a usable fashion, such as highlighting the resulting symbols in the views and generating a list of the highlighted object names.

In summary, key aspects in presenting information to users are:

- enable the user to see what is in the environment, tailoring the presentation to the objects of interest;

- expose the pertinent relationships that exist among those objects, such as dependencies, connectivity, or containment;

- provide notification of relevant changes in the environment;

- provide quick access to detailed data, such as description data, when desired;

- provide on-demand charts and graphs, as appropriate, for detailed data;

- provide extensive locate and report generation capability.

20.2.3 Providing control to the GMI user

Once users have gathered or seen enough information about a given situation to understand it, they will usually need a means of control to change it. In order to provide a graphical management interface that offers effective control of a user's environment, related functionality must be grouped together. This means that the relevant objects, object and event data, and the diagnostic and control tools required to perform specific management functions are spatially close together so they are readily at hand as needed. The following subsections explore various mechanisms for facilitating this.

Management roles

It is important for us to remember that individual users of a management system will have unique needs stemming from different responsibilities and objectives. They will be interested in managing different sets of objects and/or managing those objects differently. One user may administer systems in workgroups while another administrator may handle distributed LAN connectivity. Yet another will administer shared peripherals such as printers, plotters and disks, while a fourth may monitor performance throughout the networked environment and plan changes for optimal usage of resources.

Each such user has different goals and responsibilities. Accordingly, when they log into the management system, they desire to see maps and applications tailored to their specific responsibilities giving them appropriate access to the objects they need to control. A **management role** is a set of responsibilities and accompanying set of managed objects. *Support* for the role can be implemented via presentations, applications and services for performing a specific set of management tasks on a specified set of objects.

A restricted set of users is allowed access to a given management role. The role is configured to have access to a subset of objects and their methods in the manageable environment consistent with the objectives that have been defined for that management role. The restrictions imposed by these roles are useful because they help minimize overlap among multiple users and they help focus a given user's responsibilities by eliminating distracting mechanisms and irrelevant data. (Note that multiple users may be allowed access to any one management role and that separate roles can be configured to act on overlapping objects. Alternatively, two or more management roles may consist of identical tools, but be configured to operate on non-overlapping object domains.)

Within the management roles: tools and subtools

Moving beyond the first level of control, the management role, we next have to deal with control *within* the management role. Users need to know what actions are available and have ready access to them. Menu items under a main menu are the most prevalent means for making actions available to a user. Many GMIs also allow for pop-up menus to eliminate the need for dragging the cursor to the menu bar and searching through its items. In either case, only the actions applicable to the selected objects should be made available. Menu items under the menu bar should be grayed if they do not apply to the selected object(s), and pop-up menus should only contain applicable items. The purpose of menu graying is to focus users on what is pertinent to the context in which they are working in order to speed up their work and help direct them towards their goals.

As the number of applications integrated with the management system rises, other problems that encumber the user can arise. For example, the number of menu items will rise even faster than the number of applications (since applications can conceivably offer multiple menu items). Although the top-level menus serve to organize menu items into groups, menus are fairly general in nature, and long lists can result beneath them, making navigation difficult. Although cascading menus can be used to alleviate this problem by collecting related menu items together, there still remains a spatial problem when a user needs to frequently access a related set of applications. In such a situation, the user is forced to repeatedly traverse a long menu list to the appropriate cascade, and then down its path to the appropriate menu item. This becomes even more wearisome if sequentially accessed menu items are neither in the same cascade nor under the same top-level menu.

The concept of a **tool** can help alleviate these problems. A tool is a visual integration point for a narrowly focused and task-related set of applications. A tool is launched from its own menu item under one of the top-level GMI menus. When invoked, the tool typically spawns a window showing a view of particular objects (e.g., those previously selected) and giving access to the applications it integrates. Such applications register their actions, called **subtools**, as menu items within the tool (under *its* menus), rather than under the more general top-level menu bar of the GMI.

A number of examples illustrate the concept. For example, a performance monitoring solution would make a good candidate for a tool. A number of applications could register menu items (subtools) beneath it. Some of these subtools might be system performance monitoring, network monitoring, a threshold-setting/alarm monitoring application, a subtool for plotting performance statistics, and a correlation tool for detecting patterns and relationships across wide ranges of collected data. Other example tools could be applications collected together to provide nodal systems management, cluster management, file backup and recovery, wide-area network management, or network planning.

The purpose of the tools/subtools breakdown should be clear. It is to spatially collect a related set of functions which are frequently accessed together within the context of a certain task, so the user has them close at hand when embarking on that task.

Builders and encapsulators

Once applications are launched, a user is typically required to set or select specific parameters as input to specific actions. It is at this point that dialog boxes are used to query for user input to specifically direct the user's request, and to ensure that all necessary data is properly entered. Ideally, the GMI incorporates dialog builders, a number of which exist on the market, for simplified dialog development and to ensure consistency in their appearance and behavior.

Related to builders is the concept of encapsulation, another mechanism for simplifying user interface development for user interaction. Encapsulators can vary widely in their sophistication for taking existing applications and integrating their input and output with the rest of the GMI. Simple (but very valuable) encapsulators may merely frame an application's terminal output into a window so that the output is consistent with other GMI windows. More powerful (but far more complicated) encapsulators may actually intercept and translate an existing presentation into another form. In any case, encapsulators are a means of making user interaction for existing applications appear consistent with the GMI and other management applications.

20.2.4   Making the GMI usable: consistency and standards

A full-featured GMI is not necessarily a usable one. The same applies to applications integrated with the GMI that provide their own presentations. To achieve high usability, one of the key features a GMI must provide is consistency both in appearance and in its behavior. If consistency prevails, users will quickly pick up the GMI's interaction patterns. They will not only learn the GMI features more quickly, but they will be able to anticipate the GMI's behavior and organization.

Consistency includes, first of all, compliance with the graphics technology on which it is based. This is one of the key benefits of building on top of a standard graphics technology, such as OSF/Motif, MS Windows or OpenLook. It simply makes sense to provide a GMI based on and consistent with the same GUI technology upon which a user's other applications are based. The same interaction and presentation models are used and the user's investment in learning new tools is reduced (Open Software Foundation, 1992; IBM, 1991). This means the GMI should use the GUI of choice for each operating system platform it is implemented on.

The same principles apply at the more focused level of a GMI designed specifically for resource management. Consistency must be designed into every aspect of a GMI. This includes the appearance of menus, views, and dialog boxes, and the locations of fields, messages, and buttons. It includes the mouse and keyboard interaction models when spanning dialog boxes, and the means used for editing views or tables. Wherever models exist, they should be obeyed. When new models are required, they should be established based on usability data and testing, and then applied consistently. (One of the greatest impediments to usability is a developer who employs new techniques because he feels they are superior even though they clash with existing, standardized methods.)

Just as a GMI needs to be consistent with the graphics technology on which it is based, network and systems management applications need to be consistent with the GMI under which they integrate. A number of GMIs exist, such as HP OpenView Windows or SunNet Manager. The better GMIs include their own style guideline extensions to ensure consistency specific to management. Application developers need to follow these guidelines so their applications integrate better with other management applications and the overall management system, and thereby contribute to the overall usability. Applications that do not adhere to the guidelines will typically be deemed less usable and less friendly to users who have grown accustomed to the rest of the GMI (Hewlett-Packard Co, 1992).

Providing consistency in appearance and behavior is one of the key justifications for incorporating builders into a GMI for generating presentations on behalf of applications and objects. The applications and objects should *drive* the presentations (dictate what the presentation contains), but rely on the GMI for *creating* the actual presentation to help ensure consistency and to reduce the application developer's workload.

Integrated help

A critical GMI feature that contributes immensely to its overall usability is on-line help. Ideally, a hypertext or hypermedia system is used to provide detailed information indexed by topics, tool names, or context-sensitive selections. Management applications must integrate easily with the help system in contributing their specific help information and in launching the help system (from the application) per user requests.

The integrated help system should not be viewed solely as a tool for understanding the GMI and integrated management applications. It can also serve as a source of expertise and guidance in performing the management tasks themselves. For example, if a user receives an alarm indicating a sudden and abnormal increase in network traffic, imagine the usefulness of simply being able to click on a "Diagnostic Help" button that spawns the help system and takes it to an entry that lists possible causes for the alarm condition. Each potential cause could identify follow-up diagnostic tests for ascertaining the actual problem. If it is determined from those actions that a broadcast storm has occurred, the user could once again enter the integrated help system, this time searching for remedies for broadcast storms. To perform such functions, the help system must excel at topical search and extraction of selected information and at integration with the management applications surrounding it (Akscyn and McCracken, 1988; Martin, 1990; Kearsley and Shneiderman, 1989).

Maxims for usability

A few important rules should be kept in mind when developing a GMI in order to ensure its usability. Ignoring them may save some development time, but will likely frustrate users.

i)   Show what is relevant and hide what is not. Keep the presentation simple not fancy. Glitter only distracts from the important.

ii)   It is not enough to make things easy to do; users must also be able to do them quickly. Include accelerators and minimize required steps.

iii) Think about navigation – make it easy. Think through the most likely paths a user will have to traverse and make them easily accessible.

iv)   Set usability goals up front. If usability objectives are not set, other pressures will prevail.

v)   Apply consistent behavior and appearance at every level.

vi)   Test, test, test! Build quick prototypes and have novice users try them out. Learn from the problems they encounter and redesign. Repeat. There is no such thing as getting it "right" the first time. Only users can demonstrate whether a given design is usable.

20.3   A model for the GMI: what is inside

The requirements of a GMI that we have identified suggest a number of the key components that make up such a GMI, and we can now explore a high-level design. In doing so, we will first identify the major functional components of the GMI and then examine them in greater detail.

20.3.1   Major functional components

There are several major functional components that make up the GMI. These functional components generally fall into the three major categories: Views, Dialogs, and Roles. Figure 20.1 shows the initial breakdown of the GMI into the three major modules that correspond to these categories. These are the **Views Presentation Module**, the **Dialog Presentation Module**, and the **Roles Integration Module**. These GMI objects interact with each other, with the graphics technology used by the GMI, and with the applications integrated under the GMI. The primary interactions among the modules are also shown in the figure.

   The Views Presentation Module is responsible for generating map views and presenting the objects and the relationships among them. The Dialog Presentation Module is used to create and present dialog boxes, tables, charts and graphs as directed on demand, to present object data and to query for user input. The Roles Integration Module is used to formulate management roles with specific responsibilities out of applications, tools, and security policies.

Datastore implementation
   A large amount of object data, both presentation and non-presentation specific, must be available to a GMI. There are several datastores upon which the GMI

depends. Some of these stores are noted as inherent in the GMI while others are external; many may be implemented in either a centralized or distributed manner.

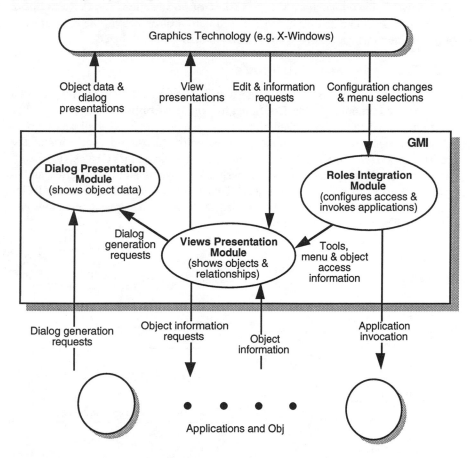

Figure 20.1 Major GMI components and interaction.

It is worth noting two extremes in implementing presentation datastores: (i) centralized storage within the GMI, and (ii) distributed storage across all the objects interacting with the GMI. An extreme case of the latter is the more object-oriented approach in which *all* information about an object is self-contained by the object. This approach simplifies the GMI, but places a greater burden on the object implementations. It also draws a cleaner boundary of responsibility in that every object-specific request is handled by the object itself. However, since the object-generated information includes a higher degree of presentation information, objects implemented in this manner are typically restricted to display by those very few GMIs that can interpret their encoded information or presentation language.

Alternatively, the centralized storage approach is (as noted earlier) more complex, yet is likely to yield higher access performance to object description data (assuming that a reasonable subset of the environment, and *not all* of it, is being managed under any one GMI). This approach draws a greater separation between actual object data (at the object) and how that data is presented to the user through various views. This allows for a greater variety of presentations (as well as GMIs), but requires more sophisticated external coordination of objects in the environment and the presentations configured with the GMI to display those objects.

20.3.2   The Roles Integration Module

The functionality of the Roles Integration Module (Figure 20.2) is primarily provided by two internal components, the **Configurator** and the **Application Invoker**. The Configurator is used to create and administer management roles. Not all users should be allowed access to the Configurator; it is a utility for the administrator of the management system itself and is used to define management roles, to install applications into the management system, to specify object domain boundaries, and to assign user access to management roles. This information is stored in the Roles Configuration Store and is used by the Application Invoker to spawn applications and enforce the security policies configured there.

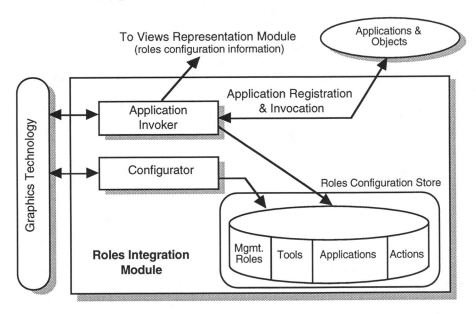

Figure 20.2 Internal breakdown of roles integration module.

The Roles Configuration Store tracks available applications and their arrangement into management roles and tools. There are four substores in the Roles Configuration Store. These are the Management Roles Substore, the Tools Substore, the Actions Substore and the Applications Substore.

Management Roles Substore
The Management Roles Substore is used to save the management roles that have been configured for the management system. Each entry identifies a management role by

name, such as "Mail Administrator" or "Network Planner". A list of system users and passwords which identifies which users are allowed access to the management role is stored with each entry.

Each management role entry specifies which application objects make up a role through lists of applications and tools/subtools which have been configured for it. The entries in these lists reference entries in the Tools and Applications Substores. Also associated with each management role is the set of manageable objects to which the solution has access. These are either listed explicitly or are referenced through rules based on object attributes. (Note that some implementations may make no distinction between applications and manageable objects, in which case the configured applications and the objects lists collapse into one.)

Tools Substore

Each tool that the GMI provides is listed in the Tools Substore. Each entry consists of actions (tool-specific menu items) supplied by each application associated with the management role. The collection of subtools (or menu items) configured to make up the tool are listed as part of the menu structure for the tool.

Actions Substore

The Actions Substore is used to store information about each menu item that can appear in any of the available management roles. An action always has a corresponding application which supplies the action functionality, but it should be noted that an application can provide multiple actions. Thus, an Actions Substore entry not only identifies the application which supplies its functionality, but also the invocation parameters required to tap that functionality. The Actions Substore also saves a list of object classes to which the action can be applied (which is used for menu graying based on the current object selection list.)

Note that the Tools and Actions Substores are called out separately to allow individual actions to show up under multiple tools if it is appropriate to do so.

Applications Substore

The Applications Substore contains data about all the applications that have been configured for access by the GMI. Each entry in the substore includes the application name, information as to how to access it for invocation (such as a file name), a list of actions that the application makes available, configurable parameters of the application and general information about the application, such as its vendor, version number, and location of help files.

The Application Invoker is the primary user of the Roles Configuration Store. The Application Invoker receives user requests to initiate specific actions referenced by menu items. It then invokes the appropriate application according to the parameters specified in the Actions, Applications and Management Roles Substores. The Application Invoker also receives requests from applications to create specific tools. The invoker builds the tools entries in the Tools Substore according to the actions and views specified by the user and/or applications.

Note that the Roles Configuration Store is implemented as a service accessible through (RPC-based) interfaces which it exposes. This provides a point of distribution enabling remote access to the store from wherever the user may be logged into the management system.

20.3.3   The Views Presentation Module

The Views Presentation Module introduced in Figure 20.1 is responsible for creating view and object presentations and giving access to object data. Its components are shown in Figure 20.3. Two major submodules make up the Views Presentation Module. They are the **View Generator** and the **Presentation Filter.** The View Generator formulates the internal representation of each object view and makes it available to the Presentation Filter for display.

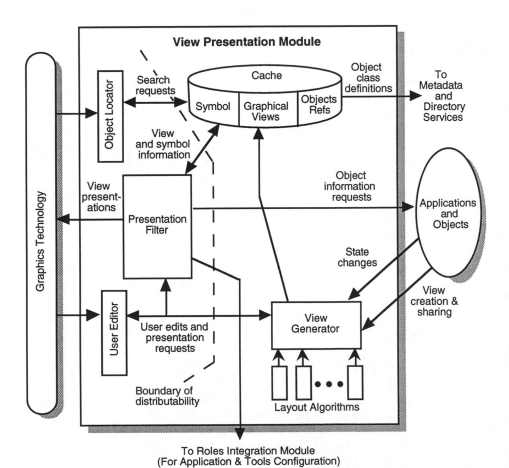

Figure 20.3 Internal breakdown of the Views Presentation Module.

View Generator

The View Generator creates views based on a specified layout algorithm,[3] a list of contained objects, and a list of relationships among those objects. Accordingly, as new objects are discovered or created, their corresponding symbols, their interconnecting relationship symbols, their positioning information within the view, their status, and the object description attributes are stored by the View Generator in the Graphical Views, Objects, and Symbols Caches of the Presentation Datastore.

- *The Graphical Views Cache* provides detailed information about an object needed to reveal its containment: the symbols it contains and what relationships exist among those contained symbols. The cache also includes presentation information pertaining to object context, such as what positional information results from the layout (and/or user editing), the background graphics associated with it, and the size and location of the view window. Each object's associated view is referenced either implicitly through the object name of the object it represents or explicitly by a view name. A view's corresponding object name is stored with the view entry.

- *The Symbols Cache* is used to save information about each symbol instance (icon or glyph) in the user's map. Each symbol represents a particular object and so each entry in the symbols cache references a given object by name or id.

    Note that there may be a many-to-one relationship among symbols and objects. Multiple symbol types – as well as multiple instances of the same symbol type – may represent a given object. This feature can be used to emphasize the particular characteristics of an object appropriate for the context presented in a given view. For example, a "high-level" object, such as a workstation acting as a diskless server *and* a network gateway, should be allowed to appear as a gateway symbol in a network segment view, as a server symbol in a diskless workgroup cluster view, and as a workstation symbol in a computer systems view. This allows the user to see the workstation according to the role it plays in each context in which it appears. Nevertheless, access to the overall workstation characteristics is still available through the symbol's link to the underlying object description data. In essence, this is the visual consequence of object class inheritance and polymorphism.

    Each Symbols Cache entry includes a symbol type by which its corresponding bitmaps can be retrieved. Additionally, since each symbol represents a potentially different aspect of an object, status is associated with each symbol (as opposed to the object) and is stored here. (For example, if the gateway functionality of the workstation noted above breaks down, the status color of the diskless server symbol need not change.)

A key component of the View Generator is the *Status Propagator*. The Status Propagator listens for incoming events to determine and propagate status changes.

---

[3] A *layout algorithm* indicates the graphical location of symbols in a view as new symbols are added to it according to a pre-established algorithm reflecting a topology. Examples include star, ring or mesh representations.

When a state change event occurs on an object, the Status Propagator looks up its associated symbols in the Symbols Cache, determines which views contain the object, and works through the status propagation changes, if any, for each symbol type representing the object. Each symbol representing an object may have its own status propagation algorithm associated with it to properly represent the status of its subcomponents. For example, a workstation that acts as both a gateway and a diskless server in the environment may be represented by different symbols in different map views. These different symbols should reflect the status of the underlying gateway or the server objects, not both. The Status Propagator works through these status propagation algorithms and presents the status changes for each affected symbol accordingly in the presentations.

Presentation Filter

The Presentation Filter forms the "center" of the Presentation Module (and the GMI) through its coordination of various presentation pieces and their formulation into what the user sees. It has primary responsibility for retrieving information and making it available to the user. It displays particular views produced by the View Generator and dictated by the management role configuration. The Presentation Filter obtains relevant role information (that is, the objects of interest and corresponding menu items for each view) from the Roles Integration Module.

When object description data is requested by the user, the Presentation Filter can respond in a couple of different ways. It can pass the request on to the object itself, which then interacts with the GMI dialog builders to display the information, assuming the object supports this functionality. Alternatively, the Presentation Filter can itself obtain the object data from the object and interact directly with the Dialog Presentation Module to provide the information.

The Presentation Filter brings forth its presentation with the help of the Object Locator and the User Editor components in the View Presentation Module.

- *The Object Locator* interacts with the user to provide location of specific objects based on description attributes. The user specifies attribute search expressions. The object locator searches through an object description store or interacts with objects directly to identify the matching object attributes. It manipulates the Presentation DataStore to indicate which symbols are highlighted as a result. (The user can then select all highlighted objects as input to a subsequent action item.)

- *The User Editor* provides editing functions through menu items, direct manipulation support, and dialog boxes to enable the user to customize the presentation as desired. Any changes are passed on to the View Generator and Presentation Filter for reflection in the actual presentation.

20.3.4   The Dialog Presentation Module

The Dialog Presentation Module (Figure 20.4) consists of two key components, the **Dialog Generator** and the **Chart, Graph and Table Generator**.

These generators (or builders) receive their instructions in several ways. One is from applications and objects which contain the instructions and depend on the generators to interpret them on their behalf. This is typically done by directly invoking generator functions and issuing "build commands" for each required dialog.

Alternatively, if higher performance is required, and the builders support it, applications can instead reference pre-established dialogs for quick display. This is especially useful for static, heavily-used dialogs.

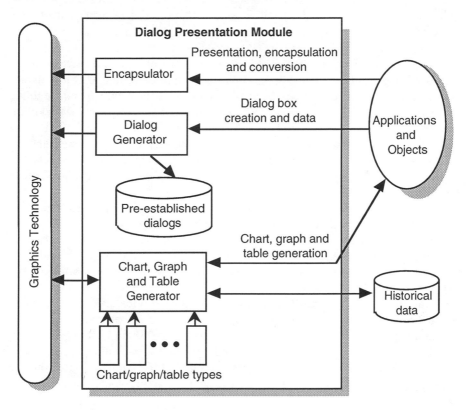

Figure 20.4 Internal breakdown of the Dialog Presentation Module.

The application user may also create dialogs directly. This is often required when the user desires to examine historical or real-time data in the form of graphs, charts or tables. The generators provide a user interface by which the user selects the type of presentation desired and specifies what data is to be shown. This usage of the generators typically demands that the data be stored in particular formats whose structure the generators understand. Otherwise, some type of conversion is required, or an extension made to the generators' set of understood formats.

The application **Encapsulator** is also included within the Dialog Presentation Object. Applications that require encapsulation, owing to an inconsistent or outdated user interface, are registered with the Encapsulator. The Encapsulator intercepts user interaction and application output on each application's behalf, translating between the native format of the encapsulated application and a format and style consistent with the GMI.

20.3.5   Additional features

A GMI is faced with meeting the needs of many different users, each demanding their own preferences in applications, features, and presentations. To meet all these needs in the best possible way, a GMI must be customizable. A number of customization requirements have already been identified, such as the creation of management roles and tools, and user editing of maps for personalized presentations. There are, however, additional ways in which the GMI needs to be extensible.

First, the GMI cannot be limited in the types of objects and corresponding symbols it can present. Users and applications must be able to add new object classes and have corresponding dialog boxes and object views automatically available to the user. This is not difficult if the creation of new object classes includes their addition to the metadata store. New symbols are also easily introduced by application developers with the addition of new symbol types and their corresponding graphical bitmaps. This applies not only to nodal symbols representing manageable objects, but also to relationship symbols, such as connections, dependencies and other relationships representable in views.

Second, the GMI needs extensibility in its basic functionality. For example, application developers should be able to add new layout algorithms to the view generator to accommodate the arrangement of symbols and their relationships in unanticipated contexts. Likewise, the dialog, chart, graph and table generators need extensibility of the dialog types they can create as well as extensibility of the recognized data structures from which the presented data is extracted.

Customization of the GMI is one of its most powerful features. It enables the GMI to become what it must so its users can meet their management objectives. Implementing the GMI components in an object-oriented fashion is perhaps the best way this can be achieved, but more important than how customization is achieved is the fact *that it is achieved.* If the appropriate hooks and mechanisms exist from the beginning, the GMI can far more readily evolve to new, previously unanticipated needs.

20.4   Integration of applications with the GMI

Now that we have discussed the major GMI components, we can examine the various resulting levels of available to developers. An application can integrate at any level. Greater levels of integration require tighter coupling and (typically) more work for the developer, but offer increased usability and value to the end user.

20.4.1   Separation of presentation from the semantics

It is important to keep in mind that a GMI generates the *presentation* of the manageable objects. The actual functionality associated with an object exists "behind" its presentation. This distinction is important because it allows the GMI functionality to be focused on general presentation capabilities and user interaction. Correspondingly, objects and applications integrating with the GMI can be freed to focus primarily on the management capabilities (or semantics) they offer rather than the presentation. This is why we distinguish between managed objects and the symbols that represent managed objects.

This separation between the presentation and the semantics of objects has several advantages. First, the distinction is valuable for application developers since it helps define their development responsibilities. Second, it makes integration of applications and manageable objects with different GMIs, or other forms of presentation, easier since any presentation means are separated from the actual objects. Third, it allows for greater customization of the presentation information to reflect what each user wants to see about the environment.

20.4.2 Levels of integration

Menu bar integration

The simplest level of integration is menu integration with the application invoker. This can be accomplished programmatically in a direct way or through a registration file which the application invoker reads. The type of information that needs to be registered is the application or object method name, its corresponding menu items and where they are to be placed in the menu structure, how to invoke the application, and the type(s) of object to which it applies.

More sophisticated forms of menu integration allow for the registration of multiple actions or methods from a particular object or application (as opposed to one) and the formulation of tools with registration of subtool actions under tool menu bars. In any case, based on this registered information, the GMI can make the actions available based on selected objects, and the application invoker can issue requests to the appropriate applications and actions as specified by the user.

Dialog integration: dialog boxes, charts, tables, graphs

The next level of integration with the GMI involves using the dialog generation capabilities to generate dialog boxes, charts, graphs and tables. Integration with the Dialog Generators can be done in a couple of ways. For preconceived dialogs and charts, the commands for building them can be installed when the application or object registers with the GMI. Then when a given dialog is required (as a result of user interaction), it need simply be referenced and the generator has it immediately available for generation and ready for any associated data to be included or presented with it. Alternatively, dynamic dialogs can be created programmatically by calling dialog generation methods directly and supplying the information to be displayed.

View and map creation

Probably the most sophisticated form of GMI integration is the creation and sharing of map views. The simplest types of view, as noted earlier, are collections of objects that share a common set of properties. These can be created arbitrarily on the basis of specific object attribute values, or by geographic or physical organization. This is the means by which users most typically create views; interacting with the attribute filters provided by the Object Locator, a resulting list of objects can be combined into a single view. This allows the users to organize objects into collections conducive to the work required and the manner in which they mentally organize their environment.

More sophisticated map generation can be achieved through applications that interact directly with the View Generator to create map views based on discovered topology information. This is the only feasible way to monitor and control the physical and logical components (which change and migrate so frequently) in medium and large-scale environments. Applications that generate map views are typically tailored to understand particular topologies, containing within them the knowledge to dynamically interpret a topology datastore and direct the GMI presentation. These applications not only generate the map views in great detail, but also keep them up to date in terms of the existence and status of the objects in their topologies.

20.4.3   Means for inter-application communication

The views presented by the GMI can serve as an integration point between applications. This can be accomplished by taking output from one application and feeding it as input to another. In its simplest form, this consists of exchanging object lists. The user may request an action to be done (such as a *locate* based on object attributes) which results in a list of objects. This list can then be leveraged as input to another application. To facilitate this, applications need to integrate with the Presentation Filter to have it highlight specific objects. Then the user must have the capability to convert *highlights* into *selections* so that the selected objects can be acted on.

In more sophisticated forms of exchange, actual data output (as opposed to a simple object listing) should be convertible as input to another application. Doing this most likely requires support of an application architecture outside of the GMI that provides data transformation services and other mechanisms for data exchange and application synchronization.

20.5   Summary

Our exploration of a Graphical Management Interface began with the three primary needs of a GMI user: appropriate information about the managed environment, access to control mechanisms for appropriately changing the environment, and tools to do this in an intuitive, effective manner. Human factors were taken into consideration as we explored the requirements of object and information presentation through map views, charts, tables and other presentation mechanisms, as well as control mechanisms, such as management roles, tools and subtools, and policies. Human factors requirements were also discussed in terms of the user interaction model, standards, maxims to follow for creating a usable GMI implementation, and extensibility of the GMI design.

The requirements that arose from the primary needs and human factors considerations led us to a model for a GMI. This model identified the major components for presenting information and making control available to the user through the Dialog Presentation, Views Presentation, and Management Roles Integration Modules. These modules, along with the primary datastores they depend on, were discussed in terms of their content, functionality and interdependencies. The culmination of these components and various datastores into a GMI resulted in a model that forms the basis and concepts for designing a sophisticated GMI implementation consistent with the usability and functional needs originally identified.

Abbreviations

GMI	Graphical Management Interface
GUI	Graphical User Interface
LAN	Local Area Network
OSF	Open Software Foundation
RPC	Remote Procedure Call

References

Akscyn R. M. and McCracken D. L. (1988). KMS: A distributed hypermedia system for managing knowledge in organizations. *Communications of the ACM,* **31**(7), 820–35

Hartson H. R. and Hix D., eds. (1988). *Advances in Human Computer Interaction, Volume 2.* Ablex Publishing Corporation

Hewlett-Packard Co. (1992). *HP OpenView Windows Application Design and Style Guide*, Part Number J2310-90002

IBM (1991). *Common User Access: Advanced Interface Design Reference.* Cary, North Carolina

Kearsley G. and Shneiderman B. (1989). *Hypertext Hands-on!* Addison-Wesley

Martin J. (1990). *Hyperdocuments and How To Create Them.* Prentice Hall

Open Software Foundation (1992). *OSF/Motif Style Guide, Version 1.2* Prentice Hall

Shneiderman B. (1987). *Designing the User Interface: Strategies for Effective Human Computer Interaction.* Addison-Wesley

Chapter 21

Artificial Intelligence in Support of Distributed Network Management

Shri K. Goyal

GTE Laboratories Incorporated,
40 Sylvan Road,
Waltham, MA 02254, USA
Email: skg0@gte.com

In this chapter, we take a look at some of the characteristics of the future networks and evaluate how artificial intelligence (AI) techniques can be used in automating the complex control, problem-solving, and decision-making tasks in a distributed network environment.

21.1   Introduction

During the past quarter of a century, and more so in the past decade, worldwide telecommunication network capabilities have rapidly advanced to meet the challenge of the information age. The pace has been further fueled by customer demand for a variety of innovative services that require the support of a high-quality reliable voice/data network. Current network technology enhancements have given rise to many sophisticated network surveillance, control, and decision-support systems. Management and administration of a complex integrated network presents a new challenge for network operators, designers, and technology innovators.

The current telecommunications environment is dynamic and transitional. The US Public Switched Telephone Network (PSTN) is currently operating with a mostly digital switching and interoffice transmission plant. Fiber optics is now the prevalent transmission growth and replacement medium, and is also penetrating the outside plant of the local exchange carriers (LECs). At a different level, SS7 out-of-band signaling is being rapidly introduced, and the hierarchical routing structure of conventional long-distance networks has been replaced by dynamic non-hierarchical routing, resulting in a marked improvement in network availability and robustness at reduced costs. At yet another level, the two-layer architecture network element (NE) and operation support system (OSS) is transitioning toward a three-layer architecture (NE, controller cluster or a mediation device and OSS) to deal with the network complexity, multivendor systems, and multiple organizations to focus on service orientation in future networks (Goyal, 1990). Those major evolutionary steps have created the need for a sophisticated OSS that supports integration of the network, information technology, and business process reengineering.

In this environment, expert systems have moved out of the laboratory and into real use. Along with their use, a whole new style of automation system design and programming is being introduced in telecommunication systems. The paradigm of rule-based knowledge representation and reasoning has been the basic technology used, and it has been successfully applied to a wide range of "real-world" problems, from basic equipment troubleshooting to global network management. Although this paradigm has been a powerful software technology, there is some evidence that more powerful tools and paradigms will be needed to handle anticipated automation requirements of what is most often referred to as the advanced intelligent network (AIN).

The academic and industrial AI communities have been pursuing research in knowledge technologies, often dubbed the second-generation expert systems. In this chapter, we take a look at some of the factors listed above and attempt to evaluate how knowledge technologies might penetrate even further in automating ever more complex control, reasoning, and decision-making tasks. We also present examples of laboratory technologies in some of the key areas of AI which will likely support telecommunication network operation and management.

21.2   Artificial intelligence (AI) technologies

Traditional algorithmic approaches have, in the past, proved satisfactory for managing networks. These approaches alone are not sufficient anymore for the management and control of complex networks (Goyal et al., 1990). They must be complemented with more potentially powerful heuristic approaches, such as are manifested in artificial intelligence (AI) systems (Goodman et al., 1989).

AI is, among other things, a set of programming methodologies that focuses on the techniques used to solve problems by generating new strategies and plans, and even generates new domain knowledge. Expert systems, a subfield of AI, provides a new, often successful, way to attack problems that previously have been considered non-solvable by machines. Utilizing human expertise and domain knowledge, the techniques focus on the use of declarative (factual) knowledge and relatively simple rules of inference for putting that knowledge to work on a specific problem. Many successful systems have emerged using this technology.

Research has shown that basic knowledge about the domain alone is not enough to get the performance exhibited by most experts. The people performing the tasks acquired another kind of knowledge, "experience" that allowed them to concentrate on the most likely causes of a problem and to adapt answers to the specific problems and even learn to improve their performance over time. The people who do this well are regarded as experts. The programs that capture their problem-solving strategies and selectively apply them under specific circumstances are called expert systems.

Most current expert systems utilize rule-based and other basic technologies. Several important technologies, which would potentially provide much-needed "power" to future AI systems, are under development in various laboratories. Some of these key technologies are targeted for providing:

i)   Transparent interoperability in heterogeneous distributed and cooperative intelligent computer systems;

ii) Higher-level knowledge representation for better utilization of a domain expert's knowledge;

iii) Techniques for distributed problem solving through knowledge sharing between intelligent agents; and

iv) Self-improving ability to the systems in a dynamic environment through machine-learning techniques. These technologies and their ramifications are further discussed in Section 21.4.

21.2.1   Expert systems in support of network operations

A variety of expert systems have been employed in telecommunications as operation support systems (OSS) and for other functions. Unfortunately, most systems are designed to solve a local and constrained problem without paying much attention to the "distributedness" of the networks. A recent survey article (Wright and Vesonder, 1990) separates the existing systems into three main functional categories: maintenance, provisioning, and network administration. The maintenance systems provide monitoring, troubleshooting, and diagnosis support to keep the networks operating efficiently and reliably. Provisioning and planning applications support development of flexible network evolution plans and designs, configuration, and execution of these plans. Network administration and management applications help manage the network traffic, and plan and execute a workable strategy when exceptions occur. Other successful miscellaneous application areas relate to sales and system configuration support, billing, facility assignment, and database management.

Table 21.1 lists some expert systems that have been tested and/or are in use in telecommunications today. Diagnostic expert systems are, by far, the most popular application in telecommunications, spanning public telephone to packet-switched networks. Well over a dozen expert systems have been reported to provide monitoring, troubleshooting, and fault diagnosis. Switch maintenance, typically for the older technology switches, is a common application. Perhaps expertise on the older switches tends to disappear as the switch technicians move on and work on the new switch types. Besides, new switches are quite sophisticated, with "intelligence" and built-in self-diagnostics to identify and report their own hardware faults.

Software faults or bugs are difficult to diagnose internally, or even by external systems. Therefore, almost no systems are currently available for the latest generation of switches, despite a clear need in this area.

Table 21.1 Examples of expert systems for telecommunication network support.

System	Task Performed	AI Method	Type, Status	Environment
Advanced Maintenance facility (AMF) British Telecom (Thandasseri, 1986)	Finds fault in TXE4A telephone exchanges	Basically a production system	Diagnostic, field tested	16-bit Micro; UNIX SAGE and LISP
Central Office Maintenance Printout Analysis and Suggestion System (COMPASS) (GTE) (Prerau et al., 1985)	Finds Faults in GTE's No 2	Mix of frames, rules, LISP and active values	Diagnostic, field tested	Xerox 11xx KEE and INTERLISP-D
Automated Cable Expertise (ACE)(Zeldin et al., 1986; Vensonder et al., 1983)	Troubleshoots telephone company local loop plant	Forward-chaining rules	Diagnostic commercial product, over 40 systems deployed	AT&T 3B2, UNIX OPS4 and LISP C
Network Management Expert System (NEMESYS)(AT&T) (Guatteru and Villarreal, 1985)	Reviews traffic completion data and suggests traffic control changes	Mix of rules, procedure and active values	Monitor, research prototype	Symbolics KEE
Network Trouble Shooting Consultant (Hannan, 1987)	Finds problems in DECnet and Ethernet LANs	Forward-chaining rules with confidence factors	Diagnostic, field tested	VAX EXPERT
Net/Advisor (BB&N) (Mantleman, 1986)	Monitors real-time network status and suggests actions to take when problems are diagnosed	Back-chaining rules (PROLOG) with LISP interface code	Diagnostic, commercial	Symbolics PROLOG and LISP
DESIGNET (BB&N) Bernstein, 1987)	Assists in building a data communications network	Object-oriented programming	Design, research prototype	Symbolics 36xx ZETALISP
MAX (NYNEX)	Analyzes local loop trouble reports and outputs dispatch recommendations	ART rules and mixed paradigm	Diagnostic, deployed in 42 NYNEX locations	SUN Inc. Workstation
IAS (Ferrara et al., 1989)	Analyzes alarm for Italian packet network	C & OPS-83	Monitoring/ diagnostic prototype under evaluation	VAX workstation
ARACHNE	Supports planning interoffice hierarchical network		Planning/ provisioning prototype	SUN communicating with IMS databases
NEC's network configurer	Planning for corporate communication and multiservice planning	OPS-83	Planning/provisioning under evaluation	32-bit workstation
AUTOTEST2 (AT&T) (Ackroff et al., 1988)	Isolates fault in Special Service Circuits using SARTS remote test system	Rule-based programming OPS-83 (and routines)	Diagnostic, deployed product	OPS-83 and C in UNIX on AT&T 3B2
SSCFI (GTE)	Isolates faults in Special Service circuits using AT2, SARTS and other test systems	ART-IM rules and "schemas", C code, CrossTalk	Diagnostic, prototype under evaluation	ART-IM and C on UNIX
Expert Message Correlation System	TRAC & Resolve "unbillable" calls		Analysis, operational	HP9000, UNIX

Expert systems have been implemented and deployed for diagnosing faults in telephone outside plant – ACE (Zeldin *et al.*, 1986) and MAX; Special Service Circuits – Autotest (Ackroff *et al.*, 1988) and SSCFI; and in specific equipment other than the switches. Some of these expert systems have had a significant impact on day-to-day operations of large networks. For example, more than 40 ACE systems are now operational in six Regional Bell Operating Companies; MAX is in use in more than 40 NYNEX locations; Autotest2 and SSCFI are going through deployment phases for use in diagnosing faults in special service circuits by automating testing.

In the provisioning arena, the focus has been support for design – for example, DESIGNET (Bernstein, 1987) – and system configuration. Only recently is expert system technology being applied to network planning – for example, ARACHNE (Gilbert *et.al.*, 1992). When dealing with provisioning, one has to model the network as a distributed system. Modeling techniques for complex systems such as telecommunication networks are still not mature. Some attention is being devoted to developing applications.

The most common application in the network administration area is traffic routing or traffic management. In the public network, experts (and thus, potentially, expert systems) monitor traffic data and install switching controls to redirect traffic and relieve congestion in the network. NEMESYS (Guattery and Villarreal, 1985) at AT&T Bell Labs is an attempt to automate some of the decision-making abilities of the traffic manager. The routine decisions NEMESYS makes are influenced by network topology and the possible cause of congestion. Several specialized billing applications, such as toll fraud detection systems, are also being developed and evaluated.

Despite the striking name "expert system", it has been recognized that expert systems should act as background processes to support and complement decision-making activities. Expert systems were originally proposed as stand-alone systems not easily integrated owing to their specialized hardware and software platforms and little intercommunication ability with existing databases. Originally, this brought about a lot of resistance from the MIS and operations personnel. The situation is changing drastically as professional workstations, lately using a UNIX environment, are becoming an acceptable development and deployment environment (to the MIS community) and as powerful tools are becoming available for these standard workstations.

Today, seamless integration of these "high tech" systems in the existing operations environment is essential for their acceptance. The deployment of many such systems has taken place recently. Figure 21.1 shows GTE's Special Service Circuit Fault Isolation (SSCFI) system integrated in the existing telephone environment. The system "acts" as an expert test technician in defining and conducting the test, evaluating the test results, and routing the report to the proper repair group. In actual operation, the system interacts with a variety of telephone operations databases and operation support systems. It picks up a trouble report from the TAS (Trouble Administrative System) queue, fetches the description of the circuit from Circuit Network Administration System (CNAS) and facility data from MARK (Mechanical Automation Record Keeping), conducts the tests using AUTOTEST 2 and SARTS (Switched Access Remote Test System), and routes the diagnosed results to the repair group through TAS (SSCFI 92). Multiple SSCFI processes are operational on IBM RS/6000 machines, with intercommunication processes running CrossTalk scripts and C code.

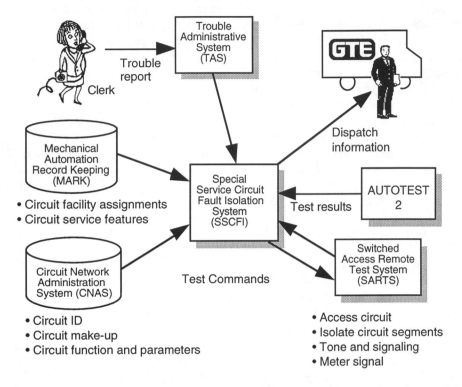

Figure 21.1 Integration of a fault isolation expert system with operations for special service circuits.

Many successful general-purpose development tools have been introduced in the past few years. Efforts to build specialized development tools with knowledge representation suitable for the telecommunications domain have met with only limited success, partly owing to lack of a formal model of network elements and their lack of interoperability between systems. For a specialized network application tool to be useful in a distributed environment, there should be a common structure or a common usable language between the problems to be solved. Owing to the lack of these facilities, large networks have been unable to use specialized, and potentially powerful, knowledge representation mechanisms – for example, model-based (Davis and Smith, 1989) and experience-based techniques. These common structures and models are slowly evolving as their value is being recognized.

Expert systems, in general, exhibit brittleness in their behavior. Generally they are built as closed systems by incorporating expert knowledge within the defined region of their expertise. As such, within the region of expertise, they perform at an expert level and totally fail just beyond these limits of expertise. Most systems today still are stand-alone, off-line, performing a well-defined and confined task. Expansion of the breadth of coverage, and, thus, their power and usefulness, is necessary to get some "real" value from these systems. This will be achieved by utilizing advanced technologies, such as are discussed in Section 21.4.

21.3   Expert system limitations and the need for enabling technologies

AI technology has delivered many successful expert systems in various industries. Most noteworthy applications are in manufacturing, scheduling, and verification applications. However, it seems that telecommunications has been less successful than other industries in fielding expert systems and reaping benefits from their use. Without detracting from the successes of the systems, we can identify limitations of existing expert system technology, and speculate as to why some of these limitations are especially critical for successful use of expert systems in the telecommunications industry.

The modern telecommunication networks in the United States have historically evolved through the combining and merging of many large and small regional networks, owned and operated by separate, often potentially competing, organizations. These mergers have created some very significant incompatibilities between interconnecting systems, operation practices, and operation support systems. Transparent operations of the interconnecting networks demand interoperability among systems. Techniques for intelligent communication between distributed objects, databases, and systems are needed for operation of large distributed networks. These will be supplemented by intelligent user and man-machine interfaces. However, several basic technologies must be developed if the industry is to reap the benefits of enhancing techniques in managing large intelligent distributed networks.

To date, most expert systems are stand-alone, working in isolation, and independent of other systems performing, often, related tasks. Most tele-communication systems are composed of a large number of distributed systems with little interoperability between subsystems that form a "complete" system. This creates an artificial boundary between intelligent (OS) systems. Also, significantly lacking from the expert system technology is a standard "knowledge interface" language and a formalism for interactive problem solving by which disparate expert systems can communicate. These are the topics of distributed systems inter-operability management and distributed AI, technologies that are especially critical in telecommunications. Such technology is crucial for an inherently distributed system domain where coordination across regions and functions is crucial for achieving any acceptable network performance.

The well-known "knowledge-acquisition bottleneck" is another kind of limitation, one that lies between the expert and the expert system. This limitation is experienced across industries, but is manifested in telecommunications in unique ways.

*   Knowledge representation schemes developed for other industries are often inappropriate for representing telecommunication knowledge. A notable

example is the kind of knowledge used by network traffic managers, which is largely experience-based, rather than derivable from precompiled heuristics or well-behaved domain models. Discussed in a later section is research on eliciting and representing this kind of "case-based" knowledge.

- The rate of technological change in telecommunication networks is remarkably high and accelerating; the expertise needed to operate the network evolves with each introduction of new hardware, signaling systems, routing strategies, or service offerings. Expert systems, as currently fielded, capture only a snapshot of this changing knowledge, and "evolve" only to the extent that they are revised by their maintainers. Machine learning is therefore a clear requirement for future systems in order to keep pace with accelerating change in network technology.

Another important feature of network operations, the time-constrained nature of decision-making, has two effects that are especially significant for the use of AI technology:

- The need for real-time response is inherent in many network operations, such as traffic control, for which the timing of an intervention is crucial to its effect on network performance. Real-time expert systems are only beginning to be evaluated, and remain an active research area.

- Because human reaction times are too long for many network operations, especially those in support of future service offerings such as dynamic reallocation of bandwidth, the human role in such tasks must be only supervisory. As automated systems perform more "closed loop" functions, the performance of the network is increasingly dependent on their reliability. For expert system technology, this requires improved verification and validation techniques. These topics have only recently begun to receive attention.

The challenges for expert systems that are posed by distributed network applications will determine the role of this technology in the future of telecommunications. The remainder of this chapter will identify some critical technologies and focus on how some of the key technology challenges identified here are being met by emerging AI technologies. We will also provide an overview of the research efforts, especially at GTE Laboratories, that apply these advanced techniques to solve telecommunication-specific problems.

21.4   Enabling knowledge technologies

The future siblings of the existing systems will be broader in scope and coverage, and more integrated with the control of the systems they monitor. Thus, rather than covering a subset of messages or alarms produced by some piece of equipment or system, they will cover a majority of meaningful messages from a variety of equipment, distributed over the entire network. Also, systems will be built for network elements not covered today. Table 21.2 lists a set of current and future operations system functions and a list of desired enabling technologies that will make the future operational capability possible.

Table 21.2 Enabling technologies in future operations support systems in distributed telecommunication systems.

Function	Future Operation	Underlying Technology
Remote Testing of Distributed System	Non-vendor-specific monitoring and data analysis systems with expert repair capability.	Standard interfaces. Intelligent interoperability, DOM. Data filtering, data correlation. Expert system, DAI.
Network Maintenance	Proactive maintenance of switches and outside plant. Mechanized trouble analysis and dispatch.	Expert system and operations research (OR) methods. Machine learning.
Traffic Management	Dynamic network reconfiguration on demand.	Expert system. Machine learning.
Performance Measurement	Support for performance enhancement and tuning. Self-healing capability.	Distributed planning, problem solving. Distributed interoperable intelligent system.
Provisioning of Special and Enhanced Services	Automatic provisioning of dynamically reconfigurable networks under software control. Mechanized design and testing of special circuits.	Network operating system (NOS), DOM. Expert system for design, analysis, and testing. Intelligent networks/services. Enhanced transaction systems. Network security.
Network Administration and Billing	Intelligent billing systems. Toll-fraud management.	Intelligent fraud-management systems. User interfaces, DOM. Knowledge discovery.
Network Management	AI-based dynamic network management. Intelligent customer and operator interfaces. Centralized customer contact systems.	Real-time AI systems. Fuzzy logic. DAI distributed problem solving. Man-machine interface. Machine learning. System integration.
Network Services Support	Dynamic service design and Provisioning	NOS, DAI, DOM. Enhanced expert systems.

Network managers must implement appropriate controls even when definite decisions cannot be made in the absence of reliable data or under time constraints.

Future intelligent systems should be able to suggest "approximate" controls under such conditions, for example, by using fuzzy logic. The knowledge and accuracy of expert systems will be enhanced by incorporating the knowledge from several experts, thus by sharing expertise or negotiating solutions. This will lead to the creation of corporate knowledge repositories or groups for each critical expertise area. This corporate resource will be updated and enhanced on a continuous basis through machine-learning technologies. Thus, the networks will manage themselves effectively by using integrated automated intelligent systems in a distributed network environment and provide performance and reliable services to the users.

The network domain is complex and difficult to manage through automation. It requires a combination of situation assessment, problem solving, planning, and control in near real time, almost on a continuous basis (Goyal *et al* .,1990; Goodman *et al* ., 1989]. It is a domain for which a **formal model does not exist** and expertise, at best, is "spotty" and often uncoordinated. What makes the situation even more difficult is that the domain has been very dynamic, with constantly changing architectures as the new generation of innovative services is being designed to meet the future services requirements. Perhaps all these factors are contributing to the slow rate of introduction of meaningful expert systems in this domain. Clearly, a new breed of more powerful techniques is needed to make a real difference. This requires significant technical developments in key technology areas. Following are some examples.

The management of large networks with intelligence, distributed among various network elements and systems, will require interoperability of heterogeneous distributed computer systems involving both programs and databases and cooperation among "intelligent agents." Issues related to distributed management and core contributing technologies are receiving a lot of attention in research laboratories and standardization organizations. Also, activities on distributed object management (DOM) at GTE Laboratories are developing tools and methods for working with such open, interoperable systems in the computing environment of the future. This work is discussed in Section 21.4.1.

Networks require a wide variety of coordinated expertise. Activities and operations of a large number and variety of disparate components must be coordinated. This demands cooperation (and negotiations) among individual intelligent systems (Durfee *et al.*, 1989; Davis and Smith, 1983) and sharing of expertise to fill in the expertise gaps. Issues such as these are being addressed under distributed AI (DAI) research. GTE Laboratories is developing a framework for cooperative problem solving and building a TEAM-CPS testbed for Customer Network Control as an application (Weihmayer *et al.*, 1990a). This activity is discussed in Section 21.4.2.

The dynamic nature of today's evolving network demands utilization of changing expertise. Model-based reasoning and experience-based reasoning support decision making based on a formal problem model or instances of successful experiences, respectively. Such knowledge representation paradigms have proven to be powerful and useful in selected application domains. A testbed for traffic management, called NETTRAC, utilizing case-based reasoning (CBR) is being developed at GTE for network traffic management (Kopeikina *et al.*,1988a). This activity is discussed in Section 21.4.3.

Network configurations and functionality change with demand on a regular basis, and so also does the needed expertise in managing the network. The ability of systems to learn from their successful experiences and mistakes is becoming an essential requirement as intelligent systems proliferate in the existing tele-communication environment. Major initiatives on machine learning research are being pursued at various universities and industrial organizations. Section 21.4.4 discusses GTE's activities in the machine-learning area and our work on knowledge discovery for extracting meaningful knowledge from large amounts of data.

21.4.1 Providing interoperability through distributed object management

With the widespread infusion of computer systems in distributed networks, the future networks will consist of vast networks of heterogeneous, autonomous, and distributed computing resources (Vittal *et al.*, 1992). These resources, properly managed, will be used as building blocks in creating systems for supporting future information technology services.

The requirements for creating and managing large distributed systems can be met in two phases. The first phase is *interconnectivity*. Most current computer systems are disjointed, and unable to communicate (exchange messages) with other systems. Even if they do, interconnectivity guarantees only communication. It does not guarantee that the two systems understand each other sufficiently to cooperate or work together in providing any service.

The second phase is the more ambitious goal of *interoperability*. Two or more systems are interoperable if they can interact to jointly execute tasks. Simple tools for achieving interoperability are increasingly being provided in the form of programming capabilities such as remote procedure call facilities. More advanced forms of interoperability require mutual understanding not only at the level of complete systems or individual programs, but also at the *data/type level*. This is necessary in order to support the integration of heterogeneous information in, for example, advanced multimedia applications, and to support the storage of such information in integrated repositories. The ultimate goal is to ensure interoperability, in order to be able to treat the complete set of resources (computers, network facilities, data, programs, and so on) available on the network as a unified system.

A further level of interoperability, which we refer to as *intelligent interoperability*, requires interaction between information systems, some of which may be intelligent themselves and capable of functioning as intelligent agents concerning their computing capabilities. Intelligent interoperability would allow the set of resources available on the network to be shared among the agents through intercommunication between agents.

The design, construction, use, and evolution of current and future intelligent distributed systems will require the extension and integration of currently disjoint technologies, rather than of any one technology. Unlike past major advances in computing, future distributed computing, whatever its form, will require knowledge from multiple disciplines. Database systems can contribute information management techniques, particularly for distributed or heterogeneous databases, as well as efficient implementation techniques for information bases. Artificial intelligence can contribute knowledge representation and reasoning techniques, on the one hand, and distributed problem solving in a multi-agent environment on the other. Operating systems can contribute resource management techniques over large distributed computer/communications networks. Programming languages can contribute languages and type/object systems for cooperative, distributed programming. Software/knowledge/information engineering can contribute design and development environments and methodologies for building intelligent cooperative distributed systems. Computer communications can provide the necessary underlying communication and interconnection technology. We refer to the combination of these technologies as *distributed object management* (DOM) technology. DOM is an essential support technology for distributed systems operations and management.

A generic architecture of distributed object managers

Just as we might think of the problem of managing distributed data as involving the development of one or more *distributed database managers*, we can think of the problem of managing distributed objects (for example, an intelligent agent) as involving the development of one or more *distributed object managers* (DOMs). DOMs are intended to deal with the problem of integrating heterogeneous data, processing, and knowledge resources residing within a network of computing systems by acting as intermediaries between these resources.

An architecture of DOMs consists of an arbitrary number of distributed (physical) nodes, each running one or more application programs, database systems, objects (if the system is object-oriented), and so on. that constitute its computing *resources*, and a collection of *clients* (which may also be application programs, software tools, objects, and so on) that make requests for operations to be performed by these resources. One or more DOMs act as *intermediaries* between these clients and resources. DOMs make the computing resources of the system appear to be *objects* (whether they are actually object-oriented or not), with the DOMs acting as object managers, permitting clients to make requests involving resources that reside anywhere in the system without having knowledge of the location, implementation details, etc. of the resources involved. Clients and resources are connected to the DOMs through software interfaces that translate requests and results passing through them to the forms required by the various components.

An architecture of DOMs includes at least the following:

- A collection of object implementations, that is, entities having both data and a set of operations that they can perform are the resources managed by a DOM.

- Client interfaces allowing clients to request objects (or the DOMs) to perform operations, provide the arguments to the operations, and receive results.

- Messaging facilities (provided by the DOMs) that forward client requests to the objects to which they are directed.

- Object interfaces allowing the DOMs to invoke the implementations of objects in support of client requests.

- A distributed collection of (physical) computer systems that provide the environments in which the above components run, and communication facilities connecting them.

DOMs may also provide other facilities, for example, name services or repositories providing information about the various objects (and their interfaces) in the system. A DOM may also provide more advanced facilities, such as support for transactions and queries.

An example distributed object management architecture

Figure 21.2 shows a specific example of such an architecture. In this example, there are two nodes, each running one system (an object-oriented database system (OODBMS) and a word-processing system), and each of these systems is interfaced through a separate DOM. The DOMs are connected by a communications network.

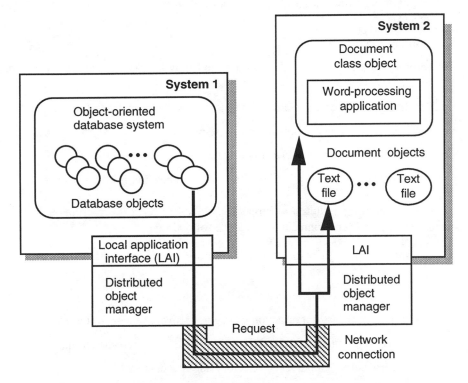

Figure 21.2 Distributed object management: an example.

An object in the OODBMS makes a request to perform some operation on what appears to it to be a document object. The request goes through the interface to the DOM at System 1, and is routed to the DOM at System 2, having an interface to the document object referenced in the request. The word-processing application at

System 2 may not be object-oriented. However, its interface to the local DOM allows that DOM to treat the text files associated with that application as document objects. In response to the request from the OODBMS, the DOM at System 2 invokes the word-processing application if it is not already executing, causes the text file corresponding to the document object referenced in the request to be loaded, and then invokes the requested operation automatically.

The DOMs, acting together, create and manage a network-wide object space. The term *object* refers to a collection of object types and associated instances, and is similar to, but a generalization of, the concept of a database schema and its associated database.

A given DOM thus provides an object-oriented interface to all resources available within the network, concealing such aspects as the location and implementation details.

The distributed object management functions performed by DOMs generally include the following:

- Maintaining information about available objects in the network and how to access them.

- Routing messages sent to objects.

- Moving objects into and out of storage, and moving objects between sites (and translating them if necessary).

- Loading procedures associated with objects into the execution environment.

- Scheduling and synchronizing request execution.

- Registering and storing intermediate or final result objects.

- Providing security, exception handling, concurrency control, and recovery.

Core technology required to support advanced features for interoperability in distributed computing environments include the following:

- Communication infrastructures – remote procedure call, peer-to-peer messaging.

- Security managers – authentication, encryption, access control.

- Reliability managers – transaction manager, recovery manager, log manager.

- Advanced/distributed operating system services – resource allocation.

- Naming services – global name directory and management.

- Control – job and request scheduling, brokering.

- Interoperability services – information and language translation, data interchange, information/object migration, copy management, other transparency services.

- Distributed computing/programming services.

- Network services.

- General services – sorting, math, data conversion.

- Repository services.

Initially, the integration of data and processing resources into DOMs will involve existing components not designed to function in this type of environment. As such, the integration may be somewhat difficult, and less than optimal in its performance. However, with the increasing use of object technology within the individual components of distributed systems, the boundaries between these components will begin to disappear, and tighter integration will be possible through the development of standard (or at least widely accepted) object models, and implementations supporting interfaces based on those models. This will make the integration of components in distributed networks possible, and should also greatly improve the interoperability of intelligent heterogeneous multivendor systems. These architectures will enable the next-generation distributed operations and information systems.

21.4.2   Distributed artificial intelligence (DAI)

The current expert system technology, for the most part, supports developing systems in small, well-constrained domains. To tackle larger, more complex problems in a distributed environment, several of these autonomous systems have to be integrated in a team to make them work cooperatively in a distributed environment. Besides, intelligent network elements integrated in distributed systems will create a natural need for DAI for coordination of intelligent activity.

A central objective for DAI research lies in the hope of, some day, creating a "society" of expert systems in which a set of selected computer programs acting as "agents" can cooperate and share their (local) expertise in much the same way as human experts do, for example, in a meeting room in an *ad hoc* consultative relationship. A metaphor for this form of cooperative problem solving can be described by a "chef and architect" interaction, each an expert in his or her domain with specific viewpoints on designing a kitchen, making decisions, and compromising through negotiations (Brandau and Weihmayer, 1989).

> *A chef wants a kitchen in which he or she can work conveniently. The chef knows all about cooking requirements, recipes, and the tools and appliances needed. The chef can read floor plans and suggest changes to suit personal preferences. The chef can design a convenient kitchen, but does not know about building codes, architectural issues, and costs associated with a design choice.*
>
> *An architect knows about the building design constraints, building codes, and architectural requirements for an "aesthetically pleasing" kitchen. The architect does not know the optimum and detail requirements that suit the cuisine style of the chef.*

The joint design process must proceed interactively. The architect proposes an initial layout. The chef fine-tunes the design to meet his or her specific requirements, and the architect considers and evaluates the proposed changes against the architectural constraints. There may be a need for a negotiating dialogue, for example, to meet the cost requirements. The optimum design requires interaction between the chef and the architect on the design process. Among the technical requirements that stand out in this example are:

i)   A language for communication between the chef and the architect;

ii) A negotiation strategy; and

iii) A framework to represent the domain expertise, for example, of the chef and the architect. It is expected that a better design, for both parties, evolves through a cooperative dialogue as their *respective expertise* is utilized.

Similar cooperative problem-solving paradigms surface in distributed network management. The following section describes an example of inter-agent problem solving in a customer (private) network control (CNC) application in telecommunications. A DAI approach was taken at GTE Laboratories to solve this problem interactively between the customer network manager and the public network manager. Some key ideas motivated the selection, including the inherent distribution of network control to the customer, the occurrence of conflicts among the controllers, and the tightly coupled interdependence of problem solutions during crisis or resource conflict.

Customer networks can include a diverse range of elements such as voice/data switches, multiplexors, digital cross-connect systems and the backbone transport network. Some facilities may be customer-owned and some public-network-owned. Currently, the key attributes of CNC are controlling network traffic through switch nodes for dynamic load balancing and network reconfiguration, and access control of external traffic inbound to the customer networks. A composite example of a private network with extensive customer network control would involve a corporate network that can reconfigure in real time to meet a demand for multipoint video sessions, temporarily off-load voice traffic to the public network, reassign incoming 800 traffic to various call-answering centers, and balance its use of "virtual" private network service and dedicated leased public facilities.

Cooperative problem solving for customer network control

TEAM-CPS (Testbed Environment for Autonomous Multi-agent Cooperative Problem Solving) is a research testbed that explores cooperative problem solving among dissimilar agents (Weihmayer *et al.,* 1990). Inter-agent cooperation in the testbed is currently demonstrated by having agents with different views of the network, but with the common purpose of implementing a self-healing network, helping each other improve their respective local solutions and **jointly** solve a facility failure problem.

Two agent types, the private or customer network manager and the public network manager, are defined. An agent in this context is a computer program with autonomous reasoning, problem solving (for example, an expert system), and communication expertise that can participate in organized joint problem solving with other agents.

In the initial version, TEAM-CPS agents were based on a blackboard inference engine which encodes local expertise, agent control knowledge, and knowledge about the cooperative environment as knowledge sources activated by a common object store. Areas of AI research involved in the design of such agents include automated reasoning, planning, meta-level control of autonomous agents, and inter-agent communications. To support a meaningful cooperative dialogue, agents need a common language, a dialogue control mechanism, knowledge and goal sharing capabilities, including explicit models of other agents' goals and strategies. Customer and public network manager agents cooperate and negotiate in TEAM-CPS, as illustrated in Figure 21.3 and discussed in the following scenario.

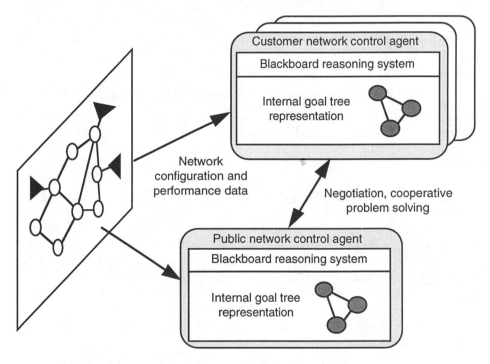

Figure 21.3 Cooperation in the customer network control domain.

In the face of a facility failure that affects both the public and the customer network, all the agents begin to plan for restoral. In this initial planning, the customer agents do not know of any resource restrictions in the public network, so they simply request that their lost capacity be restored. Each affected customer agent communicates its request, in the form of a goal tree plan, to the public agent. The public agent then combines these requests, and attempts to fairly distribute the available resources among the requesting agents, denying the remaining, infeasible parts of the customer plans. Again, these replies are communicated in the form of annotations and extensions to the respective customers' goal-tree proposals. Thus, goal trees provide the inter-agent language as well as the internal planning representation used by the agents.

Just as the public agent was able to refine the customers' plans because of its knowledge of the physical limitations of the network, the customer agents can refine the public agent's counterproposal to conform to their local knowledge of traffic loads and priorities. In addition, they may propose to exercise other control options, such as reconfiguration of existing leased trunks, rerouting of voice traffic to the public network, or retargeting 800 traffic to bypass the failed facility. When the public agent receives these updated proposals, it makes one last stage of improvement by using both its knowledge of traffic demand on the public network and of the physical implementation of existing leased trunks (to create more efficient reconfigurations than could be found by the customer alone).

As this example demonstrates, inter-agent cooperation and negotiation yield a better overall solution, superior to any that could be obtained without the dialog. This sharing of expertise and interactive exchange of partial solutions among the agents is crucial to maintaining coherent control of the customer and public networks, and is thus an important supporting technology for future networks.

TEAM-CPS: integrating planning and agent-oriented programming

Recent evolution of TEAM-CPS has focused on more general approaches to local problem solving and agent control for cooperation. This focus on communication and planning as separate but closely related functions in the process of inter agent cooperation led to the development of a new agent architecture based on the integration of two AI paradigms: classical AI planning and means-ends analysis (Weihmayer and Tan, 1991; Covo et al., 1991) and a new paradigm, agent-oriented programming (AOP) (Shoham, 1991). As described earlier, the class of problems considered here requires planning as the primary problem-solving method. AOP provides the appropriate agent models to implement a needed control structure.

In AOP (Shoham, 1991), each agent has a mental state represented by knowledge, belief, commitment (for example, *agent a* is committed to *agent b* about *action c*), and other "modalities". Agents communicate with others through specialized (prespecified) messages, such as inform, request, offer, and reject. Each agent can also invoke local functions for problem solving. The AOP framework includes two major parts:

i)   a restricted formal language with clear syntax and semantics for describing mental state; and

ii)   an interpreted programming language, AGENT0, in which to program agents, with primitive communication commands such as REQUEST and INFORM.

TEAM-CPS uses a general off-the-shelf planner from Carnegie Mellon University (CMU) called PRODIGY. PRODIGY is a domain-independent problem-solving system used primarily for planning. It has a basic means-ends analysis planner, and its search can be guided by domain-independent or domain-specific control rules. During planning, PRODIGY searches for a sequence of operators that transform an initial state (the current state) into a final state (the goal state). Before using PRODIGY, a user (or a program) must specify the operators and the specific problem.

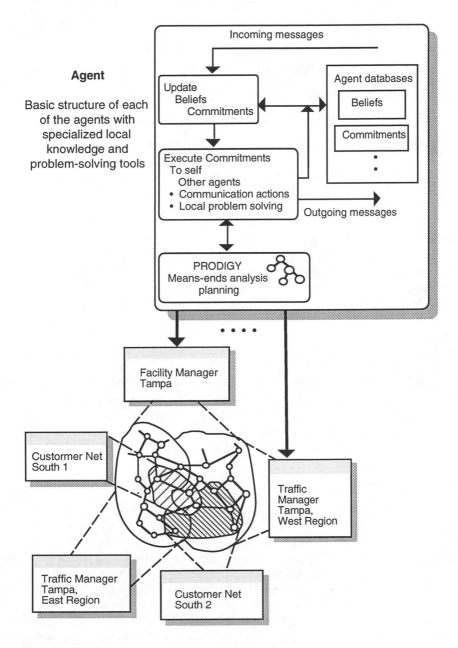

Figure 21.4 Structure of TEAM-CPS agents in a cooperative network management domain.

In TEAM-CPS, communication and planning are two separate, but interacting, layers. Agents are programmed with initial beliefs and commitments and with domain-specific functions as well as with a PRODIGY domain model. Some of the major issues involved in designing systems with coordinated agents are the following.

- How are local and non-local problem solving related in the act of cooperation?

- What language do agents use to cooperate and negotiate?

- How is the agent knowledge represented?

- How are the conflicts expressed and resolved?

- How can termination of coordination algorithms be guaranteed?

- What is the best coordination strategy for any given domain?

Figure 21.4 shows a hypothetical traffic and customer network management scenario for a local exchange area like Tampa. One of our goals with TEAM-CPS is to model such a system of operation support systems (OSS). Each OSS shown, for example, the Tampa Traffic Manager or the Customer Network Manager South 1, would be implemented as an autonomous agent in TEAM-CPS. The agent structure, shown in Figure 21.4, indicates the relationship between the belief and commitment revision mechanism in AGENT0 (that is, for each time increment, process the incoming messages, update the beliefs and commitments, and carry out the commitment rules for the current time) and the PRODIGY planning system.

This agent architecture has been shown to be extensible, computationally efficient, and simple to program (Weihmayer and Tan, 1991). There are, however, a number of issues that must be further researched before the approach can be generalized. There has been consistent progress in DAI research, but coherent applications of these results to solve meaningful problems have been slow. The need for large-problem solutions in complex networks is accelerating this pace, and we should see scaling of these techniques for managing large distributed networks.

21.4.3   Powerful knowledge representations for complex systems

Knowledge representation (KR) provides a systematic way of codifying what an expert knows about some domain. Ultimately, a computer must be able to store, process, and utilize this coded knowledge. The main criteria for assessing the power of a knowledge representational framework are (i) logical adequacy (ability to express the knowledge you wish to represent); (ii) expressive power (a language with well-defined and "complete" syntax and semantics); and (iii) notational convenience (agreed-upon conventions that make the information easy to write and read). Many representational schemes have been proposed, developed, and used in building systems (Brachman and Levesque, 1985; Koton, 1988; Kolodner et al., 1985). Most expert systems today use production rules and/or frames for knowledge representations. Rule-based paradigms offer adequate power for general-purpose work but seem to be insufficient for representing complex knowledge such as for the evolving distributed networks.

Many more sophisticated and powerful knowledge representation paradigms have been proposed. For example, model-based reasoning (MBR) (Davis and Hamscher, 1988) overcomes some limitations of these earlier approaches. The MBR technique is particularly well suited to diagnosis and troubleshooting applications, and can provide an essential KR technology for the network domain in generating a "best guess" solution when all the necessary information/data does not exist. MBR works through the interaction of observation (of the behavior of the actual device) and prediction (based on the model). It works on the presumption that if the model is correct, all the discrepancies between the observations and prediction arise from the *defect* in the device. Model-based approaches can be practically used when the device or the system can be formally modeled and the problem domain does not contain too many device interactions. As for the telecommunications domain, it is difficult to model a complete network on a consistent basis because of the wide variety of components it employs for diverse applications and their interactions. Individual devices can be modeled. However, modeling device interactions is very difficult when using this approach in the telecommunications domain. Although it is a serious area of current research, MBR still seems to suffer from performance problems, and thus applications to telecommunication systems must await more technical developments. The MBR approach has met success in process control applications.

Various representations are appropriate for specific representation of the knowledge that is required in any complex operation. Hybrid representations are likely to increase the robustness of expert systems, thereby overcoming the "brittleness" for which expert systems are criticized when unable to perform even slightly beyond their explicit domains of expertise. Several other knowledge representation paradigms have been developed. Of these, case-based reasoning (CBR), which uses analogical reasoning methods, is of particular interest. CBR, a method of problem solving, is particularly applicable to solving problems in large systems, problems such as arise in traffic congestion in large distributed network systems.

Case-based reasoning for traffic management

Analogical or case-based reasoning is a powerful mechanism for exploiting past experiences in planning and problem solving. A case-based reasoner solves problems by applying previously used solutions rather than generating a new solution to the problem from scratch. One advantage of this approach is the ability to use the large-grained knowledge representation of "cases" – the previously used solutions – rather than finer-grained rules, hence potentially enhancing the real-time performance of the systems.

Performance is surely important for real-time network applications, but there are also other requirements of the network domain, some of which stretch the capabilities of the existing CBR techniques. The need to monitor the continuous behavior of the network, and the need to aggregate problems that are distributed across the network, are two requirements that are the focus of our work at GTE. Learning new cases is also required, in order to support change in network management practices, as demanded by evolution in network technology, network elements, and support systems.

A prototype system, called NETTRAC (NETwork Traffic Routing Assistant using Cases), is being built at GTE Laboratories for traffic management (Brandau *et al.*, 1991). The system receives network performance data from a group of switches under its control, recognizes and interprets abnormal conditions that it observes, and develops plans for installing controls to alleviate network problems. With approval from the user, it installs the controls and *monitors* (Kopeikina *et al.*, 1988b) their effects, recommending fine-tuning and adjustments, when needed. Figure 21.5 shows the functional diagram of NETTRAC.

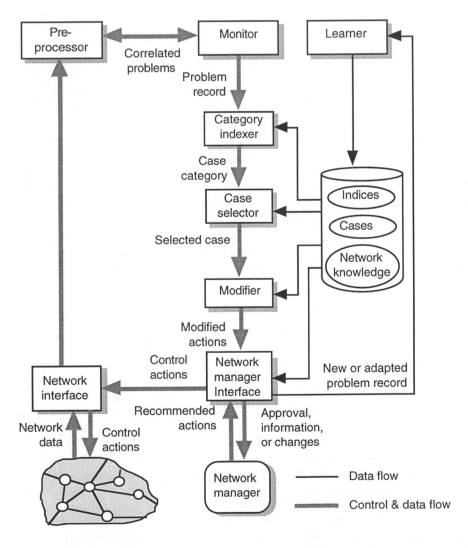

Figure 21.5 Case-based reasoning system architecture for network management.

NETTRAC currently handles the following four broad categories of network traffic problems:

- Trunk group overload (or "isolated-demand overflow")

- Focused overload

- Partial facility (trunk or switch) failure

- Complete facility failure

For NETTRAC to know how to handle a particular type of problem, we provide it with a description of how to recognize, treat, and monitor the problem. These descriptions are the "cases", "experience" or the "knowledge" in the form of past experiences, used by the case-based reasoner. To use these cases for solving network problems, NETTRAC must be able to find a relevant case when confronted with a problem. NETTRAC accomplishes this by indexing its cases according to the crucial features of a situation that together indicate the possible applicability of each case. Final selection of the specific case on which to model its response, "the problem solver," is done by evaluating the details of a situation to determine which case is most similar and most likely to lead to a favorable outcome.

Obviously, a large number of cases are required to describe all significant problems in a domain as complex as traffic management in a large network, and NETTRAC currently has only a (substantial) subset of the case knowledge it will ultimately need. We have, however, provided the system with a "case generalization" mechanism, the Modifier, that broadens the class of problems for which a case is applicable. It does this by defining specific circumstances under which a case may "borrow" attributes from another somewhat similar case. For example, a CODE-BLOCK control could be "borrowed" from some other case for any switch types that don't support the GAP control. This avoids the need to explicitly encode every possible combination of features in separate cases.

There are several advantages to be gained from this case-based approach when dealing with complex problems such as traffic management in a distributed network. Through incorporating a simple learning or case acquisition mechanism, the system can accumulate new cases as it gains experience. This makes CBR especially useful in evolving domains, or where much domain knowledge is missing or difficult to obtain, because the automatically acquired cases can adapt the system and track gradual changes in the problems of the domain. Also, CBR systems overcome the "brittleness" behavior exhibited by other approaches: rather than having to match a precise set of conditions, CBR systems are designed to handle situations that are analogous to, but not exactly like, those of which they have explicit knowledge. This feature is a result of "soft-matching" to determine case applicability, and of adapting the case to apply to a broader range of problems. There are also some efficiencies to be gained through CBR: because the system outlines a complete treatment plan, only one matching and selection cycle may be required for each network problem, compared with dozens or more for a rule-based system. This is the origin of the often-cited performance advantage of CBR (Koton, 1988) for time-constrained applications.

The ability to learn new cases from experience is an important contribution of CBR technology to NETTRAC. This feature makes use of the user's expertise as well as the system's own experience to extend its knowledge. New cases are added to the system's experience base when the user changes the system's proposed solution. As these cases accumulate, patterns emerge in the situations under which specific cases recur; the system uses these patterns to match a problem with the one in the case base. This adaptive indexing allows the system to retain reliable and fast retrieval despite an expanding set of stored cases. Together these capabilities enable NETTRAC to automatically expand its case base as it acquires experience with controlling the network.

Like all real-world CBR systems, the current NETTRAC implementation is really a hybrid of multiple knowledge representation strategies, with a large frame-based component and some simple "proto-rules." Additionally, it is a hybrid learning system because, in addition to case acquisition, it is demonstrating potential for a powerful knowledge representation paradigm for dealing with complex problems.

21.4.4   Machine learning for adapting self-improving systems

Machine-learning paradigm

'Learning denotes changes in the system that are adaptive in the sense that they enable the system to do the same tasks, drawn from the same population, more efficiently, and more effectively the next time' (Simon,1983).

Machine-learning is that branch of artificial intelligence which develops effective computational models and programs for self-improvement. Typically, learning systems require a high level of symbolic descriptions of the problem domain and the tasks to be addressed. The present-day machine-learning techniques are applicable to expert domains and expert systems.

The challenge addressed in the machine-learning work is the construction of programs that learn in various ways, including learning by training with examples and counter-examples of good performance; learning from experience (case-based reasoning, as discussed earlier); learning through deductive reasoning; and reorganizing and updating internal domain knowledge representation. The real challenge is to build an adaptive management system which effectively manages a large distributed system and improves its performance over time.

The high potential of payoff has generated a strong interest in machine-learning research and in the wealth of both symbolic methods, such as inductive or explanation-based learning, and nonsymbolic methods, such as connectionism and genetic algorithms.

Symbolic learning

A variety of machine-learning methods have been reported, for example, in knowledge-based learning (KBL) the domain knowledge base builds up incrementally. Explanation-based learning (EBL) is an example of KBL. In EBL, the learner starts with a domain theory, that is, rules or facts with which logical proofs or explanations are constructed to build up the knowledge. Inductive learning, on the other hand, is a process of acquiring knowledge by drawing inductive references from teacher- or environment-provided facts. The process attempts to derive a complete and correct description of a given phenomenon from specific observations of the phenomenon. It involves operations of generalizing, specializing, transferring, correcting, and refining knowledge. One needs a "complete" or rich set of examples to build up the inductive learning process. Several of these learning systems are discussed later under the Integrated Learning System.

Connectionist learning

Neural networks are said to be intelligent because of their ability to "learn" in response to input data by adjusting the connection weights of the interconnections throughout the network.

Neural networks are based on theoretical models of how brain cells and their interconnections are able to form and adjust to perform complex tasks and calculations. Neural networks consist of many simple neurons or processors that have densely parallel interconnections.   The processors communicate across the interconnections in terms of "activation" and "inhibitions" – signals that excite or inhibit responses by connected processors. These interconnections for signals are represented as "weight" or connection strengths that modify the makeup of the output value of the signal.   The weights "adapt" or automatically adjust themselves, controlled through the learning process.

There are primarily two types of learning: supervised and unsupervised. Supervised learning is a procedure in which the network is presented with a set of data elements represented by inputs and corresponding desired outputs. The goal of the network is to learn the association between the inputs and the desired outputs. Unsupervised learning is when a network is presented with a set of inputs but without any corresponding desired outputs. In unsupervised learning, the network adapts itself (makes adjustments to its connection weights) according to the statistical associations in the input patterns. At present, unsupervised learning is a complicated process and is primarily associated with research. Supervised learning, on the other hand, has been found to produce good results and is the more commonly used form of learning.

Learning, in a system, takes place during a training period in which the network is presented with a chosen set of data representative of the type it will process when actually deployed. Training consists of presenting input data to the network that contains a corresponding desired output. Neural networks differ from conventional processing methods and expert systems in both the type of data they process and the manner in which they do so. In general, they are extremely fault tolerant, allowing them to process incomplete, missing, or fuzzy data without crashing.

Problems associated with neural networks include a steep learning curve, lack of real development methodologies, demanding preprocessing requirements, and architectural incompatibility causing integration problems. In addition, their basis for reasoning is still somewhat unclear. However, integrated effectively, they can supplement a number of traditional numerical processing systems.

A key feature of neural networks is that information is represented in a distributed way in weighted sum of the connections rather than in a discrete string of code stored in the memory of a single processor. Neural networks have proven especially promising for organizing and identifying patterns in data, for speech recognition, robotic control and signal preprocessing. Practical adaptive systems are emerging in real applications.

Multiple learning paradigms, such as described here, are needed to meet the need for various learning requirements of systems. It is important but much less clear, however, when a particular method is appropriate. A wide variety of machine-learning applications have been proposed for telecommunication networks, for example, from alarm correlation to network planning, control, and design. A pressing need, therefore, is to identify both the appropriate application of emerging learning techniques and the means by which these techniques can be combined and used independently and together.

GTE Laboratories is developing an Integrated Learning System (ILS) testbed in an effort to address the issues of integrating learning techniques (Figure 21.6).

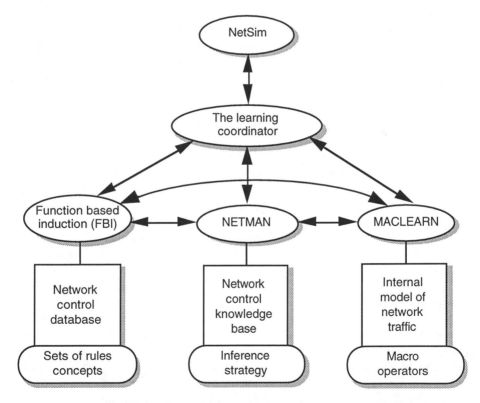

Figure 21.6 The integrated learning system.

The Integrated Learning System

A large variety of learning algorithms have been reported in the literature (Frawley, 1989; Iba, 1989; Michalski *et al.,* 1983, 1986; Silver, 1986, 1990). No one algorithm provides a totally satisfactory solution to a wide range of problems. An important issue is how to combine various learning paradigms, how to integrate different reasoning techniques, and how to coordinate distributed problem solvers. An Integrated Learning System (ILS) (Silver *et al.,* 1990) has been implemented at GTE Laboratories to provide a framework for integrating and evaluating a variety of learning algorithms distributed across a heterogeneous network of computers. For this testbed, Network Traffic Control has been chosen as the application domain.

ILS is a framework for integrating several heterogeneous, distributed learning agents that cooperate to improve problem-solving performance. ILS also includes a central controller called *The Learning Coordinator* (TLC) which manages control flow and communication among the agents, using a high-level communication protocol. The agents provide TLC with expert advice concerning the current problem; TLC then chooses which suggestion to adopt and performs the appropriate actions. The agents compete by offering possibly different advice to TLC, and they cooperate to overcome gaps in their individual knowledge. At intervals, the agents can inspect the results of the TLC's actions and use this feedback to learn. As they learn, the quality of advice given to TLC improves, leading to better performance.

The ILS integrates implementations of three learning paradigms, called agents, and TLC. The learning paradigms are inductive (FBI), macro-learning (MACLEARN), and knowledge-based learning (NETMAN).

Function Based Induction (FBI) and MACLEARN are written in Symbolics LISP and run on Symbolics LISP machines. NETMAN is written in Quintus Prolog and runs on SUN Microsystems workstations. ILS is completely distributed. Communication among instances of the agents and TLC is via TCP/IP streams with a text-based protocol.

Inductive learning. Function-Based Induction (FBI) is an extension of Quinlan's ID3 (Quinlan, 1986). FBI learns decision trees from large numbers of examples. Trees both compress and generalize the experience represented by sets of examples; the trees completely describe the examples. A decision tree can be expanded into a set of rules, one for each leaf of the tree, so that this approach generates classification rule sets from examples.

FBI can also discover potentially useful concepts that are combinations of existing functions by examining a tree and finding paths that lead to identical subtrees. The discovered concepts are then used to simplify the existing decision tree and are made available as building blocks in the construction of other decision trees. Often the concepts discovered in this way are useful because they reflect genuine features of the domain. In other cases, the concepts discovered are artifacts caused by random patterns in the example set. FBI can ask other elements of ILS, in particular NETMAN, to assess the utility of a discovered concept.

Search-based learning. MACLEARN currently performs best-first search in order to learn useful combinations of operators (called macro-operators or macros) that can be subsequently treated as a single operator. Macro-learning is a form of chunking which can improve search performance by enlarging the set of operators available for the search. The availability of a good set of macros will often drastically reduce the combinatorial explosion of a search problem. A key issue in macro learning is to be highly selective in choosing which macros to keep. MACLEARN uses various criteria to perform the filtering process.

On complex problems, MACLEARN may encounter combinatorial explosion as the search space of possible operators becomes too large. MACLEARN becomes bogged down in the search and may be unable to find a satisfactory solution. Other agents within ILS can provide assistance to MACLEARN by constraining the search and indicating which part of the search space should be explored.

Knowledge-based learning. NETMAN is an example of a knowledge-intensive learning system (Silver, 1990). Such systems have a large amount of knowledge of the domain, similar to the knowledge base of an expert system. The knowledge need be neither complete nor totally accurate. As a result, NETMAN is allowed to make mistakes. (Human experts suffer from the same limitation, of course.)

Ideally, NETMAN would be able to distinguish accurately between situations in which an action will be successful and those in which it fails. Unfortunately, the computation involved, and the stochastic nature of the domain, make this impossible to do precisely. Instead, NETMAN heuristically differentiates the cases by calling on FBI, another component of ILS. NETMAN learns four major types of information from experience.

- Stored caches: NETMAN stores as a macro the sequence of rule firings that led to advice that worked.

- Support list: The support list indicates how successful or unsuccessful a particular action proved to be. Those that have proved valuable in the past are more likely to be used in the future.

- Possible bugs: When an action fails to have the expected result, NETMAN can classify the cause and severity of this failure. This information is stored and will affect the future use of the action.

- Plans: A plan consists of a sequence of actions that has proved useful, together with the expected effect of each action.

ILS operation. ILS has tasks on two levels: the agents, although distributed, must cooperate to solve a problem in the domain, and the agents must also learn, individually and perhaps by interacting with each other, in order to further improve problem-solving performance.

The problem-solving role of a controlling agent is to monitor the state of the domain and to actuate control that the agent expects will bring the system closer to its goal. The role of a learning controller is to improve its performance over time based on experience.

The basic loop of the system, repeated every five simulated minutes, is as follows:

i) TLC issues the ADVISE message to ask the agents to propose actions to control the domain. An agent responds to this message by examining the current state of the domain (performance data) and deciding what actions would be best for improving it.

A vote (in the range 1–5) accompanies each recommendation, indicating the agent's perception of the value of that action. The exact semantics of the vote is agent-specific, since each agent has a different method for calculating it.

ii)   TLC then issues a CRITIQUE message that asks the agents to critique the proposals of the other agents. The specific pieces of advice other agents have proposed are passed along as part of this message. The response to this request is a set of votes (again in the range of 1–5), reflecting the value of each piece of advice as viewed by the responding agent.

iii) Now TLC has a list of proposed actions, and each action has, at present, a set of up to three votes associated with it. TLC has to choose them. TLC averages the votes and executes the action with the highest average, breaking ties arbitrarily. Several other possible techniques that could be used are being studied.

iv)   When new performance data are available, TLC sends a DATA-AVAILABLE message to notify agents which of the last suggested sets of actions were taken and that a sufficient period of time has passed since they were taken to allow domain data to reflect those actions. In response, agents can gather feedback from the domain to learn appropriately to affect their future problem-solving performance. Finally, they acknowledge that they have finished processing the current data.

The process then repeats from the beginning.

ILS is a framework for integrating several distributed heterogeneous learning agents that cooperate to improve performance. The initial testbed was set up with three agents, as described, then two others were added – feature learning (Zenith) and reactive planning (DYNA). The agents, in this case problem solvers, learnt both independently and cooperatively. Each agent was tested independently using telecommunication network traffic control as a domain, and each demonstrated that it can learn by interacting with that domain, and the results were encouraging. ILS, as a whole, can outperform each individual learning program. There is more work to be done, for example, in developing criteria for selecting a particular learning paradigm, a method for breaking a tie or making the decision for choosing the appropriate learner for a specific task. Another form of learning task that requires learning from a vast amount of data utilizes knowledge discovery.

Knowledge discovery

Knowledge discovery is defined as the technique of identifying "nonobvious" information from data through analysis of "interesting" patterns. Network operations generate vast amounts of data that typically get recorded in large databases. The sheer quantity of this data renders manual data analysis impossible. Knowledge discovery technology offers tools for automatically identifying and extracting meaningful information or "knowledge" from this raw data. This machine-learning subfield is a topic of much current research, and has already led to several practical applications in businesses such as banking, insurance, the airline industry, and marketing and sales.

Knowledge discovery in databases combines machine learning, statistical, and knowledge acquisition methods in an effort to automatically extract interesting and useful knowledge from raw data (Piatetsky-Shapiro and Frawley, 1991). The various algorithms and analysis methods used for discovery can be classified into the following types:

- *Clustering algorithms* divide data into meaningful subsets. The data in a given subset are clustered together because they share some thing(s) in common with one another, for example, a subset of trunk groups reporting overflows. These subsets or classes are frequently used in subsequent discovery tasks.

- *Summarization algorithms* produce a description of the common characteristics shared by all the data in a given class. For example, given the set of switches reporting overflows, it may be the case that they all carry traffic to a single called number. Summarization will discover this common characteristic.

- *Classification algorithms* take two or more classes and produce a description of characteristics that discriminate among classes. This type of description is often used to predict the classification of new data. For example, given a set of trunk groups reporting overflow and a set with no overflow, a discriminating description might be that all overflowing trunk groups have two or fewer T1s. If we were to look at an unclassified trunk group from the same network, we could use this "rule" to predict the class to which it is likely to belong.

- *Data dependency analysis* generates (from data) connected graphs that describe the interdependencies between data. For example, a dependency graph could indicate that "high traffic on Trunk Group X" is highly correlated with "overflow at another trunk group." The dependency networks depict the relational structure between data and can also indicate causal direction and strength.

- *Discovery of change:* Perhaps the most powerful technique of all is that of detecting when something has changed significantly. Detecting changes can leverage off results from previous discoveries. The change might represent an important variation in the operation of the network. Focusing only on changes is one important way of solving the difficult problem of determining what patterns are interesting.

The work on knowledge discovery at GTE Laboratories has concentrated on developing a knowledge discovery workbench (KDW) (Piatetsky-Shapiro and Matheus, 1991). Figure 21.7 shows the architecture of the workbench. The KDW combines many of the approaches described above along with techniques for representing and exploiting domain knowledge. Domain knowledge is crucial to the discovery of meaningful patterns in large databases. Without some guidance from domain experts, the indiscriminate application of the various discovery algorithms results in a plethora of statistically significant patterns having little, if any, interest or meaning to the users of the data.

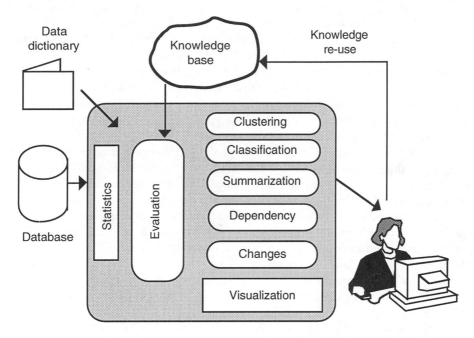

Figure 21.7 Architecture of a knowledge discovery workbench (KDW).

The KDW, and knowledge discovery in general, has the potential for uncovering useful knowledge in many significant areas. Specific areas that look particularly promising include analysis of network traffic patterns, detection of cellular fraud, and marketing and sales analysis. Another potential application area is the health-care industry, which generates vast amounts of data and makes use of a large number of distributed information systems.

21.5 Technology trends in the future network

21.5.1 The ultimate network and its evolution

Operations, Administration, Maintenance and Provisioning (OAM&P) functions are increasingly moving down toward network elements (NEs), making them self-sufficient. For most service requests, "self-provisioning" or fully automated provisioning with no external intervention will be possible. Networks will be capable of self-regulation with respect to traffic loads and self-healing or survivable with respect to failures. Functionally, networks will become increasingly distributed, by network elements taking control of their own management. This will, no doubt, require coordination of intelligent element activity for overall management of the network.

Several generic categories of knowledge engineering applications have emerged in the last several years (Wright and Vesonder, 1990; Goyal and Worrest, 1988). Some of the categories of knowledge-based systems relevant to network management capture and use expertise in design, planning, interpretation, diagnosis, monitoring, prediction, and control. The intelligent system applications for networks can be mapped into *two* broad conceptual categories. The first category deals with design and planning issues in *establishing* and *providing* network facilities. *Flexibility* of the network is built into this phase. The second category supports operations, management, administration, and control (OMAC) functions and reflects on the *reliability* aspect of the network. There are strong pressures to integrate the existing optimizing and algorithmic methods and tools with the emerging intelligence in the network. A variety of stand-alone knowledge-based systems are in field trials or in commercial use in the network. Also, algorithmic design and planning tools such as EFRAP (The Exchange Feeder Route Analysis Program), cash flow, and traffic engineering tools are available today to the network designers. There is a need for building intelligent planning tools and integrating them with currently used databases so that the same system can be used by different groups, including network planning, network engineering, and implementation planning. Expert system front ends will be providing the consolidated data environments for these groups to make intelligent decisions.

Network-management and traffic-control systems are currently used in decision-support mode to manage networks. As traffic-control expert systems become closely integrated with alarm surveillance systems and are tested sufficiently to verify the accuracy of their decisions, they can be trusted to make simple traffic-rerouting decisions and to install controls, thus making networks more automatically controlled (autonomous). At the same time, as the systems are extended with more knowledge about operations and alternative controls, they will more closely support human experts in making complex decisions.

Then there is also a question as to how the AI systems may be deployed. Will AI modules be resident in special identifiable "expert" systems? Or, will they be embedded within larger software systems? Or, do they just become another set of tools for software developers, as a library of functions providing them convenience in development? AI systems are beginning to appear in all these forms.

21.5.2   An autonomous network scenario

In an autonomous network, error-free operation is provided by hardware flexibility and intelligent diagnostic functions embedded into the network components and into the network-management system. The network-management system continuously monitors traffic demand and facility operation, adjusting the normal flow of traffic as needed. This system also has a learning component to permit it to come to anticipate the routine overloads and adjust to gradual shifts in traffic demands. One function of this system is to report on the capacity of the network to handle the demands and to warn the planning group when problems seem to be caused by design mismatch rather than by temporary demand anomalies. Operators at that stage work with the system to solve long-term operational threats – the system itself handles the small problems.

The autonomous network will also request and direct repair and maintenance functions. The overall system will have a wide variety of sensors and status display systems distributed and integrated in the network. The actions are taken by a collection of processors, with some of the monitoring and analysis functions being performed at switch level, along with some repair and maintenance actions; the rest of the repair actions will take place at regional centers serving a subset of the network (and a single roving repair crew) along with more monitoring and analysis and facility error detection and diagnosis. Regional centers will also be the first line of attack on traffic-management functions. For the sake of improved reliability and load sharing, the regions covered by a center will overlap. The centers will be individually responsible for coordinating their actions so that work is not duplicated and that answers to requests from other functions are complete. For the major operational functions, such as diagnosis of network-wide problems and overall coordination of complex problem solutions, there may be one or more central coordination centers. The function of these centers is to monitor the overall performance of the network and the other control centers, and to initiate action when it seems appropriate and is lacking. For this reason, the line between operation and design is less distinct. Operation and design are merged into one process, directing the hardware and software evolution of the network. These centers will also be responsible for interacting with the network owner to provide needed information on network operation and performance. The network owner is now a strategist, orchestrating the decision priorities to meet business objectives.

21.6 Summary

There have been significant advances on technology fronts in distributed computing environments, architectures, tools, and systems; on intelligent systems technologies in distributed AI, machine learning, and intelligent cooperative interfaces; and on processing and hardware fronts, with powerful desktop workstations available at affordable prices. In the background, the complexity in distributed system management is creating strong demands for combining these and more technologies to generate "complete" solutions. As a result, there is a push toward enterprise solutions through combining many powerful concepts and intelligent systems. More and ever, there is a need to leverage synergies between various related disciplines. Many more initiatives are on the horizon as the cooperative efforts of distributed intelligent system research comes to fruition.

Despite all these developments, it is a fair question to ask, "Are the knowledge systems real?" "Can they perform any *worthwhile* task with reliability?" Feigenbaum *et al.,* (1988) conducted an exhaustive survey of expert systems in day-to-day production use. At the AAAI Conference address several years ago, Feigenbaum reported over 3000 systems supposedly in production use. This number may well have doubled by now. DEC, Dupont, American Express, and IBM reported that their expert systems save tens to hundreds of millions of dollars per year. The advantages of knowledge systems were also established in interviews with the user groups. In many cases, these systems, besides storing the much-needed corporate expertise permanently and improving quality and performance, provide up to an order-of-magnitude productivity increase and one to two orders of magnitude speedup of operations. These gains are significant and are being recognized by the corporate management. Some companies have concentrated on building large systems for a complete task. Other companies, like Dupont, built a very large number of small systems to perform minor day-to-day tasks.

In telecommunications, knowledge systems are emerging, but slowly, primarily in diagnosis and maintenance areas. Many more powerful systems are in field-trial stage and are ready to be launched into day-to-day operations. Integration of these individual systems into a larger system is the natural next step.

The key technologies discussed here will make a marked improvement in the power and breadth of the future systems' utility and ability to handle larger and more significant tasks. Systems with distributed intelligence, with the ability to make coherent decisions under strict time constraints, with incomplete data, and with the ability to improve their performance by doing and learning will certainly change the current mode of telecommunication business.

Some final questions to ask are: Where might this new technology (AI) lead us? Will there be real benefit by using it? Should there be an autonomous network or a network without human control? Can a communication network behave and control itself effectively, using its own intelligence? Or, should the society be concerned about the "Terminator I and Terminator II" syndrome? These are interesting questions whose answers will emerge with time and with the evolution of intelligent distributed systems. For now, integration of expert systems in network management and operations is paving the way for more reliable, functionally rich, and intelligent networks, and much more is over the horizon as the technology advances.

Acknowledgments

Much of the work reported in this chapter is being conducted in several projects at GTE Laboratories. The author acknowledges the contributions of the staff of these projects. Suggestions and comments of Richard Brandau, Gregory Piatetsky, Robert Weihmayer, Michael Brodie, and John Vittal have been valuable in the preparation of this chapter and are gratefully acknowledged. Larry Bernstein, Pradeep Sen, and Ron Goodman reviewed the manuscript and gave insightful suggestions. Thanks are due to Wilfredine Chiasson, who shaped the paper in the present form. Finally, the author thanks William Griffin for encouragement and support of this work and its publication.

Abbreviations

ACE	Automated Cable Expertise
AIN	Advanced Intelligent Network
AOP	Agent-Oriented Programming
CBR	Case-Based Reasoning
CNAS	Circuit Network Administration System
CNC	Customer Network Control
DAI	Distributed Artificial Intelligence
DOM	Distributed Object Management
EBL	Explanation-Based Learning
EFRAP	Exchange Feeder Route Analysis Program
FBI	Function-Based Induction
ILS	Integrated Learning System
KBL	Knowledge-Based Learning
KDW	Knowledge Discovery Workbench
KR	Knowledge Representation
LAI	Local Application Interface
LEC	Local Exchange Carrier
MARK	Mechanical Automation Record Keeping
MBR	Model-Based Reasoning
MIS	Management Information System
NE	Network Element
NETTRAC	NETwork Traffic Routing Assistant Using Cases
NOS	Network Operating System
OAM&P	Operations, Administration, Maintenance and Provisioning.
OMAC	Operations, Management, Administration and Control
OODBMS	Object-Oriented Database Management System
OSS	Operation Support System
PSTN	Public Switched Telephone Network
SARTS	Switched Access Remote Test System
SS7	Signaling System 7
SSCFI	Special Service Circuit Fault Isolation
TAS	Trouble Administrative System
TEAM-CPS	Testbed Environment for Autonomous Multi-agent Cooperative Problem Solving
TLC	The Learning Coordinator

References

Ackroff J. M. , Surko P. T. and Wright J. R. (1988). AutoTest-2: An expert system for special services. In *Proceedings of the Fourth Annual Artificial Intelligence and Advanced Computer Technology Conference,* (Teitell M., ed.), 503–8

Bernstein S. (1987). DesignNet: an intelligent system for network design and modeling. In *International Communications Conference 1987,* (Sassa D. J. ed.), New York: IEEE, Seattle, WA

Brachman A.R. and Levesque H. (1985). *Readings in Knowledge Representation,* Morgan Kaufmann Publishers, Inc.

Brandau R. and Weihmayer R. (1989). Heterogeneous multi-agent cooperative problem solving in a telecommunications network management domain, *AAAI 9th DAI Workshop,* September 12-14, 1989, Orcas Island, Washington, Dec. 1989

Brandau R., Lemmon A. and Lafond C.V. (1991). Experience with extended episodes: cases with complex temporal structure. In *Proceedings Case-Based Reasoning Workshop,* Washington, DC, 1–12, Palo Alto: Morgan Kaufmann

Covo A., Gersht A., Kheradpir S. and Weihmayer R. (1991). New approaches to resource management in integrated long haul communication networks. IEEE Network Operations Management Symposium, Memphis, Tennessee, April 6-9 1992

Davis R. and Hamscher W. (1988). *Model Based Reasoning, Troubleshooting,* AI Labs, MIT, May 1988

Davis R. and Smith R. G. (1983). Negotiation as a metaphor for distributed problem solving, *Artificial Intelligence,* **1**, 21

Durfee E. H., Lesser V. R. and Corkill D. D. (1989). Cooperative distributed problem solving. In *The Handbook of Artificial Intelligence, Vol 4,* (Barr A., Cohen P. R., and Feigenbaum E. A. eds.), Addison-Wesley

Feigenbaum E., McCorduck P. and Nii P. (1988). *The Rise of the Expert Company,* Time Books

Ferrara F., Giovannini F. and Paschetta E. (1989). IAS: an expert system for packet-switched network monitoring and repair assistance. In *Proceedings of Conference on Artificial Intelligence, Telecommunications, and Computer Systems,* (Attard R., ed.), Nanterre, France, ECCAI, 1989, 185–97

Frawley W. J. (1989). Using functions to encode domain and contextual knowledge in statistical induction. In *Knowledge Discovery in Databases (IJCAI-89 Workshop),* International Joint Conference on Artificial Intelligence, (Piatetsky-Shapiro G. and Frawley W. J. eds.), 99–108

Gilbert E., Salgame R., Goodarzi A., Lin Y., Sardana S. and Euchner J. (1992). Arachne: weaving the telephone network at NYNEX. In *Proc. IAAI 92,* (Carlisle Scott A. and Klahr P. eds.), AAAI Press, Menlo Park, CA, 279–92

Goodman R. M., Miller J. and Smyth P. (1989). Real time autonomous expert systems in network management. In *Integrated Network Management,* (Meandzija B. and Westcott S. eds.), North Holland,

Goyal S. K. (1990). Future of OSSs Panel, *IEEE Supercomm ICC'90*, Atlanta, GA, April 1990

Goyal S. K. and Kopeikina L. (1987). *The evolution of intelligent networks*. ICC'87 Workshop on the Integration of Expert Systems into Network Operations, June 11–12, 1987, Seattle, WA

Goyal S. and Worrest R. (1988). Expert system applications to network management. In*Expert Systems Applications to Telecommunications*, (Liebowitz J., ed.), 3–44, John Wiley & Sons

Goyal S. K., Weihmayer R. and Brandau R. (1987). Intelligent systems in the future network, In *Proceedings of IEEE Networks Operations and Management Symposium*, San Diego, CA, Feb. 11–14

Guattery S. and Villarreal F. (1985). NEMESYS: an expert system for fighting congestion in the long distance network. In *IEEE Expert Systems in Government Symposium*, McLean, VA, Oct. 1985, 515–516

Hannan J. (1987). Network solutions employing expert systems. *Phoenix Computers and Communications Conference* (PCCC-87), 543–7, IEEE, Washington DC

Iba G.A. (1989). A heuristic approach to the discovery of macro-operators. *Machine Learning*, **3** (4), 285–317

Johnston A. and Ludwiczak K. (1991). Operations model and architecture for evolving telecommunication networks. Distributed Systems: Operations and Management Workshop, Santa Barbara, CA, Oct. 15–16

Kolodner J. , Simpson R. Jr., and Sycara-Cyranski K. (1985). A process model of CASE-based reasoning in problem solving. In *Proceedings IJCAI-85*, AAAI, Menlo Park, CA

Kopeikina L., Brandau R. and Lemmon A. (1988). Case-based reasoning for continuous control. In *Proceedings of Case-Based Reasoning Workshop*, Clearwater Beach, FL, Morgan Kaufmann, 250–59

Kopeikina L., Brandau R. and Lemmon A. (1988). Extending cases through time. Workshop on Case-Based Reasoning, *AAAI 88*, St. Paul, MN, Aug. 23

Koton P.A. (1988). Using experience in learning and problem solving. *Ph.D. thesis*, MIT.

Mantleman L. (1986). AI carves inroads: network design, testing, and management, *Data Communications*, July, 106–23

Michalski R. S., Carbonell J. G. and Mitchell T. M. (eds.). (1983). *Machine Learning: An Artificial Intelligence Approach*, Vol. 1, Tioga Press

Michalski R. S., Carbonell J. G. and Mitchell T. M. (eds.). (1986). *Machine Learning: An Artificial Intelligence Approach*, Vol. 2, Morgan Kaufmann

Minton S. *et al*, (1989). PRODIGY 2.0: the manual and tutorial. *Technical Report, CMU-CS-89-146*, Carnegie Mellon University

Piatetsky-Shapiro G. and Frawley W. J. (eds.). (1991). *Knowledge Discovery in Databases*, Cambridge, MA: MIT Press

Piatetsky-Shapiro G. and Matheus C. (1991). Knowledge discovery workbench: an exploratory environment for discovery in business databases. In *Proceedings of AAAI-91 KDD Workshop*, Anaheim, CA

Prerau D., Gunderson A. S., Reinke R. E. and Goyal S. K. (1985). The compass expert system: verification, technology transfer, and expansion. In *Second IEEE Conference on Artificial Intelligence Applications*, Washington DC, 597–602

Quinlan J. R. (1986). Induction of decision trees, *Machine Learning* **1** (1), 81–106

Sheth A. and Larson J. (1990). Federated database systems for managing distributed, heterogeneous, and autonomous databases. *ACM Computing Surveys,* **22**(3), 183–236

Shoham Y. (1991). AGENT0: A simple agent language and its interpreter. In *Proceedings of the Ninth National Conference on Artificial Intelligence*, July 14–19

Silver B. (1986). Precondition analysis: learning control information. In *Machine Learning: An Artificial Intelligence Approach*, (Michalski M. S., Carbonell J. G., and Mitchell T. M., eds.), Vol. 2, 647–70, Morgan Kaufmann

Silver B. (1990). NetMan: a learning network traffic controller. In *Proceedings of Third ACM International Conference on Industrial & Engineering Applications of Artificial Intelligence and Expert Systems,* (Matthews M., ed.), 923–31

Silver B., Vittal J., Frawley B., Iba G. and Bradford K. (1990). ILS: a framework for integrating multiple heterogeneous learning agents. In *Proceedings of the Second Generation Expert Systems, 10th International Workshop on Expert Systems and Their Applications*, Avignon, 1990

Simon H. (1983). In *Machine Learning: an Artificial Intelligence Approach,* Vol 1 (Michalski R. S., Carbonell J. G and Mitchell T. M., eds.). Tioga Press

Thandasseri M. (1986). Expert systems application for TXE4A exchanges. *Electrical Communication,* **60**(2)

Vesonder G. *et al*. (1983). ACE: an expert system for telephone cable maintenance. In *Proceedings of the 8th International Joint Conference on Artificial Intelligence,* 16–121, AAAI, Menlo Park, CA

Vittal J., SilverB., Frawley W., Iba G., Fawcett T., Dusseault S. and Doleac J. (1992). A Framework for Cooperative Adaptable Information Systems. In *The Next Generation of Information Systems–From Data to Knowledge*, (Papazoglou M. P. and Zeleznikow J. eds.). Springer-Verlag

Wan,H., Weissman M., Worrest R. and Goyal S. (1992). Special service circuit fault isolation expert system. GTE Laboratories, Internal Technical Note, Feb. 1992

Weihmayer R. and Brandau R. (1990). A distributed AI architecture for customer network control,. In*Proceedings of Globecom'90*, San Diego, CA, Dec. 2–5

Weihmayer R. and Tan M. (1991). TEAM-CPS: a general approach to cooperative problem solving in multiagent domains. *Technical Memo TM-0501-12-91-172*. GTE Laboratories Incorporated, Dec. 1991

Weihmayer R., Brandau R. and Shinn H. S. (1990). Modes of diversity: issues in cooperation among dissimilar agents,. In *Proceedings of Tenth Distributed AI Workshop, AAAI-sponsored*, Oct. 1990

Wright S.R. and Vesonder G.T. (1990). Expert systems in telecommunications. In *Expert Systems with Applications*, Editor-in-Chief Jay Liebowitz, **1**(2), 127–36

Zeldin P., Miller F., Siegfried E. and Wright J. (1986). Knowledge based loop maintenance: the ACE system, *ICC'86*, June 1986, 1241–43

Part VII

Case Studies

Chapter 22

Digital Equipment Corporation's Enterprise Management Architecture

Colin Strutt and Mark W. Sylor

Digital Equipment Corporation,
550 King Street,
Littleton, MA 01460-1289, USA
Email: strutt@took.enet.dec.com, sylor@blumon.enet.dec.com

The previous chapters have described some of the problems of management, management standards, management applications and specific implementation issues in management. While each of these threads can be treated separately, in a truly integrated, enterprise-wide management system these separate threads must be woven together. What results is a rich tapestry of surprising complexity. One such tapestry is Digital Equipment Corporation's Enterprise Management Architecture (EMA), and the products that implement that architecture such as the Digital Equipment Corporation Management Control Center (DECmcc). This chapter describes EMA and DECmcc and discusses how these separate issues interact in a case study of an integrated network and distributed systems management solution.

22.1 The purpose of EMA

An "enterprise" is a collection of people, working together towards some common end such as producing a television show about a starship. Those people are served by communications networks (both voice and data) and computer systems providing applications and information. Once, the computer systems and communications networks that served an enterprise were quite separate and distinct technologies. This technological difference made computer systems management and communications network management separate realms. For many years, a driving force for change has been the merger of computer and communications technologies. We call the resulting distributed system of communications networks, computer systems, applications and information, the "enterprise environment". As these technologies have merged, the realms of system and network management have merged into a single discipline, which we call *enterprise management*.

The enterprise environment exists to serve the needs of its users. The enterprise might view management of the environment as an optional overhead function. Ideally, the environment would be completely automated – the environment would manage itself. EMA embodies this ideal with the goal that each component of the environment should strive to be self-managing. Self-management is more than automating management tasks: it is the elimination of the need for management by building self-configuring, self-repairing, auto-tuning systems. Unfortunately, the reality is that for economic, technological, or other reasons, this ideal cannot be achieved by many components. Thus, certain people, called "managers", are given responsibility for ensuring that the enterprise environment in fact meets its users' needs. Enterprise management is what those managers do to ensure the users' needs are met.

Defining enterprise management as "whatever it takes for a manager to ensure that the environment serves the needs of its users" yields a very broad problem domain. The problem domain is so large it can only be solved using an architectural approach. For us, an "architecture" is a way to tackle a complex problem space. Essentially, an architecture takes a complex, difficult-to-understand problem domain, and first divides it into components. This division is often called a "model" – one of the more famous such models is the ISO reference model. If the model is "right" each of these components can be specified in a document (typically called an "architecture specification") that describes the syntax and semantics of the interfaces between those components in sufficient detail to allow the components to be developed by different groups or even to allow multiple groups to develop separate, but interoperable, implementations of the same component. Further discussion of the architectural strategy of EMA can be found in (Fehskens, 1989), which points out that the key strategic decision was to have an architecture in the first place.

22.2   The EMA model

In the EMA model, we first decided that we would use the services of the enterprise environment to support the managers. We would take advantage of the communications and computing capabilities of the environment to manage the environment as much as possible. In particular, this meant that we would incorporate effective management into every component of the environment; management would not be added on after the fact.

In the EMA model, on-line, day-to-day operational management is viewed as being essentially a monitoring/control feedback loop between the *entities* (the managed systems and components that make up the environment) and *directors* (the management systems that support the managers).

22.2.1   Directors

EMA directors present a user interface to applications that allow a manager to monitor or control entities. The user interface can be as simple as a command-line user interface, such as the EMA-defined Network Control Language (NCL) user interface, or as sophisticated as a dynamic map showing the topology and status of selected components in the network.

EMA directors also provide applications that automate management tasks. This automation can be very simple or very complex, for example, an application function could:

- take two values from an entity, add them together and present the sum to the manager (for example, to present "total errors");

- set the value of an attribute of all the entities of a particular class in the environment to have the same value;

- periodically examine the value of some attribute of an entity, and if it is greater than some manager-defined threshold, invoke a script to "correct" the problem;

- starting from a node in a communications network, use the information provided by the node to deduce what other nodes are connected to it, recursively browse the network, and from that information deduce the topology (a map) of the network.

In the EMA model we expect there will be many more entities than directors, just as there should be many more users than managers of the environment. This has two important consequences:

- Entities should generally be kept simple to keep their cost down. All other things being equal, complex management functions should be built as director functions rather than built into entities. This has led to a tendency for entities to present raw data (such as error counts) rather than refined information (such as error rates).

- Most entities are remote from a director, and thus must communicate via a management protocol. The case where the director and entity are on the same system is treated as a special case, which can be optimized by using a local interface rather than a remote protocol. One of the major things an EMA director provides is access to remote and local entities.

Management protocols are also needed between directors so that they can communicate. In EMA, director–director communications are left as flexible as possible so that multiple management styles can be supported. Some enterprises are managed in a strict hierarchy, while others are best described as loose confederations of cooperating organizations.

22.2.2   Entities

An EMA entity provides a "service" to the users of the environment and also a monitoring and control service to directors. Even the simplest PC provides many services to its user and thus comprises many entities. Some of the entities in a PC include hardware components (for example, the disks), the operating system, a communications device (for example, a LAN card), networking software (for example, DECnet), and any number of applications (for example, an application that allows a sales person to enter an order).

Because each system has many entities, we divided an EMA entity into two parts, an agent and a managed object. The agent provides services shared by all the managed objects in a system. The agent also supports the entity's end of the management protocol via protocol engines. The protocol engines allow remote management from any director in the environment able to communicate with the entity. The agent also provides a collection of other supporting services to managed object implementors.

22.2.3   Common Agent

The Common Agent is a software system that implements EMA entities. It is defined in the EMA Common Agent Architecture, and has been implemented on a number of platforms. The structure of the Common Agent (as well as DECmcc) is shown in Figure 22.1.

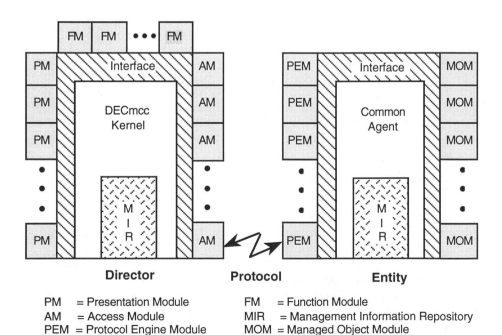

Figure 22.1 The main components of EMA.

In the Common Agent, the software implementing a managed object is called a Managed Object Module (MOM). A MOM typically implements all the managed objects of a particular class of managed objects (for example, all printers) or a group of closely related classes (such as all printers, print queues and print jobs).

In the Common Agent, the software implementing a protocol engine is called a Protocol Engine Module (PEM).

The Common Agent provides an environment that allows the MOMs and PEMs to exist and to interoperate. In addition, it provides various supporting routines to make the job of writing management MOMs and PEMs easier. By implementing the Common Agent on multiple operating system platforms, management modules can be written independent of the underlying operating system.

One of the more important supporting services provided by the Common Agent is access to a Management Information Repository (MIR). The Common Agent is described in more detail in (Newkerk *et al.*, 1993).

22.2.4 DECmcc

Digital Equipment Corporation's Management Control Center (DECmcc) is the software system that implements the EMA director. Each DECmcc comprises the following major components:

- DECmcc kernel

- Management Information Repository (MIR)

- Management Modules (MMs) as shown in Figure 22.1.

The DECmcc kernel is responsible for providing an environment that allows the management modules to exist and to interoperate. In addition, the kernel provides various supporting routines to make the job of writing management modules easier. By implementing the kernel on multiple operating system environments, the ability to operate the director in those environments is shielded from the management modules which are, for the most part, unconcerned with the underlying operating system.

The Management Information Repository (MIR) comprises the management information needed for the director to operate. There are two aspects of importance in the MIR – that of the structure of the information maintained, and that of the manner of storing and retrieving that information. In Section 22.4.2 we will look in more detail at the categories of data in the MIR.

The management modules comprise the major portion of the management director. They provide the main capabilities of an EMA director described in Section 22.2.1 above. The modules implement what is normally considered to be the management functions – or applications. It is convenient to describe three different sorts of management module and the capabilities provided by each:

- Access Modules (AMs) which provide access to remote or local entities or provide access to other directors;

- Function Modules (FMs) which provide added value or automated functions;

- Presentation Modules (PMs) which provide a user interface or provide other directors with access to the capabilities of this director.

However, as the software itself does not distinguish between the different sorts of module the differences are only in the ways one thinks about the different capabilities. In Section 22.4.1 we will expand on these different sorts of management modules.

22.3   The goals of EMA and their implications

The size of the problem domain EMA attempts to solve has a number of implications on the architecture. Some of the important goals that we set ourselves when we began the EMA model included concepts such as:

- integration;
- consistency;
- support for standards;
- extensibility;
- dynamic;
- open, vendor independence;
- policy flexibility.

22.3.1   Integration and consistency

In the past, each entity had its own management system with its own user interface, and its own style of management. The costs to the managers of such an environment are high, both in training costs to learn these utilities, and in the day-to-day costs of dealing with this complex an environment. Clearly, an EMA director had to provide a consistent, integrated user interface to the manager.

An integrated user interface means that the director should be able to bring together the management of any entity in the environment to a single user interface. A consistent user interface means that all entities, and their monitoring and control capabilities, are presented to the user in a consistent management style and yet can still support the different management policies in effect at each site or company.

While an integrated, consistent user interface is a step forward, it is not enough. Integration also means the ability to develop automatic and added-value functions that are capable of dealing with different sorts of devices or software. The developers of added-value and automatic functions need a consistent view of entities and the monitoring and control functions they provide.

In EMA, the Entity Model provides that consistent model of management operations and information and it is an object-oriented model of things that are managed. For a description of the model see (Sylor, 1989). The Entity Model is similar to OSI's SMI described in Chapters 5 and 6.

In EMA and SMI, the essential concept is that of a managed object, which is managed using defined operations, attributes and notifications. The Entity Model applies at many points in the EMA architecture. Management protocols must be able to express the concepts of managed objects, operations, attributes and notifications. The CMIP protocol was designed to express all these concepts. SNMP can express a subset of these concepts. The Common Agent MOMs and the DECmcc AMs and FMs present their functions as managed objects. Finally, the Common Agent and the DECmcc Kernel structure communications between these modules according to the same concepts.

22.3.2   Heterogeneity, standards, and interoperability

Customers no longer deal with a single vendor for the provision of their networking needs. The industry is moving to a more open, commodity marketplace. The enterprise environment is heterogeneous: multivendor, multiplatform and multi-protocol. EMA directors and entities must be able to interoperate with entities and directors in the environment that are not built according to the EMA models. In particular, an EMA director must be able to manage non-EMA entities and EMA entities must be manageable by non-EMA directors.

One way of dealing with this heterogeneity is by assuming that all entities conform to some standard. Standards in network and computer system management have burgeoned over the recent few years. We need to consider not just the *de jure* but also the *de facto* standards as well. Standards, insofar as they affect the management software, come in two flavors. The first and most obvious is the management protocol (such as SNMP or CMIP). The second, however, is probably more important and concerns the management models that underlie the management philosophies involved (such as OSI's or SNMP's SMI). The approach of choosing a standard, and assuming everyone would build to that standard seemed to us to be untenable. There was no clear winner in the standards arena. Moreover, most enterprises had a large investment in equipment and software that was developed before the advent of standards in this arena, and it would not be practical for them to replace all their systems to implement a new and different standard.

As noted above, within EMA directors and entities the Entity Model defines a consistent, standard environment. To deal with a heterogeneous world, EMA allows mapping functions that allow EMA directors and entities to interoperate with non-EMA directors and entities, to be developed. EMA provides a rich environment for developing these mapping functions; the following list describes some of the possibilities:

- A MOM that maps an existing management utility for some entity into EMA managed object(s) could be developed in the Common Agent. Such a MOM was developed to use the UNIX disk space utility (df) to determine how much free space was available on a disk.

- An AM that speaks some private protocol supported by a legacy entity could be developed in DECmcc. Some enterprising engineers at Digital Equipment

Corporation, for example, developed the capability to manage air conditioning units through an AM.

- An AM that speaks some standard protocol supported by the entity, for example, SNMP could be developed in DECmcc. A number of such AMs have been developed by Digital.

- A PEM could be developed in the Common Agent to speak a private (or standard) protocol supported by a non-EMA director. For example, an SNMP PEM for the Common Agent has been developed.

- An Agent PM that maps a standard, or private, protocol into operations on EMA managed objects could be developed for DECmcc. Such an Agent PM has been developed for the Network Management Forum (NMF) CMIP.

- A specialized management gateway that maps non-EMA entities into EMA (or vice versa) could be developed. These management gateways are called proxies, element management systems, mediation devices or service points in other architectures; in EMA, we call these mediators. A DECmcc system with an Agent PM is a mediator between the entities DECmcc manages and the non-EMA director using the Agent PM. Vendors of entities who already have developed management systems for those entities may choose to implement a mediator that is compatible with EMA on that management system rather than retrofit EMA compatibility into their entities.

The key to these mapping functions is the generality of the managed object-oriented Entity Model. Our experience is that any style of management can be mapped into some capability of managed objects. We have found that while the mapping is possible, the key ideas of managed objects are sufficiently different from traditional, procedural management that developers newly exposed to it have a difficult time adapting. Designing the managed objects has proven to be harder than actually implementing them. To make the step of designing an entity as managed objects that conform to the Entity Model easier, we have developed a number of guidelines and design techniques. Some of these techniques are described in (Sylor, 1989).

22.3.3   Dynamic extensibility

Even in a small enterprise, the environment will be ever changing. Hence the management system must be extensible to support both new managed objects and new management applications. Adding a new managed object of an already supported class is easy. Adding a new class of managed object means adding a new MOM or AM, as appropriate. It must also be possible to extend the management system with new added-value or automatic functions as well as new user interface styles and/or user interface devices.

It is also important to be able to extend the management capabilities, in a dynamic manner. We certainly would not wish to bring the management system (or worse, the environment) to a halt in order to install some new management capability.

Change is the one thing that is constant about customers' environments. An extensible director in EMA has been described in (Shurtleff and Strutt, 1990).

22.3.4   Open, architected application programming interfaces

One of the things that was clear to us, when DECmcc was being conceived, was that Digital Equipment Corporation could not hope to develop all the software needed to manage all the networks and distributed systems components. Instead we needed to define an environment whereby others could develop different pieces of the management software, particularly those that pertain specifically to their own components, and yet be able to integrate them into the management software without needing to involve Digital – we have referred to this concept as blind extensibility. One of the keys to blind extensibility is architected application programming interfaces (APIs).

The interfaces provided by the DECmcc Kernel and the Common Agent are architected APIs. In a bounded system, typically one dedicated to a single task (for example, a dedicated router), APIs are a purely internal matter for the implementation. However, in general-purpose extensible systems, such as DECmcc and the Common Agent, it is important to architect the API so other vendors can implement to it, and to provide the same API on a number of platforms. In this way, portable managed objects and management applications that can be easily ported to multiple platforms can be developed.

Taking the Common Agent and the DECmcc Kernel together provides a distributed EMA framework which provides an open set of APIs that can be used to build managed objects and applications. This framework has been designed to make it easy to integrate the various parts of the model. It has also been designed so it can be tailored, in that only the APIs needed on a particular platform need be included there.

Even better than an architected API is an open API, one defined in an open standards process. Currently, no standards group has defined a management framework with the capabilities of the EMA framework. We hope that such an open API will eventually be defined. There have been industry efforts around the DME (OSF's Distributed Management Environment) and XMP (the X/Open Management Protocols API).

22.4   DECmcc director design

In this section, we look in more detail at the design of DECmcc. The resulting design of DECmcc took all of the goals of EMA into consideration. DECmcc is designed as a distributed application, to take advantage of distributed system services (such as the OSF/DCE components).

22.4.1   Management modules

Access Modules (AMs) are used to provide the director with an access path to a particular set of entities. This set is usually some entities that share something in common, such as all the entities in a given device or all the entities that support the same protocol. An example of the former is an AM that supports DECnet Phase IV nodes. An example of the latter is an AM that supports the SNMP protocol.

In some sense, the AMs are acting as gateways to non-EMA environments – the AM for an EMA entity is trivial. One advantage of AMs as separate modules is that it allows any special handling needed for managing particular devices to be located in one place.

With an AM one has the ability to provide the basic (or primitive) management operations afforded by the entities – this might mean just the Gets, Sets, and Traps, or it might include additional operations such as Creates, Deletes, and Actions.

Function Modules (FMs) provide the value-added management applications, often building on the primitive operations provided through the AMs, to provide more sophisticated and user-oriented management operations. FMs may also implement director entities such as Trouble Tickets which are not implemented in any network entity.

The way the intermodule calling is implemented in DECmcc allows FMs to make use of each other's services in providing their own services. In this way even more sophisticated applications can be constructed using services provided by different FMs. This permits the maximum reuse of software functions in the director environment. Section 22.4.4 provides a detailed example of this capability.

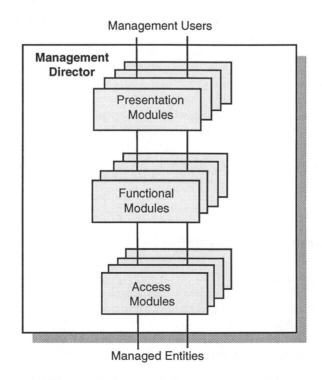

Figure 22.2 Layers of management modules.

Presentation Modules (PMs) deal with the aspects of presenting information to, and receiving information from, the environment outside the director. Typically PMs deal with the user interface, covering aspects of the style of user interface (such as iconic, forms or command-line style) as well as the user interface devices (dealing with X-Windows workstations, 3270-style screens, VT400 or equivalent terminals).

However, another use for PMs is to provide an interface to other management systems via some standard protocol – in this way DECmcc appears to the other management system as an agent for some devices, and so this style of PM is referred to as an Agent PM. Often one implements both the AM and the corresponding Agent PM capabilities for the same management protocol in one software package, as is the case with the Network Management Forum (NMF) Conformant Management Entity (CME) implementation.

The different sorts of management modules (AMs, FMs and PMs) are packaged together to form an instance of a director. Each of the modules implements one layer of management, as perceived by the user. Thus from an execution or dataflow viewpoint, one can view the director as shown in Figure 22.2.

In a later section we will look at the mechanism defined for intermodule calls.

22.4.2 Management information

It is convenient to group different portions of the management information maintained by DECmcc according to use. We have defined four categories of management information:

- class data;

- instance data;

- historical data;

- miscellaneous data.

Class data is used to maintain information about the classes of entities managed via DECmcc. The data is structured according to the EMA Entity Model, and is specified along with the supporting management modules using an appropriate specification format – for example, the Management Specification Language (MSL). The class data that is stored includes information about each class such as the class name, its attributes, operations and events, and sufficient details about each to permit other management modules to derive their processing from it.

Thus, for example, a generic iconic PM can use the class data to present valid operations for a selected icon representing an entity, and to display the appropriate attributes for that entity. Similarly, a generic alarms FM can use the class data to be able to request any data from an entity in determining if a user-specified alarm condition has occurred.

In the current DECmcc implementation, the class data is stored in a flat file format, and is replicated on each system that runs DECmcc for speed of access. Obviously, as the class data is object-oriented, an object-oriented database would be an appropriate vehicle for the class data.

Instance data is used to maintain information about the configuration being managed, specifically containing information about the instances of the classes stored in the class data. Sufficient data is kept to allow the display of a portion of the configuration (for example, on an iconic windows display) without needing to poll the network. Thus the data refers to what is believed to be the configuration, even if some portion of the real configuration is unavailable, owing perhaps to network partitioning.

One important aspect of the instance data is the desire to keep a globally consistent view of the configuration. This ensures that every manager has access (security considerations notwithstanding) to the same information about the configuration, including using the same names for the same components.

In the current DECmcc implementation, the instance data is typically stored using the DECdns (Distributed Name Service) or the CDS (Cell Directory Service) component of the OSF/DCE. Historical data is used to keep data about the entities stored over time. (Indeed, "historical" is perhaps a misnomer, as data could be future data for planning purposes as well as past data for reporting purposes – however, the phrase "temporal data" did not have the same ring to it.) This data is typically polled, or otherwise obtained, and stored away for subsequent use in many ways.

Historical data can be used as the basis for providing on-line trend analysis or off-line reports. The data can also be used to play what-if-I-had scenarios, particularly for fault diagnosis. In addition, data that has been stored is available to allow diagnosis of faults where the symptoms either revealed themselves later or the symptoms disappeared – being able to understand "why the LAN performance was so bad yesterday" is a much-needed capability.

The intermodule communication in DECmcc is defined in such a way that access to historical data is done in the same way as for current data – this means that applications, such as FMs, do not have to be rewritten in order to take advantage of historical data. Thus a module that deals with computing statistics based on raw counter values can work just as easily with live network data as with historical data.

In the current DECmcc implementation, historical data is stored either as flat files for on-line analysis through DECmcc, or it may also be exported to a relational database for off-line processing. As with the class data, the on-line data is object-oriented.

Miscellaneous data is used for all other data needed by the director or its management modules. The structure of such data is under the control of the module or modules that make use of it, unlike the previous three categories. Examples of miscellaneous data include parse tables for a command-line PM, or rules for a rules-based alarms FM. Other information that would be stored as miscellaneous data includes:

- script files;

- sample policies;

- site/company policy;

- management processes and procedures.

22.4.3   Intermodule calling (mcc_call)

The design of the mechanism by which management modules invoke each other's services is a critical part of DECmcc. It was clear to us early on that we could not rely on modules knowing *a priori* the names of the procedures they needed to invoke in other management modules – instead we had to provide an alternative means for modules to call each other.

We chose to take an approach based on a procedure call paradigm (known as mcc_call) where the parameters to the procedure are used to define the "service" that is desired, and the mechanism which implements the mcc_call determines the appropriate module, and the appropriate procedure in that module, that is capable of providing the desired service.

The services are defined in terms of operations (verbs or directives) applied to objects (entities) – hence the resulting API is in essence an object-oriented procedure call environment. The object parameter (*in_entity*) defines the entity (or entities, as multiple entities may be selected simultaneously) to which the operation is to be applied. The operation parameters (verb and partition) specify which directive is to be invoked, with the partition qualifying the verb for a non-action directive (such as an attribute-based directive, like SET).

The results of an operation are returned in: *time_stamp* which indicates the time the directive was performed, or the time for which returned data is appropriate; *out_p* which contains the encoded output parameters (encoded, as we do not know ahead of time how many actual parameters will be returned for a general call); and *out_entity* which contains the actual entity name for the directive (useful to qualify each piece of returned data where multiple entities were selected in the call).

Additional parameters provide for: encoded input parameters in *in_p* (again, we cannot predict the number of directive arguments), time-related information in *time_spec* (concerned with the scheduling and scope of interest relating to the request), and directive-independent qualifiers to the request in *in_q* such as the domain context or access control information.

One other parameter (*handle*) is used by the service requester, service provider and the calling mechanism to relate multiple calls, such as where multiple entities are involved in a request, or where a request covers a span of time.

Each management module defines the services it offers by providing dispatch entries defining each of its services, and each entry defines the verb, entity and partition and is associated with the procedure in the module that supports that service. In order to reduce the total number of such entries, wildcards may be used – this is often the case with the entity portion.

The calling mechanism assembles all dispatch entries for all modules configured in the director, and then on receipt of an mcc_call can match up the service requester with the appropriate service provider. Thus the mechanism for intermodule calling is perfectly general and dynamically extensible at runtime, facilitating the on-line addition of management modules into the DECmcc environment. Additionally, management modules can, by being data-driven using information in the class data of the MIR, adapt to new management modules in the system that were conceived and written after the first module was in use – this technique is used extensively in the suite of management modules that is available with DECmcc.

Complete details of the DECmcc mcc_call API can be found in (Digital Equipment Corporation, 1991d).

22.4.4   Reusing DECmcc management module services

As mentioned in Section 22.4.1 Function Modules can make use of each other's services in very general ways, allowing runtime combinations of modules that may not have been previously considered during development. This provides the ability to construct extremely powerful management applications through the reuse of services provided by management modules.

Consider an Access Module that provides access to some simple counter of error conditions (perhaps a count of the number of datalink errors, the number of login failures or the number of disk errors). In addition to being able to request and display the counter value via a PM to a user, one might have an Alarms FM that provides the ability to notify some manager when the attribute exceeds some predetermined threshold value. (We would presume the FM is capable of notifying a manager on many more conditions than this – the key is that the manager can specify those conditions by way of "rules".) We might also have a Performance FM that provides the ability to calculate the rate of errors by polling for two values of the counter separated by a time interval, computing the difference and dividing by the interval. (Again we would presume the FM is capable of calculating a rate for any counter specified by the manager.) Thus we have two FMs capable of using the same information (the simple error counter) for two different uses.

However, the ability to notify a manager when a counter exceeds a value is not particularly useful – of more interest is when the rate of errors exceeds some threshold. Thus by specifying a rule in terms of the error rate rather than the error counter the Alarms FM can request the rate which in turn is calculated by the Performance FM; the latter FM makes requests of the appropriate AM to gather the error counter at different time intervals. Thus we have a simple situation where one FM provides its services using the services of another FM.

Further, consider the Alarms FM maintaining a counter of the number of times an alarm condition has caused a notification to be emitted, and that this counter is available via (self) management of the FM itself. Now as well as the manager being able to request the count of alarm firings, it might be convenient to compute the rate of alarm firings, using the same Performance FM, and then perhaps to configure the Alarms FM to fire a notification when this rate exceeds some defined threshold. This notification might go to the superior of the manager receiving the original notifications, indicating that the manager has too much work to do right now!

The intermodule calling mechanism is defined in such a way that the binding between modules occurs at service invocation time rather than at compile, link or load time. Hence the system configures itself dynamically according to the actual services requested by modules and users. This capability enables the system to operate in a dynamic, extensible manner and to adapt to new modules as they are configured into DECmcc.

Thus, for the example cited above Figure 22.3 represents the logical configuration of modules that exist from a control and data flow perspective for the particular request that was made.

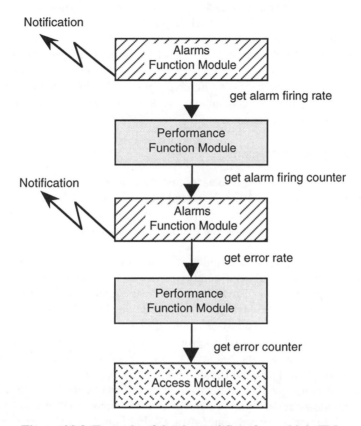

Figure 22.3 Example of data/control flow for multiple FMs.

In reality the two copies of each of the FMs represent the same module. Note also that the notifications can be treated as events passing through other management modules. This portion of the example has been omitted for clarity.

22.4.5   DECmcc as a distributed application

As described, the mcc_call provides a general-purpose management director API for procedure calls between modules of a director. It might appear that this mechanism only applies to modules executing on the same system. However, the design of DECmcc incorporated distributed processing techniques from the outset. The mcc_call is amenable to a remote procedure call – however, as the service is not defined by the procedure name, but instead by the parameters to the procedure, a different method of binding is necessary.

From a requirements standpoint, it is easy to see that in a medium or large network one would want to have AMs located close to the entities they represent, PMs located close to the user, and perhaps FMs located on other systems. Indeed for some management protocols there may be connectivity constraints that limit the separation of AM and entity.

The dispatch mechanism takes distribution into account – hence a request for a service provided by an AM is dispatched to an AM in an appropriate system. Similarly a request for other services can be dispatched to an appropriate system that might contain the required historical data, or where background processing might be taking place. This means that the same background process, perhaps one that is detecting alarm conditions, can be being used simultaneously by multiple managers on other systems – in this way, economies of scale can be realized. More information on distribution in DECmcc can be found in (Strutt, 1993).

22.4.6   Management domains

Dealing with larger configurations requires that there be some structuring paradigm to ensure that each user can cope with the attendant complexity. We chose to employ a concept referred to as management domains, whereby users can choose to group together entities in arbitrary, and often overlapping, ways that suit the management needs of their organizations.

Domains have an obvious graphic analogy when we consider how to represent views of subsets of the total configuration, as only the smallest networks can be displayed in a single window. However, there are other benefits from providing such structuring – we can associate historical data with a domain, and hence with the owner of the domain who is then responsible for the disk space taken up by this data. We can also associate the appropriate background processing with domains, such as for gathering and storing data for the historical data portion of the MIR, and for observing and detecting conditions that would be of interest to users (alarms).

Some additional detail on domains in DECmcc can be found in (Strutt, 1991). Further information on DECmcc in general can be found in (Strutt and Shurtleff, 1989; Digital Equipment Corporation, 1991a; Digital Equipment Corporation, 1991b; Strutt and Swist, 1993).

22.5   DECmcc modules

In this section we look at the features of some of the modules implemented as part of the DECmcc product family. We see how they can, individually and in combination, provide a significant set of management functions over a wide range of entities. Obviously as companies other than Digital Equipment are developing modules for DECmcc, the total capabilities of the product exceed those detailed here.

As implemented, DECmcc runs on multiple platforms, including Digital platforms such as OpenVMS and ULTRIX.

22.5.1   Access modules (AM)

- *SNMP AM* provides access to any SNMP-manageable object. Such objects might implement MIB I, MIB II, any of the many other standard MIBs (already defined or to be defined in the future) and any enterprise (that is, private) MIB extensions defined by any vendor. This module is a generic, data-driven module, and it determines dynamically from the MIR's class information everything needed to encode and decode SNMP protocol messages. Supporting this module is a MIB Translator Utility (MTU) that is capable of reading appropriately written (that is, RFC1212, conformant) MIB definitions and providing the information necessary to populate the MIR's class data. Clients of this module can retrieve (Get) or modify (Set) any MIB variable(s) in any system, can field events (Traps) from any system, and can provide a community name to specify an appropriate view of a MIB.

- *Ethernet AM* provides access to primitive 802.3 and/or Ethernet V2 datalink management. In particular a client may access information about the existence and makeup of a local area network (LAN) station (via the 802.2 XID messages) and may test a LAN station (via the 802.2 TEST messages). Ethernet V2 stations provide additional tests using the Loop and Loop With Assist messages. Suitably configured Ethernet stations that implement the Maintenance Operations Protocol (MOP) may provide additional information via the RequestID, SystemID, RequestCounters and Counters messages.

- *Bridge AM* provides access to the Digital LANbridge and DECbridge families of Ethernet/802.3/FDDI bridges. These bridges are accessed using the proprietary XLII management protocol and provide access to many different attributes which may be retrieved and set to allow monitoring and configuring of the bridges in an extended LAN environment. The forwarding databases, and address and protocol filtering are all manageable via this AM.

- *FDDI AM* and *Concentrator AM* are used to manage various FDDI components. The FDDI AM provides access to the primitive management operations of FDDI stations via the Station Management (SMT) protocol, providing access to counter and status information as well as to the Status Information Frames (SIF) for determining ring topology information. The Concentrator AM provides access to additional capabilities for the management of Digital Equipment's DECconcentrators, allowing the FDDI concentrators to be configured and tested.

- *DECnet Phase IV AM* is used to access the management capabilities of DECnet Phase IV nodes, either hosts, routers, or other servers. This module implements the DECnet Phase IV NICE (Network Information and Control Exchange) protocol. Typical DECmcc operations are Set, Show, Create, Delete, Enable and Disable as well as access to DECnet Events. This module handles permanent DECnet attributes via an "initial attributes" partition.

- *DECnet/OSI Phase V AM* implements the DECnet/OSI Phase V CMIP (Common Management Information Protocol, an early version of the OSI protocol of the same name) used to manage any entity defined for DECnet/OSI Phase V. This module, like the SNMP AM, is a generic, data-driven module, capable of adapting to new entities merely by adding the appropriate class information into the MIR. Typical operations include Set, Show, Create, Delete, Enable, Disable, Suspend, Resume, Pass and Block as well as access to DECnet/OSI events. For more details see (Sylor, 1991) and (Densmore, 1991).

- *Data Collector AM* provides non-DECmcc applications with the ability to pass events into DECmcc, without the need for a special-purpose Access Module to be developed. An API is provided for these applications to forward events to DECmcc.

- *Circuit AM* provides a synthesized view of circuits that are not directly manageable, such as datalink circuits, projecting a composite view based on data and operations for the manageable endpoints of the circuits. The definition of the objects representing the circuits is aligned with the NMF circuit definition to maximize the interoperability with FMs that deal with such circuits. By providing this additional abstraction a manager can represent the circuit on an iconic display as something that can be selected, against which management operations can be applied and for which status information can be displayed such as color changes representing alarm information.

22.5.2   Function modules (FM)

- *Registration FM* is responsible for maintaining part of the on-line management configuration information, specifically registering the components of the enterprise. This MIR Instance information is stored using DECdns typically, thus providing an enterprise-wide consistent view of the components of the enterprise. By planning the layout of the DECdns servers, the manager can ensure that information is maintained where needed and replicated as desired, but all information is available to any manager anywhere in the enterprise. While its services are often used by the manager directly, such as for the Register and Directory commands, other modules such as the Iconic Map PM make use of the services in the provision of their capabilities. This module is capable of registering and providing directory information about any class of entity that is enrolled in the class portion of the MIR.

- *Domain FM* maintains information about the various user-specified domains and the entities that comprise them (Strutt, 1991). As previously mentioned, the contents of management domains are defined solely by the manager(s) according to their management needs – some might define them on organizational boundaries, some on geographical boundaries, some according to the management functions performed, and others in a way that is meaningful to them. This module provides services for the creation and deletion of domains and setting up or changing the contents of the domains. Entities from any of the enrolled classes may be added to any domain. The domains are themselves entities, and hence have globally unique names and are maintained in the configuration. This permits domains to be members of other domains, allowing navigation from one domain to another from a map display, and in some cases also allows passing of notifications from one domain to another – these capabilities allow a manager to see a view of a large portion of the enterprise as icons representing domains, navigating "in" to a domain when desired or when an icon color indicates a problem in one area of the enterprise.

- *Historian Services* are implemented through three FMs: *Historical Data Recorder (HDR) FM, Exporter FM* and *Archive FM.* The HDR FM is responsible for gathering data, typically attribute values, for any entity for any enrolled class in the enterprise, and storing them in the Historical section of the MIR for subsequent processing as historical data via other modules. This module responds to the manager's desired policies by collecting only that data, at a specified period, that the manager desires. The Exporter FM is responsible for gathering information from either the live enterprise or from the MIR, in either case perhaps applying further processing in the management director, and then exporting it to a relational database for off-line processing by various information management tools, to produce reports. Like the HDR FM, the Exporter FM responds to the manager's policies by exporting only the information desired as often as the manager requires. The Archive FM, among other capabilities, is responsible for periodically purging from the Historical portion of the MIR data that has exceeded a manager-specified lifetime for on-line data. For more details see (Shvartsman, 1993a; 1993b).

- *Alarm Services* are implemented using an *Alarms FM* and a *Notification FM*. The former FM is responsible for evaluating "rules" specified by the manager, according to the desired policies, that represent conditions in which the manager is interested. These conditions may be error conditions requiring reactive management when they occur, warning conditions allowing proactive management when they occur, or they may be any interesting condition. The rules that can be evaluated may be based on the receipt of any event from any entity, or may be based on comparisons of attributes values against previous values of the same attribute or against constant values. The alarm expressions can also be more complex Boolean expressions. The Notification FM is responsible for forwarding events to interested clients (specifically other MMs) when alarm rules evaluate to true – for example, fire.

- *Performance Analyzer FM* provides the capability of calculating traffic and error rates for DECnet and certain LAN entities. In some cases these rates are merely computed directly from counters provided by the entities, but in other cases they may be calculated from combinations of entities that make up a single system. For more information on this module see (Anwaruddin, 1991).

- *Fault Diagnostic Assistant FM* provides symptom-directed fault diagnostics to aid a manager in determining the actual cause of a problem. Based on commonly observed symptoms, this module runs the appropriate series of tests to diagnose the situation. This module supports diagnostics for both IP-based and DECnet-based faults.

• *Spanning Tree Map FM* makes use of the services of the *Bridge AM* to determine the LANbridge and/or the 802.1d "spanning tree" configuration of an extended LAN. The information is used to construct maps of bridges for use by the Iconic Map PM.

• *FDDI Ring Map FM* makes use of the services of the FDDI FM to determine the physical configuration of an FDDI ring. The module determines the stations, including bridges and concentrators, on the ring as well as their configuration in the single or dual ring. The information is used to construct maps for use by the Iconic Map PM.

22.5.3   Presentation modules (PM)

• *Forms/Command Line (FCL) PM* is used to provide command-line access to all the management capabilities of the director. It permits the execution of command scripts either on-line or in batch. It is the preferred user interface for management experts. In some environments, a full screen (forms) mode can be employed which provides an easier-to-use interface with additional context-sensitive help facilities in the construction of commands. By using the class data in the MIR, this module is capable of adapting as new modules are enrolled in the director. The parse table information as well as all the display formats are built using the class data so the module does not need to be changed whenever new classes are added or augmented.

• *Iconic Map PM* provides a windows-based iconic interface. The PM displays maps of domains which represent views into portions of the configuration. Icons can change color according to the status of the resources they represent, based on the conditions in which the manager is interested. The manager may select an icon representing an entity (which might be another domain) and either double-click to "look into" the object represented by the icon (looking at the entities that comprise the selected entity) or single-click to select the icon (or icons) and then choose from a menu of operations that apply to objects of the class represented by the icon. A second type of window appears, requesting any operation arguments and displaying results for the operation. Displays of numeric attributes can also be provided in alternative forms such as graphs or histograms. As with the FCL PM, this module is generic and data-driven, and thus capable of adapting to newly enrolled modules, basing its input window layouts and output window layouts on the class data in the MIR. For examples of how DECmcc is used, refer to (Digital Equipment Corporation, 1991c).

• *Notification PM* allows the manager to view selected alarm notifications and events, also based on a windows user interface. The module maintains information about a manager-defined set of conditions, and displays a subset of this information on the screen. The manager may choose to vary the information displayed, without changing the information that is being collected. By judicious use of color representing the perceived severity of the conditions, the manager can concentrate on the most important problems first, and can also relate to the same colors used by the Iconic Map PM.

22.5.4   Agent PMs and AMs

- *Network Management Forum* – the AM and Agent PM together implement the software necessary to appear as a Network Management Forum defined Conformant Management Entity (CME), implementing the NMF-defined subset of the OSI CMIP protocol. With the AM, any CME managed object can be managed, using any appropriate FMs and PMs. With the Agent PM, DECmcc-managed entities can be managed from NMF managing systems.

- *IBM's System Network Architecture (SNA) Management* – the AM and Agent PM together implement the software necessary to allow interoperability between DECmcc and an EMA Agent software component in either NetView or NET/MASTER in an SNA environment. Through the AM a DECmcc manager can manage resources in an SNA environment, and can receive alert notifications from NetView or NET/MASTER. Through the Agent PM, the NetView or NET/MASTER user can manage resources from the DECmcc environment, and can receive events or alarms (that is, notifications) from DECmcc. For more information on these modules see (Fernandez and Winkler, 1993)

22.6   "What you get for free"

Owing to the nature of DECmcc, and the data-driven, extensible, dynamic implementation of a number of the management modules, addition of a new module (for example, an Access Module) to DECmcc automatically affords the newly manageable entities significant management capabilities, including the following. Consider an AM that provides access to SQUIGGLE devices – when you add the AM into DECmcc, you will be able to perform the following automatically:

- identify (that is, name or address) specific SQUIGGLE resources;

- register SQUIGGLE resources in the DECmcc environment, making them known to your DECmcc, and all other DECmccs in the network ;

- represent SQUIGGLEs on an iconic map, by adding them to the domains of your choice;

- display management data about specific named SQUIGGLEs (directly through the AM);

- modify management information in specific named SQUIGGLEs;

- request management operations be applied to specific named SQUIGGLEs;

- display information relating to events from SQUIGGLEs;

- create alarm rules that can be triggered on particular detected conditions (polled or unsolicited) about named SQUIGGLE resources. (Rule templates would be provided with the AM for convenience.) When an alarm fires, the appropriate icon's color can be changed, and information displayed in a notification window;

- arrange to store management data periodically from named SQUIGGLE resources into the MIR historical data or export it to a relational database for off-line processing. Subsequently the stored information may be presented to users or used by other DECmcc applications.

Of course, if you so desire, you may also write new, additional FMs and/or PMs that make use of specific capabilities of the SQUIGGLE devices, and perhaps other devices as well.

Additionally, where one desires to manage new devices or software accessible via one of the standard management protocols (such as SNMP), there is no need to write an Access Module. Instead, an existing AM can be "extended" by loading the appropriate management class information into the MIR's class data. Then all the above capabilities are available immediately.

22.7   Conclusions

EMA and DECmcc represent a significant investment by Digital Equipment Corporation to address the problems of managing diverse environments. EMA is an architected approach, necessitated by the complexity of the problems involved – however, as an architecture it addresses the goals of integration, consistency, heterogeneity, standards and dynamic extensibility, in the context of both the managed objects and their agents and the management director and its management applications.

By the implementation of architected, open APIs for both the Common Agent and DECmcc, we have developed open platforms for both agent systems and director systems. The modular approach to both platforms, together with the underlying design based on distributed systems principles, yields management capabilities that are capable of embracing older, legacy management components as well as incorporating new standard and *de facto* management components.

As distributed technology becomes more widespread, the usefulness of the ideas encompassed in Digital Equipment's management approach will be realized.

Abbreviations

AMs   Access Modules
API   Application Programming Interface
CDS   Cell Directory Service

CME	Conformant Management Entity
CMIP	Common Management Information Protocol
DCE	Distributed Computing Environment
DME	Distributed Management Environment
DECdns	Digital Equipment Corporation's Distributed Name Service
DECmcc	Digital Equipment Corporation's Management Control Center
EMA	Enterprise Management Architecture
FCL	Forms and Command Line
FDDI	Fiber Distributed Data Interface
FMs	Function Modules
HDR	Historical Data Recorder
LAN	Local Area Network
MIB	Management Information Base
MIR	Management Information Repository
MMs	Management Modules
MOM	Managed Object Module
MOP	Maintenance Operations Protocol
MSL	Management Specification Language
MTU	MIB Translator Utility
NCL	Network Control Language
NICE	Network Information Control and Exchange
NMF	Network Management Forum
OSF	Open Software Foundation
OSI	Open Systems Interconnection
PEM	Protocol Engine Module
PMs	Presentation Modules
RFC	Request for Comments
SIF	Status Information Frames
SMI	Structure of Management Information
SMT	Station Management
SNA	System Network Architecture
SNMP	Simple Network Management Protocol
XMP	X/Open Management Protocols API

References

Anwaruddin M. (1991). Performance management in an EMA director. In *Integrated Network Management II*. (Krishnan I. and Zimmer W., eds.), 679–89. North Holland

Densmore M. (1991). Providing CMIS services in DECmcc. In *Proc. IFIP Symposium on Integrated Network Management*, Crystal City VA, April 1991, 313–26

Digital Equipment Corporation (1991a). *EMA General Description*. Order number: AA-PD5JA-TE.

Digital Equipment Corporation (1991b). *DECmcc Introduction*. Order number: AA-PD57C-TE

Digital Equipment Corporation (1991c). *DECmcc Use*. Order number: AA-PD59C-TE

Digital Equipment Corporation (1991d). *DECmcc System Reference Manual* (two volumes). Order number: AA-PD5LC-TE, AA-PE55C-TE

Fehskens L. (1989). An architectural strategy for enterprise management. In *Integrated Network Management I*, (Meandzija B and Westcott J., eds), 41–60. North Holland

Fernandez J. and Winkler K. (1993). Modeling SNA networks using the structure of management information. *IEEE Communications*, **31**(5), 60–67

Newkerk O., Nihart M. A. and Wong S. (1993). The common agent. *IEEE JSAC Special Issue on Network Management and Control*, **11**(9), 1346–52

Shurtleff D.G. and Strutt C. (1990). Extensibility of an enterprise management director. In *Network Management and Control* (Kershenbaum A., Malek M., and Wall M., eds.), 129–41, NewYork: Plenum Press

Shvartsman A. (1993a). An historical object base in an enterprise management director. In *Integrated Network Management III*, (Hegering and Yemini Y., eds.), 123–34. North Holland

Shvartsman A. (1993b). Dealing with history and time in a distributed enterprise manager. *IEEE Network*, **7**(6), 32–43

Strutt C. (1991). Dealing with scale in an enterprise management director. In *Integrated Network Management II*, (Krishnan I. and Zimmer W., eds.), 577–93. North Holland

Strutt C. (1993). Distribution in an enterprise management director. In *Integrated Network Management III*. (Hegering H. and Yemini Y., eds.), 223–34. North Holland

Strutt C. and Shurtleff D.G. (1989). Architecture for an integrated, extensible enterprise management director. In *Integrated Network Management I*, (Meandzija B and Westcott J. eds.), 61–72. North Holland

Strutt C. and Swist J. A. (1993). Design of the DECmcc management director. *Digital Equipment Corporation Technical Journal*, **5**(1), 130–42

Sylor M.W. (1989). Guidelines for structuring manageable entities. In *Integrated Network Management I*, (Meandzija B and Westcott J. eds), 169–83. North Holland

Sylor M.W. (1991). DECnet/OSI phase V network management. In *Integrated Network Management II*, (Krishnan I. and Zimmer W., eds.), 57–69. North Holland

Chapter 23

DME Framework and Design

Matthias Autrata[†] and Colin Strutt[*]

[†]Open Software Foundation,[1]
11 Cambridge Center,
Cambridge, MA 02142, USA
Email: math@osf.org

[*]Digital Equipment Corporation,
550 King Street,
Littleton, MA 01460–1289, USA
Email: strutt@took.enet.dec.com

In its fourth request for technology, OSF solicited technologies addressing the management of networks and distributed computer systems – the DME. The diversity of management approaches used today, and the differences between network and systems management, leave much to be desired in terms of uniformity, ease of use, cost, and comprehensiveness. To address these issues, a framework was sought which encompasses the different approaches, and provides a foundation for management of the emerging distributed computing environments.

We describe the problem briefly, take a high-level look at the framework architecture, and discuss implementation concerns to develop a solution flexible enough to form the basis for integrated distributed systems management.

23.1 The DME framework

Using its open process for evaluating and acquiring technology, the Open Software Foundation (OSF) selected a set of technologies to integrate into its Distributed Management Environment (DME). The DME comprises enabling technology capable of working with any operating system and will simplify the management of stand-alone and distributed systems, reducing the costs for system administration. Thus the DME provides the functions that system administrators need while serving as a foundation for the development of management applications (OSF, 1991, 1992a).

---

[1]   Current address: OpenVision Technologies Inc., 41 North Main Street, North Grafton, MA
01536, USA, Email: Matthias.Autrata@ov.com

The DME comprises several major components in two major groupings:

i) Framework

- an object-oriented infrastructure for distributed management applications – the Object Management Framework (OMF),

- support for the Simple Network Management Protocol (SNMP) and the Common Management Information Protocol (CMIP) – the Network Management Option (NMO),

- a distributed user interface (DUI),

- distributed notification services.

ii) Distributed Services

- software distribution and installation,

- software licensing,

- personal computer integration,

- host management.

The focus of this chapter is on the framework and its components. DME is one offering in the portfolio of technologies that make up the OSF open computing environment. To meet the needs of open computing, DME fulfills several requirements.

23.1.1   Scalability

DME supports a wide range of environments, ranging from single nodes to large corporate networks. It uniformly applies the same principles and management solutions in a scalable fashion. This is possible because DME services can be located anywhere on the network. They are connected through services provided by the OSF Distributed Computing Environment (DCE), which gives users and developers a consistent means of accessing diverse systems (OSF, 1992b).

DME is a distributed system that may present a centralized view to the user, but the management operations that DME provides can be distributed to be performed where most appropriate. In this way, there is no single bottleneck to the growth of the system, nor is there a single point of failure.

A distributed approach allows both the processing and presentation of the right level of information where it is needed. Within a local area network, for example, a system administrator might want detailed data about the resources that must be managed. At a management center overlooking 10,000 networked computers, the same level of detail would be overwhelming, resulting in important information being lost. Thus data at lower levels needs to be filtered and processed to become information at a higher-level management center.

23.1.2   System and network management

The wide variety of computing resources that must be managed in a distributed environment has led to a diversity of incompatible methods for managing those resources. DME addresses this problem by providing functions and services that unify and support both network and systems management. It protects existing solutions while providing a migration path to newer technologies. Through a single management model, DME accommodates the differences between system and network management.

Network management requires functions such as monitoring, polling, and event management. Most network management involves monitoring of devices on a network. SNMP is used primarily in the management of TCP/IP networks. Simple protocols and services are used to configure or repair network connectivity, making higher-level, more complex, services available. CMIP is used for the management of OSI-based systems. In the telecommunications industry, for example, additional specialized protocols are employed. The design of DME accommodates different protocols easily and provides a uniform view on all management interactions.

System management functions are typically programs running on a computer. Security requirements are stringent, and complex relationships among managed entities must be maintained. Many important entities, such as users, systems, and printers, are long-lived. Typically, less polling activity is present.

With today's computing environments, similar entities must be managed in different ways. DME provides the mechanisms that allow entities to be viewed consistently, eliminating the need for system and network managers to learn and apply different approaches to managing similar things.

23.1.3   A coherent user interface

A unified presentation of all management information and a consistent style of invoking operations are important aspects of a consistent approach to management. The DUI integrates all interaction – dialogs, including forms and lists; groups of icons; and topology displays, including network maps – into one management user interface. The skills acquired using one application are immediately transferable to another. In addition, an administrator can invoke all DME management operations via a command-line interface.

23.1.4   Interoperability

A management framework must define and provide for interoperability of diverse resources at several levels. At the lowest level, it must define and standardize communications protocols. At higher levels, a security framework must be defined, so that communication can take place in an authenticated manner. Furthermore, the syntax and semantics of the management operations must be well defined and specified openly, so that other parties can reuse them to integrate in their solutions.

DME supports the standard management protocols SNMP and CMIP. In addition, for the development of distributed management solutions, DME builds on the foundation established by the OSF DCE and the Object Management Group

(OMG) Common Object Request Broker Architecture (CORBA). For secure communication between management application entities, DME uses the DCE Remote Procedure Call (RPC). The RPC communication is built on a set of interfaces defined in the DCE Interface Definition Language (IDL). For development of distributed objects comprising the management applications, and representing the managed objects, DME uses CORBA.

23.1.5   Distributed management as distributed objects

We explain above that DME is based on objects. Clearly not all managed objects will reside on one computer system, or even in one program. Rather the objects will be spread all over the network. So part of the problem of distributed management is involved with invoking operations on remote objects.

The approach taken in DME recognizes that objects reside where they need to be, and there is a protocol to access them and invoke operations on them from a remote site. Objects are realized in object servers – programs that implement one or more objects. Applications are formed by groups of objects collaborating and interacting to solve a management problem. The DME framework provides for the common understanding of how to deal with objects in a uniform way, and the protocols needed to access them.

Locating the objects in a distributed environment requires a directory service, providing a mapping from the object names to the locations of their servers. Objects have names, which can be used to obtain their object ids. These object ids are used by the underlying management framework and communications infrastructure to contact the server.

In addition, the framework provides services to handle the notifications being generated by the objects. Mechanisms exist to filter notifications based on criteria such as severity, and to forward them to other objects or applications. The notifications may then be displayed on the screen, change the color of an icon, trigger some automated operation, or just be logged in some file for later inspection.

23.2   High-level overview of the architecture

All management can be subsumed if we are able to deal with two kinds of things: objects and the operations that can be invoked on those objects. The DME architecture and framework provide the conceptual model, an implementation of it, and the necessary tools to build objects which can be located anywhere in the network. Management, then, is carried out by collections of objects which collaborate in order to perform a management task.

The DME Framework is built upon enhanced DCE services and provides the following fundamental components used to build management applications:

- A language to define types and their interfaces[2];

---

[2]   The DME framework defines an extended language, I4DL, which allows one to define additional operational characteristics beyond the interface.

- A set of client services and APIs to invoke operations on objects;

- A set of object services to facilitate the implementation of objects, including persistence, event services, and tools to build graphically oriented applications;

- A set of management services, which are specifically designed to simplify the development of management applications.

These components will be described in greater detail later on. Before that, however, we will look into related work and how it applies to DME.

23.2.1   Related standards and environments

There are a number of standards and efforts underway to define distributed object frameworks. Some of these standards are specific to management whereas others are of general purpose. In the following sections, we will discuss the most important standards, technologies and efforts, and explain how they are used to build the DME framework.

OSF's Distributed Computing Environment

The Distributed Computing Environment (DCE) provides an integrated set of technologies to implement distributed client-server applications based on RPCs. Included with the DCE technology are:

- RPC to make requests of servers. In order to describe a service, one uses DCE's IDL. Server descriptions in this language are translated into client and server stubs. The client stubs look almost like ordinary C function calls. The stubs serialize the data passed in and transmit them to the server, where the datastream is disassembled and passed to the function being called remotely. In that way, RPC and IDL hide most of the network complexities from the programmer.

- Directory services to register services and to provide a convenient way for clients to locate the services. In that way, clients and servers can be written without *a priori* knowledge of the location of individual servers.

- Security services enable programmers to create secure applications by providing the means to securely authenticate clients to servers and vice versa. Servers may support Access Control Lists in order to authorize clients' requests.

- Time services ensure that a consistent notion of time exists in the network. This is especially important for security (to determine the lifetime of a security certificate, for example) and for RPC (to control timeouts, for example).

- Threads facilities provide for programming parallel programs. The threads facility conforms to the Posix threads standard and is used throughout the other DCE services.

In DCE these services are all integrated into one coherent framework. However, DCE does not provide policies of how the services are to be used. For example, the namespace maintained by the directory service can be structured in any arbitrary (albeit hierarchical) fashion. Furthermore, DCE IDL does not support the concept of subtyping and definition of implementation characteristics.

Thus, DCE provides an almost completely policy-free development environment for any kind of distributed application.

OMG CORBA

OMG defined an architecture called Common Object Request Broker Architecture (CORBA, 1991). This specification comprises:

- An Interface Definition Language to define the external behavior of objects. This language can be compiled to provide client and server stubs for object implementations. In that sense it parallels DCE's IDL, but with an object-oriented syntax. In fact, the relationship between the CORBA IDL and DCE's IDL is much like the relationship between C++ and C;

- An API to build object requests dynamically;

- A basic object adapter, which is used to define the most common object server environment;

- An interface repository which contains descriptions of all interfaces in use in a given system.

CORBA is not a complete specification like the one for DCE. CORBA only specifies the most crucial external interfaces and APIs of the system. It does not address interoperability, security or naming. All of these features and services are expected to be defined in the future. However, CORBA does provide a foundation upon which one can build a distributed object system that can grow and addresses the currently missing items. It is fairly straightforward to map CORBA to DCE (see examples later in this chapter).

OSI and internet management

OSI set out to define a comprehensive management architecture in the mid and late eighties. The result of this multi-year effort is a number of formal standards defining the Common Management Information Protocol and Services (CMIP/CMIS), Guidelines and a template language for the Definition of Managed Objects (GDMO), and a number of services. Likewise, but much simpler, there exist a number of Internet standards specifying a Simple Network Management Protocol. This protocol is used as the basis for a number of network management products today. The DME framework incorporates these standards through a component called the Network Management Option. We will discuss the integration of these standards and associated efforts below.

Tivoli's management environment

Tivoli System's TME also provides a distributed object-oriented development environment. When this framework was initially developed, it defined its own object model and distributed runtime environment, as neither the CORBA specification nor DCE were available at the time.

TME provides a number of object services and management services as well as a distributed user interface toolkit. Tivoli is currently in the process of migrating its services to conform to the CORBA specifications.

23.2.2 Reconciling environments

While developing the architecture for DME, it became clear that there are a number of major requirements and forces that need to be reconciled:

- An object infrastructure is a necessary part of DME technology.

- The industry is rapidly moving towards CORBA as the *de facto* standard definition for an object infrastructure.

- DCE provides a solid platform with important services and interoperability guarantees.

- The Tivoli object and management services technology provides a good starting point for a comprehensive set of services.

Looking at these forces together, OSF concluded that it is an industry requirement to address object technology by providing an interoperable backbone definition and implementation upon which value-added object environments could be built. This technology forms an evolutionary extension of DCE, providing an object-oriented view in line with the CORBA specification.

Thus, OSF addresses the requirement for a consistent, interoperable CORBA definition while at the same time building the foundation for the management services needed to fulfill DME's goals. DME objects are implemented in object servers; these object servers are in turn DCE servers and registered with DCE's directory service. Likewise, clients requesting services of objects are DCE clients making requests on the objects that are being realized in a DCE server. That is exactly what the DME framework does: it provides the core services and tools to build objects according to the CORBA specification on top of DCE. In that sense DME does provide a toolkit which hides some of the complexities of DCE. At the same time, DME implements policy as to how things are to be structured.

In the following sections, we will approach the DME framework from a specification and developers' perspective.

23.2.3 Object framework infrastructure

The DME Framework can be depicted as shown in Figure 23.1. DCE is extended with a number of features that make it more convenient to implement distributed object-based services. Upon these extensions are built a small set of services which are in turn used by the management services that form the basis for development of management applications.

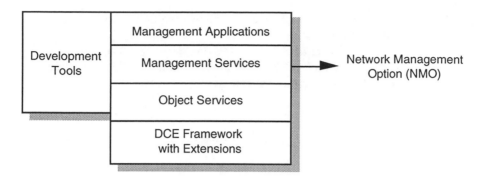

Figure 23.1 DME framework structure.

The DCE extensions cover support for a more dynamic approach to server activation. In particular, DCE will be able to start servers on demand as a procedure call arrives. This functionality will be used to implement dynamic object activation. Furthermore, the support to dynamically start servers will include a repository of server implementations which will also form the object implementation repository for the DME framework.

On the client side, extensions to DCE include support for dynamically creating RPC calls, so that clients can make calls without having necessarily all the stubs compiled into them (see Figure 23.2).

The DME Framework is built by exporting an object-oriented view to the DCE enhancements described above. In particular, the interfaces described in CORBA IDL will be mapped onto one or more corresponding DCE IDL definitions. The CORBA IDL to C mapping provides a very simple model to the programmer. All one needs to know, in order to invoke an operation on an object, is the object's reference. The DME Framework will provide the necessary stubs and libraries which take care of the interactions with the DCE namespace, and then call the DCE IDL stub derived from the CORBA IDL stub.

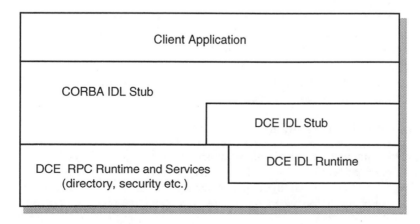

Figure 23.2 Client-side components.

Similarly, the framework will provide skeletons and libraries for the object implementation which automate the development of an object in a DCE server.

23.2.4 Object services

In order to develop management applications, there needs to be present a fundamental set of services which not only make the development task easier, but also help to ensure portability of an application across different vendors' implementations of the framework. Furthermore, the object services also define an interoperable application layer. These services can be categorized into low-level and fairly generic ones, and higher-level, management-specific ones. We call the low-level fundamental services object services and the higher-level ones management services.

The DME Framework will include a minimal set of object services which are needed to build distributed applications and services. These object services will be aligned with the definitions adopted or being worked on by OMG. They include:

- Life-cycle, in order to consistently manage creating, moving, copying and deleting objects;

- Persistence, in order to provide storage for an object's private attributes, and to be able to support objects whose lifetime is much longer than that of a single process;

- Security, in order to simplify and automate the authorization of requests on an object;

- Naming, in order to obtain an object reference, given a human-readable name of an object;

- Events, in order to support out-of-band communication between objects and administrators;

- Synchronization, in order to maintain consistency across multiple, concurrent operations on objects;

- Associations and relationships, in order to define a common foundation for higher-level services that describe complex object relationships, like network maps;

- Time, in order to provide a consistent view of time in a distributed system;

- Message catalogs, in order to support distributed internationalized presentation of messages.

The list of object services included in DME will grow over time. The list above represents the minimal set of services necessary for DME's planned set of management services.

23.2.5   Management services

The management services form the foundation for developing portable and interoperable management applications. In a distributed environment, interoperability is not only defined by common protocols and low-level services like security and naming, but also by the availability of a common set of higher-level services. DME management services define such a set of common services that should be present in every system, so that applications may be deployed assuming their presence. Also, these services form the foundation for the integration of management applications. Since many of the services help to capture common knowledge and structure, applications that use those services integrate with each other and share information in the distributed environment.

The set of services can roughly be categorized into the following:

Distributed user interface

The distributed user interface (DUI) provides applications with the capability to interact with users in a fashion that is both distributed and independent of user interface technology. Applications post dialogs and presentation information to the DUI, which takes care of mapping the presentation information to a specific toolkit, like Motif. The DUI also handles a large part of the dialog interaction with the user. For example, an application may post a dialog to enter information about a user. All the field editing and moving about the dialog is handled by the DUI. The DUI may be instructed to call the application back with information about the data entered or if other events occur (such as pressing the cancel button).

The DUI can manage multiple clients and thus also provides the integration point for applications that are distributed over the network.

Maps and collections

There is a need to structure, manage and present information according to relationships that exist between the objects. For example, various categories of printer could all be kept in collections. Likewise, a number of file systems may be managed collectively. Collection-objects provide application developers with the basic tools to manage unordered sets of references to other objects. Several subtypes of the basic collection interface allow for specialized handling.

Maps are like collections in that they maintain object references. In this case, however, the map-objects also maintain a graph that describes the relationships between the individual members of the map. This service would, for example, be used to represent the physical network structure.

This service provides the following interfaces:

- Connections, to model the fact that two objects are connected in a certain way. Objects can have more than one connection, and can play different roles in different connections.

- Maps, to model large sets of connections.

- Collections, to model unstructured relationships between objects. Collections can be thought of as being a set of object references.

There are also several variations and extensions available, and all the interfaces integrate with each other. For example, a collection may participate in a map, and there may be collections of maps.

Monitoring

Monitoring addresses the broad category of management tasks that is involved with keeping track of the status of the system and the triggering of actions in response to events that occur in the system.

In particular, the monitoring services define an infrastructure into which other objects can be installed so that there is a common way of reporting events. Likewise, there needs to be a common way of obtaining information about events that occurred in the system. Lastly, monitoring defines a common structure for triggering actions and propagating status changes within related entities. An example that ties monitoring, maps and the DUI together is the occurrence of a critical fault at some network device. A managed object would emit a notification about the fault. The notification would be examined and redistributed by the monitoring service and eventually reach an object in a map that represents the subnetwork where the device is located. Next, the object in the map would need to update its status, and inform higher-level objects about the fault. Depending on the current status of the network map display, certain icons might change color, and dialogs would appear that describe the problem.

Discovery

Discovery addresses the need to keep track of the configuration of the system. Especially in larger installations, a manual configuration of the system is very labor-intensive and error-prone, in some sense almost impossible. Additionally, the structure and components of a distributed system change over time. In order to keep track of the evolution of the environment, there needs to be a common set of rules and services about how to register and unregister new objects, where to put them (in maps, for example) and how to notify administrators about their existence.

The discovery management service provides a set of common interfaces and notification declarations for other objects to use so that they may report status changes or their creation and deletion.

Policy

Management applications need to reflect the way in which tasks are carried out in any given environment. Many of the operations that can be carried out can be subject to a local policy. Here, policy is intended to mean the sets of guidelines and rules about how operations are carried out.

These policies may be limited logically or geographically to subsets of the entire set of objects present in a system. Conventions and supporting services which maintain administrative policies across collections of managed objects are used to define administrative domains. Domains enforce, for example, which values are reasonable defaults and the sets of legal values for certain data items.

Scheduling

Many administrative tasks need to be performed during non-peak hours. Also, sometimes a host or service might be unreachable for some reason. Scheduling is the service that supports timed, off-line execution of requests, not unlike the *cron* tools in UNIX environments.

Adapter objects

There are a large number of standardized and proprietary management protocols. Given the vast differences in protocol architectures, as well as naming and security in these protocols, there cannot be a single multi-protocol architecture that hides all these differences under one common API. However, objects can be used to provide a DME Framework-conformant view on these foreign protocols and their services. The concept of adapter objects covers any access of such protocols in order to carry out (a part of) a management task. There are numerous variations and qualities of adapter objects possible. A few examples include:

- *Protocol adapter.* This type of service provides the primitives of a specific protocol in an object's interface. Effectively, this kind of adapter object provides an object-oriented API to the protocol, but nothing more. The benefit of this approach is that multiple parties can access the protocol regardless of their own location and that DME Framework security can be applied to that protocol access. This is the most generic and primitive kind of adapter object. Other adapter objects might use it as a basis.

- *Management Information Base (MIB) adapter.* This type of adapter maps a standard MIB into the DME Framework object model. In the SNMP case, such an adapter would map MIB II into a set of IDL interfaces which would export a more convenient view on the management information than the raw table- and variable-oriented one provided by SNMP alone. This kind of adapter object is still relatively primitive, but it provides already some abstraction of the protocol and its idiosyncrasies.

- *Service-oriented adapter.* This type of adapter provides a high-level view on some service that needs to be accessed by a management application. This variant provides the most convenience for the user (client) since it is the most abstract. In the SNMP case, for example, a service-oriented adapter object could address a particular vendor's router device or even internet routing on SNMP in general.

Adapter objects are, of course specific to the protocol or environment which they map into the DME Framework. The initial release of DME will provide a MIB II adapter service (for SNMP) and potentially some services for CMIP as well.

23.3   Implementation of the DME framework

The DME framework can be divided into several components and layers. In this section, we present a component view and an overview of the individual component design. Figure 23.3 shows a simplified view of the process and data structure of the DME framework implementation.

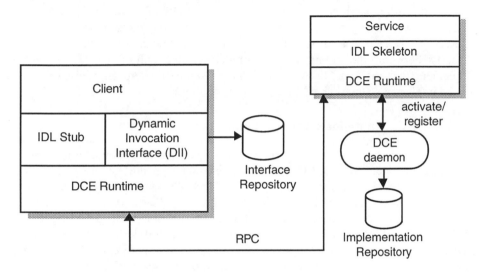

Figure 23.3 DME framework components.

In this framework, every client is directly a DCE client and there is no special process needed for the client to make its calls other than those already part of DCE. In a sense, the functionality of the Object Request Broker (ORB) is in part within the client, and in other parts provided by the DCE infrastructure. On the server side, there is an improved version of the DCE RPC daemon (RPCd), which is capable of activating servers on demand. As before, a client uses the directory service to obtain a partially bound handle to the desired server. The request then arrives at the DCE daemon (DCEd) which in turn starts the proper process. Once the process is started the interchange can continue as if the server had already been activated earlier; the client is unaware of this activation, except for the additional time required to activate the server.

23.3.1   Object references

In order to invoke operations on objects, an object reference for that particular object needs to be present. In DME, the object reference includes several data fields:

- The DCE name of the object (to locate the object adapter/DCEd responsible for the implementation). In the first release, the DCE name of an object is restricted to a Cell Directory Service (CDS) name with the last component being a string representation of the object's assigned uuid.

- The binding handle to the server(s) implementing this object. This datastructure may be more or less complete depending on previous activities.

- Security-related information.

The location of an object proceeds roughly as follows: an object reference contains the name of a server and an object-uuid. The client library can establish a connection with this server based on information in CDS. The Basic Object Adapter (BOA), after receiving the request, activates the object's implementation and passes a fully bound handle back to the client. Further communication can then take place directly between the client and the object's implementation. (In the OSF implementation, the terms BOA and DCEd are often used interchangeably, since the DCEd implements almost all of the BOA functionality.)

23.3.2   DCE client-side enhancements

A client wishing to invoke some operations on objects has two options: it uses either the stubs generated from the CORBA IDL files or the Dynamic Invocation Interface (DII). In either case, the libraries provided map the calls onto DCE remote procedure calls. Thus, the object client is always a DCE client as well.

A DCE client is currently required to link in the stub code generated by the DCE IDL compiler in order to be able to call a server. In order to support dynamic invocations of servers, where no stubs have been linked in before, the RPC runtime and IDL runtime have to be adjusted so that the DII can create calls *on the fly*. This requirement will be discussed in more detail below.

The current DCE runtime supports the return of exceptions which are encoded in integral values. It would be desirable that DCE support exceptions that can also contain user-defined structured data. This requirement is, however, not mandatory, as complex exception support can also be emulated in the CORBA IDL to DCE IDL mapping.

IDL

The CORBA IDL will be mapped into stub APIs according to the CORBA specification. These stub routines need an object reference as input, and given that, handle all further DCE interaction in order to perform the call. In particular, the CORBA IDL stub routines:

- Perform resolution of the object reference to a DCE server which implements the operation requested.

- Establish and cache binding handles to the DCE server.

- Pass authentication information (PACs) along with the calls.

- Handle exception information and structures, and map DCE exceptions (which are different from those in CORBA) into CORBA IDL exceptions. CORBA IDL interfaces are mapped to DCE IDL interfaces in such a way that all features *defined* in the CORBA IDL interface are represented in one DCE IDL interface. By defined, we mean those features that are actually introduced in that interface as opposed to those that are inherited and were already defined previously.

Table 23.1 Correspondence between CORBA and DCE IDLs.

CORBA IDL	DCE IDL
```interface A { int fA(in int a); }```	```interface A { int A_fA([in] int a); };```
```interface B: A { int fB(in int a); };```	```interface B { int B_fB([in] int a); };```
```interface C { int fC(in int a); };```	```interface C { int C_fC([in] int a); };```
```interface D: B, C { int fD(in int a); };```	```interface D { int D_fD([in] int a); };```

Using this example, Table 23.1 contains some IDL fragments that show how the mapping would turn out. Note that we leave out the interface attributes such as uuid and version number, which are irrelevant in this context. Likewise, we do not describe here the mapping of object references onto DCE handles.

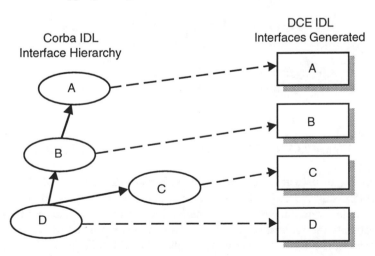

Figure 23.4 CORBA and DCE IDL relationship.

If a CORBA IDL definition references one or more interfaces from which it inherits, then these (superior) interfaces are already mapped into distinct DCE IDL interfaces. The effect of this is that CORBA IDL interface hierarchies are flattened into sets of DCE IDL interfaces as shown in Figure 23.4. The CORBA IDL compiler can use the interface uuid and version number of the CORBA IDL interface for the DCE interface. Stub routines are generated for all features *defined* in the interface. Features from an interface higher in the inheritance hierarchy are simply calls to the stub in the inherited interface.

Using the example above, we obtain the CORBA C stubs shown in Figure 23.5. Note that with C++ or an optimizing compiler, these calls could be expanded in-line and create no calling overhead.

```
/*** Stub routines for interface A ***/
        int A_fA(A o, env *ev, int a);

/*** Stub routines for interface B ***/
        int B_fA(B o, env *ev, int a) {
                return A_fA((A)o, ev, a);
        };
        int B_fB(B o, env *ev, int a);

/*** Stub routines for interface C ***/
        int C_fC(C o, env *ev, int a);

/*** Stub routines for interface D ***/
        int D_fA(D o, env *ev, int a) {
                return A_fA((A)o, ev, a);
        };
        int D_fB(D o, env *ev, int a) {
                return B_fB((B)o, ev, a);
        };
        int D_fC(D o, env *ev, int a) {
                return C_fC((C)a, ev, a);
        };
        int D_fD(D o, env *ev, int a);
```

Figure 23.5 CORBA C stubs generated from CORBA IDL.

This leaves us with a very direct and efficient mapping of CORBA IDL stubs onto DCE IDL stubs. The CORBA IDL stub structure is roughly as follows.

The object reference is used to obtain a DCE binding handle to a DCE server that implements the requested operation. This is accomplished by using the name information in the handle together with the object's uuid to query the DCE CDS and then the DCEd (or BOA). Once such a DCE handle has been obtained it is placed into the object reference for future use. After a binding handle has been obtained, the parameters passed into the CORBA IDL stub are simply passed into the DCE RPC stub and the call is made to the server. Upon return from the call, the result parameters are passed back to the caller. In case of an exception, the data is taken from the DCE stub and mapped into a CORBA exception structure and then passed back to the caller in the environment structure.

The generated DCE IDL stubs are just like other DCE stubs a programmer would create. This has the additional benefit of allowing for mixing and matching DCE interfaces and CORBA IDL-derived interfaces to some degree. If a few simple rules are followed, one can create DCE servers that can be addressed as object servers as well.

Dynamic invocation interface

The Dynamic Invocation Interface (DII) can create operation requests at runtime, without requiring that any code that was generated by the IDL compiler for the operation being requested is linked into the application. Thus the DII requires that data structures can be marshaled and unmarshaled dynamically, which in turn requires that the marshaling routines in the RPC or IDL runtime be data-driven. Furthermore, the DII needs to be able to determine which RPC interface to call, given an interface and an operation name. Thus the DII needs to consult the interface repository, in order to be able to determine which interface the operation being invoked belongs to. Furthermore, the DII needs the interface repository if it should check the correct use of parameters and data types.

Ideally, the DCE IDL runtime, the CORBA IDL runtime and the DII lower layers should share a great deal of code.

Interface repository

The interface repository is needed by the DII and is also otherwise a useful tool for browsers and debugging purposes. Its interfaces are defined in CORBA V1.1.

The DME Framework will define extensions to the current Interface Definition Repository to support the full life cycle of interface objects. In particular, it is important to also allow for runtime update and delete capabilities.

23.3.3   DCE server-side enhancements

Object implementations, unlike traditional RPC servers, may contain very large numbers of objects. Not all objects or their implementations will be active all the time. Thus the server side of the DME Framework needs to be able to manage servers and activate objects on demand. There are several activation policies which need to be supported.

Also, the framework will provide, just like on the client side, a set of libraries and routines which hide the complexity of server development from the object developer. For instance, server initialization, authorization validation and key management can be almost completely automated if certain policies are obeyed.

Lastly, the framework relies on support for delegation to securely support nested object requests.

DCE daemon (DCEd)

The DCEd will replace the RPC daemon and add automated server activation as well as remote server management. Furthermore, the DCEd will provide a number of administrative enhancements, which will make the management of a DCE host easier.

In the DME framework, the object adapter is responsible for maintaining the implementation repository and the individual object implementations. The DCEd fulfills that role. It will provide the following activation policies:

- Activate a complete object implementation on demand. If the active implementation is non-exclusive, then further requests to other objects may be passed to this implementation.

- Allow an external server process to register as an object implementation for one or more instances.

These two policies are minimally required. Ideally, the DCEd would allow arbitrary subsets of an object implementation to be present in processes. This would, however, require a change to the DCE protocols and is therefore not supported in the first release of the framework.

There is a protocol defined between the DCEd and the implementations (servers) in addition to the existing RPC protocol. This protocol allows the DCEd to:

- Activate and deactive servers;

- Activate and deactivate particular object instances within an already running server;

- Control the flow of requests between clients and the implementation via an activate/acknowledge protocol.

Implementation repository

The DCEd requires a repository in order to be able to activate implementations on demand. The implementation repository stores the knowledge about all locally available implementations and their supported interfaces. Also, the repository can map individual object uuids to separate implementations of the same interface. Thus, there may be multiple implementations of one interface present on a single system. The implementation repository basically presents a mapping function that takes an object reference, an interface id, and an operation id and maps those into a process which is to be started or contacted.

23.3.4 Object services

The object services will be implemented in such a fashion that they are as independent of the runtime environment as possible. In particular, the object services will hide the implementation details of the underlying runtime and supporting services that are being used as much as is reasonably possible.

Where there are proposals for object services currently being adopted by OMG, the implementation of these services will either follow the OMG specification or be designed so as to make it easy to provide the standard interfaces after adoption by OMG.

Life-cycle

The implementation of the life-cycle object service will follow the OMG specifications currently being adopted.

The life-cycle service and the Object Adapter (DCEd) cooperate to manufacture new object references when objects are instantiated. As mentioned above, a determinant element within an object reference in the DME framework will initially consist of the DCE name of the object adapter and a uuid identifying the object instance.

In order to create a new instance of an interface, the responsible factory object will:

- Create a new object reference;

- Collaborate with the persistence service to allocate storage for the object's persistent state;

- Instantiate a default ACL (Access Control List).

This service is a prerequisite for all other services.

Persistence

The implementation of the persistence object service will follow the OMG specifications currently being adopted. The service will make use of the persistence library which is currently planned as a DCE enhancement. At the same time, it will be architected such that an object implementation need not change if the storage service is exchanged for some other service, for example, a relational database. This service is very important for almost all management services and applications.

Security

The process of determining the authorization of a particular requester is common across all implementations. The model and corresponding object service closely follow the existing DCE guidelines for ACLs and their evaluation. A client always passes a Privilege Attribute Certificate (PAC) along with a request. The PAC contains the principal identity and group memberships of the requester in a verifiable manner.

The implementation of the security service automates the tasks that are programmed manually in current applications using DCE. A standard ACL manager is provided along with a service that obtains the PAC sent with the call, and evaluates it against the object's ACL which is maintained in a permanent ACL storage associated with the object. If the ACL evaluation does not permit the request to be carried out, a standard exception is returned to the caller.

This service's complete implementation depends on the availability of delegation in DCE in order to securely support nested object calls. Security is critical for all other services and applications.

Naming

The implementation of the naming object service will follow the OMG specifications currently being adopted. For the initial release of DME, the service will only implement a special case of federated naming, however. Object names will conform to DCE name syntax, and always contain a string representation of their object-uuid as the last component (Leser, 1993). Naming is desirable for most management services and applications.

Events

The implementation of the event object service will follow the OMG specifications currently being adopted.

There are several options for the underlying DME implementation:

- The event service is a plain implementation of the OMG specification. This would present relatively little effort but ignore the capabilities of Event Services (EVS).

- The event service uses EVS. This would add filtering capabilities either at the client or at the channel object. The problem is to make proper use of EVS in order to avoid performance penalties.

Ultimately, the event service will integrate sophisticated filtering and provide filter management as well as high performance. This service is critical for the monitoring and discovery management services and very important for most other services and applications.

Synchronization

The synchronization service allows objects to lock critical resources and sections of code. Initially, a version of this service that only operates locally on one host is probably sufficient. Synchronization is also closely related to issues about operation activation. It is desirable to be able to declare several activation policies for individual interfaces. For the implementation of these policies a local synchronization service is sufficient.

Associations and relationships

Associations and relationships form a small set of interfaces which can be used to built arbitrary, more specialized management services. This service is required as it forms the foundation of collections and maps.

Time

The time object service presents a CORBA IDL interface to DCE's distributed time service. It presents a good example of how DCE interfaces can be integrated into the DME framework.

Message catalogs

Message catalogs contain messages in a local language for display to users. A message identifier is sent to a display object which retrieves the relevant message from the catalog. Distributed message catalogs are critically important for international management applications. They form a prerequisite for the Distributed User Interface.

23.4   Development approach

The DME team is taking the following development approach:

- All services are being defined with CORBA and to some extent prototyped on other sources' ORB implementations.

- A mapping from CORBA IDL to DCE IDL is specified. This mapping defines how DME services interoperate.

- All services are then implemented on DCE (V1.02/V1.03) by implementing the CORBA-derived APIs directly on DCE. In particular, the APIs to the DME services are the CORBA IDL-derived APIs mapped to DCE RPCs according to the specification mentioned above.

Here is a very simple, incomplete example:

```
// CORBA
#pragma uuid F38F5080-2D27-11C9-A95D-12345ABCD012
#pragma version 1.0
interface foo {
      short doit (in long a, in long b);
};
```

This has a CORBA–C mapping:

```
/* C */
typedef Object foo
short foo_doit(foo o, env *ev, long a, long b);
```

and a DCE IDL mapping:

```
/* DCE IDL */
[uuid(F38F5080-2D27-11C9-A95D-12345ABCD012),
      version(1.0)]
interface foo {
short dce_foo_doit([in,out] env *ev,
      [in] long a, [in] long b);
}
```

The DME implementors now have to write a server that implements and exports the DCE interface `foo`. Additionally, the implementor has to write the `foo_doit` function such that it does the standard binding and other work and eventually calls `dce_foo_doit`, the RPC.

- The CORBA runtime is created in parallel and can make use of code from the DME services CORBA emulation.

- DME can be released with the CORBA runtime, or a prerelease of the management services on DCE can be done earlier, if needed.

This development approach decouples DME services from the availability of a CORBA development and runtime environment. The CORBA IDL to DCE IDL mapping guarantees interoperability and compatibility with future releases of DME.

Abbreviations

ACL	Access Control List
API	Application Programming Interface
BOA	Basic Object Adapter
CDS	Cell Directory Service
CORBA	Common Object Request Broker Architecture
CMIP	Common Management Information Protocol
CMIS	Common Management Information Service
DCE	Distributed Computing Environment
DCEd	DCE daemon
DII	Dynamic Invocation Interface
DME	Distributed Management Environment
DUI	Distributed User Interface
EVS	Event Services
GDMO	Guidelines for the Definition of Managed Objects
IDL	Interface Definition Language
MIB	Management Information Base
NMO	Network Management Option
OMF	Object Management Framework
OMG	Object Management Group
ORB	Object Request Broker
OSF	Open Software Foundation
PAC	Privilege Attribute Certificate
RPC	Remote Procedure Call
RPCd	RPC daemon
SNMP	Simple Network Management Protocol
TME	Tivoli's Management Environment

References

CORBA (1991). *The Common Object Request Broker: architecture and specification.* OMG Document No. 91.12.1 Revision 1.1, 10 Dec. 1991

Leser N. (1993). The distributed computing environment naming architecture. *IEE/IOP/BCS Distributed Systems Engineering,* **1**(1), Sep., 19–28

OSF (1991). *The OSF Distributed Management Environment rationale.* Open Software Foundation, 11 Cambridge Center, Cambridge, MA 02142, USA, Sep. 1991

OSF (1992a). *The OSF Distributed Management Environment architecture.* Open Software Foundation, 11 Cambridge Center, Cambridge, MA 02142, USA, May 1992

OSF (1992b). *Introduction to OSF DCE.* Open Software Foundation, 11 Cambridge Center, Cambridge, MA 02142, USA

Chapter 24

Managing Change

Branislav N. Meandzija

MetaAccess Inc.,
P.O.Box 21956,
Santa Barbara, CA 93121-1956924 , USA
Email: meandzij@ucsbuxa.ucsb.edu

The rapidly changing networking environments and applications place an ever increasing burden on current static network management platforms. Change is increasingly difficult to manage as the quantity and types of manageable objects explode. To make matters worse, a proliferating number of different management protocols, platforms, and architectures makes it increasingly necessary for management systems to include complex gateway functions, at the protocol level as well as at the application level (for example, trouble ticketing).

METAWINDOW provides a unique approach to managing change. It is built around a software development environment and as such incorporates change in its very basis. METAWINDOW combines the design, monitoring, and control functions of networking and distributed system software. This combination elevates network management from its current passive, static, data-centered, state of the art to the active, dynamic, process-oriented future.

24.1 Introduction

The understanding of network management today is tightly coupled to the issues centered around the modeling, structure, and representation of management information in general, and more specifically related to issues concerning the design and implementation of the Management Information Base (MIB). A variety of MIB issues and solutions to these issues can be found in the literature (Meandzija and Westcott, 1989; Krishnan and Zimmer, 1991; Hegering and Yemini, 1993). As we better understand management information problems our focus is slowly shifting towards the operations and control aspects of network management. Currently, most network management systems are passive and offer little more than pretty interfaces to MIBs. This is very much in contrast to the *active* nature of network management itself. Network managers need the ability to *actively* control hardware and software modules, enabling them to react quickly to the massive changes in their environment and applications which are increasingly taking place in the nineties. *Active* control should give managers the opportunity to *actively* participate in the growth of their networks and shape the networks and the management process itself in a manner best suited for their particular management task. That would provide for a natural way of taking advantage of the most valuable resource of network management – the human resource and their experience. Systems offering *active* and easy control of computer networks and distributed systems are only beginning to emerge.

There are only two ways to introduce active network management. The first is to build management systems capable of dealing with most foreseeable network management problems.   That solution is prohibitively expensive in terms of performance, development time and cost, if at all feasible. The second solution is to give network managers, as much as possible, the ability to easily alter the functioning of the network and management system. That can be accomplished through the ability to easily redesign, reimplement, reinstall, and reintegrate major software modules at run time. Computer Aided Software Engineering (CASE) tools have been created for most issues related to the design and implementation of the MIB (Krishnan and Zimmer, 1991).   The nineties will witness application of CASE principles to the areas of operations. The METAWINDOW environment is an X-windows-based object-oriented environment that combines the ARCHETYPE methodology with the popular drag-and-drop GUI paradigm and a client-server-based remote monitoring and control system.

Software generated using METAWINDOW can be linked to graphical images thus allowing **run-time monitoring** of distributed programs, protocols or applications. As the interface to METAWINDOW is a fourth-generation language (that is, **non-programming**), the network manager is not only given the capability to monitor the internals of communication processes but also to alter them through the automatic software redesign and reintegration process.

In the following sections, we first introduce ARCHETYPE in Section 24.2 and METAWINDOW in Section 24.3. In Section 24.4 we show the applicability of METAWINDOW to OSI. Section 24.5 summarizes our approach.

24.2 ARCHETYPE

The ARCHETYPE method defines two specification languages for distributed systems:

i)   ARCHETYPE Abstract Language (AAL): a "natural language" abstract specification language created for the rapid object-oriented design of networking and distributed system software and applications.

ii) ARCHETYPE Executable Language (AEL): a data-driven, concurrent, executable specification language created as a user-friendly interface to a flexible, C language inclusive, high-performance protocol engine.

METAWINDOW is the first implementation that incorporates concepts of AEL and AAL. It is used for rapid development of communications protocols and distributed systems applications, and for the maintenance and management of these systems and applications. Both ARCHETYPE languages are "graphical" languages in the sense that the structure of their programs is easily represented as graphical objects. The structure of programs of both languages is based on trees. On the abstract level, the Module Tree represents the inheritance hierarchy in a top-down design process. On the executable level the Module Tree structure can be assigned different semantics, but most commonly represents the structure of protocol and service data units (that is, the parse tree of protocol and service data units).

24.2.1   AEL Principles

AEL programs consist of Module Trees which are best understood as programmable decision trees. The Module Tree is the program that processes and generates information units (for example, frames, packets, messages) as a protocol engine. Each information unit processed by the Module Tree traverses a path in the tree from the root to a leaf. As the information unit successfully determines the next node in its traversal path, the instructions specified in the node are executed. It is possible to establish a one-to-one mapping between the decisions and the structure of information units.

Each node of the AEL Module Tree has a C function, as one of its components, that is executed whenever an information unit (such as a message or packet) visits that node. The C function can use a variety of ARCHETYPE language extensions to C to access buffering, timing, IPC, security, data representation (ASN.1, XDR), OSI, and other libraries. Each module is a tree. Modules in the same program are collections of Module Trees.

Each Module Tree has a message queue at the root node. The root node of a Module Tree fetches the next message on the queue, processes it and passes it down to one or more of its children, depending on the message processed. The messages have assigned priorities which are used as the queuing discipline. Each node in any Module Tree can generate new messages for any other Module Tree which are queued at the root of that Module Tree. In a single processor environment the queues are merged based on the priority of messages.

The interaction between modules that are not in the same program is defined by other ARCHETYPE Modules which are supplied in source form by MetaAccess and which are used in the same way as all user-generated ARCHETYPE modules.

24.2.2   AAL Principles

An AAL program is a top-down configuration and design specification that may include different object domains, systems, architectures, executable units, and module and Module Tree ARCHETYPES.

DOMAIN, SYSTEM, LINK, ARCHITECTURE and EXECUTABLE UNIT ARCHETYPES are used for specifying configuration information. A DOMAIN is to be understood as defined in Chapter 16 of this book. A SYSTEM consists of a set of

ARCHITECTURE and EXECUTABLE UNIT. A LINK is used to connect DOMAINS or SYSTEMS and allows the representation of physical connectivity in a network.

A distributed system ARCHITECTURE is specified as a sequence of AEL Modules and AAL executable units that constitute that ARCHITECTURE. The difference between an ARCHITECTURE and a SYSTEM is that an ARCHITECTURE is a static blueprint for a system that could be distributed over multiple SYSTEMS or be part of a single SYSTEM whereas a SYSTEM is a physical entity.

An EXECUTABLE UNIT is specified as a list of AEL module references. That list consists of at least two module references. The kernel module reference specifies which module will act as the I/O interface of the EXECUTABLE UNIT. The main module reference specifies which module will act as the default destination of all messages received by the kernel module. When compiled an EXECUTABLE UNIT is transformed into the executable program.

24.3   META WINDOW

METAWINDOW is used for rapid development of communications protocols and distributed systems applications, and for the maintenance and management of these systems and applications.

Major capabilities include:

* automatic generation of protocol drivers and other programs from their graphical representations;

* unique monitoring capability for network operations and management, through run-time display of communications process internals (no other product available today can offer this capability) exhibiting logical and physical protocol relationships. Managers can view network "hotspots" at run time through color or audio options; view the code processed at specific nodes at run time through recorder or step-through monitor functions; and edit code specific to individual modules or nodes during run time.

* graphical representation of programs;

* ease of learning for anybody familiar with C, as most language constructs that are different from C are graphically programmed;

* dramatically reduced development time, providing increased time and capability for prototyping and testing system performance;

* OSI stack protocols, for example, CMIP and TCP/IP stack protocols, for example, SNMP

24.3.1   Design with METAWINDOW

The AEL/AAL program to be designed and implemented in this section is a variation of the C "hello world" program. The program will recognize the words *Hello George!*, or *Hello Ethel!*, or *Hello Fred!*, or *Bye!* When one of these four inputs is recognized, this program will print out *Hello John!*, or *Howdy John!* or *Hi John!*, or *Good Bye!*, respectively.

Before using METAWINDOW to design the **hello_world** program it is necessary to create and open a module in the graphical canvas. Figure 24.1 illustrates the module **HelloWorld** at the outset of the design process.

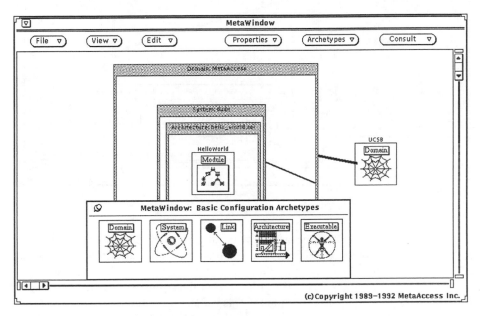

Figure 24.1 Module **HelloWorld** at the outset of the design process.

Any AEL/AAL program consists of a number of modules. Each AEL/AAL module is a tree. Each tree can be compiled as a single module into an object file. The object file will be automatically linked with other object files as part of the compilation of an AEL/AAL executable unit that consists of multiple AEL/AAL modules.

The best way to design an AEL/AAL program module is to design it around the input to be recognized and output to be generated. That can be done by assigning different inputs to different arc sequences (paths) in such a way that each arc corresponds to one input word; that is if the string *hello world* is to be recognized, one arc from the root tree node to a child will be assigned the string *hello* and one arc from that child to its own child will be assigned the string *world*. In this first design step, only the shape of the tree is considered. The actual arc information and node code are specified in subsequent steps.

There are four creatable objects relevant to trees and represented by tree icons: a node icon, a single arc icon, a virtual arc icon, and a virtual node arc icon. All creatable objects are created and manipulated by the drag-and-drop paradigm. Figure 24.2 shows the **HelloWorld** module after the initial design step.

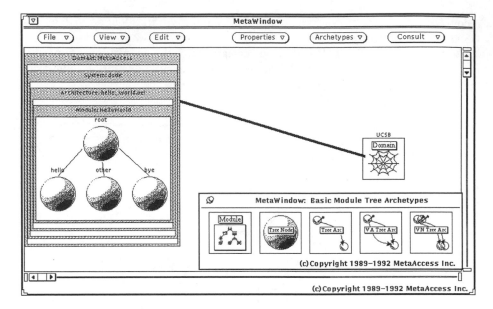

Figure 24.2 The first four nodes of the **HelloWorld** module.

The **root** node will be the starting point of any message processed by the tree. In the case of the **hello_world** program, we initially distinguish between three kinds of input: *Hello*, *Bye*, and any other input. Thus, we create a node *root* with three children: *hello*, *bye*, and *other*. After recognizing the string *Hello* it is necessary to distinguish between three kinds of input. This is done by adding three more nodes to the tree as children of the node **hello**. The final tree shape is shown in Figure 24.3.

Every message processed by the AEL tree is passed and modified from node to node, starting at the root and going down the tree until a leaf node is reached or until a node cannot pass the message to any of its children. There is a variety of different ways a message can be passed from parents to children. The most common way of deciding whether a message should be passed from a parent to a particular child is by determining whether a particular part of the message matches some data associated with the arc that combines these two nodes. That data information is specified through the arcs form. The arcs of the **root** node are shown in Figure 24.4.

Each arc has a variety of different information associated with it which will not be discussed in this chapter. The only information important for the design of the **HelloWorld** module is the arc message filters. All arcs in the designed tree should have the arc message filters for message acceptance set to **open**. That setting allows the matching of the data specified with the message.

There are two ways an AEL message can be passed, matching or indexing. Indexing is not used in the **HelloWorld** example. **Indexing** allows an explicit path specification for the tree that receives the message. A message is passed by **matching** over an arc if a matching function associated with the arc evaluates to True on the message data. The matching function can be a simple string match, an integer match, can match with a basic C type or untyped (that is, memory match), or can be user-defined through a match function specification. A match item is either defined as a call to a user-defined match function, or can be specified in three components: the position, the match value type, and the match value.

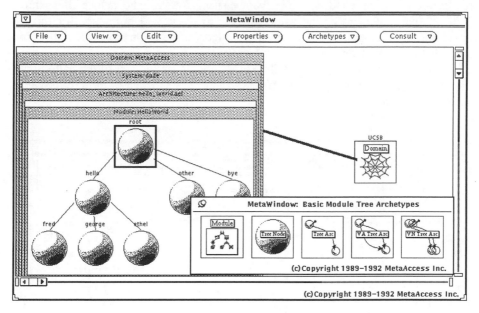

Figure 24.3 The **HelloWorld** module.

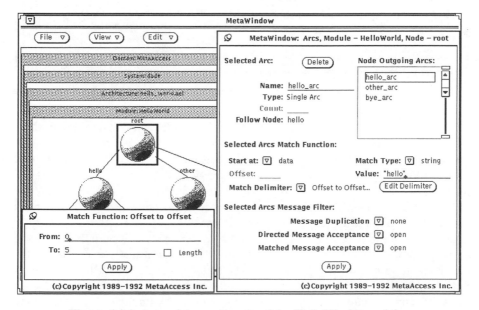

Figure 24.4 Arcs of the **root** node of the **HelloWorld** module.

The first arc of the **root** node of the **HelloWorld** module matches the string *Hello* with the first six bytes of the message evaluated. If that match yields the value true the message is passed to node **hello**. Otherwise the next arc is evaluated. The second arc of the **root** node specifies that the string *Bye! is* to be matched in position 0..3. If that match yields the value true the message will be passed for further processing by node **bye**. Otherwise the message will be evaluated against the third arc. That match will always succeed as no matching string is specified.

The only other arcs in the **HelloWorld** module are the arcs of the **hello** node. These arcs match the strings *Fred!*, *George!*, and *Ethel!*. The arcs form of the **hello** node is shown in Figure 24.5.

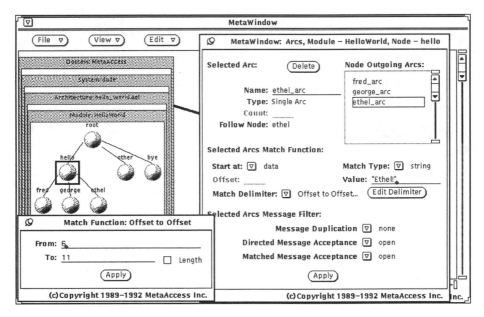

Figure 24.5 Arcs of the **hello** node of the **HelloWorld** module.

Each node consists of declarations of local variables and functions (all of these are only accessible in this one node and are static, that is, variables retain values after the node has been left), of initialization code (executed only after the first start-up of the module), of specifications of arcs to children and of the node code which is a C compound statement. Each one of these different information items of a node is edited by a different editor which is activated by selecting and clicking on the desired node and selecting the appropriate menu selection.

None of the nodes in the **HelloWorld** module have any initialization code, local functions, or data associated with them. All nodes in the tree, except for the **root** node, have their own code section. The actual C code of the different nodes is simple – it consists of a single print statement which is executed when the message visits that node. Figure 24.6 shows the forms associated with the code section of the **george** node.

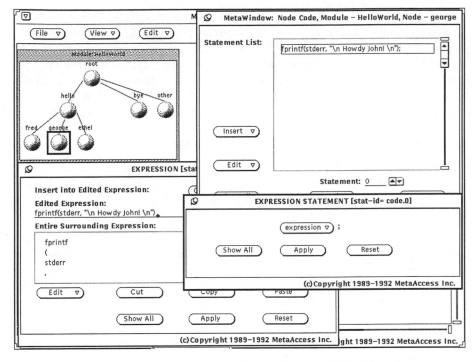

Figure 24.6 C code of the **george** node of the **HelloWorld** module.

An AEL/AAL program is called an executable unit. It is created in the same way as all other objects, by dragging and dropping its icon at the desired graphical canvas position.

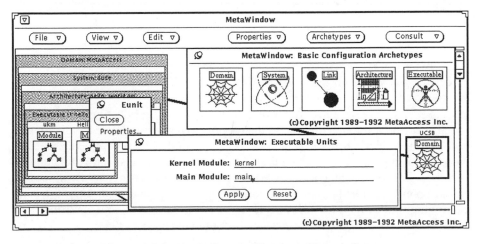

Figure 24.7 The **hello_world** executable unit form.

Each executable unit consists of at least two modules: the **kernel module** and the **main module**. The kernel module is responsible for handling any input to the program. Input is handled asynchronously. That is, it can be entered and will be accepted at any time during program execution. It will suffice to say that when the kernel module receives some input, it queues the input, as the data part of a message, for further processing in the main module. In our case the main module is the **HelloWorld** module. The executable unit form is shown in Figure 24.7.

24.3.2   Compiling and monitoring with METAWINDOW

An architecture is a collection of executable units. After the modules and executable units have been created and saved into a file representing the architecture, they can be compiled through the compile window shown in Figure 24.8.

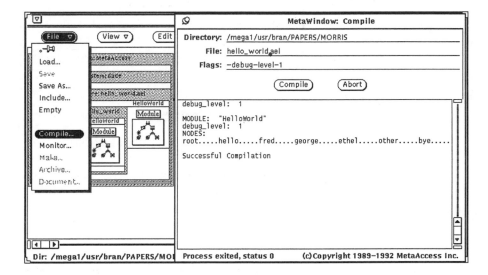

Figure 24.8 The compile window.

After the **HelloWorld** module has been compiled successfully it can be executed directly through METAWINDOW's monitor. The monitor window is shown in Figure 24.9.

METAWINDOW has a very powerful monitoring and debugging capability which is activated through the monitoring window. To select a simple highlighting of nodes while they are being executed the selection **highlight** should be made. The speed of the highlighting can be adjusted through the **display speed** regulator. To start the execution click the left mouse button on **Run**. Following is a description of the program behavior on various inputs. The inputs are entered through the main monitoring window. As each input is read, a message is created with the string as its data. This message begins its traversal at the root in the main module.

INPUT: *How does this work?*

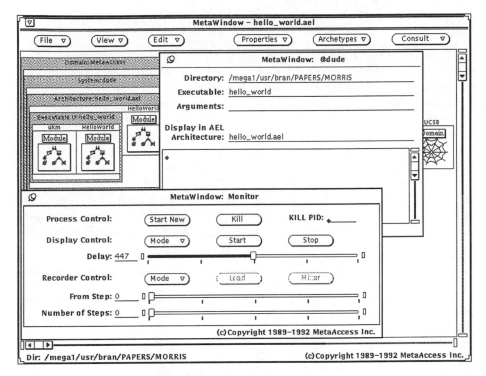

Figure 24.9 The monitor window.

The message attempts to travel down the first arc. Since the first five bytes of the data are *How d* rather than *Hello*, the message is unable to traverse this first arc. The message then attempts to travel down the second arc. Since this arc is open only to the string *Bye!* it is unable to traverse this arc also. It then attempts to traverse the third arc. This arc is open to all messages, so the message travels down this arc. The message then causes the execution of the code in this leaf node. When it finishes execution, the message is discarded.

INPUT: *Hello George!*

The message successfully travels down the first arc because bytes 0 through 4 are *Hello*. The message is now at node **hello**. It unsuccessfully attempts to make its way down arc one because bytes 6 through 12 of the data are *George!* rather than *Fred!* It is however, able to traverse arc two since *George!* is a match to this arc's match value. The code in this leaf node, which involves printing the words *Howdy, John!,* is executed and the message is then discarded.

INPUT: *Bye!*

The message attempts node arc zero unsuccessfully (arcs are numbered 0..n). It then tries the second arc and is able to traverse it. The code for this node is executed, printing *Good Bye!* and terminating the program.

24.4   OSI

Layered communications software architectures, such as the International Standardization Organization's (ISO) Open Systems Interconnection model, contain two different forms of interaction. The first type consists of interactions of the form service provider–service consumer which are typically performed on the same physical system over a Service Access Point (SAP). The second type consists of the peer-to-peer interactions for which the actual communications protocols are defined. It is convenient to represent both types of interactions as separate trees.

Each layered OSI stack is designed to function as shown in Figure 24.10. There is a flow of information from left to right (up the OSI stack) and right to left (down the OSI stack). The flows are restricted to one level at a time, for example, the transport layer subtree interacts only with the TSAP and NSAP subtrees. Each layer subtree provides the service to the next higher up SAP by communicating with the peer subtree using the services of the lower SAP.

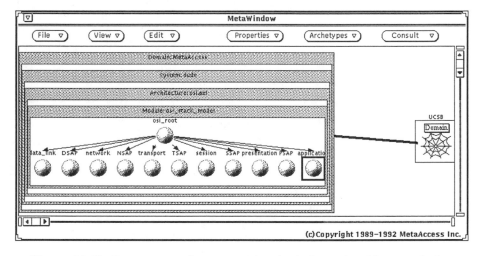

Figure 24.10 Open systems interconnection: basic layered architecture design.

The complete OSI stack can fit within one single module. However, it is much more practical and easier to design each subtree of the root as a separate module as shown in Figure 24.11.

24.4.1   Service access points (SAPs)

The basic design of an OSI Service Access Point is illustrated using the example of the Network Service Access Point (NSAP) in Figure 24.12. The NSAP module is responsible for providing an interface to all of the Network services. As can be seen from the module, all of the network primitives used by TRANSPORT are represented by leaf nodes. These primitives are N-CONNECT.request, N-DATA.request, and N-DISCONNECT.request. Whenever the **TRANSPORT** module needs to make use of one of these services, it simply sends a message down the NSAP module to the

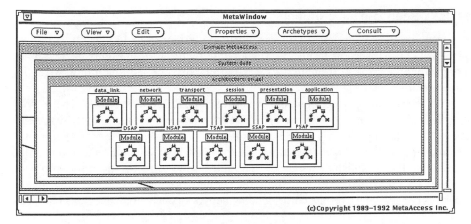

Figure 24.11 Open systems interconnection: layer implementation.

appropriate leaf. The indication primitives are also represented by leaf nodes. If the network layer needs to give an indication to the TRANSPORT module, it sends a message down the NSAP module to the appropriate leaf, which subsequently passes the indication on to the TRANSPORT module.

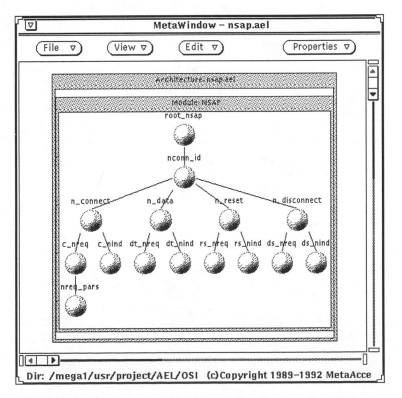

Figure 24.12 Open systems interconnection: network service access point.

24.4.2   Peer-to-peer protocols

The basic design of a protocol driver is illustrated in Figure 24.13 using the example of the ISO OSI Transport Protocol. The module represented in Figure 24.13 acts as the protocol engine. It maintains each transport connection along with the corresponding state.

The transport protocol module consist of three different subtrees. The subtree starting with the **connect** node is responsible for transport connection establishment. The subtree starting with the node **not_connect** is responsible for the distinction into different transport protocol classes and all transport protocol phases different from the connection establishment phase. The third subtree of the transport protocol module is responsible for reset and disconnect network events that occur before all transport connections over the corresponding network connection have been released.

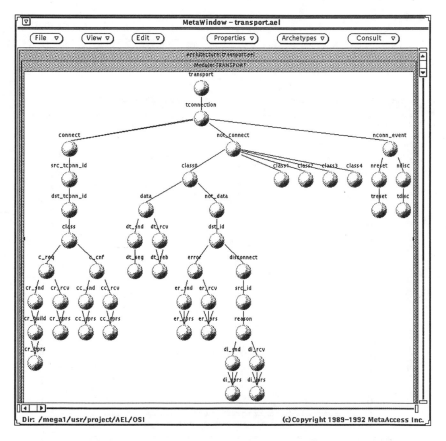

Figure 24.13 Open systems interconnection: transport protocol class 0.

24.5   Summary

It has become clear that data-centered network management paradigms, such as the ones used in the network management standards, will not be able to provide network managers with an *active* network management capability. That capability would enable network managers to quickly react to the massive changes in their environment and applications which are taking place and which will be taking place increasingly in the nineties. *Active* control should give managers the opportunity to *actively* participate in the growth of their networks and shape the networks and the management process itself in a manner best suited for their particular management task. *Active* management systems need the ability to easily redesign, reimplement, reinstall, and reintegrate major software modules at run time. The approach to *active* network management taken with METAWINDOW is that of Computer Aided Software Engineering (CASE). METAWINDOW is a CASE environment that provides *active* network management. It is based on the ARCHETYPE software engineering method for the design, specification, implementation, and monitoring of distributed software. Software generated using METAWINDOW can be linked to graphical images thus allowing run-time monitoring of protocol drivers and analysis of protocols. As MetaWindow is based on a fourth-generation language (that is, non-programming), the network manager is not only given the capability to monitor the internals of communication processes but also alter them through the automatic software redesign and reintegration process.

Abbreviations

AAL	Archetype Abstract Language
AEL	Archetype executable language
ASN.1	Abstract Syntax Notation 1
CMIP	Common Management Information Protocol
GUI	Graphical User Interface
IPC	Inter Process Communication
MIB	Management Information Base
NSAP	Network Service Access Point
OSI	Open Systems Interconnection
SAP	Service Access Point
SNMP	Simple Network Management Protocol
TSAP	Transport Service Access Point
XDR	External Data Representation

References

Hegering H.-G. and Yemini Y., eds. (1993). Integrated network management III. *Proceedings of the Third IFIP International Symposium on Integrated Network Management.* North Holland

Krishnan K. and Zimmer W., eds. (1991). Integrated network management II. *Proceedings of the Second IFIP International Symposium on Integrated Network Management.* North Holland

Meandzija B. and Ho W. P. (1987). Towards truly open systems. In *Proceedings IFIP International Symposium on Protocol Specification, Testing, and Verification.* (Rudin H. and West C., eds.), May

Meandzija B. (1988). Archetype: A unified method for the design and implementation of protocol architectures. *IEEE Transactions on Software Engineering.* **14**(6), 822–37

Meandzija B. and Westcott J., eds. (1989). Integrated network management I. *Proceedings of the First IFIP International Symposium on Integrated Network Management.* North Holland

Meandzija B. (1990). Integration through meta-communication. *Proceedings IEEE INFOCOM '90.* June, 702–9

Part VIII

Conclusions

Chapter 25

Future Directions

Liba Svobodova

IBM Research Division, Zurich Research Laboratory,
Säumerstrasse 4,
8803 Rüschlikon,
Switzerland
Email: svo@zurich.ibm.com

The preceding twenty-four chapters of this book brought up and explored a wide variety of subjects pertinent to the management of networks and distributed systems. What sort of conclusion should the reader draw from these contributions? What are the main trends? What will the network management systems of the future look like? What are the most important and most pressing problems? What are still research problems?

The management of today's and future networked environments requires far more than *network* management in the traditional sense, where the managed entities are physical lines, nodes, switching equipment, network connections, and so on. Management of distributed applications and user-oriented services adds a new dimension to the problem. On the other hand, as already pointed out in the previous material (for example, Chapters 3, 22), network management is in itself a distributed application, and the general distributed system design principles, methods, and tools are applicable in developing and running such applications. Today, the coupling between "distributed systems" and "network management" is very weak. The management functions pertaining to distributed systems and applications aspects often are disconnected from the underlying network management, and specialized software platforms and tools are used for the development of network management applications. In order to achieve a truly *integrated management of network and distributed system aspects*, both of these disparities need to be addressed. The goal of the OSF/DME (Distributed Management Environment) effort, described in Chapter 23, is to develop a common framework and a set of services for management applications. DME assumes the use of OSF/DCE (Distributed Computing Environment) technology (Schill, 1993) which has a wide acceptance in the industry.

Although there are still many technical problems to be solved (see Chapter 23), this is an important step towards a common environment for distributed applications in entirety – that is, those applications the distributed system must support for its end users, and those needed to manage the whole complex. The most intricate problem is, however, how the different aspects of managing distributed environments – systems management, network management, and application management – should be combined and integrated; this is not defined by DME nor any other standards.

It is clear to everybody that *standards* are highly important to being able to operate and manage networks built of heterogeneous components. However, the question still remains: which set of standards? In this book, the OSI concepts and standards are the primary subject of several chapters (Chapters 4, 5, and 6) and underline the subjects of several other chapters. However, this does not reflect correctly the present situation and trends in open network management; the dominance of the Simple Network Management Protocol (SNMP) can be seen especially in LAN-based environments and the Internet community in general. This trend is understandable, since the OSI standards became stable only after SNMP had already been deployed quite widely in the Internet, and are significantly more complex. In particular, the SNMP agents that need to reside in network devices can be very simple. However, simplicity also has its drawbacks. The OSI standards provide a powerful object-oriented management information model, support flexible distribution of management functionality and provide common system management functions which together make them well suited for the management of large heterogeneous networked environments and distributed applications. On the other hand, the SNMP framework and protocol are undergoing some changes. SNMPv2 fixes some of the problems of the original SNMP, and aims at enabling systems and application management; however, it strives to preserve the simplicity of the agents, and in its power and flexibility is closer to the original SNMP than the OSI standards. Both SNMP versions were addressed in Chapter 7. The motivation, process, and design principles for evolving SNMP are discussed also in (Case *et al.*, 1993). The SNMP and OSI (CMIP) standards were compared and assessed in Chapter 8[1]; other recommended readings on this subject are (Phifer and Brusil, 1993; Yemini, 1993).

The OSI standards are the basis of TMN, the Telecommunication Management Network standards (see Chapter 9), and this will drive their deployment. In distributed systems, for complex tasks such as access control and security policy management the power of the OSI object-oriented management model and CMIP is indispensable (Hauser and Zatti, 1993). A very important step in deploying the OSI standards is to specify a common base of managed object classes; GDMO (Chapter 6) is the standard notation developed for this purpose. The main work on specifying object classes for network management is carried under the auspices of the Network Management Forum, in the OMNIpoint program (Murill, 1993). In SAMSON (Security and Management Services in Open Networks), a project conducted under the European RACE program (Samson, 1993), managed objects related to security management are being described in GDMO. With appropriate tools, such

---

[1]   As in Chapter 8, *SNMP* and *CMIP* is used here to refer collectively to all the relevant services, protocols, and Management Information Base (MIB) in each set of standards.

specifications can be automatically translated into code for a variety of system platforms, thus simplifying and speeding up the development of OSI-based network management systems; several such tools and platforms are under development (Desai *et al.*, 1993; Dossogne and Dupont, 1993; Wittig and Pfeiler, 1993). Nevertheless, the effective use of the OSI network management standards will continue to present quite a challenge. The distributed structure and control of the management functions and the underlying management information (MIB) pose rather complex implementation problems; instructive examples can be found in (Aneroussis *et al.*, 1993).

SNMP-based networks will continue to exist and expand, and the problem of having to support multiple standards for a possibly unlimited time period has opened up once again. Different approaches to the integration of network management systems based on the two standards have been proposed. One possibility, which assumes the use of only CMIP-based management applications, is to create a special CMIP agent that provides a gateway into or *encapsulates* the SNMP world (Abeck *et al.*, 1993; Balazs *et al.*, 1992; Kalyanasundaram and Sethi, 1993; Zihang and Lobelle, 1993); how satisfactory such solutions will be is still uncertain. An approach that allows both SNMP and CMIP applications to work with the same management agent based on a common MIB is described in (Mazumdar *et al.*, 1993). XMP, the programming interface for management applications being standardized by X/Open, supports both SNMP and CMIP, but the application writer has to know which standard is to be used, and use the appropriate operations. In general, it would be desirable to produce an integrated architecture for the development and operations of management applications based on either standard or any proprietary legacy solution, independent of the underlying management protocols. The Multiprotocol Transport Networking (MPTN) architecture that makes application programming interfaces, and consequently applications, independent of the underlying transport/network protocols (MPTN, 1993; Britton *et al.*, 1993) offers an interesting model. However, the differences between the various management services and protocols and the representation of the underlying management information seem to be too large to fit into a common architectural framework. At the least, practical mechanisms that facilitate the implementation of the necessary mapping functions are needed. In DME, the adapter object mechanism can be used to map different management services and protocols to DME-conformant entities. Chapter 22 presented a number of possibilities for developing mapping functions in DEC's Enterprise Management Architecture.

A concept of growing importance in networked environments is the so-called *Customer Premises Network (CPN)* (Paone *et al.*, 1992). CPN is a private, possibly quite complex, network administered and managed according to the needs of the owner, that uses services provided via public networks to interconnect with remote CPNs of the same enterprise or CPNs of other organizations. For a smooth interoperation in such environments, the network management systems of CPN and public network service provider must cooperate. Such a cooperation is eased by common standards. At Telecom'91 in Geneva, IBM and Ericsson jointly demonstrated a CMIP-based interoperability of their respective proprietary network management systems to provide adaptive connectivity. An essential issue is the standardization of the management information that must be made available by each side to its partner.   Currently, the focus is on defining a Customer Network Management (CNM) service that allows customers to access management information pertaining to a public data network and issue certain management requests relevant to customer's own management needs (Sunaga and Tomita, 1993; Sher and Tesink, 1993).   The RACE project PREPARE is developing a model for cooperative service management based on the TMN architecture, where management information is exchanged both ways and coordinated in order to perform management actions with end-to-end effects (Schneider and Donnelly, 1993).

The network management systems have to be able to manage a broad range of networks of different technologies.   Clearly, many of the existing networks will continue to be used for a long time, and many more networks based on the well-established technologies will be installed.   At the same time, the ATM (Asynchronous Transfer Mode) technology is leaving field trials and ATM networks start appearing, first as LANs and MANs, forming the basis of Customer Premises Networks that will connect to public B-ISDN (Broadband Integrated Services Digital Network) (Le Boudec et al., 1993).   What impact will this technology have?   What new problems does it bring to network management? Above all, ATM-based networks have to satisfy the expectations that they can deliver multimedia information at the required Quality of Service (QoS) and acceptable cost (see Chapter 11).   Management of QoS in ATM-based broadband networks has been an important topic in the RACE program (Geihs et al., 1992).   Closer interactions between the real-time network control mechanisms and network management is being sought to provide more efficiently guaranteed QoS (Lazar, 1992).   However, the QoS needed for distributed multimedia services cannot be satisfied alone by the basic networking technology (switches, adapters, media access control protocols); *integrated management of the system and network resources* is required to achieve control over quality of service end-to-end.

Network management *tools* play an essential role in managing networks from simple LANs to complex heterogeneous networked environments.   Choosing the best network management tool from among the various product offerings is not an easy task, especially when the requirements are not sufficiently well understood.   The study by (Meyer et al., 1993) illustrates how such requirements can be defined and used to evaluate different alternatives.   A rather different set of requirements concern the user interface (Chapter 20).   Sophisticated graphics for the visualization of configuration and performance data are already a standard feature of the user interfaces to network management systems; advanced manipulation and presentation techniques utilizing the full range of information media (text, graphics, image, audio, voice) are likely to play an important role in the future (Marchisio et al., 1993). Further, groupware to assist distributed problem solving by human operators and experts may be a useful addition to the management platforms (Valta and de Jager, 1993).

Let us return to the subject of managing distributed systems and applications. This area is far less advanced than network management. Various aspects of distributed system management were presented in specific chapters: distributed system configuration (Chapter 18), distributed monitoring (Chapter 12), name management (Chapter 10), access control (Chapters 15, 17), and user administration and accounting (Chapter 14). Case studies of managing large distributed systems in practice are rare in the literature. The most frequently cited case is the Project Athena system developed and operational at MIT. This distributed system, which in 1992 encompassed about 1500 workstations and 100 servers, had been designed so that it would be manageable with limited personnel; an analysis of the support requirements are given in (Arfman and Roden, 1992). Project Athena developed a very good model for managing distributed systems in university environments, but distributed systems supporting *business* operations have more extensive and stringent requirements concerning performance, availability, security, data and workflow management, as well as application-specific management. One of the key problems is the definition of the procedures and policies for using the various management information available through network management systems and local operating systems and providing a comprehensive and understandable view to the end user from the application perspective.

Clearly, the problem is very complex. Distributed applications may potentially span the whole world, many interconnected networks based on different technologies, some private, some provided as a public service, with different costs, performance, reliability, and security characteristics. At the distributed application and services level, it may be necessary to manage and provide controlled access to millions of objects. One extremely important mechanism for dealing with this sort of size and complexity is the concept of the *domain*. The most general definition of a domain is a separately administered environment (Chapters 9, 23), but the concept of the domain can be extended to provide different views of the problem, and a mechanism for defining intra- and inter-domain policies (Chapters 16, 17, 22). In many situations, *inter-domain* management will both take place at a higher level (with many details of the intra-domain management suppressed) and require additional precautions, since it is assumed that foreign domains cannot and should not be entirely trusted. Mutual authentication of the cooperating domain management systems is a prerequisite. However, the first problem is the design of inter-domain authentication procedures that support such authentication across different security domains, which do require some minimal degree of mutual trust among the domain security managers. The problem gets further complicated when the different domains use different authentication procedures; see for example (Piessens *et al.,* 1993).

With the introduction of notebook computers into the market in 1990, a new era of computing and networking has started: *pervasive mobile computing*. The portable devices will use extensively wireless technologies to access the global networks and information services. Some portable devices will be very small and their function limited to accessing and managing information of personal interest, others will provide full-scale operating system and software development functions to their users. What sort of management support is necessary to accommodate the rapidly growing population of mobile users with very differing communication and computation capabilities and requirements? To allow them to access networks and a large variety of network-based services from anywhere and anytime? One big problem is reliable and secure authentication of legitimate users, to allow them to operate in a foreign domain and move between foreign domains that cannot be fully trusted. The emerging standards for wireless cellular networks provide only a partial solution to the authentication problem; a solution that will work across any network is proposed in (Tsudik *et al.*, 1993). A related problem is accounting and billing for the services used in the visited domain and the access to the global network and services in general. Various policies were discussed in Chapter 14. But, the future pervasive use of a great variety of information services available on networks by a vast population of general users will require new, very simple, general, flexible, yet very secure and easy to administer mechanisms for gaining access to and being properly charged for such services. Other important issues, such as mobile user tracking and location management, are discussed in (Imielinski and Badrinath, 1993; Maass *et al.*, 1993); such management functions have to be properly integrated into the overall network and distributed system management.

In general, management of networked environments will remain a challenging technical area for any foreseeable future. These environments both reflect and create complex organizational and social structures, which will pose more and more demanding requirements on the behavior of the networks and distributed systems, and, thus, on their management. Not just structuring and distribution of the management function is necessary to deal with the complexity; automation of the management tasks is of highest importance. This requires the use and cooperation of specialized expert systems and decision support systems, and in turn new knowledge technologies and methods for integrating them (see Chapter 21). Cooperation of human experts on solving complex tasks with many facets provides a basic framework for this approach to automating network management. Is it possible, when substantial progress is made in managing the ever more complex networks and distributed applications, that some useful models will emerge from this work for the management of human organizations?

Abbreviations

ATM	Asynchronous Transfer Mode
B-ISDN	Broadband Integrated Services Digital Network
CMIP	Common Management Information Protocol
CPN	Customer Premises Network
DCE	Distributed Computing Environment
DME	Distributed Management Environment
GDMO	Guidelines for the Definition of Managed Objects
MPTN	Multiprotocol Transport Networking
QoS	Quality of Service
SNMP	Simple Network Management Protocol

References

Abeck S., Clemm A. and Holberg U. (1993). Simply open network management: an approach for integration of SNMP into OSI management soncepts. In *Integrated Network Management, III* (Hegering H.-G. and Yemini Y., eds.), 361–75, North-Holland

Aneroussis N.G., Kalmanek Ch.R. and Kelly V.E. (1993). Implementing OSI network management facilities on the Xunet ATM platform. *4th IFIP/IEEE Intl. Workshop on Distributed Systems: Operations and Management (DSOM'93)*, Long Branch, New Jersey, Oct. 5–6, 1993

Arfman J.M. and Roden P. (1992). Project Athena: supporting distributed computing at MIT, *IBM Systems Journal*, **31**(8), 550–63

Balazs A., Beschoner K. and Mueller H.-J. (1992). Integration of OSI-based and SNMP-based network management systems: an example. *3rd IFIP/IEEE Intl. Workshop on Distributed Systems: Operations and Management (DSOM'92)*, Munich, Germany, Oct. 12–13, 1992

Britton K., Chen W.-S.E., Chung T.-Y.D., Edwards A., Mathew J., Pozefsky D., Sarkar S., Turner R., Doeringer W. and Dykeman D. (1993). Multi-protocol transport networking: a general internetworking solution. *IEEE Intl. Conf. on Network Protocols*, San Francisco, October 19-22, 1993

Case J. D., McCloghrie K., Rose M.T. and Waldbusser S. (1993). An introduction to the simple management protocol. In *Integrated Network Management, III* (Hegering H.-G. and Yemini Y., eds.), 261–72, North-Holland

Desai S., Joglekar S. and Westerfield P.B. (1993). An object management and communication platform for building TMN compliant operations systems. *4th IFIP/IEEE Intl. Workshop on Distributed Systems: Operations and Management (DSOM'93)*, Long, Branch, New Jersey, Oct. 5-6, 1993

Dossogne F. and Dupont M.-P. (1993). A software architecture for management information model definition, implementation, and validation. In *Integrated Network Management, III* (Hegering H.-G. and Yemini Y., eds.), 593–604, North-Holland

Geihs K., Francois P., Griffin D., Kaas-Petersen C. and Mann A. (1992). Service and traffic management for IBCN. *IBM Systems Journal*, **31**(4), 711–27

Hauser R. and Zatti S. (1993). Security, authentication, and policy management in open distributed systems. *IBM Research Report RZ 526*, Oct. 1993

Imielinski T. and Badrinath B.R. (1993). Mobile wireless computing: solutions and challenges in data management. *WINLAB/Rutgers Technical Report*, Feb. 1993

Kalyanasundaram P. and Sethi A.S. (1993). An application gateway design for OSI-internet management. *Integrated Network Management, III* (Hegering H.-G. and Yemini Y., eds.), 389–401, North-Holland

Lazar A.A. (1992). The integration of real-time control with management in broadband networks. *Proc. of the Workshop on Broadband Communications*, Estoril, Portugal, Jan. 20-22, 1992

Le Boudec J.-Y., Port E. and Truong H.L. (1993). Flight of the FALCON. *IEEE Communications Magazine, 31*(2), 69–84

Maass H., Schreyer O. and Stahl M. (1993). Directory services for mobility management in private telecommunication networks. *Proc. IEEE Intl. Conference on Communications ICC'93*, Geneva, Switzerland, May 23-26, 1993, 1252–56

Marchisio L., Ronco E. and Saracco R. (1993). Modeling the user interface. *IEEE Communications Magazine, 31*(5), 68–74

Mazumdar S., Brady S. and Levine D.W. (1993). Design of protocol independent management agent to support SNMP and CMIP queries. *Integrated Network Management, III* (Hegering, H.-G. and Yemini, Y., eds.), 377–88, North-Holland

Meyer K., Betser J., Negaard E., Persinger D., Wang S., Maltese R. and Sunshine, C. (1993). An architecture driven comparison of network management systems. *Integrated Network Management, III* (Hegering H.-G. and Yemini Y., eds.), 479–91, North-Holland

MPTN (1993). Multiprotocol transport networking (MPTN) architecture: technical overview, *GC31-7073,* IBM Corp., April 1993

Murrill, B. (1993). OMNIPoint: an implementation guide to integrated networked information systems management. *Integrated Network Management, III* (Hegering, H.-G. and Yemini, Y., eds.), 405–18, North-Holland

Phifer L. and Brusil P. (1993). Incorporating OSI management technology into the marketplace. In *Integrated Network Management, III* (Hegering H.-G. and Yemini Y., eds.), 327–41, North-Holland

Paone R., Pitt D. and Schlichthaerle D. (1992). An evolutionary customer premises network for business communications. *XIV International Switching Symposium (ISS'92)*, Yokohama, Japan, Oct. 25-30, 1992, 290–4

Piessens F., de Decker B. and Janson P. (1993). Interconnecting domains with heterogeneous key distribution and authentication protocols. *Proc. 1993 IEEE Symposium on Research in Security and Privacy*, Oakland, California, May 1993, 66–79

Samson (1993). Project R2058 Security and Management Services in Open Networks, SAMSON, abstract of the reports Functional Requirements, Top Level Specification, and Detailed Level Design Specification, available via anonymous FTP from samson.darmstadt.gmd.de directory /pub/samson.

Schill A. ed. (1993). *DCE – The OSF Distributed Computing Environment: Client/Server Model and Beyond.* Lecture Notes in Computer Science 731, Springer-Verlag.

Schneider J.M. and Donnelly W. (1993). Co-coperative management of integrated communication services over the CCITT X interface. *4th IFIP/IEEE Intl. Workshop on Distributed Systems: Operations and Management* (DSOM'93), Long, Branch, New Jersey, Oct. 5-6, 1993

Sher P. and Tesink K. (1993). Potential network management services and capabilities associated with SMDS. *Integrated Network Management, III* (Hegering H.-G. and Yemini Y., eds.), 543–54, North-Holland

Sunaga H. and Tomita S. (1993). Managed object definition for customer network management in public data networks. *Integrated Network Management, III* (Hegering H.-G. and Yemini Y., eds.), 569–80, North-Holland

Tsudik G., Molva R. and Samfat D. (1993). Authentication of mobile users. IBM Research Report RZ 2493, Sep. 1993. To be published in *IEEE Network*, Special Issue on Mobile Communications, March 1994.

Valta R. and de Jager R. (1993). Deploying group communication techniques in network management. *Integrated Network Management, III* (Hegering H.-G. and Yemini Y., eds.), 751–63, North-Holland

Wittig M. and Pfeiler M. (1993). A tool supporting the management information modeling process. *Integrated Network Management, III* (Hegering H.-G. and Yemini Y., eds.),739–50, North-Holland

Yemini, Y. (1993). The OSI network management model. *IEEE Communications Magazine*, **31**(5), 20–9

Zihang R. and Lobelle M. (1993). Network management integrating SNMP/CMIP protocol implementations. *Cracow Intl. Workshop on Requirements and Techniques for Network Management*, Cracow, Poland, May 19-21, 1993

Index